Stars and Stripes on Screen

A Comprehensive Guide to Portrayals of American Military on Film

Lawrence H. Suid
Dolores A. Haverstick

The Scarecrow Press, Inc.
Lanham, Maryland • Toronto • Oxford
2005

SCARECROW PRESS, INC.

Published in the United States of America
by Scarecrow Press, Inc.
A wholly owned subsidiary of
The Rowman & Littlefield Publishing Group, Inc.
4501 Forbes Boulevard, Suite 200, Lanham, Maryland 20706
www.scarecrowpress.com

PO Box 317
Oxford
OX2 9RU, UK

British Library Cataloguing in Publication Information Available

Library of Congress Cataloging-in-Publication Data
Suid, Lawrence H.
  Stars and stripes on screen : a comprehensive guide to portrayals of American military on film / Lawrence
H. Suid, Dolores A. Haverstick.
     p. cm.
  Includes bibliographical references.
  ISBN 0-8108-5412-0 (pbk. : alk. paper)
  1. Armed Forces in motion pictures. 2. United States—Armed Forces. 3. Motion pictures—United
States—Catalogs. I. Haverstick, Dolores A., 1948– II. Title.
PN1995.9.A72S85 2005
791.43'658—dc22

                                    2004022922

⊗™ The paper used in this publication meets the minimum requirements of
American National Standard for Information Sciences—Permanence of
Paper for Printed Library Materials, ANSI/NISO Z39.48-1992.
Manufactured in the United States of America.

To Phil Haverstick, who made this book possible

Contents

Acknowledgments

In writing both editions of *Guts & Glory* and *Sailing on the Silver Screen*, Lawrence Suid received assistance from many people, particularly the 400 or so people he interviewed. Hopefully he thanked them individually or collectively. In contrast, this guide draws upon earlier research and secondary sources. As a result, the authors have fewer people to thank, but with the same deep appreciation for the help they have rendered.

First and foremost, we acknowledge Phil Haverstick's ongoing encouragement and support of our effort. He understood the time that we required to complete the book, especially in the last weeks when we seemed to be close to the end, only to discover more titles and additional appendixes. Moreover, his great knowledge of movies enabled him to offer pungent constructive suggestions that helped to make the narratives that much more useful. We can only hope the book itself justifies his assistance.

In the past, the authors used the Library of Congress Film Studies Center primarily as a repository for movies they had to screen that were otherwise unavailable. For the guide, however, we made the Library our home, using its reference books and computers to help verify and cross-check information. More important, we drew on the knowledge of the reference librarians, Madeline Maltz, Zoran Sinobad, Rosemary Hanes, and Josie Walters-Johnston, to help locate information about the films that we wanted to include. At the same time, we continued to screen films, such as ***Old Ironsides*** and ***Riders of the Storm***, to decide whether they fell into the scope of the study. The former did; the latter did not. In any case, as he has done over the years, Joseph Balian helped make sure we were loading the movies correctly and offered his own observations, particularly about Curtis LeMay.

As had Don Baruch, his predecessor, Phil Strub, Special Assistant for Audio/Visual in the Office of Assistant Secretary of Defense for Public Affairs, has remained ever ready, either by phone or e-mail, to provide information to ensure the accuracy of our entries for productions that have crossed his desk since arriving in the Pentagon in 1989. Without Phil's interest in our work and his assistance, we very likely could not have undertaken the project, let alone have finished the guide with the detail and accuracy we have been able to.

Also in the Washington area, we would like to thank Norm Hatch, Jack Green, Don Bittner, and Bill Eldard for their willingness to answer questions about the military and film. And from a distance, Kathy Ross in the Army's Los Angeles Public Affairs Office, Chuck Davis in the Air Force's Los Angeles Public Affairs Office, Bob Anderson in the Navy's Public Affairs Office, and Mitch Marovitz, formerly in the Army's Los Angeles Public Affairs Office, were always ready to answer questions about films on which they had worked. Likewise, Dale Dye, from wherever he happened to be working on a military movie, as technical advisor, actor, or both, would quickly respond to questions about projects in which he had been involved.

Without Stephen Ryan's knowledge of films and names and his keen editing eye, this guide would undoubtedly have been less accurate and less complete. We very much appreciate his interest in the project and his continuing help in making *Stars and Stripes on Screen* the book it has become.

We would also like to thank our friends, Chuck Lieman and Jeanne Mullaney, and Chris and Don Sylvester, for their understanding that the book demanded our attention even though we would have preferred spending the time with them over a good dinner or at a play. Finally a special thanks to Larry's brother, Murray Suid, for his interest in the project and for creating a website that will enable readers of the guide to correspond with us directly.

Overview

Why war movies? Why another guide to military motion pictures?

We have a simple answer to the first question. Despite protestations that they love peace, most Americans actually love violence, at least from the safety of their theater seats or living room sofas. For them, war movies provide more violence on a larger scale than any other film genre. Motion pictures about the military have enjoyed popularity since 1898, when J. Stuart Blackton pasted pictures of American warships onto wooden blocks in a small pool of water and recreated the Battle for Santiago Bay. Only in the periods immediately following every war have filmmakers believed audiences would not want to relive recent hostilities. However, within a few years, Hollywood would again start to portray the U.S. armed services in mortal combat against enemies, real and imagined.

Along with images of men—and more recently women—on the battlefield, filmmakers have also portrayed the armed services away from combat, whether during a war period or in peacetime, often in comedic situations and in musicals. While most of these noncombat stories could take place on any civilian stage, utilizing military settings enabled Hollywood to draw upon the pageantry of uniforms and exotic locations, particularly during the 1920s and 1930s, when filmmakers regularly visited the military and naval academies. Likewise, writers turned out dramas set within the armed services portraying attempted coups, murder mysteries, accidental submarine sinkings, terrorist attacks, trials, and, of course, alien invaders from outer space.

One might ask whether since 1898 the United States has ever enjoyed a period of peace and tranquility. Between the Spanish American War and World War I, Teddy Roosevelt sent the fleet around the world and secured the Panama Canal Zone. The U.S. Army also fought Pancho Villa on the Mexican border, giving the officer corps and cavalry combat experience. And the military ultimately undertook at least moderate preparations for our involvement in World War I before actually sending troops overseas. While the nation maintained its isolationism during the 1920s and 1930s, the Army and Marines went to Central America to battle terrorists and guerrillas. The Army and the Navy also fought each other, and within each service, over the role of airplanes in any future war. Ultimately, by the late 1930s, the military had mustered out the horse cavalry and had begun preparing for the inevitable involvement in the impending global conflict, whether or not American citizens realized combat was coming.

The peace that followed World War II quickly turned into a cold war, with huge expenditures for intercontinental airplanes, ships, and nuclear weapons. The United States also fought a police action in Korea, threatened to fight a nuclear war over a small island 90 miles from Florida, and became involved in an undeclared war against a small, peasant army 10,000 miles from home—without a formal declaration of war—while supposedly at peace. And since the Vietnam War ended, the United States has invaded Grenada and Panama, sent advisors back to Nicaragua, sent peacekeepers to Somalia and Bosnia, defeated a petty despot who was threatening Middle Eastern oil reservoirs, and later launched a preemptive war to drive that dictator off his throne.

Whether fighting a declared war, a police action, or an undeclared war, the American military had always prevailed—until Vietnam. If people did not perceive Korea as a victory, they blamed politicians rather than the military for creating the stalemate. The film industry would ultimately portray all of those battles. In *Guts & Glory*, author Suid advanced the thesis that the United States fell so easily into the quagmire that the Vietnam War became because the American people had always seen their military win on the real, as well as the cinematic, battlefield.

Why would anyone question General William Westmoreland when he said he needed only another 100,000 troops to defeat the Viet Cong and the North Vietnamese Army? After all, no one then knew that the commander of the American forces in Vietnam was understating the size of the North Vietnamese Army in his reports to Washington, revealed in a 1982 CBS documentary, *The Uncounted Enemy: A Vietnam Deception* (1982). Hollywood had always portrayed the armed services winning every war, and its generals as honest, intelligent, honorable men. Military people were expected to fight bravely, never lie, and give candy to children. With very few exceptions, American combat movies had not shown soldiers committing atrocities, raping teenage girls, getting stoned, fighting each other, or burning down villages.

Hollywood had created only positive images of the military services in war and peace up to the Vietnam War because of the symbiotic relationship between the motion picture industry and the military that began in the earliest days of the medium. That relationship might best be described as one of mutual exploitation. Filmmakers wanted men, equipment, and locations to provide an authentic ambience at little or no cost, while giving up as little of their creativity as possible. The military wanted positive images to aid recruitment and obtain funding from Congress and so would provide assistance if a proposed film would benefit the service being featured.

Until the Vietnam War, only rarely would a service refuse to cooperate on a production. Even when a script might not initially provide a positive image, the service would usually negotiate away problematic details and ultimately decide it would be in its best interest to give at least some help, in order to have some input into the portrayals of its men and their mission. As described in detail in *Guts & Glory*, the negotiations between Columbia Pictures and the Army on *From Here to Eternity* (1953) provide a paradigm for how the relationship worked.

Any movie based on James Jones's novel would contain images that the Army would prefer never reach the screen, that is, brutality in the stockade, an officer promoted even after attempting to force one of his men to enter a boxing tournament, and an enlisted man making love to his officer's wife. Some of these plot lines could not be changed without destroying the power of Jones's portrayal of life in the Army before Pearl Harbor. But through negotiations, the Army was able to keep the brutality in the stockade unseen and to have the officer forced to resign his commission. So while *From Here to Eternity* would never benefit the service, providing assistance proved to be in the Army's best interest.

The Vietnam War savaged the positive images the armed services had worked so hard to create. The postwar portrayals of the war that Hollywood turned out in the late 1970s and early 1980s reinforced the idea that the United States had lost the conflict due to the incompetence of its officers, as well as to the lack of discipline and combat readiness of its men. At the same time, however, beginning with *Midway* in 1976, Hollywood began the process of rehabilitating the military's shattered image, a process that *Top Gun* completed in 1986.

Since then, filmmakers have regularly turned to the military for men, equipment, and locations to create movies depicting men in combat, as well as peacetime, much as they had done from the beginning of the relationship. Times have changed, however. Not all movies contain positive images, and the Pentagon has shown greater reluctance to provide assistance. Even when the services do agree to cooperate on a production, the completed film still may contain negative images. Nevertheless, during the 1990s and into the new millennium, the military has continued to appear, both in theaters and on television screens.

With so many military films produced (and more on the way), a compilation of titles and information about these productions has become necessary. As our bibliography illustrates, many scholars have attempted in one way or another to satisfy this need. Some have tried to include all titles; some have focused on a particular war; some have focused on a particular aspect of war, for example, the combat movie; and others have focused on a particular time period, for example, films made during a specific war. Some writers have discussed films within a narrative format; some primarily by listing titles with information including director, screenwriter, etc.; and others have combined the two, that is, some information and a brief narrative.

Why then *this* guidebook? We have tried to create the best of all possible guides. We have included all significant information: director, screenwriter, producer, stars, period, subject, service, color, and length. Beyond this information, three features make this guide unique. First, we have provided review dates to delineate when a film appeared. Second, to the extent possible, we have indicated whether a particular theatrical film sought assistance from one or another of the armed services and if that assistance was granted, in part or fully. Third, where relevant, we have discussed the military and historical accuracy of the film.

RELEASE DATES

Until the recent blanket opening of films all over the country on the same date, Hollywood often released new movies on different days in different locations. Moreover, studios sometimes opened a film the last week of a year in New York and Los Angeles to qualify for the upcoming Academy Awards. The general release then occurred sometime in the new year, which leads to the assumption that a film appeared in that year. For example, *Twelve O'Clock High* and *Sands of Iwo Jima* actually opened in December 1949, although most people believe they debuted in 1950. Film festivals in the United States and abroad further complicate the identification of release dates.

In an attempt to bring order to this potential confusion, we have provided two review dates, whenever possible. We have included the reviews from the *Weekly Variety,* which usually contains the first review of any film, and from the *New York Times,* which coincides with either a film's Academy Award qualifying release or with the movie's general release.

This approach has a further benefit of providing sources for additional information about a particular film; both the *Weekly Variety* and the *New York Times* have collected and published their reviews up to 1998 and these are available in most major libraries. In cases in which neither publication reviewed the film—usually a low budget production with little to recommend it visually or dramatically—we have used the date provided by either the American Film Institute's catalogue of films or the Internet Movie Data Base (IMDB) (www.imdb.com). The earliest release date appears in parentheses next to each movie's title in chapter 1.

In a very few cases, usually for films produced before 1920, we have used another film publication such as *Daily Variety* (identified as DV in the key to abbreviations) if it provides the complete date, that is, month, day, and year. For recent films, whose reviews have not yet been put in the Library of Congress clipping file, we have used the *Variety* website "posted" date, which is usually a few days before the film's release date and the first published review. On the other hand, the *New York Times* includes the publication date of its reviews online. Finally, when the *Times* has run two reviews, usually during the week and then in its Sunday "Arts & Leisure" section, we have tried to include both dates, again as a source of additional information about the film. Feature films that went straight to video seldom have reviews, but of course they are included if found.

For each film, we have provided a narrative abstract that, at a minimum, describes the plot in one or two sentences. For the majority of films, we have written three or four sentences. For significant productions, we have gone into some depth in regard to the subject, the cooperation the film did or did not receive, and its place in the history of military movies. We admit to having taken an eclectic approach to the narratives, and they do not follow any particular pattern or style, since both authors did the writing. The films themselves have usually dictated the tone and approach. Obviously a "B" or "C" film receives less attention and may be dismissed with a cursory comment.

MILITARY ASSISTANCE

Before the unification of the services into the Department of Defense (DoD) in 1947, each military branch dealt with studios separately, with one or more officers handling requests, usually in the service's public affairs office. Since 1949, the DoD has had its own public affairs office, which serves as a liaison with the film industry. From 1949 to 1989, Donald Baruch headed the office. Mr. Baruch compiled a list of films and television programs that received cooperation from 1949 to 1968. The National Archives has the records of the first four years of his office, and most of his other records (up to 1962) were deposited in the Georgetown University Special Collections Library. Since 1989, Philip Strub has served as the special assistant of the Assistant Secretary of Defense for Public Affairs.

In doing the research for the first edition of *Guts & Glory*, Suid compiled information about the relationship between the film industry and the military from a multitude of sources. These included the Library of Congress, the National Archives, the University of Southern California Film Studies Center, the Academy of Motion Pictures Arts and Sciences Library in Beverly Hills, presidential libraries, and other repositories. He also conducted more than 400 relevant interviews. His collection is now in the Georgetown University Special Collections Library. In addition, Mr. Strub has continued Mr. Baruch's practice of preserving retired records by depositing them at Georgetown University. Author Suid drew upon these collected records to create for the Department of Defense a database of those motion pictures that have received assistance or were denied help. The database became the starting point for this guide.

In 1954, the DoD issued Instruction 5122.3, "Function of Pictorial Branch and Cooperation Policies," which formalized the criteria for providing cooperation to the film industry. It assigned responsibility for supervising the policies and procedures to the DoD public affairs office. The instruction stipulated that to qualify for assistance the completed film had to achieve three goals:

1. Benefits the Department of Defense and is in the best interest of national defense and the public good.
2. Adheres to the general policy of the Department of Defense regarding operations, morale, and discipline of its components and complies with standards of dignity and propriety.
3. Portrays accurately and authentically military operations, historical incidents, persons, or places, depicting a true interpretation of military life, and/or has educational and public relations values from a Department of Defense viewpoint.

With minor changes in language, this instruction has remained in effect to the present, although not always followed strictly. Comedies, such as the Dean Martin and Jerry Lewis vehicle *Jumping Jacks*, often exceed the limits of dramatic license. The Navy had significant problems with *The Caine Mutiny*, claiming, wrongly, that it had never experienced a mutiny aboard one of its ships. However, the Navy found that it was in its best interest to provide assistance, since it gained leverage to improve the negative portrayal of Captain Queeg. *Pearl Harbor* lacked any accuracy in its portrayal of history and military operations but received full cooperation because producer Jerry Bruckheimer sold Secretary of Defense William Cohen on the project. In all cases, however, the armed services have hoped the completed films would aid recruiting, help force retention, and inform the viewers of their mission and abilities to defend and protect the nation.

The degree and kind of military assistance varied with the requirements of the particular production. For example, William Wellman spent nine months shooting *Wings* in Texas and had full use of soldiers and virtually every military airplane in the Army Air Corps. The film still holds the record for the amount of cooperation and length of filming on military facilities. In contrast, on the nonmilitary *Random Hearts* (1999), the Navy provided an underwater rescue team, so that the director could film a rescue operation on a civilian jet that had crashed off the shore of the Patuxent Naval Air Station. The filmmakers spent only a few days there, but the Navy considered the movie to be a ten-minute commercial for one of its missions. We classify both films as having received full cooperation.

The Pentagon defines limited cooperation as providing assistance for two or three days at a locale with shots of nonmoving equipment as background to on-screen action, for example, actors walking past a docked ship, action in the recruiting office on Times Square, or a guard checking passes at a base entrance. Courtesy assistance consists of a tour of a military facility, stock footage, or providing instruction for the blowing of a bosun's whistle. If the script did not meet the military's regulations and negotiations could not resolve the problems, the service would simply deny the request for assistance.

Those decisions often came after public relations officers had provided considerable information, and in many instances they maintained that the production had actually received assistance. Consequently, we have included an information-only category (Inform), which includes films that only needed or received information but no material help. For example, the Army public affairs office in Los Angeles provided the makers of *Forrest Gump* significant advice, which helped correct inaccuracies in the script. However, the Army denied the request for actual assistance because the script still did not satisfy the service's criteria for assistance. In this case, we have indicated the film received informational assistance but was denied material help.

Finally, we have the category of "Not Requested, Not Required," shown as NR. This includes productions for which the filmmakers did not request assistance because a) they realized they could not receive help given the nature of the script, b) the film was to be made overseas where the United States had no resources to make available, or c) assistance was not needed or could readily be obtained from private sources without the hassle of submitting a formal request to the Pentagon.

ORGANIZATION OF THE GUIDE

Chapter 1 covers feature films, that is, movies intended for theatrical release. To be sure, some may never have made it that far, going straight to cable or video because of their lack of dramatic quality or poor production values. However, if our research indicated that they intended to make a theatrical feature, we gave the filmmakers the benefit of the doubt. We would like to think that we have found and listed every single military feature portraying the U.S. armed services, though we acknowledge that we may have missed a very few. At the same time, as explained in chapter 5, we did not include films in which the only military presence was a man in uniform who did not perform any on-screen military duty, unless the characters are seen in a military setting. For example, the three Navy buddies in *On the Town* begin and end their shore excursion in the Brooklyn Navy Ship Yard by walking down an actual warship's gangplank. Therefore, the film qualifies. We do hope we have included all of the reader's favorites and not omitted any significant portrayals.

Chapter 2 contains a representative sample of movies made for television, cable, and video release. Unlike feature films that had a shelf life in theaters of at least a week and subsequently can be screened in cinema repositories such as the Library of Congress, TV movies may appear only once. Moreover, television movies have become, for the most part, the old Hollywood "B" movies, ones made on a low budget, using newcomers to the industry and actors on their way up or down the professional ladder. So, for purely practical reasons, the authors have listed as many of the TV films as they could find. These include series pilots, even if many of those films failed to spawn the planned series. Moreover, a pilot has a beginning, middle, and end, whereas a series episode might contain ongoing story lines.

Although television series are not intrinsically a part of this study, we included appendix X, "Select List of Television Series Featuring Significant Military Characters/Themes," because of the close relationship between TV movies and TV series. In discussing the series themselves in appendix X, we have included only those that focused specifically on one or another of the armed services or characters performing their military duties. However, we have also listed *The West Wing* since Marine guards appear regularly performing their White House duties, military brass meet with the president, and one episode features the burial of a Korean War veteran at Arlington National Cemetery. Likewise, we have included *American Dreams* because the older brother of the heroine joins the Marines and fights in Vietnam, which is adequately portrayed, and the war itself creates the framework in which the characters live in the second half of the 1960s. As with TV films, we have simply listed as many as we could find, recognizing that readers will probably be aware of others.

In chapter 3, "Documentaries," we have again included a representative sample that portrayed the U.S. armed services in action, from the Spanish American War to the present. This is not the place to debate what constitutes a documentary. Most people believe that a documentary portrays real events as they are happening. However, even in the greatest or most significant documentaries, the filmmakers have often manipulated the visual truth. In *The Memphis Belle*, director William Wyler reversed the B-17 Flying Fortress's 24th and 25th missions, since he wanted to end the film with the dramatic bombing of Germany, rather than the bombing of the German submarine pens on the French coast. In *December 7*, John Ford re-created much of the Japanese attack on Pearl Harbor because very little actual footage existed. Nevertheless, scenes from Ford's film have regularly appeared in documentaries as if they were the real thing. Likewise, in *The Battle of San Pietro*, John Huston staged some of the combat sequences while removing some of the more graphic shots of dead American soldiers.

Then there is Frank Capra's Why We Fight series. These seven films were intended only as indoctrination tracts to be shown to American servicemen during their basic training to explain why they had to go off to war, on the assumption they might not otherwise understand. While the series might be considered only propaganda tracts, we have included it as well as *Know Your Enemy, Japan*, and *The Negro Soldier*, because they do provide insights into the period in which they were made. Admittedly, in this chapter as in the others, we have had to make tough decisions about which titles to include and which to leave out.

Chapter 4 addresses "unseen" military appearances, in which the service and the assistance remains unidentified or unrecognized, usually in nonmilitary films. For example, despite longstanding regulations against American servicemen appearing in foreign garb, the USS *Salem* portrayed the German battleship in *Pursuit of the Graf Spee*. Twentieth Century Fox filmed the wedding scene in *Hello, Dolly!* at West Point. And the Navy provided the original plans for the USS *Constitution* to the filmmakers when they built a replica of "Old Ironsides" for the film of the same name. *San Francisco* would have been included in this section because active duty Marines appeared as civilians during the earthquake sequence. In fact, some Marines in uniform appeared performing duties they would have done in an actual disaster, so we have included *San Francisco* in "Feature Films."

APPENDIXES

Finally, we have created 10 appendixes, the first of which may prove to be the most valuable part of this guide. People often have asked the authors to identify a particular film by providing one or two details, such as "It was about submarines and I saw it as a boy," etc. By listing each service's cinematic appearances by year, the authors hope that a reader, who knows which service a movie portrayed and the approximate year in which he or she saw it in a theater, may have his or her memory jogged by seeing the titles of the movies that appeared in that time frame. The reader can then go back to the appropriate title entry in chapter 1 to confirm it was the long-remembered movie.

We recognize that our choices for best and worst military movies may not be the ones all readers would have selected. With that in mind, we have tried to include in the narrative of each film why we considered it good or bad. In *Guts & Glory*, author Suid made it abundantly clear why he does not consider *Saving Private Ryan* a good or honest film, and we were sorely tempted to list it as one of the worst movies. However, we do recognize that Steven Spielberg's portrayal of D-Day has become one of the most praised and honored military films of all time. Consequently, we created a special category for "Significant, but Highly Flawed" movies. In our lists of the best, worst, or significant but flawed, we do not elaborate why we have designated a film as such. Readers can discern our reasons in the individual discussions of those films.

In Chapter 5, we have provided a representative sampling of films that were considered for inclusion in the main section but did not make the cut. We provide reasons for our decisions.

More than a few could have gone either way, and we remain open to arguments to include other titles in future editions.

CRITERIA FOR INCLUDING FILMS

1. The film has to portray American servicemen or servicewomen in uniform from 1898 to the present, doing their assigned jobs, in combat, in the cold war, in POW camps, or in a peace-time environment.

Why 1898? This year stands as a watershed in the evolution of the nation's armed forces, the nature of the wars it was to fight, and how their actions would be portrayed to the American people. Until then, the military had served to create, preserve, and expand the United States within the continent. At the same time, the infant movie industry first portrayed the American military in combat during the Spanish–American War. Subsequently, filmmakers began to use the armed services as subjects for drama, comedy, and pure action-adventure stories. By the 1920s, the military was regularly appearing as a subject for all manner of stories. Consequently, 1898 stands as a well-defined historical starting point for this guide, the year in which the American military entered the modern world and began its appearance on movie screens, which has continued with few interruptions ever since.

We do not include *A Yank in the RAF* because Tyrone Power flies for the British in an RAF uniform. We do include D. W. Griffith's Revolutionary War epic *America* because the cavalrymen and their horses are in fact members of the 1923 U.S. Army, albeit wearing period costumes. However, we do not include *Gettysburg* because the soldiers on both sides are re-enactors or extras, not U.S. soldiers on active duty. We include *The Day the Earth Stood Still* because the contemporary Army confronts the alien flying saucer. *Aliens* does not fall into the scope of the study since the Marines are from some future time with no connection to today's Marine Corps.

2. The film must have been marketed in the United States. However, the movie's country of origin is of no importance in deciding whether to include it. Argentine, Australian, Canadian, English, Filipino, French, and Japanese filmmakers, among others, have contributed to the portrayal of American fighting men. For example, we include Australia's *Siege of Firebase Gloria* because it portrays American Marines in action.

3. Length of the military's portrayal on the screen or the realism of a military sequence does not govern the decision whether to include the film. In fact, a great majority of the movies that fall into the scope of the guide lack authenticity or plausibility, which the authors usually discuss. In any case, even short appearances, such as in *Random Hearts,* may well contribute to the viewer's perception of the military.

4. POWs, by definition, remain on active duty during their incarceration. Consequently, any film portraying the rescue of prisoners by former soldiers, such as Rambo in *Rambo: First Blood, Part II*, falls into the scope of the study.

5. In lists of Vietnam war films, many scholars include movies that portray veterans returning from Vietnam, trying to adjust to the real world. Since the men are no longer in the service and the films do not show any military activity, we have not included them–unless they have a flashback to active duty, as in *Heroes*, *Rolling Thunder*, and *Cease Fire*.

6. We have not included movies set entirely in veterans hospitals since the Department of Veterans Affairs is not a part of the DoD. If, however, the film opens with a combat scene that results in the soldier's injury, as in *The Men*, or the hospitalized veteran has a flashback to the

event that injured him, then the film falls into the scope of the study. We include **Coming Home** because Bruce Dern was a Marine on active duty and the Marine recruiter at the end of the film was in uniform, not because Jon Voight had been a Marine, since he was never seen in combat.

7. Even though author Suid discussed at some length in *Guts & Glory* home front movies that made a comment on the American experience in Vietnam, we have not included movies such as **Running on Empty** in "Feature Films" unless they also contained visual images of the war.

8. We have included musicals and comedies whose stories are set on military facilities or whose characters are in uniform, since these films convey, especially to young viewers, that life in the service is fun and games. We have not included movies that might depict a service-man on leave but which has no other portrayal of the military, such as **The Clock** (1945). Likewise, we ultimately deleted **For Me and My Gal** (1942), because the doughboys being en-tertained were undoubtedly extras simply dressed in WWI costumes. Moreover, although Gene Kelly wipes out a German machine gun nest, he does it as a civilian, not as a soldier.

9. Given the guide's purpose to list films portraying the U.S. armed services since 1898, it in-cludes few movies about American wars of the eighteenth and nineteenth centuries. Exceptions are those that contain twentieth-century servicemen as extras, as in **America**, or equipment that a service may have provided, as in **Birth of a Nation**. **John Paul Jones** falls into the scope of the study because it opens and closes aboard an aircraft carrier. We include **Ten Gentlemen from West Point**, but barely, because it ends with a brief scene of cadets marching at West Point as background to the listing of famous Academy graduates. **Gettysburg** and **Gods and Generals** do not qualify since the filmmakers received help from the Interior Department and civilian re-enacters—not the Army.

10. If the military appears in a science fiction film, courtesy of one of the U.S. services, or is portrayed by actors and extras, we include the title. Discussing a request for cooperation on the 1986 **Invaders from Mars**, the director of the Marine Corps Public Affairs Office in Los Angeles stated that Leathernecks had no problem killing Martians. Likewise, the services have been willing to cooperate on science fiction films portraying all manner of fanciful enemies— from giant ants, to mutant grasshoppers, to space travelers. Hollywood has usually ignored the likelihood that the same superior intelligence and technology that enabled aliens to reach the earth would also allow them to easily defeat humans, if they came intent on conquest.

In any event, the Air Force usually would not help on stories portraying flying saucers, since the service has denied the existence of flying saucers for more than 50 years. Likewise, the Navy de-nied assistance to **The Philadelphia Experiment**, since the service had said for years that no time travel experiment had ever taken place in the Philadelphia Navy Yard (as writers had claimed). In contrast, the Navy provided full cooperation on **Final Countdown**, since the service saw the film for what it was, a pure fantasy as well as a sales pitch for additional aircraft carriers.

11. In selecting titles for inclusion in "Documentaries," we have excluded newsreels whose only purpose was to inform their audiences of specific, current events. Nor have we listed training films of the sort that Ronald Reagan narrated during World War II, as they were in-tended only to educate servicemen during basic training. As a general rule, we have avoided "short" documentaries of less than 20 minutes, the sort that often were shown in schools. At the same time, we have included **Battle of Santiago Bay** as representative of the earliest non-fiction films, even though early documentaries were usually only a few minutes in duration. We also included the Marine film **Bombs Over Tokyo** since it told a story and was intended to inform its audience, Congress.

A few words about how we identified the armed forces. Until the 1947 unification of the services into the Department of Defense, the U.S. military was divided into the War Department, the official name of the Army, and the Navy Department, which included the Marine Corps as a subordinate branch. Whatever the time frame, we use the term "Army" when discussing the nation's ground forces. The Air Force began as the Army Air Corps, a subordinate branch of the Army. In 1941 it was designated as the Army Air Force and became the Air Force after unification. For simplicity, we have used the term "Air Force" when discussing any movie portraying the nation's principle air power and air logistics force, whatever the year. Until unification, the Navy Department included the surface, undersea, and aviation branches, with the Marine Corps functioning as a subordinate service. While the Marines nominally remain under the auspices of the Secretary of the Navy, since 1947 the Corps has functioned as an independent service. However, we have treated the Marines as a separate entity from the beginning of its relationship with the film industry during WWI. Finally, since unification, we have used the terms "the armed services," the "Pentagon," "DoD," and "the military" interchangeably.

The authors acknowledge they have not seen all of the 1,300 plus movies included in the guide. Many of the early fiims no longer exist, and the total number of films that fall into the scope of the study made it impossible to screen more than a few of the ones that the authors had not seen previously. Nevertheless, we have read about each film listed in two or more sources cited in the bibliography. In particular, we have utilized the collected reviews in *Weekly Variety* and the *New York Times* as well as the narratives in the *American Film Institute Catalogue* (AFI catalogue). In addition, we have cross-checked our information on the Internet Movie Data Base and on other Internet tools, including Yahoo and Google. Where a conflict existed, we have regularly relied on the *Weekly Variety* review information, since the industry's bible usually did the first review of a film (before the studio decided to cut its length for one reason or another). If needed, we used the AFI catalogue as the final arbitrator.

The authors decided early on not to indicate whether a movie was available on video or DVD. Most early films have still not made it to the marketplace, but most recent films have. At the same time, more titles are regularly being resurrected from studio film vaults. Consequently, we decided that readers wanting to know the availability of a particular movie can check to see if it is listed as available on IMDB or directly from Amazon, Borders, or Barnes and Noble.

On the other hand, we have indicated which movies author Suid discussed in depth in *Guts & Glory* [G&G] or *Sailing on the Silver Screen* [SSS]. Both books are narrative histories, the former of the relationship between the film industry and the military and the latter of that between Hollywood and the Navy. In each, he focused on the most significant films, explaining how and why they were produced, with or without military assistance, in contrast to this filmography of all movies portraying the military.

Ideally, we have created the definitive filmography of military movies. As realists, we recognize that we may have missed a film or two in our widely flung nets, and we would like to receive comments, corrections, and suggestions. Contact us at www.lawrencesuid.com.

Key to Abbreviations

Because of space limitations, we have used abbreviations for historical period/type of film, military and other government organizations, types of cooperation provided by the military, film companies, and television networks, and reviewing publications and additional sources. Reviews that appeared on or after January 1, 2000, are shown, for example, as 01/01/2000, while an earlier review for the same film could be shown as 12/31/99. The earliest reviews we discovered were in the second decade of the twentieth century.

Abbreviation	Historical Period/Type of Film
Bosnia	Balkan wars, 1990s
Civil War	American Civil War, 1861–1865
Cold War	1943–1989
Gulf Wars	1991–present
Korea	Korean War, 1950–1953
Mexican Border	1914–1917, Pancho Villa vs. the U.S. Army
Peace	U.S. armed forces not engaged in combat
Preparedness	1938–1941
Revolutionary	1775–1783
SciFi	Science fiction
Somalia	1992–1993
SpAmer	Spanish–American War
Terrorists	Ongoing
Vietnam	1962–1975
WWI	World War I, U.S. participation, 1917–1919
WWII	World War II, 1941–1945

Abbreviation	Military Organizations
Air Force	Includes Army Air Corps and Army Air Force
Army	U.S. Infantry and includes the War Department
Coast Guard	While currently a part of the Department of Homeland Security, the service has a defense role in support to its sister, armed services
Marines	Considered a separate entity although the Corps remains a part of the Navy Department; includes aviation arm

Navy	Includes the air arm, the surface fleet, and submarines as well as the SEALS
NG	National Guard (Army and/or Air Force)

Abbreviation	**Types of DoD Cooperation**
Cour	Courtesy
Deny	Requested but could not be granted
Full	Requested and granted
Inform	Provided information but cooperation could not be granted
Ltd	Limited cooperation granted
NR	Not required and/or not requested
Unkn	Unknown; do not know type of cooperation or if requested

Abbreviation	**Government Entities**
DoD	Department of Defense
OWI	Office of War Information (during WWII)
USIA	United States Information Agency

Abbreviation	**Cast and Crew**
DIR	Director(s)
PRO	Producer(s); does not include executive or assistant producers. When a name is shown in brackets, for example, [William Jacobs], the producer's name is not credited on the film but is shown as the producer in the American Film Institute's catalog or other source.
SW	Includes screenwriter, titles (for silent films), adaptation, scenario (for silent films), etc.
STARS:	Usually those individuals who receive the leading roles, although we have also included individuals who later became "stars" or were once "stars."

Abbreviation	**Company**
Action Intl	Action International
Amer-Intl	American International
Artisan Enter	Artisan Entertainment
Avco	Avco Embassy
BxOfIntl	Boxoffice International Pictures
Brtsh Natl	British National Film
Cin	Cinerama Releasing Corp.
Cine-Fund	Cinequity Funding Corporation
Crown	Crown International Pictures
Excel Enter	Excel Entertainment
FBO	Film Booking Office of America, later merged with RKO
Film Ventures	Film Ventures International
First Natl	First National
FPL	Famous Players Lasky
Fox	Twentieth Century Fox and its predecessors
Goldwyn	Samuel Goldwyn Company/Films

Green Dolphin	Green Dolphin Productions
Hemis Flm	Hemisphere Films
Lubin	Lubin Manufacturing Company
MGM	Metro-Goldwyn-Mayer
New Era–Natl Pic	New Era–National Pictures Co.
New World	New World Pictures
PRC	Producers Releasing Corp.
Quantum Enter	Quantum Entertainment
Renaissance Pic	Renaissance Pictures
Reyn Pict Inc	Reynolds Pictures Incorporated
Roach	Hal Roach Studios
UA	United Artists
Vitagraph	Vitagraph Picture Company of America
WB	Warner Brothers
White Line Pro	White Line Productions
World Enter	World Entertainment

Abbreviation	Television, including cable, network
A&E	Arts and Entertainment Network
ABC	American Broadcasting Company
CBS	Columbia Broadcasting System
Discv	Discovery Channel
Disney	The Disney Channel (cable)
HBO	Home Box Office (cable)
History	History Channel (cable)
NBC	National Broadcasting Company
PBS	Public Broadcasting System
SFN	Science Fiction Network
Showt	Showtime
TNT	Turner Network Television
USA	USA Network

Abbreviation	Reviewing Publication/Additional Source
DNR	Did not review
DV	*Daily Variety*
DVP	website of *Daily Variety*; date is the date "posted" to the website
G&G	*Guts & Glory, The Making of the American Military Image* by Lawrence H. Suid
NYT	*New York Times*
SSS	*Sailing on the Silver Screen* by Lawrence H. Suid
VTR	*Variety Television Reviews*
WP	*Washington Post*
WV	*Weekly Variety*
Unkn	Unknown information

Feature Films

About Face (1942)

Peace	Army	NR	B&W	43 mins
UA	WV: 04-15-42		NYT: DNR	

DIR: Kurt Neumann. SW: Eugene Conrad, Edward E. Seabrook. PRO: Hal Roach, Fred Guiol. STARS: William Tracy, Joe Sawyer, Jean Porter.

Historical events caught up with this short comedy, which had gone into production before Pearl Harbor. It depicts two Army sergeants getting into juvenile scrapes, one of which occurs at an Army/Navy dance.

Above and Beyond (1952) [G&G]

WWII	Air Force	Full	B&W	122 mins
MGM	WV: 11-19-52		NYT: 01-31-53	

DIR: Melvin Frank, Norman Panama. SW: Melvin Frank, Norman Panama, Beirne Lay Jr. PRO: Melvin Frank, Norman Panama. STARS: Robert Taylor, James Whitmore, Jim Backus, Eleanor Parker.

This docudrama portrays Paul Tibbets, who commanded the 509th Composite Group, which dropped the two atomic bombs on Japan. Based on Lay's magazine article, the film becomes part history and part domestic soap opera as Tibbets's wife complains bitterly about his refusal to confide to her his secret assignment. The filmmakers somewhat fictionalized the account of how Tibbets received his assignment because of the flier's ongoing feud with a top Air Force general.

The training sequences capture the reality of the long hours practicing maneuvers and bombing techniques for an operation about which only Tibbets knew. However, the cinematic mission lacks historical accuracy. The movie B-29 has turrets, the name is painted on the wrong side of the fuselage, and it takes off in daylight. In fact, the *Enola Gay*'s turrets were removed to give it more speed, it had its name on the left side, and it took off at 2:00 A.M., leaving from a brightly lit tarmac.

In any case, the *Enola Gay* and Tibbets successfully complete their mission with the nuclear destruction of Hiroshima and the pilot returns to the United States, where his now-understanding wife
greets him. Nevertheless, the flier's place in history outlasted his marriage.

Above the Clouds (1934)

Peace	Navy	Full	B&W	68 mins
Columbia	WV: 01-09-34		NYT: DNR	

DIR: Roy William Neill. SW: Albert de Mond. PRO: Columbia Pictures. STARS: Robert Armstrong, Richard Cromwell, Dorothy Wilson.

A poorly done story of an early newsreel cameraman who films the crash of a dirigible and wins
the girl. The Navy provided airplanes and a dirigible.

Abroad with Two Yanks (1944)

WWII	Marine	NR	B&W	80 mins
UA	WV: 07-26-44		NYT: 10-26-44	

DIR: Allan Dwan. SW: Edward Seabrook, Tedwell Chapman. PRO: Edward Small. STARS: William
Bendix, Helen Walker, Dennis O'Keefe, John Abbott.

A trite, low-budget comedy in which two Marines in Australia pursue the same girl.

The Abyss (1989)

SciFi	Navy	NR	Color	146 mins
Fox	WV: 08-09-89		NYT: 08-09-89	

DIR: James Cameron. SW: James Cameron. PRO: Gale Anne Hurd. STARS: Ed Harris, Mary Elizabeth Mastrantonio, Michael Biehn, Leo Burmester, Todd Graff.

A U.S. nuclear submarine sinks, apparently the result of an encounter with an unidentified object.
Thinking the Soviets may be responsible, the Navy turns to a nearby underwater oil well platform
drilling team for help in locating the wreck and recovering the nuclear missiles before the Russians do. A SEAL team joins the search, and friction develops between the military men and the
civilians, which is compounded when it becomes clear that there is something inexplicable in the
abyss.

Ace of Aces (1933)

WWI	Air Force	Full	B&W	76 mins
RKO	WV: 11-14-33		NYT: 11-11-33	

DIR: J. Walter Ruben. SW: John Monk Saunders, H. W. Haneman. PRO: Sam Jaffe. STARS: Richard
Dix, Elizabeth Allan, Ralph Bellamy.

An unoriginal WWI portrayal of aerial combat. Dix is a sculptor whose girlfriend shames him into enlisting in the Air Corps by calling him a coward. He becomes a wanton killer in the skies, and the transformation shocks the girl.

Across the Pacific (1942)

WWII	Army	NR	B&W	97 mins
WB	WV: 08-19-42		NYT: 09-05-42	

DIR: John Huston. SW: Richard Macaulay. PRO: Jerry Wald. STARS: Humphrey Bogart, Mary Astor, Sydney Greenstreet, Charles Halton.

Based on Robert Carson's serial "Aloha Means Goodbye," the feature became, along with *Men Without Women*, one of the most mistitled films—Bogart never gets past the Panama Canal Zone. Court-martialed for being a traitor, he is actually an Army counterintelligence officer on the trail of Japanese agents trying to blow up the Panama Canal shortly before Pearl Harbor. He naturally foils the plot and wins the girl.

Action in the North Atlantic (1943) [SSS]

WWII	Navy	Full	B&W	127 mins
WB	WV: 05-19-43		NYT: 05-22-43	

DIR: Lloyd Bacon. SW: John Howard. PRO: Jerry Wald. STARS: Humphrey Bogart, Raymond Massey, Alan Hale, Julie Bishop.

Bogart, serving in the Merchant Marines on the highly dangerous Mirmansk run, takes over command when the ship's captain is wounded in a fight with a U-boat. The Navy assisted by providing gunners aboard the merchant ships.

Adventures in Iraq (1943)

WWII	Air Force	Cour	B&W	64 mins
WB	WV: 09-22-43		NYT: DNR	

DIR: D. Ross Lederman. SW: George R. Bilson, Robert E. Kent. PRO: Warner Bros. STARS: John Loder, Ruth Ford, Warren Douglas, Paul Cavanagh.

A former Flying Tiger pilot and his two passengers become prisoners of a sheik following their crash landing in the desert. The film features stock footage of American planes coming to the rescue. William Jacobs was the uncredited producer.

Aerial Gunner (1943)

WWII	Air Force	Full	B&W	78 mins
Paramount	WV: 03-24-43		NYT: 06-26-43	

DIR: William Pine. SW: Maxwell Shane. PRO: William Pine, William Thomas. STARS: Richard Arlen, Chester Morris, Lita Ward, Jimmy Lydon.

The Air Force provided assistance at its aerial gunner school, and the film portrays in great detail the training of bomber gunners. The story is a typical melodrama in which two men, enemies in civilian life, become friends during training and pursue the same girl. After graduating, the men are sent to the South Pacific and during a bombing raid against a Japanese base, crash land on an enemy island. One man sacrifices his life so that his friend and plane can return to friendly territory.

Air Cadet (1951)

Korea	Air Force	Full	B&W	93 mins
Universal	WV: 02-21-51		NYT: 05-11-51	

DIR: Joseph Pevney. SW: Robert L. Richards, Joseph Hoffman, Robert W. Soderberg. PRO: Aaron Rosenberg. STARS: Stephen McNally, Alex Nicol, Richard Long, Rock Hudson.

A routine story of flight training, this time in jet fighters. Some men live and some die in this unexceptional melodrama. Pevney filmed the exteriors at Randolph Field in Texas and Williams Field in Arizona.

Air Devils (1938)

Peace	Marines	Full	B&W	70 mins
Universal	WV: 05-11-38		NYT: DNR	

DIR: John Rawlins. SW: Harold Buckley, George Waggner. PRO: Trem Carr. STARS: Larry Blake, Dick Purcell.

A class "C" potboiler featuring Marines in the air and on the land in the South Pacific.

Air Force (1943) [G&G]

WWII	Air Force, Marines	Full	B&W	124 mins
WB	WV: 02-03-43		NYT: 02-04-43	

DIR: Howard Hawks. SW: Dudley Nichols. PRO: Hal Wallis. STARS: John Garfield, Gig Young, Harry Carey, Arthur Kennedy.

A war effort story that showed how the Army Air Corps was winning World War II. It begins with the re-creation of the historical flight of B-17s from San Francisco to Hawaii on the evening of December 6 and follows the B-17 bomber the *Mary Ann*, the film's real star, through the early days of the war. In the climactic battle, the plane leads the slaughter of the entire Japanese fleet by the Air Force. Marines appear in the sequence when the *Mary Ann* lands briefly on Wake Island, where the beleaguered Leathernecks are trying to hold off the Japanese onslaught. The film remains one of the very best movies about how Americans have fought the nation's enemies in the air.

Air Force One (1997)

Terrorism	Air Force	Full	Color	125 mins
Sony	WV: 07-21-97		NYT: 07-25-97	

DIR: Wolfgang Petersen. SW: Andrew Marlowe. PRO: Wolfgang Petersen, Gail Katz. STARS: Harrison Ford, Glenn Close, Gary Oldman, William H. Macy, Dean Stockwell.

Russian terrorists seize Air Force One, forcing Ford, as the president, to wage a one-man war to save his plane and his family. The Air Force provided a rescue aircraft with special forces, who tether their plane to Air Force One, creating an escape route for the president and his family.

Air Strike (1955)

Korea	Navy	Full	B&W	63 mins
Lippert	WV: 7-13-55		NYT: DNR	

DIR: Cy Roth. SW: Cy Roth. PRO: Cy Roth. STARS: Stanley Clements, Richard Denning, James Courtney, Don Haggerty.

A minor imitation of such films as **Wing and a Prayer** and **Twelve O'Clock High** in which a commander tries to weld together a flying unit, this time a jet plane squadron aboard the USS *Essex*, off the Korean coast.

Airplane! (1980)

WWII	Navy, Army	NR	Color	88 mins
Paramount	WV: 07-02-80		NYT: 07-02-80	

DIR: Jim Abrahams, David Zucker, Jerry Zucker. SW: Jim Abrahams, David Zucker, Jerry Zucker. PRO: Jon Davison, Howard W. Koch. STARS: Robert Hays, Julie Hagerty, Lloyd Bridges, Leslie Nielsen, Robert Stack, Peter Graves, Kareem Abdul-Jabbar.

This is an over-the-top satire of Hollywood's many disaster airplane movies as well as being one of the funniest films ever made. Why include it? Hays has become paralyzed by his perceived failure as an Navy aviator in World War II (or was it Korea?) with the loss of his men briefly portrayed through grainy combat footage. Suffering from post-traumatic stress syndrome, Hays ends up in an Army hospital comforted by Hagerty. In fact, a Navy pilot would no more end up in another service's medical facility than Ben Affleck and Josh Hartnett would have taken physicals in a Navy hospital in Pearl Harbor. At least here, the implausibility was probably intended, as was the reality that Hays was too young to have fought in either war, but who cares?

Airport '75 (1974)

Peace	Air Force	Full	Color	106 mins
Universal	WV: 10-16-74		NYT: 10-19-74	

DIR: Jack Smight. SW: Don Ingalls. PRO: William Frye. STARS: Charlton Heston, Karen Black, George Kennedy, Gloria Swanson, Dana Andrews.

After verifying that an Air Force helicopter could match the speed of a 747, the service provided a helicopter to portray Heston coming to rescue a 747, whose pilots had been killed in a collision with a private plane.

Airport '77 (1977)

Peace	Navy	Full	Color	113 mins
Universal	WV: 03-23-77		NYT: 03-26-77	

DIR: Jerry Jameson. SW: Michael Scheff, David Spector. PRO: William Frye. STARS: Jack Lemmon, George Kennedy, James Stewart, Joseph Cotton.

The Navy provided divers and equipment to portray the rescue of passengers from a private 747 that had crashed into the sea. The service believed the assistance informed audiences of its undersea rescue ability.

All Hands on Deck (1961)

WWII	Navy	Full	Color	98 mins
Fox	WV: 04-05-61		NYT: 04-01-61	

DIR: Norman Taurog. SW: Donald Morris, Jay Sommers. PRO: Oscar Brodney. STARS: Pat Boone, Buddy Hackett, Dennis O'Keefe.

A lightweight comedy set aboard a landing ship transport (LST) that the Navy provided at a dock in San Diego, California.

All the Young Men (1960)

Korea	Marines	Full	B&W	87 mins
Columbia	WV: 08-03-60		NYT: 08-27-60	

DIR: Hall Bartlett. SW: Hall Bartlett. PRO: Hall Bartlett. STARS: Alan Ladd, Sidney Poitier, James Darren, Mort Sahl.

A cliché-ridden story of Marines fighting in Korea. Dying commander of ambushed unit gives the command to Poitier, who has to win over bigots in order to save his men.

Amazing Grace and Chuck (1987)

Cold War	Air Force	Deny	Color	115 mins .
Tri-Star	WV: 04-01-87		NYT: 05-22-87	

DIR: Mike Newell. SW: David Field. PRO: David Field. STARS: Jamie Lee Curtis, Alex English, Gregory Peck, William Petersen.

Chuck, a Montana Little Leaguer, visits a Minuteman 3 Silo and the horror of its warhead causes him to refuse to pitch in an important game. His protest brings him national attention and support from Amazing Grace, a Boston Celtic basketball player, and other athletes. Ultimately, the president shows up to hear Chuck's advice on a disarmament treaty. The Air Force wanted nothing to do with a story that "does not accurately portray U.S. efforts to maintain nuclear deterrence, to seek arms reductions, and to keep the peace."

Ambush Bay (1966)

WWII	Marines	Full	Color	109 mins
UA	WV: 08-31-66		NYT: 09-15-66	

DIR: Ron Winston. SW: Marve Feinberg, Ib Melchior. PRO: Hal Klein. STARS: Hugh O'Brian, Mickey Rooney, James Mitchum, Harry Lauter.

A nine-man Marine patrol on a Japanese-held island tries to rescue a spy with important information. Eight of the men die.

America (1924)

Revolutionary	Army	Full	B&W	93 mins
UA	WV: 02-28-24		NYT: 02-22-24	

DIR: D. W. Griffith. SW: Robert W. Chambers, John L. E. Pell. PRO: D. W. Griffith. STARS: Lionel Barrymore, Neil Hamilton, Frank McGlynn Jr., Frank Walsh.

Griffith's American revolutionary story that attempted to duplicate his success with *Birth of a Nation*. The director received assistance from the U.S. Army cavalry, enabling him to create realistic battle scenes. The Army believed the cooperation would allow its officers to better study the Revolutionary War battles.

The American Consul (1917)

Peace	Marines	Ltd	B&W	5 reels
Paramount	WV: 02-16-17		NYT: DNR	

DIR: Rollin S. Sturgeon. SW: Thomas J. Geraghty, Harvey F. Thew. PRO: Jesse Lasky. STARS: Theodore Roberts, Ernest Joy, Maude Fealy, Charles West.

Peacetime Marines rescue the American consul and his daughter from an unnamed Central American nation.

American Guerrilla in the Philippines (1950)

WWII	Navy	Ltd	Color	105 mins
Fox	WV: 11-08-50		NYT: 11-08-50	

DIR: Fritz Lang. SW: Lamar Trotti. PRO: Lamar Trotti. STARS: Tyrone Power, Tom Ewell, Bob Patten, Tommy Cook.

Based on Ira Wolfert's novel of the same name, the film tells the story of a survivor of PT-boat Squadron 3, which wages a one-man war against the Japanese until the return of General MacArthur. The Navy provided a destroyer and other equipment to help re-create the American return.

The American President (1995)

Peace	Marines	Ltd	Color	115 mins
Castle Rock	WV: 11-06-95		NYT: 11-17-95	

DIR: Rob Reiner. SW: Aaron Sorkin. PRO: Rob Reiner. STARS: Michael Douglas, Martin Sheen, Annette Bening, Michael J. Fox.

The Marine band appears as background in a story about the president of the United States, who falls in love with a lobbyist.

The Americanization of Emily (1964) [G&G]

WWII	Navy	NR	B&W	117 mins
MGM	WV: 10-28-64		NYT: 10-28-64	

DIR: Arthur Hiller. SW: Paddy Chayefsky. PRO: Martin Ransohoff. STARS: James Garner, Melvyn Douglas, Julie Andrews, James Coburn.

Loosely based on a William Bradford Huie novel, the film tells the story of Andrews, an English widow, who first scorns and then falls in love with Garner, a dashing Navy officer, whose greatest appeal is his cowardice. Andrews believes his antiwar sentiments will keep him out of harm's way, but when he is mistakenly hailed as a hero, she insists he not tell the truth about how he was wounded on Omaha Beach and so go to prison. Her change in philosophy and thus her American-ization happens so rapidly, audiences may miss the film's sudden change in philosophy. Knowing the Navy would want nothing to do with a film portraying one of its men as a coward, the producer did not even submit a script to the service.

Anchors Aweigh (1945)

WWII	Navy	Ltd	Color	140 mins
MGM	WV: 07-18-45		NYT: 07-20-45	

DIR: George Sidney. SW: Isobel Lennart. PRO: Joseph Pasternak. STARS: Frank Sinatra, Gene Kelly, Kathryn Grayson, Dean Stockwell.

A typical wartime service musical, designed simply to entertain. Navy ships provided atmospheric background.

The Andromeda Strain (1971)

SciFi	Air Force/Army	NR	Color	130 mins
Universal	WV:03-10-71		NYT:03-22-71	

DIR: Robert Wise. SW: Nelson Gidding. PRO: Robert Wise. STARS: Arthur Hill, David Wayne, James Olson, Kate Reid.

Based on Michael Crichton's novel, the film opens with an acknowledgment of assistance from Vandenburg Air Force Base. Not really, given the story in which the military supports a project to create a biological weapon from material that an orbiting Army satellite collects. The deadly strain of virus, which returns to earth courtesy of the service, proves to be more complicated than antici-pated and the plans to contain it do not work. The scientists who devised the program ultimately find the solution, but barely in time. The military comes across as ineffectual and the government as the ultimate villain for approving the effort to produce a weapon of mass destruction.

Annapolis (2005)

Peace	Navy	Inform/Deny	Color	Unkn
Buena Vista	WV:		NYT:	

DIR: Justin Lin. SW: David Collard. PRO: Damien Saccani, Mark Vahradian. STARS: James Franco, Jordana Brewster, Donnie Wahlberg, Vicellous Reon Shannon.

An Officer and a Gentleman meets *Rocky* and every Naval Academy movie made during the 1920s and 1930s. The resulting story focused on a young man from the wrong side of the tracks whose dream of attending Annapolis came true, but with unexpected results. The Navy met with the filmmakers after receiving an initial script containing a plethora of factual and procedural errors. The second script was even worse and the Navy denied a request for assistance. Buena Vista then abandoned plans to shoot at the Naval Academy despite the authenticity that the campus would have provided. They instead filmed the story in Philadelphia because of the tax incentives that Pennsylvania offered.

Annapolis (1928–AFI Catalogue)

Peace	Navy	Full	B&W	63 mins
Pathé	WV: 02-06-29		NYT: DNR	

DIR: Christy Cabanne. SW: Royal Pease, F. McGrew Willis. PRO: F. McGrew Willis. STARS: John Mack Brown, Hugh Allan, Jeanette Loff, Maurice Ryan.

A story of Academy life in which two midshipmen pursue the same girl. The campus background and Navy assistance cannot overcome a poor script.

Annapolis Farewell (1935)

Peace	Navy	Full	B&W	75 mins
Paramount	WV: 08-28-35		NYT: 08-24-35	

DIR: Alexander Hall. SW: Dale Van Every, Frank Craven. PRO: Louis Lighton. STARS: Guy Standing, Rosalind Keith, Tom Brown, Richard Cromwell.

Based on the short story "Target," the film follows two midshipmen pursuing the same girl, with the usual complications. A retired commodore living on campus complains about the current state of the Navy and reminisces about the Battle of Manila Bay, when he served as commander of a battleship. Ultimately, the old man dies aboard his old ship when the Navy uses it for target practice. He is eulogized for not giving up the ship.

Annapolis Salute (1937)

Peace	Navy	Full	B&W	65 mins
RKO	WV: 10-06-37		NYT: 10-02-37	

DIR: Christy Cabanne. SW: John Twist. PRO: Robert Sisk. STARS: James Ellison, Marsha Hunt, Harry Carey, Van Heflin.

A weak portrayal of everyday life at Annapolis, owing its images to the Navy, which allowed the filmmakers access to the Academy.

An Annapolis Story (1955)

Korea	Navy	Full	Color	81 mins
Allied Artists	WV: 03-23-55		NYT: 04-09-55	

DIR: Don Siegel. SW: Daniel Ullman, Geoffrey Homes. PRO: Walter Mirisch. STARS: John Derek, Kevin McCarthy, Pat Conway, Alvy Moore.

Hollywood returned to the Academy for the first time since World War II, albeit only briefly with a second unit to film background shots. Given the story, the Navy insisted that "The" in the original title be changed to "An." While the movie has the mandatory love triangle, this time with two brothers pursuing the girl, the focus is on aerial operations off an aircraft carrier during the Korean War.

Antwone Fisher (2002)

Peace	Navy	Ltd	Color	120 mins
Fox	WV: 09-23-2002		NYT: 12-19, 22 & 29-2002	

DIR: Denzel Washington. SW: Antwone Fisher. PRO: Todd Black, Denzel Washington, Randa Haines. STARS: Denzel Washington, Derek Luke, Joy Bryant, Salli Richardson.

Based on Fisher's life and his autobiography *Finding Fish*, the story follows a young black man's journey from early abuse, to lashing out as a Navy enlisted man, to maturity with the help of Washington as a Navy psychiatrist. The service provided the San Diego naval base as background for the military scenes.

Anybody's War (1930)

WWI	Army	Unkn	B&W	90 mins
Paramount	WV: 07-16-30		NYT: 07-11-30	

DIR: Richard Wallace. SW: Lloyd Corrigan. PRO: Paramount. STARS: George Moran, Charles Mack, Joan Peers, Neil Hamilton.

Based on the novel *The Two Black Crows in the A. E. F.*, Moran and Mack, in black face, end up in the Army in France, where they rescue a buddy trapped behind German lines. The film offends everyone without being funny.

Anzio (1968)

WWII	Army	Full	B&W	117 mins
Columbia	WV: 06-19-68		NYT: 07-25-68	

DIR: Edward Dmytryk. SW: Harry Craig. PRO: Dino De Laurentis. STARS: Robert Mitchum, Peter Falk, Arthur Kennedy, Robert Ryan.

Based on the W. Vaughan-Thomas novel, the film follows a small patrol caught up in the fiasco that followed the American landing at Anzio in 1944. Because the story paid no attention to the actual landings 55 miles north of the German lines, it became a generic war movie.

Apocalypse Now (1979) [G&G]

Vietnam	Army	Deny	Color	153 mins
UA	WV: 05-16-79		NYT: 08-15-79	

DIR: Francis Ford Coppola. SW: John Milius, Francis Ford Coppola. PRO: Francis Ford Coppola. STARS: Martin Sheen, Marlon Brando, Robert Duvall, Dennis Hopper.

Loosely based on Joseph Conrad's *Heart of Darkness*, Coppola's film became the Vietnam movie against which all others have been measured. In fact, it is a surrealistic morass that contains everything horrible, real and imagined, about the war in Southeast Asia. The Army refused to assist the director despite his visit to the Pentagon in 1975 with an unfinished script for which he could never create a satisfactory ending. At the heart of the service's problem with the story was the springboard: the Army and the CIA order one officer to terminate another officer, something the military said would never happen.

The film does contain some brilliant filmmaking, most particularly the helicopter assault on a Vietnam village. However, Sheen's dialogue with Brando about the meaning of life and of war makes little if any sense. Nevertheless, some veterans maintain that of all the Vietnam films, Coppola's best evokes their memories of their experiences in the war. Others, however, dismiss it as a surrealistic nightmare.

Probably the best critique of **Apocalypse Now** came from *Saturday Night Live* the week the film opened. Sheen, this time a studio executive, is ordered to go up the river to terminate Coppola's production, which was over budget and over time. When the director says he still does not have his ending, Sheen informs him that B-52s will be arriving in 30 seconds to bomb the set. The director responds, "My ending, one of my endings."

Apocalypse Now Redux (2001)

Vietnam	Army	Deny	Color	203 mins
UA	WV: 05-14-01		NYT: 05-13-01	

DIR: Francis Ford Coppola. SW: John Milius, Francis Ford Coppola. PRO: Francis Ford Coppola. STARS: Martin Sheen, Marlon Brando, Robert Duvall, Dennis Hopper.

The 50 additional minutes do not make the expanded version any more satisfactory or provide any better understanding of the American experience in Vietnam. This time around, Sheen and Brando launch into a much longer climactic dialogue about something or other, before Sheen finally butchers Brando.

Apollo 13 (1995)

Peace	Navy, Air Force	Full	Color	139 mins
Universal	WV: 06-26-95		NYT: 06-30-95	

DIR: Ron Howard. SW: William Broyles Jr., Al Reinert. PRO: Brian Grazer. STARS: Tom Hanks, Bill Paxton, Kevin Bacon, Ed Harris.

Based on J. Lovell and J. Kluger's *Lost Moon*. The Navy provided an aircraft carrier to replicate the ocean landing of the ill-fated *Apollo 13*.

Armageddon (1998)

Peace	Air Force	Ltd	Color	144 mins
Touchstone	WV: 06-29-98		NYT: 07-01-98	

DIR: Michael Bay. SW: Jonathan Hensleigh, J. J. Abrams. PRO: Jerry Bruckheimer. STARS: Bruce Willis, Ben Affleck.

The Air Force provided limited assistance, with its men doing their normal jobs in face of impending disaster from outer space.

Armored Command (1961)

WWII	Army		Full	B&W		99 mins
Allied Artists	WV: 08-08-61			NYT: 10-07-61		

DIR: Byron Haskin. SW: R. W. Alcorn. PRO: R. W. Alcorn. STARS: Howard Keel, Tina Louise, Burt Reynolds, Warner Anderson.

An Army unit becomes trapped in a town during a German counterattack. Louise plays a German spy who provides the German army with military information until Keel exposes her.

Army Girl (1938)

Preparedness	Army		Unkn	B&W		90 mins
Republic	WV: 07-20-38			NYT: 08-12-38		

DIR: George Nicholls Jr. SW: Barry Trivers, Samuel Ornitz. PRO: Sol C. Siegel. STARS: Madge Evans, Preston Foster, James Gleason.

Film could be subtitled, "Here come the tanks," since the story focuses on the Army's replacement of horses by light tanks. A contest between tanks and horses over a planned course provides most of the action, along with a love story subplot featuring the commanding officer's daughter.

Army Surgeon (1942)

WWI	Army		Ltd	B&W		63 mins
RKO	WV: 11-11-42			NYT: 11-05-42		

DIR: A. Edward Sutherland. SW: Everett Lavery, Barry Trivers. PRO: Bert Gilroy. STARS: James Ellison, Jane Wyatt, Kent Taylor.

Based on an original story about a doctor and his love for a nurse, the film lacks any socially or artistically redeeming features or insights into medicine at the front.

Atlantic Convoy (1942)

WWII	Marines, Navy		Ltd	B&W		66 mins
Columbia	WV: 07-08-42			NYT: 07-06-42		

DIR: Lew Landers. SW: Robert Lee Johnson. PRO: Colbert Clark. STARS: Bruce Bennett, Virginia Field, John Beal.

Low-budget story of Marine flying patrols from Iceland, guarding the shipping lanes in the early days of WWII—with a required love interest and German spies.

Atomic Submarine (1960)

SciFi	Navy	NR	B&W	72 mins
Allied Artists	WV: 02-17-60		NYT: 04-20-60	

DIR: Spencer Bennet. SW: Orville Hampton. PRO: Alex Gordon. STARS: Arthur Franz, Dick Foran, Tom Conway, Brett Halsey.

A bland science fiction story of a U.S. submarine looking for an alien flying saucer under the North Pole. The use of newsreel footage of an American nuclear submarine provides the only authenticity.

Attack (1956) [G&G]

WWII	Army	Deny	B&W	107 mins
UA	WV: 09-12-56		NYT: 09-20-56	

DIR: Robert Aldrich. SW: James Poe. PRO: Robert Aldrich. STARS: Jack Palance, Eddie Albert, Lee Marvin.

A cowardly officer leads a unit in the Battle of the Bulge. The Army refused to cooperate because an enlisted man ultimately kills the officer. The film was the first major production since the unification of the services into the DoD in 1947 to be denied cooperation.

At War with the Army (1950)

Peace	Army	Full	B&W	93 mins
Paramount	WV: 12-13-50		NYT: 01-25-51	

DIR: Hal Walker. SW: Fred Finklehoffe. PRO: Fred Finklehoffe, Abner Greshler. STARS: Dean Martin, Jerry Lewis, Polly Bergen, Angela Greene.

Based on the Broadway play, the film contained the first screen appearance of the comic duo who find themselves in the Army. Despite the absurd situations, the service cooperated because, like all military comedies, it suggested that young men would see life in the Army as a fun experience and enlist.

Away All Boats (1956)

WWII	Navy, Marines	Full	Color	114 mins
Universal	WV: 05-16-56		NYT: 08-17-56	

DIR: Joseph Pevney. SW: Ted Sherdeman. PRO: Howard Christie. STARS: Jeff Chandler, George Nader, Richard Boone, David Janssen.

Based on Kenneth Dodson's novel, the film explores the logistics side of the war in the Pacific as Chandler tries to provide discipline and motivation for his crew during the landings on Japanese-held islands. The Marines appear as themselves during assault sequences.

Baby Blue Marine (1976)

WWII	Marines	Full/Deny	Color	90 mins
Columbia	WV: 04-28-76		NYT: 05-06-76	

DIR: John Hancock. SW: Stanford Whitmore. PRO: Aaron Spelling, Leonard Goldberg. STARS: Jan-Michael Vincent, Richard Gere, Glynnis O'Connor, Katherine Helmond.

The story of a Marine recruit who washes out of boot camp during WWII and later acquires the uniform of a Marine raider while hitchhiking home to Missouri. Along the way, he impresses the people he encounters. In a small California town, he meets a girl and becomes a hero. The Marines initially permitted filming at the San Diego Recruit Depot but withdrew assistance when the actor playing a drill sergeant refused to cut his hair.

Back at the Front (1952)

Peace	Army	Ltd	B&W	87 mins
Universal	WV: 10-01-52		NYT: DNR	

DIR: George Sherman. SW: Lou Breslow, Don McGuire, Oscar Brodney. PRO: Leonard Goldstein. STARS: Tom Ewell, Harvey Lembeck, Mari Blanchard, Barry Kelley.

Also known as *Willie and Joe Back at the Front*, the film featured Bill Maudlin's characters. Called back to active duty, the Army sends Willie and Joe to Japan, where they test new equipment, accidentally become involved with weapons smugglers, and somehow turn into heroes, only to be reassigned to the states to save friendly relations with Japan.

Back Door to Hell (1964)

WWII	Army	NR	B&W	75 mins
Lippert	WV: DNR		NYT: DNR	

DIR: Monte Hellman. SW: Richard Guttman, John Hackett. PRO: Fred Roos. STARS: Jimmie Rodgers, Jack Nicholson, John Hackett.

A low-budget but effective story of a three-man Ranger unit sent to blow up a Japanese communications center before MacArthur returns to the Philippines. Good acting, including a very young Nicholson, lends believability to the film.

Back to Bataan (1945)

WWII	Army	Full	B&W	95 mins
RKO	WV: 05-30-45		NYT: 09-13-45	

DIR: Edward Dmytryk. SW: Ben Barzman, Richard Landau. PRO: Robert Fellows. STARS: John Wayne, Anthony Quinn, Richard Loo.

John Wayne, playing an American colonel, creates a guerrilla force in the Philippines to harass the Japanese until the Army returns to liberate the country. The fictional story intended to arouse patriotism by showing underdogs fighting against huge odds.

Bailout at 43,000 (1957)

Peace	Air Force	Full	B&W	78 mins
UA	WV: 05-15-57		NYT: 06-08-57	

DIR: Francis Lyon. SW: Paul Monash. PRO: Howard Pine, William Thomas. STARS: John Payne, Karen Steele, Paul Kelly, Richard Eyer.

A slow-moving film portraying the Air Force's attempt to develop an ejection seat for its B-47 bomber. The only question is whether Payne will refuse to carry out the test jump. However, like all such minor military stories, the viewer knows the answer before the end.

Bamboo Blonde (1946)

WWII	Air Force	Full	B&W	68 mins
RKO	WV: 06-19-46		NYT: DNR	

DIR: Anthony Mann. SW: Olive Cooper, Lawrence Kimble. PRO: Herman Schlom, Sid Rogell. STARS: Francis Langford, Ralph Edwards, Russell Wade, Iris Adrian.

A predictable story of a B-29 pilot who has a brief interlude with a singer the night before he leaves for the Pacific. His plane gains fame when the crew paints the singer's picture on the fuselage. When the crew is sent back to the States for a bond drive, the pilot and singer fall in love and, after the usual complications, love triumphs.

Bamboo Prison (1954)

Korea	Army	Ltd	B&W	80 mins
Columbia	WV: 12-15-54		NYT: DNR	

DIR: Lewis Seiler. SW: Edwin Blum, Jack DeWitt. PRO: Bryan Foy. STARS: Robert Francis, Brian Keith, E. G. Marshall, Dianne Foster.

A story about American POWs during the Korean War. Francis pretends to be an informer to confuse his jailers. Film has the usual prison camp antics, but *Weekly Variety* thought that it contained less brutality than other POW films.

Bamboo Saucer (1968)

SciFi	Air Force	Ltd	Color	100 mins
World Enter	WV: 11-06-68		NYT: DNR	

DIR: Frank Telford. SW: Frank Telford. PRO: Charles Burns, Jerry Fairbanks. STARS: Dan Duryea, John Ericson, Lois Nettleton, Nan Leslie.

The Air Force provided limited assistance to a convoluted story of a joint U.S.–USSR expedition searching for a flying saucer that may have landed in China. The help was provided even though the service has always denied that flying saucers exist and so generally refused to become involved with stories portraying alien visitors in round spaceships.

Baroque A Nova (1969)

WWII	Army	NR	Color	Unkn
Independent	WV: DNR		NYT: DNR	

DIR: Michael Armstrong. SW: Michael Armstrong. PRO: Michael Armstrong. STARS: Dirk Brandts, Brad Clements, Eric Lehman, Christopher Silagyi.

A low-budget production about a group of U.S. soldiers whose plane crashes in the Baroque A Nova Desert and immediately become prisoners of a unit of German soldiers. To survive the desert, the enemies must learn to coexist while maintaining their status as combatants. The Santa Barbara area stood in for the African desert.

Basic (2003)

Peace	Army	Inform	Color	98 mins
Columbia	DV: 03-24-2003		NYT: 04-20-2003	

DIR: John McTiernan. SW: James Vanderbilt. PRO: Mike Medavoy. STARS: John Travolta, Connie Nielson, Samuel L. Jackson, Tim Daly.

Travolta investigates the disappearance of Special Forces trainees on a routine exercise in the jungles of Panama and the murder of Jackson, a universally hated senior sergeant. The filmmakers inquired about using Camp Blanding in Florida, but the Army showed no interest in providing material assistance given the story line. However, the service's Los Angeles public affairs office gave the production costumer a very limited amount of information.

Basic Training (1985)

Peace	DoD	NR	Color	88 mins
The Movie Store	WV: 11-20-85		NYT: DNR	

DIR: Andrew Sugerman. SW: Bernard Kahn. PRO: Otto Salamon, Gil Adler. STARS: Ann Dusenberry, Rhonda Shear, Angela Aames.

Probably all one needs to know about the film is that The Playboy Channel produced it and that its original title was *Up the Pentagon*. Dusenberry gets an entry-level job in the DoD public affairs office, is fired for insubordination, and gets her job back so she can make the world safe for democracy, while getting rid of the Pentagon boobs. She uses her body to work her way to the top but without losing her virtue. About as bad as a film can get.

Bat-21 (1988) [G&G]

Vietnam	Air Force	Full	Color	105 mins
Tri-Star	WV: 10-05-88		NYT: 10-21-88	

DIR: Peter Markle. SW: William Anderson, George Gordon. PRO: David Fisher, Gary A. Neill, Michael Balson. STARS: Gene Hackman, Danny Glover, Jerry Reed, David Marshall Grant.

Based on Anderson's book, the film provides a highly fictionalized account of the rescue of a downed Air Force officer in Vietnam, late in the American involvement. By then, all the services saw as their de facto primary missions rescuing their downed or lost comrades. The effort to recover Hackman, playing Lt. Col. Iceal Hambleton, became the largest such operation in American history, during which 11 men died. However, in the cinematic version, Hackman's character has only one rescuer, Glover, who guides the downed officer toward freedom.

The project took many years to reach the screen, and, although the Air Force gave full assistance during production, it did not approve the completed film because it contained scenes the service found inaccurate and negative. This included a key dramatic sequence: the napalming of a Vietnamese village, which brought Hackman face-to-face with the reality of the war, which he had before only experienced from a distance.

Bataan (1943) [G&G]

WWII	Army	Cour	B&W	114 mins
MGM	WV: 05-26-43		NYT: 06-04-43	

DIR: Tay Garnett. SW: Robert Andrews. PRO: Dore Schary. STARS: Robert Taylor, George Murphy, Desi Arnaz, Lloyd Nolan.

Inspired by the fall of Bataan, *Bataan* became one of the first films to go into production after Pearl Harbor. Schary wanted to stimulate patriotism and unite the whole nation against the Japanese threat. As a result, he included a black soldier in the group of Americans fleeing the Japanese. Taylor's death provided a powerful heroic image. The Army read the script and offered informational assistance to the production, which was shot wholly at the studio.

Battle Beneath the Earth (1968)

Cold War	Navy, Army, Air Force	Cour	Color	91 mins
MGM	WV: 05-15-68		NYT: 09-12-68	

DIR: Montgomery Tully. SW: Lance Hargreaves. PRO: Charles Reynolds. STARS: Kerwin Mathews, Robert Ayres, Peter Arne.

A fantasy in which the U.S. military thwarts tunneling Chinese from invading the United States. The only visible assistance is footage of Air Force transports landing with equipment and men to interdict and destroy the tunnels. Given the Cold War situation, the film blames a rogue general, not the Communist government, for the invasion operation. The general, from a long line of Chinese warlords, has used his tunneling equipment to place two atomic bombs under Peking to keep the present Chinese leadership from aborting his plans.

Battle Circus (1953)

Korea	Army	Full	B&W	90 mins
MGM	WV: 01-28-53		NYT: 05-28-53	

DIR: Richard Brooks. SW: Allen Rivkin, Laura Kerr. PRO: Pandro Berman. STARS: Humphrey Bogart, June Allyson, Keenan Wynn.

The original *M*A*S*H* portrayal, essentially a romance between Dr. Bogart and nurse Allyson set on the Korean battlefield. The Army provided helicopters and medical tents.

Battle Cry (1955) [G&G]

WWII	Marines	Full	Color	147 mins
WB	WV: 02-02-55		NYT: 02-03-55	

DIR: Raoul Walsh. SW: Leon Uris. PRO: Raoul Walsh. STARS: Van Heflin, Aldo Ray, James Whitmore, Tab Hunter, Raymond Massey, Anne Francis, Dorothy Malone.

Based on Uris's best-selling novel of the same name, the Marine epic focuses more on the noncombat experiences of the men than on combat. Although most Marines have viewed John Wayne as the quintessential fighting man as portrayed in *Sands of Iwo Jima*, they said that *Battle Cry* better captured their lives in the Corps. Nevertheless, the Production Code Office and the Marines had problems with the sexuality portrayed in Hunter's relationships with Francis, his girl back home, and in San Diego with Malone, the wife of a Navy officer.

In particular, the Marines observed that although Hunter represented the type of young man they wanted to recruit, showing him "humping a married woman twice his age will have many detrimental aftermaths." Despite this then-risqué image, the Corps provided full cooperation at the Recruit Depot in San Diego and at Camp Pendleton and allowed Walsh to film a landing assault on Vieques, Puerto Rico. The assistance helped provide an authentic ambience to the movie even though Uris never identified actual battles. Ultimately, Warner Bros received Code approval despite retaining some of the romantic interludes, but the Marines decided not to help promote the film because of Hunter's affair. Of course, its portrayal undoubtedly helped with recruitment.

Battle Cry of Peace (1915)

WWI	Army, Navy	Full	B&W	90 mins
Vitagraph	WV: 08-13-15		NYT: 08-07-15	

DIR: J. Stuart Blackton, Wilford North. SW: J. Stuart Blackton, Hudson Maxim. PRO: J. Stuart Blackton. STARS: Charles Richman, L. Rogers Lytton, James Morrison, Mary Maurice.

The film depicted a near-future military invasion of the United States by an unspecified dictatorship. The theme was considered very timely in the period before the United States entered WWI. In addition to the military's material assistance, Admiral George Dewey and Army Chief of Staff General Leonard Wood appeared as themselves, although the enemy overran the United States with surprising ease.

Battle Flame (1959)

Korea	Marines	Ltd	B&W	78 mins
Allied Artists	WV: 05-13-59		NYT: DNR	

DIR: R.G. Springsteen. SW: Lester Sansom, Elwood Ullman. PRO: Lester Sansom. STARS: Robert Blake, Scott Brady, Gordon Jones, Elaine Edwards, Wayne Heffley.

The Marines rescue five American nurses whom the Chinese army had captured.

Battle Force (1978)

WWII	Army	NR	Color	101 mins
Imersion Pictures	WV: DNR		NYT: DNR	

DIR: Umberto Lenzi. SW: Cesare Frugoni, Umberto Lenzi. PRO: Mino Loy, Luciano Martino. STARS: John Huston, Stacy Keach, Henry Fonda, Helmut Berger, Guy Doleman, Orson Welles.

A low budget, made-in-Italy film that plowed no new ground in showing WWII from both sides, with combat footage lifted from earlier movies. The only real question is how the producers managed to hire so many top caliber American actors.

Battleground (1949) [G&G]

WWII	Army		Full	B&W	118 mins
MGM	WV: 09-28-49			NYT: 11-12-49	

DIR: William Wellman. SW: Robert Pirosh. PRO: Dore Schary. STARS: Van Johnson, John Hodiak, George Murphy, Ricardo Montalban, Marshall Thompson, Denise Darcel, Richard Jaeckel.

Set during the Battle of the Bulge, the film provides one of the most realistic portrayals of small-unit combat. Pirosh based his screenplay on his own experiences during the fighting. However, Wellman shot most of the film on a sound stage. The Army loaned soldiers to serve as extras and to train the actors to look like infantrymen in order to lend authenticity to the action. As a result, many critics and veterans consider *Battleground* one of the best WWII movies.

Schary waged his own battle against studio executives, who thought the time was not yet right to look back on the recent conflict. However, the producer wanted to make the film in order to remind Americans why they had to fight the war. A chaplain delivers Schary's message to the soldiers during a lull in combat.

Battle Hymn (1956)

Korea	Air Force		Full	Color	108 mins
Universal	WV: 12-19-56			NYT: 02-16-57	

DIR: Douglas Sirk. SW: Vincent Evans, Charles Grayson. PRO: Ross Hunter. STARS: Rock Hudson, Dan Duryea, Martha Hyer.

The film mixed even parts of religion and warrior in a cute "true" story of Col. Dean Hess, a WWII fighter pilot turned minister, who returns to aerial combat during the Korean War. In his free time, he starts an orphanage in which live surprisingly clean and plump Korean children. In the end, Hess and the Air Force evacuate the orphans in the face of an enemy attack.

Battle of Blood Island (1960)

WWII	Army		NR	B&W	64 mins
Filmgroup	WV: 05-16-60			NYT: DNR	

DIR: Joel Rapp. SW: Joel Rapp. PRO: Stanley Bickman. STARS: Richard Devon, Ron Kennedy.

The only two survivors of a U.S. assault on a Japanese-held island hide in a cave until the end of the war, which is indicated by the suicide of the Japanese soldiers. The GIs then turn on one another until a Navy ship shows up to rescue them.

Battle of the Bulge (1965)

WWII	Army		NR	Color	163 mins
WB	WV: 12-22-65			NYT: 12-18-65	

DIR: Ken Annakin. SW: Philip Yordan, Milton Sperling. PRO: Philip Yordan, Milton Sperling. STARS: Henry Fonda, Robert Shaw, Robert Ryan, Dana Andrews, Charles Bronson, Telly Savalas, and thousands of Spanish soldiers.

A fictionalized story of the Battle of the Bulge, shot entirely in Spain with the Spanish Army and its tanks. Consequently the Pentagon had no means to cooperate. The movie lacked any credibility from the opening scene, in which Fonda as an intelligence officer flies in a small plane over the Belgian Alps looking for the German army. The film tries to capture combat from both sides and shows the German massacre at Malmedy, which provided the first significant postwar cinematic images of "bad" Germans. Unfortunately, the dusty Spanish countryside looked very little like snowy Belgium.

Battle of the Coral Sea (1959)

WWII	Navy	Ltd	B&W	80 mins
Columbia	WV: 10-14-59		NYT: DNR	

DIR: Paul Wendkos. SW: Stephen Kandel, Daniel Ullman. PRO: Charles Schneer. STARS: Cliff Robertson, Gia Scala, L. Q. Jones, Gene Blakely.

A submarine crew captured and imprisoned on a Japanese-held island manages to escape and sends information about an impending battle back to the American fleet. The story has almost nothing to do with the battle in the film's title.

Battle Stations (1956)

WWII	Navy	Full	B&W	81 mins
Columbia	WV: 02-01-56		NYT: DNR	

DIR: Lewis Seiler. SW: Crane Wilbur. PRO: Bryan Foy. STARS: John Lund, William Bendix, Richard Boone, James Lydon.

Slightly fictionalized story of the March 1945 attack on the USS *Franklin*, the most heavily damaged ship in WWII to return to the United States. The film contains an excellent re-creation of life aboard a WWII aircraft carrier. The Navy provided a carrier and original footage of the *Franklin*'s heroic struggle to survive.

Battle Taxi (1955)

Korea	Army	Full	B&W	82 mins
UA	WV: 01-12-55		NYT: DNR	

DIR: Herbert Strock. SW: Art Arthur, Malvin Wald. PRO: Art Arthur, Ivan Tors. STARS: Sterling Hayden, Arthur Franz, Marshall Thompson.

An unexceptional story of Army helicopters during the Korean War.

Battle Zone (1952)

Korea	Marines	Full	B&W	82 mins
Allied Artists	WV: 10-15-52		NYT: 12-01-52	

DIR: Lesley Selander. SW: Steve Fisher. PRO: Walter Wanger. STARS: John Hodiak, Linda Christian, Stephen McNally, Charles Bronson (uncredited).

The film focused on the experiences of Marine combat photographers, but ironically, the actual combat footage is not well integrated into a trite story of two Marines in pursuit of the same nurse. The director shot most of the film at Camp Pendleton. It also benefited from a segment shot on Vieques, Puerto Rico during a Marine training exercise.

Beachhead (1954)

WWII	Marines	Deny	B&W	89 mins
UA	WV: 02-03-54		NYT: 04-17-54	

DIR: Stuart Heisler. SW: Richard Alan Simmons. PRO: Howard Koch. STARS: Tony Curtis, Frank Lovejoy, Mary Murphy, Eduard Franz.

Based on Richard Hubler's novel, *I've Got Mine.* The Marines refused to cooperate on the story portraying a four-man patrol sent out to obtain information about enemy positions. Why? Because two of the men die along the way, and the service did not want to be associated with a 50 percent casualty rate during a new recruiting campaign following the end of the Korean War. However, the Corps liked the completed film and provided the Marine Band at the premiere.

Beach Red (1967) [G&G]

WWII	Marines	Cour	Color	105 mins
UA	WV: 08-02-67		NYT: 08-04-67	

DIR: Cornel Wilde. SW: Clinton Johnston, Donald Peters. PRO: Cornel Wilde. STARS: Cornel Wilde, Rip Torn, Burr DeBenning.

Based on Peter Bowman's novel, although it is not about the Marines. The gritty action film, set on a South Pacific island, showed that combatants on both sides were not all that different. The Corps initially agreed to cooperate and provided Wilde with stock footage, which the director/producer restored. Later, as the war in Vietnam was escalating, the Marines withdrew from the project because the service saw the film as making an antiwar statement. In fact, **Beach Red** remains a rare example of a combat movie in which the antiwar message survived the excitement of cinematic battle.

Because You're Mine (1952)

Peace	Army	NR	Color	103 mins
MGM	WV: 09-03-52		NYT: 09-26-52	

DIR: Alexander Hall. SW: Ruth Brooks Flippen, Sy Gomberg, Karl Tunberg. PRO: Joseph Pasternak. STARS: Mario Lanza, Doretta Morrow, James Whitmore, Dean Miller.

The uninspiring musical uses the Army only as a background. Opera singer Lanza gets drafted and falls in love with his sergeant's sister.

The Bedford Incident (1965) [G&G]

Cold war	Navy	Deny	B&W	102 mins
Columbia	WV: 10-13-65		NYT: 12-03-65	

DIR: James Harris. SW: James Poe. PRO: James Harris. STARS: Richard Widmark, Sidney Poitier, Martin Balsam, Wally Cox.

The film focuses on an obsessed American destroyer captain who, Ahab-like, tracks a Soviet submarine in international waters. Ultimately, a misunderstood order on the destroyer's bridge results in the destruction of both the pursuer and the pursued. The Navy gave the director and screenwriter an informational/research trip aboard a destroyer. However, the service considered the portrayal of the captain to be unacceptable and refused an additional request for assistance. The British provided a destroyer and helicopter to the filmmakers for the sequence in which Poitier, playing a journalist, arrives aboard the *Bedford*. Harris created the subsequent external shots of the destroyer sailing among icebergs in the British model ship test basin on Malta. Despite the improvisations, the film portrays very well the burdens of leadership during the Cold War and the dangers of accidental nuclear warfare.

The Beginning of the End (1957)

SciFi	Air Force, Army	Ltd	B&W	73 mins
Republic	WV: 07-03-57		NYT: 07-04-57	

DIR: Bert Gordon. SW: Fred Freiberger, Lester Gorn. PRO: Bert Gordon. STARS: Peter Graves, Peggie Castle, Morris Ankrum, Thomas Browne Henry.

Giant grasshoppers, mutated by Agriculture Department radiation experiments, eat everything in their path on the way to Chicago. The military, in the form of stock footage and limited National Guard help, ultimately saves the city by luring the beasts into Lake Michigan.

The Beginning or the End (1947) [G&G]

WWII	Air Force, Army	Full	B&W	112 mins
MGM	WV: 02-19-47		NYT: 02-21-47	

DIR: Norman Taurog. SW: Frank Wead. PRO: Sam Marx. STARS: Brian Donlevy, Robert Walker, Hume Cronyn.

MGM made the movie to inform the American people how the atomic bomb was built and used. Marx actually visited President Harry Truman in the White House to discuss his decision to drop the bomb. At the end of the meeting, Truman warned that the bomb could be the beginning of a new world order or the end of humankind. The producer asked for permission to use the comment as the film's title. The president agreed but stipulated that the studio could not credit him with the idea.

Although the film identified Gen. Leslie Groves, other military people, and scientists by name, and received military assistance, the resulting movie lacked any veracity and provided little understanding of the technical achievement. Perhaps the most egregious falsification occurred when a fictional cinematic scientist accidentally suffered a fatal radiation dosage while preparing the bomb for delivery to the plane. Never happened. Likewise, filmmakers painted the name *Enola Gay* on the wrong side of the bomb-carrying B-29; used a superfortress with turrets, although they had been removed from the plane; and had the mission begin in daylight although actual takeoff time was 2:00 A.M. However, the Army liked the special-effects creation of the atomic explosion over Hiroshima and borrowed the footage for their own use.

Behind Enemy Lines (2001) [G&G]

Bosnia	Navy, Marines	Full	Color	93 mins
Fox	WV: 11-26-2001		NYT: 11-30-2001	

DIR: John Moore. SW: David Veloz, Zak Penn. PRO: Stephanie Austin. STARS: Owen Wilson, Gene Hackman.

The rescue of Air Force flier Scott O'Grady inspired the film, which portrays the escape of Wilson, a Navy navigator, shot down over Bosnia while photographing the burial of victims of ethnic cleansing. After seeing a civilian assassin execute his pilot, Wilson flees cross-country with the Serbian army and the assassin in hot pursuit. Ultimately a Marine Tactical Recovery of Aircraft and Personnel (TRAP) team rescues him and the digital camera disk containing the evidence of the atrocities.

The Pentagon initially objected to a scene in the script in which Hackman, as an admiral, notifies a news network about the downed airman and the Navy's deferral to a French NATO officer who refuses to authorize an American rescue attempt. After the filmmakers agreed to change the scenes, the Navy and Marines provided full cooperation, including an aircraft carrier and helicopters. However, during filming the director tried to shoot the original scene. After a DoD threat to withdraw assistance, he shot Hackman only looking at the news reporter's business card, which left nothing to the imagination since the next scene showed the story on TV. In the end, the film realistically shows how Marines would stage a rescue operation, although an admiral would not take part in an actual TRAP mission as Hackman did.

Behind the Door (1920)

WWI	Navy	Unkn	B&W	7 reels
Famous Players	WV: 01-31-20		NYT: 01-05-20	

DIR: Irvin Willat. SW: Luther Reed. PRO: Thomas Ince. STARS: Hobart Bosworth, Jane Novak, Wallace Beery.

Gouverneur Morris's short story "Behind the Door" in *McClure's Magazine* (July 1918) provided the inspiration for this anti-German propaganda film. Bosworth, as a German American, enlists in the U.S. Navy to demonstrate his loyalty to the United States. A German U-boat sinks his ship, leaving him and his wife as the only survivors. Another German U-Boat picks her off the raft, the crew gang-rapes her, and she dies. A year later, Bosworth captures the sub captain and starts to skin him alive, and he dies. Powerful stuff for filmgoers of the time.

Behind the Front (1926)

WWI	Army	Ltd	B&W	61 mins
Famous Players	WV: 02-10-26		NYT: 02-10-26	

DIR: A. Edward Sutherland. SW: Ethel Doherty. PRO: Adolph Zukor, Jesse L. Lasky. STARS: Wallace Beery, Richard Arlen, Raymond Hatton, Tom Kennedy, Mary Brian, Chester Conklin.

Adapted from Hugh Wiley's story "The Spoils of War," which appeared in *The Saturday Evening Post*, the comedy, set in WWI, provided laughs by burlesquing the Army from the highest ranks to the lowest. Brian, as the girl, tricks 25 men into volunteering in her brother's company by telling each he is her hero, while she then marries a rich boy. The men go through basic training, find buddies, and end up in the mud of the French trenches, with Sutherland directing for comedy instead of combat.

A Bell for Adano (1945)

WWII	Army, Navy	Ltd	B&W	103 mins
Fox	WV: 06-20-45		NYT: 07-06-45	

DIR: Henry King. SW: Lamar Trotti. Pro: Louis Lighton. STARS: Gene Tierney, John Hodiak, William Bendix, Richard Conte, Henry Morgan.

An almost literal translation of John Hersey's novel about the U.S. liberation of an Italian town. The military provided limited assistance, and filmmakers toned down the martinet character of the Army general.

The Best Years of Our Lives (1946)

Peace	Air Force	Ltd	B&W	172 mins
RKO	WV: 11-27-46		NYT: 11-22-46	

DIR: William Wyler. SW: Robert Sherwood. PRO: Samuel Goldwyn. STARS: Myrna Loy, Fredric March, Dana Andrews, Hoagy Carmichael, Harold Russell, Teresa Wright.

From the MacKinlay Kantor novel, *Glory for Me,* the movie depicts the challenges returning WWII veterans faced. The Air Force provided assistance in filming a brief sequence at a WWII airplane graveyard.

Between Heaven and Hell (1956)

WWII	Army	Full	Color	94 mins
Fox	WV: 10-10-56		NYT: 10-12-56	

DIR: Richard Fleischer. SW: Harry Brown. PRO: David Weisbart. STARS: Robert Wagner, Terry Moore, Broderick Crawford, Buddy Ebsen.

Based on Francis Gwaltney's novel, the film creates a realistic rendering of the way things were during WWII. Wagner begins as a naive young man and becomes a mature person because of his combat experiences.

Beyond Glory (1948)

WWII/Peace	Army	Full	B&W	82 mins
Paramount	WV: 06-16-48		NYT: 08-04-48	

DIR: John Farrow. SW: William Wister Haines. PRO: Robert Fellows. STARS: Alan Ladd, Donna Reed, George Macready, Henry Travers, Audie Murphy.

In a complex story, Ladd enters West Point with encouragement of the widow of his WWII commander, whose death he thinks he may have caused in Tunisia. His guilt feelings, revealed in flashbacks, cause him trouble at the Academy, but all ends well, particularly with the film's positive portrayal of officer development. The film concludes with Gen. Dwight D. Eisenhower himself delivering the commencement speech to graduating cadets in what was Murphy's first movie.

Beyond the Call of Duty (1992)

Vietnam	Army	NR	Color	85 mins
New Horizon	WV: DNR		NYT: DNR	

DIR: Cirio Santiago. SW: R. G. Davis, Beverly Gray. PRO: Cirio Santiago, Joan Barnett, Steven Rabiner. STARS: Jan-Michael Vincent, Eb Lottimer, Jillian McWhirter, Vic Trevino.

A typical Santiago, Philippine/American production that uses high-speed action and violence to mask the lack of substance. In this case, a free-wheeling U.S. officer and his men venture in a high-speed river gunboat behind enemy lines to kill as many North Vietnamese as possible. Along the way, he rescues a beautiful journalist and then beats a hasty retreat with the enemy in hot pursuit.

Beyond Victory (1931)

WWI	Army	Unkn	B&W	70 mins
RKO	WV: 04-08-31		NYT: 04-06-31	

DIR: John Robertson. SW: Horace Jackson, James Gleason. PRO: E. B. Derr. STARS: Bill Boyd, Zasu Pitts, Lew Cody, Fred Scott, James Gleason.

Four survivors of an American battalion recall how they joined the Army and arrived on the French battlefield. Two die and two survive to the armistice. The film contains a strong antiwar message.

Big Jim McLain (1952)

Cold War	Navy, Marines	Ltd	B&W	90 mins
WB	WV: 08-27-52		NYT: 09-18-52	

DIR: Edward Ludwig. SW: James Edward Grant, Richard English, Eric Taylor. PRO: Robert Fellows. STARS: John Wayne, James Arness, Nancy Olson, Alan Napier.

An espionage movie in which Wayne plays a civilian House Un-American Activities Committee investigator hunting communists in Hawaii. The Navy provided locations in Pearl Harbor for background shots of ships and Wayne aboard a vessel in one of his politically correct, but lesser, roles.

The Big Lift (1950) [G&G]

Cold War	Air Force	Full	B&W	120 mins
Fox	WV: 04-12-50		NYT: 04-27-50	

DIR: George Seaton. SW: George Seaton. PRO: William Perlberg. STARS: Montgomery Clift, Paul Douglas, Bruni Löbel. O. E. Hasse.

This fictional story portrayed the airmen who participated in the Berlin Airlift of 1948. The Air Force allowed the filmmakers to shoot flight operations at actual locations in West Berlin and West Germany, which helped create a realistic ambience.

The Big Parade (1925) [G&G]

WWI	Army	Full	B&W	140 mins
MGM	WV: 11-11-25		NYT: 11-20-25	

DIR: King Vidor. SW: Harry Behn. PRO: King Vidor. STARS: John Gilbert, Renée Adorée, Hobart Bosworth.

The first great movie about the U.S. Army in World War I. Most viewers saw it as an antiwar story, but it actually ended happily with the boy reuniting with the girl. Vidor shot most of the film in and around Los Angeles. However, to create the great advance to the front, he sent his second unit director to Texas to shoot a long line of troops, equipment, and planes in a straight line moving into battle. The base commander claimed that France did not have any straight lines and provided help to shoot the advance on a curved road.

Vidor did not accept the commander's claim or the resulting images and went back to Texas, convincing the officer to again give him use of men and equipment. In the end, the director used both sequences and created a film that allows people to see in it different messages. It remains one of the most significant representations of the U.S. experience during WWI.

The Big Red One (1980) [G&G]

WWII	Army	NR	Color	113 mins
UA	WV: 05-14-80		NYT: 07-18-80	

DIR: Samuel Fuller. SW: Samuel Fuller. PRO: Gene Corman. STARS: Lee Marvin, Mark Hamill, Robert Carradine, Kelly Ward.

Fuller tried for many years to make a semi-autobiographical film about his experiences in the "Big Red One," the First Division. By the time he finally received the funding, the Army had no more WWII equipment, so he had to make the film in Israel. It contained highly positive images of the Army, the first such portrayals of the service in the post-Vietnam period, with audiences cheering in the right places. Fuller did violate his own thesis, that in a war movie one or more main characters must die, since Marvin's cinematic squad survives to the end intact.

Biloxi Blues (1988)

WWII	Army	Full	Color	106 mins
Universal	WV: 03-28-88		NYT: 03-25-88	

DIR: Mike Nichols. SW: Neil Simon. PRO: Ray Stark. STARS: Matthew Broderick, Christopher Walken, Matt Mulhern, Corey Parker.

Based on a Neil Simon play, the film follows the coming of age of Broderick as a young recruit from Brighton Beach. The Army provided Fort Chaffee for basic training sequences.

Birdy (1984)

Vietnam	Army	Inform	Color	120 mins
Tri-Star	WV: 12-12-84		NYT: 12-21-84	

DIR: Alan Parker. SW: Sandy Kroopf, Jack Behr. PRO: Alan Marshall. STARS: Matthew Modine, Nicolas Cage, John Harkins.

Although set during Vietnam, the film is based on William Wharton's WWII novel. Modine brilliantly plays Birdy, who has a fascination with birds and ends up in a VA hospital in a mute, catatonic state as a result of his teenage obsession and combat experiences. His boyhood friend, Nicolas Cage, who received disfiguring facial wounds in the war, arrives at the direction of the Army to see if he can draw out Birdy from his silence. *Birdy* ranks with the best of the soldier-returning-from-Vietnam films, although perhaps the darkest as Modine's obsession sends him in a descent into hell. Although the script contains a strong antiwar message, the Army reportedly gave informal approval for material assistance. While the filmmakers did not follow up their request, the production received informational help from Letterman Army Medical Center in Los Angeles.

Black Hawk Down (2001)

Peace	Army	Full	Color	143 mins
Columbia	WV: 12-10-2001		NYT: 12-28-2001	

DIR: Ridley Scott. SW: Ken Nolan. PRO: Jerry Bruckheimer, Ridley Scott. STARS: Josh Hartnett, Ewan McGregor, Tom Sizemore, Eric Bana.

Based on Mark Bowden's nonfiction book, the film portrays the ill-fated October 1993 mission in Mogadishu, Somalia, when U.S. Army Special Forces and Rangers set out to snatch two warlords. The plan began to unravel when the first Black Hawk helicopter was shot down. Then the Somali militia began to attack the Americans on the ground. Ultimately 18 men died, and President Bill Clinton withdrew the military almost immediately.

Most people saw the mission as a disaster. However, the Army said their men understood the danger and expected to take casualties, carried out their assignments, captured two warlords, and followed their contingency plan to extricate themselves from the center of the city. Perhaps, but if war is diplomacy by other means and perceptions count as much as reality, then the United States did suffer a significant loss, because American forces left the country to the warlords and because, until the movie appeared, most people thought the United States had experienced an embarrassing defeat.

The film itself benefited from considerable assistance from the Army, including the sending of men and helicopters to Morocco where shooting took place. As a result, the movie contained a pseudo-documentary portrayal of urban warfare that ranks with the *Battle of Algiers*. It may have lacked much character development of the men who went into harm's way, but in the end the American spirit was the real hero.

Black Sunday (1977)

Peace	Navy	NR	Color	143 mins
Paramount	WV: 03-30-77		NYT: 04-01-77	

DIR: John Frankenheimer. SW: Ernest Lehman, Kenneth Ross. PRO: Robert Evans. STARS: Bruce Dern, Robert Shaw, Marthe Keller, Fritz Weaver.

Based on a Thomas Harris novel. Bruce Dern plays a former Navy pilot and Vietnam POW whose experiences have ruined his life. He joins a terrorist group and pilots the TV blimp that is aimed at the Super Bowl stadium.

Blockade (1929)

| Peace | Army, Navy, Marines | Full | B&W | 70 mins |
| RKO | WV: 05-22-29, 07-31-29 | | NYT: DNR | |

DIR: George Seitz. SW: John S. Twist, Louis Sarecky, Harvey Thew. PRO: RKO. STARS: Wallace MacDonald, James Bradbury, Walter McGrail.

Adapted from the story by Louis Sarecky, the film was cut to 60 minutes for rerelease of the completely silent version. A few Marines come to the rescue, helping capture rum runners in Florida.

Block-Heads (1938)

| WWI | Army | Unkn | B&W | 55 mins |
| Fox | WV: 08-31-38 | | NYT: 08-30-38 | |

DIR: John Blystone. SW: Charles Rogers, Felix Adler. PRO: Hal Roach. STARS: Stan Laurel, Oliver Hardy, Patricia Ellis.

Laurel guards his WWI trench for 20 years after the armistice because no one ever told him that the war had ended. On a tour of the battlefield, Hardy discovers his old Army buddy and brings him home.

Blood and Steel (1959)

| WWII | Navy | NR | B&W | 63 mins |
| Fox | WV: 12-16-59 | | NYT: DNR | |

DIR: Bernard Kowalski. SW: Joseph Gilette. PRO: Gene Corman. STARS: John Lupton, James Edwards, Brett Halsey, Ziva Rodann.

A native girl helps Navy Seabees free her village from the Japanese.

Blood Warriors (1993)

| Peace | Marines | NR | Color | 95 mins |
| Imperial (video) | WV: DNR | | NYT: DNR | |

DIR: Sam Firstenberg. SW: Jon Stevens, David Bradley. PRO: Gope Samtani, Samuel Sax. STARS: David Bradley, Frank Zagarino, Jennifer Campbell, Frans Tumbuan.

The story begins with Bradley being accused of shooting his brother in the back during a training exercise and being dishonorably discharged from the Marines. The rest of the movie, shot in Indonesia, has Bradley fighting mercenaries, whose leader actually shot the brother.

The Bloody Child (1996)

| Gulf | Marines | NR | Color | 85 mins |
| Mirage | WV: 02-26-96 | | NYT: 05-02-97 | |

DIR: Nina Menkes. SW: Nina Menkes, Tinka Menkes. PRO: Nina Menkes. STARS: Russ Little, Tinka Menkes, Robert Muller, Jack O'Hara.

Set in the vicinity of the Marine base at Twenty-Nine Palms, this is a strange little film about a Gulf War Marine who kills his pregnant wife. Despite its low budget and the director's esoteric approach to filmmaking, Stephen Holden wrote in his *New York Times* review that the movie provides "a suffocating vision of American military life as a lethal social malignancy."

Blue Eagle (1926)

WWI	Navy	Ltd	B&W	7 reels
Fox	WV: DNR		NYT: DNR	

DIR: John Ford. SW: L. G. Rigby. PRO: John Ford. STARS: George O'Brien, Janet Gaynor, William Russell, Robert Edeson.

Based on Gerald Beaumont's story "The Lord's Referee" in the July 1923 **Red Book**, the film portrays rival gang leaders aboard the World War I battleship USS *Rivalry*, mostly held in check by wartime discipline. A shipboard fight begins but abates when a submarine attacks. Tensions between the sailors are resolved after the battle.

Blue Sky (1994)

Peace	Army	NR	Color	101 mins
Orion	WV: 09-12-94		NYT: 09-16-94	

DIR: Tony Richardson. SW: Rama Stagner, Arlene Sarner, Jerry Leichtling. PRO: Robert Solo. STARS: Tommy Lee Jones, Jessica Lange, Powers Boothe, Dale Dye.

Jones, as a dedicated, tough, controlled career officer, endures continual embarrassment from Lange as an unstable, manic-depressive, but sexy wife. He stays with her out of love and belief that marital problems should be kept within the family. Jones's competence as an expert on the lethal effects of nuclear testing masks the strain of caring for his wife, whose volatility regularly humiliates him and their children. Although the subplot dealing with Jones's concerns about nuclear testing intrude upon the family drama, the film remains a powerful portrayal of life in the pre-Vietnam Army. To be sure, the service would have preferred it would not have been made, any more than it appreciated Deborah Kerr's portrayal of Karen Holmes in **From Here to Eternity**.

Blue Thunder (1983) [G&G]

Vietnam	Army	Deny	Color	108 mins
Columbia	WV: 02-02-83		NYT: 05-13-83	

DIR: John Badham. SW: Dan O'Bannon, Don Jakoby. PRO: Gordon Carroll. STARS: Roy Scheider, Malcolm McDowell, Warren Oates.

The movie portrayed a futuristic helicopter the Los Angeles Police Department buys to combat a growing crime wave. The Army turned down a request for assistance in a short scene set in Vietnam because a soldier throws a Vietcong out of a helicopter (which did happen).

The Bob Mathias Story (1954)

Peace	Marines	Full	B&W	80 mins
Allied Artists	WV: 10-06-54		NYT: 10-16-54	

DIR: Francis Lyon. SW: Richard Collins. PRO: James Fallon, William Selwyn. STARS: Bob Mathias, Ward Bond, Melba Mathias, Ann Doran.

The cinematic biography tells the story of the two-time Olympic Decathlon gold medal winner who served with the Marines.

Body Snatchers (1993)

SciFi	Army	NR	Color	87 mins
WB	WV: 05-03-93		NYT: 05-18-93, 02-04-94	

DIR: Abel Ferrara. SW: Stuart Gordon, Dennis Paoli, Nicholas St. John. PRO: Robert H. Solo. STARS: Gabrielle Anwar, Terry Kinney, Billy Wirth, Meg Tilly, R. Lee Ermey.

The third cinematic rendering of Jack Finney's novel *The Body Snatchers*, this time set on an Army base. Although the film maintains the same story of alien pods taking over humans as they sleep, the theme of loss of identity has become a staple theme of the genre. Moreover, setting the action on a military base creates a fundamental dramatic problem. Since the soldiers already have poker faces, how can viewers tell humans from the soulless, emotionless pod people?

The Bold and the Brave (1956)

WWII	Army	NR	B&W	87 mins
RKO	WV: 03-21-56		NYT: 05-26-56	

DIR: Lewis Foster. SW: Robert Lewin. PRO: Hal Chester. STARS: Wendell Corey, Mickey Rooney, Don Taylor, Nicole Maurey.

The film follows the battle for three men's souls during the war in Italy: one a preacher, one an idealist who lives off his wife, and one a seeker of money.

Bolshevism on Trial (1919)

Peace	Navy, Marines	Ltd.	B&W	70 mins
Mayflower	WV: 05-02-19		NYT: DNR	

DIR: Harley Knoles. SW: Harry Chandlee. PRO: Mayflower. STARS: Robert Frazer, Leslie Stowe, Howard Truesdale, Jim Savage.

Based on Thomas Dixon's novel *Comrades*, the film portrays a failed effort to establish a utopia on an island off the Florida coast. In the end, the Marines arrive aboard a Navy ship to restore order to the island.

Bombardier (1943)

WWII	Air Force	Full	B&W	99 mins
RKO	WV: 05-12-43		NYT: 07-02-43	

DIR: Richard Wallace. SW: John Twist. PRO: Robert Fellows. STARS: Pat O'Brien, Randolph Scott, Eddie Albert, Robert Ryan.

Wallace shot the story, which portrays the training of bombardiers and shows bombers in combat, at the Air Force bombardier training facility in Arizona.

Bombers B-52 (1957)

Cold War	Air Force	Full	Color	106 mins
WB	WV: 10-30-57		NYT: 11-23-57	

DIR: Gordon Douglas. SW: Irving Wallace. PRO: Richard Whorf. STARS: Natalie Wood, Karl Malden, Efrem Zimbalist Jr.

A Strategic Air Command (SAC) film made with full support of Gen. Curtis LeMay. The film portrayed the Air Force's transition from B-47s to B-52s as the primary intercontinental deterrent. Blatant propaganda for the SAC mission, but still dramatic because of full access to Air Force facilities at Castle Air Force base in California.

Born on the Fourth of July (1989) [G&G]

Vietnam	Marines	NR	Color	144 mins
Universal	WV: 12-20-89		NYT: 12-20-89, 01-21-90	

DIR: Oliver Stone. SW: Oliver Stone, Ron Kovic. PRO: A. Kitman Ho. STARS: Tom Cruise, Willem Dafoe, Abbie Hoffman, Caroline Kava.

Based on his book of the same name, the film portrays Kovic's journey from gung ho Marine, who joined the Corps as a result of watching *Sands of Iwo Jima*, to an embittered, paralyzed veteran who survives in part because of the toughness he learned in the service. After extended negotiations in 1978, the Marines agreed to provide assistance to the production. However, the project fell apart when Al Pacino began work on another film.

Despite using virtually the same script when he resurrected the project in 1988, Stone did not return to the Marines for assistance, claiming the service would not have helped him, even when he was shown the original approval letter. Whatever its historical inaccuracies, the film captured well Kovic's odyssey from gung ho Marine to antiwar activist.

The Boys in Company C (1978) [G&G]

Vietnam	Marines	NR	Color	126 mins
Columbia	WV: 01-25-78		NYT: 02-02-78, 02-19-78	

DIR: Sidney J. Furie. SW: Rick Natkin, Sidney Furie. PRO: André Morgan. STARS: Stan Shaw, Andrew Stevens, Craig Wasson, James Whitmore Jr., Lee Ermey.

Given the negative image of the Marines and the anti-Vietnam, antimilitary story, the producers did not bother to send the script to the Pentagon requesting assistance. Instead, they made the movie in the Philippines using assistance that its military provided. The film helped create the postwar image of American incompetence in Vietnam.

Brady's Escape (1984)

WWII	Air Force	NR	Color	96 mins
Satori	WV: 06-20-84		NYT: 06-24-84	

DIR: Pál Gábor. SW: William Lewis. PRO: Robert Halmi. STARS: John Savage, Kelly Reno, Ildikó Bánsági.

A Hungarian/American production portraying an Air Force bomber pilot shot down over the Hungarian outback and his efforts to survive and reach safety with the help of Tito's partisans in Yugoslavia. The only combat sequence is one bombing mission and bail out from a damaged plane by Savage and his navigator, the only surviving crew members. Their efforts to escape, of course, constitute expected military behavior.

Brass Target (1978)

Peace	Army	NR	Color	112 mins
UA	WV: 12-13-78		NYT: 12-22-78	

DIR: John Hough. SW: Alvin Boretz. PRO: Arthur Lewis. STARS: John Cassavetes, George Kennedy, Robert Vaughn, Patrick McGoohan.

Based on Frederick Nolan's novel *The Algonquin Project*, the film hypothesizes the assassination of Gen. George Patton instead of his actual death resulting from a car accident. The cinematic killing is part of a plot to steal German gold, but the film's blurring of the line between truth and fantasy is to no avail, dramatically or historically.

Breakthrough (1950)

WWII	Army	Full	B&W	91 mins
WB	WV: 11-01-50		NYT: 11-18-50	

DIR: Lewis Seiler. SW: Bernard Girard, Ted Sherdeman. PRO: Brian Foy. STARS: David Brian, John Agar, Frank Lovejoy, Paul Picerni.

A rambling and disjointed portrayal of fighting after the Normandy landing. On one hand, the film shows the grimness of war, and on the other, the "glamour" of combat, the camaraderie of the men, the thrill of success, and the beautiful women they liberate. Some men die, but the main characters survive to fight another day.

The Bridge (1959-in Germany)

WWII	Army	NR	B&W	102 mins
AA	WV: 02-03-60		NYT: 05-02-61	

DIR: Bernhard Wicki. SW: Bernhard Wicki, Michael Mansfeld. PRO: Jochen Severin. STARS: Folker Bohnet, Fritz Wepper, Michael Hinz, Frank Glaubrecht, Karl Michael Balzer.

Based on Manfred Gregor's *The Bridge*. U.S. tanks attack an unimportant bridge that German teenagers defend in the last two days of the war. A massacre occurs as it must, but not before the boy soldiers inflict serious damage on the American tanks and soldiers.

The Bridge at Remagen (1969) [G&G]

WWII	Army	NR	Color	115 mins
UA	WV: 06-25-69		NYT: 08-28-69	

DIR: John Guillermin. SW: Richard Yates, William Roberts. PRO: David Wolper. STARS: George Segal, Robert Vaughn, Ben Gazzara.

A highly fictionalized account of the capture on March 7, 1945, of the last remaining undestroyed bridge over the Rhine River. Although based on military historian and later Congressman Ken Hechler's *The Bridge at Remagen,* neither the bridge nor the story much resembles what happened when the U.S. Army found the bridge still standing and managed to put troops across the river before the Germans were able to blow it up.

The filmmakers found a bridge in Czechoslovakia that vaguely resembled the Ludendorff Bridge, and the Czech Army provided men and tanks to re-create the crossing, until Soviet forces arrived to put down anticommunist demonstrations throughout the country. Filming was then completed in Italy. The technical advisor, a retired Army officer, later said that the men who had fought at Remagen and crossed the bridge would recognize the actual soldiers being loosely portrayed. However, because most of the audience had not been there, they would have a difficult time separating fact from fiction.

The Bridge on the River Kwai (1957)

WWII	Navy	NR	Color	161 mins
Columbia	WV: 11-20-57		NYT: 12-19-57	

DIR: David Lean. SW: Michael Wilson, Carl Foreman (credited on screen to Pierre Boulle). PRO: Sam Spiegel. STARS: William Holden, Alec Guinness, Jack Hawkins, Sessue Hayakawa, James Donald.

Based on Boulle's novel, this film has two focuses. Guinness, as a British colonel in a Japanese POW camp, enters into a conflict of wills with Hayakawa, the camp commander, over the building of a railroad bridge spanning the River Kwai. At the same time, the cinematic narrative has an American military presence in the person of Holden, who represents himself as a Navy commander who survived the sinking of his ship. Although captured, he manages to escape from the camp and reach the safety of British territory.

Unfortunately, his ruse is exposed after the English request that the U.S. Navy assign him to Hawkins's mission to blow up the bridge. Given a choice of being court-martialed for posing as an officer or accepting the order with the British rank of major, former Navy seaman Holden "volunteers" for the mission and ultimately shares in the destruction of the bridge, although at the cost of his life. Nevertheless, the film provides the message that the British and U.S. military jointly won the war.

A Bridge Too Far (1977) [G&G]

WWII	Army	Full	Color	175 mins
UA	WV: 06-08-77		NYT: 06-17-77	

DIR: Richard Attenborough. SW: William Goldman. PRO: Joseph E. Levine, Richard P. Levine. STARS: Michael Caine, Sean Connery, Robert Redford, Ryan O'Neal, Elliot Gould, Gene Hackman, James Caan, Dirk Bogarde, Laurence Olivier, Anthony Hopkins, Maximilian Schell.

Based on Cornelius Ryan's journalistic book of the same name, this vastly underrated movie portrays well the tragedy and courage of the men who tried to capture the Dutch bridges over the Rhine in September 1944, so that the Allies could push into Germany and end the war before the New Year. The Pentagon considered the script to be excellent and contributed men and material to the American segments of the British production.

Although the film did capture the essence of Operation Market Garden, it illustrates the problems of telling history within a feature film. The director could not slap a map onto the screen every five minutes or stop the action to explain what was happening. Consequently, in portraying events that happened over so wide an area and from the perspective of both sides in the battle, the audience could easily become confused. Nevertheless, people left the theater fully understanding why the Allies tried to go to a bridge too far and suffered greater losses than at Normandy.

The Bridges at Toko-Ri (1954) [SSS]

Korea	Navy	Full	Color	103 mins
Paramount	WV: 12-29-54		NYT: 01-21-55	

DIR: Mark Robson. SW: Valentine Davies. PRO: William Seaton. STARS: William Holden, Grace Kelly, Fredric March, Mickey Rooney.

Based on James Michener's novel, the film attempted to justify the U.S. defense of South Korea. The Navy provided a carrier task force to re-create the service's aerial operations, culminating in the attack on the bridges at Toko-Ri, created with Navy jets performing for the cameras, miniatures, and special effects. The service liked the film because it showed jets doing their job, although the image of Holden lying dead in a ditch contained a powerful antiwar message.

The Brig (1964)

Peace	Marines	Unkn	B&W	60 mins
White Line Pro	WV: DNR		NYT: 09-21-64	

DIR: Adolfas Mekas, Jonas Mekas, SW: Kenneth Brown. PRO: David Stone. STARS: Warren Finnerty, Jim Anderson, Henry Howard.

Condensed cinematic version of Kenneth Brown's one-act play portraying regimented sadism in a Marine brig. The film contained unrelenting violence, which the author said re-created his personal experiences.

Bright Victory (1951)

WWII	Army	Unkn	B&W	96 mins
Universal	WV: 07-21-51		NYT: 08-01-51	

DIR: Mark Robson. SW: Robert Buckner. PRO: Robert Buckner. STARS: Arthur Kennedy, Peggy Dow, Julia Adams, James Edwards.

Based on Raynard Kendrick's novel, the film portrays a veteran's fight to overcome blindness with the help of a young woman he meets at a Veterans hospital in Valley Forge, Pennsylvania.

Broken Arrow (1996)

Terrorism	Air Force	Deny	Color	108 mins
Fox	WV: 02-12-96		NYT: 02-09-96	

DIR: John Woo. SW: Graham Yost. PRO: Mark Gordon, Bill Badalato. STARS: John Travolta, Christian Slater, Samantha Mathis.

A renegade Air Force (Slater) pilot steals two nuclear weapons to sell to the highest bidder. For obvious reasons, the Air Force flatly refused to cooperate.

Buck Privates (1928)

Peace	Army	Unkn	B&W	60 mins
Universal	WV: 02-01-28		NYT: 01-30-28	

DIR: Melville Brown. SW: Melville Brown, John Clymer. PRO: Universal. STARS: Lya de Putti, Malcolm McGregor, Zasu Pitts, James Marcus.

Comedy and romance combine in post–WWI Europe as members of the American Expeditionary Force head home through Luxemburg. Two soldiers pursue the same girl despite the villagers' prohibition against doughboys fraternizing with their young maidens. The usual comedic complications take place before a happy ending.

Buck Privates (1941)

Peace	Army	Full	B&W	41 mins
Universal	WV: 02-05-41		NYT: 02-14-41	

DIR: Arthur Lubin. SW: Arthur Horman. PRO: Alex Gottlieb. STARS: Bud Abbott, Lou Costello, Lee Bowman, Andrews Sisters.

Basic training as experienced by Abbot and Costello is riotously funny, but raises questions as to the Army's preparedness for the coming war.

Buck Privates Come Home (1947)

Peace	Army	Full	B&W	77 mins
Universal	WV: 03-12-47		NYT: 04-12-47	

DIR: Charles Barton. SW: John Grant, Frederic Rinaldo, Robert Lees. PRO: Robert Arthur. STARS: Bud Abbott, Lou Costello, Tom Brown.

Comics Abbott and Costello come home, six years after they went off to war in *Buck Privates*, and try to adjust to civilian life, with flashbacks to their wartime training.

Buffalo Soldiers (2001)

Cold War	Army	NR	Color	95 mins
Miramax	WV: 09-24-2001		NYT: 07-25-2003	

DIR: Gregor Jordan. SW: Eric Weiss, Nora Maccoby. PRO: Rainer Grupe, Ariane Moody. STARS: Joaquin Phoenix, Ed Harris, Scott Glenn, Anna Paquin, Gabriel Mann.

Based on Robert O'Connor's novel, the film turned the Army's recruiting slogan: "Be All You Can Be" into Sergeant Bilko's philosophy: "Steal All You Can Steal." As many of the Vietnam films portrayed that war, *Buffalo Soldiers* portrays all the worst things, real and imagined, that might occur in the peacetime Army. Although the military reflects the society that creates it, on balance most soldiers have always done their jobs responsibly—not as shown here. After several delays, the film was initially released in 2001 but was immediately withdrawn after 9/11. Ultimately rereleased in August 2003, it quickly disappeared without a trace.

The Bugle Sounds (1941)

Preparedness	Army	Full	B&W	101 mins
MGM	WV: 12-17-41		NYT: 04-03-42	

DIR: S. Sylvan Simon. SW: Cyril Hume. PRO: J. Walter Ruben. STARS: Wallace Beery, Marjorie Main, Lewis Stone, George Bancroft.

The portrayal of the American mechanized cavalry in the days leading up to Pearl Harbor intended to show how the Army was preparing for war at an unidentified post. The service provided hundreds of armored cars, trucks, and tanks during training exercises as background for the story of Beery as an old cavalry sergeant who rebels against modern technology. His personal conflict creates a tale of sabotage, the Army's secret service, and vindication and honor, with the resulting patriotic flag-waving needed so badly in the aftermath of Pearl Harbor.

Bye Bye Birdie (1963)

Peace	Army	Ltd	Color	112 mins
Columbia	WV: 04-10-63		NYT: 04-05-63	

DIR: George Sidney. SW: Irving Brecher. PRO: Fred Kohlmar. STARS: Dick Van Dyke, Ann-Margret, Bobby Rydell, Janet Leigh, Paul Lynde.

Based on the play of the same name, a famous rock and roll star (guess who?) gets drafted into the Army and makes one last tour before entering the service, where he still finds time for romance and performances.

Cadence (1990)

Peace	Army	NR	Color	97 mins
Republic	WV: 11-05-90		NYT: 03-15-91	

DIR: Martin Sheen. SW: Dennis Shryack. PRO: Richard Davis, Glennis Liberty. STARS: Charlie Sheen, Martin Sheen, Laurence Fishburne, Michael Beach.

Based on Gordon Weaver's novel, the film is a formalistic portrayal of life in a military brig, this time with Charlie Sheen as a rebellious inmate in an Army stockade. Martin Sheen directs for the only time in his career and also plays a standard issue bigoted, bullying commandant. In the course of events, the younger Sheen joins a group of black inmates who bring some order to his life at the expense of further enmity from his father.

Cadet Girl (1941)

Preparedness	Army	Full	B&W	69 mins
Fox	WV: 11-19-41		NYT: 12-11-41	

DIR: Ray McCarey. SW: Stanley Rauh, H. W. Hanemann. PRO: Sol Wurtzel. STARS: Carole Landis, George Montgomery, John Shepperd, William Tracy, Janis Carter.

A musical in which West Point cadet Montgomery falls in love with singer Landis but ultimately gives her up and follows family tradition, returning to the Academy.

Cage (1989)

Vietnam	Marines	NR	Color	101 mins
New Century	WV: 09-13-89		NYT: DNR	

DIR: Lang Elliott. SW: Hugh Kelley. PRO: Lang Elliott. STARS: Lou Ferrigno, Reb Brown, Michael Dante, Mike Moroff.

In the opening scene, a Marine patrol hastily retreats to the landing zone where a rescue helicopter is waiting. As Ferrigno pulls Brown aboard, he is shot in the head but does not drop his friend. The scene dissolves to 20 years later. Mentally diminished Ferrigno, with Brown as his handler, fights opponents to the death, noting, "It doesn't matter. . . . I died a long time ago."

The Caine *Mutiny* (1954) [G&G]

WWII	Navy, Marines	Full	Color	125 mins
Columbia	WV: 06-09-54		NYT: 06-25-54	

DIR: Edward Dmytryk. SW: Stanley Roberts, Michael Blankfort. PRO: Stanley Kramer. STARS: Humphrey Bogart, Robert Francis, José Ferrer, Van Johnson, Fred MacMurray, May Wynn, Lee Marvin.

In truth, World War II serves only as the background for Herman Wouk's rite of passage novel and the film it inspired. Mama's boy Willie Keith, a recent Princeton and OCS graduate, joins the USS *Caine*, an aging minesweeper. Ultimately, the strange machinations of Capt. Queeg cause Steve Maryk, the executive officer, to take command of the *Caine* in the midst of a typhoon. In the book's introduction, Wouk wrote that the action "was not a mutiny in the old-time sense . . . with flashing of cutlasses, a captain in chains, and desperate sailors turning outlaws." Nevertheless, the Navy convenes a court-martial for Maryk and the officers who supported him. Under cross-examination, Queeg breaks down, playing senselessly with ball bearings, and an acquittal follows quickly. Having matured from his experiences, Keith returns to the *Caine* and ultimately becomes her last captain.

Although the film ends after the court-martial, the cinematic Keith has also matured and is prepared to lead his own life after the war. Despite the positive portrayal of how the Navy has contributed to the change in Keith, the service initially refused to even consider a request for assistance in making *The Caine Mutiny*, claiming the Navy had never had a mutiny on any of its ships. In fact, a mutiny aboard a frigate in 1842 had led to the creation of the Naval Academy. The Navy also objected to the portrayal of Queeg as a Capt. Bligh. Ultimately, producer Kramer wore down the Navy during 30 months of negotiations, and the service agreed to provide men and two ships to portray the *Caine* in San Francisco and in Hawaii, and access to an aircraft carrier for a key sequence.

In return, Kramer changed Queeg from an incompetent, out-of-control captain into a worn-out officer who did not receive his officers' support. While Queeg's actions aboard ship and his breakdown still did not burnish the Navy's image, by providing assistance and a technical advisor, the service was able to ameliorate the negative portrayals of Queeg in the novel and in the original script. The Navy's concerns aside, *The Caine Mutiny* contained a fine portrayal of life aboard an unglamorous ship that received no glory but made a contribution to the winning of the war.

Marines appeared briefly in the scene in which the *Caine* is escorting Leathernecks to the beach during the assault on a South Pacific island. In one of the crucial moments in the film, Queeg orders the *Caine* to turn and run before reaching the demarcation point, earning him the nickname "Old Yellow Stain," which would damn him during his court-martial testimony.

Calling All Marines (1939)

Peace	Marines	Unkn	B&W	67 mins
Republic	WV: 09-27-39		NYT: 10-26-39	

DIR: John Auer. SW: Earl Felton. PRO: Armand Schaefer. STARS: Donald Barry, Helen Mack, Robert Kent.

In this insignificant spy melodrama, Barry starts out as a small-time mobster, who joins the Marines to steal secret torpedo plans. He changes direction as he learns the Corps esprit, breaks up the spy ring, and becomes a Marine hero. B. B. Cristler observed in the *New York Times* that the Corps "will probably survive the tribute paid to it by Republic Pictures."

Call Me Mister (1951)

Peace	Army	Ltd	Color	95 mins
Fox	WV: 01-24-51		NYT: 02-01-51	

DIR: Lloyd Bacon. SW: Albert Lewin. PRO: Fred Kohlmar. STARS: Betty Grable, Dan Dailey, Danny Thomas.

Based on the stage musical review of the same name, this trite story focuses on Grable as an entertainer whom the Army employs in postwar Japan.

Call Out the Marines (1942)

Peace	Marines	Ltd	B&W	67 mins
RKO	WV: 01-14-42		NYT: 01-26-42	

DIR: Frank Ryan. SW: Frank Ryan, William Hamilton. PRO: Howard Benedict. STARS: Victor McLaglen, Edmund Lowe.

A preparedness Marine story with the heroes reenlisting after 15 years and foiling a spy ring, while having fun and games.

Captain Eddie (1945)

WWII	Air Force	Ltd	B&W	107 mins
Fox	WV: 06-20-45		NYT: 08-09-45	

DIR: Lloyd Bacon. SW: John Tucker Battle. PRO: Winfield Sheehan. STARS: Fred MacMurray, Charles Bickford, Thomas Mitchell.

Despite the title, the film does not focus on Eddie Rickenbacker's WWI exploits, except for brief flashbacks. Instead, it portrays him as a young man courting his future wife. The film does contain a brief sequence aboard a life raft in the South Pacific, during the three weeks he awaited rescue. The Air Force assisted with this sequence.

Captain Milkshake (1970)

Vietnam	Marines	Unkn	Color & B&W	89 mins
Richmark Productions	WV: 12-09-70		NYT: DNR	

DIR: Richard Crawford. SW: Richard Crawford, Barry Leichtling. PRO: Richard Crawford. STARS: Geoff Gage, David Korn, Andrea Cagan, Ronald Barca.

A young Marine on emergency leave from Vietnam falls in love with a hippie. The film is a small budget, cliché-ridden production in which the Marine returns to Vietnam, with a predictable ending.

Captain Newman, M.D. (1963)

WWII	Army	Full	Color	106 mins
Universal	WV: 10-23-63		NYT: 02-21-64	

DIR: David Miller. SW: Richard Breen, Phoebe Ephron, Henry Ephron. PRO: Robert Arthur. STARS: Gregory Peck, Tony Curtis, Eddie Albert, Bobby Darin, Robert Duvall.

Based on a Leo Rosten novel, the film combines Army hospital drama with comedy, telling the story of a psychiatrist's efforts to heal the emotional injuries combat sometimes inflicts on men as severely as it does physical wounds.

Captive Hearts (1987)

WWII	Air Force	NR	Color	97 mins
MGM	WV: 06-10-87		NYT: DNR	

DIR: Paul Almond. SW: John Kuri, Patrick Morita. PRO: John Kuri. STARS: Pat Morita, Chris Makepeace, Mari Sato, Michael Sarrazin.

Two U.S. fliers shot down over Northern Japan become prisoners of a local village. Sarrazin, the Jap-hating sergeant, wanders off into the winter cold. Makepeace, the gentle officer, befriends the villagers and embarks on an innocent romance with a local girl. The war intrudes only briefly when two Japanese soldiers come looking for the fliers.

Captured (1933)

WWI	Air Force	Full	B&W	72 mins
MGM	WV: 08-22-33		NYT: 08-18-33	

DIR: Roy Del Ruth. SW: Philip Gibbs, Edward Chodorov. PRO: Edward Chodorov. STARS: Leslie Howard, Douglas Fairbanks Jr., Paul Lukas.

Based on Gibbs's novel *Fellow Prisoners*, the film takes place in a German prison camp close to the front in which American, British, and French captives plot their escape using German planes from a nearby aerodrome. The Army Air Corps gave assistance at the Burbank airport.

The Cassandra Crossing (1977)

Cold War	Army	NR	Color	127 mins
Avco	WV: 02-02-77		NYT: 02-20-77	

DIR: George Pan Cosmatos. SW: Tom Mankiewicz, Robert Katz, George Pan Cosmatos. PRO: Carlo Ponti. STARS: Richard Harris, Burt Lancaster, Martin Sheen, O. J. Simpson, Sophia Loren, Martin Sheen.

Lancaster, as an Army officer, must destroy a train carrying civilians infected by a virus by sending it over a rickety Polish bridge. Apart from the spectacular collapse of the bridge, the film has only one other virtue: It makes a significant comment on the image of the American military in the post-Vietnam period. After Lancaster is informed that the virus is contained, he explains he must still carry out his mission to eliminate the "very idea" that it existed. To a doctor's repulsion, Lancaster responds, "I know you must see me as some sort of monster. . . . I realize it is no longer fashionable to be a military man. But it's my job and I do it well."

Cast a Giant Shadow (1966)

WWII	Army	NR	Color	146 mins
Batjac	WV: 03-30-66		NYT: 03-31-66	

DIR: Melville Shavelson. SW: Melville Shavelson. PRO: Melville Shavelson, Michael Wayne. STARS: Kirk Douglas, Frank Sinatra, John Wayne, Yul Brynner, Senta Berger.

Based on Ted Berkman's biography, the film portrays Douglas as Mickey Marcus, an American colonel, whom the nascent Jewish state recruits to help create the Israeli army as independence looms. Wayne, in his only portrayal as a general, offers advice to Marcus about his decision to join the Jewish fighters against the numerically superior Arab armies. The movie includes scenes of Douglas during WWII.

Castle Keep (1969)

WWII	Army	NR	Color	105 mins
Columbia	WV: 07-23-69		NYT: 07-24-69	

DIR: Sydney Pollack. SW: Daniel Taradash, David Rayfiel. PRO: Martin Ransohoff. STARS: Burt Lancaster, Peter Falk, Patrick O'Neal, Tony Bill, Scott Wilson.

Based on a William Eastlake novel, the film begins as a satire of war and ends up glorifying the madness of combat. Soldiers holed up in a castle during the Battle of the Bulge face the prospect of destroying the historic fortress to defeat the enemy.

Casualties of War (1989) [G&G]

Vietnam	Army	NR	Color	113 mins
Columbia	WV: 08-16-89		NYT: 08-18 & 27-89	

DIR: Brian De Palma. SW: David Rabe. PRO: Art Linson. STARS: Michael J. Fox, Sean Penn, Don Harvey, John C. Reilly.

Based on Daniel Lang's October 16, 1969, article in the *New Yorker* and his subsequent book, the film relates the true story of a five-man patrol that kidnapped a young Vietnamese girl. Four of the men raped and then killed her. In the movie, Fox, as the fifth man, refuses to take part and reports the atrocity, which stands as a metaphor for what the United States did to Vietnam. Ironically, the four men, who were found guilty and sentenced to long terms in Fort Leavenworth, served little time, while the soldier who turned in his comrades still lives under an assumed name somewhere in the Midwest.

The filmmakers did not approach the Army for cooperation, probably recognizing that the service would want to distance itself from revisiting the atrocity. De Palma used Thailand as a stand-in for Vietnam. Only *Go Tell the Spartans* captures the reality of the war as well as *Casualties of War.* Nevertheless, it has failed to attract much attention because of its unsparing look at the American experience in Vietnam.

Catch-22 (1970) [G&G]

WWII	Air Force	NR	Color	121 mins
Paramount	WV: 06-10-70		NYT: 06-25-70	

DIR: Mike Nichols. SW: Buck Henry. PRO: John Calley. STARS: Alan Arkin, Martin Balsam, Richard Benjamin, Orson Welles, Buck Henry, Anthony Perkins, Bob Newhart.

People whose only knowledge of the film came from the ads went to see another WWII story of aerial combat. People who had read Joseph Heller's novel went to see *Catch-22* for its black humor and comment on the nature of survival. Both groups left disappointed. The B-25s that the producer collected from all over the world served only to provide a distant background to a story about the helplessness of men in combat. Nichols was not able to fully capture Heller's satirical look at war and by implication the absurdity of society as a whole. As a result, the film may best be described as a noble failure.

Caught in the Draft (1941)

WWII	Army	Full	B&W	82 mins
Paramount	WV: 05-28-41		NYT: 06-26-41	

DIR: David Butler. SW: Harry Tugend. PRO: B. G. De Sylva. STARS: Bob Hope, Dorothy Lamour, Eddie Bracken, Lynne Overman.

Movie star Hope gets drafted and frantically tries to survive in the Army, which provided men and equipment, including a tank and parachute drop, as background for this preparedness comedy.

Cease Fire! (1953)

Korea	Army	Full	B&W	75 mins
Paramount	WV: 11-23-53		NYT: 11-25-53	

DIR: Owen Crump. SW: Walter Doniger. PRO: Hal Wallis. STARS: Roy Thompson, Richard Elliott, Albert Cook.

Best categorized as a semidocumentary, the film used real U.S. soldiers in Korea, with military cooperation, to reenact an actual military operation.

Cease Fire (1985)

Vietnam	Army	NR	Color	97 mins
Cineworld	WV: 07-10-85		NYT: 10-18-85	

DIR: David Nutter. SW: George Fernandez. PRO: William Grefe. STARS: Don Johnson, Lisa Blount, Chris Noel, Robert Lyons.

Adapted by Fernandez from his play *Vietnam Trilogy*, the film follows Johnson's efforts to survive his Vietnam experiences. The key to his recovery from post-Vietnam stress syndrome is acknowledging his actions following a Vietcong ambush of his unit. The short combat sequence, created in Florida without Army cooperation, reveals the source of Johnson's anguish. The story is very similar in structure and climax as Henry Winkler's struggle in **Heroes**. In each film, a woman provides the sustenance that enables the veteran to find himself.

Chain Lightning (1950)

WWII/Peace	Air Force	Full	B&W	94 mins
WB	WV: 02-08-50		NYT: 02-20-50	

DIR: Stuart Heisler. SW: Liam O'Brien. PRO: Anthony Veiller. STARS: Humphrey Bogart, Eleanor Parker, Raymond Massey, Richard Whorf.

The film opens with an American bombing mission over Germany in which newly developed enemy jets successfully attack the bombers. It then tells the story of the postwar development of American jet fighters.

Chasers (1994)

Peace	Marines	Deny	Color	102 mins
Morgan Creek	WV: 05-02-94		NYT: 04-22-94	

DIR: Dennis Hopper. SW: John Batteer, John Rice, Dan Gilroy. PRO: James Robinson. STARS: Tom Berenger, William McNamara, Erika Eleniak, Gary Busey, Crispin Glover, Dean Stockwell, Dennis Hopper.

A poor remake of *The Last Detail*, this time with a female Marine transported to prison after a conviction for assault. The filmmakers did request use of a National Guard motor pool, but after informal negotiations, the company acknowledged that it could not make the script changes that the DoD wanted.

Chesty Anderson—U.S. Navy (1976)

Peace	Navy	NR	Color	89 mins
Atlas Films	WV: 05-09-84		NYT: DNR	

DIR: Ed Forsyth. SW: H. F. Green, Paul Pompian. PRO: Paul Pompian. STARS: Shari Eubank, Dorrie Thomson, Rosanne Katon, Marcie Barkin, Fred Willard, Frank Campanella.

Chesty and three of her fellow WAVEs head out to find Chesty's missing sister. Silly gags and beautiful women populate this sexploitation mystery.

China Doll (1958)

WWII	Air Force	NR	B&W	88 mins
UA	WV: 08-20-58		NYT: 12-04-58	

DIR: Frank Borzage. SW: Kitty Buhler, James Benson Nablo, Thomas F. Kelly. PRO: Frank Borzage. STARS: Victor Mature, Stuart Whitman, LiLi Hua, Ward Bond, Bob Mathias, Johnny Desmond, Denver Pyle.

China in 1943 provides the background for this strange but dull story in which Mature flies the "hump" to provide supplies to China after Japan seals off all other access. He accidentally buys a Chinese girl, whom he comes to love and marry. When they are killed in a Japanese air raid, their daughter spends 13 years in an orphanage and then emigrates to the United States to live with Mature's family. Stock footage creates the limited combat images.

China Venture (1953)

WWII	Marines/Navy	Unkn	Color	83 mins
Columbia	WV: 08-26-53		NYT: DNR	

DIR: Don Siegel. SW: George Worthing Yates, Richard Collins. PRO: Anson Bond. STARS: Edmond O'Brien, Barry Sullivan, Philip Ahn.

Late in the war, a small unit of Marines and Navy personnel attempt "to spirit" an injured Japanese admiral from the Chinese coast to obtain intelligence.

China's Little Devils (1945)

WWII	Air Force	Unkn	B&W	74 mins
Monogram	WV: DNR		NYT: DNR	

DIR: Monta Bell. SW: Samuel Ornitz. PRO: Grant Withers. STARS: Harry Carey, Paul Kelly, Ducky Louie.

The film is an unworthy successor to *The Flying Tigers*, this time seen through the eyes of Chinese children carrying the war to the Japanese before Pearl Harbor, side by side with the Flying Tigers. In the end, as in *Air Force*, the American fliers, now in the Air Force, bomb Tokyo.

Cinderella Liberty (1973) [G&G]

Peace	Navy	Deny	Color	117 mins
Fox	WV: 12-12-73		NYT: 12-19-73	

DIR: Mark Rydell. SW: Darryl Ponicsan. PRO: Mark Rydell. STARS: James Caan, Marsha Mason, Eli Wallach, Dabney Coleman.

Based on Ponicsan's novel. Caan plays a sailor who falls in love with a prostitute who has a mixed race son. When she departs, Caan goes AWOL to take care of the boy. Rydell undertook lengthy negotiations to obtain access to a Naval base. For the service, the sticking point was Caan's going AWOL, but tentative agreement was finally reached. Then, the chief of information disapproved assistance, saying the movie would perpetuate the post-Vietnam negative image of the Navy and military as a whole, although Vietnam was not specifically mentioned. After the turn down, Rydell returned to his original script. Nevertheless, the film actually benefited the Navy since it showed its sailors sympathetically.

Cipher Bureau (1938)

Preparedness	Navy, Marines	Unkn	B&W	64 mins
Grand National	WV: 12-21-38		NYT: 12-14-38	

DIR: Charles Lamont. SW: Arthur Hoerl. PRO: Franklyn Warner. STARS: Leon Ames, Charlotte Wynters, Don Dillaway, Jason Robards Sr.

The film portrays how spies, those with guttural accents, transmit our secrets to their handlers. A young Navy officer falls for a Mata Hari type, but in the end love conquers all, with a little help from the Marines.

Classmates (1914)

Peace	Army	Full	B&W	4 reels
Biograph	WV: 02-27-14		NYT: DNR	

DIR: James Kirkwood. SW: Margaret Turnbull, William De Mille. PRO: Biograph. STARS: Blanche Sweet, Henry Walthall, Marshall Neilan, Gertrude Robinson.

Based on a 1907 play by Margaret Turnbull and William De Mille, the film follows a poor Southern boy who goes to West Point and experiences all the trials and heartaches of a cinematic plebe. The movie contains scenes of drills and a dance at the Academy. D. W. Griffith worked as the supervising manager on the film.

Classmates (1924)

Peace	Army	Full	B&W	74 mins
Inspirational/FN	WV: 12-31-24		NYT: 12-30-24	

DIR: John Robertson. SW: Josephine Lovett, Margaret Turnbull. PRO: John Robertson. STARS: Richard Barthelmess, Charlotte Walker, Madge Evans, Reginald Sheffield.

A remake of the 1914 film shot at the Academy, using the historical setting as background for a typical plebe love story. It captured well the discipline cadets had to endure to become officers as well as the rewards, including a wedding at the Academy chapel.

Clear and Present Danger (1994) [G&G]

Peace	Navy, Army	Ltd	Color	141 mins
Paramount	WV: 08-01-94		NYT: 08-03-94	

DIR: Phillip Noyce. SW: Donald Stewart, Steven Zaillian, John Milius. PRO: Mace Neufeld, Robert Rehme. STARS: Harrison Ford, Willem Dafoe, Anne Archer, James Earl Jones.

Based on the Tom Clancy novel, the filmmakers initially requested that an Air Force airplane bomb a cinematic drug lords' meeting in an unidentified country, but the service declined. After extended script negotiations, the Navy approved the use of an aircraft carrier to launch a plane with a special guided bomb that destroyed the building. The story ignored the reality that the ship's crew witnessed the top-secret mission because the plane returned without the bomb.

The Client (1994)

Peace	Air Force	Cour	Color	122 mins
WB	WV: 06-13-94		NYT: 07-20-94	

DIR: Joel Schumacher. SW: Akiva Goldsman, Robert Getchell. PRO: Arnon Milchan, Steven Reuther. STARS: Susan Sarandon, Tommy Lee Jones, Brad Renfro, Anthony Edwards.

Based on the John Grisham novel, the director used a National Guard hanger and Guardsmen as extras for the scene in which the "client" is accepted into the federal witness protection program under heavy FBI and National Guard security.

Clipped Wings (1938)

Peace	Air Force	Ltd	B&W	62 mins
Ace Pictures	WV: 05-04-38		NYT: DNR	

DIR: Stuart Paton. SW: Harry Forbes. PRO: Kier Philips. STARS: Lloyd Hughes, Rosalind Keith, William Janney, Jason Robards Sr.

A "C" movie about a soldier who disappears during WWI and his half brother, who years later is training to become an Army flyer until he "washes out" because he has a storm phobia. The two re-unite to fight oil thieves. The film has many flying sequences as well as aerial combat.

Clipped Wings (1953)

Peace	Air Force	Ltd	B&W	65 mins
Allied Artists	WV: 11-25-53		NYT: DNR	

DIR: Edward Bernds. SW: Charles R. Marion. PRO: Ben Schwalb. STARS: Leo Gorcey, Huntz Hall, Bernard Gorcey, Renie Riano.

The Bowery Boys join the Air Force in a slapstick comedy, for which the service provided limited use of men and equipment, ensues.

Close Encounters of the Third Kind (1977)

Peace	Air Force	Deny	Color	135 mins
Columbia	WV: 11-09-77		NYT: 11-17 & 20-77	

DIR: Steven Spielberg. SW: Steven Spielberg. PRO: Julia Phillips, Michael Phillips. STARS: Richard Dreyfuss, François Truffaut, Teri Garr, Melinda Dillon.

The studio requested the use of an Air Force hangar to shoot the film's final sequence, in which a saucerlike alien spaceship lands. The Air Force refused to assist, explaining that the service had denied the existence of UFOs and aliens for more than 30 years and that to cooperate on a film that showed them would be inappropriate.

Cock-Eyed World (1929)

Peace	Marines	Ltd	B&W	118 mins
Fox	WV: 08-07-29		NYT: 09-07-29	

DIR: Raoul Walsh. SW: Maxwell Anderson, William Wells. PRO: William Fox. STARS: Victor McLaglen, Edmund Lowe, Lili Damita.

The Marines provided assistance to this sequel of **What Price Glory?** in which Flagg and Quirt receive orders to go to a South Seas island and predictably compete for a local girl's affection.

Cocoon (1985)

SciFi	Air Force	Deny	Color	117 mins
Fox	WV: 06-19-85		NYT: 01-25-85	

DIR: Ron Howard. SW: Tom Benedek. PRO: Richard D. Zanuck, David Brown, Lili Fini Zanuck. STARS: Don Ameche, Wilford Brimley, Hume Cronyn, Brian Dennehy, Maureen Stapleton, Jessica Tandy.

The story of senior citizens discovering the fountain of youth in a sci-fi fantasy. The Air Force denied assistance because the film portrayed the service unrealistically and posited the existence of UFOs, which ran contrary to Air Force policy.

Colossus. See *The Forbin Project.*

Combat Squad (1953)

Korea	Army		Full	B&W	72 mins
Columbia	WV: 09-30-53			NYT: DNR	

DIR: Cy Roth. SW: Wyott Ordung. PRO: Jerry Thomas. STARS: John Ireland, Lon McCallister, Hal March.

Typical "B" army film set in Korea for which the service provided men and equipment pro forma.

Come on Leathernecks (1938)

Peace	Marines		Unkn	B&W	65 mins
Republic	WV: 08-24-38			NYT: 09-15-38	

DIR: James Cruze. SW: Sidney Salkow. PRO: Herman Schlom. STARS: Richard Cromwell, Leon Ames, Edward Brophy.

The film portrays a Naval Academy star football player who decides on a career as a Marine rather than one as a professional athlete.

Come on Marines (1934)

Peace	Marines		Full	B&W	64 mins
Paramount	WV: 03-27-34			NYT: 03-24-34	

DIR: Henry Hathaway. SW: Byron Morgan, Joel Sayre. PRO: Albert Lewis. STARS: Richard Arlen, Ida Lupino, Roscoe Karns, Monte Blue.

Typical Depression-era escapist film in which Arlen leads a small Marine unit to rescue a group of glamorous female tourists on a Pacific island.

Come See the Paradise (1990)

WWII	Army		Deny	Color	138 mins
Fox	WV: 05-16-90			NYT: 12-23-90	

DIR: Alan Parker. SW: Alan Parker. PRO: Robert Colesberry. STARS: Dennis Quaid, Tamlyn Tomita, Sab Shimono.

The Army denied assistance because soldiers appear only in the background in a story about the U.S. internment of Japanese in WWII.

Coming Home (1978) [G&G]

Vietnam	Marines	Deny	Color	127 mins
UA	WV: 02-15-78		NYT: 02-16 & 19-78	

DIR: Hal Ashby. SW: Nancy Dowd, Waldo Salt, Robert Jones. PRO: Jerome Hellman. STARS: Jane Fonda, Jon Voight, Bruce Dern, Robert Carradine, Penelope Milford.

The Marines refused to assist based on the original script, which portrayed Leathernecks in Vietnam cutting ears off dead Vietcong. In addition, the story showed an officer suffering a mental breakdown from his war experiences and committing suicide. Moreover, a paralyzed veteran criticized the Corps and the war. In fact, if the producers had submitted the final revised script, the Marines might have provided some help. In any case, the film helped convince the Marines that it was better to assist than to ignore projects, even those with "warts." At least Dern's haircut would have been regulation.

Command Decision (1948)

WWII	Air Force	Full	B&W	112 mins
MGM	WV: 12-29-48		NYT: 01-20-49	

DIR: Sam Wood. SW: William Laidlaw, George Froeschel. PRO: Sidney Franklin. STARS: Clark Gable, Walter Pidgeon, Van Johnson, Brian Donlevy, John Hodiak.

Based on William Wister Haines's play of the same name, this was the first postwar movie to portray the bombing of Germany. However, it loses credibility with the appearance of a congressional committee seeking answers to combat losses. The Air Force provided planes and combat footage.

Commandos (1968) a.k.a. *Sullivan's Marauders* (U.S.)

WWII	Army	NR	Color	82 mins (U.S.)
Heritage	WV: DNR		NYT: DNR	

DIR: Armando Crispino. SW: Menahem Golan, Don Martin, Dario Argento, et. al. PRO: Artur Brauner, Alfonso Sansone. STARS: Lee Van Cleef, Jack Kelly, Giampiero Albertini, Marino Masé, Helmut Schmid.

An Italian/American production portraying a standard search-and-destroy mission done many times before and since, but here with fine action sequences and good characterizations. Seven Italian American GIs disguise themselves as Italian soldiers to infiltrate and kill the Italian troops and hold the position until the arrival of an American battalion.

Con Air (1997)

Gulf	Army	NR	Color	115 mins
Touchstone	WV: 06-02-97		NYT: DNR	

DIR: Simon West. SW: Scott Rosenberg. PRO: Jerry Bruckheimer. STARS: Nicolas Cage, John Cusack, John Malkovich, Monica Potter.

The film contains a brief opening sequence of U.S. Rangers fighting in the first Gulf War, with a voice-over praising their fighting ability, and then a discharge ceremony back in the United States.

Contact (1997)

SciFi	Army	Ltd	Color	142 mins
WB	WV: 07-14-97		NYT: 07-11-97	

DIR: Robert Zemeckis. SW: James V. Hart, Michael Goldenberg. PRO: Steve Starkey, Robert Zemeckis. STARS: Jodie Foster, Matthew McConaughey, Tom Skerritt, John Hurt, David Morse.

Based on Carl Sagan's novel, the original script contained a silly depiction of the military. As a result of negotiations between the producer and the Army, the military portrayal was greatly improved. Consequently, the National Guard provided vehicles and helicopters for this story of the first human contact with other life forms.

Convoy (1927)

WWI	Navy	Full	B&W	circa 75 mins
FN	WV: 05-11-27		NYT: 05-09-27	

DIR: Joseph Boyle. SW: Willis Goldbeck. PRO: Robert Kane, Victor H. Hakperin, Edward R. Hakperin. STARS: Lowell Sherman, Dorothy Mackaill, William Collier Jr.

Adapted from John Taintor Foote's novel, *The Song of the Dragon*, the film served as the Navy's response to the 1920s Army and Marine films portraying their men in action during the recent war. *Variety* described **Convoy** as the Navy's **Big Parade**. It combined footage from the service's film archives of actual naval exploits during WWI with a melodramatic secret service story.

The Core (2003)

SciFi	Army, Air Force, Navy	Full	Color	135 mins
Paramount	WV: 03-24-2003		NYT: 03-28-2003	

DIR: Jon Amiel. SW: Cooper Layne, John Rogers. PRO: David Foster, Cooper Layne, Sean Bailey. STARS: Aaron Eckhart, Hilary Swank, Delroy Lindo, Stanley Tucci, Richard Jenkins.

Dumb, clichéd, often-repeated account of the day the earth's core stops spinning, which will cause the world to be fried in a year. Film combines **Fantastic Voyage**, **Towering Inferno**, and **Journey to the Center of the Earth** with scientists and astronauts burrowing into the earth to plant two atomic bombs, which will hopefully set the world spinning again. DoD provided men, equipment, and the carrier USS *Constellation*.

Corregidor (1943)

WWII	Army	Ltd	B&W	74 mins
PRC	WV: 06-02-43		NYT: 05-28-43	

DIR: William Nigh. SW: Doris Malloy. PRO: Dixon R. Harwin, Edward Finney. STARS: Otto Kruger, Elissa Landi, Donald Woods.

Using stock footage to create the combat background, the film attempts to exploit the military disaster of Corregidor through a low-budget, no stars production focusing on a love triangle.

Counter Measures (1998) a.k.a. *Crash Dive* 2 (on video)

Cold War	Navy	Inform	Color	90 mins
Warhead Films	WV: DNR		NYT: DNR	

DIR: Fred Olen Ray. SW: Steve Latshaw. PRO: Ashok Amritraj, Andrew Stevens. STARS: Michael Dudikoff, James Horan, Alexander Keith.

An old-fashioned B-movie in which U.S. Navy medical officer Dudikoff visits a Russian submarine on a goodwill mission that is interrupted when terrorists kidnap the sub and threaten to launch nuclear missiles. Dudikoff comes to the rescue. The cinematic sub is a WWII veteran, now a tourist attraction on the San Francisco waterfront. Amritraj received a ride aboard the USS *Abraham Lincoln*, which she described as "an invaluable experience," and information about naval nuclear procedures from the service's L.A. Public Affairs office, but no material assistance. Probably nothing could have helped the film, which was released in Europe in 1997 but went onto cable and video almost immediately in the United States.

The Courage of Lassie (1946)

WWII	Army	Full	Color	92 mins
MGM	WV: DNR		NYT: 07-25-46	

DIR: Fred Wilcox. SW: Lionel Houser. PRO: Robert Sisk. STARS: Lassie, Elizabeth Taylor, Frank Morgan, Tom Drake, Bill Wallace.

Lassie here plays Bill, a long-suffering collie who goes from a stray puppy to a home with Taylor, has an accident, and then is drafted to become a K-9 dog. There, he is wounded, faces the Japs in the trenches, suffers battle fatigue, becomes psychotic, and ultimately finds his way back to Taylor. Although aimed at a young audience, the film does show how the Army used dogs in the war.

Courage Under Fire (1996) [G&G]

Gulf	Army	Inform/Deny	Color	115 mins
Fox	WV: 06-24-96		NYT: 07-12-96	

DIR: Edward Zwick. SW: Patrick Duncan. PRO: John Davis, Joseph Singer, David Friendly. STARS: Denzel Washington, Meg Ryan, Lou Diamond Phillips, Michael Moriarty, Matt Damon.

Based on Patrick Duncan's novel of the same name, Washington searches for evidence to support awarding a Medal of Honor to helicopter pilot Ryan, who was killed during the first Gulf War while on a supply mission. Did she die from friendly or enemy fire? Washington has his own issues, a drinking problem and being under investigation for his role in a friendly-fire incident, when his tank destroyed another American tank.

The filmmakers submitted a request to the Army for use of armored vehicles, installations, etc., but the producers were unable to resolve many of the service's concerns, including a mutiny against Ryan by some of her men, their lying and a cover-up, Washington's drinking, etc. Although refusing material assistance, the Army did provide information and allowed Washington to make an overnight visit to Fort Irwin to learn about tank operations. As a result, the actor was able to create a more accurate portrayal of an officer, and he later made favorable comments about the service during publicity interviews for the film.

The Court-Martial of Billy Mitchell (1955)

Peace	Air Force	Ltd	Color	100 mins
WB	WV: 12-14-55		NYT: 12-23-55	

DIR: Otto Preminger. SW: Milton Sperling, Emmet Lavery. PRO: Milton Sperling. STARS: Gary Cooper, Charles Bickford, Ralph Bellamy, Rod Steiger.

A re-creation of Mitchell's court-martial for insubordination in his strong advocacy of air power during the 1920s. The film goes out of its way to vindicate Mitchell for opposing traditional Army and Navy officers, who could not visualize the importance of aerial bombardment.

Crash Dive (1943) [SSS]

WWII	Navy	Full	Color	105 mins
Fox	WV: 04-21-43		NYT: 04-29-43	

DIR: Archie Mayo. SW: Jo Swerling. PRO: Milton Sperling. STARS: Tyrone Power, Anne Baxter, Dana Andrews, James Gleason.

The first major submarine movie of WWII contained pure fantasy, with a U.S. sub on a combat cruise in the Atlantic, sinking German ships and destroying a mythical Nazi submarine supply base on an island in the North Atlantic. The Navy provided a submarine and exterior scenes at the New London, Connecticut sub base. In fact, U.S. subs made only one combat cruise in the Atlantic, going as far as the Bay of Biscay with very limited success, due in part to a problem with defective torpedoes. (See John Wayne's *Operation Pacific*.) All subs were then transferred to the Pacific theater.

Crazylegs (1953)

WWII	Marines	Unkn	B&W	87 mins
Republic	WV: 09-30-53		NYT: DNR	

DIR: Francis Lyon. SW: Hall Bartlett. PRO: Hall Bartlett. STARS: Elroy Hirsch, Lloyd Nolan, Bob Waterfield.

Typical sports biography of Elroy Hirsch's football career with the Los Angeles Rams. The film includes his Marine career.

Crimson Romance (1934)

WWI	Air Force	Unkn	B&W	70 mins
Mascot	WV: 10-16-34		NYT: 10-13-34	

DIR: Davis Howard. SW: Al Martin, Sherman Lowe, Milton Krims. PRO: Nat Levine. STARS: Ben Lyon, Sari Maritza, Eric von Stroheim, James Bush.

An independent film with a real twist: Lyon and Bush join the German air force. When the United States enters the war, Lyon changes sides to avoid facing the Americans, but Bush remains with the Germans because of the discrimination he faced as a German child growing up in the United States. The film contains strong German sympathies.

Crimson Tide (1995) [G&G]

Terrorism	Navy	Deny	Color	115 mins
Disney	WV: 05-08-95		NYT: 05-12-95	

DIR: Tony Scott. SW: Michael Schiffer. PRO: Jerry Bruckheimer, Don Simpson. STARS: Denzel Washington, Gene Hackman, Matt Craven.

A post–Cold War film in which the United States orders a nuclear submarine to launch missiles against Russian nationalists who have seized nuclear weapons. The Navy refused to cooperate because the service said the script did not portray launch system safeguards accurately and included a minimutiny by the executive officer, Washington. Compounding its inaccuracies, the film had Washington exonerated and given command of a submarine. In reality, he would probably have been jailed or, at the least, given a dishonorable discharge.

The Crowded Sky (1960)

Peace	Navy	NR	Color	105 mins
WB	WV: 08-24-60		NYT: 02-11-61	

DIR: Joe Pevney. SW: Charles Schnee, PRO: Michael Garrison. STAR: Dana Andrews, Rhonda Fleming, John Kerr, Anne Francis.

Based on Hank Searls's novel, the film became one of the first airplane disaster movies and the model for all future portrayals. A Navy jet with a defective radio system heads toward a collision with an airliner, filled with uninteresting people. The service could not have been happy with the portrayal of Navy pilot Andrews with personal problems, and with the expected ending.

Cry for Happy (1961)

Peace	Navy	Ltd	Color	110 mins
Columbia	WV: 01-11-61		NYT: 03-04-61	

DIR: George Marshall. SW: Irving Brecher. PRO: William Goetz. STARS: Glenn Ford, Donald O'Connor, Miiko Taka.

Based on George Campbell's novel, this silly comedy follows four sailors in Japan who chase four geisha girls while on leave.

Cry Havoc (1943)

WWII	Army	Ltd	B&W	97 mins
MGM	WV: 11-10-43		NYT: 11-24-43	

DIR: Richard Thorpe. SW: Paul Osborn. PRO: Edwin Knopf. STARS: Margaret Sullavan, Ann Sothern, Joan Blondell, Fay Bainter.

Based on the Allan R. Kenward play *Proof Thro' the Night*, the film tells the story of American nurses on Bataan who minister to the wounded soldiers as the Japanese steadily advance. One of the few Hollywood films of the period that lacked a major male presence.

The Cuban Love Song (1931)

Peace	Marines	Unkn	B&W	80 mins
MGM	WV: 12-08-31		NYT: 12-05-31	

DIR: W. S. Van Dyke. SW: C. Gardner Sullivan, Bess Meredith. PRO: Albert Lewin. STARS: Lawrence Tibbett, Jimmy Durante, Lupe Velez.

A lightweight musical comedy set for the most part in Cuba, with the Marines going to Cuba to have a good time.

Cutaway (2000)

Peace	Army	Full	Color	104 mins
Open Book	WV: DNR		NYT: DNR	

DIR: Guy Manos. SW: Greg Manos, Guy Manos. PRO: David Glasser. STARS: Tom Berenger, Stephen Baldwin, Dennis Rodman.

The only good aspect of this action-adventure movie is the exciting appearance of the Army's Golden Knights precision parachutists.

Darby's Rangers (1958)

WWII	Army	Full	B&W	121 mins
WB	WV: 01-22-58		NYT: 02-13-58	

DIR: William Wellman. SW: Guy Trosper. PRO: Martin Rackin. STARS: James Garner, Jack Warden, Edward Byrnes, Torin Thatcher.

A romantic adventure story, featuring friendly women for all the guys, while ostensibly describing the founding and training of Army rangers. The film served as a great recruiting advertisement for the service.

Dave (1993)

Peace	Navy	Ltd	Color	105 mins
WB	WV: 04-26-93		NYT: 05-07 & 09-93	

DIR: Ivan Reitman. SW: Gary Ross. Pro: Lauren Shuler-Donner, Ivan Reitman. STARS: Kevin Kline, Sigourney Weaver, Frank Langella, Ben Kingsley, Kevin Dunn.

Bad guys inside the White House substitute a look-alike for a stroke-stricken president. The Navy allowed the filmmakers to shoot a brief exterior scene at Bethesda Naval Hospital. However, the producer had to rent a commercial helicopter to re-create the landing scene on the White House lawn.

The Day After Tomorrow (2004)

Peace/SciFi	Army	Full	Color	124 mins
Fox	WV: 05-25-04		NYT: 05-28-04	

DIR: Roland Emmerich. SW: Roland Emmerich, Jeffrey Nachmanoff. PRO: Roland Emmerich, Mark Gordon. STARS: Dennis Quaid, Jake Gyllenhaal, Sela Ward, Ian Holm, Emmy Rossum.

Art Bell and Whitley Strieber's cautionary fantasy **The Coming Global Superstorm** provided the inspiration for Emmerich to undertake the project. Quaid, a world-renowned climatologist, tries to save the earth as it first undergoes abrupt global warming and then a new ice age. The 10th Mountain Division provided the director with a few Black Hawk helicopters, Humvees, and men, while Fort Bliss gave additional support to portray the Army performing its usual job during any natural disaster.

The Day the Earth Stood Still (1951)

Cold War/SciFi	Army	Ltd	B&W	92 mins
Fox	WV: 09-05-51		NYT: 09-19-51	

DIR: Robert Wise. SW: Edmund North. PRO: Julian Blaustein. STARS: Michael Rennie, Patricia Neal, Sam Jaffe, Hugh Marlowe, Billy Gray.

A classic science fiction story for which the Army provided men and materiel because in an actual alien landing, the army would have been mobilized. However the military acts rashly, attempting to kill the alien, without success. Unlike the Air Force, which denied the existence of flying saucers, the Army and National Guard had no problem challenging aliens even though the service proved no match for the visitor's technology.

D-Day, the Sixth of June (1956)

WWII	Army	Ltd	Color	106 mins
Fox	WV: 05-30-56		NYT: 05-30-56	

DIR: Henry Koster. SW: Ivan Moffat, Harry Brown. PRO: Charles Brackett. STARS: Robert Taylor, Richard Todd, Dana Wynter, Edmond O'Brien, John Williams.

Departing from novelist Lionel Shapiro's in-depth descriptions of the military planning for the D-Day invasion in *The Sixth of June*, most of this film follows the extramarital affair of an Army captain and the British family his dalliance affects. The battle scene is mercifully brief.

The Deadly Mantis (1957)

SciFi	Air Force, Army	Cour	B&W	78 mins
Universal	WV: 03-27-57		NYT: DNR	

DIR: Nathan Juran. SW: Martin Berkeley. PRO: William Alland. STARS: Craig Stevens, William Hopper, Alix Talton.

The film features the "Continental Air Defense" forces and equipment fighting a gigantic insect, freed from its polar cap home during an earthquake and on a predictable rampage. The military finally does its job, using "poison gas mines" to kill the insect in a tunnel under the Hudson River. No wonder the *New York Times* did not review it.

Dead Men Can't Dance (1997)

Korea	Army	NR	Color	97 mins
Live Entertainment	WV: DNR		NYT: DNR	

DIR: Steve Anderson. SW: Paul Sinor. PRO: Elaine Hastings Edell. STARS: Kathleen York, Adrian Paul, Michael Biehn, R. Lee Ermey.

Anticipating future headlines, the film posits a story of an elite Army unit sent into North Korea to destroy its nuclear facility; the unit is captured. In the end, an all-women Ranger unit comes to the rescue and completes the mission. Only the *Jakarta Post* ever reviewed this ludicrous film, and it went almost immediately to video.

Dead Presidents (1995)

Vietnam	Marines	NR	Color	119 mins
Buena Vista	WV: 10-2-95		NYT: 09-29-95	

DIR: Albert Hughes, Allen Hughes. SW: Albert Hughes, Allen Hughes, Michael Henry Brown. PRO: Allen Hughes, Albert Hughes. STARS: Larenz Tate, Keith David, Chris Tucker, Bokeem Woodbine.

The film is mostly set in the black community during the late 1960s and early 1970s, with 20 intense minutes of combat in Vietnam, where the hero comes of age under fire. He operates with great efficiency as part of an elite unit. The most grotesque incidents involve the obsessive blood lust of a maniacal corpsman, who carries around the chopped off head of an enemy for good luck, which was enough to disqualify the film for cooperation. Dale Dye served as civilian technical advisor, and the Florida outback stood in for Vietnam.

Death Before Dishonor (1987)

Peace	Marines	NR	Color	95 mins
New World	WV: 02-04-87		NYT: 02-20-87, 03-01-87	

DIR: Terry Leonard. SW: John Gatliff, Lawrence Kubik. PRO: Lawrence Kubik. STARS: Fred Dryer, Brian Keith, Paul Winfield.

This movie portrays a Marine's fight against Arab terrorists in a fictional Middle Eastern country. The credo "Death Before Dishonor" establishes the connection to the Marines. Dryer wages a one-man war against the stereotypical, ruthless Arabs to rescue his commanding officer. Filmed in Israel.

Death of a Soldier (1986)

WWII	Army	NR	Color	93 mins
Suatu	WV: 05-07-86		NYT: 05-16 & 25-86	

DIR: Philippe Mora. SW: William Nagle. PRO: William Nagle, David Hannay. STARS: James Coburn, Bill Hunter, Reb Brown, Maurie Fields.

In this Australian production, based on a true story, Coburn plays a U.S. Army lawyer in wartime Australia who oversees the relationship between the growing number of U.S. soldiers and the local population. When Aussie girls begin to die, Coburn helps the local police capture Brown, a psychotic soldier, and then defends him. Although the soldier confesses to his crimes, he is clearly insane. Nevertheless, Gen. Douglas MacArthur approves the soldier's execution to placate the Aussies, not too different from the British executing Breaker Morant to maintain good relations with Germany.

Decision Before Dawn (1951)

WWII	Army	Full	B&W	119 mins
Fox	WV: 12-19-51		NYT: 12-22-51	

DIR: Anatole Litvak. SW: Peter Viertel. PRO: Anatole Litvak, Frank McCarthy. STARS: Richard Basehart, Gary Merrill, Oskar Werner, Hildegarde Knef.

Based on George Howe's novel *Call It Treason*, the film portrays a German POW who agrees to spy for the U.S. Army. McCarthy sought script approval before filming in war-torn Germany using an extensive German cast. The movie features unreconstructed ruins, rubble, and other war-related artifacts to depict the behind-the-scenes crumbling of the Third Reich's infrastructure and proud citizens.

Deep Impact (1998)

SciFi	Army	Full	Color	120 mins
WB	WV: 05-11-98		NYT: 05-08-98	

DIR: Mimi Leder. SW: Michael Tolkin, Bruce Joel Rubin. PRO: Richard Zanuck, Darryl Brown. STARS: Robert Duvall, Elijah Wood, Vanessa Redgrave, Maximilian Schell, Morgan Freeman.

This movie beat **Armageddon** to theaters with a similar threat from outer space, this time a comet. Freeman, the president, uses every instrument available to avoid human extinction from the collision. After changes in script, the Army provided National Guard helicopters and other equipment performing as they would in any major disaster. An outstanding cast is wasted in a mundane portrayal saved only by good special effects.

The Deep Six (1958)

WWII	Navy	Full	Color	110 mins
WB	WV: 01-01-58		NYT: 01-16-58	

DIR: Rudolph Maté. SW: John Twist, Martin Rackin, Harry Brown. PRO: Martin Rackin. STARS: Alan Ladd, Dianne Foster, William Bendix, James Whitmore.

Based on a Martin Dibner novel. Ladd portrayed a Quaker serving as a gunnery officer aboard a destroyer in the Pacific. The director used combat footage and interactions among the officers to create a realistic ambience of the war at sea.

The Deer Hunter (1978) [G&G]

Vietnam	Army	Deny	Color	183 mins
Universal	WV: 11-29-78		NYT: 12-15-78	

DIR: Michael Cimino. SW: Louis Garfinkle, Quinn Redeker, Deric Washburn, Michael Cimino. PRO: Barry Spikings, Michael Deeley, Michael Cimino, John Peverall. STARS: Robert De Niro, John Cazale, Meryl Streep, John Savage, Christopher Walken.

Although most people believe the movie is commenting on the American experience in Vietnam, Garfinkle and Redeker, who wrote the original script, did not initially use the war as their stage. Ultimately, they decided their story served as a metaphor for the U.S. involvement in Vietnam. In fact, their script only portrayed a game of Russian roulette in which a brain-damaged enlisted POW played at the direction of his officer and companion, first in a North Vietnamese prison and then in Saigon after they escape. Spikings and Deeley, who bought the script, realized it contained too much violence and hired Cimino to moderate the story. The director initially tried to eliminate the roulette, saying he did not understand its significance. Later, he and cowriter Washburn grafted their story of steel workers onto the original script and portrayed them hunting in the wilds of Pennsylvania with its 10,000-foot mountain. Although the three main characters volunteer for Vietnam, Cimino was to claim that the film was not about that war.

When the Army received the script by way of the Pennsylvania Film Bureau with a request that the DoD provide assistance, the service rejected it. The public affairs office cited numerous inaccurate portrayals, including POWs being forced to play Russian roulette and De Niro's bearded character returning to Vietnam in a Green Beret uniform as Saigon fell.

When the film first appeared, critics and audiences accepted the Russian roulette as having occurred. The truth came out too late to influence the Academy Awards voters. In any event, the portrayal and the closing scene, in which the surviving characters, zombie-like, sing "God Bless America," invalidate any claim the film might have to explaining the nature of the Vietnam War and its impact on the American people.

The Delta Force (1986)

Peace	Army	NR	Color	126 mins
Cannon	WV: 02-19-86		NYT 02-14 & 23-86	

DIR: Menahem Golan. SW: James Bruner, Menahem Golan. PRO: Menahem Golan, Yoram Globus. STARS: Chuck Norris, Lee Marvin, Martin Balsam, Joey Bishop.

Inspired by the 1985 TWA hijacking and filmed in Israel. The Delta Force, a crack U.S. commando unit, led by Lee Marvin and Chuck Norris, rescues passengers from an airliner hijacked by Arab terrorists.

Delta Force 2: Operation Stranglehold (1990)

Peace	Marines, Army	NR	Color	105 mins
Cannon	WV: 05-23-90		NYT: 08-25-90	

DIR: Aaron Norris. SW: Lee Reynolds. PRO: Menahem Golan, Christopher Pearce. STARS: Chuck Norris, Billy Drago, Richard Jaeckel, John Ryan.

In this heroic depiction of the U.S. war on international drug rings, Norris's brother uses the energy and charisma of his leading man along with missile-firing helicopters and other exploding devices to depict good versus evil. The Marines and the Army combine to break up a Colombian drug ring.

Delta Force 3: The Killing Game (1991)

Terrorists	Army	NR	Color	Unkn
Global Pictures	WV: DNR		NYT: DNR	

DIR: Sam Firstenberg. SW: Boaz Davidson, Andrew Deutsch. PRO: Christopher Pearce. STARS: Nick Cassavetes, Eric Douglas, Mike Norris, Matthew Penn.

The president calls in the Delta Force to find an atomic bomb, which terrorists have hidden somewhere in the United States. Chuck Norris's son appears in this one.

Delta Force Commando (1987-Italy)

Terrorists	Army	Deny	Color	90 mins
Realta	WV: DNR		NYT: DNR	

DIR: Pierluigi Ciriaci. SW: Dardano Sacchetti. PRO: Fabrizio De Angelis. STARS: Brett Baxter Clark, Fred Williamson, Mark Gregory, Bo Svenson.

This is the first of a "rip off" series of films, along with *Operation Delta Force*, that capitalized on the success of three Chuck Norris (and family) action-adventure movies that loosely portrayed the elite Delta Force. The Norris *Delta Force* films popularized the elite force's unique status in the military, even as they exaggerated the reality of the special forces operations. In contrast, the "rip off" movies contained virtually no resemblance to the manner in which the U.S. special forces actually operated. Made quickly and with low budgets, one as a television movie and the others nominally feature films, they went almost immediately to cable and video. For the most part, the clichéd, ludicrous plots simply became the vehicles for almost nonstop violence. Nevertheless, the films provided images of special forces activities that viewers might have accepted as reality, at least until the release of *Black Hawk Down* in 2001.

In this film, the Delta Force is sent to recover a nuclear bomb that Latin American revolutionaries seized from a military base in Puerto Rico. The DoD denied a request for assistance, saying that the story was unrealistic and provided no benefit to the Pentagon or the nation.

Delta Force Commando II: Priority Red One (1991-Italy)

Terrorism	Army, Air Force	NR	Color	Unkn
Realta	WV: DNR		NYT: DNR	

DIR: Pierluigi Ciriaci. SW: Unkn. PRO: Unkn. STARS: Richard Hatch, Fred Williamson, Giannina Facio, Van Johnson.

In this virtually incomprehensible film that went directly to video, the Delta Force receives orders to find and bring back six missing nuclear missiles that may be aimed at Russia.

Destination Gobi (1953)

WWII	Navy	Ltd	Color	89 mins
Fox	WV: 02-18-53		NYT: 05-30-53	

DIR: Robert Wise. SW: Everett Freeman. PRO: Stanley Rubin. STARS: Richard Widmark, Don Taylor, Martin Milner, Ross Bagdasarian.

Navy meteorologists travel to the Gobi Desert, of all places, to send back weather information to the military planners preparing for Pacific island invasions.

Destination Tokyo (1943) [G&G]

WWII	Navy	Full	B&W	135 mins
WB	WV: 12-22-43		NYT: 01-01-44	

DIR: Delmer Daves. SW: Delmer Daves. PRO: Jerry Wald. STARS: Cary Grant, John Garfield, Alan Hale, John Ridgely.

Widely considered to be one of the best WWII submarine stories ever, this movie portrays a U.S. sub that goes into Tokyo Bay to collect weather information for the Doolittle raid on Japan in April 1942. The Navy provided a submarine at Mare Island, California, for exterior filming. The cliché of an appendicitis operation aboard ship by a corpsman began with this movie. Despite Daves's claim that he wanted to make an accurate film, he showed the submarine leaving on its mission on December 24, 1941, more than two weeks before the Navy conceived the plan to bomb Japan. Daves also created a nonexistent submarine net protecting Tokyo Bay. On the other hand, his "radar" scope initially caused the Navy some security concerns. In any case, the film provided the images of submarine warfare that became the reality for most people during the war and for years afterward.

Destroyer (1943) [SSS]

WWII	Navy	Full	B&W	99 mins
Columbia	WV: 08-18-43		NYT: 09-02-43	

DIR: William Seiter. SW: Frank "Spig" Wead, Lewis Weltzer, Borden Chase. PRO: Louis F. Edelman. STARS: Edward G. Robinson, Glenn Ford, Edgar Buchanan.

Old-salty-dog Robinson, playing a WWI Navy veteran, learns new tricks when reenlisting onto the "new" *John Paul Jones* and drives the "youngsters" crazy describing how "it used to be." Robinson's courage during combat has not waned the second time around.

Devil Dogs of the Air (1935) [G&G]

Peace	Marines, Navy	Full	B&W	86 mins
WB	WV: 02-12-35		NYT: 02-07-35	

DIR: Lloyd Bacon. SW: Malcolm Boylan, Earl Baldwin. PRO: Cosmopolitan. STARS: James Cagney, Pat O'Brien, Margaret Lindsay.

Jack Warner and Hal Wallis served as executive producers on this clichéd Marine comedy in which Cagney and O'Brien chase the same girl. While filming for three weeks at the Marine flying base on North Island, San Diego, Bacon obtained spectacular flying sequences, including the climactic 10-minute portrayal of a Marine landing exercise supported by ships and planes. The movie remains the only one ever to show Marine planes taking off from an aircraft carrier to fly close air support for Leathernecks on the ground. However, the film does not explain the ongoing debate over the role of Marine planes aboard carriers: Should they only fly close air support or should they help protect the carrier from aerial attack?

The Devil Makes Three (1952)

Peace	Air Force	NR	B&W	90 mins
MGM	WV: 08-13-52		NYT: 08-30-52	

DIR: Andrew Marton. SW: Jerry Davis. PRO: Richard Goldstone. STARS: Gene Kelly, Pier Angeli, Richard Rober, Richard Egan.

Air Force officer Kelly returns to Germany in 1947 to thank the family who hid him after he was shot down over Munich. However, he finds that U.S. bombs have killed his benefactors, except for Angeli. As expected, she initially hates him, but they soon fall in love. Complications intrude in the form of surviving Nazis who are smuggling gold in an effort to continue the Third Reich. Ultimately, love triumphs over such evil.

The Devil's Brigade (1968) [G&G]

WWII	Army	Full	Color	130 mins
UA	WV: 05-01-68		NYT: 05-23-68	

DIR: Andrew McLaglen. SW: William Roberts. PRO: David Wolper. STARS: William Holden, Cliff Robertson, Vince Edwards, Dana Andrews.

Like Lee Marvin in *The Dirty Dozen* and Gregory Peck in *Twelve O'Clock High*, Holden molds a group of misfits into a crack unit, which fights alongside a Canadian contingent during the Italian campaign. To create the combat sequences, including the assault on a mountaintop German fortification (filmed in Utah), the Army provided soldiers, as extras, and military equipment.

The Devil's Playground (1937) [G&G]

Peace	Navy	Full	B&W	74 mins
Columbia	WV: 02-17-37		NYT: 02-15-37	

DIR: Erle Kenton. SW: Norman Springer, Liam O'Flaherty, Jerome Chodorov, Dalton Trumbo. PRO: Columbia. STARS: Richard Dix, Dolores Del Rio, Chester Morris, Pierre Watkin.

A remake of Frank Capra's **Submarine**. Although the Navy had assisted on the original film, the model for all future submarine disaster movies, the service had great reluctance to become involved with the sound version. Neither film offered any benefit to the Navy because of the images of sunken submarines, unfaithful service wives, and a Navy diver who at first refuses the assignment to help rescue the submarine crew because his best friend, who unwittingly slept with the diver's wife, is aboard. Ultimately the cuckolded diver does go down to the stricken submarine with an air hose. Given the depth of the sub, no rescue would have been possible, but the film ends with the two friends together and the unfaithful wife back to bar-hopping. Despite such problems of accuracy and image, the Navy agreed to provide full cooperation after much negotiation and some script revisions.

The D.I. (1957)

Peace	Marines	Full	B&W	106 mins
WB	WV: 05-29-57		NYT: 06-06-57	

DIR: Jack Webb. SW: James Lee Barrett. PRO: Jack Webb. STARS: Jack Webb, Don Dubbins, Lin McCarthy.

Filmed at Paris Island. Webb created the classic portrayal of how Marine drill instructors turn recruits into fighting Leathernecks.

Dirigible (1931) [SSS]

Peace	Navy	Full	B&W	93 mins
Columbia	WV: 04-08-31		NYT: 04-06-31	

DIR: Frank Capra. SW: Frank "Spig" Wead, Jo Swerling. PRO: Harry Cohn. STARS: Jack Holt, Ralph Graves, Fay Wray.

A Navy dirigible floats to the rescue after the explorers' plane crashes while landing to plant "the flag" at the South Pole. The film features a midair dirigible crack-up inspired by actual dirigible disasters. Navy planes and a dirigible at Lakehurst, New Jersey, created authentic ambience.

The Dirty Dozen (1967)

WWII	Army	NR	Color	150 mins
MGM	WV: 06-21-67		NYT: 06-16-67	

DIR: Robert Aldrich. SW: Nunnally Johnson, Lukas Heller. PRO: Kenneth Hyman. STARS: Lee Marvin, Charles Bronson, Jim Brown, John Cassavetes, Richard Jaeckel, Clint Walker, Trini Lopez, Telly Savalas, Donald Sutherland, George Kennedy, Ralph Meeker, Robert Ryan, Ernest Borgnine.

From the E. M. Nathanson novel. The all-star cast provide a classic rendering of the molding of military misfits, in this case, convicted rapists, murders, and deserters, into a crack special forces-type unit. It then receives the pre-D-Day mission of killing German officers in France to disrupt any enemy counterattack. Aldrich said that since he shot the film in England, he had no reason to request Army support.

Distant Thunder (1988)

Vietnam	Army	NR	Color	114 mins
Paramount	WV: 09-07-88		NYT: 11-11-88	

DIR: Rick Rosenthal. SW: Robert Stitzel. PRO: Robert Schaffel. STARS: John Lithgow, Ralph Macchio, Kerrie Keane, Reb Brown, Janet Margolin.

Vietnam in 1969 appeared in the prologue to this story about the problems some Vietnam veterans faced when they returned home. Some reviewers found the film sympathetic to the vets, while others thought it stigmatized them as they had been in movies 10 years earlier.

Dive Bomber (1941) [G&G]

Preparedness	Navy	Full	Color	130 mins
WB	WV: 08-13-41		NYT: 08-30-41	

DIR: Michael Curtiz. SW: Frank "Spig" Wead, Robert Buckner. PRO: Warner Bros. STARS: Errol Flynn, Fred MacMurray, Ralph Bellamy, Alexis Smith.

The film focuses on the role of Navy flight surgeons in the development of aviation medicine. This preparedness film contains Technicolor shots of rows of planes on the field, on the decks of carriers, and in the sky and backgrounds shot at Eglin Air Force Base in Florida, Pearl Harbor, Hawaii, and the U.S. Naval Base San Diego, California. In addition, Curtiz filmed aboard the carriers *Enterprise* and *Saratoga*. Despite this assistance, some viewers thought the film provided a negative image of the Navy because some of the fliers died in crashes.

Dogfight (1991)

Vietnam	Marines	NR	Color	89 mins
WB	WV: 09-16-91		NYT: 09-13 & 15-91	

DIR: Nancy Savoca. SW: Bob Comfort. PRO: Peter Newman, Richard Guay. STARS: River Phoenix, Lili Taylor, Richard Panebianco, Anthony Clark, Mitchell Whitfield, Holly Near, Sue Morales.

This feminist nightmare follows four Marines on the night before their departure for Vietnam and portrays their contest to bring the ugliest woman to a party. Phoenix's character becomes attracted to the girl he finds. He is the only one who returns from the war, and a hippie taunts him with the greeting: "How many babies did you kill?"

Dog Tags (1990)

Vietnam	Army	NR	Color	100 mins
Cinevest Enter.	WV: DNR		NYT: DNR	

DIR: Romano Scavolini. SW: Romano Scavolini. PRO: Alain Adams, Dalu Jones. STARS: Gigi Dueñas, Peter Elich, Robert Haufrecht, Chris Hilton.

Army commandos rescue POWs from tiger cages but then discover their real mission was to liberate a cache of gold. The film contains every cliché and inaccuracy from earlier Vietnam movies. The Philippines stood in for Vietnam one more time.

Dondi (1961)

Peace	Army	Cour	B&W	80 mins
Allied Artists	WV: 08-23-61		NYT: DNR	

DIR: Albert Zugsmith. SW: Gus Edson, Irwin Hasen. PRO: Albert Zugsmith. STARS: David Janssen, Patti Page, Walter Winchell, Mickey Shaughnessy.

Diabetics beware! Based on the Edson and Irwin Hasen comic strip, the movie simply creates a too sweet version of GIs rescuing an Italian orphan. Originally released at 100 minutes, the studio cut it to 80 minutes for scheduling as a companion piece to main features, and most of the actors' roles suffered under the knife.

Don't Cry, It's Only Thunder (1982) [G&G]

Vietnam	Army	Full	Color	108 mins
Sanrio	WV: 03-10-82		NYT: 12-03-82	

DIR: Peter Werner. SW: Paul G. Hensler. PRO: Walt de Faria, Paul Hensler. STARS: Dennis Christopher, Roger Aaron Brown, Susan Saint James, James Whitmore Jr.

Based on a true story, this is one of the first movies set in Vietnam in which the leading character is a good guy. Christopher fulfills a promise to his dying friend to support a Vietnamese orphanage in Saigon. The Army loaned equipment and men to the production in the Philippines.

Don't Give Up the Ship (1959)

Peace	Navy	Ltd	Color	89 mins
Paramount	WV: 06-03-59		NYT: 07-09-59	

DIR: Norman Taurog. SW: Herbert Baker, Edmund Beloin, Henry Garson. PRO: Hal Wallis. STARS: Jerry Lewis, Dina Merrill, Diana Spencer, Mickey Shaughnessy.

Taurog created a better-than-average comedy in which Lewis, as an ensign, loses a battleship during WWII.

Don't Go Near the Water (1957)

WWII	Navy	Full	Color	107 mins
MGM	WV: 11-13-57		NYT: 11-15-57	

DIR: Charles Walters. SW: Dorothy Kingsley, George Wells. PRO: Lawrence Weingarten. STARS: Glenn Ford, Gia Scala, Anne Francis, Keenan Wynn.

Ford stars in a silly Navy comedy set in the South Pacific showing that WWII was actually fun and games and little combat.

Doughboys (1930)

WWI	Army	NR	B&W	80 mins
MGM	WV: 09-24-30		NYT: 09-30-30	

DIR: Edward Sedgwick. SW: Al Boasberg, Sidney Lazarus. PRO: MGM. STARS: Buster Keaton, Sally Eilers, Cliff Edwards, Frank Mayo, Victor Potel, Arnold Korff.

Keaton based the story on his own experiences in WWI but played it here as a comedy in which he accidentally enlists in the Army and finds himself in France. Eilers, who had repulsed Keaton's earlier courting, becomes a troop entertainer, and their romance is kindled.

Down Periscope (1996)

Peace	Navy	Cour	Color	92 mins
Fox	WV: 03-04-96		NYT: 03-01-96	

DIR: David Ward. SW: Hugh Wilson, Andrew Kurtzman, Eliot Wald. PRO: Robert Lawrence. STARS: Kelsey Grammer, Lauren Holly, Bruce Dern, Rob Schneider, Rip Torn, Harry Dean Stanton, William H. Macy.

Grammer's movie debut took place in this lackluster comedy focusing on misfits at sea. The Navy allowed a mothballed submarine to be towed in front of the cameras despite the less-than-positive image of the service.

Dr. Strangelove or: How I Learned to Stop Worrying and Love the Bomb (1964) [G&G]

Cold War	Air Force	NR	B&W	93 mins
Columbia	WV: 01-22-64		NYT: 01-31-64	

DIR: Stanley Kubrick. SW: Stanley Kubrick, Terry Southern, Peter George. PRO: Stanley Kubrick. STARS: Peter Sellers, George C. Scott, Keenan Wynn, Slim Pickens, James Earl Jones, Tracy Reed, Sterling Hayden, Peter Bull.

Based on Peter George's 1958 novel *Red Alert*. Kubrick initially intended to make a serious comment on the possibility of a nuclear accident that might trigger World War III. However, he confronted the absurdities inherent in the story, noting, "How the hell could the President ever tell the Russian Premier to shoot down American planes? Good Lord, it sounds ridiculous." As a result, he turned the film into a satirical nightmare, with its surrealistic portrayal of men blundering through war rooms, engaging in absurd dialogues, and committing all manner of lunacy while the world moves rapidly to absolute destruction.

In the end, Kubrick created the first movie about SAC that questioned the value of nuclear weapons designed to keep peace between the United States and the Soviet Union. While Kubrick made some tentative inquiries about possible Air Force assistance, he never submitted a script and made the film in England, using models for his flying sequences. The characters of Generals Turgidson and Ripper were drawn on the perceived image of SAC's creator, Curtis LeMay, and the filmmakers modeled Dr. Strangelove on Herman Kahn and Edward Teller.

ICBMs and Polaris missiles were to take over much of the nuclear deterrent from the Air Force bombers, and the Soviet Union was to collapse. Nevertheless, **Dr. Strangelove** has not become dated or its satire lessened. However, the very nature of the satiric portrayals diluted Kubrick's original message, and most people still appreciate the film more for its comedic images than for its warning about nuclear weapons.

Draft 258 (1918)

WWI	Army	Full	B&W	7 reels
MGM	WV: 02-08-18		NYT: DNR	

DIR: Christy Cabanne. SW: Christy Cabanne. PRO: MGM. STARS: Mabel Taliaferro, Walter Miller, Earl Brunswick, Eugene Borden.

A dysfunctional family takes different approaches to WWI. The sister patriotically supports the war. One brother, Matthew, takes to a soapbox avowing pacifism and becomes a patsy for German spies. The other brother, George, refuses to report for induction when his draft number, 258, comes up but enlists after his sister shames him by offering to go in his place. When the German spies capture the girl and plan to blow up an airplane factory, Matthew realizes the perfidy of his associates. As he tries to save his sister and the factory, her officer-boyfriend John leads the cavalry to their rescue. Matthew then joins the Army and the brothers head to France. A war-effort film of the most rabid kind.

Dragonfly Squadron (1954)

Korea	Air Force	NR	B&W	82 mins
Allied Artists	WV: 02-03-54		NYT: DNR	

DIR: Lesley Selander. SW: John Champion. PRO: John Champion. STARS: John Hodiak, Barbara Britton, Bruce Bennet, Jess Barker.

American fliers train their South Korean counterparts before the North Korean invasion in 1950. While on the ground, they pursue romance.

Dress Parade (1927) [G&G]

Peace	Army	Full	B&W	66 mins
Pathé	WV: 11-02-27		NYT: 10-31-27	

DIR: Donald Crisp. SW: Major Robert Glassburn, Major Alexander Chilton, Herbert Walters. PRO: Cecil De Mille. STARS: William Boyd, Bessie Love, Hugh Allan.

Filmed on location at West Point, this coming-of-age movie uses academy life and the spirit of Gen. "Black Jack" Pershing to chronicle the development of a gentleman-soldier.

Duke of West Point (1938)

Peace	Army	Unkn	B&W	107 mins
UA	WV: 12-21-38		NYT: 12-16-38	

DIR: Alfred E. Green. SW: George Bruce. PRO: Edward Small. STARS: Louis Hayward, Joan Fontaine, Tom Brown, Richard Carlson.

A Cambridge (England) man sent to West Point by his father attempts to uphold his family's honor and win the girl. Hockey replaces football in this coming-of-age film.

The Eagle Has Landed (1976)

WWII	Army	NR	Color	123 mins
Columbia	WV: 12-22-76		NYT: 03-26-77	

DIR: John Sturges. SW: Tom Mankiewicz. PRO: Jack Wiener, David Niven. STARS: Michael Caine, Donald Sutherland, Robert Duvall, Donald Pleasence, Larry Hagman.

Based on a Jack Higgins novel, the film follows the efforts of a crack German commando unit to assassinate Winston Churchill during his visit to the English countryside. When their identities are revealed, the Germans seize the small town in which they had been waiting for the prime minister's arrival. A nearby U.S. Army unit responds to the threat and launches an attack. Hagman, as an incompetent captain, almost allows the Germans to win the day before he receives his just rewards and the Americans liberate the town.

Earth vs. the Flying Saucers (1956)

SciFi	All	NR	B&W	82 mins
Columbia	WV: 06-06-56		NYT: 08-02-56	

DIR: Fred F. Sears. SW: George Worthing Yates, Raymond Marcus. PRO: Charles Schneer. STARS: Hugh Marlowe, Joan Taylor, Donald Curtis, Morris Ankrum, Grandon Rhodes, Tom Browne Henry.

Creatures on flying saucers knock down a scientist's artificial satellites, launched for the military. Then these space beings capture one of our generals and threaten to take over the entire earth.

Earthquake (1974)

Disaster	Army	NR	Color	122 mins
Universal	WV: 11-13-74		NYT: 11-16-14	

DIR: Mark Robson. SW: George Fox, Mario Puzo. PRO: Mark Robson. STARS: Charlton Heston, Ava Gardner, George Kennedy, Lorne Greene, Geneviève Bujold, Richard Roundtree.

A big one hits Los Angeles, affecting a cross section of the population. Robson saw no advantage to obtaining Army cooperation and used actors to portray National Guardsmen doing their usual jobs in the face of a natural disaster. The TV version had an additional 17 minutes.

Easy Come, Easy Go (1967)

Peace	Navy	Ltd	Color	95 mins
Paramount	WV: 03-22-67		NYT: 06-15-67	

DIR: John Rich. SW: Allan Weiss, Anthony Lawrence. PRO: Hal Wallis. STARS: Elvis Presley, Dodie Marshall, Pat Priest.

Elvis, a Navy underwater demolition expert, discovers sunken treasure and leaves the service to recover it, with requisite songs and dance.

Eight Iron Men (1952)

WWII	Army	NR	B&W	80 mins
Columbia	WV: 10-22-52		NYT: 01-02-53	

DIR: Edward Dmytryk. SW: Harry Brown. PRO: Stanley Kramer. STARS: Bonar Colleano, Lee Marvin, Richard Kiley.

Based on Brown's play *A Sound of Hunting*, the film is an interior portrayal of men in combat who spend most of their time talking while holed up in an Italian town. The film has little to say about the experience of men in combat.

84 Charlie Mopic (1989)

Vietnam	Army	NR	Color	95 mins
New Century	WV: 01-25-89		NYT: 03-22-89	

DIR: Patrick Duncan. SW: Patrick Duncan. PRO: Michael Nolin, Jill Griffith. STARS: Jonathan Emerson, Nicholas Cascone, Jason Tomlins, Christopher Burgard.

Made in documentary style, the movie portrays a combat cameraman following a patrol on its two-day mission. Duncan was able to create a sense of realism in a fictional film. Compare to the documentary *The Anderson Platoon* (see chapter 3).

The Enemy Below (1957) [G&G]

WWII	Navy	Full	Color	98 mins
Fox	WV: 11-27-57		NYT: 12-26-57	

DIR: Dick Powell. SW: Wendell Mayes. PRO: Dick Powell. STARS: Robert Mitchum, Curt Jürgens, Al Hedison, Theodore Bikel.

Based on the British novel by D. A. Rayner, the film portrays an American destroyer waging mortal war against a German submarine in the South Atlantic. The two captains become warriors in arms, not advocates of the political systems that have sent them to war. One of the very best Navy movies, any time or any war.

The service provided a destroyer and men and helped create a scene in which torpedoes from the submarine bracket the American ship. The film's only flaw is the model sequence showing the destruction of both ships after Mitchum rams his crippled destroyer into the submarine, which he has forced to the surface. Unlike the novel's ending, in which the two captains die in the explosion after meeting face to face, the movie has the officers talk on the fantail of a rescue ship about their confrontations with each other and with death.

Ensign Pulver (1964)

WWII	Navy	Deny	Color	104 mins
WB	WV: 02-26-64		NYT: 08-01-64	

DIR: Joshua Logan. SW: Joshua Logan, Peter Feibleman. PRO: Joshua Logan. STARS: Robert Walker Jr., Burl Ives, Walter Matthau, Tommy Sands, Larry Hagman.

The Navy refused to assist with this sequel to *Mister Roberts* because the cinematic images of the officers were highly negative. Even though *Mister Roberts* also contained those same images, the Navy had cooperated on that earlier movie because John Ford was the original director.

Ernest in the Army (1998)

Peace	Army	NR	Color	85 mins
Active Enter	DV: DNR		NYT: DNR	

DIR: John Cherry. SW: John Cherry, Joseph Dattorre. PRO: John Cherry, Kenneth Badish. STARS: Jim Varney, Haley Tyson, David Müller, Christo Davids.

A comic mess in which Varney, as Ernest, ends up in the Army and becomes involved in military action against a petty Middle Eastern tyrant. The lack of reviews attests to the film's "artistic merit."

Ernest Saves Christmas (1988)

Peace	Air Force	Cour	Color	89 mins
Touchstone	WV: 11-16-88		NYT: 11-11-88	

DIR: John Cherry. SW: B. Kline, Ed Turner. PRO: Stacy Williams, Doug Claybourne. STARS: Jim Varney, Douglas Seale, Oliver Clark.

The Pentagon approved the request for Air Force stock footage of planes and uniformed personnel since the film portrayed the service in a positive manner. Ernest helps Santa find his successor.

Escape from the Planet of the Apes (1971)

SciFi	Marines	NR	Color	97 mins
Fox	WV: 05-26-71		NYT: 05-29-71	

DIR: Don Taylor. SW: Paul Dehn. PRO: Arthur P. Jacobs. STARS: Roddy McDowall, Kim Hunter, Bradford Dillman, Sal Mineo.

The Apes flee their home planet as it explodes and land in California, only to be "secured" by Marine guards.

The Eternal Sea (1955) [SSS]

WWII	Navy		Full	B&W	103 mins
Republic	WV: 04-06-55			NYT: 06-10-55	

DIR: John Auer. SW: Allen Rivkin. PRO: Herbert Yates. STARS: Sterling Hayden, Alexis Smith, Dean Jagger, Ben Cooper.

Inspired by the life of Admiral John Hoskins, who lost a leg in the sinking of the USS *Princeton* the day before he was to assume command of the aircraft carrier. Citing Navy regulations, he then fought to remain on active duty. Ultimately, he obtained command of the new *Princeton,* and after the war he paved the way for carrier-based jets, flying the first Navy jet off a carrier despite his handicap.

The Eve of St. Mark (1944)

WWII	Army		Unkn	B&W	96 mins
Fox	WV: 05-17-44			NYT: 05-31-44	

DIR: John M. Stahl. SW: George Seaton. PRO: William Perlberg. STARS: Anne Baxter, William Eythe, Michael O'Shea, Vincent Price, Henry Morgan.

Adapted from Maxwell Anderson's play, the story followed a group of all-American young men from their basic training, which occurred before Pearl Harbor, until their final days in the Philippines. The filmmakers revised the ending to intentionally leave moviegoing relatives and sweethearts of the troops a modicum of hope that some American defenders in the Philippines were still alive, despite being classified as missing in action.

Executive Decision (1996)

Terrorism	Army		Full	Color	134 mins
WB	WV: 03-11-96			NYT: 03-15-96	

DIR: Stuart Baird. SW: Jim Thomas, John Thomas. PRO: Joel Silver. STARS: Kurt Russell, Halle Berry, John Leguizamo, Joe Morgan, Oliver Platt, Steven Seagal.

A prescient story of terrorists who seize a 747 and threaten to blow it up with its cargo of nerve gas over Washington. A crisis management team wrestles with the decision to shoot down the plane before it reaches the coast. Ultimately Russell, as an electronics expert, with help of stewardess Berry, outwits the terrorists and lands the plane, barely. The Air Force supplied a stealth plane as the vehicle to deliver Russell and his men to the underside of the passenger plane. Perhaps the best aspect of the film is the timely death of Seagal during the transfer from the stealth to the airliner.

The Expendables (1988)

Vietnam	Army	NR	Color	89 mins
Concorde	WV: DNR		NYT: DNR	

DIR: Cirio Santiago. SW: Philip Alderton. PRO: Christopher Santiago, Anna Roth. STARS: Anthony Finetti, Peter Nelson, Loren Haynes, William Steis, Kevin Duffis, Vic Diaz.

The Dirty Dozen set in Vietnam. A squad of misfits becomes a cohesive unit sent to Cambodia to rescue American hostages in a "C" movie that went immediately to cable and tape.

The Exterminator (1980)

Vietnam	Army	NR	Color	101 mins
Avco	WV: 09-17-80		NYT: 09-11-80	

DIR: James Glickenhaus. SW: James Glickenhaus. PRO: Mark Buntzman. STARS: Samantha Eggar, Christopher George, Robert Ginty, Steve James.

This vigilante film opens with a brief precredit sequence set in Vietnam with a Ranger team attempting a helicopter rescue but captured after a firefight that lacks any reality. After torture, one soldier escapes, kills the captors, saves his surviving team members, boards a rescue helicopter, and ends up back in New York fighting gangs during the rest of movie.

The Extraordinary Seaman (1969)

WWII	Navy	Ltd	Color	79 mins
MGM	WV: 01-22-69		NYT: DNR	

DIR: John Frankenheimer. SW: Phillip Rock, Hal Dresner. PRO: Edward Lewis, John Cushingham. STARS: David Niven, Faye Dunaway, Alan Alda, Mickey Rooney.

A second-rate comedy that uses stock combat footage to set the period. Three lost U.S. sailors join a British ghost who is trying to salvage his family's honor by sinking an enemy ship before WWII ends.

Eye of the Eagle (1988)

Vietnam	Army	NR	Color	82 mins
Concorde	WV: 01-06-88		NYT: DNR	

DIR: Cirio H. Santiago. SW: Joseph Zucchero, Nigel Hogge. PRO: Cirio Santiago. STARS: Brett Clark, Robert Patrick, Ed Crick, William Steis.

One of a series of "C" movies made in the Philippines with an imported American cast, intended to go directly to the emerging video market. The plot this time portrays a rogue unit of listed MIAs and POWs who have banded together to engage in massacres and other unauthorized missions.

Eye of the Eagle II: Inside the Enemy **(1989)**

Vietnam	Army	NR	Color	79 mins
Concorde	WV: 07-05-89		NYT: DNR	

DIR: Carl Franklin. SW: Carl Franklin, Dan Gagliasso. PRO: Catherine Santiago. STARS: William Field, Ken Jacobson, Ronald William Lawrence, Shirley Tesoro.

Little relationship to the earlier film except for the crew and management. This time a soldier is involved with a Vietnamese girl whom his commanding officer turns into a drug addict and forces into prostitution.

Eye of the Eagle III **(1990)**. See *Last Stand at Lang Mei*.

Fail Safe **(1964) [G&G]**

Cold War	Air Force	Deny	B&W	111 mins
Columbia	WV: 09-16-64		NYT: 09-16-64	

DIR: Sidney Lumet. SW: Walter Bernstein. PRO: Max Youngstein. STARS: Henry Fonda, Dan O'Herlihy, Walter Matthau, Frank Overton, Larry Hagman.

A cautionary tale about the possibility of accidental nuclear warfare, based on a book by Eugene Burdick and Harvey Wheeler. Youngstein rejected the Air Force's claim that its fail safe procedures would prevent the launching of a nuclear strike against the Soviet Union. Consequently, he made the leap of faith that if an accidental strike was not absolutely impossible, then it became probable. Therefore, the film portrays a computer failure initiating a U.S. attack against Moscow. When the Soviet capital is destroyed, the U.S. president orders an American plane to drop two hydrogen bombs on New York City, to support his claim that the attack was an accident. The brilliance of Stanley Kubrick's *Dr. Strangelove,* which essentially told the same story but as satire rather than docudrama, overshadowed Youngstein's film.

Farewell to the King **(1989)**

WWII	Navy	NR	Color	115 mins
Orion	WV: 02-15-90		NYT: 03-03-89	

DIR: John Milius. SW: John Milius. PRO: Andre Morgan. STARS: Nigel Havers, Frank McRae, Nick Nolte, Richard Morgan, Michael Nissman, John Bennett Perry.

Milius adapted Pierre Schoendorffer's novel into an interesting, if implausible, often inexplicable movie. Nolte, as a U.S. sailor, escapes the Japanese execution of his shipmates on Borneo and becomes the leader of a tribe of headhunters in a pastoral existence. However, when the Japanese intrude upon his paradise, he launches a war of vengeance against the enemy.

Father Goose **(1964)**

WWII	Navy	Ltd	Color	115 mins
Universal	WV: 11-18-64		NYT: 12-11-64	

DIR: Ralph Nelson. SW: Peter Stone, Frank Tarloff. PRO: Robert Arthur. STARS: Cary Grant, Leslie Caron, Trevor Howard, Jack Good, Sharyl Locke.

The war in the Pacific plays only a supporting role in this film, which headlines Grant as an Australian coast watcher. Quickly, his remote island becomes populated with Caron as a French schoolteacher and her female students. Man versus drink becomes man versus woman, with expected results.

Fat Man and Little Boy (1989) [G&G]

WWII	Army		Deny	Color	126 mins
Paramount	WV: 10-18-89			NYT: 10-20-89	

DIR: Roland Joffé. SW: Bruce Robinson, Roland Joffé. PRO: Tony Garnett. STARS: Paul Newman, Dwight Schultz, Bonnie Bedelia, John Cusack, Laura Dern, Natasha Richardson.

On one level, the film purports to portray the building of the atomic bomb at Los Alamos, New Mexico, with a focus on the allegedly difficult relationships in that rather small world: Groves and Oppenheimer, Oppenheimer and his wife, Oppenheimer and his mistress, etc. In fact, Joffé stated that he made the movie to warn about the dangers the bomb and radiation posed to the world. However, in creating his message, the director completely misrepresented the history of the Manhattan Project. Newman's portrait of Gen. Grove did not help matters because the actor was not able to capture the portly general's mannerisms or character.

Fear and Desire (1953)

WWII	Army		NR	B&W	68 mins
Kubrick	WV: 04-01-53			NYT: 04-01-53	

DIR: Stanley Kubrick. SW: Howard Sackler, Stanley Kubrick. PRO: Stanley Kubrick. STARS: Frank Silvera, Kenneth Harp, Paul Mazursky, Steve Coit.

Kubrick's first feature, made on a shoestring budget of $100,000, follows the efforts of four GIs, trapped in enemy territory, to escape. The director showed early signs of brilliance in portraying the men's mental and physical reactions to their situation.

A Few Good Men (1992) [G&G]

Peace	Marines		Deny, Ltd	Color	140 mins
Castle Rock	WV: 11-16-92			NYT: 12-11-92	

DIR: Rob Reiner. SW: Aaron Sorkin. PRO: David Brown, Rob Reiner, Andrew Scheinman. STARS: Tom Cruise, Jack Nicholson, Demi Moore, Kevin Bacon, Kiefer Sutherland.

Based on Sorkin's stage play, the film is simply a genre courtroom drama. Navy lawyer Cruise defends two Marine grunts against a murder charge for accidentally killing a fellow Marine during a harassment that Nicholson, as the commander of the Marine facility at Guantanamo Bay, ordered. The colonel initially denies giving the order, then argues it was necessary for the defense of the country, and finally cracks up on the witness stand à la Capt. Queeg in the face of Cruise's withering attack. The Marines refused to have anything to do with production, but the Navy allowed filming at Point Mugu, where filmmakers created the Guantanamo exteriors.

55 *Days at Peking* (1963)

China	Marines	Cour	Color	150 mins
Allied Artists	WV: 05-01-63		NYT: 05-30-63	

DIR: Nicholas Ray. SW: Philip Yordan, Bernard Gordon. PRO: Samuel Bronston. STARS: Charlton Heston, David Niven, Ava Gardner, Flora Robson, John Ireland, Leo Genn.

An historical drama of Marines in China during the Boxer Rebellion, more epic than history.

Field of Fire (1991)

Vietnam	Army	NR	Color	96 mins
New Horizon	WV: DNR		NYT: DNR	

DIR: Cirio Santiago. SW: Thomas Cleaver. PRO: Christopher Santiago, Roger Corman. STARS: Joe Mari Avellana, Don Barnes, David Carradine, Eb Lottimer, Jim Moss.

This time, Philippine action director Santiago follows a special forces unit into the Vietnam jungle to recover a secret U.S. fighter helicopter and its pilot. While there, they fight the Vietcong and a traitor in their ranks. As always, nonstop combat with bodies flying everywhere.

Fighter Attack (1953)

WWII	Air Force	Full	Color	80 mins
Allied Artists	WV: 11-25-53		NYT: DNR	

DIR: Lesley Selander. SW: Shimon Wincelberg. PRO: William Calihan Jr. STARS: Sterling Hayden, J. Carrol Naish, Joy Page.

The movie used actual air combat footage to create the ambience for a story set in Corsica and Italy during the 1944 campaign against the Nazis in Italy.

Fighter Squadron (1948)

WWII	Air Force	Full	Color	94 mins
WB	WV: 11-24-48		NYT: 11-20-48	

DIR: Raoul Walsh. SW: Seton I. Miller, Martin Rackin. PRO: Seton I. Miller. STARS: Edmond O'Brien, Robert Stack, James Holden, Rock Hudson.

Set in England during the air war in the spring of 1944, leading up to D-Day and the subsequent fighting. Black cats but no women interfere with the American aerial combat defending U.S. bombers against the remains of the German air force, and after June 6, attacking enemy troops and armaments on the ground. Walsh used Air Force color combat footage for the first time in a feature film and Michigan Air National Guard planes to portray the role of the P-47 Thunderbolts, the "tank busters," in winning the war.

Fighting Coast Guard (1951)

WWII	Coast Guard	Full	B&W	86 mins
Republic	WV: 05-02-51		NYT: 05-12-51	

DIR: Joseph Kane. SW: Kenneth Garmet. PRO: Republic. STARS: Brian Donlevy, Forrest Tucker, Ella Raines, John Russell, Richard Jaeckel.

One of the few WWII films portraying the Coast Guard, in this case showing how the service trained its men to help win the war.

Fighting Devil Dogs (1938) (serial)

Peace	Marines	Full	B&W	30 min segments
Republic	WV: 05-11-38		NYT: DNR	

DIR: John English, William Witney. SW: Barry Shipman, Franklyn Adreon. PRO: Robert Beche. STARS: Lee Powell, Herman Brix, Eleanor Stewart, Montagu Love, Hugh Sothern, Sam Flint.

A film in 12 chapters depicting the Marines fighting a death ray in the tropics.

The Fighting Roosevelts (1919)

SpAmer, WWI	Army	Full	B&W	6 reels
First Natl	WV: 01-24-19		NYT: 01-20-19	

DIR: William Nigh. SW: Charles Towne, Porter Browne. PRO: Frederick Collins. STARS: Francis Noonan, Herbert Bradshaw, E. J. Ratcliffe.

A docudrama portraying Theodore Roosevelt from his youth through WWI, made with TR's approval. Includes the charge up San Juan Hill and scenes from his sons' participation in WWI.

The Fighting Seabees (1944) [G&G]

WWII	Navy	Full	B&W	100 mins
Republic	WV: 01-19-44		NYT: 03-20-44	

DIR: Edward Ludwig. SW: Borden Chase, Aeneas McKenzie. PRO: Albert J. Cohen. STARS: John Wayne, Susan Hayward, Dennis O'Keefe, William Frawley.

The film details the evolution of the Navy Seabees from its origins as a naval construction organization to an armed engineering fighting force. The Navy approved the shooting of a Seabee training exercise at Camp Pendleton, including the building of an airfield, which was then integrated into the completed film. The idea for the movie came from a studio truck driver, who gave it to Wayne, who passed it on to a studio producer. One of only two of Wayne's military films in which the actor's character died.

***The Fighting 69th* (1940)**

WWI	Army	NR	B&W	90 mins
WB	WV: 01-10-40		NYT: 01-27-40	

DIR: William Keighley. SW: Norman Reilly Raine, Fred Niblo Jr., Dean Franklin. PRO: Jack Warner, Hal Wallis. STARS: Pat O'Brien, James Cagney, George F. Brent, Alan Hale.

The story of the New York Irish Regiment from its training as unruly recruits to its combat in France during WWI. Cagney plays an arrogant braggart, troublemaker, and coward under fire but redeems himself before dying as a hero. The studio built, in California, a replica of Camp Miles, on Long Island, where the regiment had trained.

The Fighting Sullivans. See *The Sullivans*

***Final Approach* (1991)**

SciFi	Air Force	NR	Color	103 mins
Intercontinental	WV: 06-17-91		NYT: 03-13-92	

DIR: Eric Steven Stahl. SW: Eric Steven Stahl, Gerald Laurence. PRO: Eric Steven Stahl. STARS: James B. Sikking, Hector Elizondo, Kevin McCarthy, Madolyn Smith-Osborne.

This film is notable only for its use of new digital sound recording technology. Air Force officer Sikking crashes a secret stealth plane after it is hit by lightning. Where he is after that is the essence of the film, which must have drawn its inspiration from ***Incident at Owl Creek Bridge***.

***The Final Countdown* (1980) [G&G]**

SciFi/WWII	Navy, Marines	Full	Color	103 mins
United Artists	WV: 07-16-80		NYT: 08-01-80	

DIR: Don Taylor. SW: David Ambrose, Gerry Davis, Thomas Hunter, Peter Powell. PRO: Peter Douglas. STARS: Kirk Douglas, Martin Sheen, Katharine Ross, James Farentino.

A sci-fi movie set aboard the aircraft carrier *Nimitz,* which goes back in time to the day before Pearl Harbor. Since the story was pure fantasy, the Navy had no problem assisting, especially when the aircraft carrier became the star of the film. Marines appear briefly trying to secure a captured Japanese pilot, whom they kill after he wreaks havoc. As with all time travel stories, if the travelers from the future change history, in this case, stop the Japanese attack on December 7, they would cease to exist. However, if they cease to exist, they could not have come back to change the future. A dilemma that such films tend to ignore. In any case, only the *Nimitz* provides any interest to an otherwise insipid story. (See ***The Philadelphia Experiment*** and the Navy's treatment of the script.)

***The Finest Hour* (1991)**

Persian Gulf	Navy	Full	Color	105 mins
MGM	WV: DNR		NYT: DNR	

DIR: Shimon Dotan. SW: Shimon Dotan, Stuart Schoffman. PRO: Menahem Golan. STARS: Rob Lowe, Gale Hansen, Tracy Griffith, Eb Lottimer.

Lowe and Hansen become best friends while training to become Navy SEALS. Griffith comes between the two men when she marries Lowe, but the friends are reunited when they undertake a mission to destroy an Iraqi biological weapons site during Desert Shield. Although the Navy assisted during filming in and around San Diego, the authentic ambience did not prevent the movie from going straight to cable and video—since people had recently seen the first Persian Gulf war so up close and personal.

Fire Birds (1990)

Peace	Army, Air Force	Full	Color	85 mins
Touchstone	WV: 05-23-90		NYT: 05-25-90	

DIR: David Green. SW: Nick Thiel, Paul F. Edwards. PRO: William Badalato. STARS: Nicolas Cage, Tommy Lee Jones, Sean Young, Bryan Kestner, Dale Dye.

The film is a throwback to the 1930s portrayals of U.S. involvement in the affairs of Latin American countries. In this case, Apache assault helicopters are the weapons of choice against drug lords. Young, as a female flight instructor, is the love interest. None of this helps instill interest in the story.

Firefox (1982) [G&G]

Cold War	Air Force	Full	Color	137 mins
WB	WV: 06-16-82		NYT: 06-18-82	

DIR: Clint Eastwood. SW: Alex Lasker, Wendell Wellman. PRO: Clint Eastwood. STARS: Clint Eastwood, Freddie Jones, David Huffman.

Based on Craig Thomas's novel. Eastwood steals a Soviet secret spy plane (not surprisingly resembling our X-15) from its guarded hangar and flies it out of the USSR, refueling in the Arctic, with the help of one of our nuclear subs. He then successfully does battle with the sister plane, chasing the purloined plane in a video game-like dogfight. Neither story nor portrayal makes any sense, and this is certainly one of Eastwood's lesser efforts. Some scenes were filmed in an Edwards Air Force Base hangar.

First Blood (1982)

Peace, Vietnam	Army	Deny	Color	97 mins
Orion	WV: 10-27-82		NYT: 10-22-82	

DIR: Ted Kotcheff. SW: Michael Kozoll, William Sackheim, Sylvester Stallone. PRO: Buzz Feitshans. STARS: Sylvester Stallone, Richard Crenna, Brian Dennehy, David Caruso, Jack Starrett.

The Army denied assistance to this story of an ex-Green Beret who wages war on a small town that has harassed him. The service said the script depicted the Army "in a totally negative manner and had factual inaccuracies such as portraying the National Guard performing a mission that would be performed by state police." The Army also said it would not be in its best interest to support a film of "overwhelming violence with a character portrayed as a killer only because of his Army training."

First to Fight (1967)

WWII	Marines	Full	Color	97 mins
WB	WV: 01-25-67		NYT: 03-30-67	

DIR: Christian Nyby. SW: Gene Coon. PRO: William Conrad. STARS: Dean Jagger, Chad Everett, Marilyn Devin, Gene Hackman.

A typical Marine World War II South Pacific melodrama in which a Medal of Honor recipient on Guadalcanal freezes during the landing on Saipan, apparently because he had married.

First Yank into Tokyo (1945)

WWII	Army	Ltd	B&W	82 mins
RKO	WV: 09-05-45		NYT: 10-25-45	

DIR: Gordon Douglas. SW: J. Robert Bren, Gladys Atwater. PRO: J. Robert Bren. STARS: Tom Neal, Barbara Hale, Marc Cramer, Leonard Strong.

Although the shooting was completed before the atomic bombs were dropped in August 1945, this prescient film used a secret gigantic bomb as the weapon of choice to subdue Japan. To draw on the recent events, the filmmakers used newsreel footage of the actual atomic bomb explosions to begin and end the movie.

Fixed Bayonets (1951)

Korea	Army	Ltd	B&W	92 mins
Fox	WV: 11-21-51		NYT: 11-21-51	

DIR: Samuel Fuller. SW: Samuel Fuller. PRO: Jules Buck. STARS: Richard Basehart, Gene Evans, Michael O'Shea, Richard Hylton.

Lacking originality and reality, including lack of visible breath in the winter scenes, the story followed a small unit defending the retreat of a regiment during the darkest hours of the Korean police action.

Flat Top (1952)

WWII	Navy	Full	Color	83 mins
Allied Artists	WV: 11-19-52		NYT: 12-06-52	

DIR: Lesley Selander. SW: Steve Fisher. PRO: Walter Mirisch. STARS: Sterling Hayden, Richard Carlson, Bill Phipps, John Bromfield.

Shot on the USS *Princeton* and featuring some of its personnel, the production also used actual combat footage to tell the story of a seasoned commanding officer training a new group of carrier pilots.

The Fleet's In (1928)

Peace	Navy	Full	B&W	75 mins
Paramount	WV: 10-03-28		NYT: 10-01-28	

DIR: Malcolm St. Clair. SW: George Marion, Monte Brice, J. Walter Ruben. PRO: Paramount. STARS: Clara Bow, James Hall, Jack Oakie, Eddie Dunn.

A sailor meets a "taxi" dancer, insults her, protects her, and wins her as she defends his behavior before police.

The Fleet's In (1942)

Peace	Navy	Full	B&W	93 mins
Paramount	WV: 01-21-42		NYT: 03-12-42	

DIR: Victor Schertzinger. SW: Walter de Leon, Sid Silvers. PRO: Paul Jones. STARS: Dorothy Lamour, William Holden, Eddie Bracken, Betty Hutton.

A musical version of the earlier 1920s film. Loverboy sailor Holden pursues and wins Lamour. Hutton's film debut.

Flight (1929) [G&G]

Peace	Marines	Full	B&W	110 mins
Columbia	WV: 09-18-29		NYT: 09-14-29	

DIR: Frank Capra. SW: Howard Green, Frank Capra. PRO: Harry Cohn. STARS: Jack Holt, Ralph Graves, Lila Lee.

Two Marines chase the same girl in the United States and Nicaragua. The heroes use close air support to help their comrades on the ground, which provided an early portrayal of the Corps's development of tactical bombing in close air support of ground forces that the Corps put to good use in WWII. Capra filmed the aerial sequences at the Naval Air Station Pensacola. (See ***Devil Dogs of the Air*** and ***Flying Leathernecks.***)

Flight Command (1940) [SSS]

Preparedness	Navy	Full	B&W	113 mins
MGM	WV: 12-18-40		NYT: 01-17-41	

DIR: Frank Borzage. SW: Wells Root, Commander Harvey Haislip. PRO: J. Walter Ruben, Frank Borzage. STARS: Robert Taylor, Ruth Hussey, Walter Pidgeon.

The Navy in San Diego assisted on the production, including staging carrier takeoffs from the USS *Enterprise*, formation flying, and weaponry training. The story itself focused on the development of equipment for poor-visibility flying.

Flight for Freedom (1943)

WWII	Navy	Ltd	B&W	101 mins
RKO	WV: 02-03-43		NYT: 04-16-43	

DIR: Lothar Mendes. SW: Oliver Garrett, S. K. Lauren. PRO: David Hempstead. STARS: Rosalind Russell, Fred MacMurray, Herbert Marshall, Eduardo Ciannelli.

The exploits of Amelia Earhart and her unexplained disappearance inspired this story. Russell plays a globe-circling flyer. At the request of the Navy she flies the Pacific to help uncover possible Japanese fortifications. Ultimately she dies a heroic death when she crashes her plane into the sea. The film included a brief prologue showing the contemporary bombing of Japanese bases.

Flight from Ashiya (1964)

Peace	Air Force	Ltd	Color	102 mins
UA	WV: 04-01-64		NYT: 04-23-64	

DIR: Michael Anderson. SW: Elliott Arnold, Waldo Salt. PRO: Harold Hecht. STARS: Yul Brynner, Richard Widmark, George Chakiris, Suzy Parker, June Shelley.

In this joint American–Japanese production, the Air Rescue Corps provided the background for a story that explored, through flashbacks, the lives of the plane's crew.

Flight Lieutenant (1942)

Preparedness	Air Force	Ltd	B&W	80 mins
Columbia	WV: 08-05-42		NYT: 07-31-42	

DIR: Sidney Salkow. SW: Michael Blankfort. PRO: B. P. Schulberg. STARS: Pat O'Brien, Glenn Ford, Evelyn Keyes.

Tired formula story, this time of a flying father who takes the place of his flying son and ultimately saves his life.

Flight Nurse (1953)

Korea	Air Force	Full	B&W	90 mins
UA	WV: 11-04-53		NYT: 01-30-54	

DIR: Allan Dwan. SW: Alan LeMay. PRO: Herbert Yates. STARS: Joan Leslie, Forrest Tucker, Arthur Franz, Jeff Donnell, James Holden.

The film portrays the heroic work of Air Force flight nurses and includes vivid reminders of Communist Chinese war crimes against UN soldiers, conveying a clear propagandistic message. The Air Force provided combat footage, planes, and men as background to a bevy of nurses bravely treating and transporting the wounded.

Flight of the Intruder (1991) [G&G]

Vietnam	Navy	Full	Color	115 mins
Paramount	WV: 01-21-91		NYT: 01-18-91	

DIR: John Milius. SW: Robert Dillon, David Shaber. PRO: Mace Nuefeld, Robert Rehme. STARS: Danny Glover, Willem Dafoe, Brad Johnson, Rosanna Arquette, Tom Sizemore.

Based on Stephen Coonts's novel and set in 1972, on an aircraft carrier in the last months of the Vietnam War, the film contained a rather positive image of Navy fliers and officers. However, the heroes' "feel good" bombing of Hanoi could not help the movie at the box office because the first Gulf War debuted simultaneously with the film's release. Why spend money on tickets when CNN was broadcasting the real thing?

Flight to Fame (1938)

SciFi	Army, Air Force	Unkn	B&W	67 mins
Columbia	WV: 12-14-38		NYT: DNR	

DIR: C. C. Coleman Jr. SW: Michael L. Simmons. PRO: Columbia. STARS: Charles Farrell, Jacqueline Wells, Hugh Sothern, Jason Robards Sr.

The movie contained experimental planes and death rays. Robards, a former combat pilot, tries to kill off his old WWI buddies using the ray.

Flirtation Walk (1934)

Peace	Army	Full	B&W	100 mins
WB	WV: 12-04-34		NYT: 11-29-34	

DIR: Frank Borzage. SW: Delmer Daves, Lou Edelman. PRO: Frank Borzage. STARS: Dick Powell, Ruby Keeler, Pat O'Brien.

The Army responded to the spate of Annapolis movies by giving the filmmakers complete access to West Point, with marching cadets and beautiful scenery as background to a predictable love story.

Fly Away Home (1996)

Peace	Air Force	Full	Color	110 mins
Sony	WV: 09-02-96		NYT: 09-13-96	

DIR: Carroll Ballard. SW: Robert Rodat, Vince McKewin. PRO: John Veitch, Carol Baum. STARS: Jeff Daniels, Anna Paquin, Dana Delany.

Based on the autobiography of Bill Lishman, who used his ultralight plane to lead orphaned geese on their migration south from Canada. Along the way, the flier had to make an emergency landing at an Air Force base. The service men fed the geese and refueled the plane. The National Guard and AF provided their planes as background on land and in flight for several days to re-create the actual events.

The Flying Fleet (1929) [SSS]

Peace	Navy		Full	B&W	72 mins
Pathé	WV: 02-23-29			NYT: 02-11-29	

DIR: George Hill. SW: Frank Wead, Byron Morgan, Richard Schayer. PRO: George Hill. STARS: Ramon Navarro, Ralph Graves, Anita Page.

Lt. Commander Frank "Spig" Wead, a record-setting Navy flier turned writer after suffering a disabling spinal injury, drew on his own experiences to create the film's authentic ambience. The story chronicles the adventures of six Annapolis graduates aspiring to get their wings. A Navy aircraft carrier, the USS *Langley*, appears in a Hollywood feature for the first time.

Flying Leathernecks (1951) [G&G]

WWII	Marines		Full	Color	103 mins
RKO	WV: 07-25-51			NYT: 09-20-51	

DIR: Nicholas Ray. SW: James Edward Grant, Beirne Lay Jr. PRO: Edmund Granger, Howard Hughes. STARS: John Wayne, Robert Ryan, Don Taylor, Janis Carter.

The film provides a study of leadership and command and control similar to that portrayed in *Twelve O'Clock High* and *A Wing and a Prayer,* among many others. Granger was trying to duplicate his success with *Sands of Iwo Jima* and the resulting popularity of Wayne. Originally, the producer had intended to set his story in Korea, but the Marines had more important things to do during the fighting then taking place there. Consequently, the filmmakers used combat footage and a few WWII fighters to illustrate how close air support had been used during the recent war.

The Flying Marine (1929)

Peace	Marines		Full	B&W	60 mins
Columbia	WV: 08-07-29			NYT: DNR	

DIR: Albert Rogell. SW: John Natteford. PRO: Harry Cohn. STARS: Jason Robards Sr., Ben Lyon, Shirley Mason.

The flying sequences, which were the only aspect of the film to remember, portrayed the development of Marine aviation.

The Flying Missile (1950) [SSS]

Cold War	Navy		Full	B&W	91 mins
Columbia	WV: 12-27-50			NYT: 12-25-50	

DIR: Henry Levin. SW: Richard English, James Gunn. PRO: Jerry Bresler. STARS: Glenn Ford, Viveca Lindfors, Jerry Paris, Henry O'Neill.

The footage shot at the Naval Air Test Missile Center in Point Mugu, California, helped Levin portray the development of missile-firing submarines. Some submariners considered this an important film because it showed how submarines could win the next war. The movie also displayed the vulnerability of surface ships to missiles fired from beyond the horizon. Nevertheless, the film provided some comfort to the public as the arms race continued to accelerate.

Flying Tigers (1942)

WWII	Air Force	Full	B&W	102 mins
Republic	WV: 09-23-42		NYT: 10-23-42	

DIR: David Miller. SW: Kenneth Gamet, Barry Trivers. PRO: Edmund Grainger. STARS: John Wayne, John Carroll, Anna Lee, Paul Kelly.

This docudrama created a fictionalized account of the American volunteer fliers who fought under Gen. Claire Chennault in the Chinese theater before Pearl Harbor and then joined the U.S. Air Force. The service provided the planes and Wayne began to create his military persona.

The Flying Torpedo (1926)

SciFi	Army	Unkn	B&W	5 reels
Triangle	WV: 03-17-16		NYT: DNR	

DIR: John B. O'Brien, Christy Cabanne. SW: John Emerson, Robert M. Baker, D. W. Griffith. PRO: D. W. Griffith. STARS: John Emerson, Spottiswoode Aitken, William E. Lawrence, Raymond Wells.

In the early 1920s, several foreign nations threaten to invade the United States, and the government offers a million dollar prize to anyone who can invent a weapon capable of defeating the enemy. Spies kill Aitken, the scientist, as he is finishing the weapon, but his friend Emerson retrieves the plans and builds the flying torpedo. The Army uses the torpedo to repel the foreign fleet, in a tremendous battle off the California Coast. This is one of the earliest films, along with *Battle Cry of Peace*, set in the near future.

Follow the Fleet (1936)

Peace	Navy	Full	B&W	110 mins
RKO	WV: 02-26-36		NYT: 02-21-36	

DIR: Mark Sandrich. SW: Dwight Taylor, Allan Scott. PRO: Pandro S. Berman. STARS: Fred Astaire, Ginger Rogers, Randolph Scott, Betty Grable, Lucille Ball.

The musical features Astaire, who joins the Navy when Rogers refuses to marry him. During shore leave, he tries again.

Fools in the Dark (1924)

Peace	Marines	Unkn	B&W	65 mins
R-C Pictures	WV: 08-20-24		NYT: 08-18-24	

DIR: Alfred Santell. SW: John Grey, Bertram Millhauser. PRO: R-C Pictures. STARS: Patsy Ruth Miller, Matt Moore, Bert Grassby.

The hero escapes from imprisonment by a mad scientist and then saves his girlfriend, with the help of the Marines.

For Me and My Gal (1942)

WWI	Army	NR	B&W	104 mins
MGM	WV: 09-09-42		NYT: 10-22-42	

DIR: Busby Berkeley. SW: Richard Sherman, Fred Finklehoffe, Sid Silvers. PRO: Arthur Freed. STARS: Judy Garland, George Murphy, Gene Kelly, Ben Blue, Keenan Wynn.

Actually a war-preparedness movie, this musical provided a patriotic uplift for the country during the first year of hostilities. Kelly and Garland entertain doughboys at the front. Having avoided service by slamming a trunk lid on his hand, Kelly wipes out a German machine gun nest as a civilian but ends up in uniform anyway.

The Forbin Project (1970) a.k.a. *Colossus*

SciFi	Army, Air Force	NR	Color	100 mins
Universal	WV: 04-01-70		NYT: 05-05-70	

DIR: Joseph Sargent. SW: James Bridges. PRO: Stanley Chase. STARS: Eric Braeden, Susan Clark, Gordon Pinsent.

Based on D. F. Jones's novel *Colossus*, the film features a giant computer, to which the United States gave control over all nuclear weapons to ensure the ability to launch a response to any Soviet attack. Unfortunately for humankind, Colossus takes over the world with the help of its Soviet counterpart. The U.S. military is portrayed as helpless to disarm the rogue computers.

For the Boys (1991)

WWII	All	NR	Color	145 mins
Fox	WV: 11-18-91		NYT: 11-22-91, 01-19 &	
			02-23-92	

DIR: Mark Rydell. SW: Marshall Brickman, Neil Jimenez, Lindy Laub. PRO: Bette Midler, Bonnie Bruckheimer, Margaret South. STARS: Bette Midler, James Caan, George Segal.

Fifty years of entertaining U.S. troops provides the cultural background for this relationship story of two aging USO performers. The producers initially requested use of military installations and personnel but ultimately decided they did not need assistance. In fact, the DoD would have denied help based on negative depictions of the military in the script.

Force of Arms (1951)

WWII	Army	Ltd	B&W	98 mins
WB	WV: 08-15-51		NYT: 08-14-51	

DIR: Michael Curtiz. SW: Orin Jannings, Richard Tregaskis. PRO: Anthony Veiller. STARS: William Holden, Nancy Olson, Frank Lovejoy, Gene Evans, Dick Wesson.

A love story set against the background of the Italian theater in which Holden, as the officer, is pulled from the San Pietro front for a brief rest and meets Olson, a WAC lieutenant. In his next battle, Holden is wounded and believes he is at fault for the death of his friends because he had been in a hurry to return to his lover. The film uses a small amount of combat footage.

Force Ten from Navarone (1978)

WWII	Army	NR	Color	118 mins
Amer-Intl	WV: 11-29-78		NYT: 12-22-78	

DIR: Guy Hamilton. SW: Robin Chapman, Carl Foreman. PRO: Oliver Unger. STARS: Robert Shaw, Harrison Ford, Edward Fox, Carl Weathers.

Based on Alistair MacLean's novel. American soldiers participate in a special forces mission to blow up a bridge in Yugoslavia.

Forever Young (1992)

Peace	Army, Air Force	Ltd	Color	102 mins.
WB	WV: 12-07-92		NYT: 11-06-92	

DIR: Steve Miner. SW: Jeffrey Abrams. PRO: Bruce Davey. STARS: Mel Gibson, Jamie Lee Curtis, Elijah Wood, Isabel Glasser, George Wendt.

Two 10-year-olds provide the springboard for a love story when they thaw an Army cryogenics experiment, releasing Gibson from his long, accidental state of suspended animation. The DoD approved the use of an Army Reserve facility as background for creating an air show sequence, which provided an opportunity to showcase military airplanes.

The Forgotten Warrior (1986)

Vietnam	Army	NR	Color	76 mins
Interwood Films	WV: DNR		NYT: DNR	

DIR: Nick Cacas, Charlie Ordonez. SW: Tom McKenzie. PRO: Unkn. STARS: Ronald Marchini, Quincy Frazer, Sam Lapuz, Joe Meyer.

A low-budget film shot in the Philippines follows a POW who escapes into the jungle and goes primitive. The soldier then becomes the object of pursuit by U.S. and North Vietnam soldiers. As the lack of reviews suggests, the convoluted story makes little sense, except as a vehicle for violence.

Forrest Gump (1994) [G&G]

Vietnam	Army	Inform/Deny	Color	142 mins
Universal	WV: 07-11-94		NYT: 07-06-94	

DIR: Robert Zemeckis. SW: Eric Roth. PRO: Wendy Finerman, Steve Tisch, Steve Starkey. STARS: Tom Hanks, Robin Wright, Gary Sinise, Sally Field, Mykelti Williamson.

Based on Winston Groom's novel about a mentally challenged, naive Southern boy, the film follows Forrest's trials and tribulations as he appears at many historical milestones of the 1960s, with the help of computer-generated graphics. In the course of events, Gump joins the Army, where he becomes a hero and sees the world. The studio requested assistance from the Army to re-create basic training and Vietnam combat sequences. Saying that the early script contained a nihilistic view of the Army and the Vietnam War, the service declined to assist.

However, the military found a subsequent script much better, thanks to input from technical advisor Dale Dye and the Army's Los Angeles public affairs office, which provided extensive courtesy assistance in the form of script advice, information for set designers and dressers, uniform advice for costumers, and a TV clip from the American Forces Vietnam network. A key change corrected the erroneous portrayal of the existence of a unit of mentally challenged soldiers. In fact, Secretary of Defense Robert McNamara and the Army had created a program in which inductees who scored low on mental tests were assimilated into regular units.

Ultimately, however, the service refused to provide material help, citing Gump's appearance at an antiwar rally wearing his uniform and recently awarded Medal of Honor, which violated regulations. It also objected to Forrest's antiwar comments at the rally (subsequently deleted from the film when a police officer pulled the plug on the speaker system). In truth, given Gump's mental limitations, he undoubtedly would not have remembered the regulations even if he had once learned them. In any case, despite its denial of full assistance to the production, the Army benefited from the portrayal of how the service treated Gump.

Four in a Jeep (1951)

Cold War	Army	Ltd	B&W	100 mins
UA	WV: 04-11-51		NYT: 06-12-51	

DIR: Leopold Lindtberg, Elizabeth Montagu. SW: Richard Schweizer. PRO: Lazar Wechsler. STARS: Viveca Lindfors, Ralph Meeker, Yoseph Yodin, Michael Medwin.

A melodrama set in postwar Vienna with Russian, English, French, and U.S. military police patrolling the city together before the Cold War escalated.

Four Jills in a Jeep (1944)

WWII	Army	Unkn	B&W	68 mins
Fox	WV: 03-15-44		NYT: 04-06-44	

DIR: William Seiter. SW: Robert Ellis, Helen Logan, Snag Werris. PRO: Irving Starr. STARS: Kay Francis, Carole Landis, Martha Raye, Mitzi Mayfair, Phil Silvers, Alice Faye, Dick Haymes.

The film was based on actual experiences of actresses during a USO tour, with some additional romance thrown in. Performers, including Jimmy Dorsey and his band, made cameo appearances.

Four Sons (1928)

WWI	Army	Unkn	B&W	100 mins
Fox	WV: 02-15-28		NYT:02-14-28	

DIR: John Ford. SW: I. A. R. Wylie, Philip Klein. PRO: John Ford. STARS: Margaret Mann, James Hall, Francis X. Bushman Jr., Charles Morton, George Meeker, Earle Foxe.

A German mother loses three sons to the German war effort while a fourth, having moved to the United States before the war, survives his American Expeditionary Forces enlistment. The mother and son reunite in New York City.

The Fourth War (1990) [G&G]

Cold War	Army	NR	Color	91 mins
Kodiak	WV: 03-14-90		NYT: 03-24-90	

DIR: John Frankenheimer. SW: Stephen Peters, Kenneth Ross. PRO: Wolf Schmidt. STARS: Roy Scheider, Jürgen Prochnow, Tim Reid, Lara Harris, Harry Dean Stanton, Dale Dye, Bill MacDonald.

The film portrays a Cold War confrontation in which a U.S. Army officer confronts a Soviet officer on the German–Czech border as the East–West antagonism is thawing. The title came from Albert Einstein's comment that the third world war would be fought with atomic weapons and the fourth with sticks and stones. The climactic battle between the two men, which takes place in front of soldiers from both sides, does not escalate into war, thanks to the cooler heads, perhaps a parable for the end of the Cold War.

Francis (1949)

WWII	Army	Full	B&W	91 mins
UA	WV: 12-14-49		NYT: 03-16-50	

DIR: Arthur Lubin. SW: David Stern. PRO: Robert Arthur. STARS: Donald O'Connor, Patricia Medina, Zasu Pitts, Ray Collins.

In this first in a series of talking mule films, Francis teams up with O'Connor in Burma behind enemy lines, saves his life, and wins them awards and O'Connor time with an Army medical corps psychiatrist as he tries to explain his and Francis's exploits.

Francis Goes to West Point (1952)

Peace	Army	Full	B&W	81 mins
Universal	WV: 06-18-52		NYT: 08-23-52	

DIR: Arthur Lubin. SW: Oscar Brodney. PRO: Leonard Goldstein. STARS: Donald O'Connor, Lori Nelson, Alice Kelley, Palmer Lee.

Francis helps O'Connor succeed at West Point and provides advice to the football coach for the traditional Army–Navy game. Perhaps he is afraid the teams will switch from pigskin to mule skin.

Francis in the Navy (1955)

Peace	Navy	Full	B&W	80 mins
Universal	WV: 06-29-55		NYT: 08-06-55	

DIR: Arthur Lubin. SW: Devery Freeman. PRO: Stanley Rubin. STARS: Donald O'Connor, Martha Hyer, Richard Erdman, Jim Backus, Clint Eastwood, David Janssen.

Plethora of great actors makes this a wonderful film for movie trivia buffs.

Francis Joins the WACS (1954)

Peace	Army	Full	B&W	94 mins
Universal	WV: 07-07-54		NYT: 07-31-54	

DIR: Arthur Lubin. SW: Devery Freeman, James Allardice. PRO: Ted Richmond. STARS: Donald O'Connor, Julia Adams, Chill Wills, Mamie Van Dorn, Lynn Bari, Zasu Pitts.

Francis's voice, actor Chill Wills, gets a human role as the general in this chapter of the Francis series. O'Connor reenlists, but due to an administrative error ends up in the WACs.

Fräulein (1958)

WWII	Army	Ltd	Color	95 mins
Fox	WV: 05-07-58		NYT: 06-09-58	

DIR: Henry Koster. SW: Leo Townsend. PRO: Walter Reisch. STARS: Dana Wynter, Mel Ferrer, Dolores Michaels, Maggie Hayes, Theodore Bikel.

Based on a James McGovern novel, the film portrays an American officer who escapes from a German POW camp and receives help from a "good" German professor and his adolescent daughter. After the war, the girl struggles to survive in postwar Germany, before ultimately finding happiness with the flier. The Army provided men and equipment for filming in Germany.

Frogmen (1951) [SSS]

WWII	Navy	Full	B&W	96 mins
Fox	WV: 06-13-51		NYT: 06-30-51	

DIR: Lloyd Bacon. SW: John Tucker Battle. PRO: Samuel Engel. STARS: Richard Widmark, Dana Andrews, Gary Merrill, Jeffrey Hunter, Robert Wagner.

Naval installations at Norfolk, Virginia, and in the Virgin Islands provided realism to this all-male story of one of the Navy's WWII underwater demolition teams. The organization later evolved into the secretive and mythical Navy SEALS, but here lots of swimming makes for a dull movie.

From Headquarters (1929)

Peace	Marines	Unkn	B&W	7 reels
WB	WV: 07-17-29		NYT: DNR	

DIR: Howard Bretherton. SW: Harvey Gates. PRO: WB. STARS: Monte Blue, Guinn Williams, Gladys Brockwell.

Marines fight rebels in the jungle of an unidentified South American country, with few surviving.

From Here to Eternity (1953) [G&G]

Peace	Army	Full	Color	118 mins
Columbia	WV: 07-29-53		NYT: 08-06-53	

DIR: Fred Zinnemann. SW: Daniel Taradash. PRO: Buddy Adler. STARS: Burt Lancaster, Deborah Kerr, Montgomery Clift, Frank Sinatra, Donna Reed, Ernest Borgnine.

Based on James Jones's best-selling novel, which guaranteed that Hollywood would turn it into a major movie, whatever the obstacles. The Army desperately did not want to provide assistance to the production, given the negative portrayals of an officer, brutality in the stockade administered by a sadistic warden, and the adultery of an officer's wife with an enlisted man. The Motion Picture Code Office had its own concerns: the language, the whorehouse, the sex, and the violence.

Columbia Pictures head Harry Cohn was not about to take no for an answer, and the studio embarked upon a long series of negotiations that ultimately produced a script that softened the images of the brutality and called for the removal of the incompetent officer. Although the movie would never benefit the service, the changes were in its best interest. As a result, the Army gave the studio access to Schofield Barracks in Hawaii, which lent the production an authentic ambience, and the film became one of the very best portrayals of the American armed services in peace or war.

Full Metal Jacket (1987) [G&G]

Vietnam	Marines	NR	Color	116 mins
WB	WV: 06-17-87		NYT: 06-26-87, 07-05-87	

DIR: Stanley Kubrick. SW: Stanley Kubrick, Michael Herr, Gustav Hasford. PRO: Stanley Kubrick. STARS: Matthew Modine, Adam Baldwin, Vincent D'Onofrio, R. Lee Ermey.

Based on the Gustav Hasford novel *The Short-Timers,* this movie contains two parts, which do not connect. The first half is an excellent portrayal of Marine boot camp thanks to technical advice and the acting of Ermey, a retired drill instructor. In reality, the Marines would have undoubtedly thrown out the insane recruit, D'Onofrio, long before he killed Ermey and himself to end the first half of the film.

The second part, set in Vietnam, is only an impressionistic portrayal of the war because Kubrick had limited knowledge of or understanding of what happened in Southeast Asia. What he knew came from watching television news. The director filmed the combat scenes in an abandoned gas works on the Thames (now Canary Wharf), and all the palm trees in the world could not make the then-derelict area of London look like Vietnam. Nor did the story provide any realistic insights into the American experience in Southeast Asia.

Gallant Bess (1946)

WWII	Navy	Full	Color	100 mins
MGM	WV: 09-04-46		NYT: 12-06-46	

DIR: Andrew Marton. SW: Jeanne Bartlett. PRO: Harry Rapf. STARS: Marshall Thompson, George Tobias, Clem Bevans, Donald Curtis, Silvership (as Bess).

In this melodrama, Thompson plays an orphan farm boy whose horse has become his companion as he runs a stud farm that his father left him. Despite doubts about leaving his friend, the young man joins the Seabees, the Navy's newly created armed engineering and construction outfit. (See John Wayne's *The Fighting Seabees*, above.) Leaving Bess with a friend, Thompson goes to the Seabees training base at Port Hueneme, California. While he is there, the mare contracts pneumonia and dies. Brokenhearted, Thompson goes to the South Pacific. There he saves a horse injured in a Japanese bombing attack, and the "new" Bess saves him and becomes the unit's mascot. The Navy allowed Marton to shoot at its training facility, which infused the film with authenticity and provided audiences with information about Seabee training and combat ability.

The Gallant Hours (1960)

WWII	Navy	Full	B&W	115 mins
UA	WV: 05-18-60		NYT: 06-23-60	

DIR: Robert Montgomery. SW: Beirne Lay Jr., Frank D. Gilroy. PRO: Robert Montgomery, James Cagney. STARS: James Cagney, Dennis Weaver, Ward Costello, Vaughn Taylor.

In dramatizing Adm. William "Bull" Halsey's victory at the Battle of Guadalcanal Sea in November 1942, Montgomery claimed he had created a historically accurate account of the decisive engagement, which sealed the American victory for Guadalcanal. The director cited his service on the admiral's staff as the basis for his knowledge. However, the film ends with the shooting down of Adm. Isoroku Yamamoto, the architect of the Japanese attack on Pearl Harbor, although the incident actually took place five months later. Consequently, the gratuitous error raises questions about the veracity of anything that preceded the climax. Moreover, the docudrama contained no visualized action or even combat footage, which limited the movie's appeal. The military ambience came only from a few sailors listening to the battle over loudspeakers and some Navy planes used as props.

Gardens of Stone (1987) [G&G]

Vietnam	Army	Full	Color	111 mins
Tri-Star	WV: 05-06-87		NYT: 05-08-87	

DIR: Francis Coppola. SW: Ronald Bass. PRO: Michael I. Levy, Francis Coppola. STARS: James Caan, Anjelica Huston, James Earl Jones, D. B. Sweeney, Dean Stockwell, Mary Stuart Masterson, Sam Bottoms.

Based on Nicholas Proffitt's novel, the film demonstrated the Pentagon's willingness to assist a filmmaker who previously had been denied cooperation. Although the Army had refused Coppola's request for help on *Apocalypse Now*, the service provided the director full access to Arlington National Cemetery to tell a story about members of the Ft. Meyer's burial detail during the height of the Vietnam War. The resulting film contains a powerful antiwar and anti-Vietnam War message, one of the strongest ever put on the screen.

A Gathering of Eagles (1963) [G&G]

Cold War	Air Force	Full	Color	115 mins
Universal	WV: 06-05-63		NYT: 07-11-63	

DIR: Delbert Mann. SW: Robert Pirosh. PRO: Sy Bartlett. STARS: Rock Hudson, Rod Taylor, Mary Peach, Barry Sullivan.

Another Strategic Air Command (SAC) propaganda film portraying the Air Force's Cold War mission. Assistant Secretary of Defense Arthur Sylvester tried to prevent the service from providing assistance during the period in which he was examining the cooperation process. However, Air Force Chief of Staff Curtis LeMay sent the secretary a short memo stating that he wanted the film made, and Sylvester immediately gave his approval. The story naturally contained a positive portrayal of SAC when compared to *Fail Safe* and *Dr. Strangelove*, both then in production.

The Gay Deceivers (1969)

Vietnam	Army	NR	Color	97 mins
Fanfare Films	WV: 06-11-69		NYT: 07-31-69	

DIR: Bruce Kessler. SW: Jerome Wish, Gil Lasky, Abe Polsky. PRO: Joe Solomon. STARS: Kevin Coughlin, Brooke Bundy, Lawrence Casey, Jo Ann Harris.

Two friends attempt to avoid the draft and the war by pretending to be gay. The recruiting officer apparently accepts the claim but then spies on them. Ultimately, they try to retract their story and accept induction, but they have maintained their ruse so well, the Army refuses to induct them.

The General's Daughter (1999)

Peace	Army	NR	Color	116 mins
Paramount	WV: 06-14-99		NYT: 06-18-99	

DIR: Simon West. SW: Christopher Bertolini, William Goldman. PRO: Mace Neufeld. STARS: John Travolta, Madeleine Stowe, James Cromwell, Timothy Hutton.

This soap opera, murder mystery film was adapted from Nelson DeMille's best-selling novel about a famous general's cover-up of his daughter's gang rape while a cadet at West Point. Given the negative portrayal of the military, the filmmakers did not even consider requesting assistance.

Geronimo (1939)

Indian Wars	Army	Full	B&W	89 mins
Paramount	WV: 11-22-39		NYT: 02-08-40	

DIR: Paul Sloane. SW: Paul Sloane. PRO: Paramount. STARS: Preston Foster, Ellen Drew, Andy Devine, William Henry, Gene Lockhart.

The film portrays the Army's effort to stop Geronimo's attacks on settlers. The Army allowed Sloane to shoot background footage at Fort Bliss in Texas and provided cavalry soldiers who appeared in period uniforms, in much the same way as the service gave D. W. Griffith 1,000 men and horses to shoot battle scenes for the Revolutionary War film *America*. The Screen Actors Guild complained about the loss of work for their members, but the Army responded that since the filming occurred more than 300 miles from Los Angeles, regulations against the military's taking jobs from actors did not apply.

Giant (1956)

WWII	Army	Ltd	Color	198 mins
WB	WV: 10-10-56		NYT: 10-11-56	

DIR: George Stevens. SW: Fred Guiol, Ivan Moffat. PRO: George Stevens, Henry Ginsberg. STARS: Elizabeth Taylor, Rock Hudson, James Dean.

The Army provided a burial detail in the cinematic rendering of Edna Ferber's epic novel.

G.I. Blues (1960)

Peace	Army	Full	Color	115 mins
Paramount	WV: 10-19-60		NYT: 11-05-60	

DIR: Norman Taurog. SW: Edmund Beloin, Henry Garson. PRO: Hal Wallis. STARS: Elvis Presley, Juliet Prowse, Robert Ivers, Letitia Román.

Presley plays a singing GI tank-gunner on an Army base in postwar Germany.

G.I. Jane (1951)

Peace	Army	Unkn	B&W	62 mins
Lippert	WV: 07-31-51		NYT: DNR	

DIR: Reginald Le Borg. SW: Jan Jeffries (Henry Blankfort), Murray Lerner. PRO: Murray Lerner. STARS: Jean Porter, Tom Neal, Iris Adrian.

This "B" musical features a dream sequence showing what *Weekly Variety* described as "highly unorthodox phases of Army life." Neal, stationed on a remote desert radar post, intentionally mixes up orders to get a group of WACs assigned to the location.

G.I. Jane (1997) [G&G]

Peace	Navy	Deny	Color	124 mins
Buena Vista	WV: 08-22-97		NYT: 09-21-97	

DIR: Ridley Scott. SW: David Twohy, Danielle Alexandra. PRO: Ridley Scott, Roger Birnbaum, Demi Moore, Suzanne Todd. STARS: Demi Moore, Viggo Mortensen, Anne Bancroft, Jason Beghe, Kevin Gage.

At the insistence of a female senator, the Navy recruits Moore to become the first female SEAL (Sea, Air, and Land Specialist). Although 60 percent of her male counterparts wash out during training, Moore succeeds and participates in what was to be the final training exercise before graduation. Instead, the class is diverted to help extricate American troops in a Mideast crisis and she helps save her seriously wounded commander.

Initially, the filmmakers did not think they would need Navy assistance. As a result, when they finally came to the Pentagon, they did not have sufficient time to resolve the Navy's "over attention" to the smaller issues. At one point, Moore tried to take matters into her own hands by calling the

White House, but with no perceptible result. The media suggested that the company's problems focused on the portrayal of a female SEAL, whom the Navy said did not exist. Of course, this ignored the story line that Moore was to become the first female SEAL. Scott himself pointed out that Moore could be in an experimental program in which she did SEAL-like training. When negotiations finally broke down, Scott simply portrayed Moore working side by side with her fellow trainees and taking part in a successful, if fanciful, mission.

A Girl, a Guy, and a Gob (1941)

| Peace | Navy | Full | B&W | 90 mins |
| RKO | WV: 03-05-41 | | NYT: 04-24-41 | |

DIR: Richard Wallace. SW: Frank Ryan, Bert Granet. PRO: Harold Lloyd. STARS: George Murphy, Lucille Ball, Edmund O'Brien.

A slapstick comedy in which the hero leaves his girlfriend and reenlists in the Navy. Navy ships provided the background for the exterior scenes.

The Girl He Left Behind (1956)

| Peace | Army | Full | Color | 97 mins |
| WB | WV: 10-31-56 | | NYT: 10-27-56 | |

DIR: David Butler. SW: Guy Trosper. PRO: Frank P. Rosenberg. STARS: Tab Hunter, Natalie Wood, David Janssen, Jim Backus, James Garner.

A young man's coming-of-age story in the military, set on an Army base, in peacetime America of the 1950s.

A Girl in Every Port (1928)

| Peace | Navy | Full | B&W | 64 mins |
| Fox | WV: 02-22-28 | | NYT: 02-20-28 | |

DIR: Howard Hawks. SW: Howard Hawks, Seton I. Miller, James K. McGuinness. PRO: William Fox. STARS: Victor McLaglen, Maria Casajuana, Robert Armstrong, Louise Brooks.

Lots of girls and sex appeal but no romance in this buddy silent film.

A Girl in Every Port (1951)

| Peace | Navy | Full | B&W | 86 mins |
| RKO | WV: 12-26-51 | | NYT: 02-14-52 | |

DIR: Chester Erskine. SW: Chester Erskine. PRO: Irwin Allen, Irving Cummings Jr. STARS: Groucho Marx, Marie Wilson, William Bendix.

Why would the Navy cooperate on a film portraying two always-in-hot-water lifers whose latest hijinks involved hiding horses on their ship? Maybe it was the casting of Groucho and Bendix. Or maybe it was the "join the Navy, have fun and meet pretty girls" imagery. Although a Marx Brothers-like comedy, the film made the service look like fun for young viewers. Although the action all took place on a sound stage, the final scene showed Navy ships at sea.

The Girls of Pleasure Island (1953)

Peace	Marines	Full	Color	95 mins
Paramount	WV: 02-25-53		NYT: 02-25-53	

DIR: F. Hugh Herbert, Alvin Ganzer. SW: F. Hugh Herbert. PRO: Paul Jones. STARS: Don Taylor, Leo Genn, Philip Ober, Elsa Lanchester, Dorothy Bromiley, Audrey Dalton.

Based on William Maier's novel, the comedy involves three girls on a South Seas island with 1,500 Marines. Great odds.

The Glenn Miller Story (1954)

WWII	Air Force	Full	Color	115 mins
Universal	WV: 01-06-54		NYT: 02-11-54	

DIR: Anthony Mann. SW: Valentine Davies, Oscar Brodney. PRO: Aaron Rosenberg. STARS: James Stewart, June Allyson.

Although the film focuses on how Miller created his band's special sound and musical success, it includes his enlistment during WWII, his performing for the troops, and his mysterious disappearance on a flight from England to Paris.

Glory Alley (1952)

Korea	Army	NR	B&W	79 mins
MGM	WV: 05-21-52		NYT: 07-30-52	

DIR: Raoul Walsh. SW: Art Cohn. PRO: Nicholas Nayfack. STARS: Ralph Meeker, Leslie Caron, Kurt Kasznar, Gilbert Roland.

Boxer Meeker runs from the ring seconds before he is to fight for the middleweight championship. After being accused of cowardice, he joins the Army; fights in Korea, where he receives the Medal of Honor; and returns home to New Orleans, where he finds redemption in the ring.

Glory Brigade (1953)

Korea	Army	Full	B&W	81 mins
Fox	WV: 05-13-53		NYT: 08-15-53	

DIR: Robert D. Webb. SW: Franklin Coen. PRO: William Bloom. STARS: Victor Mature, Lee Marvin, Richard Egan, Alexander Scourby.

In Korea, U.S. combat engineers accompany a UN Greek unit and overcome cultural differences to successfully complete an important mission. The production was shot at the Army's Ft. Leonard Wood, in Missouri, which provided a reasonable facsimile of the Korean countryside.

Go for Broke (1951)

WWII	Army	Full	B&W	90 mins
MGM	WV: 03-28-51		NYT: 05-25-51	

DIR: Robert Pirosh. SW: Robert Pirosh. PRO: Dore Schary. STARS: Van Johnson and the heroes of the 442nd Regimental Combat Team.

The movie followed the exploits of a Japanese American combat team, which fought bravely in Italy. Along with soldiers as extras, Pirosh used combat footage to create the battlefield environment.

Go Tell the Spartans (1978) [G&G]

Vietnam	Army	Deny	Color	114 mins
Avco	WV: 06-14-78		NYT: 09-23-78	

DIR: Ted Post. SW: Wendell Mayes. PRO: Allan F. Bodoh, Mitchell Cannold. STARS: Burt Lancaster, Craig Wasson, Jonathan Goldsmith, Marc Singer.

Based on Daniel Ford's novel *Incident at Muc Wa.* Mayes set the story in 1964, during the American advisory period in Vietnam. After he optioned the book, the screenwriter needed more than 10 years to film his script due to Hollywood's antipathy to Vietnam-related subjects. Lancaster, an aging major, receives orders to take his men to the abandoned village of Muc Wa, which had been the scene of a French defeat during its Indochina war. He points out to his superior that the village has no strategic value and the American presence will only attract the Vietcong. The command ignores his advice, and despite his efforts to win hearts and minds, once Lancaster sets up his headquarters in Muc Wa, the enemy arrives on schedule, as he had predicted.

Although the DoD public relations office advised the Army that Mayes's script contained the best portrayal of the U.S. involvement in Vietnam that had come into the Pentagon, the service also found many problems. It objected to the inclusion of a draftee in country because the United States sent only volunteers to Southeast Asia in 1964. In addition, it said the script contained negative images of some American officers, South Vietnamese soldiers torturing prisoners, and venality by our Vietnamese allies.

However, the Army expressed its greatest concern over the Lancaster character. The service noted that he was too old to still be a major and found the explanation of why he had not been promoted or retired unacceptable. At the film's high point, Lancaster describes to his exec officer his relationship with his general's wife and how at an embassy party the general, the ambassador, and the president discovered the couple in the gazebo *in flagrante delicto*, with the wife performing oral sex on him. In answer to the question of what he did, Lancaster explained he did the only thing he had been trained to do: he saluted.

If the producers had understood the process of negotiating with the Pentagon, the problems might have been resolved. After the story, Lancaster could have paused and then said, "If you believe that, I can sell you the Brooklyn Bridge," followed by the real reason he was still a major. As in the book, he could have explained that he had received a battlefield promotion to officer in Korea and so would probably have not risen higher in rank.

In any case, the director of the Army's L.A. public affairs office refused to discuss changes in the script with the filmmakers, saying soldiers did not use four-letter words in Vietnam as Mayes had included. The filmmakers then recruited the office's second in command, who liked the script and took 30 days' leave to serve as a "civilian" technical advisor. His advice helped create one of the two best portrayals of the American experience in Vietnam, one which could have served as a cautionary tale if Mayes had been able to make the movie in the mid-1960s.

Gobs and Gals (1952)

Cold War	Navy	NR	B&W	86 mins
Republic	WV: 04-30-52		NYT: DNR	

DIR: R. G. Springsteen. SW: Arthur T. Horman. PRO: Sidney Picker. STARS: George Bernard, Bert Bernard, Robert Hutton, Cathy Downs, Gordon Jones, Florence Marly, Leon Belasco.

Two sailors on a South Sea island weather station use their officer's photographs in letters to their pen pals. The scheme gets the officer in trouble with his own sweetheart when they all return stateside. Worse, one of the correspondents turns out to be a Russian spy. In the end, the two enlisted men help foil an espionage plot and love conquers all.

God Is My Co-Pilot (1945)

WWII	Air Force	Full	B&W	83 mins
WB	WV: 02-21-45		NYT: 03-24-45	

DIR: Robert Florey. SW: Peter Milne, Abem Finkel. PRO: Robert Buckner. STARS: Dennis Morgan, Dane Clark, Raymond Massey, Alan Hale.

Using a few by then obsolete P-40 fighters, which the Army loaned to the filmmakers, the movie, through a series of flashbacks, highlighted the life of Air Force ace Col. Robert Lee Scott Jr., who flew with Gen. Chennault's Flying Tigers over China and then wrote the book on which the movie was based.

Godzilla (1998)

SciFi	Army, Navy, AF	NR	Color	140 mins
Tri-Star	WV: 05-25-98		NYT: 05-18&19-98	

DIR: Roland Emmerich. SW: Dean Devlin, Roland Emmerich, Ted Elliott, Terry Rossio. PRO: Dean Devlin. STARS: Matthew Broderick, Jean Reno, Maria Pitillo, Hank Azaria, Michael Lerner.

French nuclear fallout creates a mutant lizard with a taste for fishing boats in this re-creation of the Japanese *Godzilla* films of the 1950s. The military whisks away a famous U.S. Nuclear Regulatory Agency scientist from his research on earthworms near Chernobyl to determine the genesis of the huge claw mark on the remains of a shipwrecked Japanese fishing boat. Destruction, not science, provides the movie's raison d'être, with the military, as always, waging war against the beast.

Goldeneye (1995)

Peace	Army	Full	Color	130 mins.
MGM	WV: 11-20-95		NYT: 11-17-95	

DIR: Martin Campbell. SW: Jeffrey Caine, Bruce Feirstein. PRO: Michael G. Wilson, Barbara Broccoli. STARS: Pierce Brosnan, Sean Bean, Joe Don Baker, Judi Dench, Izabella Scorupco, Famke Janssen, Robbie Coltrane.

Marines and National Guard helicopters come to the belated rescue of Brosnan. The military sequence was filmed in Puerto Rico.

Goldfinger (1964)

Peace	Army	Ltd	Color	112 mins
UA	WV: 09-23-64		NYT: 12-22-64	

DIR: Guy Hamilton. SW: Richard Maibaum, Paul Dehn. PRO: Harry Saltzman, Albert R. Broccoli. STARS: Sean Connery, Honor Blackman, Gert Fröbe, Shirley Eaton.

The Army provided filmmakers access to Fort Knox and men and equipment from Fort Campbell in this James Bond thriller.

Good Guys Wear Black (1978)

Vietnam	Army	Full	Color	96 mins
Cannon	WV: 06-28-78		NYT: 06-30-79	

DIR: Ted Post. SW: Bruce Cohn, Mark Medoff. PRO: Allan F. Bodoh. STARS: Chuck Norris, Anne Archer, Lloyd Haynes, James Franciscus, Dana Andrews.

Karate-kicking Norris investigates what happened behind the scenes to prevent U.S. helicopters from showing up during his last uniformed assignment in Vietnam to rescue American POWs. Post's film was one of the first set in Vietnam to receive Army cooperation in the form of helicopters and equipment.

Good Morning, Vietnam (1987) [G&G]

Vietnam	Air Force	Deny	Color	120 mins
Buena Vista	WV: 12-23-87		NYT: 12-23-87	

DIR: Barry Levinson. SW: Mitch Markowitz. PRO: Mark Johnson, Larry Brezner. STARS: Robin Williams, Forest Whitaker, Tung Thanh Tran.

The first cinematic comedy set in Vietnam portrayed the Armed Forces Vietnam Network DJ Adrian Cronauer, but wildly exaggerated his experiences for dramatic effect and box office success. The DoD found the script highly unrealistic and Cronauer later said that the film did not in any way portray his on-the-air or off-duty actions. In the end, the war was only the stage on which Williams could perform his comedic act.

Gray Lady Down (1978) [G&G]

Peace	Navy	Full	Color	111 mins
Universal	WV: 03-08-78		NYT: 03-10-78	

DIR: David Greene. SW: James Whittaker, Howard Sackler. PRO: Walter Mirisch. STARS: Charlton Heston, David Carradine, Stacy Keach, Ned Beatty.

One of our nuclear submarines collides with a Norwegian freighter and sinks to the edge of the continental shelf. The Navy provided assistance to the production on the theory that it showed how the service would rescue sailors from a doomed submarine, as long as it did not fall off the edge. Of course, the sinking of the sub, as in previous such stories, did not provide a very positive image for the Navy or its senior officers.

The Great Escape (1963)

WWII	Army	Ltd	Color	169 mins
UA	WV: 04-17-63		NYT: 08-08-63	

DIR: John Sturges. SW: James Clavell, W. R. Burnett. PRO: John Sturges. STARS: Steve McQueen, James Garner, Richard Attenborough, James Coburn, Charles Bronson.

Inspired by Paul Brickhill's book, the film portrays the escape of British and American airmen from a Nazi maximum-security stalag (prisoner of war camp). The Army provided some stock footage.

The Great Mail Robbery (1927)

Peace	Marines	Ltd	B&W	60 mins
FBO	WV: 07-20-27		NYT: 07-20-27	

DIR: George Seitz. SW: J. Hawks, Peter Milne. PRO: FBO. STARS: Theodore Von Eltz, Frank Nelson, Jeanne Morgan, Lee Shumway.

The Marines defeat mail robbers with men, bombs, and guns.

The Great Raid (2005)

WWII	Army	Inform	Color
Miramax	WV: Unkn		NYT: Unkn

DIR: John Dahl. SW: Carlo Bernard, Doug Miro, Hossein Amini, Kevin Lund, T. J. Scott. PRO: Marty Katz, Lawrence Bender. STARS: Benjamin Bratt, James Franco, Connie Nielsen, Joseph Fiennes, Mark Consuelos.

A true story provides the plot for this account of how Army rangers in 1945 rescued more than 500 Americans from the Cabanatuan Japanese POW camp in the Philippines—30 miles behind enemy lines. The Japanese had orders to execute the prisoners before American forces reached the camp, and the rescue was a race against time. The film's release was postponed several times.

The Great Santini (1979) [G&G]

Peace	Marines	Full	Color	115 mins
BCP	WV: 10-31-79		NYT: 07-14 & 20-80	

DIR: Lewis John Carlino. SW: Lewis John Carlino. PRO: Charles A. Pratt. STARS: Robert Duvall, Blythe Danner, Michael O'Keefe.

Pat Conroy's autobiographical novel provided the plot for this film, which focused on the relationship between a Marine flier father and his family. The service manifested very great reluctance to become involved with production because the "Great Santini," Bull Meechum, was a warrior Marine out of his element during peacetime. In particular, the public affairs office took exception to a confrontation he had with naval officers, a scene in which a Marine jet takes off from a docked aircraft carrier (suggesting how little the filmmakers knew about military operations), and his treatment of his wife and children. However, the script arrived at a time when the service was reexamining its policies on cooperation. Consequently, during the protracted negotiations, both sides compromised and the Marines agreed to provide cooperation at the Marine Air Station in Beaufort, South Carolina. The resulting film humanized Marines and undoubtedly benefited the Corps.

The Green Berets (1968) [G&G]

Vietnam	Army	Full	Color	141mins
WB	WV: 06-09-68		NYT: 06-20-68	

DIR: John Wayne, Ray Kellogg. SW: James Lee Barrett. PRO: Michael Wayne. STARS: John Wayne, Aldo Ray, David Janssen, Jim Hutton.

John Wayne was willing to put his money where his mouth was and made the film based on the Robin Moore novel about the Green Berets during the advisory phase of the war in Vietnam. Because Wayne had written to President Lyndon B. Johnson about how he intended to create a movie supporting the administration's involvement in Southeast Asia, the Army enthusiastically supported the production. However, before the Waynes could receive cooperation at Fort Benning, Georgia, producer Wayne had to agree to change the location of a Green Beret mission from North to South Vietnam since the service denied that its men had ever crossed the border into the North. Although Moore said he had accompanied a special forces team across the border, the producer said his father would have called him a dumb son of a bitch and kicked him in the ass if the Army had turned down his request for help.

In fact, Georgia looked like Georgia—not Vietnam—and the film remained primarily a John Wayne shoot-'em-up with some prowar propaganda thrown in for good measure. The wrong-headedness of *The Green Berets* can best be seen in the final scene, in which Wayne senior walked down a beach with a Vietnamese boy as the sun set in the East, into the South China Sea, but shot at Point Mugu Naval Air Station in California. Of course, when Wayne told the Vietnamese orphan boy that "he" was what the war was all about, he undoubtedly believed it.

The Green Dragon (2001)

Vietnam	Marines	Full	Color	115 mins
Franchise Pictures	WV: 02-05-2001		NYT: 07-19-2002	

DIR: Timothy Linh Bui. SW: Timothy Linh Bui. PRO: Elie Samaha, Tony Bui, Tajamika Paxton, Andrew Stevens. STARS: Patrick Swayze, Forest Whitaker, Don Duong.

The film portrayed Vietnamese refugees held at Camp Pendleton after their escape from Vietnam. The Marines allowed the company to shoot on base.

Guadalcanal Diary (1943)

WWII	Marines	Full	B&W	93 mins
Fox	WV: 10-27-43		NYT: 11-18-43	

DIR: Lewis Seiler. SW: Lamar Trotti, Jerome Cady. PRO: Bryan Foy. STARS: Preston Foster, Lloyd Nolan, William Bendix.

Based on journalist Richard Tregaskis's book, this docudrama portrayed the Marine fight to take Guadalcanal. Filmed at Camp Pendleton and on the beaches of San Clemente, the movie provided an eloquent depiction of the heroic struggle very similar to that in *The Story of G.I. Joe*, based on Ernie's Pyle's writing on the Italian campaign. The film contained no lofty speeches about bravery or the glory of death in combat, just the accounts of men in combat doing their jobs in a necessary war.

Guarding Tess (1994)

Peace	Army	Ltd	Color	96 mins
Tri-Star	WV: 03-07-94		NYT: 03-11-94	

DIR: Hugh Wilson. SW: Hugh Wilson, Peter Torokvei. PRO: Ned Tanen, Nancy Graham Tanen. STARS: Shirley MacLaine, Nicolas Cage, Austin Pendleton, Edward Albert, Dale Dye, James Rebhorn, Richard Griffiths, John Roselius.

Maryland Army National Guard helicopters appeared in a scene depicting the rescue of the former first lady.

Gung Ho! (1943)

WWII	Marines, Navy	Full	B&W	88 mins
Universal	WV: 12-22-43		NYT: 01-26-44	

DIR: Ray Enright. SW: Lucien Hubbard. PRO: Walter Wanger. STARS: Randolph Scott, Robert Mitchum, J. Carrol Naish.

In this docudrama, the filmmakers changed the names (including that of the president's son Maj. James Roosevelt, who was second in command), but otherwise created a reasonably accurate account of the Marine Raiders's assault on Makin Island and the first capture of Japanese territory. The Corps assisted in the production, providing men and equipment and technical advice from then Lt. Col. Evans Carlson, who had led the mission.

A Guy Named Joe (1943)

WWII	Air Force	Full	B&W	120 mins
MGM	WV: 12-29-43		NYT: 12-24-43, 01-09-44	

DIR: Victor Fleming. SW: Dalton Trumbo, Frederick Hazlitt Brennan. PRO: Everett Riskin. STARS: Spencer Tracy, Irene Dunne, Van Johnson.

Tracy dies, and his ghost helps to train another pilot, who also replaces Tracy in the affections of Tracy's grieving girlfriend.

Hail the Conquering Hero (1944)

WWII	Marines	Unkn	B&W	101 mins
Paramount	WV: 06-07-44		NYT: 08-10-44	

DIR: Preston Sturges. SW: Preston Sturges. PRO: Preston Sturges. STARS: Eddie Bracken, Ella Raines.

A Marine, medically discharged after one month in the Corps because of hay fever, returns home as an ersatz hero. He ultimately confesses the deceit, but all's well that ends well.

Hair (1979) [G&G]

Vietnam	Army	Full	Color	118 mins
UA	WV: 03-14-79		NYT: 03-14 & 25-79	

DIR: Milos Forman. SW: Michael Weller. PRO: Lester Persky, Michael Butler. STARS: John Savage, Treat Williams, Beverly D'Angelo, Annie Golden, Nicholas Ray, Cheryl Barnes.

Although the film was based on Gerome Ragni, James Rado, and Galt MacDermot's antiwar, antiestablishment Broadway musical hit, Weller nevertheless radically changed the scenario. While keeping most of the songs, the writer created a thematic story of friendship and innocence lost. Initially, the Army flatly refused to even discuss cooperation because of the antiwar message of the play. However, the filmmakers wanted a military presence to juxtapose with the surrealistic hippie life in New York. After long negotiations with the DoD, the California National Guard allowed Forman to film on a closed base and use an airplane for the climactic military sequence in which Williams marched into the bowels of a transport plane and flew off to Vietnam in place of Savage. Unlike the ending of *The Deer Hunter*, in which the characters have learned nothing, the young people in *Hair* have gained knowledge from their experiences and have let the sunshine in.

Half Shot at Sunrise (1930)

WWI	Army	Unkn	B&W	75 mins
RKO	WV: 10-15-30		NYT: 10-11-30	

DIR: Paul Sloane. SW: James Creelman, Ralph Spence, Anne Caldwell. PRO: William Le Baron. STARS: Bert Wheeler, Robert Woolsey.

Two American doughboys in Paris who are AWOL have comedic adventures while keeping one step ahead of the MPs chasing them. One small combat sequence provides action.

Halls of Montezuma (1950)

WWII	Marines	Full	Color	113 mins
Fox	WV: 02-13-50		NYT: 01-06-51	

DIR: Lewis Milestone. SW: Michael Blankfort. PRO: Robert Bassler. STARS: Richard Widmark, Karl Malden, Robert Wagner.

Fox's effort to duplicate the success of *Sands of Iwo Jima*, this time looking at officers and issues of command and control. Widmark is suffering from combat fatigue while trying to lead his men. Malden, as a medic, ministers to Widmark, whose men try to capture Japanese soldiers to obtain intelligence. The Marines provided men and equipment during filming at Camp Pendleton.

Ham and Eggs at the Front (1927)

WWI	Army	NR	B&W	Unkn
WB	WV: 03-14-28		NYT: DNR	

DIR: Roy Del Ruth. SW: Darryl F. Zanuck, James A. Starr, Robert Dillon. PRO: WB. STARS: Tom Wilson, Myrna Loy, William Irving, Noah Young.

A blackface comedy about two doughboys in France who pursue Loy, also in blackface, and after the usual comedic hijinks, capture a German general. Both Loy and Zanuck regretted their involvement in the racist images.

Hamburger Hill (1987) [G&G]

Vietnam	Army	Full	Color	110 mins
Paramount	WV: 08-12-87		NYT: 08-28-87	

DIR: John Irvin. SW: Jim Carabatsos. PRO: Marcia Nasatir, Jim Carabatsos. STARS: Anthony Barrile, Michael Patrick Boatman, Don Cheadle, Michael Dolan, Don James, Dylan McDermott.

This was the first Hollywood rendering of the American experience in Vietnam to receive major assistance from the Army. The film, with the Philippines standing in for Vietnam, portrayed the infantry's efforts to seize Hamburger Hill and the Army's subsequent abandonment of the height, which became a metaphor for the war itself. In fact, the battle kept the Ashau Valley relatively quiet for several years, although the movie did not explain this. As a result, most people saw *Hamburger Hill* as making an antiwar statement even though the Army had assisted.

Hannibal Brooks (1969)

WWII	Army	NR	Color	101 mins
UA	WV: 03-05-69		NYT: 05-01-69	

DIR: Michael Winner. SW: Dick Clement, Ian La Frenais. PRO: Michael Winner. STARS: Oliver Reed, Michael J. Pollard, John Alderton.

During the last months of the war, the Germans assign Reed, a British POW, to take care of Lucy, a 15-year-old elephant, in the Munich zoo. Ordered to escort Lucy to Innsbruck, Austria, after the zoo is bombed, Reed ends up heading to Switzerland, joined by Pollard, an escaped American POW, and his guerrilla band of fellow escapees. At the border, Lucy breaks down the barrier and the men and the beast reach safety.

The Hanoi Hilton (1987) [G&G]

Vietnam	Air Force, Navy	Full	Color	123 mins
Cannon	WV: 03-25-87		NYT: 03-27-87	

DIR: Lionel Chetwynd. SW: Lionel Chetwynd. PRO: Menahem Golan, Yoram Globus. STARS: Michael Moriarty, Jeffrey Jones, Paul LeMat, David Soul, Stephen Davies, Lawrence Pressman, Aki Aleong.

The film recounted how American POWs survived in the infamous "Hanoi Hilton" prison, home of captured fliers during most of the war. Although the men were visible victims of the war, the story said nothing about the wives and parents waiting for an occasional word from the prisoners. Nor did the movie provide any balance by explaining the suffering of the North Vietnamese people at the hands of American bombing, a fault Chetwynd acknowledged. It also took a cheap shot at the antiwar movement by including a naive Jane Fonda lookalike, who aborted an effort by the prisoners to give her a message when she turns it over to the North Vietnamese. The Navy provided an aircraft carrier to re-create the launch of bombers attacking North Vietnam.

Hanover Street **(1979)**

WWII	Air Force	NR	Color	109 mins
Columbia	WV: 05-16-79		NYT: 05-18 & 27-79	

DIR: Peter Hyams. SW: Peter Hyams. PRO: Paul N. Lazarus, III. STARS: Harrison Ford, Lesley-Anne Down, Christopher Plummer, Alec McGowen.

A soap opera love affair set in WWII England between B-25 pilot Ford and a married British woman. Ford ultimately embarks upon a secret mission into German-held France with the husband, whom he rescues, and then nobly gives up the wife. For the flying sequences, the filmmakers ferried five bombers across the Atlantic. In fact, the Air Force used B-25s in other theaters, not in the 8th Air Force in England.

The Happiest Millionaire **(1967)**

WWI	Marines	Ltd	Color	164 mins
Disney	WV: 06-28-67		NYT: 12-01-67	

DIR: Norman Tokar. SW: A. J. Carothers. PRO: Bill Anderson. STARS: Fred MacMurray, Greer Garson, Tommy Steele.

Based on the book and play by Kyle Crichton and Cordelia Drexler Biddle. Marines appear as background in this musical set during WWI.

Hart's War **(2002)**

WWII	Army	NR	Color	128 mins
MGM	WV: 02-11-2002		NYT: 02-15-2002	

DIR: Gregory Hoblit. SW: Billy Ray, Terry George. PRO: David Ladd, David Foster, Arnold Rifkin, Gregory Hoblit. STARS: Bruce Willis, Colin Farrell, Terence Howard, Cole Hauser, Marcel Iures.

John Katzenbach's novel provided the story for the film, which *Weekly Variety* described as **Stalag 17** meets **A Soldier's Story** because it portrays racial prejudice among U.S. soldiers against two black airmen imprisoned with them in a German POW camp. Iures, as the commandant, may be the most sympathetic character.

Heartbreak Ridge (1986) [G&G]

Grenada	Marines	Full	Color	128 mins
WB	WV: 12-03-86		NYT: 12-05-86	

DIR: Clint Eastwood. SW: James Carabatsos. PRO: Clint Eastwood. STARS: Clint Eastwood, Marsha Mason, Mario Van Peebles.

The Army refused to cooperate on this story of the Grenada invasion because of the raw language and an historically inaccurate portrayal of the event. In contrast, the Marines jumped at the chance for a positive portrayal of their contribution to the victory against an overmatched militia composed mostly of Cuban soldiers. In their eagerness, the Marines failed to ensure that the completed film would contain positive images and so provide the expected benefit. Apart from errors in re-creating the Marines' contribution to the successful operation, in one scene, Eastwood shoots a wounded Cuban soldier and takes a cigar from the dead man. After Eastwood screened the movie in the Pentagon, the Marines requested their screen credits be removed because of their dissatisfaction with their portrayal.

Hearts of the World (1918)

WWI	Army	NR	B&W	117 mins
Artcraft	WV: 04-12-18		NYT: 04-05-18; 08-12-19	

DIR: D. W. Griffith. SW: D. W. Griffith. PRO: D. W. Griffith. STARS: Lillian Gish, Adolph Lestina, Robert Harron, Noël Coward.

The British and French military provided assistance to Griffith near the front in France for this story of German troops fighting the French in and around a small village. Only at the end do the Americans make a brief appearance to symbolically forecast the Allied victory. In 1918, the film provided propaganda to support the Allied war effort. Upon its rerelease, after the war had ended, it appealed to the audience more as a dramatic story about people trying to survive during war.

Heaven and Earth (1993)

Vietnam	Marines	NR	Color	135 mins
WB	WV: 12-27-93		NYT: 12-24-93	

DIR: Oliver Stone. SW: Oliver Stone. PRO: Oliver Stone, Arnon Milchan, Robert Kline, A. Kitman Ho. STARS: Hiep Thi Le, Tommy Lee Jones, Joan Chen, Haing S. Ngor, Debbie Reynolds, Dale Dye.

Based on the books *When Heaven and Earth Changed Places* and *Children of War, Women of Peace*, the story focuses on efforts of a Vietnamese woman to become an American. Tommy Lee Jones plays an ex-Marine married to the woman.

Heaven Knows, Mr. Allison (1957)

WWII	Marines	Cour	Color	107 mins
Fox	WV: 03-20-57		NYT: 03-15-57	

DIR: John Huston. SW: John Huston, John Lee Mahin. PRO: Buddy Adler. STARS: Robert Mitchum, Deborah Kerr.

Based on Charles Shaw's novel. A Marine and a nun find themselves marooned on a desert island during World War II. A few Marines provided unofficial assistance to create the assault of the island and rescue of the two people before forbidden romance can occur.

Hell Below (1933) [SSS]

WWI	Navy, Air Force	Full	B&W	103 mins
MGM	WV: 05-02-33		NYT: 04-26-33	

DIR: Jack Conway. SW: Laird Doyle, Raymond Schrock, John Lee Mahin, John Meehan. PRO: Jack Conway. STARS: Robert Montgomery, Walter Huston, Madge Evans, Jimmy Durante, Robert Young.

Based on Cdr. Edward Ellsberg's novel *Pig Boats*, this last significant WWI naval movie has three intersecting plot lines in a story that once again features death aboard a submarine and heroic missions against the enemy. Initially, the Navy wanted nothing to do with a story it considered "entirely unfit for production." After MGM hired a retired submariner and produced a significantly revised script, the Navy approved assistance, and the completed film provided positive images of its men and hardware.

Hell Divers (1931) [SSS]

Peace	Navy	Full	B&W	110 mins
MGM	WV: 12-29-31		NYT: 12-23-31	

DIR: George Hill. SW: Harvey Gates, Malcolm S. Boylan. PRO: George Hill. STARS: Wallace Beery, Clark Gable, Conrad Nagel, Dorothy Jordan, Robert Young.

A typical Navy recruiting film of the 1930s loaded with planes, dirigibles, and an aircraft carrier, the USS *Saratoga*. The film shows planes landing on carriers, "new" dive bombing techniques, and the only cinematic portrayal of a dirigible landing aboard a carrier.

Hell in the Pacific (1968)

WWII	Marines	Unkn	Color	103 mins
Selmur	WV: 12-11-68		NYT: 02-11-69	

DIR: John Boorman. SW: Alexander Jacobs, Eric Bercovici. PRO: Reuben Bercovitch. STARS: Lee Marvin, Toshirô Mifune.

A Marine and a Japanese soldier find themselves trapped on a South Pacific island and work together to survive. They build a raft to escape the desolate piece of land, but when they arrive at another island, their mutual animosity resurfaces, despite having become soul brothers. At the end, they head in opposite directions to uncertain futures.

Hell Is for Heroes (1962)

WWII	Army	Full	B&W	90 mins
Paramount	WV: 05-30-62		NYT: 07-12-62	

DIR: Don Siegel. SW: Robert Pirosh, Richard Carr. PRO: Henry Blanke, Robert Pirosh. STARS: Steve McQueen, Bobby Darin, Fess Parker, Harry Guardino, Nick Adams, James Coburn.

Inspired by a historical but classified event. Steve McQueen plays an unconventional, busted NCO who sacrifices himself to hold off a large German force along the Siegfried Line. Pirosh backed out of producing this one halfway through the filming.

Hell on the Battleground (1989)

Cold War	Army	NR	Color	86 mins
Action Intl	WV: 04-12-89		NYT: DNR	

DIR: David A. Prior. SW: David A. Prior. PRO: Fritz Matthews. STARS: William Smith, Fritz Matthews, Ted Prior, Chet Hood.

Formerly titled *Battleground*, this direct-to-video release envisions a U.S.–Soviet conflict (time, place, and reasons are not revealed), with infantry and tank battles.

Hell Squad (1958)

WWII	Army	NR	B&W	64 mins
Amer-Intl	WV: 10-29-58		NYT: DNR	

DIR: Burt Topper. SW: Burt Topper. PRO: Burt Topper. STARS: Wally Campo, Brandon Carroll, Fred Galvin, Gregg Stuart, Cecil Addis.

An original story with an unusual ending. The film follows a small patrol lost in the Tunisian desert, trying to find its way back to base, during the early days of the U.S. involvement in WWII. The film bears some resemblance to the 1943 *Sahara*.

Hell to Eternity (1960)

WWII	Marines	Full	B&W	132 mins
Allied Artists	WV: 08-03-60		NYT: 10-13-60	

DIR: Phil Karlson. SW: Ted Sherdeman, Walter Schmidt. PRO: Irving Levin. STARS: Jeffrey Hunter, David Janssen, Vic Damone, Sessue Hayakawa, George Takei.

Based on the true story of Guy Gabaldon, who was raised by a Japanese family and became a Marine during World War II. Using his knowledge of Japanese, he managed to persuade a huge number of Japanese soldiers to surrender on Saipan.

Hellcats of the Navy (1957) [SSS]

WWII	Navy	Full	B&W	81 mins
Columbia	WV: 05-01-57		NYT: DNR	

DIR: Nathan Juran. SW: David Lang, Raymond Marcus. PRO: Charles H. Schneer. STARS: Ronald Reagan, Nancy Davis, Arthur Franz, Robert Arthur, William Leslie, Harry Lauter.

Adm. Chester Nimitz provided a forward to the filming of ***Hellcats of the Sea*** by submariners Adm. Charles Lockwood and Hans Christian. The movie attempted to capture the angst of submariners sacrificing one or more crew members to ensure the survival of the others. It also explored the clash between Capt. Reagan and his executive officer Franz over his readiness for command. This was the only occasion on which Reagan starred with his second wife, Nancy Davis.

Hello Annapolis (1942)

Preparedness	Navy	Full	B&W	62 mins
Columbia	WV: DNR		NYT: DNR	

DIR: Charles Barton. SW: Donald Davis, Tom Reed. PRO: Wallace MacDonald. STARS: Tom Brown, Jean Parker, Larry Parks, Phil Brown, Joseph Crehan, Thurston Hall.

A rich boy, a poor boy, and a female Navy brat create a coming-of-age story set at the Naval Academy before the war. Parker prefers the rich boy, Brown, who belittles the Navy but goes to Annapolis when the girl says she will only marry a Navy man. On the other hand, Parks is an enlisted man trying to work his way into the Academy. After misadventures, a boiler room accident, and suitable heroics, Parker agrees to marry Brown after graduation.

Hell's Horizon (1955)

Korea	Air Force	Ltd	B&W	78 mins
Columbia	WV: 11-23-55		NYT: DNR	

DIR: Tom Gries. SW: Tom Gries. PRO: Wray Davis. STARS: John Ireland, Marla English, Bill Williams, Hugh Beaumont.

The story of a single-plane bombing mission using bad weather to cover it during its mission to attack a bridge over the Yalu River. When the clouds unexpectedly open up, North Korean MIGs attack. The disliked pilot manages to hold the crew together and the plane returns to base, crash landing with an empty fuel tank. Done before and will be done again.

Her Man o'War (1926)

WWI	Army	Full	B&W	61 mins
PDC	WV: 09-15-26		NYT: DNR	

DIR: Frank Urson. SW: Charles Logue, Jeanie Macpherson. PRO: Cecil B. DeMille. STARS: William Boyd, Jimmie Adams, Jetta Goudal.

Two Yanks volunteer to pose as deserters to spy upon the German placement of a "big gun" that is impeding their unit's progress. The German officer does not trust their disinformation and keeps them under surveillance. A girl informs the German officer of the espionage but then realizes she loves one of the men and continues his work until they are all captured and sentenced to die. U.S. troops arrive in the nick of time.

Here Come the Jets (1959)

Peace	Air Force	Ltd	B&W	72 mins
Fox	WV: 06-03-59		NYT: DNR	

DIR: Gene Fowler Jr. SW: Louis Vittes. PRO: Richard Einfeld. STARS: Steve Brodie, Lyn Thomas, Mark Dana, John Doucette, Jean Carson.

Brodie plays an alcoholic Korean War hero, whom plane manufacturer Doucette works to rehabilitate so that he can test fly new jet airliners. The film features a "flight simulator."

Here Come the Marines (1952)

Peace	Marines	Ltd	B&W	66 mins
Monogram	WV: 05-28-52		NYT: DNR	

DIR: William Beaudine. SW: Jack Crutcher, Charles Marion, Tim Ryan. PRO: Jerry Thomas. STARS: Leo Gorcey, Huntz Hall, Bernard Gorcey.

The comedic "Bowery Boys" find themselves in the Marines.

Here Come the Waves (1944)

WWII	Navy	Ltd	B&W	99 mins
Paramount	WV: 12-20-44		NYT: 12-28-44	

DIR: Mark Sandrich. SW: Allan Scott, Ken Englund, Zion Myers. PRO: Mark Sandrich. STARS: Bing Crosby, Betty Hutton, Sonny Tufts.

A musical play within a play, with Crosby playing a crooner who is initially passed over when he tries to join the Navy because he is color-blind. When he is finally allowed to enlist, he is assigned to sing and act in shows targeted for WAVE recruiting.

Here Comes the Navy (1934)

Peace	Navy	Full	B&W	88 mins
WB	WV: 07-24-34		NYT: 07-21-34	

DIR: Lloyd Bacon. SW: Ben Markson, Earl Baldwin. PRO: Warner Bros. STARS: James Cagney, Pat O'Brien, Gloria Stuart.

Warner Bros. "borrowed" the Brooklyn Navy Yard for the Broadway premiere of a movie showing "gobs" doing their everyday jobs. Originally intended to be a comedy when first released, in its 1940 rerelease it became a patriotic preparedness film. Ironically the on-board footage was shot on the USS *Arizona*. Jack Warner and Hal Wallis served as executive producers.

Hero of Submarine D-2 (1916) [SSS]

Peace	Navy	Full	B&W	5 reels
Vitagraph	WV: 03-10-16		NYT: DNR	

DIR: Paul Scardon. SW: Cyrus Townsend Brady, Jasper Ewing Brady. PRO: Paul Scardon. STARS: Charles Richman, James Morrison, Anders Randolf.

A war-preparedness melodrama in which the hero is an Annapolis instructor who refuses to reinstate a politician's son who has flunked out. As a result, the officer finds himself reassigned to commanding a submarine. He then suffers serious wounds during a battle to foil a Russian plot to blow up the U.S. fleet. The disgraced midshipman rescues his teacher-nemesis and becomes a hero, while the officer marries the young man's sister. The Navy allowed filming for the first time at the Naval Academy as well as shooting at the Newport, Rhode Island naval base.

Heroes (1977) [G&G]

Vietnam	Army	Ltd	Color	113 mins
Universal	WV: 11-02-77		NYT: 11-05-77	

DIR: Jeremy Paul Kagan. SW: James Carabatsos, David Freeman. PRO: David Foster, Lawrence Turman. STARS: Henry Winkler, Sally Field, Harrison Ford.

Winkler plays a deranged Vietnam vet who escapes from a VA hospital and heads cross-country to start a worm business with a Vietnam buddy. Field stars as his companion. When they arrive at the buddy's home, the shocked parents tell Winkler that their son was killed in Vietnam, causing him to experience a flashback to the battlefield action that explains his craziness. The Army allowed the director to film a scene at the Times Square Recruiting station, in which Winkler tries to keep young men from enlisting despite the recruiter's claim that war is better than sex. Despite its antiwar tone, *Heroes* was the first Vietnam-related film after the end of the war to receive Pentagon assistance.

Heroes Die Young (1960)

WWII	Army	Unkn	B&W	76 mins
AA	WV: DNR		NYT: DNR	

DIR: Gerald Shepard. SW: Gerald Shepard. PRO: Gerald Shepard, Frank Russell. STARS: Erika Peters, Scott Borland, Robert Getz, Bill Browne, James Strother.

The film draws on the Air Force's massive raid against the Ploesti oil field, intended to deprive Germany of fuel to continue the war. Strother leads an eight-man unit into Rumania to set signal fires, which will guide the bombers to their target. The mission and the raid succeed, but at great cost.

Hey, Rookie (1944)

WWII	Army	Unkn	B&W	71 mins
Columbia	WV: 04-12-44		NYT: DNR	

DIR: Charles Barton. SW: Henry Myers, Edward Eliscu, Jay Gorney. PRO: Irving Briskin. STARS: Joe Besser, Ann Miller, Larry Parks, Joe Sawyer.

Based on an army musical play, the story portrays a musical comedy producer, then in the army, who was assigned to develop a show to entertain his fellow soldiers.

High Barbaree (1947)

WWII	Navy	Full	B&W	91 mins
MGM	WV 03-12-47		NYT 06-06-47	

DIR: Jack Conway. SW: Anne Morrison Chapin, Whitfield Cook, Cyril Hume. PRO: Everett Riskin. STARS: Van Johnson, June Allyson, Thomas Mitchell, Marilyn Maxwell.

Based on a novel by Charles Nordhoff and James Norman Hall, the film removes much of the novel's imaginative fantasy and the film becomes a love story between Navy flier Johnson and Allyson, interrupted by WWII. When the Japanese shoot down Johnson's Catalina flying boat, *High Barbaree*, in the South Pacific, he tells his life's story to sustain hope of rescue as he and one surviving crewman float on the empty ocean.

High Crimes (2002)

Peace	Marines	Deny	Color	115 mins
Fox	WV: 04-05-2002		NYT: 04-05-2002	

DIR: Carl Franklin. SW: Yuri Zeltser, Cary Bickley. PRO: Arnon Milchan, Janet Yang, Jesse B. Franklin. STARS: Ashley Judd, Morgan Freeman, Jim Caviezel.

Based on Joseph Finder's novel, the film tells a muddled story of an ex-Marine, Caviezel, accused of war crimes in Central America. His lawyer wife, Judd, and a broken down former military lawyer, Freeman, try to clear the husband, with the resulting climax rendering everything that has come before nonsensical. A poor image of Marines and high military authority in the script caused the service to deny cooperation.

Hit the Deck (1930)

Peace	Navy	Full	B&W	93 mins
RKO	WV: 01-22-30		NYT: 01-15-30	

DIR: Luther Reed. SW: Luther Reed. PRO: William LeBaron. STARS: Jack Oakie, Polly Walker, Harry Sweet, Franker Wood, Roger Gray.

Based on Hubert Osborne's play *Shore Leave*, this musical contains a comedy recruiting sequence. Reed filmed the last 31 minutes in color, a first for the armed services.

Hold Back the Night (1956)

Korea	Marines	Full	B&W	80 mins
Allied Artists	WV: 07-25-56		NYT: DNR	

DIR: Allan Dwan. SW: John C. Higgins, Walter Doniger. PRO: Hayes Goetz. STARS: John Payne, Mona Freeman, Peter Graves, Chuck Connors.

The film portrays the same story as the 1952 **Retreat, Hell!** about the Marine retreat from the Yalu River in 1950. This time, however, the service had a negative reaction to the script. After suitable revisions, the Marines gave full cooperation at their cold-weather training base in northern California in real snow. Despite this, the film created less of a sense of the bitter Korean cold than did the earlier portrayal at Camp Pendleton north of San Diego, which used whitewashed hills to create the wintry background.

Hold 'em Navy (1937)

Peace	Navy	Full	B&W	62 mins
Paramount	WV: 11-10-37		NYT: 11-06-37	

DIR: Kurt Neumann. SW: Erwin Gelsey, Lloyd Corrigan, Albert Le Vino. PRO: Charles Rogers. STARS: Lew Ayres, Mary Carlisle, John Howard, Benny Baker.

A stereotypical midshipmen story, with the Navy winning the traditional big game on the last play. The movie included shots of the Naval Academy and the game itself.

Hollywood Canteen (1944)

WWII	All	Full	B&W	124 mins
WB	WV: 12-06-44		NYT: 12-16-44	

DIR: Delmer Daves. SW: Delmer Daves. PRO: Alex Gottlieb. STARS: Robert Hutton, Joan Leslie, Dane Clark, and a plethora of Hollywood stars.

The Los Angeles version of *Stage Door Canteen*, with Hutton portraying a Purple Heart recipient on leave who visits the L.A. Canteen and becomes the millionth guest. Better yet, romance flourishes amid the Cole Porter tunes featured.

The Holy Terror (1937)

Peace	Navy	Unkn	B&W	66 mins
Fox	WV: 01-27-37		NYT: 01-30-37	

DIR: James Tinling. SW: Lou Breslow, John Patrick. PRO: Fox. STARS: Jane Withers, Anthony Martin, Leah Ray, El Brendel, Joe E. Lewis.

A song and dance comedy/love story featuring a good-looking Navy balladeer, goofy gobs, and a young woman who creates mischief at a naval air station.

Home of the Brave (1949)

WWII	Army	NR	B&W	88 mins
UA	WV: 05-04-49		NYT: 05-13-49	

DIR: Mark Robson. SW: Carl Foreman. PRO: Stanley Kramer. STARS: Douglas Dick, Steve Brodie, Jeff Corey, Lloyd Bridges, Frank Lovejoy, James Edwards.

Based on Arthur Laurent's Broadway play of the same name but with the original anti-Semitism theme changed to a racial theme. Kramer and Foreman place the action in WWII, on a Japanese-held island.

Homecoming (1948)

WWII	Army	Ltd	B&W	113 mins
MGM	WV: 04-07-48		NYT: 04-30-48	

DIR: Mervyn LeRoy. SW: Paul Osborn. PRO: Sidney Franklin. STARS: Clark Gable, Lana Turner, Anne Baxter, John Hodiak.

Although the film showcased the heroic work the Medical Corps did during the war, the story centered on Gable as a happily married doctor who goes to war and falls in love with Turner, his nurse partner, patching up wounded soldiers in Italy. The Production Code Office solved the potential problem of adultery by requiring that Turner die of her combat wounds.

The Hook (1963)

Korea	Army	NR	B&W	98 mins
MGM	WV: 01-16-63		NYT: 02-16-63	

DIR: George Seaton. SW: Henry Denker. PRO: William Perlberg. STARS: Kirk Douglas, Robert Walker Jr., Nick Adams.

Three soldiers wrestle with their combat experiences and consciences when ordered to kill a prisoner. From Vahé Katcha's novel *L'Hamecon*.

The Horizontal Lieutenant (1962)

WWII	Navy	NR	Color	90 mins
MGM	WV: 04-04-62		NYT: 05-12-62	

DIR: Richard Thorpe. SW: George Wells. PRO: Joseph Pasternak. STARS: Jim Hutton, Paula Prentiss, Jack Carter, Miyoshi Umeki, Jim Backus.

In this comedy, Hutton is ordered to capture a Japanese soldier still at large on a South Sea island. Seems he's been stealing gefilte fish.

Hornet's Nest (1970)

WWII	Army	NR	Color	109 mins
UA	WV: 09-02-70		NYT: 12-10-70	

DIR: Phil Karlson, Franco Cirino. SW: S. S. Schweitzer. PRO: Stanley Canter. STARS: Rock Hudson, Sylva Koscina, Sergio Fantoni, Jacques Sernas.

This Italian/American production trods well-traveled ground in which soldiers are inserted into enemy territory to blow up menacing coastal artillery, high-ranking officers, bridges, and in this case, a huge Italian dam. Hudson loses his entire unit in an ambush but is rescued by a group of youngsters seeking revenge against the German military, which took over their town and killed their families. They agree to help him if he helps them. The ending contains an inexplicable antiwar message.

Hot Shots! (1991)

Peace	Navy	NR	Color	85 mins
Fox	WV: 08-05-91		NYT: 07-31-91	

DIR: Jim Abrahams. SW: Pat Proft, Jim Abrahams. PRO: Bill Badalato. STARS: Charlie Sheen, Cary Elwes, Valeria Golino, Lloyd Bridges.

This film resulted from crossing **Top Gun**, **Navy Seals**, and **An Officer and a Gentleman**. No wonder the studio did not request cooperation from the military.

Hot Shots! Part Deux (1993)

Gulf Wars	Army	NR	Color	89 mins
Fox	WV: 05-24-93		NYT: 05-21-93	

DIR: Jim Abrahams. SW: Jim Abrahams, Pat Proft. PRO: Bill Badalato. STARS: Charlie Sheen, Lloyd Bridges, Valeria Golino, Richard Crenna, Brenda Bakke.

A sequel, this time with Sheen as a Rambo type, recalled to the Army to rescue soldiers who were sent to rescue soldiers left behind in the first Gulf War. The film contains an over-the-top parody of POW rescue movies.

House (1986)

Vietnam	Army	NR	Color	93 mins
New World	WV: 01-22-86		NYT: 02-26-86	

DIR: Steve Miner. SW: Fred Dekker, Ethan Wiley. PRO: Richard Brophy, Sean Cunningham. STARS: William Katt, George Wendt, Richard Moll, Kay Lenz.

The film combines war and horror genres as horror novelist Katt tries to write about his experiences in Vietnam. When he moves into a Victorian house of his aunt, who recently committed suicide, all hell breaks loose both from evil forces within the house and his evil nightmares about Vietnam. Flashbacks to war contain the usual clichéd images of soldiers using drugs and refusing to obey orders, but the combat itself lacks the horror of the house.

House of Bamboo (1955)

Peace	Army	Ltd	Color	102 mins
Fox	WV: 07-06-55		NYT: 07-02-55	

DIR: Samuel Fuller. SW: Harry Kleiner, Samuel Fuller. PRO: Buddy Adler. STARS: Robert Ryan, Robert Stack, Shirley Yamaguchi, Cameron Mitchell.

This detective story is set in postwar, occupied Japan. It features Stack as an MP seeking the murderer of a GI among a gang of Yanks.

How Sleep the Brave (1981)

Vietnam	Army	NR	Color	Unkn
Lindsay Shonteff	WV: DNR		NYT: DNR	

DIR: Lindsay Shonteff. SW: Unkn. PRO: Unkn. STARS: Lawrence Day, Daniel Foley, Luis Manuel, Thomas Pollard.

This British exploitation movie follows the travails of an infantry squad newly arrived in Vietnam. In its first action, the men find themselves surrounded by the Vietcong and lose two men during the fighting. Returning to base, they immediately receive new orders to destroy an enemy village. The mission is accomplished with predictable violence, explosions, and dead bodies before the men reach safety. Filmed in England using British actors, with expected impact of the visual images and language.

Hulk (2003)

SciFi	Army	Deny	Color	138 mins
Universal	WV: 06-12-2003		NYT: 06-20-2003	

DIR: Ang Lee. SW: John Turman, Michael France, James Schamus. PRO: Larry Franco, Gale Anne Hurd, Avi Arad. STARS: Eric Bana, Jennifer Connelly, Sam Elliot, Nick Nolte.

The Army, not liking the portrayal of its officers, denied cooperation to this Marvel Comic hero film. Ironically, the completed film had more benign portrayals of the military. The Army was particularly concerned with the presence of a secret military lab that was up to no good under the direct supervision of the bad general.

The Human Comedy (1943)

WWII	Army	NR	B&W	118 mins
MGM	WV: 03-03-43		NYT:03-03-43	

DIR: Clarence Brown. SW: Howard Estabrook. PRO: Clarence Brown. STARS: Mickey Rooney, Frank Morgan, Van Johnson, James Craig, Donna Reed, Robert Mitchum.

Based on William Saroyan's original book and draft screenplay, the film focuses on life in a small California town during wartime. Teenage Rooney matures as he accepts responsibilities at home, while his brother Johnson goes off to war. The film shows soldiers on leave and others on base before heading off to combat.

The Hunt for Red October (1990) [G&G]

Cold War	Navy	Full	Color	137 mins
Paramount	WV: 02-28-90		NYT: 03-02-90	

DIR: John McTiernan. SW: Larry Ferguson, Donald Stewart. PRO: Mace Neufeld, Jerry Sherlock. STARS: Sean Connery, Alec Baldwin, Scott Glenn, Sam Neil, James Earl Jones, Tim Curry, Fred Dalton Thompson.

Appearing at the end of the Cold War and based on Tom Clancy's blockbuster novel of the same title, the film opens with a disclaimer that leads the viewer to believe in the reality of the story. Hoping the film would become the Submarine Service's *Top Gun,* the Navy assisted in the development of the ship's "bridge" and provided a carrier and a submarine for exterior scenes.

The Hunters (1958)

Korea	Air Force	Full	Color	108 mins
Fox	WV: 08-06-58		NYT: 08-27-58	

DIR: Dick Powell. SW: Wendell Mayes. PRO: Dick Powell. STARS: Robert Mitchum, Robert Wagner, May Britt, Richard Egan, Lee Philips.

This trite love triangle uses excellent aerial combat footage to create the images of jet fighters over Korea. The filmmakers contrive to lose three planes in order to advance a story line featuring an odyssey by the three pilots through North Korea to safety.

I Aim at the Stars (1960) [G&G]

WWII, Cold War	Army	Full	B&W	107 mins
Columbia	WV: 09-07-60		NYT: 10-20-60	

DIR: J. Lee Thompson. SW: Jay Dratler. PRO: Charles Schneer. STARS: Curt Jürgens, Victoria Shaw, Herbert Lom, Gia Scala, James Daly.

With encouragement and full support from the Army, the film turned Nazi hero Wernher von Braun, builder of the V-2 rocket, into an American hero, builder of rockets to defend the United States against the Soviet Union. NASA refused to cooperate because it did not want to be associated with the man whose rockets had been used to hit London. Ironically, NASA later hired von Braun when the agency needed his irreplaceable skills to design and build the Saturn rocket, which would launch the astronauts to the moon.

I Live in Grosvenor Square (1945) a.k.a. *A Yank in London*

WWII	Army	Unkn	B&W	106 mins
Pathé	WV: 05-30-45		NYT: 04-20-46	

DIR: Herbert Wilcox. SW: William D. Bayles, Nicholas Phipps. PRO: Herbert Wilcox. STARS: Anna Neagle, Rex Harrison, Dean Jagger, Robert Morley, Elliott Arluck.

This British production portrays a love triangle in which American sergeant Jagger and English officer Harrison pursue Neagle, then England's biggest female star. GIs in London on leave provide background for the film, which may also serve as a thank you to the United States for saving the free world.

I Wanted Wings (1941) [G&G]

Preparedness	Air Force	Full	B&W	131 mins
Paramount	WV: 03-26-41		NYT: 03-27-41	

DIR: Mitchell Leisen. SW: Richard Maibaum, Beirne Lay Jr., Sig Herzig, Frank Wead. PRO: Arthur Hornblow Jr. STARS: Ray Milland, William Holden, Wayne Morris, Brian Donlevy, Veronica Lake.

From Lt. Lay's novel of the same name, the film salutes the Army Air Corps with a story that plays second fiddle to the flying sequences. Set at Randolph and Kelly airfields outside San Antonio, Texas, the West Point of the air, the movie makes full use of Air Corps planes and facilities to portray the adventures of three young men who want to fly. While melodrama and romance sometimes intrude, including Lake's absurd presence aboard a B-17 during a night training flight, the story does its best to help prepare the nation for an anticipated war by showing how the air service will defend the country from outside threats.

I Was a Male War Bride (1949)

Peace	Army	Ltd	B&W	105 mins
Fox	WV: 08-10-49		NYT: 08-27-49	

DIR: Howard Hawks. SW: Charles Lederer, Leonard Spigelgass, Hagar Wilde. PRO: Sol Siegel. STARS: Cary Grant, Ann Sheridan, Bill Neff, Marion Marshall.

A comedy with Grant, as a French army officer, posing as a war bride to accompany his American WAC wife back to the United States. The Army and the Production Code Office placed obstacles in the way of the couple being able to consummate their marriage.

I Was an American Spy (1951)

WWII	Army	Ltd	B&W	84 mins
Allied Artists	WV: 03-28-51		NYT: 07-04-51	

DIR: Lesley Selander. SW: Sam Roeca. PRO: David Diamond. STARS: Ann Dvorak, Gene Evans, Leon Lontoc.

Claire Phillips based her novel *Manila Espionage* on her own experiences. The cinematic heroine in this film version saw her GI husband killed on the Bataan Death March and became a spy in Manila during the war. The Army helped create the Death March sequence.

Iceland (1942)

WWII	Marines	Unkn	B&W	79 mins
Fox	WV: 08-12-42		NYT: 10-15-42	

DIR: Bruce Humberstone. SW: Robert Ellis, Helen Logan. PRO: William Le Baron. STARS: John Payne, Sonja Henie, Jack Oakie.

Song and dance comedy romance set in Iceland during the Marines' occupation before the U.S. entry into World War II.

Ice Station Zebra (1968) [G&G]

Cold War	Navy, Marines	Full	Color	148 mins
MGM	WV: 10-23-68		NYT: 12-21-68	

DIR: John Sturges. SW: Douglas Heyes, Harry Julian Fink. PRO: Martin Ransohoff. STARS: Rock Hudson, Tony Bill, Jim Brown, Patrick McGoohan, Ernest Borgnine, Lloyd Nolan.

Incomprehensible story about a race between a U.S. submarine and Soviet paratroopers to recover photographs taken by a Russian spy satellite, which accidentally directed the recovery capsule to earth near the North Pole, or something like that. Brown, as a Marine officer, is supposed to lead the American unit to the photos, but he is shot, intentionally or by accident. Who knows or cares? Nevertheless, the Navy's submarine service received some benefit from the portrayal of life aboard a nuclear undersea craft.

Imitation General (1958)

WWII	Army	Unkn	B&W 88 mins
MGM	WV: 06-25-58		NYT: 08-21-58

DIR: George Marshall. SW: William Bowers. PRO: William Hawks. STARS: Glenn Ford, Red Buttons, Taina Elg, Dean Jones.

Farcical comedy, but with combat drama, about a private who assumes his general's guise after the officer dies, but not before telling Ford, the enlisted man, to lead from the front. His courage provides the inspiration needed to regroup the soldiers, who stop the German advance.

In & Out (1997)

Vietnam	Army	NR	Color 90 mins
Paramount	WV: 09-15-97		NYT: 09-19-97

DIR: Frank Oz. SW: Paul Rudnick. PRO: Scott Rudin. STARS: Kevin Kline, Joan Cusack, Tom Selleck, Matt Dillon, Debbie Reynolds.

The Army appears in two brief scenes in a war film set within the feature movie portraying the "outing" of teacher Kline. Projected during the Oscar presentation for best actor, the first excerpt shows Dillon professing his love for his wounded buddy. In the second, he faces a court-martial and is discharged for being gay. The excerpts portray well the military's homophobia.

In Country (1989)

Vietnam	Army	NR	Color 120 mins
WB	WV: 09-13-89		NYT: 09-15-89

DIR: Norman Jewison. SW: Frank Pierson, Cynthia Cidre. PRO: Norman Jewison, Richard Roth. STARS: Bruce Willis, Emily Lloyd, Joan Allen, Kevin Anderson.

Based on Bobbie Ann Mason's novel, the film tries to capture the impact of Vietnam on those who fought in country and those who also suffered back home. The brief combat sequences filmed in a wildlife recreation area in Kentucky do not look like Vietnam, but the ending at the Vietnam Memorial is touching and authentic.

Inchon (1981) [G&G]

Korea	Navy, Marines	Full	Color 140 mins, 106 mins
One-Way	WV: 05-06-81		NYT: 09-17-82

DIR: Terence Young. SW: Robin Moore, Laird Koening, Paul Savage. PRO: Mitsuhari Ishii. STARS: Laurence Olivier, Ben Gazzara, Toshirô Mifune, Richard Roundtree, David Janssen, Jacqueline Bisset.

The Marines provided men and equipment, and the Navy provided ships, to re-create the 1950 landing at Inchon during the Korean War. The Pentagon did not realize until the production ended that Reverend Moon was financing the film as anticommunist propaganda with a religious message thrown in. *Inchon* remains one of the worst films ever made.

To be sure, Olivier's performance as MacArthur is far better than Gregory Peck's in *MacArthur*. Nevertheless, Olivier's characterization of MacArthur as weak-willed is absurd. Watching Olivier's MacArthur crawl into bed to ask his wife if he is still capable of leading men into battle simply boggles the mind. (See James Sikking's portrayal in the HBO film *In Pursuit of Honor* as an antidote for Olivier's MacArthur.) Would-be filmmaker Moon further reduced any credibility the movie might have had when he eliminated Janssen's character after the actor died. Of course, shortening the world premiere length considerably made the pain of watching *Inchon* somewhat less.

The Incredible Mr. Limpet (1964)

WWII	Navy	Full	Color	99 mins
WB	WV: 01-22-64		NYT: 03-26-64	

DIR: Arthur Lubin. SW: Jameson Brewer, John Rose. PRO: John Rose. STARS: Don Knotts, Carole Cook, Jack Weston, Andrew Duggan.

Based on Theodore Pratt's novel. Lubin created a half-cartoon, half-live comedy about a talking dolphin who helps the Navy rid the U.S. coast of Nazi submarines. Although seen as a fantasy at the time, the concept became a reality as the Navy began to train dolphins to seek out mines and human intruders. While an entertaining cinematic notion at that time, the service was to have little success with the dolphins during the second Gulf War.

Independence Day (1996) [G&G]

SciFi	All	Deny	Color	135 mins
Fox	WV: 07-01-96		NYT: 07-02-96	

DIR: Roland Emmerich. SW: Roland Emmerich, Dean Devlin. PRO: Dean Devlin. STARS: Will Smith, Bill Pullman, Jeff Goldblum, Judd Hirsch, Randy Quaid, Adam Baldwin, Brent Spiner.

The Air Force turned down a request for assistance, pointing out that the service had been saying for almost 50 years that flying saucers did not exist and so believed that it would be inappropriate to become involved in a production positing the arrival of saucers over the earth. The service also maintained that no aliens were being held at a U.S. military facility, as described in the script. On its part, the Marines objected to the script's characterization of the Marine pilot, whom Smith was to play. Although he would bravely attack the alien saucers, the Marines did not see him as a positive character because he had a stripper girlfriend.

Without service assistance, the filmmakers turned to computer-generated graphics to create their airplanes. Consequently, the film became a crucial benchmark in the Hollywood/military relationship because computer-generated graphics now replaced the need to seek Pentagon assistance. In the future, if one of the armed services wanted to appear on screen at all or to improve its images in films, it would have to relax some of its regulations to reach agreements on suitable scripts.

In Enemy Country (1968)

WWII	Army	Ltd	Color	108 mins
Universal	WV: 05-22-68		NYT: DNR	

DIR: Harry Keller. SW: Edward Anhalt. PRO: Harry Keller. STARS: Tony Franciosa, Guy Stockwell, Tom Bell, Paul Hubschmid.

A wartime espionage story in which an American flier works with the British and French to kidnap a new type of German torpedo, which had been wreaking havoc on Allied shipping.

In Enemy Hands (2004)

WWII	Navy	NR	Color	Unkn
Artisan Enter	WV:		NYT:	

DIR: Tony Giglio. SW: John Deaver, Tony Giglio. PRO: John Brister, Julius Nasso. STARS: William H. Macy, Til Schweiger, Scott Caan.

A cross between *U-571* and *The Hunt for Red October*, this is a completely implausible story about crew members from an American sub who become prisoners of the U-boat that sank their ship. The enemies must join together to avoid being destroyed. Among other problems, U.S. subs made only one cruise in the Atlantic, and none were sunk. A long delay in releasing the film led to its appearance on television abroad before it opened in the United States, going immediately to video.

In Harm's Way (1965) [G&G]

WWII	Navy, Marines	Full	Color	165 mins
Paramount	WV: 03-31-65		NYT: 04-07-65	

DIR: Otto Preminger. SW: Wendell Mayes. PRO: Otto Preminger. STARS: John Wayne, Kirk Douglas, Henry Fonda, Patricia Neal, Dana Andrews.

Based on James Bassett's novel, the film depicts fictionalized early naval combat in the South Pacific. The Navy assisted at Pearl Harbor with ships and men. The director created the cinematic battles using absurd-looking ship models, which spout naval gunfire that looks more like sparklers on the Fourth of July. Despite full cooperation, the film does contain some highly negative images of the Navy. Douglas's wife has a one-night stand with an Air Force officer the evening of December 6 and is conveniently killed by a Japanese fighter the next morning. Douglas is then derailed to a dead-end logistics assignment, but when Wayne becomes an admiral, he makes him his chief of staff.

Douglas later rapes Wayne's son's fiancé, who immediately commits suicide. Seeking redemption, Douglas undertakes a suicide reconnaissance mission that helps Wayne's armada win a major battle. Nevertheless, Wayne refuses to award Douglas a posthumous medal. *In Harm's Way* did not much better portray the Marines because it depicts para-Marines landing on an enemy-held island—even though the two battalions of Leatherneck paratroopers never undertook an airborne assault during World War II and instead were employed as traditional assault forces.

For Wayne's character, the film offers a mixed bag. He makes admiral (Wayne rarely achieved flag rank in films), finds love with Neal, and displays professionalism, courage, decisiveness, and caring—qualities inherent in all successful commanders. On the other hand, he also demonstrates a complete lack of common sense by flying into battle to observe the para-Marines landing, knowing the Japanese might have obtained plans if his plane were shot down. He loses a leg and his ship during one of the early battles, and his son dies in combat. Still, at the end, he returns to active duty and wins a generic battle, perhaps a fusion of the naval sea battles of Guadalcanal and Leyte Gulf.

In Love and War (1958)

WWII	Marines	Ltd	Color	107 mins
Fox	WV: 10-29-58		NYT: 11-01-58	

DIR: Philip Dunne. SW: Edward Anhalt. PRO: Jerry Wald. STARS: Robert Wagner, Jeffrey Hunter, Dana Wynter, Hope Lange.

Marines in love and combat going through their rites of passage as a result of their experiences.

In the Army Now (1994)

Gulf War	Army	Full	Color	91 mins
Disney	WV: 08-15-94		NYT: 08-12-94	

DIR: Daniel Petrie Jr. SW: Ken Kaufman, Stu Krieger, Daniel Petrie Jr., Fax Bahr, Adam Small. PRO: Michael Rotenberg. STARS: Pauly Shore, Andy Dick, Lori Petty, David Grier, Esai Morales, Lynn Whitfield.

Shore and Dick join the reserves to make some money and end up in the first Gulf War, where they save the day for their comrades. The Army gave full cooperation for this silly comedy.

In the Line of Fire (1993)

Peace	Air Force	Ltd	Color	128 mins
Columbia	WV: 07-19-93		NYT: 07-09 & 11-93	

DIR: Wolfgang Petersen. SW: Jeff Maguire. PRO: Jeff Apple. STARS: Clint Eastwood, John Malkovich, Rene Russo, Dylan McDermott.

Eastwood plays a secret service agent trying to prevent a demented assassin, Malkovich, from killing the president. The Air Force permitted the filming of service personnel during arrivals and departures of the president at military installations.

In the Meantime, Darling (1944)

WWII	Army	Full	B&W	72 mins
Fox	WV: 09-20-44		NYT: DNR	

DIR: Otto Preminger. SW: Arthur Kober, Michael Uris. PRO: Otto Preminger. STARS: Jeanne Crain, Frank Latimore, Eugene Pallette, Mary Nash, Stanley Prager, Gale Robbins.

This film cannot decide whether it tells the story of a bride's adjustment to military life, of her efforts to keep her officer husband from being shipped overseas, of misunderstandings about her possible pregnancy, or of her recognition that she has home front obligations. In the end, she becomes a proper Army wife. The service allowed Fox to film exterior scenes at Camp Callan near San Diego and at Camp Cooke near Lompoc.

In the Navy **(1941)**

Peace	Navy	Full	B&W 85 mins
Universal	WV: 06-04-41		NYT: 06-12-41

DIR: Arthur Lubin. SW: Arthur Horman, John Grant. PRO: Alex Gottlieb. STARS: Bud Abbott, Lou Costello, Dick Powell, the Andrew Sisters.

A typical Abbott and Costello comedy, this time set aboard a battleship. The Navy supplied background shots for the boys' cavorting, including training in San Diego and aboard the battleship *Alabama* on its way to Pearl Harbor.

Into the Sun **(1992)**

Middle East	Air Force	NR	Color 100 mins
Trimark	WV: 01-27-92		NYT: DNR

DIR: Fritz Kiersch. SW: John Brancato, Michael Ferris. PRO: Kevin M. Kallberg, Oliver G. Hess. STARS: Anthony Michael Hall, Michael Paré, Deborah Maria Moore, Terry Kiser.

In this comedy, Air Force officer Paré receives an assignment to show movie star Hall how to portray a jet pilot in his next movie. When skirmishes begin with an unidentified Arab state, Paré disobeys orders and takes the actor along for the ride. The film is ridiculous but fun.

Invaders from Mars **(1953)**

SciFi	Marines	Ltd	B&W 73 mins
Fox	WV: 04-08-53		NYT: 05-30-53

DIR: William Cameron Menzies. SW: Richard Blake. PRO: Edward Alperson. STARS: Helena Carter, Arthur Franz, Jimmy Hunt.

The Marines perform the job expected of them if earth were to be invaded—kill, kill, kill.

Invaders from Mars **(1986)**

SciFi	Marines	Full	Color 93 mins
Cannon	WV: 05-21-86		NYT: 06-06-86

DIR: Tobe Hooper. SW: Dan O'Bannon, Don Jakoby. PRO: Menahem Golan, Yoram Globus. STARS: Karen Black, Hunter Carson, Timothy Bottoms, James Karen, Louise Fletcher.

A remake of the 1953 classic. During negotiations for assistance, Fred Peck, director of the services' Los Angeles Public Affairs office, told Hooper, "Marines have no qualms about killing Martians." Hooper liked the comment so much he put it into the film, and the Marines perform the job expected of them if earth were to be invaded—kill, kill, kill, redux, redux, redux.

Invasion USA (1952)

Cold War	Army, Air Force, Navy	Ltd	B&W	73 mins
Columbia	WV: 12-10-52		NYT: 04-30-53	

DIR: Alfred Green. SW: Robert Smith. PRO: Albert Zugsmith, Robert Smith. STARS: Gerald Mohr, Peggie Castle, Dan O'Herlihy, Robert Bice.

A cautionary tale warning of the danger of weakness in the face of a vicious enemy, unidentified but obvious, who invades and subjugates the United States using atomic bombs. The film makes significant use of old WWII stock combat footage, obtained from the services, but also contains a few newly shot scenes of the military in action. Green, probably unaware that he was being accurate, used shots of American B-29s to represent the enemy's heavy bombers. In fact, the Soviets had designed their first generation of atom bomb-carrying planes based on an interned B-29. In the end, the foreign conquest proves to be only a dream.

Invasion USA (1985)

Peace	Army	Full	Color	107 mins
Cannon	WV: 09-25-85		NYT: 09-27 & 29-85	

DIR: Joseph Zito. SW: James Bruner, Chuck Norris. PRO: Menahem Golan, Yoram Globus. STARS: Chuck Norris, Richard Lynch, Melissa Prophet, Alexander Zale.

A purported warning to Americans against becoming soft, the film portrays pseudo-Russian agents leading ruthless Cuban and Arab mercenaries, who land in south Florida, turn neighbor against neighbor, and head north. Norris leads the counterattack and defeats the invaders in downtown Atlanta. In fact, the film served primarily as a vehicle in which Norris displayed his particular form of violence. Nevertheless, the National Guard supplied men and equipment since the Guard would act as the movie portrayed and the good guys did win—although it was a close call.

The Invisible Menace (1938)

Peace	Army	Unkn	B&W	54 mins
WB	WV: 01-26-38		NYT: 02-14-38	

DIR: John Farrow. SW: Crane Wilbur. PRO: Warner Bros. STARS: Boris Karloff, Marie Wilson, Eddie Craven, Eddie Acuff, Henry Kolker.

A "C" murder mystery, from a Ralph Spencer Zink play, set on an Army post. Jack Warner and Hal Wallis served as executive producers.

Iron Eagle (1986)

Peace	Air Force	Deny	Color	116 mins
Tri-Star	WV: 01-22-86		NYT: 01-18-86	

DIR: Sidney Furie. SW: Kevin Elders, Sidney Furie. PRO: Ron Samuels, Joe Wizan. STARS: Louis Gossett Jr., Jason Gedrick, David Suchet, Tim Thomerson.

A teenage version of the Rambo films. Gedrick, with the help of retired Air Force officer Gossett, carries out the rescue of his flier father, who was shot down when he accidentally violated an un-named Arab country's air space. The U.S. military does virtually nothing to save the pilot from ex-ecution. Given the negative images of the military and the country, the Pentagon turned down the request for assistance, and the filmmakers borrowed the Israeli Air Force.

Iron Eagle 2 **(1988)**

Peace	Air Force	Deny	Color	105 mins
Tri-Star	WV: 11-16-88		NYT: 11-12-88	

DIR: Sidney Furie. SW: Kevin Elders, Sidney Furie. PRO: Jacob Kotzky, Sharon Harel, John Ke-meny. STARS: Louis Gossett Jr., Mark Humphrey, Stuart Margolin.

In this installment, the cinematic Pentagon orders Gossett to put together a joint Soviet–U.S. strike force to destroy an unnamed Middle Eastern country's nuclear missile site, to some degree predict-ing the end of the Cold War and the later conflicts in the Gulf region. The Pentagon refused to provide any assistance since the script contained negative images of the American military estab-lishment and portrayed a preemptive strike, which then violated long-standing U.S. policy. As a re-sult, Furie again shot the entire film in Israel.

The Iron Major **(1943)**

WWI	Army	Unkn	B&W	90 mins
RKO	WV: 10-20-43		NYT: 11-01-43	

DIR: Ray Enright. SW: Aben Kandel, Warren Duff. PRO: Robert Fellows. STARS: Pat O'Brien, Ruth Warrick, Robert Ryan.

The story of Frank Cavanaugh, a WWI hero who became a famous football coach (Dartmouth, Fordham, and Boston College). The film includes a scene of Cavanaugh as a doughboy in France.

Iron Triangle **(1989)**

Vietnam	Army	NR	Color	91 mins
Scotti Brothers	WV: 02-08-89		NYT: 02-03-89	

DIR: Eric Weston. SW: Eric Weston, John Bushelman, Larry Hilbrand. PRO: Tony Scotti, Angela Schapiro. STARS: Beau Bridges, Haing S. Ngor, Johnny Hallyday, Liem Whatley.

A then-unique look at the Vietnam War equally from the perspective of an American GI and a North Vietnamese soldier. The film presents, 25 years too late, the argument that the Vietnamese people simply wanted all foreigners out of their country.

Island in the Sky **(1953)**

WWII	Air Force	Ltd	B&W	108 mins
WB	WV: 08-12-53		NYT: 10-10-53	

DIR: William Wellman. SW: Ernest K. Gann. PRO: John Wayne, Robert Fellows. STARS: John Wayne, Lloyd Nolan, Walter Abel, James Arness.

The Air Force provided help in creating the rescue sequences for the story, based on Ernest Ganns's novel about the rescue of downed fliers.

Isle of Destiny (1940)

Preparedness	Marines	Unkn	Color 83 mins
RKO	WV: 04-10-40		NYT: 04-08-40

DIR: Elmer Clifton. SW: Arthur Hoerl, M. Coates Webster, Robert Lively, Allan Vaughn Elston. PRO: Franklyn Warner. STARS: William Gargan, Wallace Ford, June Lang, Gilbert Roland, Etienne Girardot.

Question: What do you get when you mix the Marines with a gun-running gang in the South Seas and a beautiful, rich, young aviatrix? Answer: This "B" melodrama.

Is Paris Burning? (1966)

WWII	Army	Full	B&W 173 mins
Paramount	WV: 10-26-66		NYT: 11-11-66

DIR: René Clément. SW: Gore Vidal, Francis Coppola. PRO: Paul Graetz. STARS: Jean-Paul Belmondo, Charles Boyer, Orson Welles, Gert Fröbe, Kirk Douglas, Glenn Ford, Alain Delon, Robert Stack.

A cast of thousands helped create confusing visual images that fail to explain why Paris did not burn despite Hitler's orders. Writers Vidal and Coppola did not transfer Larry Collins and Dominque LaPierre's journalistic history to the screen with any coherence. Under command of Omar Bradley and George Patton, the U.S. Army liberated Paris in 1944; the service helped re-create its accomplishment with a limited number of men and some equipment.

It Came from Beneath the Sea (1955)

SciFi	Navy	Full	B&W 79 mins
Columbia	WV: 06-22-55		NYT: DNR

DIR: Robert Gordon. SW: George Yates, Hal Smith. PRO: Charles Schneer. STARS: Kenneth Tobey, Donald Curtis, Ian Keith, Dean Maddox Jr.

The Navy provided a nuclear sub, other ships, and men to tell the story of a mutated giant squid, the result of testing hydrogen bombs, that attacks San Francisco. The service was featured prominently and positively in efforts to stop the squid.

It Started with a Kiss (1959)

Peace	Air Force	Ltd	Color 104 mins
MGM	WV: 08-19-59		NYT: 08-20-59

DIR: George Marshall. SW: Charles Lederer. PRO: Aaron Rosenberg. STARS: Glenn Ford, Debbie Reynolds, Eva Gabor, Fred Clark.

A romantic comedy in which Air Force sergeant Ford wins the girl and travels to his next assignment in Spain. The service provided backgrounds.

The Jackal (1997)

Peace	Marines	Full	Color	124 mins
Universal	WV: 11-10-97		NYT: 11-14-97	

DIR: Michael Caton-Jones. SW: Chuck Pfarrer, Kenneth Ross. PRO: James Jacks, Sean Daniel, Kevin Jarre, Michael Caton-Jones. STARS: Bruce Willis, Richard Gere, Sidney Poitier, Diane Venora, Mathilda May.

An inferior remake of the 1973 Fred Zinnemann thriller in which a professional assassin stalks President Charles DeGaulle, this time set in the United States, with the intended victim unknown to the audience until the moment of truth. The Marines appear performing an assault from the air in an effort to stop the Jackal.

Jacknife (1989)

Vietnam	Air Force	Full	Color	102 mins
Cineplex	WV: 03-01-89		NYT: 03-10-89	

DIR: David Jones. SW: Stephen Metcalfe. PRO: Robert Schaffel, Carol Baum. STARS: Robert De Niro, Ed Harris, Kathy Baker, Charles Dutton, Loudon Wainwright, III.

Based on Metcalfe's play *Strange Snow*, the film contained the requisite flashbacks to Vietnam while exploring the relationship between two surviving Vietnam War buddies and the evolving love interest of one with the other's sister.

Jacob's Ladder (1990)

Vietnam	Army	NR	Color	115 mins
TriStar	WV: 11-05-90		NYT: 11-02 & 11-90	

DIR: Adrian Lyne. SW: Bruce Joel Rubin. PRO: Alan Marshall. STARS: Tim Robbins, Elizabeth Peña, Danny Aiello, Matt Craven.

Intended to be a psychological thriller, the story focuses on Robbins as a Vietnam veteran suffering from posttraumatic shock. The movie opens on the battlefield and has flashbacks to combat as Robbins begins to experience strange visions. Ultimately, he concludes that he and his comrades were victims of secret chemical warfare experiments. Given such negative images of the military, the filmmakers did not bother to even submit a script to the Pentagon.

Jet Attack (1958)

Korea	Air Force	Full	B&W	68 mins
Amer-Intl	WV: 03-26-58		NYT: DNR	

DIR: Edward L. Cahn. SW: Orville H. Hampton. PRO: Israel Berman, Alex Gordon. STARS: John Agar, Audrey Totter, Gregory Walcott, James Dobson.

The director used stock war footage to give authenticity to the story of a fighter pilot, shot down behind enemy lines, who is able to rescue a famous scientist with the help of a Russian nurse.

Jet Pilot (1957)

Korea	Air Force	Full	Color	112 mins
Universal	WV: 09-25-57		NYT: 10-05-57	

DIR: Josef von Sternberg. SW: Jules Furthman. PRO: Jules Furthman. STARS: John Wayne, Janet Leigh, Jay C. Flippen, Paul Fix.

Howard Hughes's fingerprints can be found on this Cold War tussle between the United States and the Soviet Union. The absurd love story between Wayne, an American flier, and Leigh, a Russian jet ace, is only one of the film's low lights. Chuck Yeager did some of the stunt flying, which added only a modicum of visual appeal. Although the film was completed in 1950, Hughes delayed the release for seven years, probably because neither he nor the studio could figure out what to do with this lemon.

Joe Butterfly (1957)

WWII	Army	Full	Color	90 mins
Universal	WV: 04-24-57		NYT: 05-30-57	

DIR: Jesse Hibbs. SW: Sy Gomberg, Marion Hargrove, Jack Sher. PRO: Aaron Rosenberg. STARS: Audie Murphy, George Nader, Keenan Wynn, Burgess Meredith.

The story opens with the newsreel footage of the Japanese formal surrender on the USS *Missouri*. It then turns its attention to well-meaning GIs in the Army of Occupation who use their cunning to outwit the service's system of red tape in order to accomplish good deeds. The film made good use of Japanese locations.

The Joe Louis Story (1953)

WWII	Army	NR	B&W	88 mins
UA	WV: 12-30-53		NYT: 11-04-53	

DIR: Robert Gordon. SW: Robert Sylvester. PRO: Stirling Silliphant. STARS: Coley Wallace, Paul Stewart, Hilda Simms, James Edwards.

This biography of the Brown Bomber's pugilistic career included scenes of Louis as a sergeant in the Army, giving exhibitions on military bases.

Johanna Enlists (1918)

WWI	Army	Full	B&W	5 reels
FPL	WV: 09-13-18		NYT: 09-16-18	

DIR: William D. Taylor. SW: Frances Marion. PRO: Mary Pickford. STARS: Mary Pickford, Anne Schaefer, Monte Blue.

In the movie, based on Rupert Hughes's short story "The Mobilization of Johanna" in *Hearst's Magazine*, Pickford plays a young girl, stifled on her father's backwoods Pennsylvania farm. One day an Army regiment arrives to train on the land before deploying to France, which results in the usual complications of the heart and the comedy. The Army provided the soldiers and equipment of the 143rd Artillery Regiment, and Pickford became its honorary captain and godmother when it went overseas.

John Paul Jones (1959)

Revolutionary	Navy	Full	Color	126 mins
WB	WV: 06-17-59		NYT: 06-17-59	

DIR: John Farrow. SW: John Farrow, Jesse Lasky Jr. PRO: Samuel Bronston. STARS: Robert Stack, Marisa Pavan, Charles Coburn, Bette Davis.

The Navy loaned an aircraft carrier for the opening and closing scenes of this film, with other contemporary ships in the background for the film's salute to the father of the U.S. Navy. While not a completely accurate rendering of Jones's life, the story conveys the message that the United States must continue to have a strong Navy to protect it from all outside threats.

Johnny Got His Gun (1971)

WWI	Army	NR	Color	111 mins
World Enter	WV: 05-19-71		NYT: 08-05-71	

DIR: Dalton Trumbo. SW: Dalton Trumbo. PRO: Bruce Campbell. STARS: Timothy Bottoms, Jason Robards, Marsha Hunt, Diane Varsi.

Based on his novel of the same name, Trumbo brought his antiwar story to the screen, in his sole directing stint. A soldier who has lost his arms and legs, as well as his ability to see, hear, and speak, lies in a military hospital at the mercy of a zealous Army doctor who sees in Johnny the opportunity to experiment on a person who has apparently lost all humanity. Ultimately, however, the young man breaks through his wall of silence with the help of a nurse who recognizes the "basket case" does have life and feelings. Unlike most other filmmakers, who tried to use violence to create their antiwar messages, Trumbo made his antiwar statement by showing the man as a victim of war, not as a hero.

Join the Marines (1937)

Peace	Marines	Full	B&W	70 mins
Republic	WV: 02-17-37		NYT: DNR	

DIR: Ralph Staub. SW: Joseph Krumgold, Olive Cooper. PRO: Nat Levine. STARS: Paul Kelly, June Travis, Purnell Pratt, Reginald Denny.

Kelly, a New York policeman innocently involved in an Olympic scandal, joins the Marines to start life anew after he is fired from the police force. As a Marine, he rapidly moves up the ladder, winning a commission, and after helping put down a native revolt in some unidentified country, marries the girl who initially had little use for the Corps.

Jud (1971)

Vietnam	Marines	NR	Color	80 mins
Prism Pictures	WV: 09-01-71		NYT: DNR	

DIR: Gunther Collins. SW: Gunther Collins. PRO: Igo Kantor. STARS: Joseph Kaufmann, Robert Deman, Alix Wyeth, Norman Burton.

A veteran returns from Vietnam to find that Los Angeles is worse than combat. Realistic flashbacks to combat do not mesh with home-front images.

Judgment at Nuremberg (1961)

Peace	Army	Full	B&W	190 mins
UA	WV: 10-18-61		NYT: 12-20-61	

DIR: Stanley Kramer. SW: Abby Mann. PRO: Stanley Kramer. STARS: Spencer Tracy, Maximilian Schell, Richard Widmark, Burt Lancaster, Judy Garland, Montgomery Clift, William Shatner.

The Army provided men and equipment on location in West Germany to help establish the ambience of early postwar Germany. The film portrays the trial of Nazi judges who had legitimized Hitler's decrees. Widmark, as an Army prosecutor, and Schell, as the defense attorney, oppose each other, with Tracy serving as the presiding judge. The closing dialog between Lancaster, a convicted judge, and Tracy says it all. When the German maintains he did not know Hitler's rule would lead to the gas chambers, Tracy responds, "It came to that the first time you sentenced to death a man you knew to be innocent."

Judgment in Berlin (1988)

Cold War	Air Force	Ltd	Color	92 mins
New Line Cinema	WV: 05-04-88		NYT: 05-06-88	

DIR: Leo Penn. SW: Joshua Sinclair, Leo Penn. PRO: Joshua Sinclair, Ingrid Windisch. STARS: Martin Sheen, Sam Wanamaker, Max Gail, Jürgen Heinrich, Heinz Honig, Harris Yulin, Sean Penn.

This small but good film concerns itself with the hijacking of a jet and a defection from behind the iron curtain to West Germany. The courtroom drama that follows focuses on whether the hijacking can be justified because the hijackers are fleeing from communism. Penn was allowed to shoot the landing sequence at Tempelhof Air Force base in West Berlin. The film appeared on TV as *Escape to Freedom*.

Jumping Jacks (1952)

Peace	Army	Full	B&W	96 mins
Paramount	WV: 06-04-52		NYT: 07-24-52	

DIR: Norman Taurog. SW: Robert Lees, Fred Rinaldo, Herbert Baker. PRO: Hal Wallis. STARS: Dean Martin, Jerry Lewis, Mona Freeman.

This Martin and Lewis comedy takes place in a paratrooper training camp. Because it was a a comedy, the Army was not as concerned with technical accuracy as if it had been a serious drama. As a result, the Army allowed Lewis to land on Martin's parachute canopy, which does not collapse, as it would have in actuality.

Jungle Patrol (1948)

WWII	Air Force	Ltd	B&W	71 mins
Fox	WV: 09-22-48		NYT: DNR	

DIR: Joseph Newman. SW: Francis Swann. PRO: Frank Seltzer. STARS: Kristine Miller, Arthur Franz, Ross Ford, Tom Noonan, Richard Jaeckel.

Based on a William Bowers play, the action takes place during the Pacific campaign on New Guinea. Miller plays a visiting USO entertainer at a temporary airstrip. Aerial combat skirmishes are heard, not seen.

Jurassic Park III (2001)

SciFi	Navy, Marines	Full	Color	91 mins
Universal	WV: 07-23 & 29-2001		NYT: 07-18-2001	

DIR: Joe Johnston. SW: Peter Buchman, Alexander Payne, Jim Taylor. PRO: Kathleen Kennedy, Larry Franco. STARS: Sam Neill, William H. Macy, Téa Leoni.

Navy helicopters, Marine Corps amphibious assault vehicles, and military extras arrive in the nick of time to rescue scientists from prehistoric creatures. They accomplish their mission without firing a single shot, but the service did get its assault techniques on the screen.

K-19: The Widowmaker (2002)

Cold War	Navy	Deny	Color	140 mins
Paramount	WV: 07-21-2002		NYT: 05-12, 07-19-2002	

DIR: Kathryn Bigelow. SW: Christopher Kyle. PRO: Kathryn Bigelow, Sigurjon Sighvatsson, Chris Whitaker, Edward Feldman. STARS: Harrison Ford, Sam Spruell, Peter Stebbings, Liam Neeson.

The Navy turned down a request for assistance because the film recounted the initial, ill-fated cruise of the K-19, the Soviet Union's first nuclear submarine. Consequently, for the sequence in which a U.S. destroyer and helicopter hover around the stricken submarine, the producers turned to the Canadian Navy, which provided the required hardware.

Keep 'Em Flying (1941)

Preparedness	Air Force	Full	B&W	86 mins
Universal	WV: 11-26-41		NYT: 11-27-41	

DIR: Arthur Lubin. SW: True Boardman, Nat Perrin, John Grant. PRO: Glenn Tryon. STARS: Bud Abbott, Lou Costello, Martha Raye, Carol Bruce, William Gargan, Dick Foran.

An Air Corps comedy melds Abbott and Costello's burlesque routines with flying sequences, courtesy of the service.

Keep 'Em Rolling (1934)

WWI	Army	Full	B&W
RKO	WV: 06-26-34		NYT: DNR

DIR: George Archainbaud. SW: Albert Shelby LeVino. PRO: RKO. STARS: Walter Huston, Frances Dee, Minna Gombell.

A horse named Rodney saves Huston's life in France, and the soldier comes to love him. When they are separated, Huston goes AWOL in anger. However, when the U.S. president retires Rodney, he makes Huston the horse's caretaker. The Army allowed Archainbaud to shoot exteriors at Fort Myer, Virginia, with assistance from the 16th Field Artillery.

Keep Your Powder Dry (1945)

WWII	Army	Full	B&W 93 mins
MGM	WV: 02-21-45		NYT: 03-12-45

DIR: Edward Buzzell. SW: George Bruce, Mary C. McCall Jr. PRO: George Haight. STARS: Lana Turner, Laraine Day, Susan Peters, Agnes Moorehead, Bill Johnson.

The story of three women from very different social backgrounds who join the Women's Army Corps. The film includes scenes of basic and officer candidate training.

Kelly's Heroes (1970)

WWII	Army	Deny	Color 148 mins
MGM	WV: 06-17-70		NYT: 06-24-70

DIR: Brian G. Hutton. SW: Troy Kennedy-Martin. PRO: Gabriel Katzka, Sidney Beckerman. STARS: Clint Eastwood, Telly Savalas, Don Rickles, Carroll O'Connor, Donald Sutherland.

Shot in Yugoslavia, this comedy revolves around the efforts of some American soldiers, led by Eastwood, who plan to steal $16 million in gold bullion from a German bank deep inside enemy territory during a three-day R&R. In the process, they open up a new front through which the Army attacks. Still, the story offered no benefit for the service.

Kill Zone (1993)

Vietnam	Army	DNR	Color 81 mins
New Horizon	WV: DNR		NYT: DNR

DIR: Cirio Santiago. SW: Frederick Bailey. PRO: Roger Corman, Steven Rabiner, Cirio Santiago. STARS: David Carradine, Archie Adamos, Ronald Asinas, Tony Dorsett.

A typical Santiago Vietnam shoot 'em up that portrays Carradine's pathological efforts to kill as many Vietcong as graphically as possible.

The Killing Fields (1984) [G&G]

Vietnam	Marines	Full	Color 141 mins
Enigma	WV: 10-31-84		NYT: 11-02-84

DIR: Roland Joffé. SW: Bruce Robinson. PRO: David Puttnam. STARS: Sam Waterston, Haing S. Ngor, John Malkovich.

Based on Sydney Schanberg's *New York Times* article "The Death and Life of Dith Pran." The Marines provided men and equipment to re-create the American evacuation of the U.S. Embassy in Cambodia as the Khmer Rouge advanced on the capital.

King Kong (1933) [G&G]

Peace	Navy, Marines	Deny	B&W 96 mins
RKO	WV: 03-07-33		NYT: 02-03-33

DIR: Merian C. Cooper, Ernest B. Schoedsack. SW: James Creelman, Ruth Rose. PRO: Merian C. Cooper, Ernest B. Schoedsack. STARS: King Kong, Fay Wray, Robert Armstrong, Bruce Cabot, Frank Reicher.

The Navy turned down the request for the use of its fighters, citing regulations concerning non-competition with private enterprises, pointing out that the planes were available from commercial sources. However, Cooper did not tell the commander of the naval station on Long Island that the service had denied his request for help, and the officer permitted four of his planes to attack Kong as he clung to the Empire State Building. A Marine, flying a Navy plane, was one of the four pilots who shot King Kong off his perch. The Navy probably did not suffer a black eye from its actions since the capturer of Kong observed, "No, beauty killed the beast."

King Kong (1976)

Peace	Air Force	Full	Color 134 mins
Paramount	WV: 12-15-76		NYT: 12-18-76

DIR: John Guillermin. SW: Lorenzo Semple Jr., James Creelman, Ruth Rose. PRO: Dino De Laurentis. STARS: Jeff Bridges, Charles Grodin, Jessica Lange, John Randolph, Rene Auberjonois.

This time around the Air Force provided jet planes to kill Kong.

Kings Go Forth (1958)

WWII	Army	Full	B&W 109 mins
UA	WV: 06-11-58		NYT: 07-04-58

DIR: Delmer Daves. SW: Merle Miller. PRO: Frank Ross. STARS: Frank Sinatra, Tony Curtis, Natalie Wood.

Based on Joe David Brown's *Kings Go Forth*, the story is set in southern France during the Seventh Army's mop-up of German units. Sinatra and Curtis pursue Wood until they discover she is half black. Curtis then turns his back on her and dies on a mission with Sinatra, who loses an arm but returns to the girl.

Kiss Them for Me (1957)

WWII	Navy	NR	Color	102 mins
Fox	WV: 11-06-57		NYT: 11-09-57	

DIR: Stanley Donen. SW: Julius Epstein. PRO: Jerry Wald. STARS: Cary Grant, Jayne Mansfield, Suzy Parker, Larry Blyden.

Adapted from Luther Davis's Broadway play, based on the Frederic Wakeman novel *Shore Leave*, the film follows three Navy aces on their three-day leave in San Francisco, after their Pacific aerial heroics.

Kissin' Cousins (1964)

Cold War	Air Force	NR	Color	96 mins
MGM	WV: 03-04-64		NYT: 04-02-64	

DIR: Gene Nelson. SW: Gerald Drayson Adams, Gene Nelson. PRO: Sam Katzman. STARS: Elvis Presley, Arthur O'Connell, Glenda Farrell, Pamela Austin, Jack Albertson.

Elvis plays an Air Force officer who is sent into a rural area to convince his kith and kin (one of whom is played by a blonde-wigged Elvis) to allow the building of an Intercontinental Ballistic Missile (ICBM) installation.

Korea Patrol (1951)

Korea	Army	NR	B&W	59 mins
Eagle Lion Classics	WV: 01-03-51		NYT: DNR	

DIR: Max Nosseck. SW: Kenneth G. Brown, Walter Shenson. PRO: Walter Shenson. STARS: Richard Emory, Benson Fong, Al Eben, Danny Davenport.

Filmed entirely in California, with some UN meeting clips and actual war footage spliced in, the movie portrayed a single mission of a six-man unit and its Korean scout.

Ladies Courageous (1944)

WWII	Air Force	Full	B&W	95 mins
Universal	WV: 03-22-44		NYT: 03-16-44	

DIR: John Rawlins. SW: Norman Reilly Raine, Doris Gilbert. PRO: Walter Wanger. STARS: Loretta Young, Geraldine Fitzgerald, Diana Barrymore, Anne Gwynne.

The story featured the WAFS (Women's Auxiliary Ferrying Squadron), and the exteriors were filmed at a ferrying airfield. The movie portrayed the squadron leader's efforts to get the unit seriously recognized by Army Air Corps brass.

Lafayette, We Come (1918)

WWI	Army	NR	B&W 6 reels
Affiliated	WV: 10-25-18		NYT: 11-04-18

DIR: Léonce Perret. SW: Léonce Perret. PRO: Léonce Perret. STARS: E. K. Lincoln, Dolores Cassinelli, Emmett C. King, Ernest Maupain.

An American studying music in France returns home and enlists. Wounded in the trenches, he writes to his parents while recovering in the hospital. To portray the battlefield action, the film-makers used combat footage and newsreels. The movie's release barely beat the armistice.

Larger Than Life (1996)

Peace	Air Force	Ltd	Color 93 mins
MGM	WV: 10-28-96		NYT: 11-01-96

DIR: Howard Franklin. SW: Roy Blount Jr. PRO: Richard B. Lewis, John Watson, Pen Densham. STARS: Bill Murray, Janeane Garofalo, Matthew McConaughey, Keith David.

A disappointing story portraying Murray's efforts to transport to the West Coast, and from there to Sri Lanka, an elephant he received as his clown father's bequest. Along the way, man bonds with beast. The comedic effort more often than not fails. However, the Air Force provided a C-5 aircraft on the ground at a base in Southern California as the elephant prepares for a flight to its new home in an elephant sanctuary.

Last Action Hero (1993)

Peace	Army	Cour	B&W 130 mins
Columbia	WV: 06-28-93		NYT: 06-18-93

DIR: John McTiernan. SW: Shane Black, David Arnott, Zak Penn, Adam Leff. PRO: Stephen Roth, John McTiernan. STARS: Arnold Schwarzenegger, F. Murray Abraham, Art Carney, Robert Prosky.

Although the film had no military theme, the producer requested permission to place a prop promotional movie sign, ultimately a balloon, atop the military recruiting station in Times Square. The DoD approved the request because the scene provided a minor plug for the recruitment station.

The Last Blitzkrieg (1958)

WWII	Army	NR	B&W 85 mins
Columbia	WV: 12-17-58		NYT: 01-31-59

DIR: Arthur Dreifuss. SW: Lou Morheim. PRO: Sam Katzman. STARS: Van Johnson, Kerwin Mathews, Dick York, Larry Storch, Lise Bourdin.

Inspired by actual events, the film portrays the German Army's attempt during the Battle of the Bulge to create chaos in the American ranks by infiltrating behind U.S. lines American-educated German soldiers who speak excellent English. There, the Germans, dressed as GIs, are supposed to disrupt transportation and communications. Johnson plays the leader of the German elite force, most of whom are caught and, being in the wrong uniforms, are executed as spies. Filmed in Holland, the picture used stock footage to re-create the combat sequences. See also **Battle of the Bulge,** which contains a sequence showing how the Germans switched signposts and shot American soldiers.

The Last Castle (2001)

Peace	Army	NR	Color 131 mins
Dreamworks	WV: 10-19-2001		NYT: 10-16-2001

DIR: Rod Lurie. SW: David Scarpa. PRO: Robert Lawrence. STARS: Robert Redford, James Gandolfini, Mark Ruffalo, Steve Burton.

Redford portrays a three-star general whom the Army court-martialed for disobeying an executive order, an act that resulted in the death of some of his men. He pleads guilty and is imprisoned in the maximum-security castle. There he organizes the inmates against the brutal prison commander, Gandolfini, with predictable results. The film contains negative images of military justice and requires the audience to ignore the reality that most of the prisoners may be guilty as charged.

The Last Detail (1973) [G&G]

Peace	Navy, Marines	Deny	Color 103 mins
Columbia	WV: 12-05-73		NYT: 02-11 & 24-74

DIR: Hal Ashby. SW: Robert Towne. PRO: Gerald Ayres. STARS: Jack Nicholson, Otis Young, Randy Quaid, Michael Moriarty.

Based on Daryl Ponicsan's novel, the story portrayed the transport of Quaid, a Navy enlisted man, sentenced to serve eight years for attempting to steal $40 from a church charity box, from the naval base in Norfolk, Virginia, to the naval brig in Portsmouth, New Hampshire. Along the way, MPs Nicholson and Young introduce their naive prisoner to the ways of the world and manhood. Given their frequent use of vulgarities and circumvention of "rules" and "procedures," the Navy rejected all efforts from the filmmakers to obtain even limited assistance. However, Ashby shot the actual entrance to the Norfolk naval base, which enabled him to create a sense of authenticity for the rest of the picture.

The Last Escape (1970)

WWII	Army	Unkn	Color 90 mins
UA	WV: 07-01-70		NYT: 07-02-70

DIR: Walter Grauman. SW: Herman Hoffman. PRO: Irving Temaner. STARS: Stuart Whitman, John Collin, Pinkas Braun, Martin Jarvis.

At the war's end in Europe, an American unit rescues British military personnel, German rocket scientists, and other refugees as German SS troops and Soviet tanks pursue.

The Last Hunter (1980)

Vietnam	Army	NR	Color 97 mins
Vestron Video	WV: DNR		NYT: DNR

DIR: Anthony M. Dawson (Antonio Margheriti). SW: Dardano Sacchetti. PRO: Gianfranco Couy-oumdjian. STARS: David Warbeck, Tony King, Tisa Farrow, Bobby Rhodes.

This spaghetti (i.e., Italian) war movie was shot in the Philippines with American actors. In it, a squad of soldiers set out to rescue a buddy trapped behind enemy lines. The film uses combat only as a vehicle to put on the screen graphic violence rivaling that in *Saving Private Ryan* and *Black Hawk Down*.

Last Stand at Lang Mei (1990) a.k.a. *Eye of the Eagle III*

Vietnam	Army	NR	Color 90 mins
Concorde	WV: DNR		NYT: DNR

DIR: Cirio H. Santiago. SW: Carl Franklin, Dan Gagliasso, M. A. Solomon. PRO: Roger Corman, Christopher R. Santiago. STARS: Frederick Bailey, Marilyn Bautista, Ramon D'Salva, Carl Franklin.

One in a long line of Santiago's made-in-the-Philippines films that in the United States went straight to video. This one concerns an Army unit deep behind enemy lines on an American fire base, surrounded by the attacking enemy and written off as missing in action by the Army.

The Last Time I Saw Archie (1961)

Peace	Army	Cour	B&W 103 mins
UA	WV: 05-31-61		NYT: 05-29-61

DIR: Jack Webb. SW: William Bowers. PRO: Jack Webb. STARS: Jack Webb, Robert Mitchum, Martha Hyer, Louis Nye, Don Knotts.

This Army comedy portrays a private whose mannerisms in a WWII Civilian Pilot Training outfit convince the others that he is a general investigating a spy.

Latino (1985)

Nicaragua	Army	NR	Color 108 mins
Lucasfilm	WV: 05-22-85		NYT: 02-28-86

DIR: Haskell Wexler. SW: Haskell Wexler. PRO: Benjamin Berg. STARS: Robert Beltran, Annette Cardona, Tony Plana.

The film tells the story of Green Beret veterans from Vietnam who are now advising Contras in their fight against Sandinistas. Wexler shot on location in Nicaragua, and the movie became the direc-tor's propaganda statement about American support of antigovernment forces, arguing that the United States was repeating the mistakes it had made in Vietnam.

The Leatherneck (1929)

China	Marines	Unkn	B&W 76 mins
Pathé	WV: 04-24-29		NYT: 04-22-29

DIR: Howard Higgin. SW: Elliott Clawson. PRO: Ralph Block. STARS: Alan Hale, William Boyd, Robert Armstrong, Diane Ellis.

The film tells the story of three Marines stationed in China and classified as missing in action. One is insane, another dead, and the third charged with murder. The movie's centerpiece, a court-martial, follows.

Leathernecking (1930)

Peace	Marines	Ltd	B&W/Color 72 mins.
RKO	WV: 09-17-30		NYT: 09-13-30

DIR: Edward Cline. SW: Alfred Jackson, Jane Murfin. PRO: RKO. STARS: Benny Rubin, Eddie Foy Jr., Irene Dunne, Ken Murray.

Based on *Present Arms*, this musical comedy features Marines on the loose, with a private pretending to be a captain. Although the production looked expensive, with 20 minutes in color, more often than not the comedy went AWOL.

Leathernecks aka Colli di cuoio (1988)

Vietnam	Marines	NR	Color 87 mins
Unkn	WV: DNR		NYT: DNR

DIR: Ignazio Dolce. SW: Unkn. PRO: Gianfranco Couyoumdjian. STARS: Richard Hatch, Vassili Karis, Antonio Marsina, James Mitchum.

Spaghetti Vietnam film shot in the Philippines on a very low budget, which shows. Hatch, as a Marine officer, and his patrol locate a cache of U.S. weapons in the hands of the North Vietnamese. He alerts an intelligence officer and joins him in tracking down the arms dealer, returning to base just in time for the climactic battle, the story's only raison d'être.

The Leathernecks Have Landed (1936)

Peace	Marines	Full	B&W 67 mins
Republic	WV: 03-25-36		NYT: 03-23-36

DIR: Howard Bretherton. SW: Seton I. Miller. PRO: Ken Goldsmith. STARS: Lew Ayres, Jimmy Ellison, Maynard Holmes.

Ayres plays a Marine thrown out of the service for indirectly causing the death of his friend. He redeems himself in a shoot-out between the Marines and Chinese rebels. The Marines appear in stock footage, including scenes in Shanghai. Marine Corps Reserves assisted in production, and active Marines in dress uniforms drilled in the lobby when the film opened.

Let It Rain (1927)

Peace	Navy, Marines	Ltd	B&W 67 mins
Paramount	WV: 03-09-27		NYT: 03-09-27

DIR: Edward Cline. SW: Wade Boteler, George Crone, Earl Snell. PRO: Douglas MacLean. STARS: Douglas MacLean, Shirley Mason, Wade Boteler, Frank Campeau, James Bradbury Jr.

A comedy set aboard ship, with Marines in constant conflict with sailors.

Let's Go Navy (1951) [SSS]

Peace	Navy	NR	B&W	68 mins
Monogram	WV: 08-01-51		NYT: DNR	

DIR: William Beaudine. SW: Max Adams. PRO: Jan Grippo. STARS: Leo Gorcey, Huntz Hall, Allen Jenkins, Tom Neal, Charlita.

A "Bowery Boys" film in which "sailors" rob the boys. Seeking the criminals, the boys, in a mix up, enlist in the Navy. While serving they fail to find the crooks, but when they return home a year later, they find the perpetrators and deal with them appropriately.

Lieutenant Danny, U.S.A. (1916)

Mexican Border	Army	Full	B&W	5 reels
Triangle	WV: 08-11-16		NYT: DNR	

DIR: Walter Edwards. SW: J. G. Hawks. PRO: Thomas Ince. STARS: William Desmond, Enid Markey, Gertrude Claire, Thornton Edwards.

Desmond, as a newly minted lieutenant from West Point, receives orders to go to the Mexican border and join the fight against Mexican bandits. In the course of events, he falls in love with a Mexican girl, rescuing her from a gang, which in turn captures him and puts him in front of a firing squad. Saved when the bullet hits his St. Christopher medal, he routs the bandits and marries the girl. While explaining to the nation how its Army was defeating the bandits, the film stirred up patriotism.

Lt. Robin Crusoe, U.S.N. (1966)

Vietnam	Navy	Full	Color	115 mins
Disney	WV: 05-18-66		NYT: 07-14-66	

DIR: Byron Paul. SW: Bill Walsh, Don DaGradi. PRO: Bill Walsh, Ron Miller, Walt Disney. STARS: Dick Van Dyke, Nancy Kwan, Akim Tamiroff.

A carrier takeoff and a helicopter rescue figure in this updated Defoe classic.

The Lieutenant Wore Skirts (1956)

Peace	Army	Full	Color	98 mins
Fox	WV: 01-11-56		NYT: 01-12-56	

DIR: Frank Tashlin. SW: Albert Beich, Frank Tashlin. PRO: Buddy Adler. STARS: Tom Ewell, Sheree North, Rita Moreno, Rick Jason, Les Tremayne.

When a WWII hero is recalled, his wife, a former WAC, rejoins her service. The husband ends up being rejected, but the wife likes her uniform and decides to remain a WAC.

Life Is Beautiful (1997—in Italy)

WWII	Army	NR	Color	116 mins
Miramax	WV: 01-04-98		NYT: 05-18-98, 10-23-98	

DIR: Roberto Benigni. SW: Vincenzo Cerami, Roberto Benigni. PRO: John Davis, Elda Ferri, Gianluigi Braschi. STARS: Roberto Benigni, Nicoletta Braschi, Giustino Durano, Lidia Alfonsi, Sergio Bini Bustric, Horst Bucholz.

Benigni tells the story of a Jewish man who married, had a child, and was madly in love. His idyllic life is shattered by WWII, and he finds himself in a concentration camp, where he protects his son from the evil around them through comedy and games. U.S. tanks arrive to liberate the camp, too late to save Benigni, but not his wife and son.

Limbo (1972) [G&G]

Vietnam	Navy	Deny	Color	111 mins
Universal	WV: 11-08-72		NYT: 01-27-73	

DIR: Mark Robson. SW: Joan Silver, James Bridges. PRO: Linda Gottlieb. STARS: Kate Jackson, Katherine Justice, Stuart Margolin, Hazel Medina.

The film follows the trials and tribulations of a group of Navy POWs' wives during the Vietnam War. The service turned down a request for limited assistance because the movie showed one of the wives being unfaithful. The Navy believed the completed film would be shown in North Vietnam as soon as it was released in the United States, and the cinematic wife's infidelity would hurt POW morale, especially if the film had received military support.

The Line (1980)

Vietnam	Army	NR	Color	95 mins
Astral Films	WV: DNR		NYT: DNR	

DIR: Robert J. Siegel. SW: Patricia Maxwell, Reginald Shelborne. PRO: Robert Siegel, Virginia Largent. STARS: Ray Baker, Don Blakely, Jacqueline Brookes, Robert Capece, Gil Rogers, Russ Thacker.

Parents of a son who returns home AWOL from Vietnam turn him in to military authorities, who imprison him at the Presidio, the setting for the movie. The filmmakers claimed that the prison scenario was based on a true story of 27 prisoners who staged a sit-down strike, refusing to take part in a military execution.

Little Mister Jim (1946)

Peace	Army	Full	B&W	92 mins
MGM	WV: 06-05-46		NYT: DNR	

DIR: Fred Zinnemann. SW: George Bruce. PRO: Orville O. Dull. STARS: Jackie "Butch" Jenkins, James Craig, Frances Gifford, Luana Patten, Spring Byington, Ching Wah Lee.

On an Army base somewhere in the United States in 1938, an officer's son experiences the loss of his mother and sees the grief of his drinking father. A Chinese manservant provides sage advice to the boy, until he reveals his true identity as a general and returns to China to fight the Japanese, accompanied by the father as a combat observer. The Army allowed Zinnemann to film exterior scenes on an Army base.

Lone Star (1996)

Peace	Army	Inform	Color 134 mins
Sony	WV: 03-18-96		NYT: 06-21-96

DIR: John Sayles. SW: John Sayles. PRO: Maggie Renzi, R. Paul Miller. STARS: Chris Cooper, Elizabeth Peña, Joe Morton, Kris Kristofferson.

The Army public affairs office in Los Angeles provided informational assistance during preproduction for the few scenes that take place on an Army base. However, the filmmakers would not sign the cooperation agreement, which permitted a PA officer to supervise the Army scenes for technical accuracy. Therefore, the Army denied access to its facilities. With no service presence on the set, the colonel wore his insignia upside down.

The Longest Day (1962) [G&G]

WWII	Army, Navy, Marines Full	B&W 180 mins
Fox	WV: 10-03-62	NYT: 10-05-62

DIR: Ken Annakin, Bernhard Wicki, Andrew Marton. SW: Cornelius Ryan, Jack Sedon, Romain Gary, James Jones, David Pursall. PRO: Darryl F. Zanuck. STARS: John Wayne, Red Buttons, Richard Burton, Robert Ryan, Peter Lawford, Henry Fonda, Robert Mitchum, Sal Mineo, Jeffrey Hunter, Sean Connery, etc.

Based on Ryan's journalistic history *The Longest Day*, the film became the last and greatest of the first cycle of films about World War II. It also became the model for all subsequent war epics and remains the standard against which to judge all movies about men in mortal combat. Zanuck also created a movie that compares to any of his earlier Academy Award-winning movies, although it only won an Oscar for special effects.

Since the weather on June 6, 1944, had prevented the air forces of both sides from supporting or defending against the invasion, Zanuck did not have to acquire an air force to provide cover for the ground troops he accumulated. However, he built replicas of the gliders used in the assault. He also used actual locales to re-create the battles both on the beaches and inland, particularly at Pointe du Hoc and Ste. Mere-Eglise.

Zanuck received full cooperation from the armed services of the United States, France, and England, particularly in the re-creation of the Normandy landings. U.S. Marines, wearing Army uniforms, helped stage the Omaha Beach sequence filmed on Corsica. Although the Army had approved the script, the service ultimately refused to acknowledge its support because the producer refused to remove a scene in which GIs shoot German soldiers trying to surrender.

The film has none of the attributes usually associated with great movies. The actors do not remain on the screen long enough to create characters with whom the audience can empathize. The story has no beginning, middle, or end. Rather, as a docudrama, the film simply re-created D-Day with all the confusion, tragedy, and drama of the actual event, albeit with significant dramatic license. Nevertheless, it provides a stunning portrayal of the day that changed the history of the twentieth century and perhaps of all time.

The Long Gray Line (1955)

Peace	Army	Full	Color	135 mins
Columbia	WV: 02-09-55		NYT: 02-11-55	

DIR: John Ford. SW: Edward Hope. PRO: Robert Arthur. STARS: Tyrone Power, Maureen O'Hara, Robert Francis, Donald Crisp, Ward Bond.

Filmed at West Point with full cooperation, the story is as much about a man's love of an institution as about a man's love for a woman. Power plays Irish immigrant Marty Maher, who served for 50 years as the Military Academy's athletic trainer and instructor of its traditions to the long line of cadets that passed through its halls, classrooms, and playing fields. Ford manages, but barely, to avoid submerging the film in sentiment while capturing the essence of West Point.

The Lost Battalion (1919)

WWI	Army	Full	B&W	6–8 reels
McManus Corp.	WV: DNR		NYT: 07-03-19	

DIR: Burton King. SW: Charles Logue. PRO: Edward A. MacManus. STARS: Helen Ferguson, Marion Coakley, Sidney D'Albrook, Gaston Glass.

Beginning with the formation of the 77th Division in September 1917, the film follows the doughboys to France and then the advance of one battalion deep into the Argonne Forest in September 1918. After being surrounded for six days, another battalion of the division penetrates German lines to rescue the men. General Robert Alexander, who had led the division, provided personal supervision of the production, and the U.S. Army Signal Corps rendered full cooperation, including men from the units that had fought in the battle.

Lost Boundaries (1949)

WWII	Navy	NR	B&W	99 mins
Film Classics	WV: 06-29-49		NYT: 07-01-49	

DIR: Alfred Werker. SW: Eugene Ling, Virginia Shaler. PRO: Louis de Rochemont. STARS: Beatrice Pearson, Mel Ferrer, Richard Hylton, Canada Lee.

Ferrer plays Dr. Howard Carter, a light-skinned black who passes for white during his medical career until he tries to enlist as a doctor during World War II. In a brief scene, after he acknowledges his Negro background, the Navy rejects him on the grounds that he failed "to meet physical qualifications." Ironically, by the time the docudrama appeared, President Truman had ordered the armed services to integrate. Nevertheless, the film highlighted the Navy's racist past.

The Lost Idol (1990)

Vietnam	Army	NR	Color	103 mins
Unkn	WV: DNR		NYT: DNR	

DIR: Philip Chalong. SW: James Phillips, Tony Suvat. PRO: Unkn. STARS: Myra Chason, Pierre Delalande, Erik Estrada, James Phillips, Sorapong Chatree, Christoph Klüppel.

As with **The Deer Hunter**, filmmakers cannot get it right, placing U.S. troops still in Vietnam when Saigon fell in 1975. The stranded soldiers head to safety in Thailand, finding a gold statue along the way. The greedy lieutenant shoots his men in hopes of keeping the treasure for himself. But when he returns eight years later to dig up the idol, the officer, now a major, learns that one of his men has survived as a farmer, and he must decide how to deal with his past.

The Lost Missile (1958)

SciFi	All	Ltd	B&W	70 mins
UA	WV: 12-03-58		NYT: DNR	

DIR: Lester William Berke. SW: John McPartland, Jerome Bixby, Lester William Berke. PRO: Lee Gordon. STARS: Robert Loggia, Ellen Parker, Larry Kerr, Kitty Kelly.

Quick, a killer missile from outer space is headed to Ottawa! This U.S.–Canadian production uses a Nike-like missile to save the world. Thank goodness.

Lucky Jordan (1942)

WWII	Army	Unkn	B&W	83 mins
Paramount	WV: 11-18-42		NYT: 01-25-43	

DIR: Frank Tuttle. SW: Darrell Ware, Karl Tunberg. PRO: Fred Kohlmar. STARS: Alan Ladd, Helen Walker, Sheldon Leonard, Mabel Paige.

The film was based on Charles Leonard's short story "Prelude to Glory," in *The Saturday Evening Post*. Ladd, a mobster, gets drafted, despite efforts to avoid induction. As to be expected, he rebels at Army discipline and ends up in the brig. He escapes and kidnaps Walker when she tries to persuade him not to go AWOL. Back at his gang's headquarters, he discovers his replacement is involved with enemy agents bent on stealing Army tank plans. Ladd foils their plot and returns to the Army.

MacArthur (1977) [G&G]

WWII	Army, Marines	Full	Color	122 mins
Universal	WV: 06-29-77		NYT: 07-01-77	

DIR: Joseph Sargent. SW: Hal Barwood, Matthew Robbins. PRO: Frank McCarthy. STARS: Gregory Peck, Ed Flanders, Dan O'Herlihy, Marj Dusay, Sandy Kenyon.

McCarthy attempted to repeat his success with **Patton** by doing the biography of another controversial general, this time covering not only WWII but also Korea. Peck refused to portray the general with his warts or even use makeup to look his character's age. One reviewer probably said it best: MacArthur was a better actor than Peck. The Marines appear fleetingly in combat sequences.

Madame Butterfly (1915) [SSS]

Peace	Navy	Deny	B&W 5 reels
FPL	WV: 11-12-15		NYT: 11-08-15

DIR: Sidney Olcott. SW: John Luther Long. PRO: Daniel Frohman. STARS: Mary Pickford, Olive West, Jane Hall.

The Navy refused to cooperate given the image of an officer who pretends to marry a Japanese girl, abandons her and their child, returns to the United States, and marries an American woman. Navy Secretary Josephus Daniels told the studio that the actions of the officer did not "reflect credit on the service."

Madame Butterfly (1932)

Peace	Navy	NR	B&W 85 mins
Paramount	WV: 12-27-32		NYT: 12-26-32

DIR: Marion Gering. SW: Josephine Lovett, Joseph M. March. PRO: B. P. Schulberg. STARS: Sylvia Sidney, Cary Grant, Charles Ruggles, Irving Pichel.

Based on David Belasco's play, the film does not re-create Puccini's tragic opera but tells the story as a simple drama of an American naval officer's seduction and abandonment of a Japanese maiden. This version contains no more positive image of the sailor than the 1915 rendering with which the Navy had no interest in becoming involved.

Madame Spy (1918)

WWI	Navy	Ltd	B&W 5 reels
Universal	WV: 01-11-18		NYT: DNR

DIR: Douglas Gerrard. SW: Harvey Gates. PRO: Jack Mulhall. STARS: Jack Mulhall, Donna Drew, Wadsworth Harris, George Gebhart, Jean Hersholt.

This espionage drama portrays a young man who fails his Annapolis entrance exam to the horror and shame of his admiral father. The man redeems himself by foiling a plot to hand over to the enemy his father's plans for the U.S. Atlantic Coast defenses. The film contains scenes of the Naval Academy and warships.

Major Payne (1995)

Peace	Marines	Deny	Color 97 mins
Universal	WV: 03-20-95		NYT: 03-24-95

DIR: Nick Castle. SW: Dean Lorey, Damon Wayans, Gary Rosen, William Roberts, Richard Alan Simmons. PRO: Eric Gold, Michael Rachmil. STARS: Damon Wayans, Orlando Brown, Michael Ironside.

A clichéd warrior in a peacetime story in which Wayans portrays a Marine killing machine without a war, poorly adjusting to civilian life. Although he undergoes a slow transformation as a junior ROTC instructor when assigned to a military academy, the Marines refused to assist since they believed the retired hero did not present a good image of the Corps.

A Man from Wyoming (1930)

WWI	Army	Unkn	B&W 70 mins
Paramount	WV: DNR		NYT: 07-12-30

DIR: Rowland V. Lee. SW: Albert S. Le Vino, John V. A. Weaver. PRO: Paramount. STARS: Gary Cooper, June Collyer, Regis Toomey, Morgan Farley.

Cooper portrays an engineer from Wyoming who is building bridges in France during the war when he meets rich girl and occasional Red Cross worker Collyer. They marry, he disappears at the front, she resumes her gay ways, and at the armistice, guess what happens?

The Man in the Gray Flannel Suit (1956)

WWII	Army	Unkn	Color 152 mins
Fox	WV: 04-04-56		NYT: 04-13-56

DIR: Nunnally Johnson. SW: Nunnally Johnson. PRO: Darryl F. Zanuck. STARS: Gregory Peck, Jennifer Jones, Fredric March, Lee J. Cobb, Keenan Wynn.

Based on Sloan Wilson's novel about Madison Avenue, the film says more about the long-term impact of war on its participants than about war per se. In flashbacks, Peck relives his combat experiences in Italy and on a South Pacific island. His killing of a young German soldier and later one of his own men in a friendly-fire incident in the Pacific continue to haunt him, even as he is becoming a corporate executive 10 years later. However, until one of his wartime soldiers recognizes him and informs him of the consequences of his wartime adulterous affair, he seems to have forgotten the Italian girl with whom he had a brief but passionate relationship and who he knew was pregnant before he returned to combat.

The film remains one of the few Hollywood productions that dared show the down side of a necessary war. No record exists that Fox approached the Pentagon for military assistance. Nevertheless, the film contains some staged battle scenes and some stock combat footage. However, Johnson gave little attention to the timing of events or the historical reality that the Army did not engage in any assault from the sea in the last weeks of the Pacific war or undertake an airborne parachute drop to support a landing, which Peck's character did.

Man in the Middle (1964)

WWII	Army	NR	B&W 94 mins
Fox	WV: 01-15-64		NYT: 03-05-64

DIR: Guy Hamilton. SW: Keith Waterhouse, Willis Hall. PRO: Walter Seltzer. STARS: Robert Mitchum, France Nuyen, Barry Sullivan, Keenan Wynn.

Based on Howard Fast's novel *The Winston Affair*, this slow, tedious courtroom drama is centered on the sanity or insanity of an American officer who has murdered a British soldier in the China-Burma-India theater. No fireworks, and the fate of the officer remains unclear at the end of the film. Obviously, not a story that would benefit the Army.

The Man Who Was Afraid (1917)

WWI	Army	Unkn	B&W	4–5 reels
Essanay	WV: 07-06-17		NYT: DNR	

DIR: Fred Wright. SW: H. Tipton Steck. PRO: Jesse D. Hampton. STARS: Bryant Washburn, Mark Ellison, Ernest Maupain.

From Mary Pulver's story in *The Saturday Evening Post,* the film follows a young man, the victim of an overprotective mother, who resigns from the National Guard rather than go to France. His comrades call him a coward and his girlfriend spurns him. Naturally, he has no choice but to go to France, where he rejoins his unit, becomes a hero, and wins the girl.

The Manchurian Candidate (1962)

Korea, Cold War	Army	Ltd	B&W	126 mins
Columbia	WV: 10-17-62		NYT: 10-25-62	

DIR: John Frankenheimer. SW: George Axelrod. PRO: John Frankenheimer, George Axelrod. STARS: Frank Sinatra, Laurence Harvey, Janet Leigh, Angela Lansbury.

Based on Richard Condon's novel of the same name, the film offers many possible interpretations: social and political satire, dramatic thriller, Cold War propaganda. Ultimately the story focuses on a former Korean War POW whom the enemy brainwashed to become an assassin upon his return to the United States.

The Manchurian Candidate (2004)

Gulf War	Army	NR	Color	130 mins
Paramount	WV: 7-17-04		NYT: 7-30-04	

DIR: Jonathan Demme. SW: Dean Georgaris, Daniel Pyne. PRO: Scott Rudin, Tina Sinatra, Ilona Herzberg. STARS: Denzel Washington, Meryl Streep, Liev Schreiber, Jon Voight, Kimberly Elise.

The pale remake of the 1962 classic opens in Kuwait just before Operation Desert Storm is to begin. On patrol, Washington's men are ambushed, kidnapped, and brainwashed by an unidentified enemy. The military action that serves as the film's springboard is confused and generic. Washington's character would have been given a medical discharge, given his apparent mental problems in the years following the war. More to the point, his being in the military has little bearing on the story or the ending, which only a complete cynic would even begin to understand.

The Manhattan Project (1986)

Cold War	Army, Air Force	NR	Color	120 mins
Fox	WV: 05-14-86		NYT: 06-13-86	

DIR: Marshall Brickman. SW: Marshall Brickman, Thomas Baum. PRO: Jennifer Ogden, Marshall Brickman. STARS: John Lithgow, Christopher Collet, Cynthia Nixon, Jill Eikenberry, John Mahoney.

The film portrays a brilliant teenager who builds the first private atomic bomb as an entry in a science fair. The story attempts to combine comedy with serious drama, but it ends without a disaster, which diminishes the warning about the dangers of nuclear proliferation. The anti-bomb message in this and similar movies such as *Fail Safe* and *WarGames* did not thrill the Pentagon and military planners.

Marching On (1943)

WWII	Army	Full	B&W 63 mins
Sack	WV: DNR		NYT: DNR

DIR: Spencer Williams. SW: Spencer Williams. PRO: H. W. Keir. STARS: Hugo Martin, George T. Sutton, Myra D. Hemmings, Georgia Kelly.

Son and grandson of U.S. soldiers of previous wars, Martin, a young black man, does not believe the United States is in danger and thinks that Europeans should defend themselves. However, he is drafted and undergoes basic training at Fort Huachuca in Arizona, where the movie was shot, using regular soldiers as extras. In the course of the story, he changes his opinion about the war. Re-released as *Where's My Man To-night?*, it became a more marketable feature-length film in the 1950s by adding 20 minutes of orchestra and dance performance. The film was found in Tyler, Texas, in the 1980s, in a cache of "black" films made for then-segregated audiences.

Marianne (1929)

WWI	Army	Unkn	B&W 84 mins
MGM	WV: 10-23-29		NYT: 10-19-29

DIR: Robert Z. Leonard. SW: Gladys Unger, Laurence Stallings. PRO: Marion Davies, Robert Z. Leonard. STARS: Marion Davies, Oscar Shaw, Robert Castle, Robert Ames.

A romantic musical comedy that takes place after the Armistice when an American unit is billeted in a French town. There, an officer pursues Marianne's piglet, which she claims is her pet. A doughboy joins the effort to keep the little porcine out of the pot. The private, who has been smitten by the girl, ends up in the stockade, while the girl sacrifices the petite pig for 200 francs to help four war orphans. In the end, the soldier leaves the girl to her prewar fiancé, who returns home blind and in love with his nurse. So, the girl takes her four orphans to the United States for a reunion with the private. Released in both silent and sound versions.

Maria's Lovers (1984)

WWII	Army	NR	Color 94 mins
MGM	WV: 05-23-84		NYT: DNR

DIR: Andrei Konchalovsky. SW: Gérard Brach, Andrei Konchalovsky, Paul Zindel. PRO: Bosko Djordjevic, Lawrence Taylor-Mortoff. STARS: Nastassja Kinski, John Savage, Robert Mitchum, Keith Carradine.

One of the few films to explore the negative effect WWII had on its returning veterans. A brief excerpt from John Huston's Army Signal Corps documentary *Let There Be Light* (see chapter 3) serves as the springboard for the story and provides the only U.S. military presence.

Marine Battleground (1963)

Korea	Marines	NR	B&W	88 mins (US)
Daewon Prod.	WV: DNR		NYT: DNR	

DIR: Man-hui Lee, Manli Lee, Milton Mann. SW: Kook-jin Jang, Milton Mann, Han-chul Yu. PRO: Paul Mart, Seon Won. STARS: Jock Mahoney, Pat Yi, David Lowe, Lloyd Kino.

In this Korean/American production, the Marines wage a pitched battle against the advancing Chinese communists and then find themselves stranded behind enemy lines without communications to their headquarters. A bloody retreat follows.

Marine Raiders (1944)

WWII	Marines, Army, Navy	Full	B&W	90 mins
RKO	WV: 06-21-44		NYT: 07-01-44	

DIR: Harold Schuster. SW: Martin Rackin, Warren Duff. PRO: Robert Fellows. STARS: Robert Ryan, Pat O'Brien, Frank McHugh.

The film combines fictional drama with scenes of combat from Guadalcanal and other islands as well as training sequences. The Marines provided men, equipment, and combat footage. Guadalcanal scenes show how the Army relieved the Marines.

The Marines Are Coming (1935)

Peace	Marines	Unkn	B&W	70 mins
Mascot	WV: 02-27-35		NYT: 02-23-35	

DIR: David Howard. SW: James Gruen. PRO: Nat Levine. STARS: William Haines, Esther Ralston, Conrad Nagel.

An annoying and witless young Marine officer chases women and is thrown out of the Marines for gambling. He then rehabilitates himself by enlisting as a private and ultimately rescuing his rival from bandits.

The Marines Are Here (1938)

Peace	Marines	Full	B&W	61 mins
Monogram	WV: 07-06-38		NYT: DNR	

DIR: Phil Rosen. SW: Jack Knapp, J. Benton Cheney. PRO: Scott R. Dunlap. STARS: Gordon Oliver, June Travis, Ray Walker.

The film idealizes Marines as real men who carry the white man's burden against bandits. The hero is a bad-boy Marine who reforms himself in the process of becoming a worthy Leatherneck.

Marines Come Through (1943)

WWII	Marines	Ltd	B&W 60 mins
Astor Pictures	WV: 07-14-43		NYT: DNR

DIR: Louis Gasnier. SW: D. S. Leslie, Jack Kofoed, Lawrence Meade. PRO: George Hirliman. STARS: Wallace Ford, Toby Wing, Grant Withers, Sheila Lynch.

Originally released as **Fight on Marines**, this "C" film shows Nazis trying to steal a new bombsight. Marine aviation mechanics foil the plot. The New York Board of Review denied the film an export license because it portrayed the Marines as amateurish and lacking discipline.

The Marines Fly High (1940)

Peace	Marines	Full	B&W 68 mins
RKO	WV: 03-06-40		NYT: 03-05-40

DIR: George Nichols Jr., Ben Stoloff. SW: Jerry Cady, Lt. Cdr. A. J. Bolton. PRO: Robert Sisk. STARS: Lucille Ball, John Eldredge, Richard Dix, Chester Morris.

A "B" movie in which two Marine officer pilots pursue the same girl and fight in Central America against bandits. Like **Flight** before it, the film shows Marines developing air-to-ground tactical support against rebels.

Marines, Let's Go (1961)

Korea	Marines	Ltd	B&W 103 mins
Fox	WV: 08-16-61		NYT: 08-16-61

DIR: Raoul Walsh. SW: John Twist. PRO: Raoul Walsh. STARS: Tom Tryon, David Hedison, Tom Reese, Linda Hutchins.

Walsh's dated, corny, predictable, and juvenile homage to the Marines, one more time. The service did not want to cooperate given the poor screenplay but relented because of the director's long service to the Marines, beginning with **What Price Glory** in 1926. The film portrays a group of Marines transferred from Korea to Japan to serve as a regimental reserve and then back to combat in Korea.

Mars Attacks! (1996)

SciFi	Air Force	Deny	Color 110 mins
WB	WV: 12-02-96		NYT: 12-13-96

DIR: Tim Burton. SW: Jonathan Gems. PRO: Tim Burton, Larry Franco. STARS: Jack Nicholson, Glenn Close, Annette Bening, Jim Brown.

Although the film was clearly a comedic fantasy, the Air Force denied cooperation because the service has always refused to become involved with any story that suggests flying saucers are real.

M*A*S*H (1970) [G&G]

Korea	Army	NR	Color 116 mins
Fox	WV: 01-21-70		NYT: 01-26-70, 02-01-70

DIR: Robert Altman. SW: Ring Lardner Jr. PRO: Ingo Preminger. STARS: Elliott Gould, Donald Sutherland, Tom Skerritt, Sally Kellerman, Robert Duvall, Jo Ann Pflug, Rene Auberjonois.

From Richard Hooker's novel, Altman created a battlefield hospital in which blood flowed and doctors had fun. Supposedly a comment on Vietnam and the absurdity of war, but no combat appeared or was even heard. The doctors might as well have been operating on the side of a Los Angeles freeway.

Matinee (1993)

Cold War	Navy, NG	Full	Color 99 mins
Universal	WV: 02-01-93		NYT: 01-29-93

DIR: Joe Dante. SW: Charles Haas. PRO: Michael Finnell. STARS: John Goodman, Cathy Moriarty, Simon Fenton, Omri Katz, Kevin McCarthy.

A send-up of the Cold War horror films set in Key West during the Cuban Missile Crisis. For the production, the Navy provided ships as background to portray the naval blockade of Soviet ships heading to Cuba and a Navy helicopter flying overhead. The National Guard set up a hawk missile battery as it had done in 1962, to add to the ambience.

The McConnell Story (1955)

WWII/Korea	Air Force	Full	Color 106 mins
WB	WV: 08-17-55		NYT: 09-30-55

DIR: Gordon Douglas. SW: Ted Sherdeman, Sam Rolfe. PRO: Henry Blanke. STARS: Alan Ladd, June Allyson, James Whitmore, Frank Faylen.

The cinematic biography of Joseph McConnell, who served as a navigator aboard a B-17 in WWII, became a jet ace in Korea, and died while testing a new F-86 jet fighter. On the ground, the story plods. In the air, the film soars with drama.

McHale's Navy (1964)

WWII	Navy, Marines	Ltd	Color 93 mins
Universal	WV: 07-01-64		NYT: 07-11-64

Dir: Edward Montagne. SW: Frank Gill Jr., George Carleton Brown. PRO: Edward Montagne. STARS: Ernest Borgnine, Joe Flynn, Tim Conway, Gary Vinson.

In a slapstick comedy spawned by the television series, Montagne filled the screen with zany gags, on and off Borgnine's PT-boat. Given his philosophy of his way first and the Navy's way second, the service reluctantly provided minor assistance.

McHale's Navy (1997)

Peace	Navy	NR	Color	109 mins
Universal	DV: 04-21-97		NYT: DNR	

DIR: Bryan Spicer. SW: Peter Crabbe. PRO: Tom Arnold, Conrad Hool, Bill Sheinberg, Jon Sheinberg, Sid Sheinberg. STARS: Tom Arnold, Dean Stockwell, Debra Messing, David Alan Grier, Tim Curry, Ernest Borgnine.

McHale, recalled to active duty, musters his former crew to take on a rogue terrorist who is building a nuclear device right under the eyes of Stockwell, as Capt. Binghampton, the new commander of the Naval station. With this rendition, the franchise ceased being very funny.

McHale's Navy Joins the Air Force (1965)

WWII	Navy, Air Force	Ltd	Color	92 mins
Universal	WV: 06-09-65		NYT: DNR	

DIR: Edward Montagne. SW: John Fenton Murray. PRO: Edward Montagne. STARS: Joe Flynn, Tim Conway, Bob Hastings, Gary Vinson.

The second rendering of the TV series onto the big screen, with less success due to the absence of Borgnine. In addition to occasionally riotous comedy, the film portrays the sinking of a Japanese fleet and FDR awarding medals.

Mean Johnny Barrows (1976)

Vietnam	Army	NR	Color	90 mins
Dimension Pictures	WV: DNR		NYT: DNR	

DIR: Fred Williamson. SW: Jolivett Cato, Charles Walker. PRO: Fred Williamson. STARS: Fred Williamson, Roddy McDowall, Stuart Whitman, Jenny Sherman, Elliot Gould.

The Army discharged Williamson for striking a racist officer. The veteran ends up as a gas station attendant until a mobster offers him a job as a hit man. The film cannot even get the uniforms correct in the Vietnam combat scenes.

Memphis Belle (1990) [G&G]

WWII	Air Force	Deny	Color	106 mins
WB	WV: 09-10-90		NYT: 10-12-90	

DIR: Michael Caton-Jones. SW: Monte Merrick. PRO: David Putnam, Catherine Wyler. STARS: Matthew Modine, Eric Stoltz, Sean Astin, Harry Connick Jr., John Lithgow.

Knowledgeable viewers could only ask why Wyler would sully her father William's superb 1944 documentary, *The Memphis Belle*. The script lacks any credibility beginning with the explosion of a crippled B-17 as it returns from a mission with no fuel, bombs, or ammunition left to explode and includes a drunken navigator being hoisted aboard his plane to guide a mission to its target. The only valid images come from the use of actual combat footage, some taken by the senior Wyler and his cameramen during WWII.

The Men (1950) [G&G]

WWII	Army	Full	B&W 85 mins
UA	WV: 05-24-50		NYT: 07-21-50

DIR: Fred Zinnemann. SW: Carl Foreman. PRO: Stanley Kramer. STARS: Marlon Brando, Teresa Wright, Everett Sloane, Jack Webb.

This docudrama portrayed the rehabilitation of paralyzed WWII veterans. Brando, in his first movie role, spent time in a ward with the veterans so that he could better create his character, a young soldier whose fiancé still wants to marry him despite his crippling injury. Zinnemann used actual paralyzed veterans as extras in the hospital sequences. Despite its antiwar images, the Army and then the Veterans Administration saw the value of a film that informed Americans of the sacrifice young men had made and how they adjusted to their new lives confined to beds or wheelchairs.

Men in War (1957)

Korea	Army	NR	B&W 102 mins
UA	WV: 01-23-57		NYT: 03-20-57

DIR: Anthony Mann. SW: Philip Yordan. PRO: Sidney Harmon, Anthony Mahn. STARS: Robert Ryan, Aldo Ray, Robert Keith, Vic Morrow.

Based on Van Van Praag's novel *Day Without End*, the film portrayed an infantry platoon during combat in Korea. The small-scale battle sequences did not require Army cooperation, which would have been problematic, given the portrayal of the officers and men.

Men of Honor (2000) [G&G]

Peace	Navy, Marines	Full	Color 129 mins
Fox	WV: 09-18-2000		NYT: 11-10-2000

DIR: George Tillman Jr. SW: Scott Marshall Smith. PRO: Robert Teitel, Bill Badalato. STARS: Robert De Niro, Cuba Gooding Jr., Charlize Theron.

The story follows Carl Brashear, the first black Navy master chief diver, and his trials and tribulations, including the loss of a leg during a dive. The Navy gave full cooperation within the limits of its resources—even though the film portrays the commander of the diving school as a bigoted fool. In the end, Brashear emerges as a larger than life hero who helped integrate the Navy. A Marine performs his duty as a guard at the Navy's hearing to determine Brashear's fitness to remain a Navy diver.

Men of the Fighting Lady (1954) [SSS]

Korea	Navy	Full	B&W 79 mins
MGM	WV: 05-12-54		NYT: 05-08-54

DIR: Andrew Marton. SW: Art Cohen. PRO: Henry Berman. STARS: Van Johnson, Walter Pidgeon, Louis Calhern, Dewey Martin.

Based on James Michener's *Saturday Evening Post* article "The Forgotten Heroes of Korea" and Harry Burns's article "The Case of the Blind Pilot," the film, in a quasi-documentary format, portrayed the combat experiences of Navy jet pilots flying dangerous missions over Korea. Many of the characters were actual people who had performed the exploits visualized on the screen. In writing *The Bridges at Toko-Ri*, Michener drew on the same stories he had recounted in his article, which caused problems when Paramount bought the film rights to the novel.

Men with Wings (1938)

Preparedness	Air Force	Unkn	Color 102 mins
Paramount	WV: 10-26-38		NYT: 10-27-38

DIR: William A. Wellman. SW: Robert Carson. PRO: William A. Wellman. STARS: Fred MacMurray, Ray Milland, Louise Campbell, Andy Devine, Lynne Overman, Porter Hall, Kitty Kelly, Donald O'Connor.

The movie focused on the development of a new, superior bomber. The *New York Times* reviewer wrote that the filmmakers eliminated the original pacifist ending due to the growing threat of fascism.

Men Without Women (1930) [G&G]

Peace	Navy	Full	B&W 76 mins
Fox	WV: 02-05-30		NYT: 02-01-30

DIR: John Ford. SW: Dudley Nichols. PRO: John Ford. STARS: Kenneth MacKenna, Frank Albertson, Paul Page, John Wayne.

The film adhered to the plot of most peacetime submarine stories from *Submarine* and *Submarine D-1* to *Gray Lady Down*. A sub sinks in a collision or due to a malfunction, a terrible image for the Navy. But the sub service finds a benefit where it can by demonstrating how it would rescue the trapped men. Wayne jumps into the sea to rescue sailors as they pop to the surface from the stricken sub. Along with *Across the Pacific*, one of the two most inaccurate titles ever given a film since the sub's sailors spend their free time ashore in Shanghai at the longest bar in the world, with the local women offering their unique form of companionship.

Merrill's Marauders (1962)

WWII	Army	Full	Color 98 mins
WB	WV: 05-09-62		NYT: 06-14-62

DIR: Samuel Fuller. SW: Milton Sperling, Samuel Fuller. PRO: Milton Sperling. STARS: Jeff Chandler, Ty Hardin, Peter Brown, John Hoyt.

The story is drawn from former marauder Charlton Ogburn Jr.'s *The Marauders*, which details Gen. Frank Merrill's exploits in Burma. The film portrays how his marauders worked with the

British to stop the Japanese advance toward India. Fuller shot the movie in the Philippines with help from the Army and technical advice by Gen. Sam Wilson, who had served as Merrill's executive officer.

A Midnight Clear (1992)

WWII	Army	Deny	Color	107 mins
Interstar	WV: 03-30-92		NYT: 04-24-92	

DIR: Keith Gordon. SW: Keith Gordon. PRO: Dale Pollock, Bill Borden. STARS: Peter Berg, Kevin Dillon, Arye Gross, Ethan Hawke, Gary Sinise.

Based on William Wharton's novel about a confrontation between a U.S. intelligence squad and a German unit in the Ardennes Forest in December 1944, with the Germans wanting to surrender. After spending Christmas together, the agreement falls apart and the two sides return to combat. The Army declined to assist production, stating that the film contained a "completely negative nihilistic depiction of military personnel and operations" and that support would have competed with commercial sources.

The Midshipman (1925) [SSS]

Peace	Navy	Full	B&W	74 mins
MGM	WV: 10-14-25		NYT: 10-13-25	

DIR: Christy Cabanne. SW: F. McGrew Willis. PRO: MGM. STARS: Ramon Novarro, Harriet Hammond, Wesley Barry, Margaret Seddon.

One of the earliest Annapolis films in a series that Hollywood shot at the Naval Academy in the 1920s and 1930s to capture the atmosphere and excitement of midshipmen marching, drilling, and socializing. As always, the Navy and the Academy provided full cooperation.

Midshipman Jack (1933) [SSS]

Peace	Navy	Full	B&W	70 mins
Radio	WV: 11-21-33		NYT: 11-20-33	

DIR: Christy Cabanne. SW: Frank Wead, F. McGrew Willis. PRO: RKO. STARS: Bruce Cabot, Betty Furness, Frank Albertson, Arthur Lake.

The Academy setting along the Severn, the uniforms, the pageantry, and naval ships set the stage for a clichéd Annapolis love story that served as a recruiting poster for the Navy.

Midway (1976) [G&G]

WWII	Navy	Full	Color	132 mins
Universal	WV: 06-16-76		NYT: 06-19-76	

DIR: Jack Smight. SW: Donald Sanford. PRO: Walter Mirisch. STARS: Charlton Heston, Henry Fonda, James Coburn, Glenn Ford.

A failed epic intended as a 200th birthday present for the United States. At a time when Hollywood was still not ready to renew its traditional relationship with the Pentagon, the film began the rehabilitation of the military's image so savaged by Vietnam. The Navy provided use of the USS *Lexington* to serve as a stand-in for the American carriers that defeated the Japanese off Midway and changed the course of the war.

To re-create the flying sequences, the filmmakers used footage from ***Thirty Seconds Over Tokyo***, ***Tora! Tora! Tora!***, and Navy combat film. Despite the drama inherent in the visual images, the story itself could not rise above trite soap opera, and the characters remained wooden caricatures. Among other plot lines, Heston's aviator-son falls in love with a Japanese girl and seeks his father's help. Perhaps the best thing in the movie is Heston's crash onto the carrier deck, during which his WWII-vintage dive bomber morphs into a Korean War jet as it explodes. Why the switch in planes? The editor said he needed a fiery crash, and the type of plane was irrelevant.

Mike (1926)

Peace	Marines	Full	B&W	74 mins
MGM	WV: 01-13-26		NYT: 01-11-26	

DIR: Marshall Neilan. SW: Marion Jackson. PRO: Louis B. Mayer. STARS: Sally O'Neill, William Haines, Charlie Murray, Ned Sparks.

A comedy in which Marines come to the rescue with precise bombing to help capture a gang of outlaws.

The Military Air Scout (1911) [G&G]

Peace	Air Force	Informal	B&W	Unkn length
Vitagraph	WV: DNR		NYT: DNR	

DIR: William Humphrey. SW: Unkn. PRO: Unkn. STARS: Earle Williams, Edith Storey, Alec Francis, Lt. "Hap" Arnold.

At an air show on Long Island, the director asked Lt. Henry H. (Hap) Arnold if he would fly his Army biplane in front of a camera to provide footage for this movie. Arnold agreed and liked the experience so much that he even considered leaving the army and becoming an actor. Instead, he began a long relationship with Hollywood that produced most of the positive portrayals of the U.S. Air Force into the 1950s.

Minesweeper (1943)

WWII	Navy	Full	B&W	67 mins
Paramount	WV: 11-10-43		NYT: DNR	

DIR: William Berke. SW: Edward Lowe, Maxwell Shane. PRO: William Pine, William Thomas. STARS: Richard Arlen, Jean Parker, Russell Hayden, Guinn Williams.

A typical wartime story with a typical love triangle that is solved when one of the heroes, a disgraced Annapolis grad, gets killed while trying to capture a new and deadly Japanese mine.

Miracle of the White Stallions (1963)

WWII	Army	Unkn	Color 117 mins
Buena Vista	WV: 03-27-63		NYT: 05-23-63

DIR: Arthur Hiller. SW: A. J. Carothers. PRO: Walt Disney. STARS: Robert Taylor, Lilli Palmer, Curt Jürgens, Eddie Albert, James Franciscus.

Based on Col. Alois Podhajsky's *The Dancing White Horses of Vienna,* the film depicts the evacuation, with Gen. George Patton's help, of the famous equines as the U.S. 3rd Army approached Vienna.

Mission Over Korea (1953)

Korea	Air Force	Ltd	B&W 85 mins
Columbia	WV: DNR		NYT: 09-19-53

DIR: Fred F. Sears. SW: Jesse L. Lasky Jr., Eugene Ling, Martin Goldsmith. PRO: Robert Cohn. STARS: John Hodiak, John Derek, Maureen O'Sullivan, Audrey Totter, Rex Reason, Richard Erdman.

Appearing after the armistice and using combat footage showing the Korean topography and the long lines of refugees, this low-budget, older-officer-versus-younger-warrior tale did not need to be told. Perhaps the producer's relationship as a nephew of strong man Harry Cohen, president of Columbia, had something to do with the casting and all the other resources necessary to produce a film.

Miss Sadie Thompson (1953)

Peace	Marines	Ltd	B&W 90 mins
Columbia	WV: 12-23-53		NYT: 12-04-53

DIR: Curtis Bernhardt. SW: Harry Kleiner. PRO: Jerry Wald. STARS: Rita Hayworth, José Ferrer, Aldo Ray, Russell Collins, Charles Bronson.

The picture is based on John Colton's play, which in turn was based on Somerset Maugham's story "Rain." Sex, sin, and salvation in the South Seas, with Ray as a Marine who makes Hayworth an honest woman.

Missing in Action (1984)

Vietnam	Army	NR	Color 101 mins
Cannon	WV: 11-21-84		NYT: 11-17-84, 12-02-84

DIR: Joseph Zito. SW: James Bruner, Lance Hool. PRO: Menahem Golan, Yoram Globus. STARS: Chuck Norris, M. Emmet Walsh, David Tress, James Hong.

Norris, as a colonel who had been a POW during the war, returns to Vietnam seeking to rescue other prisoners.

Missing in Action 2: The Beginning (1985)

Vietnam	Army	NR	Color	96 mins
Cannon	WV: 03-06-85		NYT: 03-02-85	

DIR: Lance Hool. SW: Arthur Silver, Larry Levinson, Steve Bing. PRO: Menahem Golan, Yoram Globus. STARS: Chuck Norris, Steven Williams.

This time around, the film reveals what Norris went through as a POW in Vietnam and shows how he escaped, which set the stage for the first movie in the series.

Mister Roberts (1955) [SSS]

WWII	Navy	Full	Color	120 mins
WB	WV: 05-25-55		NYT: 07-15-55	

DIR: John Ford, Mervyn Le Roy. SW: Frank Nugent, Joshua Logan. PRO: Leland Haywood. STARS: Henry Fonda, James Cagney, William Powell, Jack Lemmon, Ward Bond.

Based on Thomas Heggen's novel and subsequent stage play, the film portrays life aboard a Navy cargo ship in the Pacific backwaters of WWII. The Navy had significant problems with the script and its portrayal of the captain's stupidity and tyrannies. The fact that Ford would be directing the film and Cagney would be portraying the captain tipped the balance in favor of providing a ship and material support. The high comedy ultimately overcame Cagney's negative character. Le Roy replaced a "sick" Ford during the shooting.

Mr. Winkle Goes to War (1944)

WWII	Army	Ltd	B&W	78 mins
Columbia	WV: 07-12-44		NYT: 08-03-44	

DIR: Alfred Green. SW: Waldo Salt, George Corey, Louis Solomon. PRO: Jack Moss. STARS: Edward G. Robinson, Ruth Warrick, Ted Donaldson, Bob Haymes.

The film tells the story of a 38-year-old draftee who becomes a hero in the South Pacific. The Army provided limited combat footage and helped stage a short battle sequence.

Monkey on My Back (1957)

WWII	Marines	NR	B&W	94 mins
UA	WV: 05-15-57		NYT: 05-30-57	

DIR: André DeToth. SW: Paul Dudley, Anthony Veiller, Crane Wilbur. PRO: Edward Small. STARS: Cameron Mitchell, Dianne Foster, Jack Albertson, Kathy Garver, Lisa Golm.

This docudrama is based on champion boxer Barney Ross's autobiography, *No Man Stands Alone*. Early in WWII Ross enlists in the Marines, and the film shows his experiences in Guadalcanal, including the heroics leading to the award of a Silver Star, malaria, his medical dependence on morphine, and his eventual addiction. No punches pulled.

The Monster That Challenged the Earth (1957)

SciFi	Navy	NR	B&W 83 mins
UA	WV: 05-22-57		NYT: DNR

DIR: Arnold Laven. SW: Pat Fielder. PRO: Jules Levy, Arthur Gardner. STARS: Tim Holt, Audrey Dalton, Hans Conried, Harlan Warde.

An earthquake in the California desert frees prehistoric monsters, who set out to feast on humans. Navy officers from a nearby research center help local police save the world one more time.

Moon Pilot (1962)

SciFi	Air Force	Ltd	Color 98 mins
Disney	WV: 01-17-62		NY: 04-06-62

DIR: James Neilson. SW: Maurice Tombragel. PRO: Walt Disney. STARS: Tom Tryon, Brian Keith, Edmond O'Brien, Dany Saval.

Disney had fun with the astronaut corps, as a chimpanzee becomes the first living creature to circle the moon. However, no human spaceman wants the honor of following the monkey, in direct contrast to the exploring mentality of real astronauts. In the end, a visiting alien falls in love with Tryon, who "volunteers" for the second orbital mission and accompanies him on his trip to the moon. The chimp had better lines than the humans.

Moran of the Marines (1928)

Peace	Marines	Ltd	B&W 63 mins
Paramount	WV: 10-17-28		NYT: 10-15-28

DIR: Frank Strayer. SW: Agnes Brand Leahy, Sam Mintz, Ray Harris, George Marion. PRO: Paramount. STARS: Richard Dix, Ruth Elder, Roscoe Karns, Brooks Benedict.

Dix, as Moran, a well-to-do young man with a bad attitude, is arrested for fighting, disinherited by his family, and jobless. What else can he do but enlist in the Corps? Soon he and his Marine unit are dispatched to 1920s China to try to keep peace. Moran rescues the commander's daughter from bandits, but he is captured. Fear not. The girl leads his buddies to rescue him and all ends well.

More American Graffiti (1979)

Vietnam	Marines	NR	Color 111 mins
Universal	WV: 07-25-79		NYT: 08-17-79

DIR: B. W. L. Norton. SW: B. W. L. Norton. PRO: Howard Kazanjian. STARS: Bo Hopkins, Ron Howard, Paul Le Mat, Candy Clark.

The ill-conceived sequel to the 1973 **American Graffiti**. The *New York Times* reviewer described the Vietnam sequences as "revoltingly flippant." Terry the Toad finds himself in a Marine helicopter unit with no respect for command.

The Mountain Road (1960)

WWII	Army	Full	B&W 102 mins
Columbia	WV: 03-23-60		NYT: 06-30-60

DIR: Daniel Mann. SW: Alfred Hayes. PRO: William Goetz. STARS: James Stewart, Lisa Lu, Glenn Corbett, Henry Morgan.

Based on Theodore White's novel, the film contains a small, slow Army story about an officer commanding a demolition team that blocks the path of the advancing Japanese in a remote part of China as the war is winding down.

The Mouse That Roared (1959)

Cold War	All	NR	Color 83 mins
Columbia	WV: 08-05-59		NYT: 10-27-59

DIR: Jack Arnold. SW: Roger MacDougall, Stanley Mann. PRO: Walter Shenson, Carl Foreman, Jon Penington. STARS: Peter Sellers, Leo McKern, Jean Seberg, David Kossoff.

A precursor to **Dr. Strangelove**, adopted from Leonard Wibberley's novel, the film satirizes nuclear weapons and the Cold War, with Sellers playing three roles, including the commander of the invading army of the world's smallest country, which declares war on the United States, hoping to lose and become wealthy. Instead, Sellers and his band of bow-and-arrow carrying warriors win by capturing a secret nuclear weapon, ultimately revealed to be a dud. The film portrays U.S. generals and the secretary of defense as ineffectual in trying to respond to the "attack" and the loss of the bomb.

Murder in the Air (1940)

Preparedness	Navy	Unkn	B&W 55 mins
WB	WV: 07-10-40:		NYT: 07-04-40

DIR: Lewis Seiler. SW: Raymond Schrock. PRO: Bryan Foy. STARS: Ronald Reagan, John Litel, James Stephenson, Eddie Foy Jr.

Secret Service agent Reagan foils an enemy plot to steal the Navy's super-secret "inertia projector" ray gun, which has the ability to incapacitate or destroy invaders. Edmund Morris, in **Dutch**, attributed President Reagan's idea for "Star Wars" to his role in the film. Others disagree with the thesis, but the movie did offer the possibility of a new generation of weapons that appeared during the war, including radar and the atomic bomb.

Murder in the Fleet (1935) [SSS]

Peace	Navy	Full	B&W 70 mins
MGM	WV: 06-05-35		NYT: 06-03-35

DIR: Edward Sedgwick. SW: Joseph Sherman, Frank Wead. PRO: Lucien Hubbard. STARS: Robert Taylor, Jean Parker, Ted Healy, Una Merkel.

This well-done murder melodrama takes place almost entirely aboard a U.S. Navy cruiser. The service allowed Sedgwick and his camera into every nook and cranny of the ship, which provided authenticity that benefited both the service and the filmmakers.

Mystery Submarine (1950)

Peace	Navy	Ltd	B&W 78 mins
Universal	WV: 11-22-50		NYT: 02-02-51

DIR: Douglas Sirk. SW: George W. George, George Slavin. PRO: Ralph Dietrich. STARS: Macdonald Carey, Märta Torén, Robert Douglas.

The Navy pursues a U-boat that has survived the war and is now in the service of an unidentified enemy country. The film contains a good depth-charging scene but little else.

The Naked and the Dead (1958)

WWII	Army	Full	Color 131 mins
WB	WV: 07-09-58		NYT: 08-07-58

DIR: Raoul Walsh. SW: Denis Sanders, Terry Sanders. PRO: Paul Gregory. STARS: Aldo Ray, Cliff Robertson, Raymond Massey, Richard Jaeckel, Joey Bishop.

Culled from Norman Mailer's best-selling novel, the film did not rise above the standard portrayal of men trying to survive in combat, this time on a Pacific island. However, using the skills he had developed in directing such war movies as *What Price Glory* and *Battle Cry*, Walsh did create battle scenes of terrifying authenticity, in this case with help from the Army. The service first negotiated script changes to abbreviate the anti-Semitism and misogynism found in Mailer's book.

Nam Angels (1989)

Vietnam	Army	NR	Color 93 mins
Concorde	WV: 07-19-89		NYT: DNR

DIR: Cirio H. Santiago. SW: Dan Gagliasso. PRO: Christopher R. Santiago. STARS: Brad Johnson, Vernon Wells, Kevin Duffis, Rick Dean.

The Hell's Angels come to the rescue of two soldiers held prisoner behind enemy lines. It seems only those bikers can help the young lieutenant recover his buddies.

Navy Blue and Gold (1937) [SSS]

Peace	Navy	Full	B&W 93 mins
MGM	WV: 11-17-37		NYT: 12-24-37

DIR: Sam Wood. SW: George Bruce. PRO: Sam Zimbalist. STARS: Robert Young, James Stewart, Florence Rice, Billie Burke, Lionel Barrymore, Tom Brown.

Another Annapolis film provides great images for recruitment of new plebes. Stewart enrolls in Annapolis under a false name because he is embarrassed to be the son of a disgraced man. This act almost causes his dismissal when discovered. The predictable football game provides a happy ending.

Navy Blues (1930)

Peace	Navy	NR	B&W 75 mins
MGM	WV: 01-15-30		NYT: 01-11-30

DIR: Clarence Brown. SW: J. C. Nugent, Elliott Nugent, W. L. River, Dale Van Every. PRO: Clarence Brown. STARS: William Haines, Anita Page, Karl Dane, J. C. Nugent.

The sailor wins a beautiful girl during a 24-hour leave in this early "talkie." Unfortunately, he is not the marrying kind.

Navy Blues (1937)

Peace	Navy	Full	B&W 68 mins
Republic	WV: 05-12-37		NYT: DNR

DIR: Ralph Staub. SW: Gordon Kahn, Eric Taylor. PRO: Burt Kelly. STARS: Dick Purcell, Mary Brian, Warren Hymer, Joseph Sawyer.

A convoluted story in which Purcell pursues librarian Brian falsely claiming to be first an aspiring Academy candidate and then a naval intelligence agent. The latter misrepresentation ensnares him and the girl in an investigation of an assassination attempt. Love wins, as usual.

Navy Blues (1941)

Peace	Navy	Full	B&W 108 mins
WB	WV: 08-10-41		NYT: 09-20-41

DIR: Lloyd Bacon. SW: Jerry Wald, Richard Macaulay, Arthur T. Horman, Sam Perrin. PRO: Jerry Wald, Jack Saper. STARS: Ann Sheridan, Jack Oakie, Martha Raye, Jack Haley.

A Navy musical set in Honolulu included U.S. destroyers in the background and scenes filmed aboard the USS *Cleveland*.

Navy Born (1936)

Peace	Navy	Full	B&W 70 mins
Republic	WV: 06-24-36		NYT: DNR

DIR: Nate Watt. SW: Albert DeMond, Olive Cooper, Marcus Goodrich, Claire Church, Mildred Cram. PRO: Nat Levine. STARS: William Gargan, Claire Dodd, Douglas Fowley, George Irving.

A Naval aviator fights a baby's aunt for the right to raise a deceased pal's son. With the help of his flier pals, he rescues the child (who is mistakenly seized by a mobster), marries the aunt, and raises a Navy brat.

Navy Bound (1951)

Peace	Navy	Full	B&W 60 mins
Monogram	WV: 02-21-51		NYT: DNR

DIR: Paul Landres. SW: Sam Roeca. PRO: William F. Broidy. STARS: Tom Neal, Wendy Waldron, Regis Toomey, John Abbott.

From Talbert Josselyn's *Collier's Magazine* short story. A fleet boxing champion leaves the Navy to help save his family's fishing boat. To raise needed money, he fights a pro challenger, gets the money, and reenlists.

The Navy Comes Through (1942) [SSS]

WWII	Navy	Full	B&W 81 mins
RKO	WV: 10-14-42		NYT: 11-12-42

DIR: A. Edward Sutherland. SW: Roy Chanslor, Aeneas MacKenzie, Earl Baldwin, John Twist. PRO: Islin Auster. STARS: Pat O'Brien, George Murphy, Jane Wyatt, Jackie Cooper, Max Baer.

The film portrays the Navy protecting Merchant Marine ships, in this case utilizing a captured German submarine tender, which the sailors turn into a Q-boat. Rather than waste a torpedo on an apparently helpless ship, the submarine surfaces to use its deck gun to sink the small craft. Instead, the Q-boat opens fire with its hidden guns and destroys the German U-boat. Newsreel footage creates the battle scenes. The Navy provided brief images of its ships for the prologue.

Navy SEALS (1990) [G&G]

Peace	Navy	Ltd	Color 113 mins
Orion	WV: 07-18-90		NYT: 07-20-90

DIR: Lewis Teague. SW: Chuck Pfarrer, Gary Goldman. PRO: Brenda Feigen, Bernard Williams. STARS: Charlie Sheen, Michael Biehn, Joanne Whalley-Kilmer.

With some reluctance, the SEALS emerged from behind their veil of secrecy and revealed some of their modus vivendi. Exterior location filming at the Norfolk, Virginia Naval Base and a script and technical assistance from ex-SEAL Pfarrer provided some insights and authenticity in this action picture, which included scenes of SEAL training. Naturally, the SEALS use their acquired skills against Arab terrorists to rescue prisoners and destroy arsenals.

Navy Secrets (1939)

Peace	Navy	Full	B&W 60 mins
Monogram	WV: 03-22-39		NYT: DNR

DIR: Howard Bretherton. SW: Harvey Gates. PRO: William Lackey. STARS: Fay Wray, Grant Withers, William von Brincken.

This "C" movie follows two Naval investigators to track down the stealing of Navy secrets by an unidentified foreign power.

Navy Spy (1937)

Peace	Navy	Ltd	B&W 56 mins
Grand National	WV: 03-24-37		NYT: 03-22-37

DIR: Crane Wilbur. SW: Crane Wilbur. PRO: George Hirliman. STARS: Conrad Nagel, Eleanor Hunt, Judith Allen, Howard Lang.

A small-scale melodrama set within the Navy. Shots of battleships off San Pedro gave a sense of authenticity. The *AFI Catalogue* stated that the film was the second in the George Hirliman/Grand National Federal Agent series.

The Navy Way (1944)

WWII	Navy	Full	B&W 74 mins
Paramount	WV: 03-01-44		NYT: DNR

DIR: William Berke. SW: Maxwell Shane. PRO: William Pine, William Thomas. STARS: Robert Lowery, Jean Parker, Bill Henry, Roscoe Karns.

To highlight naval training, Berke received full cooperation in filming most of the exterior shots at the Great Lakes Naval Training Center in Illinois. Lowery plays a boxer who resents being inducted just as he was to fight the champion. Nevertheless, he becomes an exemplary graduate from the Training Center and heads off to sea on a new ship.

Navy Wife (1936)

Peace	Navy	Ltd	B&W 72 mins
Fox	WV: 01-08-36		NYT: DNR

DIR: Allan Dwan. SW: Sonya Levien, Edward T. Lowe. PRO: Sol M. Wurtzel. STARS: Claire Trevor, Ralph Bellamy, Warren Hymer.

Based on Kathleen Norris's novel *Beauty's Daughter*, the film explores the marriage of Navy doctor Bellamy, a widower, and Navy nurse Trevor. In addition to the problems inherent in a service relationship, Trevor must share her new husband with his handicapped daughter.

Navy Wife (1956)

Peace	Navy	NR	B&W 83 mins
Allied Artists	WV: 06-13-56		NYT: DNR

DIR: Edward Bernds. SW: Kay Lenard. PRO: Walter Wanger. STARS: Joan Bennett, Gary Merrill, Judy Nugent, Maurice Manson.

On the screen, Tate Blain's novel *Mother Sir* became a bland story of how the wife of a Navy officer stationed in a Japanese village influenced the local women to demand the same freedom as their American counterparts during the occupation.

The Net (1995)

Peace	Air Force	Cour	Color 112 mins
Columbia	WV: 07-24-95		NYT: 07-28-95

DIR: Irwin Winkler. SW: John Brancato, Michael Ferris. PRO: Irwin Winkler, Rob Cowan. STARS: Sandra Bullock, Jeremy Northam, Dennis Miller, Diane Baker, Ken Howard.

Bullock plays a computer nerd who receives mysterious and possibly deadly information. The studio requested one day's filming at a missile launch facility at Vandenberg Air Force Base. Although not a military story, the Air Force thought the sequence was innoculous and offered a brief reminder that the Air Force was in the missile-launching business.

Never Say Never Again (1983)

Cold War	Navy	Deny	Color 137 mins
WB	WV: 10-05-83		NYT: 10-07 & 16-83

DIR: Irvin Kershner. SW: Lorenzo Semple Jr. PRO: Jack Swartzman. STARS: Sean Connery, Klaus Maria Brandauer, Max Von Sydow, Kim Basinger, Edward Fox, Alec McCowen, Barbara Carrera, Bernie Casey.

This remake of **Thunderball** was the only James Bond film on which the Pentagon refused to assist. The studio wanted stock footage and an undersea shot of a nuclear submarine, which it would film. However, the script depicted a drug-addicted U.S. Air Force officer and other negative military images as well as negative portrayals of the British military. As a result, the Navy denied help for the story of a tycoon arcade game collector who intends to use two nuclear-tipped Tomahawk missiles to manipulate and control the world.

Never So Few (1959)

WWII	Army	NR	Color 126 mins
MGM	WV: 12-09-59		NYT: 01-22-60

DIR: John Sturges. SW: Millard Kaufman. PRO: Edmund Grainger. STARS: Frank Sinatra, Gina Lollobrigida, Peter Lawford.

Based on Tom Chamales's book. Sinatra leads a U.S./British/native Kachin force that strays into China and wipes out some of Chiang Kai-Shek's troops in retaliation for earlier losses.

Never Wave at a WAC (1952)

Peace	Army	Full	B&W 87 mins
RKO	WV: 12-17-52		NYT: 04-24-53

DIR: Norman Z. McLeod. SW: Ken Englund. PRO: Frederick Brisson, Gordon Griffith. STARS: Rosalind Russell, Paul Douglas, Marie Wilson.

General Omar Bradley appears as himself in one scene in this film set at Ft. Lee, Virginia, the Women's Army Corps (WAC) training camp.

The New World (Le Nouveau Monde) (1995)

Cold War	Army	Deny	Color	127 mins
Bar Films	WV: 03-06-95		NYT: DNR	

DIR: Alain Corneau. SW: Alain Corneau, Pascal Quignard. PRO: Jean-Louis Livi. STARS: Nicolas Chatel, Alicia Silverstone, James Gandolfini.

Based on Pascal Quignard's novel, *L'Occupation a Americaine*, the movie explores what the French call U.S. "occupation" of their country in the 1950s because of American impact on their culture and life. The filmmakers requested that the U.S. Army provide a military band to show the influence of jazz-playing soldiers. The service refused, saying that the film would portray soldiers smoking marijuana and drinking heavily, with no GI shown in a "particularly positive" light.

The Next Karate Kid (1994)

Peace	Army	Ltd	Color	104 mins
Columbia	WV: 08-22-94		NYT: 09-10-94	

DIR: Christopher Cain. SW: Mark Lee. PRO: Jerry Weintraub. STARS: Noriyuki (Pat) Morita, Hilary Swank, Michael Ironside.

The Army approved filming of a cinematic military awards ceremony at Fort Myer because of a positive portrayal of the military in the short opening scene.

Night People (1954)

Cold War	Army	NR	Color	93 mins
Fox	WV: 03-17-54		NYT: 03-13-54	

DIR: Nunnally Johnson. SW: Nunnally Johnson. PRO: Nunnally Johnson. STARS: Gregory Peck, Broderick Crawford, Rita Gam, Buddy Ebsen, Walter Abel.

From an original story by Jedd Harris and Thomas Reed, the film provides a lively piece of Cold War espionage set in Berlin. Peck plays an Army counterintelligence colonel, who spars with his Russian counterpart over the return of a kidnapped GI son of an American manufacturer.

Night Wars (1988)

Vietnam	Army	NR	Color	90 mins
WB	WV: 09-28-88		NYT: DNR	

DIR: David Prior. SW: David Prior. PRO: Fritz Matthews. STARS: Dan Haggerty, Brian O'Connor, Chet Hood, Steve Horton, Cameron Smith.

Two veterans have "realistic" nightmares about their wartime experiences which produce real wounds. Ultimately, they return to Vietnam in their sleep, rescue their buddy, kill an American turncoat who had tortured them as POWs, and rejoin the real world and normality.

1941 (1979)

WWII	Army	NR	Color	118 mins
Universal	WV: 12-19-79		NYT: 12-14-79	

DIR: Steven Spielberg. SW: Robert Zemeckis, Bob Gale. PRO: Buzz Feitshans. STARS: Dan Aykroyd, Ned Beatty, John Belushi, Treat Williams, Robert Stack, Toshirô Mifune, Slim Pickens, John Candy.

The comedy spoofs the consequences that the Pearl Harbor bombing had on Hollywood. The film has some funny vignettes, but even the 26 minutes added for network television did little to improve the whole. Not be confused with that other bomb, *Pearl Harbor*.

The Ninth Configuration (1980)

Peace	Army	NR	Color	105 mins
WB	WV: 02-06-80		NYT: 08-08-80	

DIR: William Peter Blatty. SW: William Peter Blatty. PRO: William Peter Blatty. STARS: Stacy Keach, Scott Wilson, Jason Miller, Ed Flanders.

Based on Blatty's novel *Twinkle, Twinkle Killer Kane.* He assumed all the responsibility for this production, best described as *One Flew Over the Cuckoo's Nest* meets *Catch-22*. Set in a military insane asylum somewhere in the United States, although it used a European castle for exterior scenes. Keach, the institution's new psychiatrist, is more disturbed than his patients.

No Man Is an Island (1962)

WWII	Navy	Full	Color	114 mins
Universal	WV: 08-08-62		NYT: 10-11-62	

DIR: John Monks Jr., Richard Goldstone. SW: John Monks Jr., Richard Goldstone. PRO: John Monks Jr., Richard Goldstone. STARS: Jeffrey Hunter, Barbara Perez, Marshall Thompson, Ronald Remy.

Filmed in the Philippines, the story of George Tweed reveals how he heroically signaled U.S. Navy ships from his hilltop hideout on Guam for over a year during the Japanese occupation. The production became significant for the Pentagon's cooperation policy, which was then under heavy scrutiny, because an off-duty sailor died as a result of an explosion aboard one of the Navy ships taking part in the filming.

No Man's Land (1918)

WWI	Navy	Ltd	B&W	5 reels
MGM	WV: 07-19-18		NYT: DNR	

DIR: Will Davis. SW: Bert Lytell; Albert Le Vino. PRO: MGM. STARS: Bert Lytell, Anna Nilsson, Charles Arling, Mollie McConnell.

Based on Joseph V. Louis's novel of the same name, the film portrays a German spy who frames Lytell, marries his girl, and retreats to a small island, from which he sinks Allied ships. In the end, Lytell is exonerated and, with the help of a Navy ship, kills the spy and rescues the girl. The story obviously provided an anti-German propaganda message to help the U.S. war effort.

No Time for Sergeants (1958)

Peace	Air Force	Unkn	B&W	111 mins
WB	WV: 05-07-58		NYT: 05-30-58	

DIR: Mervyn LeRoy. SW: John Lee Mahin. PRO: Mervyn LeRoy, Alex Segal. STARS: Andy Griffith, Myron McCormick, Nick Adams, Murray Hamilton, Howard Smith, Don Knotts.

A novel, a teleplay, a Broadway play, then this movie featuring Griffith as an enlisted man in the Air Force. Full of generic gags, the script could have taken place in any of the services.

No Way Out (1987) [G&G]

Cold War	Navy	NR	Color	116 mins
Universal	WV: 08-12-87		NYT: 08-14-87	

DIR: Roger Donaldson. SW: Robert Garland. PRO: Mace Neufeld, Laura Ziskin, Robert Garland. STARS: Kevin Costner, Gene Hackman, Sean Young, Will Patton, Iman, Fred Dalton Thompson.

In this remake of *The Big Clock,* based on Kenneth Fearing's novel, Costner, a decorated Navy officer, receives orders to investigate the murder of a young woman, his new lover, but also the mistress of the secretary of defense, who had killed her in a fit of jealousy. Worse, Costner turns out to be a Soviet deep mole. Although the producers did not request military assistance for obvious reasons, they did receive permission from the General Services Administration to film on the Pentagon's then public main concourse. However, while shooting there after hours, the director talked his way past the security guards and also shot a scene on the innermost "A" Ring, at the NATO corridor. This added an authentic ambience to the film, but the duplicity angered DoD officials. Nevertheless, this did not affect the Navy's decision to provide full cooperation to Neufeld's 1990 *The Hunt for Red October*.

Nobody's Perfect (1968)

Peace	Navy	Ltd	Color	103 mins
Universal	WV: 01-10-68		NYT: 04-04-68	

DIR: Alan Rafkin. SW: John D. F. Black. PRO: Howard Christie. STARS: Doug McClure, Nancy Kwan, James Whitmore, David Hartman, Gary Vinson, James Shigeta.

A Navy comedy set aboard a U.S. submarine rescue vessel and in Japan.

None But the Brave (1965)

WWII	Marines	Ltd	Color	105 mins
WB	WV: 02-10-65		NYT: 02-25-65	

DIR: Frank Sinatra. SW: John Twist, Katsuya Susaki. PRO: Frank Sinatra, Kikumaru Okuda. STARS: Frank Sinatra, Clint Walker, Tommy Sands.

A Marine plane crashes on a small Japanese-held island forgotten by the war. The two sides arrange a truce because there seems to be no hope of rescue. However, when an American destroyer arrives on the scene, the enemies renew the war, with only five Leathernecks surviving.

Not with My Wife, You Don't (1966)

Peace	Air Force	Ltd	Color	118 mins
WB	WV: 09-21-66		NYT: 11-03-66	

DIR: Norman Panama. SW: Norman Panama, Larry Gelbart, Peter Barnes. PRO: Norman Panama. STARS: Tony Curtis, Virna Lisi, George C. Scott, Carroll O'Connor, Richard Eastham, Eddie Ryder.

An aimless, silly romantic comedy in which two Korean War Air Force buddies, Curtis and Scott, now peacetime colonels on assignment in Europe, compete for the affection of Lisi, Curtis's bored wife.

The Notebook (2004)

WWII	Army	NR	Color	124 mins
New Line	WV: 05-18-04		NYT: 06-25-04	

DIR: Nick Cassavetes. SW: Jeremy Leven, Jan Sardi. PRO: Mark Johnson, Lynn Harris. STARS: Ryan Gosling, Rachel McAdams, James Garner, Gena Rowlands, Sam Shepard.

Based on Nicholas Sparks's novel, the film is an old-fashioned love story spanning six decades and includes brief sequences in an Army induction center in North Africa, in the Battle of the Bulge, and an Army hospital.

Nowhere to Hide (1987)

Peace	Marines	NR	Color	90 mins
New Century	WV: 09-09-87		NYT: DNR	

DIR: Mario Azzopardi. SW: Alex Rebar, George Goldsmith. PRO: Andras Hamori, Julie Corman. STARS: Amy Madigan, Daniel Hugh Kelly, Robin MacEachern, John Colicos.

Marine officer Kelly discovers that defective parts have been used in the new helicopters his unit has just received, but before he can go public, a corrupt general arranges his death. Then the general and his hooligans begin chasing Kelly's wife, who is also a Marine, and her son, in whose toy is hidden the incriminating documents. Neither the Marine base nor the story as a whole has any reality.

The Nun and the Sergeant (1962)

Korea	Marines	NR	B&W 73 mins
UA	WV: 07-11-62		NYT: DNR

DIR: Franklin Adreon. SW: Don Cerveris. PRO: Eugene Frenke. STARS: Robert Webber, Anna Sten, Leo Gordon, Hari Rhodes.

A *Dirty Dozen*-like story set in Korea, where Marines in the brig are recruited for a dangerous demolition mission. They are hampered by having to take along a nun and several Korean schoolgirls.

Objective, Burma! (1945)

WWII	Army	Ltd	B&W 142 mins
WB	WV: 01-31-45		NYT: 01-27-45

DIR: Raoul Walsh. SW: Ranald MacDougall, Lester Cole. PRO: Jerry Wald. STARS: Errol Flynn, William Prince, James Brown, George Tobias.

Flynn leads American paratroopers into Burma to destroy an important Japanese base. The problem is that the United States did not have troops in Burma at that time, and this film angered the British forces that fought there.

Off Limits (1953)

Peace	Army	Full	B&W 87 mins
Paramount	WV: 02-04-53		NYT: 03-30-53

DIR: George Marshall. SW: Hal Kanter, Jack Sher. PRO: Harry Tugend. STARS: Bob Hope, Mickey Rooney, Marilyn Maxwell, Eddie Mayehoff.

Boxing manager/trainer Hope enlists when his best fighter is drafted. The fighter returns to civilian life after the Army finds him unfit, and Hope tries desperately to join him. Meanwhile draftee Rooney gets Hope to coach him, and mayhem ensues.

An Officer and a Gentleman (1982) [G&G]

Peace	Navy, Marines	Deny/Ltd	Color 126 mins
Paramount	WV: 07-21-82		NYT: 07-28-82, 08-08-82

DIR: Taylor Hackford. SW: Douglas Day Stewart. PRO: Martin Elfand. STARS: Richard Gere, Debra Winger, Louis Gossett Jr., David Keith, Robert Loggia.

The Navy refused to cooperate because of the four-letter words, a washed-out naval aviation cadet who commits suicide, and steamy sex. However, the Marines provided a drill instructor as a technical advisor to Louis Gossett Jr. and off-duty Marines to serve as extras. This coming-of-age story of motorcycle-riding Gere and factory worker Winger resembled the cinematic Navy romances of the 1930s. Gossett Jr. received an Oscar for his consummate portrayal of a Marine D.I.

Okinawa (1952)

WWII	Navy	Full	B&W 67 mins
Columbia	WV: 02-27-52		NYT: 04-24-52

DIR: Leigh Jason. SW: Jameson Brewer, Arthur Ross. PRO: Wallace MacDonald. STARS: Pat O'Brien, Cameron Mitchell, Richard Denning.

This "B" film used combat footage to tell a stock story of life aboard a destroyer during the fight for the island. The crew included the typical sailors: the gruff old lifer, the homesick kid, the hard-talking but actually good-hearted guy, etc. Only the combat footage makes viewing bearable.

On an Island with You (1948)

Peace	Navy	NR	Color 107 mins
MGM	WV: 04-28-48		NYT: 07-30-48

DIR: Richard Thorpe. SW: Dorothy Kingsley, Charles Martin, Hans Wilhelm, Dorothy Cooper. PRO: Joseph Pasternak. STARS: Esther Williams, Peter Lawford, Ricardo Montalban, Jimmy Durante.

Lawford plays a Navy technical advisor assigned to work on a song, dance, and swim musical. This may well be the only film to show how the military worked on a Hollywood movie or at least how the industry perceived how the services provided assistance.

On the Beach (1959) [G&G]

Cold War	Navy	Cour	B&W 134 mins
UA	WV: 12-02-59		NYT: 12-18-59

DIR: Stanley Kramer. SW: John Paxton. PRO: Stanley Kramer. STARS: Gregory Peck, Ava Gardner, Fred Astaire, Anthony Perkins.

Based on Neville Shute's novel. Kramer created a nuclear nightmare in which a deadly radiation cloud is inexorably approaching Australia from an unexplained war fought somewhere in the Northern Hemisphere. Submarine captain Peck takes his ship from Australia to the West Coast of the United States seeking the source of a mysterious radio signal that was reaching Australia but finds only death, the fate that will soon arrive down under. Still, the director seemed to want it both ways, because the film ends with a Salvation Army banner waving in the breeze with the message "It is not too late . . . Brother." In any case, the film's warning about the threat of a nuclear holocaust was the first of several similar antibomb cinematic portrayals, including **Dr. Strangelove** and **Fail Safe**.

The Navy gave Kramer a ride aboard a nuclear sub and gave his art department limited access to the submarine to obtain information on building the sets. As always, the Pentagon had great problems with any story suggesting an accidental nuclear war might occur. Nevertheless, the service ultimately and with great reluctance agreed to route a nuclear submarine to Australia for exterior shots of the ship docked, on the surface, and submerging. When it did not arrive on time, Kramer used an Australian sub.

On the Double (1961)

WWII	Army	Cour	Color	92 mins
Paramount	WV: 05-17-61		NYT: 05-20-61	

DIR: Melville Shavelson. SW: Jack Rose, Melville Shavelson. PRO: Jack Rose. STARS: Danny Kaye, Dana Wynter, Wilfred Hyde-White.

Filmed in London. Kaye, an American PFC, happens to be an exact double for a British general, who is key to planning the upcoming invasion. To protect the general, they switch identities.

On the Threshold of Space (1956)

Cold War	Air Force	Full	Color	98 mins
Fox	WV: 03-07-56		NYT: 03-30-56	

DIR: Robert Webb. SW: Shimon Wincelberg, Francis Cockrell. PRO: William Bloom. STARS: Guy Madison, Virginia Leith, John Hodiak, Dean Jagger.

The Air Force provided assistance to portray the service's testing of new equipment and technology of supersonic flight. The film showed men riding rocket sleds, ballooning to the edge of space, and parachuting from great heights.

On the Town (1949)

Peace	Navy	Ltd	Color	98 mins
MGM	WV: 12-07-49		NYT: 12-09-49	

DIR: Stanley Donen, Gene Kelly. SW: Adolph Green, Betty Comden. PRO: Arthur Freed. STARS: Gene Kelly, Frank Sinatra, Jules Munshin, Betty Garrett, Ann Miller.

Based on the Green and Comden play. Three sailors, Kelly, Sinatra, and Munshin, spend a wild 24 hours in New York. Their spree begins and ends in the Brooklyn Navy Yard, with permission from the service to film their departure from and their later return to their ship.

Once Before I Die (1965)

WWII	Army	NR	Color	97 mins
WB	WV: DNR		NYT: DNR	

DIR: John Derek. SW: Anthony March, Vance Skarstedt. PRO: John Derek. STARS: John Derek, Ursula Andress, Richard Jaeckel.

American soldiers and their families, caught in the countryside when the Japanese attack the Philippines on December 8, return to Manila. During the trip, a young soldier confides to Andress, his officer's fiancée, that he wants to lose his virginity before he dies. Guess what happens.

One Minute to Zero (1952) [G&G]

Korea	Army	Full	B&W	105 mins
RKO	WV: 07-16-52		NYT: 09-20-52	

DIR: Tay Garnett. SW: Milton Krims, William Wister Haines. PRO: Edmund Grainger. STARS: Robert Mitchum, Ann Blyth, William Talman.

This is a rare instance in which the armed services solicited Hollywood to make a movie. In this case, the Air Force and Army asked Howard Hughes to portray the close air support that fliers were providing to ground forces in the early months of the Korean War. Garnett shot his story at Camp Carson in Colorado, but despite its origins within the Pentagon, the Army refused to approve the completed film because of the climactic scene. In it, Mitchum orders his artillery to fire on a line of refugees infiltrated with North Korean soldiers. Once Hughes ascertained from his Pentagon contacts that the military would not rescind his government contracts, the studio head released the film with the scene intact, making it one of the very few movies that received full cooperation but not DoD approval.

Onionhead (1958)

WWII	Coast Guard	Full	B&W 110 mins
WB	WV: 09-24-58		NYT: 10-02-58

DIR: Norman Taurog. SW: Nelson Gidding. PRO: Jules Schermer. STARS: Andy Griffith, Felicia Farr, Walter Matthau, Erin O'Brien, Joe Mantell, Joey Bishop.

Based on Weldon Hill's novel, in what amounts to a more serious sequel to *No Time for Sergeants*, Griffith flips a coin and joins the Coast Guard because he is getting nowhere in college or with women. Once in the service, he becomes a lowly shipboard cook. But he also experiences the drama of combat against a German sub, comedy, and romance. Perhaps the film tried to touch too many bases, but Griffith manages some good humor even when facing serious combat.

Operation Bikini (1963)

WWII	Navy	NR	B&W/Color 84 mins
Amer-Intl	WV: 04-10-63		NYT: DNR

DIR: Anthony Carras. SW: John Tomerlin. PRO: James Nicholson, Lou Rusoff. STARS: Tab Hunter, Frankie Avalon, Scott Brady, Jim Backus, Gary Crosby, Michael Dante, Jody McCrea, Eva Six.

As might be expected, American-International advertised the film with shots of buxom girls in bikinis. In fact, the Bikini of the title is the Pacific island, which provided the location for the action in this portrayal of an underwater demolition team at work. In this instance, the unit must explode a sunken U.S. submarine to thwart the Japanese from recovering still-secret radar equipment. In addition to action at sea, the UDT lands on the Japanese-infested island, where the expected guerrilla support turns out to be an old man, a teenager, and those buxom women in bikinis.

Operation Bottleneck (1961)

WWII	Army	NR	B&W 77 mins
UA	WV: DNR		NYT: DNR

DIR: Edward Cahn. SW: Orville Hampton. PRO: Robert Kent. STARS: Ron Foster, Miiko Taka, Norman Alden, John Clarke, Ben Wright.

A paratrooper unit attempts to rescue an injured comrade whom the Japanese have captured during an American mission into Burma.

Operation C.I.A. (1965)

Vietnam	Army, Marines	NR	B&W 90 mins
Allied Artists	WV: DNR		NYT: DNR

DIR: Christian Nyby. SW: Bill Ballinger, Peer Oppenheimer. PRO: Peer Oppenheimer. STARS: Bill Catching, Burt Reynolds, Danielle Aubry, Cyril Collick, Vic Diaz, John Hoyt, Kieu Chinh.

A CIA espionage, action-adventure story set in Saigon, with the Communists as really bad guys. The U.S. military is visible, but still only in the background, as would have been the case in the early 1960s.

Operation Dames (1959)

Korea	Army	NR	B&W 74 mins
Amer-Intl	WV: 03-04-59		NYT: DNR

DIR: Louis Clyde Stoumen. SW: Ed Lakso. PRO: Stanley Kallis. STARS: Alice Allyn, Chuck Henderson, Don Devlin, Ed Craig.

Story follows voluptuous (this is American-International, after all) members of a USO troop caught behind enemy lines in Korea.

Operation Delta Force (1997)

Terrorism	Army	NR	Color 93 mins
Nu World	WV: DNR		NYT: DNR

DIR: Sam Firstenberg. SW: David Sparling. PRO: Danny Lerner. STARS: Jeff Fahey, Ernie Hudson, Rob Stewart, Frank Zagarino.

Along with the **Delta Force Commando** films, this is the first of yet another series that capitalized on the Chuck Norris (and family) **Delta Force** films. In this film, the Army's Special Operations Delta Force tracks down terrorists who have seized a deadly virus. This was followed by a made for television movie, **Operation Delta Force II: Mayday** (1998) and three more sequels.

Operation Delta Force 3: Clear Target (1998)

Terrorism	Army, Navy	NR	Color 94 mins
NU World	WV: DNR		NYT: DNR

DIR: Mark Roper. SW: David Sparling. PRO: Danny Lerner. STARS: Jim Fitzpatrick, Bryan Genesse, Kevin Scannell, Greg Collins.

The Delta Force is sent to rescue a nuclear sub, this time hijacked by a drug kingpin, who threatens to launch mustard gas–tipped rockets.

Operation Delta Force 4: Deep Fault (2001)

Balkans	Army	NR	Color 96 mins
Nu Image	WV: DNR		NYT: DNR

DIR: Mark Roper. SW: David Sparling. PRO: Danny Lerner, David Varod. STARS: Greg Collins, Joe Lara, Hayley DuMond.

The Delta Force is sent to rescue seismologists who have witnessed Serbian atrocities; the government fears the Serbs will capture and execute them.

Operation Delta Force 5: Random Fire (1999)

Terrorism	Army	NR	Color 91 mins
Nu Image	WV: DNR		NYT: DNR

DIR: Yossi Wein. SW: Bernard Stone. PRO: Danny Lerner, Brigid Olen. STARS: Todd Jensen, Trae Thomas, Anthony Bishop, Tony Caprari.

The Delta Force is sent to stop terrorists who are turning hostages, including members of the team, into human bombs for sale to the highest bidders.

Operation Dumbo Drop (1995)

Vietnam	Army	NR	Color 107 mins
Buena Vista	WV: 07-31-95		NYT: 07-28-95

DIR: Simon Wincer. SW: Gene Quintano, Jim Kouf. PRO: Diane Nabatoff, David Madden. STARS: Danny Glover, Ray Liotta, Denis Leary.

In the middle of the war, a new captain arrives in a strategic Vietnamese village and immediately faces the problem of replacing the villagers' elephant. As a Disney Company family release, the film lacked realism, not the least of which was the soldiers' lack of four-letter words. Because the movie was filmed in Thailand, the DoD lost the opportunity to provide assistance on a positive portrayal of the Army during the Vietnam War.

Operation Haylift (1950)

Peace	Air Force	Full	B&W 73 mins
Lippert	WV: 04-19-50		NYT: DNR

DIR: William Berke. SW: Dean Riesner, Joe Sawyer. PRO: Joe Sawyer. STARS: Bill Williams, Tom Brown, Ann Rutherford, Jane Nigh.

Filmed at Ely, Nevada, the second half of this film is practically a documentary of how the U.S. Air Force helped ranchers feed their stock during the blizzards of 1949. The service provided its flying boxcars to help create an authentic atmosphere.

Operation Mad Ball (1957)

Peace	Army	Ltd	Color 105 mins
Columbia	WV: 09-04-57		NYT: 11-21-57

DIR: Richard Quine. SW: Arthur Carter, Jed Harris, Blake Edwards. PRO: Jed Harris. STARS: Ernie Kovacs, Jack Lemmon, Kathryn Grant, Mickey Rooney.

Based on Arthur Carter's play, this military comedy is set in Normandy at the end of WWII. There, GIs demonstrate their ingenuity in having a good time, showing once again that life in the Army can be exhilarating without the violence of combat.

Operation 'Nam (1985) a.k.a. *Cobra Mission*

Vietnam	Army	NR	Color 85 mins
Fulvia	WV: DNR		NYT: DNR

DIR: Larry Ludman (Fabrizio De Angelis). SW: Fabrizio De Angelis, Gianfranco Clerici, Vincenzo Mannino. PRO: Farbrizio De Angelis, Erwin Dietrich. STARS: Oliver Tobias, Christopher Connelly, Manfred Lehmann, John Steiner.

An Italian-made Vietnam story with no authenticity of dress, visuals (shot in Rome), or insight into the American experience in country. Four vets return to Vietnam 10 years after the war to rescue proverbial POWs, in this case being held with full knowledge and complicity of the United States. For the most part, the film serves simply as a vehicle for putting violence on the screen.

Operation Pacific (1951) [SSS]

WWII	Navy	Full	B&W 111 mins
WB	WV: 01-10-51		NYT: 02-08-51

DIR: George Waggner. SW: George Waggner. PRO: Louis Edelman. STARS: John Wayne, Patricia Neal, Ward Bond.

This was the first post-WWII submarine movie, although the Navy was not happy that it featured the service's efforts to solve the problem it had with defective torpedoes during the first year of the war. Wayne and his men fix the problem, rescue a nun and children, and help to win the war.

Operation Petticoat (1959)

WWII	Navy, Army	Full	B&W 124 mins
Columbia	WV: 09-30-59		NYT: 12-04-59

DIR: Blake Edwards. SW: Stanley Shapiro, Maurice Richlin. PRO: Robert Arthur. STARS: Cary Grant, Tony Curtis, Arthur O'Connell, Joan O'Brien, Dina Merrill.

Although set in the chaos of the Philippines after the December 1941 Japanese attack, the filmmakers managed to create a comedy based on seemingly improbable but actual events. The USS *Seadragon* did sail from the combat zone with a pinkish hue because it had been undergoing repairs and its paint job was not completed when the war started. Several submarines did evacuate Americans, including nurses, from Corregidor before the island fell on May 6, 1942. In the movie, Grant captains a pink submarine with a contingent of shapely nurses, which provided the opportunity for sight gags and double entendres, within the limits of the still existing Code Office. All ended well, with Grant and Curtis, his executive officer, marrying two of the nurses.

The Navy liked the project and acknowledged that the script contained incidents described in its *U.S. Submarine Operations in World War II*. However, the service said the studio should find a WWII submariner to help correct technical inaccuracies. On the other hand, the Army had problems with the appearance of its nurses in a "slapstick" comedy, saying, "Such a portrayal of serious professional women . . . would not be taken lightly by these women, their friends, and families." Ultimately, the producer submitted a script that satisfied both services, and the Navy even allowed the filmmakers to paint the USS *Balao* pink during shooting. Arthur admitted, "We blushed when we asked for it and almost fainted when the Navy said okay." In the end, the opportunity to portray a lighter side of life aboard a submarine, even in wartime, undoubtedly benefited the service.

Operation War Zone (1990)

Vietnam	Army	NR	Color	86 mins
Action Intl	WV: DNR		NYT: DNR	

DIR: David Prior. SW: David Prior, Ted Prior. PRO: Fritz Matthews. STARS: Joe Spinell, Fritz Matthews, William Zipp, John Cianetti.

A corrupt Army general is selling armaments to North Vietnam, both for profit and to keep the war going, because if the United States wins, the Pentagon budget will shrink. Americans on both sides of the "plan" fight each other as well as the Vietnamese in what is probably the worst war film about Vietnam and perhaps about any war.

Opposing Force (1986)

Peace	Air Force	NR	Color	100 mins
Orion	WV: DNR		NYT: DNR	

DIR: Eric Karson. SW: L. J. Cowgill. PRO: Daniel Berk, Tamar Glaser. STARS: Tom Skerritt, Lisa Eichhorn, Anthony Zerbe, Richard Roundtree.

A group of soldiers and Air Force pilot Eichhorn volunteer for an escape and evasion course in the Philippines. The commandant has no use for women in the military, and when the class parachutes onto a remote island, he has Eichhorn raped, after which the training becomes real as the trainees try to reach safety.

Ordinary Heroes (1986)

Vietnam	Army	NR	Color	95 mins
Juniper Releasing	WV: DNR		NYT: DNR	

DIR: Peter Cooper. SW: Unkn. PRO: Unkn. STARS: Richard Dean Anderson, Richard Baxter, Valerie Bertinelli, Dixie Jones.

A blinded soldier has a difficult time adjusting to his injury, despite help from a girl. A historically inaccurate scene set in Vietnam shows the Fifth Mechanized Infantry Brigade fighting in 1973, two years after the unit returned to the United States. However, the film does contain a positive view of veterans, a rarity in stories set in the aftermath of the Vietnam War.

Out of the Depths (1946)

WWII	Navy	NR	B&W 61 mins
Columbia	WV: 03-20-46		NYT: DNR

DIR: D. Ross Lederman. SW: Martin Berkeley, Ted Thomas. PRO: Wallace MacDonald. STARS: Ross Hunter, Jim Bannon, Ken Curtis.

A U.S. submarine in the Sea of Japan picks up an intelligence officer and learns that Japan is defeated. The officer also has information that will prevent the bombing of the USS *Missouri* during the surrender ceremony. As the torpedo-deficient sub speeds to Japan, it encounters a maverick suicide-carrier. The captain prepares to ram the carrier to prevent it from disrupting the surrender. Pure fantasy.

Outbreak (1995)

Peace	Army	Deny	Color 127 mins
WB	WV: 03-13-95		NYT: 03-10-95

DIR: Wolfgang Petersen. SW: Laurence Dworet, Robert Roy Pool. PRO: Arnold Kopelson, Wolfgang Petersen, Gail Katz. STARS: Dustin Hoffman, Rene Russo, Morgan Freeman, Kevin Spacey, Cuba Gooding Jr.

The film showed the military being responsible for developing biological weapons. Army senior officers then conspired to cover up the virus's earlier history, which dated back to the 1960s. The filmmakers were unwilling to make key changes and withdrew their request for DoD assistance.

The Outsider (1961)

WWII	Marines	Full	B&W 108 mins
Universal	WV: 12-20-61		NYT: 12-08-61

DIR: Delbert Mann. SW: Stewart Stern, William Bradford Huie. PRO: Sy Bartlett. STARS: Tony Curtis, James Franciscus, Bruce Bennett.

The movie tells the story of Ira Hayes, the reluctant hero of the Mount Surabachi flag-raising on Iwo Jima. Hayes was overwhelmed by his fame and ultimately died of alcoholism and exposure. Nevertheless, the Marines provided full cooperation at the Recruit Depot in San Diego and at Camp Pendleton. The film shows how the Marines and the military used Hayes to sell bonds for the war effort but did not help him fight his alcoholism. General Victor Krulak, the commander of the San Diego Recruit Depot during the shooting of the movie there, believed the Marines were partially responsible for his death because of this. Director Mann acknowledged toning down the scene in which Hayes dies.

Over the Top (1918)

WWI	Army	Full	B&W 9 reels
Vitagraph	WV: 04-05-18		NYT: 04-01-18

DIR: Wilfrid North, Arthur Guy Empey (trench scenes). SW: Robert Gordon Anderson. PRO: Albert Smith. STARS: Arthur Guy Empey, Lois Meredith, James Morrison, Arthur Donaldson.

Based on Empey's best-selling novel of the same name, which turned into a convoluted, bloated story on the screen. It begins on the Mexican border, where the author/director/film's hero receives an honorable discharge from the U.S. Army. After the sinking of the *Lusitania*, Empey joins the British Army, is wounded, and is mustered out. Back home, he falls in love, returns to the U.S. Army, fights in France, is captured by a villainous German spy whom he ultimately kills, and lives happily ever after. Despite the mess, the film contains realistic scenes of trench warfare, which the Army helped stage at Camp Wheeler near Macon, Georgia.

Over There (1917)

WWI	Army	NR	B&W 6 reels
Select Pictures	WV: 10-19-17		NYT: DNR

DIR: James Kirkwood. SW: Charles Richman, Eve Unsell. PRO: Charles Richman. STARS: Charles Richman, Anna Nilsson, Walter McGrail, Gertrude Berkeley.

Young man Richman fears bloodshed and initially refuses to enlist, but after his girlfriend calls him a coward and becomes a nurse, he enlists and fights bravely in France, rescuing the girl's officer father before being wounded. The girl nurses him and things end happily. However, the story serves only as framework on which to hang official combat footage. An officer in the Canadian Expeditionary Force provided technical advice.

Pacific Inferno (1979)

WWII	Navy	NR	Color 90 mins
Nathaniel Prod	WV: DNR		NYT: DNR

DIR: Rolf Bayer. SW: Rolf Bayer. PRO: Cassius Weathersby, Spencer Jourdain, Jim Brown, B. Sherry-Greenwood. STARS: Jim Brown, Richard Jaeckel, Timothy Brown, Rik Van Nutter.

On the supposition that Gen. Douglas MacArthur ordered millions of dollars in silver dumped in Manilla Bay to avoid its capture, the Japanese occupiers order two captured U.S. Navy deep-sea divers to find the treasure. No big return on his investment for Jim Brown with this one.

The Package (1989)

Cold War	Army	Cour	Color 108 mins
Orion	WV: 08-23-89		NYT: 09-24-89

DIR: Andrew Davis. SW: John Bishop. PRO: Beverly J. Camhe, Tobie Haggerty. STARS: Gene Hackman, Joanna Cassidy, Tommy Lee Jones, Dennis Franz, John Heard, Pam Grier, Kevin Crowley, Reni Santoni.

Geopolitical thriller in which career Army NCO Hackman transports prisoner Jones to the states. Jones escapes to Chicago to assassinate a visiting Russian leader. The DoD and the Air Force provided courtesy assistance, which included a visit to an Air Force base and the photographing of a transport plane.

Pack Up Your Troubles (1932)

WWI	Army	Unkn	B&W 68 mins
MGM	WV: 10-04-32		NYT: 10-01-32

DIR: George Marshall, Ray McCarey. SW: H. M. Walker. PRO: Hal Roach. STARS: Stan Laurel, Oliver Hardy, Don Dillaway, Jacqueline Taylor, James Finlayson.

Laurel and Hardy's buddy dies in the French trenches, and the boys spend the rest of the film trying to find the grandparents of their friend's orphaned daughter. Comedy emanates from the search.

Pack Up Your Troubles (1939)

WWI	Army	Unkn	B&W 75 mins
Fox	WV: 11-01-39		NYT: 10-27-39

DIR: H. Bruce Humberstone. SW: Lou Breslow, Owen Francis. PRO: Sol Wurtzel. STARS: Jane Withers, Al Ritz, Harry Ritz, Jimmy Ritz.

The Ritz brothers cannot find work in vaudeville and join the Army. In France, they are assigned to a mule battalion and meet Withers, playing a local maiden. The film focuses on slapstick, with comedy flowing out of military situations.

Panama Hattie (1942)

WWII	Navy	Ltd	B&W 80 mins
MGM	WV: 07-22-42		NYT: 10-02-42

DIR: Norman Z. McLeod. SW: Jack McGowan, Wilkie Mahoney. PRO: Arthur Freed. STARS: Red Skelton, Ann Sothern, Lena Horne.

Adapted for the screen from Cole Porter's musical, the film, according to the critics, unsuccessfully features sailors at play.

Panama Patrol (1939)

Peace	Army	Unkn	B&W 67 mins
General National	WV: 08-16-39		NYT: DNR

DIR: Charles Lamont. SW: Arthur Hoerl. PRO: Charles Lamont. STARS: Leon Ames, Charlotte Wynters, Weldon Hayburn, Abner Biberman.

An Army intelligence officer tracks down a spy ring involving an interpreter in the army intelligence office. The interpreter, though portrayed by an Oriental, is named Johnson, and his ring of

Orientals are very interested in our Panama Canal. Very similar to Grand National's *Cipher Bureau*.

Pancho Villa (1972)

Mexican border	Army	NR	Color	92 mins
Scotia Intl	WV: DNR		NYT: DNR	

DIR: Eugenio Martín. SW: Julian Zimet. PRO: Bernard Gordon. STARS: Telly Savalas, Clint Walker, Chuck Connors, Anne Francis, Ben Tatar.

Not to be taken seriously, but the film does provide a modern take on Pancho Villa's war with the U.S. cavalry, which served in some measure as preparedness training for the American involvement in WWI.

Parades (1972)

Vietnam	Army	NR	Color	95 mins
Confron Co	WV: 05-24-72		NYT: 07-25-72	

DIR: Robert Siegel. SW: George Tabori. PRO: Robert Siegel. STARS: Russ Thacker, Brad Sullivan, David Doyle, Erik Estrada.

Set in a fictitious military prison, the film portrays brutality that an incompetent commander and sadistic guards mete out to prisoners. In turn, the prisoners vent their anger at their captors, Vietnam, and the armed forces. The film clearly did not provide a cautionary warning to the current generation of commanders and prison guards.

Parachute Battalion (1941)

Preparedness	Army	Full	B&W	75 mins
RKO	WV: 07-16-41		NYT: 08-29-41	

DIR: Leslie Goodwins. SW: John Twist, Major Hugh Fite, US Army Air Corps. PRO: Howard Benedict. STARS: Robert Preston, Nancy Kelly, Edmund O'Brien, Harry Carey, Buddy Ebsen.

Or, "How Our Army Trains Parachute Troops." This preparedness film was made with the assistance of the 501st Parachute Battalion at Fort Benning, Georgia.

Parachute Nurse (1942)

WWII	Army	Full	B&W	63 mins
Columbia	WV: 07-29-42		NYT: 07-27-42	

DIR: Charles Barton. SW: Rian James. PRO: Wallace MacDonald. STARS: Marguerite Chapman, William Wright, Kay Harris.

A "B" film that shows how the nurses packed their chutes and trained so that they could parachute, if necessary, from disabled Medivac planes. Nurses frequently staffed these air ambulances, which flew severely wounded troops, primarily senior officers, back to the States for treatment.

Paratroop Command (1959)

WWII	Army	NR	B&W 77 mins
Amer-Intl	WV: 01-28-59		NYT: DNR

DIR: William Witney. SW: Stanley Shpetner. PRO: Stanley Shpetner. STARS: Richard Bakalyn, Ken Lynch, Jack Hogan, Jimmy Murphy.

An atypical military film that does not include a heterogeneous mixture of men from all backgrounds, religions, and military experiences. The hero's accidental killing of one of the members of his unit creates tensions that ultimately dissipate as the men fight their way through North Africa, into Sicily, and finally into Italy.

Parrish (1961)

Peace	Navy	Ltd	Color 140 mins
WB	WV: 03-22-61		NYT: 05-05-61

DIR: Delmer Daves. SW: Delmer Daves. PRO: Delmer Daves. STARS: Troy Donahue, Claudette Colbert, Karl Malden, Dean Jagger.

A soap opera set in Connecticut's tobacco country. Donahue joins the Navy and goes to sea on a nuclear submarine. The Navy allowed Daves to film the submarine at the New London, Connecticut, sub base and on its way out to sea.

Patent Leather Kid (1927) [G&G]

WWI	Army	Full	B&W 110 mins
FN	WV: 08-17-27		NYT: 08-16-27

DIR: Alfred Santell. SW: Gerald C. Duffy, Adela Rogers St. Johns, Winifred Dunn. PRO: Alfred Santell. STARS: Richard Barthelmess, Molly O'Day, Lawford Davidson, Matthew Betz.

A young "flashy, conceited, cowardly" prizefighter and his trainer are drafted, and during combat in France, the trainer dies. This motivates the boxer to shed his arrogance and perform heroically on the battlefield. Returning home, he reunites with his nurse girlfriend, and his war-paralyzed hand slowly rises to a salute as the Stars and Stripes passes during a parade. After considerable negotiations, the Army provided men, tanks, and equipment. The filmmakers believed they were making a movie of "great military, educational, historical, and patriotic value," and the Army did benefit from the portrayal of tank battles and the maturing of a young soldier. However, the release of *Wings* three days earlier greatly diminished the film's appeal.

The Patriot (1986)

Terrorism	Navy	NR	Color 88 mins
Crown	WV: 09-17-86		NYT: 12-13-86

DIR: Frank Harris. SW: Andy Ruben, Katt Shea, John Kingswell. PRO: Michael Bennett, Victor Hwang, Julius Nasso, Nile Niami, Steven Seagal. STARS: Gregg Henry, Simone Griffeth, Michael J. Pollard, Jeff Conaway, Stack Pierce, Leslie Nielsen.

The Navy has a nuclear bomb stolen and recruits Henry, a dishonorably discharged SEAL, to retrieve the weapon before the bad guys destroy three cities. The rest of the film makes no more sense, with action its only justification.

The Patriot (1998)

Terrorism	Army	NR	Color	90 mins
Buena Vista	WV: DNR		NYT: DNR	

DIR: Dean Semler. SW: M. Sussman. PRO: Howard Baldwin. STARS: Steven Seagal, Gailard Sartain, L. Q. Jones, Silas Mitchell.

A distinctly un-Seagal film, lacking action and martial arts. Instead, the hero plays a father and a retired CIA agent turned country doctor. Sartain, leader of an Aryan militia group, releases a deadly virus, which threatens to spread beyond the small town. The militia wipes out a National Guard unit in an ambush, leaving Seagal to save the day, this time by finding an anecdote to the virus (in a flower then dropped by helicopter—seriously!) rather than fists. No wonder the film endangered Seagal's career and went straight to video.

Patriot Games (1992)

Peace	Navy	Ltd	Color	116 mins
Paramount	WV: 06-08-92		NYT: 06-05-92	

DIR: Phillip Noyce. SW: W. Peter Iliff, Donald Stewart. PRO: Mace Neufeld, Robert Rehme. STARS: Harrison Ford, Anne Archer, Patrick Bergin, Sean Bean, James Fox, Samuel L. Jackson, James Earl Jones, Richard Harris.

From Tom Clancy's novel, the film provided an opportunity for Hollywood to return to the Naval Academy with a few shots of the campus, its classrooms, and a few Navy helicopters in flight. Otherwise, no military presence.

Patton (1970) [G&G]

WWII	Army, Navy	Ltd	Color	173 mins
Fox	WV: 01-21-70		NYT: 02-05-70	

DIR: Franklin J. Schaffner. SW: Francis Ford Coppola, Edmund North. PRO: Frank McCarthy. STARS: George C. Scott, Karl Malden, Michael Bates, Tim Considine.

The classic cinematic biography of a controversial general, made in Spain, where that government rented their army's tanks and soldiers. Although the Patton family tried to prevent the production for 15 years, the Pentagon finally advised it that Patton was in the "public domain" and approved the script, which Gen. Omar Bradley had vetted. Cooperation approval was smoothed because Frank McCarthy had served as Army Chief of Staff General George Marshall's secretary during the war. The U.S. Navy helped restage Patton's landing on Sicily, which was about the only American military assistance to the production.

The film captured Patton's tactical brilliance and his warts, perhaps most particularly his love of war. Men, who had served under the general or knew him, all attested to the accuracy of Scott's portrayal, despite the two men's physical differences; for most people, Scott became Patton. The film does compress events. In fact, Patton slapped two soldiers and apologized twice. The opening scene, replicating Patton's pep talk to his men before D-Day, also inaccurately portrayed him as a four-star general with all his medals, even though he did not receive his fourth star until later in the war. Nevertheless, *Patton* remains one of the most historically accurate Hollywood military movies and probably the best rendering of military leadership in any motion picture ever made.

The Peacemaker (1997)

Terrorism	Army	NR	Color	123 mins
Dreamworks	WV: 09-22-97		NYT: DNR	

DIR: Mimi Leder. SW: Michael Schiffer. PRO: Walter Parkes, Branko Lustig. STARS: George Clooney, Nicole Kidman, Marcel Iures.

An idealized portrayal of how the U.S. military pursued stolen Russian missiles. Clooney stars as a U.S. Army Special Forces lieutenant colonel.

Pearl Harbor (2001) [G&G]

WWII	Air Force, Navy	Full	Color	182 mins
Disney	WV: 05-23-2001		NYT: 05-25-2001	

DIR: Michael Bay. SW: Randall Wallace. PRO: Jerry Bruckheimer, Michael Bay. STARS: Ben Affleck, Josh Hartnett, Kate Beckinsale, Cuba Gooding Jr., Jon Voight, Alec Baldwin.

Based on the fertile imagination of Wallace and the cinematic creativity of Bay, the film owed virtually nothing to Cleo, the muse of history. To obtain cooperation, Bruckheimer and Bay visited Secretary of Defense William Cohen and showed him an animated 20-minute short detailing how they intended to tell the story of December 7, 1941. Perhaps flattered by such famous people or the technology exhibited, Cohen announced his support of the project and the DoD approved the script within two weeks, even though each service had provided a detailed analysis of the script listing pages of historical and factual errors as well as the implausibilities of time and place.

Why then, apart from Cohen's support, did the Navy, the primary source of assistance, agree to loan Pearl Harbor to the filmmakers? The service most likely hoped for its own *Saving Private Ryan*. On their part Bruckheimer and Bay wanted to create a mixture of *Titanic*'s love story, an epic of historical proportions, a repeat of *Top Gun*'s aerial sequences, *Private Ryan*'s combat excitement, and Bay's propensity for blowing things up. Instead, the military and the filmmakers ended up with a tepid love triangle set in the months before Pearl Harbor with no respect for historical events, military procedures, or actions. Unlike the visual reality of *Top Gun*, Bay's computer-generated graphics of Japanese planes flying at low level between battleships and airplane hangars and the Spitfire battles with German fighters and bombers over the white cliffs of Dover looked like video games and computer-generated graphics, and so had virtually no believability.

Worse, the film contained a multiplicity of factual and historical inaccuracies. For a historian or knowledgeable viewer, the only pleasure was finding them. What follows must suffice. Navy nurses did not treat Army fliers. No mountains, especially the same California mountains that appeared in the film, exist either on Long Island or around Eglin AFB in the Florida panhandle, where Doolittle's fliers trained. Americans in the Eagle Squadron joined the RAF and did not wear their American uniforms. Admiral Kimmel received the war-warning telegram on November 27, not after the attack. Admiral Yamamoto did not accompany the task force to Pearl Harbor. FDR received word of the attack in his study relaxing with his stamp collection. The Air Force had tested the feasibility of taking a B-25 bomber off a carrier, contrary to what Doolittle tells his fliers. The planes flew to Japan and dropped their bombs individually, not in formation. Only the ashes of the dead fliers were returned to the United States, and not until the end of the war. Bay could not even get the date of the attack right. With ominous music in the background, a Japanese officer pulls a leaf off the calendar and December 7 has arrived. Alas, for the Japanese it would have been December 8.

Before beginning shooting in Pearl Harbor, Bay had dismissed *Tora! Tora! Tora!* as simply being a documentary that did not capture the events of December 7. The director demonstrated well that a soap-opera drama, on whatever scale he made it, had no chance of providing any understanding of the American experience at Pearl Harbor. He could not bring the love story to life. His portrayal of the Doolittle Raid in April 1942 became a disconnected postscript that added nothing to an understanding of the Japanese attack and our rapid mobilization in response to it. *Pearl Harbor* may have reminded viewers what those friendly people, who now sell us cars, television sets, VCRs, and Play Stations, did to the United States on a quiet, peaceful Sunday morning long ago and far away. But at what cost in time, money, and truth?

The Perez Family (1995)

Cold War	Army	Ltd	Color	112 mins
Goldwyn	WV: 05-15-95		NYT: 05-12-95	

DIR: Mira Nair. SW: Robin Swicord. PRO: Michael Nozik, Lydia Dean Pilcher. STARS: Marisa Tomei, Alfred Molina, Anjelica Huston.

The Florida Army National Guard provided tanks and trucks to reenact the humanitarian aid it provided to Cuban refugees during the 1980 Mariel exodus from Cuba. The National Guard appears mainly in the background but was important to the story, and the Army felt the depiction was positive and accurate.

The Perfect Furlough (1958)

Peace	Army	Ltd	Color	93 mins
Universal	WV: 10-08-58		NYT: 01-22-58	

DIR: Blake Edwards. SW: Stanley Shapiro. PRO: Robert Arthur. STARS: Tony Curtis, Janet Leigh, Keenan Wynn, Linda Cristal.

A comedic tale of soldiers at an Arctic outpost, one of whom wins a three-week furlough in Paris with a beautiful woman and the accompanying psychologist who will supervise the encounter.

The Perfect Storm (2000)

Peace	Air Force	Ltd	Color	129 mins
WB	WV: 06-26-2000		NYT: 04-30-2000	

DIR: Wolfgang Petersen. SW: Bill Wittliff. PRO: Paula Weinstein, Wolfgang Petersen, Gail Katz. STARS: George Clooney, John C. Reilly, Mark Wahlberg, Diane Lane, William Fichtner.

Based on Sebastian Junger's best-selling book, the film speculates about what happened to a fishing boat caught in the unprecedented storm in the North Atlantic. The Air Force provided helicopters and a plane in a brief scene portraying the search and rescue operation.

The Philadelphia Experiment (1984) [SSS]

WWII/Sci-Fi	Navy	Deny	Color	102 mins
New World	WV. 08-01-84		NYT: 08-17-84	

DIR: Stewart Raffill. SW: William Gray, Michael Janover. PRO: Douglas Curtis, Joel B. Michaels. STARS: Michael Paré, Nancy Allen, Eric Christmas, Bobby Di Cicco, Kene Holliday.

The Navy refused to cooperate on this time-travel story because the service denied that any time-travel experiments had ever taken place at the Philadelphia Navy Yard. As a result, the filmmakers shot aboard the USS *Yorktown*, now a museum at Patriot's Point, Charleston, South Carolina.

The Philadelphia Experiment II (1993)

WWII/Sci-Fi	Army	NR	Color	97 mins
Trimark	WV: 11-29-93		NYT: 11-13-93	

DIR: Stephen Cornwell. SW: Kevin Rock, Nick Paine. PRO: Mark Levinson, Doug Curtis. STARS: Brad Johnson, Gerrit Graham, Marjean Holden, James Greene.

Time-travel back to Nazi-era Germany with all the problems inherent in such fantasies.

The Pigeon That Took Rome (1962)

WWII	Army	Ltd	B&W	101 mins
Paramount	WV: 07-04-62		NYT: 08-23-62	

DIR: Melville Shavelson. SW: Melville Shavelson. PRO: Melville Shavelson. STARS: Charlton Heston, Elsa Martinelli, Harry Guardino.

Moses in Italy, disguised as a U.S. Infantry officer, using pigeons instead of chariot horses to facilitate the Allied capture of Rome.

Pilot No. 5 (1943)

WWII	Air Force	Ltd	B&W	70 mins
MGM	WV: 04-07-43		NYT: 06-25-43	

DIR: George Sidney. SW: David Hertz. PRO: P. B. Fineman. STARS: Franchot Tone, Marsha Hunt, Gene Kelly, Van Johnson.

The only military action appears near the end of the movie when Tone, a Navy aviator, flies against a Japanese task force; when his bomb does not release, he suicidally dives his plane into a Japanese carrier. Never happened, of course, but good for the war effort.

Plan Nine from Outer Space (1959)

SciFi	Army, Air Force	NR	B&W 78 mins
Reyn Pic Inc	WV: DNR		NYT: DNR

DIR: Ed Wood Jr. SW: Ed Wood Jr. PRO: Ed Wood Jr. STARS: Bela Lugosi, Vampira.

Generally agreed that this is one of the worst movies ever made, regardless of genre or budget. Although Wood never approached the Pentagon, he managed to acquire some stock combat footage of soldiers firing artillery and rockets and jet fighters in flight, which he used in portraying the military's futile attack on the flying saucers. An Army colonel commands the effort.

Platoon (1986) [G&G]

Vietnam	Army	Deny	Color 120 mins
Orion	WV: 12-03-86		NYT: 12-19-86

DIR: Oliver Stone. SW: Oliver Stone. PRO: Arnold Kopelson. STARS: Tom Berenger, Willem Dafoe, Charlie Sheen, Forest Whitaker.

Supposedly based on his own experiences in Vietnam. Stone claimed that he was simply portraying the men and events he had witnessed with his platoon. However, he filled the screen with the worst things real and imagined that may or may not have happened even one time. Sheen and his voice-over speak for the director. The Army refused to provide any assistance to the production, saying that the script lacked any balance. Although acknowledging that some men had used drugs in Vietnam, the Army and veterans pointed out that soldiers in the field needed all their faculties unimpaired.

Stone's company commander, Bob Hemphill, wrote to him after seeing *Platoon*, pointing out that none of the things the director had shown happening in Bravo company had ever taken place. Stone answered that he may have seen such things during times he spent in other units. Perhaps. But Stone and the film represent that they happened in a specific unit, his unit, Bravo Company. Consequently, his commander's assessment: "There's no reality in *Platoon*" remains more accurate than Stone's claim that in the film he captured "the true meaning" of his experiences. Unfortunately, those who were not in Vietnam and whose only knowledge of the war comes from films such as Stone's do not understand that leaders did not engage in disputes that led to physical combat, and that most soldiers did their jobs and did them well—even in the quagmire of Vietnam or they did not survive their tour.

Platoon Leader (1988)

Vietnam	Army	NR	Color 100 mins
Cannon	WV: 10-12-88		NYT: DNR

DIR: Aaron Norris. SW: Rick Marx, Andrew Deutsch, David Walker, Harry Alan Towers. PRO: Harry Alan Towers. STARS: Michael Dudikoff, Robert F. Lyons, Michael DeLorenzo, Rick Fitts, Jesse Dabson.

Based on James R. McDonough's novel, this exploitative film needed Chuck Norris badly. However, the cinematic West Point-educated lieutenant did not know how to lead, to the severe detriment of his troops.

Pork Chop Hill (1959) [G&G]

Korea	Army	Full	B&W 97 mins
UA	WV: 05-06-59		NYT: 05-30-59

DIR: Lewis Milestone. SW: James R. Webb. PRO: Sy Bartlett. STARS: Gregory Peck, Harry Guardino, Rip Torn, George Peppard, James Edwards, Bob Steele, Woody Strode, George Shibata.

Based on Gen. S. L. A. Marshall's history of the fight for a tactically unimportant hill, the film provides one of the best portrayals of the American combat experience in Korea and of men in battle. Bartlett wanted to make the movie to counter reports that the black soldiers had not done their jobs in Korea. He also wanted to make a comment about the absurdity of war, showing soldiers having to take a hill for political/diplomatic purposes, only to then give it up. Bartlett believed no soldier should ever be put in that position. Nevertheless the Army assisted on the production because it showed the soldiers performing their jobs bravely.

POW, the Escape (1986)

Vietnam	Army	NR	Color 90 mins
Cannon	WV: 04-09-86		NYT: 04-05-86

DIR: Gideon Amir. SW: Jeremy Lipp, James Bruner, Malcolm Barbour, John Langley, Avi Kleinberger. PRO: Menahem Golan, Yoram Globus. STARS: David Carradine, Charles R. Floyd, Mako, Steve James, Phil Brock.

Carradine strikes a bargain with his Vietcong jailor and leads a group of POWs through the jungles to safety in the days before the fall of Saigon. Originally titled *Behind Enemy Lines*.

Practically Yours (1944)

WWII	Navy	Unkn	B&W 99 mins
Paramount	WV: 12-20-44		NYT: 03-29-45

DIR: Mitchell Leisen. SW: Norman Krasna. PRO: Mitchell Leisen. STARS: Claudette Colbert, Fred MacMurray.

Radioing a moving farewell to "Peggy," Navy flier MacMurray dives his plane into a Japanese carrier, and in a million to one shot, survives to return home as a hero. In fact, "Peggy" was his dog, but the publicity links him to another Peggy, a former coworker, Colbert, and the two of them go along with the misunderstanding, with predicable results.

Predator (1987)

SciFi	Army	NR	Color 107 mins
Fox	WV: 06-17-87		NYT: 06-12-87

DIR: John McTiernan. SW: Jim Thomas, John Thomas. PRO: Lawrence Gordon, Joel Silver, John Davis. STARS: Arnold Schwarzenegger, Carl Weathers, Bill Duke, Elpidia Carrillo, Jesse Ventura.

American commandos, not otherwise identified, receive orders to go to the Central American jungle to rescue downed airmen from terrorists but arrive too late. After eliminating the terrorists, the commandos realize that an invisible alien is stalking and killing them one at a time. With Arnold leading the way, the men fight their way back to civilization and rescue.

The Presidio (1988) [G&G]

Peace	Army, Air Force	Full	Color 97 mins
Paramount	WV: 06-15-88		NYT: 06-10-88

DIR: Peter Hyams. SW: Larry Ferguson. PRO: D. Constantine Conte. STARS: Sean Connery, Mark Harmon, Meg Ryan, Jack Warden.

Hyams made good use of the scenic Presidio, on San Francisco Bay, then an Army fort, in a murder mystery with Vietnam War overtones. In solving the case, Connery discovers that his best friend from Vietnam was a member of a gang smuggling diamonds into the United States on Air Force planes and is involved with the murder.

Pride of the Army. See *War Dogs.*

Pride of the Marines (1936)

Peace	Marines	Full	B&W 64 mins
Columbia	WV: 04-29-36		NYT: 04-27-36

DIR: D. Ross Lederman. SW: Harold Shumate. PRO: Columbia. STARS: Charles Bickford, Florence Rice, Billy Burrud, Robert Allen, Ward Bond.

A Marine adopting a young orphan provides the cinematic opportunity for displaying parades, battleships, etc., in this flag-waving story.

Pride of the Marines (1945)

WWII	Marines	Full	B&W 119 mins
WB	WV: 08-08-45		NYT: 08-25-45

DIR: Delmer Daves. SW: Albert Maltz. PRO: Jerry Wald. STARS: John Garfield, Eleanor Parker, Dane Clark.

Adapted from Roger Butterfield's book, the film tells the story of Al Schmid, a Marine blinded on Guadalcanal, detailing his rehabilitation, with the help of his fiancée, who insists upon marrying him despite his injury.

Pride of the Navy (1939)

Peace	Navy	Full	B&W 65 mins
Republic	WV: 02-01-39		NYT: DNR

DIR: Charles Lamont. SW: Ben Markson, Saul Elkins, Joseph Hoffman. PRO: Republic. STARS: James Dunn, Rochelle Hudson, Gordon Oliver.

This low-budget, "C" film follows the escapades of a young man kicked out of Annapolis who designs a small, fast torpedo boat and wins another naval appointment, this time to the reserves.

Prisoner of Japan (1942)

WWI	Navy	Unkn	B&W 54 mins
PRC	WV: 12-02-42		NYT: DNR

DIR: Arthur Ripley. SW: Robert Chapin, Arthur Ripley. PRO: Seymour Nebenzal, Edgar G. Ulmer. STARS: Alan Baxter, Gertrude Michael, Ernest Dorian.

American naval officers try to find a Japanese spy's communications center on a small Pacific island. The Navy loses a battleship, which was not to happen again after Pearl Harbor, but then defeats the enemy's fleet, in this trashy "C" stab at aiding the war effort. The filming took Ripley six days, and he could have used at least one more.

Prisoner of War (1954)

Korea	Army	Ltd	B&W 80 mins
MGM	WV: 03-24-54		NYT: 05-10-54

DIR: Andrew Marton. SW: Allen Rivkin. PRO: Henry Berman. STARS: Ronald Reagan, Steve Forrest, Dewey Martin, Harry Morgan.

Rivkin crafted his screenplay from interviews with many Korean War POW returnees, and the studio claimed that all the film's incidents and dialogues had actually occurred. Reagan parachutes behind enemy lines to join a gaggle of prisoners to confirm stories of atrocities.

Private Benjamin (1980) [G&G]

Peace	Army	Deny	Color 109 mins
WB	WV: 10-08-80		NYT: 10-10-80

DIR: Howard Zieff. SW: Nancy Meyers, Charles Shyer, Harvey Miller. PRO: Nancy Meyers, Charles Shyer, Harvey Miller. STARS: Goldie Hawn, Eileen Brennan, Armand Assante, Robert Webber, Albert Brooks.

The Army objected to the image of a general sexually harassing Hawn as Private Benjamin. When she freezes and refuses to make a parachute jump, the general gives her the alternative of having sex with him. She jumps! The service also had a problem with the portrayal of an Army recruiter describing basic training as being like Club Med. In any case, Hawn leaves her life of leisure and wealth and, like countless generations of male recruits, she undergoes a rite of passage in the military and becomes all she can be as an independent woman, which includes the abandonment of her French doctor fiancé at the altar.

Private Buckaroo (1942)

WWII	Army	Unkn	B&W 68 mins
Universal	WV: 06-03-42		NYT: 06-25-42

DIR: Edward Cline. SW: Edmund Kelso, Edward James. PRO: Ken Goldsmith. STARS: Harry James and his Band, the Andrews Sisters, Dick Foran, Donald O'Connor.

A musical featuring James and his band, who move from the night club circuit to the USO theater. The slight story puts Foran in the Army, opposing Army regulations, but he has the right attitude by the end of the film, which closes with a patriotic march to stimulated flag-waving.

Private Jones (1933)

WWI	Army	NR	B&W 70 mins
Universal	WV: 03-28-33		NYT: 03-25-33

DIR: Russell Mack. SW: William N. Robson, Prescott Chaplin. PRO: Carl Laemmle. STARS: Lee Tracy, Donald Cook, Gloria Stuart, Shirley Grey, Russell Gleason.

A wartime slacker, drafted against his will, has comic misadventures, including falling in love with his commander's wife and KP duty. However, during combat he demonstrates heroism and sacrifice, seeing "the light."

The Private Navy of Sgt. O'Farrell (1968)

WWII	Navy	Ltd	Color 92 mins
UA	WV: 05-08-68		NYT: 05-09-68

DIR: Frank Tashlin. SW: Frank Tashlin. PRO: John Beck. STARS: Bob Hope, Phyllis Diller, Jeffrey Hunter, Gina Lollobrigida, Mako.

Hope plays a seasoned noncom on an out-of-the-way South Pacific island that has avoided the chaos of war. Army–Navy shenanigans prevail, and the film includes a parody of the beach scene in *From Here to Eternity*.

Private War (1990)

Cold War	Army	NR	Color 94 mins
Smart Egg Pictures	WV: 07-04-90		NYT: DNR

DIR: Frank De Palma. SW: Terry Borst, Bjorn Carlstein, Frank De Palma. PRO: Luigi Cingolani. STARS: Joe Dallesandro, Martin Hewitt, Kimberly Beck, Reggie Johnson.

In this Yugoslav/American production, Dallesandro, a former POW in Vietnam, now a sergeant stationed in Northern Italy, suffers flashbacks to the war. Relieved of his assignment, his demons push him over the edge, where he wages a war against his corrupt officers, who are selling guns to terrorists, while hoping one of his men will put him out of his misery.

The Private War of Major Benson (1955)

Peace	Army	Ltd	Color	105 mins
Universal	WV: 06-01-55		NYT: 08-03-55	

DIR: Jerry Hopper. SW: William Roberts, Richard Alan Simmons. PRO: Howard Pine. STARS: Charlton Heston, Julie Adams, William Demerest, Tim Considine, Sal Mineo.

Here, Heston plays a tough, old-school officer who mouths off one time too many to his superiors and is sent to run a private school, which he discovers is a Catholic military boarding institution. He gains a little humanity from the students and love with Adams.

A Private's Affair (1959)

Peace	Army	Ltd	Color	92 mins
Fox	WV: 07-22-59		NYT: 08-15-59	

DIR: Raoul Walsh. SW: Winston Miller. PRO: David Weisbart. STARS: Sal Mineo, Christine Carère, Barry Coe, Barbara Eden, Gary Crosby, Jim Backus, Terry Moore.

In this silly service comedy, the base commander sends four Army buddies to New York to compete on a TV talent show. Many complications follow, both with their act and with the women they meet. Idiotic.

Project X (1987)

Cold War	Air Force	Deny	Color	108 mins
Fox	WV: 04-15-87		NYT: 04-17-87	

DIR: Jonathan Kaplan. SW: Stanley Weiser. PRO: Walter F. Parkes, Lawrence Lasker. STARS: Matthew Broderick, Helen Hunt, Stephen Lang, Bill Sadler, and several chimpanzees.

Because the movie showed a wayward pilot being sent to babysit monkeys used for experiments at a fictional Strategic Weapons Center, the Air Force refused to cooperate, saying the punishment did not reflect well on the Air Force. Nor did killing the chimps upon completion of the experiments benefit the service's image. Broderick ultimately came to the rescue.

The Proud and Profane (1956)

WWII	Marines	Full	B&W	111 mins
Paramount	WV: 05-30-56		NYT: 06-14-56	

DIR: George Seaton. SW: George Seaton. PRO: William Perlberg. STARS: Willliam Holden, Deborah Kerr, Thelma Ritter.

Based on Lucy Herndon Crockett's novel *The Magnificent Bastards*, the film contains a convoluted story of romance between Holden, a Marine colonel, and Kerr, a widowed Red Cross worker, set in the wartime South Pacific. Any attempted resemblance to *From Here to Eternity* misses by a mile.

PT-109 (1963) [G&G]

WWII	Navy	Full	Color	140 mins
WB	WV: 03-20-63		NYT: 06-27-63	

DIR: Leslie H. Martinson. SW: Richard L. Breen. PRO: Bryan Foy. STARS: Cliff Robertson, Ty Hardin, James Gregory, Robert Culp, Grant Williams.

A pseudo-propaganda film intended to help President John F. Kennedy's reelection. Fred Zinnemann, for one, refused to accept the directing job because of the political overtones. The Navy provided a destroyer and other hardware as background during shooting in the Florida Keys. The studio had to replicate a PT-boat because it could not find a real one. In the end, the story failed because the film-makers were portraying a sitting president and could not show warts or native girls. Still, Kennedy's heroism comes through, and the French loved the film, according to the president's press secretary, Pierre Salinger.

The Puppet Masters (1994)

SciFi	Army	Deny	Color	109 mins
Buena Vista	WV: 10-24-94		NYT: 10-22-94	

DIR: Stuart Orme. SW: Ted Elliott, Terry Rossio, David Goyer. PRO: Ralph Winter. STARS: Donald Sutherland, Eric Thal, Julie Warner, Keith David.

Based on Robert Heinlein's novel of the same name, which preceded most similar stories of alien invasion and seizure of human bodies such as in *Invasion of the Body Snatchers*. As usual in these stories, the military joins with scientists in an attempt to defeat the enemy. After reading the script, the DoD turned down an informal request for help, saying that "military assistance was not going to be forthcoming."

Purple Haze (1982)

Vietnam	Army	Deny	Color	97 mins
Universal	WV: 11-17-82		NYT: 11-11-83	

DIR: David Morris. SW: Victoria Wozniak, David Morris. PRO: Thomas Fucci. STARS: Peter Nelson, Chuck McQuary, Bernard Baldan, Susanna Lack.

The producers sought DoD help on the story of young men seeking the meaning to life during the traumatic events of 1968. The Army turned down the request because it saw no benefit in "providing assistance to this production in its present form. Even with liberal license for satire and humor, we cannot support a script which consistently emphasizes the portrayal of Army personnel (and members of Congress) as buffoons and subjects of ridicule." In turn, the studio advised the Army that it could not "accommodate the major script revisions" required. In fact, only the Army induction ceremony at the end of the film contained any military imagery.

The Purple Heart (1944) [G&G]

WWII	Air Force	NR	B&W	99 mins
Fox	WV: 02-23-44		NYT: 03-09-44	

DIR: Lewis Milestone. SW: Jerome Cady. PRO: Darryl F. Zanuck. STARS: Dana Andrews, Richard Conte, Farley Granger, Kevin O'Shea, Donald Barry, Sam Levene, Charles Russell, John Craven.

The Jimmy Doolittle raid on Japan in April 1942 inspired this fictional depiction of the capture of eight of the fliers. The film contained the typical war effort anti-enemy propaganda. In this case, it offered images of the Japanese torturing Americans and heroic portrayals of the fliers. Even though the War Department, in November 1943, had directed Hollywood to stop showing Japanese atrocities, the Office of War Information approved the completed movie, saying the studio had toned down the negative images by putting the torture and subsequent executions off-screen. In fact, the Japanese only executed three of Doolittle's fliers, not the eight who received death sentences in the film.

Purple Hearts (1984) [G&G]

Vietnam	Navy, Marines	Full	Color	116 mins
WB	WV: 05-09-84		NYT: 05-04-84	

DIR: Sidney Furie. SW: Rick Natkin, Sidney Furie. PRO: Sidney Furie, Lope Juban Jr. STARS: Ken Wahl, Cheryl Ladd, Stephen Lee, David Harris, R. Lee Ermey.

One of the first films that did not trash the American military in Vietnam. Instead, it contained a traditional wartime love story between Wahl as a Navy doctor and Ladd as a Navy nurse. Wahl goes on a secret mission with a Marine unit, although the movie does not explain the reason. In fact, the Marine Corps does not have doctors, because all Marines must be prepared to fight and the conventions of war prohibit doctors from becoming combatants. When the doc returns from combat, he is told that Ladd has died in a mortar attack. As in all such films, of course, Wahl finds her alive in her stateside hospital, which he has joined following his tour. Tears flow, as might be expected.

Purple Heart Diary (1957)

WWII	Army	Cour	B&W	72 mins
Columbia	WV: 11-27-57		NYT: DNR	

DIR: Richard Quine. SW: William Sackheim. PRO: Sam Katzman. STARS: Frances Langford, Judd Holdren, Ben Lessy, Tony Romano.

This is a minor docudrama of singer Langford's tour to the far Pacific in WWII, which includes a plane crash and sneak Japanese attack, benefit of stock combat footage.

The Purple V (1943)

WWII	Air Force	NR	B&W	58 mins
Republic	WV: 03-24-43		NYT: DNR	

DIR: George Sherman. SW: Curt Siodmak, Bertram Millhauser. PRO: Herbert Yates. STARS: John Archer, Mary McLeod, Fritz Kortner, Rex Williams, Peter Lawford.

This is a rare, wartime "good German" movie. Kortner portrays a man *Variety* describes as the "pre-Hitler German liberal schoolmaster." He not only helps Archer, a downed American flyer, return to the Allied lines but also sends with the flier "secret" information concerning the North African campaign. Unfortunately, the teacher dies fighting Nazism.

Q-Ships (1928)

WWI	Navy	Unkn	B&W	92 mins
New Era–Natl Pic	WV: 07-11-28		NYT: 09-17-28	

DIR: Geoffrey Barkas, Michael Barringer. SW: Michael Barringer. PRO: E. Gordon Craig. STARS: Lt.-Commander Harold Auten, Johnny Butt, Roy Travers.

This British-made film re-created the historic meeting between British Adm. John Jellicoe and American Adm. William Sims in which they decided to use Q-ships against the German U-boats. The Q-ships, old tubs, and ships barely afloat, disguised as merchant ships and manned with small but fearless gunnery crews, opened fire on the German submarines when they surfaced to use their deck gun upon the apparently vulnerable ships, rather than waste torpedoes. The film also contains an episode involving the stopping of the USS *Juliana,* whose skipper berates the German U-boat commander. The Imperial War Museum provided footage, including the arrival of the first American soldiers to land in England.

The Quick and the Dead (1963)

WWII	Army	NR	B&W	92 mins
Beckman	WV: 03-06-63		NYT: DNR	

DIR: Robert Totten. SW: Sheila Lynch, Robert Totten. PRO: Sam Altonian. STARS: Larry Mann, Victor French, Jon Cedar, Sandy Donigan.

A depleted squad of U.S. soldiers joins up with Italian partisans to rid the immediate northern Italian area of the Nazis in this low-budget film.

Quicksand (2001)

Peace	Marines	NR	Color	92 mins
Quantum Enter	WV: DNR		NYT: DNR	

DIR: Sam Firstenberg. SW: Steve Schoenberg, Ruben Gordon. PRO: Frank DeMartin, Rafael Primorac. STARS: Michael Dudikoff, Brooke Theiss, Douglas Weston, Michael O'Hagan, Dan Hedaya.

This is the only known American military movie filmed in India. Sandi, a female Marine sergeant, is suspected of murdering her father, the commanding general of her assigned base. Bill, the new base psychiatrist, who had been treating her, discovers that an unusually high number of suicides have occurred on the base. He sets out to investigate the cause and the murder, while falling in love with his patient, which causes him to wonder if he wants to find out the truth.

Quicksands (1923)

Mexican Border	Army	Full	B&W	70 mins
American Releasing	WV: 03-29-23		NYT: DNR	

DIR: Jack Conway. SW: Howard Hawks, Oliver Hardy. PRO: Howard Hawks. STARS: Helene Chadwick, Richard Dix, Alan Hale, Noah Beery.

The film portrays the American efforts to break up a drug-smuggling ring on the Mexican border, with the Army and Customs Service working together. The U.S. cavalry rides to the rescue of the hero, his girl, and her customs official father.

Race to Space (2002)

Peace	Air Force	Full	Color	104 mins
Lion Gate Films	WV: 03-25-2002		NYT: DNR	

DIR: Sean McNamara. SW: Eric Gardner, Steve H. Wilson. PRO: David Brookwell, Sean McNamara, Glenn Greene. STARS: James Woods, Annabeth Gish, Alex D. Linz, William Devane.

Weekly Variety thought the film looked like a commercial for the Air Force and NASA, as *Top Gun* was for the Navy. Woods plays a German scientist who works in NASA's early space program. Devane wants to stop the chimp test flight, and Woods's son is called a Nazi and communist by kids at school.

The Rack (1956)

Korea	Army	Ltd	B&W	99 mins
MGM	WV: 04-18-56		NYT: 11-06-56	

DIR: Arnold Laven. SW: Stewart Stern. PRO: Arthur M. Loew Jr. STARS: Paul Newman, Wendell Corey, Walter Pidgeon, Lee Marvin.

Taken from Rod Serling's teleplay, the film depicts the court-martial of a collaborationist, a victim of psychological torture who had also served heroically in WWII.

The Raiders of Leyte Gulf (1963)

WWII	Army	NR	B&W	80 mins
Hemis Flm	WV: 08-28-63		NYT: DNR	

DIR: Eddie Romero. SW: Carl Kuntze, Eddie Romero. PRO: Eddie Romero. STARS: Jennings Sturgeon, Michael Parsons, Efren Reyes.

A not-unfamiliar wartime Philippines story line. This time Army officer Parsons and his Filipino comrades, a.k.a. guerrillas, fight hand-to-hand with the Japanese remainders of a garrison to free Sturgeon, an American intelligence officer. Eventually the entire population of the little captured village rises up to join the guerrillas. Lots of cheap production values do nothing to make an awful film better.

Rain (1932)

Peace	Marines	Ltd	B&W	92 mins
UA	WV: 10-18-32		NYT: 10-13-32	

DIR: Lewis Milestone. SW: Maxwell Anderson. PRO: Lewis Milestone. STARS: Joan Crawford, Walter Huston, William Gargan.

Adapted from the short story by Somerset Maugham and the stage play of the same name, in which Sadie Thompson, a prostitute, quarantined with other passengers on a South Seas island, befriends Marines but becomes entangled with a missionary who forces her to repent and then rapes her. After her rapist commits suicide, she accepts the love of a Marine sergeant.

Raise the Titanic! (1980) [G&G]

Cold War	Navy	Full	Color	112 mins
Marble Arch	WV: 08-06-80		NYT: 08-01-80	

DIR: Jerry Jameson. SW: Adam Kennedy. PRO: William Frye. STARS: Jason Robards, Richard Jordan, David Selby, Anne Archer.

Based on a Clive Barnes novel. The subsequent discovery of the *Titanic* and its condition (broken into two pieces) instantly rendered the book and this movie pure fantasy. The Navy provided assistance in the form of a diving support ship and deep rescue submersibles. The service had requested a change in the script's ending, which suggested the United States might be duplicitous because it might choose to use the rare mineral aboard the *Titanic* for offensive instead of the stated defensive purposes. The director of Navy public affairs thought the filmmakers had agreed to use the ending he had written. The filmmakers were to deny any such commitment, and the completed film had the original ending. As a result, the service asked that its credit be removed.

Rambo: First Blood, Part II (1985)

Vietnam	Army	NR	Color	95 mins
Tri-Star	WV: 05-22-85		NYT: 05-22-86	

DIR: George Pan Cosmatos. SW: Sylvester Stallone, James Cameron. PRO: Buzz Feitshans. STARS: Sylvester Stallone, Richard Crenna, Charles Napier, Julia Nickson, Steven Berkoff, Martin Kove.

Although the film does not portray the U.S. military in action, the story fantasizes the continuing existence of Vietnam POWs who, by definition, remain on active duty until Rambo, a former Special Operations veteran, rescues them.

Random Hearts (1999)

Peace	Navy	Full	Color	133 mins
Columbia	DV: 10-04-99		NYT: 10-03-99	

DIR: Sydney Pollack. SW: Kurt Luedtke, Darryl Ponicsan. PRO: Sydney Pollack, Marykay Powell. STARS: Harrison Ford, Kristin Scott Thomas, Charles Dutton, Bonnie Hunt, Peter Coyote.

Although the film contained only a soap-opera romance, the Navy provided assistance to portray how it would undertake a recovery operation on a plane crash, in this case a commercial jet down in Chesapeake Bay near the Patuxent Naval Air Station in Maryland. The service considered that the rescue scene provided information on how it responded to emergencies and might well become a Navy recruiting commercial.

Rascel Marine (1958)

WWII	Marines	NR	B&W 106 mins
Unkn	WV: DNR		NYT: DNR

DIR: Guido Leoni. SW: Unkn. PRO: Unkn. STARS: Ernesto Calindri, Mario Carotenuto, Célina Cély, Kaida Horinki.

A spaghetti war comedy set on a South Seas island, where Japanese soldiers and Marines cease fire to pursue the hearts of two native sisters.

The Ravager (1970)

Vietnam	Army	NR	Color 76 mins
Green Dolphin	WV: DNR		NYT: DNR

DIR: Charles Nizet. SW: Unkn. PRO: Dave Ackerman. STARS: Darlene Dawes, Pierre Gaston, Lynn Hayes, Ann Hollis, Jo Long.

Gaston enters the Army and serves in Vietnam as a demolition expert. While in country, he witnesses the Vietcong brutally rape and murder a young Vietnamese woman, and his trauma requires hospitalization, rehabilitation, and ultimately discharge. His memories of the rape cause him to murder those he sees engaging in sex.

The Real Glory (1939)

Peace	Army	NR	B&W 95 mins
UA	WV: 09-13-39		NYT: 09-15-39

DIR: Henry Hathaway. SW: Jo Swerling, Robert R. Presnell. PRO: Samuel Goldwyn. STARS: Gary Cooper, Andrea Leeds. David Niven.

United States troops, in 1906, prepare to hand over military authority to the locals and to leave the Philippines. Released as the war in the Pacific continued to spread, the film reminded people of our long-standing involvement in the Philippines.

Red Ball Express (1952)

WWII	Army	Full	B&W 83 mins
Universal	WV: 04-30-52		NYT: 05-30-52

DIR: Budd Boetticher. SW: John Michael Hayes. PRO: Aaron Rosenberg. STARS: Jeff Chandler, Alex Nicol, Charles Drake, Sidney Poitier, Judith Braun.

Filmed at Fort Eustis, Virginia, the movie portrays the Army's Transportation Corps' truck supply line as it scrambled to keep delivering fuel and other material to Patton's fast-moving tank Corps as it sped through France. As ***Patton*** revealed, the trucks did not always make it on time, but the film remains one of the few Hollywood productions that portrayed military logistics, without which an Army has no chance of winning.

Red Dawn (1984)

Cold War	Army, Air Force	NR	Color	114 mins
MGM/UA	WV: 08-08-84		NYT: 08-10-84	

DIR: John Milius. SW: Kevin Reynolds, John Milius. PRO: Buzz Feitshans, Sidney Beckerman. STARS: Patrick Swayze, C. Thomas Howell, Ron O'Neal, William Smith, Powers Boothe, Charlie Sheen.

Following a successful Cuban/Soviet nonnuclear attack on the United States, a band of American teens somewhere in the Midwest successfully use guerrilla tactics to defend their country until betrayed by some of their own supporters. The ultimate victory is left to a postscript. Perhaps the Iraqi insurgents watched the movie. Milius sought Pentagon cooperation, which was ultimately approved, but he decided not to use it because he would have had to pay too much for the transportation of tanks and other equipment to the shooting location of his low-budget production near Las Vegas, New Mexico.

Reflections in a Golden Eye (1967)

Peace	Army	NR	Color	109 mins
WB	WV: 10-11-67		NYT: 10-12-67	

DIR: John Huston. SW: Chapman Mortimer, Gladys Hill. PRO: Ray Stark, John Huston. STARS: Elizabeth Taylor, Marlon Brando, Brian Keith, Julie Harris.

From Carson McCullers's novel of the same name, this melodrama seemed to have all the ingredients needed to attract audiences, in addition to a star-studded cast. A murder takes place on a peacetime Army post while licentious characters and their assorted relationships steam up the screen. Brando is a homosexual officer whose wife is having an affair with her officer neighbor, while the latter's wife is having her own affair, while Brando stalks a handsome soldier. Who had any time to kill someone? Too much was happening for Huston to have a strong focus. The Army would have been hard-pressed to find any benefit in cooperating on this story.

Remember Pearl Harbor (1942)

WWII	Army	Ltd	B&W	75 mins
Republic	WV: 05-13-42		NYT: 06-04-42	

DIR: Joseph Santley. SW: Malcolm Stuart Boylan, Isabel Dawn. PRO: Albert J. Cohen. STARS: Donald M. Barry, Alan Curtis, Fay McKenzie.

This buddy film depicted two young American soldiers in the Philippines; one of whom has trouble staying out of the brig. After the Pearl Harbor attack, he uncovers a Japanese spy ring and dives his plane into a Japanese troop transport ship. The only surprise is that Republic needed five months to get the movie ready for release even though it used the same script, with only superficial revisions, for the fifth time since ***The Marines Have Landed*** in 1937.

Renaissance Man **(1994)**

| Peace | Army | | Full | | Color | 129 mins |
| Disney | WV: 05-30-94 | | | | NYT: 06-03-94 |

DIR: Penny Marshall. SW: Jim Burnstein. PRO: Sara Colleton, Elliot Abbott, Robert Greenhut, Andrew G. Vajna. STARS: Danny DeVito, Gregory Hines, James Remar, Cliff Robertson.

DeVito, an unemployed advertising executive, takes a job with the U.S. Army to work with under-achievers in hopes of making them better soldiers. After successful script negotiations, the Army felt it had obtained an outstanding rewrite and approved full assistance, consisting of filming on a military installation and active duty soldiers as extras.

The Rescue **(1988)**

| Cold War | Navy | | NR | | Color | 98 mins |
| Buena Vista | WV: 08-10-88 | | | | NYT: 08-05-88 |

DIR: Ferdinand Fairfax. SW: Jim Thomas, John Thomas. PRO: Laura Ziskin. STARS: Kevin Dillon, Marc Price, Ned Vaughn.

Teenagers of Navy families stationed in South Korea plan and carry out the Rambo-like rescue of their SEAL fathers imprisoned in North Korea. Not your typical Disney feature, nor one of which the studio should have been proud. Only teenagers could have found any merit in the film.

Retreat, Hell! **(1952) [G&G]**

| Korea | Marines | | Full | | B&W | 94 mins |
| WB | WV: 02-13-52 | | | | NYT: 02-20-52 |

DIR: Joseph H. Lewis. SW: Milton Sperling, Ted Sherdeman. PRO: Milton Sperling. STARS: Frank Lovejoy, Richard Carlson, Rusty Tamblyn, Anita Louise.

The film portrayed the Marine retreat from the Yalu River after the Chinese Communist army crossed into North Korea and joined the conflict in the first winter of the war. The press reported that a Marine general had denied his men were retreating, saying they were simply advancing in another direction. He later denied the quote, but the public affairs office used it to promote the courage of the Marines.

The film industry's Code Office initially refused to approve the film because it had the word "hell" in the title, but the Marines pressured the studio to stand firm because the phrase had become part of the historical record. The company shot the film at Camp Pendleton north of San Diego, painting the hills white to create the winter environment, which does convey the sense of the bitter cold the Marines faced, unlike *Hold Back the Night*, shot in snow at the Corps' cold-weather training facility in Northern California, which told virtually the same story but strangely lacked a sense of the cold and the suffering of the men.

The Right Stuff **(1983)**

| Cold War | Navy, Air Force, Marines | Full | | Color | 192 mins |
| WB | WV: 10-12-83 | | | NYT: 10-21-83, 11-06-83 |

DIR: Philip Kaufman. SW: Philip Kaufman. PRO: Robert Chartoff, Irwin Winkler. STARS: Sam Shepard, Scott Glenn, Ed Harris, Dennis Quaid, Fred Ward, Barbara Hershey, Kim Stanley, Scott Paulin, Charles Frank.

The Pentagon loaned facilities and an aircraft carrier to help replicate the early days of the American Mercury space program. Based on Tom Wolfe's book, the film tells the story of the first astronauts, who were far more interesting than the sanitized heroes NASA and *LIFE* magazine allowed the public to see.

The Rock (1996) [G&G]

Terrorism	Navy, Marines	NR	Color	131 mins
HP	WV: 06-03-96		NYT: 06-06-96	

DIR: Michael Bay. SW: David Weisberg, Douglas Cook, Mark Rosner. PRO: Don Simpson, Jerry Bruckheimer. STARS: Sean Connery, Nicolas Cage, Ed Harris, David Morse.

A renegade Marine general and his rouge followers seize Alcatraz and threaten to kill the tourist hostages and fire gas-tipped rockets at San Francisco unless the government pays restitution to the families of special forces killed in covert actions. In fact, no Marine general would position himself without an avenue of escape—at least, the Corps would hope not. Of course, plausibility has never been Bay's trademark, as he uses his stories simply as vehicles for action sequences, in this case, with Navy SEALS and Connery leading the assault against the rebels. As a result, people may miss the dramatic incongruity inherent in the story. Harris is using bad means to achieve good ends, but it remains difficult to believe an honorable person, a military man at that, would actually launch a missile attack against innocent civilians. See also *Twilight's Last Gleaming*, which has a similar structure and asks the audience to believe an officer with good intentions would actually use a weapon of mass destruction—which would render his purpose moot.

Rolling Thunder (1977) [G&G]

Vietnam	Air Force	Deny	Color	99 mins
Amer-Intl	WV: 10-05-77		NYT: 10-15-77	

DIR: John Flynn. SW: Paul Schrader, Heywood Gould. PRO: Norman T. Herman. STARS: William Devane, Tommy Lee Jones, Linda Haynes, Lisa Richards, Dabney Coleman, James Best, Cassie Yates.

Devane, a longtime POW, returns home to a grand Texas welcome, a young son he has never known, an unfaithful wife, and a changed society in which women work, go braless, and wear miniskirts. And it goes downhill fast from there. A gang of thugs comes looking for the silver dollars Devane received as a welcome-home gift. He has a flashback to his interrogation in Vietnam at which he only recites his name, rank, and serial number. In response, the gang puts his hand in a garbage disposal, shoots him, and kills his wife and son.

Once the Air Force doctors heal his wounds, including replacing his hand with a hook, Devane seeks revenge, not for the murder of his wife but for the loss of his son. He receives help on his mission from a POW groupie and Jones, a fellow POW, who has his own problems with a wife who does not understand what he experienced and why he has changed. The slaughter that follows serves as a catharsis for their Vietnam and back-home experiences.

Rolling Thunder may have been the most violent movie ever to come out of Hollywood, at least until ***Saving Private Ryan*** and ***Black Hawk Down***. Flynn recalled that during previews large numbers of the audiences ran out of the theater when Devane had his hand forced into the garbage disposal, later, when he stuck his hook into one man's groin, and when he put it into another man's hand while seeking information on the whereabouts of the gang. The Air Force considered Devane's character and actions as defaming the images of Vietnam vets. The service maintained that most men returned home normal, did not find that their wives had cheated on them, and did not go about killing people in droves. As a result, the service refused to provide assistance—even though the film portrayed Air Force doctors in a most positive fashion.

Devane's killing spree may well have contributed to Hollywood's negative images of returning Vietnam vets as demented and violent. In this case, however, his actions are perfectly explicable. The gang serves as a surrogate for his Vietnamese jailers and his retribution, which takes place in a whorehouse in a brilliantly executed montage of unrestrained slaughter, provides him with some measure of closure. At the end, Devane and Jones leave the battlefield after having killed "a few people," hanging on to one another, finally ready to head home.

To create these dances with death, Flynn combined sound, music, dialogue, and images of blood and bodies strewn everywhere that remain etched in the minds of people who did not leave the theater or turn off their cable channel or VCRs. What they saw remains perhaps the best movie ever made about the plight of Vietnam POWs and surely one of the very best movies about American military men.

Rookies (1927)

| Peace | Marines | Ltd | B&W   7 reels |
| MGM | WV: 04-25-27 | | NYT: 04-25-27 |

DIR: Sam Wood. SW: Byron Morgan, Joe Farnham. PRO: Unkn. STARS: Karl Dane, George Arthur, Frank Currier, Marceline Day.

This comedy portrays George Arthur attending a "Citizens Training Camp," run by the Army, in lieu of 30 days in the "workhouse" for using a fire hose on a squad of parading Marines.

Rookies in Burma (1943)

| WWII | Army | Unkn | B&W   61 mins |
| RKO | WV: 12-08-43 | | NYT: DNR |

DIR: Leslie Goodwins. SW: Edward James. PRO: Bert Gilroy. STARS: Wally Brown, Alan Carney, Erford Gage.

This "comedy" portrayed the Japanese capturing two bumbling soldiers in Burma and then their escape from a POW camp before American forces had actually arrived in country. The Office of War Information asked the studio to end the series after this, the second release, because it showed GIs as imbeciles.

The Rough Riders (1927)

| SpAmer | Army, Navy | NR | B&W   137 mins |
| Paramount | WV: 03-30-27 | | NYT: 03-16-27 |

DIR: Victor Fleming. SW: John Fish Goodrich, Robert N. Lee, Keene Thompson. PRO: Lucien Hubbard. STARS: Frank Hopper, Charles Farrell, Charles Emmett Mack, Mary Astor, Noah Beery, Col. Fred Lindsay, George Bancroft.

The action here focuses on the Texas training camp where Teddy Roosevelt's men prepared for war and from which they left to fight in Cuba. The film features the charge up San Juan Hill. According to contemporaneous reviews of the movie, audiences came expecting to see Roosevelt, not an actor, playing Roosevelt, even though the former president had died in 1919.

Rules of Engagement (2000) [G&G]

Peace	Marines, Navy	Full	Color	128 mins
Paramount	WV: 03-30-2000		NYT: 04-02 & 07-2000	

DIR: William Friedkin. SW: Stephen Gaghan. PRO: Richard Zanuck, Scott Rudin. STARS: Tommy Lee Jones, Samuel L. Jackson, Guy Pearce.

A decorated Marine officer, Jackson, and his troops rescue an ambassador and his family from an embassy in Yemen during a political crisis. When shots are apparently fired from the mob in front of the embassy, Jackson orders his men to return fire in self-defense, killing many civilians. Fearing a backlash in the face of diplomatic and media criticism, the Marines at the direction of the National Security Advisor order Jackson to face a court martial for violating rules of engagement because no direct proof apparently exists to show that the Marines were taking fire from within the crowd.

Jackson asks Jones, a Marine lawyer and comrade from Vietnam, to defend him. Jones, who became a lawyer after being seriously wounded, is about to retire after a rather undistinguished legal career but accepts the case because Jackson had saved his life during a firefight. The trial reveals that Jackson is being used as a scapegoat. He is acquitted of the most serious charges, but his career is ended. Only in the closing titles does the film reveal that the national security advisor, who withheld a videotape that would have exonerated Jackson, received his just reward.

Given the portrayals, the filmmakers did not initially approach the Marines for help. Ultimately they did go into the Marine public affairs office in Los Angeles to discuss the script, and after negotiations, Friedkin received use of a helicopter assault carrier and a helicopter to help stage the rescue mission. Despite problems with the story, which contained many implausibilities, the film did raise important questions about rules of engagement when the United States intervenes in foreign countries, whatever the provocation or lack thereof.

Run for Your Life (1988)

Vietnam	Army	NR	Color	Unkn
Unkn	WV: DNR		NYT: DNR	

DIR: Terence Young. SW: Unkn. PRO: Unkn. STARS: Sabine Sun, Jill Pearson, Gregg Stewart, Christine Cox.

An officer who was fragged in Vietnam, currently stationed at a base near Rome, continues to vent his anger by beating his wife. In turn, she trains to run the Rome Marathon, a race her husband had won twice. The less said the better.

Run Silent, Run Deep (1958) [SSS]

WWII	Navy	Full	B&W 93 mins
UA	WV: 03-26-58		NYT: 03-28-58

DIR: Robert Wise. SW: John Gay. PRO: Harold Hecht. STARS: Clark Gable, Burt Lancaster, Jack Warden, Brad Dexter, Don Rickles.

Based on Capt. Ed Beach's respected novel about submarine warfare in the Pacific, the film focuses on the conflict between the captain and his executive officer. The Navy provided a research tour of a submarine and assistance in building the set to actual size to help create the claustrophobic ambience. However, the film's opening does not explain how Gable survived the sinking of his previous submarine nor how he returned from the South China Sea to Hawaii. Beach objected to this sequence because he had not included it in his novel and he found it ludicrous and inexplicable. He also objected to air bubbles coming from the miniature submarine, pointing out that if real subs generated bubbles, they would pinpoint the location of the boat for the enemy. However, Wise explained that people expected to see some sign of motion from the undersea craft, so he took dramatic license.

Running Brave (1983)

Peace	Marines	Ltd	Color 106 mins
Buena Vista	WV: 10-05-83		NYT: DNR

DIR: Donald Shebib credited as D. S. Everett. SW: Henry Bean, Shirl Hendryx. PRO: Ira Englander. STARS: Robby Benson, Pat Hingle, Claudia Cron, Jeff McCracken.

This sports biography of Billy Mills portrays the Native American Marine who won the 10,000 meters race in the 1964 Tokyo Olympics, still considered one of the greatest upsets in track and field history. The film includes scenes of Mills training in the Marines.

The Russians Are Coming, the Russians Are Coming (1966)

Cold War	Navy, Air Force	Ltd	Color 124 mins
UA	WV: 05-25-66		NYT: 05-26-66

DIR: Norman Jewison. SW: William Rose. PRO: Norman Jewison. STARS: Carl Reiner, Eva Marie Saint, Alan Arkin, Brian Keith, Jonathan Winters, Theodore Bikel, Paul Ford.

Based on Nathaniel Benchley's novel *The Off-Islanders*, this film's action takes place on a mythical Massachusetts island (actually filmed in northern California) when a Russian submarine accidentally runs aground and the summer residents believe they are being invaded. The Navy loaned a submarine for a few establishing shots but then backed off as it became concerned about being criticized for being portrayed as failing to detect a Soviet submarine so close to U.S. territory. However, an Air Force jet did a brief fly-over for the cameras.

Sabre Jet (1953)

Korea	Air Force	Full	Color 96 mins
UA	WV: 09-09-53		NYT: 11-03-53

DIR: Louis King. SW: Dale Eunson, Katherine Albert. PRO: Carl Krueger. STARS: Robert Stack, Coleen Gray, Richard Arlen, Julie Bishop, Leon Ames, Amanda Blake, Reed Sherman, Jerry Paris.

Squadron leader Stack flies an F-86 Sabre jet over Korea from a Japanese base and wants Gray, his reporter wife, to stay at home where he thinks women belong. One might ask why she even married him. But the film has many more problems, most particularly the combining of combat footage from WWII and Korea. Watch carefully and see a WWII P-38 and a German BF-109 go down in flames and shots of F-80 and F-100 jets substituting for the Sabres in aerial combat, and the strafing of a MIG airfield populated with WWII German, Japanese, and even American planes. Probably worst of all is a scene in which Stack is ordered to blow up an ammunition dump hidden in a house. He locates it by simply shooting up all the houses along the road until he finds the right one—we know it is the right one because of the explosion.

The Sad Sack (1957)

Cold War	Army	Full	B&W	98 mins
Paramount	WV: 10-23-57		NYT: 11-28-57	

DIR: George Marshall. SW: Edmund Beloin, Nate Monaster. PRO: Hal B. Wallis. STARS: Jerry Lewis, David Wayne, Phyllis Kirk, Peter Lorre, Joe Mantell, Gene Evans.

Lewis, without Martin, stationed in Morocco, innocently becomes involved with local criminals and then spends the rest of the film trying to disengage from them, while surviving his corporal, WACs, and the base psychiatrist.

Sadie Thompson (1928)

Peace	Marines	NR	B&W	97 mins
UA	WV: 02-08-28:		NYT: 02-06-28	

DIR: Raoul Walsh. SW: Raoul Walsh. PRO: Raoul Walsh, Gloria Swanson. STARS: Gloria Swanson, Lionel Barrymore, James Marcus, Raoul Walsh.

Prostitute Swanson arrives on a South Seas island, where she meets Walsh playing a Marine sergeant stationed there with a detachment. A missionary persuades her to repent but then rapes her and commits suicide. In turn, she and Walsh leave for Australia and a new life. Remade as *Rain* in 1932 and *Miss Sadie Thompson* in 1954.

Sahara (1943) [G&G]

WWII	Army	Full	B&W	95 mins
Columbia	WV: 09-29-43		NYT: 11-12-43	

DIR: Zoltan Korda. SW: John Howard Lawson, Zoltan Korda. PRO: Harry Joe Brown. STARS: Humphrey Bogart, Bruce Bennett, Lloyd Bridges, J. Carrol Naish, Kurt Krueger.

The Army provided a tank and personnel in this fantasy about Americans fighting with the British against the Germans in Libya in the early days of WWII, albeit before U.S. forces had actually arrived in Africa. Filming took place at the Army's Camp Young desert training facility along the

California–Nevada border. On his way through the desert to the safety of Allied lines, Bogart picks up a diverse group of soldiers representing the coalition opposing the Axis, as well as an evil Nazi flier and a pro-American Italian soldier. Despite long-standing regulations prohibiting American men and equipment from portraying an enemy, U.S. soldiers played Germans and a P-40 fighter, disguised as a German plane, strafed Bogart's tank.

Sailor Beware (1951)

Peace	Navy	Full	B&W	104 mins
Paramount	WV: 12-05-51		NYT: 02-01-52	

DIR: Hal Walker. SW: James Allardice, Martin Rackin, John Grant. PRO: Hal Wallis. STARS: Jerry Lewis, Dean Martin, Corinne Calvet, Marion Marshall, Robert Strauss, Leif Erickson, Vince Edwards.

The movie version of the Kenyon Nicholson and Charles Robinson play provides Lewis an opportunity to wreak havoc on the Navy, when he and Martin are inducted. Training sequences, Lewis on the conning tower of a diving sub, and a WAVE or two appear in this formula piece.

A Sailor-Made Man (1921)

Peace	Navy	Ltd	B&W	4 reels
Roach	WV: 11-25-21		NYT: 11-06-23	

DIR: Fred Newmeyer. SW: Hal Roach, Sam Taylor, H. M. Walker. PRO: Hal Roach. STARS: Harold Lloyd, Mildred Davis, Noah Young, Dick Sutherland.

Lloyd, a rich young man, joins the Navy to win his rich, young girlfriend, who challenges him to do something with his life. Naval personnel appeared in scenes when Lloyd was aboard his ship.

Sailor's Lady (1940)

Peace	Navy	Ltd	B&W	67 mins
Fox	WV: 07-03-40		NYT: 06-29-40	

DIR: Allan Dwan. SW: Frank Wead, Frederick Hazlitt Brennan, Lou Breslow, Owen Francis. PRO: Fox. STARS: Nancy Kelly, Jon Hall, Joan Davis, Dana Andrews, Mary Nash, Larry "Buster" Crabbe, Wally Vernon.

In this comedy, two sailors vie for the affections of Kelly, who is serving as a guardian to a baby named "Skipper." Several scenes portray the baby aboard a Navy warship, crying as the ship commences target practice.

Sailor's Luck (1933)

Peace	Navy	Ltd	B&W	64 mins
Fox	WV: 03-21-33		03-17-33	

DIR: Raoul Walsh. SW: Charlotte Miller, Marguerite Roberts. PRO: William Fox. STARS: James Dunn, Sally Eilers, Victor Jory, Sammy Cohen.

Standard issue Navy comedy mixed with romance. Harrigan, on shore leave, meets Eilers, but cannot accept her promise of love since she enters a dance marathon after his ship heads for San Francisco.

Sailors on Leave (1941)

Peace	Navy	Cour	B&W 71 mins
Republic	WV: 10-08-41		NYT: DNR

DIR: Albert S. Rogell. SW: Art Arthur, Malcolm Stuart Boylan. PRO: Albert J. Cohen, Adam Abel. STARS: William Lundigan, Shirley Ross, Chick Chandler, Ruth Donnelly, Mae Clarke.

Battleships and cafes are backgrounds in this comedy, which also features Jule Styne and Frank Loesser musical numbers. Lundigan, as the sailor, wants to avoid marriage but owes big bucks to his crew members. One possible solution is to find a rich wife. Easier said than done, especially for a destitute sailor.

Saints and Soldiers (2003)

WWII	Army	NR	Color 90 mins
Excel Enter	DVP: 11-24-2003		NYT: 10-15-2003

DIR: Ryan Little. SW: Geoffrey Panos, Matt Whitaker. PRO: Ryan Little. STARS: Corbin Allred, Larry Bagby, Kirby Heyborne, Peter Asle Holden.

Five American soldiers, captured by the Germans with more than 100 others near Malmedy, in Belgium, escape during a moment of confusion and panic when German soldiers fire on the unarmed prisoners. Without water and food, in bitter cold, the GIs struggle to get back to Allied lines.

Salute (1929)

Peace	Navy	Full	B&W 83 mins
Fox	WV: 08-21-29		NYT: 10-05-29

DIR: John Ford. SW: James K. McGuinness, John Stone, Wilbur Morse Jr. PRO: John Ford. STARS: George O'Brien, William Janney, Helen Chandler, Ward Bond, Frank Albertson, John Wayne.

The film follows the same pattern of other military academy stories, subordinating the characters to the background in which they marched, played, and fell in love. In this case, brothers oppose each other in the Army–Navy game. *Salute* does have two claims to fame: It was the first sound movie to feature Annapolis, and John Wayne, a midshipman, spoke on screen for the first time.

Salute to the Marines (1943)

WWII	Marines	Full	Color 101 mins
MGM	WV: 07-26-43		NYT: 08-30-43

DIR: S. Sylvan Simon. SW: George Bruce. PRO: John Considine Jr. STARS: Wallace Beery, Fay Bainter, Reginald Owen, William Lundigan.

Based on an original story, the movie opens during a medal ceremony at the San Diego Marine base and then flashes back to portray how Beery, a retired Marine, waged war on the Japanese in the Philippines in the early days of the conflict. At the end, the film returns to the ceremony, in which Beery's daughter accepts his medal for heroism. Marines appeared in the San Diego scenes and the picture exuded patriotism, helping the war effort and the Corps's recruiting.

San Francisco (1936)

Peace	Marines	Ltd	B&W	115 mins
MGM	WV: 07-01-36		NYT: 06-27-36	

DIR: W. S. Van Dyke. SW: Anita Loos. PRO: John Emerson, Bernard Hyman. STARS: Clark Gable, Spencer Tracy, Jack Holt, Jeanette MacDonald.

Director Van Dyke, a Marine reserve officer, used active-duty Marines as unidentified extras during earthquake scenes because of their ability to obey orders quickly. Marines also appear in uniform performing duties, as they would do in a real emergency, to bring order out of chaos.

The Sand Pebbles (1966)

China	Navy	NR	Color	179 mins
Fox	WV: 12-21-66		NYT: 12-21-66	

DIR: Robert Wise. SW: Robert Anderson. PRO: Robert Wise. STARS: Steve McQueen, Richard Attenborough, Richard Crenna, Candice Bergen, Mako.

Based on Richard McKenna's novel, the film can be seen as predicting the morass that Vietnam would shortly become, if it was not already one. In this case, a U.S. Navy gunboat on the Yangtze River in 1926 becomes involved with the unrest in China, while trying to rescue some American missionaries who do not really want to be rescued.

Sands of Iwo Jima (1949) [G&G]

WWII	Marines	Full	B&W	110 mins
Republic	WV: 12-14-49		NYT: 12-31-49	

DIR: Allan Dwan. SW: Harry Brown, James Grant. PRO: Herbert Yates. STARS: John Wayne, John Agar, Forrest Tucker, Arthur Franz, Richard Jaeckel.

Based on Grainger's original idea after he saw the phrase "sands of Iwo Jima" in a newspaper. *Sands of Iwo Jima* remains to this day the classic WWII Marine story and one of the most influential war movies ever made. The film follows the travails of Sgt. Stryker's rifle company from New Zealand to Tarawa to Iwo Jima. In Stryker, a hard-bitten, bitter Marine, Wayne created the quintessential image of the American fighting man who passes his combat wisdom to the next generation of young men who will protect the nation. Stryker and his company help take Tarawa and Iwo Jima in realistic combat scenes that combine live action at Camp Pendleton with Marine footage taken on Tarawa (originally used in *With the Marines at Tarawa,* which won an Oscar for best documentary) and at Iwo Jima. As the squad pauses just before reaching the summit of Mount Surabachi, a Japanese sniper shoots Stryker in the back. However, Wayne has trained his men well to do their jobs, and they carry on to victory as Marines raise the flag, with the surviving participants taking part in the scene that would help create the mythic image for all time.

The Corps naturally loved the story and provided full assistance at Pendleton, where Dwan had use of Marines and equipment for several weeks. The Corps also assigned then-Capt. Leonard Fribourg as technical advisor to ensure the accuracy of the portrayal of procedures and appearance of the actors, who actually trained with Marines before shooting began. Fribourg's only objection was to a scene in which Stryker hits one of his men in the face with a rifle butt while instructing him in hand-to-hand combat. After consulting with Marine Headquarters, Fribourg approved the scene with slight changes.

Wayne's portrayal influenced several generations of young American males to enlist in the Marines. However, in Vietnam, these newly minted Leathernecks discovered that war did not resemble the sanitized version contained in **Sands of Iwo Jima**. Ron Kovic wrote in the book **Born on the Fourth of July** that he could not wait to enlist in the Corps after watching John Wayne run up Mount Surabachi, but he then lamented his lost innocence and paralyzed body. Still, Wayne's persona continues to pervade contemporary American society, including beer commercials.

The Satan Bug (1965)

Terrorism	Army	NR	Color	114 mins
United Artists	WV: 03-10-65		NYT: 04-15-65	

DIR: John Sturges. SW: James Clavell, Edward Anhalt. PRO: John Sturges. STARS: Dana Andrews, Richard Basehart, George Maharis.

Based on Ian Stuart's novel, this is an early terrorist film showing the military's effort to find stolen death germs. The movie contained bad images of the Army, including the portrayal of military scientists developing biological weapons. Still, it was better than most of the genre.

Saved from the Harem (1915)

Peace	Navy	Ltd	B&W	4 reels
Lubin	WV: DNR		NYT: DNR	

DIR: Wilbert Melville. SW: Julian Louis LaMothe, Wilbert Melville. PRO: Lubin. STARS: Melvin Mayo, Adelaide Bronti, Violet MacMillan, Adda Gleason, Lee Shumway.

After a change in presidential administrations, a family from Kankakee, Illinois, travel to Vergania, an Eastern kingdom, to represent U.S. interests. Upon meeting the daughter, Amy, the king decides he wants her for his harem. Amy's boyfriend, Navy Lt. Robert Brice, sails into the harbor and rescues the family—just in time.

Saving Private Ryan (1998) [G&G]

WWII	Army	Cour	Color	170 mins
Dreamworks	WV: 09-13-98		NYT: 07-24 & 09-04-98	

DIR: Steven Spielberg. SW: Robert Rodat. PRO: Steven Spielberg, Ian Bryce, Mark Gordon, Gary Levinsohn. STARS: Tom Hanks, Tom Sizemore, Edward Burns, Barry Pepper, Matt Damon, Dale Dye.

Extravagantly praised portrayal of the landing of the 29th Division on Omaha Beach on Day-D and the subsequent fighting inland. Using scenes borrowed from ***The Longest Day*** and clichéd images from other combat films, Spielberg effectively staged his version of hell in 24 minutes of unrelenting violence. The director was to claim that only he could portray the reality of combat by using extreme violence. Most D-Day veterans acknowledge that Spielberg captured the essence of their experiences and the horror that Omaha Beach became. Nevertheless, however brilliant the filmmaking, the bloody montage has virtually no relationship to the rest of the movie. Using ***A Walk in the Sun*** as his inspiration, Spielberg then follows the trek of a ranger unit through enemy territory to find and retrieve Private Ryan, whose three brothers have died in combat, two on D-Day and one in the Pacific.

In fact, the springboards of the story lack any credibility. In the movie's opening sequence, the veteran kneeling at an unidentified grave at the American cemetery overlooking the English Channel has a flashback to a landing craft approaching Omaha Beach. Only at the end of the movie does Spielberg reveal that Private Ryan, not Captain Miller, survived the war and had the flashback to the assault. However, Ryan, a paratrooper with the 101st Airborne, landed 15 miles inland and could not have had the flashback since he would have no firsthand knowledge of the events that took place on Omaha Beach.

Moreover, as the Army advised Spielberg after reading the script, the Pentagon and Gen. George Marshall could not have known two days after the landing that Ryan's two brothers had died on D-Day as the film portrays. Nor could the death notices have arrived at the Ryan farm in Iowa the same day that Marshall learns of the deaths. Neither faxes nor e-mails existed on June 6, 1944, and notifications of next of kin did not begin for at least a month after the landing, in contrast to the almost immediate arrival of the news in the movie.

From the scenes in the Pentagon onward, all veracity and plausibility rapidly disappear. The Army would not have sent elite Rangers on the mission portrayed; a Ranger observed that if such an effort would have even been attempted, the Army would have sent a chaplain in a jeep. Moreover, hedgerows, invisible in the movie, actually hindered all movements off the beaches after the initial landings.

Although Hanks's Captain Miller clearly suffers from battle fatigue, Spielberg never explains the cause, and in any event, neither Miller nor his men would have been in combat for quite some time, if at all, before D-Day. In any case, if his condition had been spotted, the Army would certainly have kept him back in England recuperating, not leading his men on the mission. Given their special training and selection for the hazardous assignment, it is incomprehensible that Miller's men would have staged a minimutiny to protest his handling of a German soldier. If Spielberg was seeking accuracy, he would have had Miller shoot the German instantly, given the circumstances, rather than allowing him to wander off. This happened on occasion, and in Spielberg and Hanks's TV miniseries ***Band of Brothers***, American soldiers did shoot a group of POWs rather than continue to guard them. But fear not, the German will return to fight another day.

The rest of the movie is no more believable, particularly Miller's climactic defense of a bridge against German tanks. First, he ignores the prime directive: bring Ryan home safely. Second, he tries to deny the enemy a bridge he has no means of defending. He has no antitank weapons, only a few surviving Rangers and a few lightly armed paratroopers. Then there is the irony Spielberg tries to create by having the freed German reappear to first kill gruesomely (and gratuitously) the Jewish soldier and then shoot Miller. However, the director is not done with the irony. While the cowardly Upham had sat quivering on the stairs while the German killed the Jewish soldier, he finally finds courage and kills the German soldier up close and personal.

In the end, Spielberg returns to his Hollywood roots and has the cavalry, in the guise of P-51 "tank-busters," arrive to save the day, sort of: the bridge survives, Miller dies, and Ryan lives. Even here, Spielberg cannot get it right, factually or dramatically. P-47 Thunderbolts, not the film's P-51 Mustangs, which flew over the cinematic bridge, had the nickname "tank busters." And, although a critic has no right to tell a director how to create his film, only whether he succeeds or not, here goes: dramatically, Miller should have lived to have the flashback, while Ryan should have died to remind people that surviving in combat remains a crap shoot.

Sayonara (1957)

Korea	Air Force	Full	Color 147 mins
WB	WV: 11-13-57		NYT: 12-06-57

DIR: Joshua Logan. SW: Paul Osborn. PRO: William Goetz. STARS: Marlon Brando, Red Buttons, Miyoshi Umeki, James Garner, Ricardo Montalban, Patricia Owens.

Based on the James Michener novel, the film explores racial prejudice within the U.S. military. In the end, love could not conquer all, and Buttons and Umeki commit suicide. Although not a positive image of the Air Force, the service cooperated by allowing the filming of planes at one of its Japanese bases.

Screaming Eagles (1956)

WWII	Army	Full	B&W 80 mins
Allied Artists	WV: 05-30-56		NYT: DNR

DIR: Charles Haas. SW: David Lang, Robert Presnell Jr. PRO: Samuel Bischoff, David Diamond. STARS: Tom Tryon, Jan Merlin, Alvy Moore, Martin Milner.

A surly private replacement joins a 101st Airborne platoon and parachutes behind enemy lines on D-Day.

The Search (1948)

Peace	Army	Full	B&W 105 mins
MGM	WV: 03-24-48		NYT: 03-24-48

DIR: Fred Zinnemann. SW: David Wechsler, Richard Schweizer, Paul Jarrico. PRO: Lazar Wechsler. STARS: Montgomery Clift, Jarmila Novotna, Wendell Corey, Ivan Jandl.

Zinnemann filmed exteriors on the outskirts of Munich and Nuremberg in the American zone of occupied Germany. The Army provided jeeps, a barracks, and other background material for this story of displaced children following the end of WWII hostilities in Europe. In his first film role, Clift plays a GI who wants to adopt one of the children, until his mother succeeds in finding him.

Search and Destroy (1979)

Vietnam	Army	NR	Color 93 mins
Film Ventures	WV: DNR		NYT: DNR

DIR: William Fruet. SW: Don Enright. PRO: James Margellos. STARS: Perry King, Don Stroud, Tisa Farrow, Park Jong Soo, Kirk McOll.

Someone is murdering, one by one, the veterans from a squad who fought together in Vietnam. Full of "B" movie Vietnam War clichés. Similar story to *Good Guys Wear Black*.

The Seas Beneath (1931)

WWI	Navy	Full	B&W 98 mins
Fox	WV: 02-04-31		NYT: 01-31-31

DIR: John Ford. SW: James Parker Jr., Dudley Nichols. PRO: W. M. Fox, John Ford. STARS: George O'Brien, Marion Lessing, Warren Hymer, Walter C. Kelly.

Men Without Women again, with women shown as active rather than reactive. However, no tension this time, even though the women are actually spies.

The Secret War of Harry Frigg (1968)

WWII	Army	Unkn	Color 110 mins
Universal	WV: 02-28-68		NYT: 03-05-68

DIR: Jack Smight. SW: Peter Stone, Frank Tarloff. PRO: Hal E. Chester. STARS: Paul Newman, Sylva Koscina, Tom Bosley, Andrew Duggan, John Williams, Werner Peters, James Gregory.

In this comedy, Newman portrays a goof-off, unsophisticated private sent to rescue five Allied generals held by the Axis.

See Here, Private Hargrove (1944)

WWII	Army	Full	B&W 101 mins
MGM	WV: 02-23-44		NYT: 03-22-44

DIR: Wesley Ruggles. SW: Harry Kurnitz. PRO: George Haight. STARS: Robert Walker, Donna Reed, Keenan Wynn, Robert Benchley.

From Marion Hargrove's book, the film tells the romantic story of a young man who enlists in the Army, which serves as background for the attendant comedy episodes shot, in part, at Fort Bragg, North Carolina.

The Sergeant (1968)

Peace	Army	NR	Color 107 mins
WB	WV: 10-30-68		NYT: 12-26-68

DIR: John Flynn. SW: Dennis Murphy. PRO: Richard Goldstone. STARS: Rod Steiger, John Phillip Law, Frank Latimore.

Based on Dennis Murphy's novel *The Sergeant*. A WWII heroic sergeant descends on a small post in southern France and, for all practical purposes, takes over command from a lax and alcoholic officer. He then pursues a young private, both physically and psychologically. WWII prologue scenes in B&W.

Sgt. Bilko (1996)

Peace	Army	Deny	Color 94 mins
Universal	WV: 04-01-96		NYT: 03-29-96

DIR: Jonathan Lynn. SW: Andy Breckman. PRO: Brian Grazer. STARS: Steve Martin, Dan Aykroyd, Phil Hartman, Glenne Headly.

The big screen version of the television character that Nat Hiken created and Phil Silvers made infamous. This version, with its conniving noncommissioned officer, did nothing to benefit the Army even though Bilko was following the Army's recruiting slogan of the 1990s of being all he could be. Consequently, the service declined to provide assistance.

Sergeant Mike (1945)

WWII	Army	Full	B&W 60 mins
Columbia	WV: 02-07-45		NYT: DNR

DIR: Henry Levin. SW: Robert Lee Johnson. PRO: Jack Fier. STARS: Larry Parks, Jeanne Bates, and the dogs, Mike and Pearl.

 A soldier transferred from machine guns to canines is disgruntled until he learns that a war orphan donated one of his charges. The dogs definitely have the starring roles as they wipe out gun nests and carry messages. Guess who the soldier marries?

Sergeant Murphy (1937)

Peace	Army	Ltd	B&W 57mins
WB	WV: 12-22-37		NYT: DNR

DIR: B. Reeves Eason. SW: Sy Bartlett, William Jacobs. PRO: Bryan Foy. STARS: Ronald Reagan, Mary Maguire, Donald Crisp, Ben Hendricks, Max Hoffman Jr.

Private Reagan plays second fiddle to his buddy Sgt. Murphy, a rambunctious cavalry horse. When the Army discharges Sarge because of his intransigence, he embarks, with Reagan's assistance, upon a racing career culminating in a victory in the Grand National at Aintree. Filmed at the Presidio in Monterey with cavalry soldiers as extras. The Army forbade the men to accept pay, but Reagan treated them to dinner at a local hotel.

Sergeant Ryker (1968)

Korea	Army	NR	Color 85 mins
Universal	WV: DNR		NYT: 03-21-68

DIR: Buzz Kulik. SW: Seeleg Lester, William D. Gordon. PRO: Frank Telford. STARS: Lee Marvin, Bradford Dillman, Vera Miles, Peter Graves.

Based on a 1963 TV movie. Marvin disappears from his unit for two months and then returns, claiming that an officer, now dead, had ordered him to spy. Was he collaborating with the Chinese communists or telling the truth? Only the court-martial can decide, after talk and more talk, much of it interesting, which makes Marvin's Ryker so unique.

Sergeant York (1941)

WWI	Army	Ltd	B&W	134 mins
WB	WV: 07-02-41		NYT: 07-03-41	

DIR: Howard Hawks. SW: Abem Finkel, Harry Chandlee, Howard Koch, John Huston. PRO: Jesse L. Lasky, Howard Hawks, Hal B. Wallis. STARS: Gary Cooper, Walter Brennan, Joan Leslie, George Tobias, Stanley Ridges.

The patriotic story of a plain citizen from the hills of Tennessee who reluctantly went off to France, killed 26 Germans, captured 132 more in the Argonne sector, and received the Medal of Honor. When he returned home, York eschewed all monetary rewards and refused to give permission to make a film about his heroism.

Only as another war loomed did York agree to support the production after receiving assurances that he would receive substantial funds for his educational work and that Cooper agreed to play York. While the film stirs up patriotism and the need to defend democracy, it acknowledges York's pacifism and how the Army convinced him of the necessity for a strong military. Ultimately, the movie became one of the preparedness, antifascist films American isolationists cited as part of Hollywood's effort to draw the United States into World War II.

Seven Days in May (1964) [G&G]

Cold War	Marines, Navy	NR	B&W	120 mins
Paramount	WV: 02-05-64		NYT: 02-20-64	

DIR: John Frankenheimer. SW: Rod Serling. PRO: Edward Lewis. STARS: Burt Lancaster, Kirk Douglas, Fredric March, Edmond O'Brien.

Based on the Fletcher Knebel and Charles Bailey novel. Douglas plays a Marine colonel who foils a coup attempt by Lancaster, playing the chairman of the Joint Chiefs of Staff. Although President John F. Kennedy liked the book and thought it should become an important movie, the filmmakers chose not to request cooperation. However, the producer talked his way onto an aircraft carrier anchored at the San Diego Naval Base and took several shots, which later helped give the film an authentic ambience. The Navy and DoD protested the deception, but the producer said he would do anything necessary to get the director his needed scenes.

Seven Sinners (1940)

Peace	Navy	Full	B&W	85 mins
WB	WV: 10-30-40		NYT: 11-18-40	

DIR: Tay Garnett. SW: John Meehan, Harry Tugend. PRO: Joseph Pasternak. STARS: Marlene Dietrich, John Wayne, Broderick Crawford, Mischa Auer, Billy Gilbert, Anna Lee, Samuel S. Hinds.

Wayne is a Navy lieutenant who falls for Dietrich, a café singer living beyond a singer's means. *La Traviata* without a tragic end as the lady gives up Wayne to safeguard his career and settles for the ship's doctor.

Sharkfighters (1956)

WWII	Navy	Full	Color	74 mins
UA	WV: 10-31-56		NYT: DNR	

DIR: Jerry Hopper. SW: Lawrence Roman, Jonathan Robinson. PRO: Samuel Goldwyn Jr. STARS: Victor Mature, Karen Steele, James Olson.

The film depicts the Navy's attempt to develop a repellent that would protect downed fliers, and others, from shark attacks.

She Goes to War (1929)

WWI	Army	Unkn	B&W	87 mins
UA	WV: 06-12-29		NYT: 06-10-29	

DIR: Henry King. SW: Howard Estabrook, John Monk Saunders, Mme. Fred De Gresac. PRO: Victor Halperin, Edward R. Halperin. STARS: Eleanor Boardman, John Holland, Edmund Burns, Alma Rubens.

A rich socialite obtains an overseas Red Cross position and then disguises herself in order to fight at the front in place of her friend, who got drunk to avoid the draft. She falls in love with her commander, the garage owner from her hometown, with whose affections she had previously toyed.

She's in the Army (1942)

WWII	Army	NR	B&W	63 mins
Monogram	WV: 06-24-42		NYT: DNR	

DIR: Jean Yarbrough. SW: Sidney Sheldon, George Bricker. PRO: T. H. Richmond. STARS: Lucile Gleason, Veda Ann Borg, Marie Wilson, Lyle Talbot, Robert Lowery, Warren Hymer.

The film creates a patriotic atmosphere as women go through service training, etc., for the Ambulance and Defense Corps.

Shipmates (1931) [SSS]

Peace	Navy	Full	B&W	71 min
MGM	WV: 05-27-31		NYT: 05-23-31	

DIR: Harry Pollard. SW: Lou Edelman, Delmer Daves, Malcolm Stuart Boylan. PRO: MGM. STARS: Robert Montgomery, Ernest Torrence, Dorothy Jordan, Hobart Bosworth.

The Navy provided ships and Annapolis locales for this love story between a gob and an admiral's daughter. As usual, everything turns out fine: the gob gets an Annapolis appointment, saves an arsenal ship, and wins both the gal's and the admiral's hearts.

Shipmates Forever (1935) [SSS]

Peace	Navy	Full	B&W 109 mins
WB	WV: 10-23-35		NYT: 10-17-35

DIR: Frank Borzage. SW: Delmer Daves. PRO: Frank Borzage. STARS: Ruby Keeler, Dick Powell, Lewis Stone, Ross Alexander, Eddie Acuff.

An admiral's son wants to croon (providing a chance for Powell and Keeler to sing and dance) and does not do well at Annapolis until he rescues his buddy from an exploding boiler. While recuperating in the hospital, Powell determines to make something of himself in the Navy. Filming at the Naval Academy included focus on midshipmen's daily lives.

Shoulder Arms (1918)

WWI	Army	NR	B&W 36 mins
First Natl	WV: 10-25-18		NYT: 10-21-18

DIR: Charlie Chaplin. SW: Charlie Chaplin. PRO: Charlie Chaplin. STARS: Charlie Chaplin, Sydney Chaplin.

In the Army, Chaplin goes through basic training, during which time he dreams of fighting in Europe, capturing the kaiser and the crown prince, and becoming a hero. In one priceless scene, Chaplin disguises himself as a tree while behind enemy lines. Despite its comic intent, the film does convey some idea of training routines and life in the trenches of France.

The Siege (1998)

Terrorism	Army	NR	Color 109 mins
Fox	WV: 11-06-98		NYT: 11-06-98

DIR: Edward Zwick. SW: Lawrence Wright, Menno Meyjes, Edward Zwick. PRO: Lynda Obst, Edward Zwick. STARS: Denzel Washington, Annette Bening, Bruce Willis, Tony Shalhoub.

Zwick did not request assistance—perhaps still smarting from the Army's refusal to assist on *Courage Under Fire* and perhaps also recognizing the service's likely antipathy toward the script, which showed a general trying to establish martial law in the center of New York City.

Siege of Firebase Gloria (1989)

Vietnam	Army, Marines	NR	Color 100 mins
Fries Entertainment	WV: 03-22-89		NYT: DNR

DIR: Brian Trenchard-Smith. SW: William Nagle, Tony Johnston. PRO: Howard Grigsby, Rudolfos Confesor. STARS: Wings Hauser, R. Lee Ermey, Albert Popwell.

An Australian portrayal of American Marines defending a fire base during the Tet Offensive.

Silent Raiders (1954)

WWII	Army	NR	B&W 65 mins
Lippert	WV: DNR		NYT: DNR

DIR: Richard Bartlett. SW: Richard Bartlett. PRO: Richard Bartlett, Earle Lyon. STARS: Richard Bartlett, Earle Lyon, Jeanette Bordeaux, Earl Hansen, Robert Knapp.

This low-budget film features the director and producer in two of the starring roles. The story follows a commando team that lands just before D-Day to take out a Nazi communications center. Been there before, done that many times.

The Singing Marine (1937)

Peace	Marines	Full	B&W	105 mins
WB	WV: 07-07-37		NYT: 07-01-37	

DIR: Ray Enright. SW: Delmer Daves. PRO: WB. STARS: Dick Powell, Doris Weston, Lee Dixon.

A typical 1930s escapist musical, with Dick Powell as a bashful Marine who goes to New York for an amateur hour tryout and is unprepared for success. The film features the San Diego Marine base.

Situation Hopeless . . . But Not Serious (1965)

WWII	Air Force	NR	B&W	97 mins
Paramount	WV: 10-06-65		NYT: 10-14-65	

DIR: Gottfried Reinhardt. SW: Jan Lustig, Silvia Reinhardt. PRO: Gottfried Reinhardt. STARS: Alec Guinness, Robert Redford, Mike Connors, Paul Dahlke, Frank Wolff.

Based on Robert Shaw's novel, this little comedy tells the story of a lonely German clerk who "captures" two downed American fliers and keeps them as POWs in his bomb shelter. The war ends, but their jailer does not want to lose their companionship by telling them.

Skirts Ahoy! (1952)

Peace	Navy	Ltd	Color	109 mins
MGM	WV: 04-16-52		NYT: 05-29-52	

DIR: Sidney Lanfield. SW: Isobel Lennart. PRO: Joseph Pasternak. STARS: Esther Williams, Joan Evans, Vivian Blaine, Barry Sullivan.

A musical in which three women, all with men problems, join the WAVEs. Williams performs two swim numbers, and the film includes lots of music and a precision drill dance by a squad of WAVEs. Sullivan plays a Great Lakes Naval Training Base medical officer who becomes Williams's target.

Ski Troop Attack (1960)

WWII	Army	Unkn.	B&W	63 mins
Filmgroup	WV: 05-04-60		NYT: DNR.	

DIR: Roger Corman. SW: Charles B. Griffith. PRO: Roger Corman. STARS: Michael Forest, Frank Wolff, Richard Sinatra, Wally Campo.

U.S. ski troops are sent behind enemy lines to blow up a German-held bridge. Tensions between Wolff, a seasoned sergeant, and Forest, a newly minted OCS lieutenant, jeopardize the mission. But in the end, the bridge falls down. Except for Remagen and Nijmegen, don't they always in war films? Corman shot the movie, allegedly in two weeks, outside Deadwood, South Dakota.

Sky Commando (1953)

WWII/Korea	Air Force	Ltd	B&W 69 mins
Columbia	WV: 08-26-53		NYT: DNR

DIR: Fred F. Sears. SW: Samuel Newman. PRO: Sam Katzman. STARS: Dan Duryea, Frances Gifford, Mike Connors, Michael Fox.

This formula action film uses combat footage and a lengthy flashback to tell the story of the commanding officer's flying career.

Sky Devils (1932)

WWI	Air Force	Cour	B&W 90 mins
UA	WV: 03-08-32		NYT: 03-04-32

DIR: A. Edward Sutherland. SW: Robert Benchley, Carroll Graham, Garrett Graham, James A. Starr, A. Edward Sutherland. PRO: A. Edward Sutherland, Howard Hughes. STARS: Spencer Tracy, William Boyd, George Cooper, Ann Dvorak.

A war comedy portraying two phony lifeguards who join up, develop a common enemy (who becomes their top sergeant), and fight in France. Tracy accidentally blows up his own airfield and Cooper, as the mechanic, takes a couple of dicey solo flights, before these two team up to save the day. The film features footage of a WWI aerial armada.

The Sky's the Limit (1943)

WWII	Air Force	Ltd	B&W 90 mins
RKO	WV: 09-08-43		NYT: 09-03-43

DIR: Edward H. Griffith. SW: Frank Fenton, S. K. Lauren, Lynn Root. PRO: David Hempstead. STARS: Fred Astaire, Joan Leslie, Robert Benchley.

Astaire this time plays a returning Flying Tigers hero, on a 10-day leave filled with music and dancing, and, of course, romance.

Slattery's Hurricane (1949)

Peace	Navy	Ltd	B&W 83 mins
Fox.	WV: 08-03-49		NYT: 08-13-49

DIR: André DeToth. SW: Herman Wouk, Richard Murphy. PRO: William Perlberg. STARS: Richard Widmark, Linda Darnell, Veronica Lake.

Widmark, a former highly skilled Navy aviator, is flying for a candy manufacturer, ironically involved in drug smuggling, which our hero does not discover until one of the company's partners has a heart attack. The film uses flashbacks of Widmark's WWII career as part of a buildup to the portrayal of hurricane-hunting Naval pilots.

Sniper's Ridge (1961)

Korea	Army	NR	B&W 61 mins
Fox	WV: 02-08-61		NYT: 08-24-61

DIR: John Bushelman. SW: Tom Maruzzi. PRO: John Bushelman. STARS: Jack Ging, Stanley Clements, John Goddard, Douglas Henderson.

An uptight captain orders a unit to undertake a dangerous mission in the waning moments before the truce in Korea. The patrol pauses when the unlikable captain steps on a mine, adding to the men's problems.

So Proudly We Hail (1943)

WWII	Army	Ltd	B&W 126 mins
Paramount	WV: 06-23-43		NYT: 09-10-43

DIR: Mark Sandrich. SW: Allan Scott. PRO: Mark Sandrich. STARS: Claudette Colbert, Paulette Goddard, Veronica Lake, George Reeves.

The classic portrayal of wartime nurses struggling to escape the Japanese as they capture Bataan, Corregidor, and the rest of the Philippines. This film set the standard for appearances of women in WWII movies (see also *Cry Havoc*).

Soldiers in the Rain (1963)

Peace	Army	Ltd	B&W 87 mins
Allied Artists	WV: 11-20-63		NYT: 11-28-63

DIR: Ralph Nelson. SW: Blake Edwards, Maurice Richlin. PRO: Blake Edwards, Martin Jurow. STARS: Jackie Gleason, Steve McQueen, Tuesday Weld, Tom Poston, Paul Hartman, Ed Nelson, Lew Gallo, Tony Bill.

Gleason plays a career sergeant whom McQueen, a supply sergeant, idolizes and hopes to convince to leave the military with him and begin a business together. The scene in which MPs beat up McQueen did not benefit the Army, but the service still provided some assistance.

A Soldier's Story (1984)

WWII	Army	Full	Color 101 mins
Columbia	WV: 09-05-84		NYT: 09-14-84

DIR: Norman Jewison. SW: Charles Fuller. PRO: Norman Jewison, Ronald L. Schwary. STARS: Howard E. Rollins Jr., Adolph Caesar, Dennis Lipscomb, Art Evans, Denzel Washington, Larry Riley, David Alan Grier, "Wings" Hauser, Patti LaBelle.

Charles Fuller adapted his Pulitzer Prize–winning *A Soldier's Play* for the screen. A murder at a black army base near the end of WWII is the setting for the plot, which explores racial attitudes in the WWII military. The Army sends Washington, playing a black officer-attorney and outsider, to investigate. When he arrives on post, the white officers hold him in contempt while the black soldiers respect and admire him. Depicts racial strife and bigotry as Washington solves the murder. The DoD felt the film could give audiences an understanding of the origins of integration in the military and so allowed the company to shoot on Fort Chafee to provide an authentic ambience.

The Soldier's Story (1981)

Vietnam	Army	NR	B&W/color 91 mins
Cine-Fund	WV: 06-03-81		NYT: DNR

DIR: Ian McLeod. SW: Ian McLeod. PRO: Ian McLeod, Mike Feheley. STARS: Geoffrey Bowes, Tom Do-Trong Chau.

Using combat footage from both the United States and North Vietnam, the film follows the war from the fictional perspective of two soldiers: one U.S. and one North Vietnamese (see also *The Iron Triangle*).

A Soldier's Sweetheart (1998)

Vietnam	Army	NR	Color 112 mins
Paramount	WV: 06-22-98		NYT: DNR

DIR: Thomas Michael Donnelly. SW: Thomas Michael Donnelly. PRO: William Gilmore. STARS: Kiefer Sutherland, Georgina Cates, Skeet Ulrich, Daniel London.

Based on Tim O'Brien's short story "Sweetheart of the Song Tra Bong," the movie views Vietnam from a woman's perspective when a girlfriend of an Army medic shows up at a remote base in Vietnam and experiences the horrors of war close up. Filmed in New Zealand.

Some Kind of Hero (1982)

Vietnam	Army	NR	Color 88 mins
Paramount	WV: 03-31-82		NYT: 04-02-82

DIR: Michael Pressman. SW: James Kirkwood Jr., Robert Boris. PRO: Howard W. Koch. STARS: Richard Pryor, Margot Kidder, Ray Sharkey, Ronny Cox, Lynne Moody.

Based on Kirkwood's novel, which portrayed his first day in country. Pryor, literally caught with his pants down, spends the next five years as a POW. To obtain better medical care for his fellow prisoner and friend, Pryor signs a statement denouncing U.S. involvement in Vietnamese affairs. When he comes home he faces a wife, a mother, and other life problems, including forfeiture of back pay for his prison camp "confession." The movie has a sympathetic portrayal of an Army colonel trying to help Pryor adjust. Pryor's performance rises above the material and the production values, including the Vietnam section, which looks like a dead ringer for California.

Somebody Up There Likes Me (1956)

WWII	Army	Ltd	B&W 112 mins
MGM	WV: 07-04-56		NYT: 09-25-56

DIR: Robert Wise. SW: Ernest Lehman. PRO: Charles Schnee. STARS: Paul Newman, Pier Angeli, Eileen Heckart, Sal Mineo.

Based on middleweight boxer Rocky Graziano's life, the movie includes his dishonorable discharge and time in Leavenworth. The Army allowed filming at a military facility as background for his military service.

Something for the Boys (1944)

WWII	Army	Unkn	Color	87 mins
Fox	WV: 11-01-44		NYT: 11-30-44	

DIR: Lewis Seiler. SW: Robert Ellis, Helen Logan, Frank Gabrielson. PRO: Irving Starr. STARS: Phil Silvers, Carmen Miranda, Michael O'Shea, Vivian Blaine.

Based on Herbert and Dorothy Fields's Broadway musical, the film tells the story of three distant cousins who inherit a plantation and, for tax purposes, with the cooperation of a nearby Army camp, make the place into a home for Army wives and put on shows to raise additional funds.

Son of a Sailor (1933)

Peace	Navy	Full	B&W	73 mins
WB	WV: 12-05-33		NYT: 11-30-33	

DIR: Lloyd Bacon. SW: Alfred Cohn, Ernest Pagano, H. M. Walker. PRO: WB. STARS: Joe E. Brown, Jean Muir, Frank McHugh, Thelma Todd.

A comedy in which Brown is a sailor on the USS *Saratoga* and stumbles through many misadventures, including preventing spies from stealing the Navy's new autopilot. Apart from watching Brown steal the show, the film gave the service the opportunity to present its third aircraft carrier (after the *Langley* and the *Lexington*) to the nation.

Son of the Navy (1940)

Peace	Navy	Unkn	B&W	71 mins
Monogram	WV: 04-10-40		NYT: DNR	

DIR: William Nigh. SW: Marion Orth, George Waggner. PRO: Scott Dunlap. STARS: James Dunn, Jean Parker, Martin Spellman.

An orphan schemes and succeeds in adopting a Navy noncommissioned officer as his father, to the gob's embarrassment. But, as these films usually end, the gob not only legally adopts the boy but also gets a great gal as a wife.

Sound Off (1952)

Peace	Army	Ltd	Color	83 mins
Columbia	WV: 04-09-52		NYT: DNR	

DIR: Richard Quine. SW: Blake Edwards, Richard Quine. PRO: Jonie Taps. STARS: Mickey Rooney, Anne James, Sammy White.

A nightclub entertainer is inducted and sent overseas in an entertainment troop, providing ample opportunity for songs, dances, and the usual comedic scamps.

South Pacific (1958)

WWII	Navy, Marines	Full	Color	171 mins
Fox	WV: 03-26-58		NYT: 03-20-58	

DIR: Joshua Logan. SW: Paul Osborn. PRO: Buddy Adler. STARS: Rossano Brazzi, Mitzi Gaynor, John Kerr, Ray Walston.

Adapted for the screen from the classic Rogers and Hammerstein musical play, which was based on James Michener's Pulitzer prize–winning *Tales of the South Pacific*. Marines and sailors on the island serve as background for the love story of the Navy nurse and the French planter. The services provided men and material and helped to create the brief combat sequence.

South Sea Woman (1953)

WWII	Marines	NR	B&W	98 mins
WB	WV: 06-03-53		NYT: 06-04-53	

DIR: Arthur Lubin. SW: Edwin Blum, Earl Baldwin, Stanley Shapiro. PRO: Samuel Bischoff. STARS: Burt Lancaster, Virginia Mayo, Chuck Connors.

Adapted from the Arthur Rankin play *General Court Martial*, told on the screen in a flashback. Two Marine rivals miss their ship back to Pearl Harbor following shore leave, and they spend the rest of the movie battling each other and the Japanese as they try to return to their unit. One man becomes a hero and the other gets the girl.

Southern Comfort (1981) [G&G]

Vietnam	Army	Ltd	Color	100 mins
Fox	WV: 09-23-81		NYT: 09-25-81	

DIR: Walter Hill. SW: Michael Kane, Walter Hill, David Giler. PRO: David Giler. STARS: Keith Carradine, Powers Boothe, Fred Ward, Franklyn Seales, Peter Coyote.

A non-Vietnam, Vietnam movie, which replaces the Vietnamese jungles with a Southern bayou and the Vietcong with the local Cajuns. The Louisiana National Guard provided some support for the tale of a Guard unit lost in the swamps during a training exercise and trying to find its way back to civilization, with the restless natives in hot pursuit.

Sphere (1998)

SciFi	Army, Navy	Ltd	Color	120 mins
WB	WV: 02-13-98		NYT: 02-13-98	

DIR: Barry Levinson. SW: Stephen Hauser, Paul Attanasio. PRO: Barry Levinson, Michael Crichton, Andrew Wald. STARS: Dustin Hoffman, Sharon Stone, Samuel L. Jackson, Peter Coyote, Liev Schreiber.

Drawn from Crichton's novel, this underwater thriller was filled with aliens and futuristic aircraft. After negotiations produced a script satisfactory to the Navy, the service allowed Levinson to take shots of ships to provide a realistic ambience, at least on the surface.

The Spirit of St. Louis (1957)

Peace	Air Force	Ltd	Color 135 mins
WB	WV: 02-20-57		NYT: 02-22-57

DIR: Billy Wilder. SW: Wendell Mayes, Billy Wilder. PRO: Leland Hayward. STARS: James Stewart, Murray Hamilton, Patricia Smith.

In flashback, the film shows Charles Lindbergh's first encounter with the Air Force. The service provided a cargo plane to transport one of the replica *Spirits* to Paris for the landing scene.

The Spirit of West Point (1947)

Peace	Army	Full	B&W 77 min
Classic Pictures	WV: 10-08-47		NYT: 10-03-47

DIR: Ralph Murphy. SW: Tom Reed. PRO: Harry Joe Brown, John Rogers. STARS: Felix Blanchard, Glenn Davis, Robert Shayne, Anne Nagel, Alan Hale Jr., George O'Hanlon.

The story of West Point's All-American football greats, Mr. Inside (Blanchard, a fullback) and Mr. Outside (Davis, a halfback), who appear as themselves, winning back-to-back Heisman Trophies. Filmed in part at the U.S. Military Academy. Blanchard completed a career in the Army, retiring as a colonel. Davis played professional football for the Los Angeles Rams.

Stage Door Canteen (1943)

WWII	All	Full	B&W 132 mins
UA	WV: 05-12-43		NYT: 06-25-43

DIR: Frank Borzage. SW: Delmer Daves. PRO: Sol Lesser. STARS: Cheryl Walker, William Terry, Marjorie Riordan, Lon McCllister.

Although the film contained a thin plot of the romances between the canteen workers and the servicemen who stopped in, its real function was as a fund-raiser to support the canteen's work of entertaining the military personnel in New York. Hollywood and Broadway stars, including Tallulah Bankhead, Katharine Hepburn, George Jessel, Alfred Lunt, Lynn Fontanne, and Paul Muni, made appearances. Actual military personnel were extras in the canteen scenes. *Variety* praised Lesser for incorporating salutes to the Aussies, Chinese, and Russians.

Stalag 17 (1953)

WWII	Air Force	Ltd	B&W 119 mins
Paramount	WV: 05-06-53		NYT: 07-02-53

DIR: Billy Wilder. SW: Billy Wilder, Edwin Blum. PRO: Billy Wilder. STARS: William Holden, Don Taylor, Otto Preminger, Peter Graves, Robert Strauss.

Based on Donald Bevan and Edmund Trzcinski's play, the film is a comedic melodrama in which Holden is suspected of being an informer by his fellow GIs inside a POW camp. The stage actors reprise their supporting roles, and Preminger plays the camp commander. The problem with the film, as with any POW story, is that reality was much grimmer than what appears on the screen. The prisoners bordered on desperation, portrayals of which lack appeal. Moreover, the actors could never physically become prisoners. Even in the best of camps, men gradually wasted away, becoming virtually skin and bones, barely surviving. Filmmakers could never duplicate this reality.

Stand By for Action (1942)

WWII	Navy	Ltd	B&W 109 mins
MGM	WV: 12-09-42		NYT: 03-12-43

DIR: Robert Z. Leonard. SW: George Bruce, John L. Balderston, Herman J. Mankiewicz. PRO: Robert Z. Leonard, Orville O. Dull. STARS: Robert Taylor, Charles Laughton, Walter Brennan, Brian Donlevy.

Young sailors and tested, veteran officers rise to the occasion as the Navy confronts enemies of the U.S. at sea. In this patriotic film, the aged destroyer, left over from WWI, is assigned convoy duty following Pearl Harbor, rescues a lifeboat full of children from a torpedoed ship, and ultimately attacks a Japanese battleship.

The Starfighters (1964)

Peace	Air Force	Ltd	Color 78 mins
Riviera	WV: DNR		NYT: DNR

DIR: Will Zens. SW: Will Zens. PRO: Will Zens. STARS: Robert Dornan, Steve Early, Richard Jordahl, Joan Lougee.

A trite story of an Air Force F-104 Starfighter pilot who tries to prove his worthiness to his father. Future Congressman Dornan played the hero.

Stargate (1994)

SciFi	Air Force	NR	Color 121 mins
MGM	WV: 10-24-94		NYT: 10-28-94

DIR: Roland Emmerich. SW: Dean Devlin, Roland Emmerich. PRO: Joel B. Michaels, Oliver Eberle, Dean Devlin. STARS: Kurt Russell, James Spader, Viveca Lindfors, Jaye Davidson, French Stewart, John Diehl.

A Stargate provides the springboard for a juvenile story featuring space travel, not by a spaceship, but by a transporter discovered in the Egyptian desert in the 1920s. More than 50 years after its discovery, an American archaeologist and language expert deciphers the symbols on the huge structure.

Along with contemporary Air Force troops, he travels across the universe to a strange new world where the troops battle the evil inhabitants to save the earth. Or something like that.

Starlift (1951)

Korea	Army, Air Force	Ltd	B&W	103 mins
WB	WV: 11-07-51		NYT: 12-15-51	

DIR: Roy Del Ruth. SW: John Klorer, Karl Kamb. PRO: Robert Arthur. STARS: Doris Day, Gordon MacRae, Virginia Mayo, Gene Nelson, Gary Cooper.

The actors play themselves in this musical romance film that features an all-star show providing entertainment for servicemen leaving for Korea from Travis Air Force Base and others returning there for rehabilitation from their wounds.

Starman (1984)

SciFi	Army, Air Force	NR	Color	115 mins
Columbia	WV: 12-05-84		NYT: 12-14-84	

DIR: John Carpenter. SW: Bruce A. Evans, Raynold Gideon. PRO: Larry J. Franco. STARS: Jeff Bridges, Karen Allen, Charles Martin Smith.

As in many other sci-fi movies, the U.S. military because the villain of the piece. In this case, the Army chases Bridges and Allen halfway across the country as Bridges tries to rendezvous with his fellow aliens for a return home. The Pentagon would undoubtedly have looked unfavorably on a request for assistance because of portrayal of the military leadership and of the alien spaceship as a flying saucer.

Star Spangled Banner (1917) [G&G]

WWI	Marines	Full	B&W	3 reels
Edison	WV: DNR		NYT: DNR	

DIR: Edward Griffith. SW: Sumner Williams. PRO: Edison. STARS: Nellie Grant, Herbert Evans, Paul Kelly, Fred Gleason, Cyril Hughes.

Based on Mary Raymond Shipman Andrews's story of the same name from her 1916 book *Old Glory*. A teenager, whose British officer father died in WWI, moves to the United States when his American mother marries a Marine colonel, who takes command of the Marine barracks at Bremerton, Washington. The boy dismisses all things American and scorns Marines. Ultimately, after he has a hiking accident and the Marines rescue him, he prepares to enlist in the Corps to fight alongside the British in France. The Corps provided full cooperation at the Marine barracks, and the film showed Leathernecks in training as background to the story. The film's release coincided with a Marine WWI recruiting campaign.

Stars and Stripes Forever (1952)

Peace	Marines	Full	Color	89 mins
Fox	WV: 11-19-52		NYT: 12-23-52	

DIR: Henry Koster. SW: Lamar Trotti. PRO: Lamar Trotti. STARS: Clifton Webb, Debra Paget, Robert Wagner.

Fictionalized story of John Philip Sousa and the Marine Corps band, which appears as itself albeit in period uniforms.

Star Trek: First Contact (1996)

SciFi	Air Force	Cour	Color	110 mins
Paramount	WV: 11-18-96		NYT: 11-22-96	

DIR: Jonathan Frakes. SW: Brannon Braga, Ronald D. Moore. PRO: Rick Berman. STARS: Patrick Stewart, Jonathan Frakes, Brent Spiner, LeVar Burton, Michael Dorn, Gates McFadden.

The Air Force allowed the studio to film at an inactive Titan missile silo with a missile on exhibit at the Pima Air Museum in Green Valley, Arizona. The only visible military was the "USAF" painted on the missile.

Star Trek IV: The Voyage Home (1986) [SSS]

SciFi	Navy	Full	Color	119 mins
Paramount	WV: 11-19-86		NYT: 11-26-86	

DIR: Leonard Nimoy. SW: Harve Bennett, Steve Meerson, Peter Krikes, Nicholas Meyer. PRO: Harve Bennett. STARS: William Shatner, Leonard Nimoy, DeForest Kelley, James Doohan, George Takei, Walter Koenig, Nichelle Nichols.

Bennett requested use of the USS *Enterprise* as the location for the heroes' efforts to obtain nuclear fuel for their spaceship, marooned in a San Francisco park. When the famous TV spaceship's namesake was unavailable, the Navy provided the *Ranger*. The service had concerns that the film would show the visitors from the future breaching security to gain access to the nuclear reactor. However, Bennett defused the issue by pointing out that the *Star Trek* trademark transporter system did not constitute a circumvention of security since it was a future form of transportation and so did not represent a contemporary threat. Bennett also transformed the Navy police, who mistreat the space travelers, into civilian police.

Stateside (2004)

Peace	Marines	NR	Color	97 mins
Goldwyn	DVP: 05-24-04		NYT: 05-21-04	

DIR: Reverge Anselmo. SW: Reverge Anselmo. PRO: Robert Greenhut, Bonnie Wells-Hlinomaz. STARS: Rachael Leigh Cook, Jonathan Tucker, Agnes Bruckner, Val Kilmer, Joe Mantegna.

The film provides two stories for the price of one, to some extent, director Anselmo's own story. It opens and closes with Marine Tucker in a VA hospital, after being injured in the terrorist bombing at the Marine barracks in Beirut, Lebanon, in 1983. In a flashback, the rest of the movie explains how he found himself at the wrong place at the wrong time. He had joined the Marines under duress after causing an accident that badly injured two of his friends. There, he had come under the tutelage of Kilmer as the DI While not the towering martinet of such cinematic DIs as Jack Webb in *The D.I.*, Louis Gossett Jr. in *An Officer and a Gentleman*, or R. Lee Ermey in *Full Metal Jacket*, Kilmer, in his insistently prodding manner, achieves his goal of turning boys, including Tucker, into men ready to face the world.

With a limited budget and without Marine assistance, Anselmo, who went through basic training himself, makes the physical ambience and the military culture believable. Meanwhile, in the other half of the story, while on leave Tucker visits his maimed friend, now in a mental institution because of her mother's conniving. There he meets the girl's roommate, Cook, an ex-child star/singer and budding schizophrenic. In this case, love does not conquer all, despite his best efforts, and Tucker heads off to Beirut and a date with history.

Stealth (2005)

SciFi	Navy	Full	Color
Columbia	WV:?		NYT:?

DIR: Rob Cohen. SW: Rob Cohen, W. D. Richter. PRO: Mike Medavoy, Laura Ziskin. STARS: Josh Lucas, Jessica Biel, Jamie Foxx, Sam Shepard.

In the near future, three Navy pilots struggle to bring an artificial intelligence program under control before it starts the next world war. Shades of *The Forbin Project* and *WarGames*. Although set in the near future, the Navy provided a contemporary carrier, planes, etc.

Stealth Fighter (2000)

Peace	Navy, Air Force	NR	Color	88 mins
Artisan Enter	WV: DNR		NYT: DNR	

DIR: Jim Wynorski. SW: Lenny Juliano. PRO: Jim Wynorski. STARS: Ice-T, Mark Adair-Rios, Paul Terrell Clayton, Sarah Dampf, Andrew Divoff, Steve Eastin.

Navy pilot Ice-T fakes his own death, goes to work for a Latin American arms dealer, steals a Stealth fighter from an Air Force base, and starts attacking military bases around the world. A reserve Navy officer is called out of retirement to put an end to the silliness, which he does after aerial combat created with footage from *Flight of the Intruder*. The filmmakers probably should have used the *Firefox* dogfight instead. A terrible movie made worse by terrible acting.

The Steel Claw (1961)

WWII	Marines	NR	Color	96 mins
WB	WV: 05-17-61		NYT: 09-21-61	

DIR: George Montgomery. SW: George Montgomery, Ferde Grofé Jr. PRO: George Montgomery, Ferde Grofé Jr. STARS: George Montgomery, Charito Luna, Mario Barri.

A superficial war story filmed in the Philippines, in which Marine Capt. Montgomery loses a hand and is discharged because of his injury. After fabricating a clawlike replacement, he attempts to rescue a general the Japanese had captured at the beginning of the war. In fact, the general is dead and

Montgomery almost loses his life in the effort but is helped to safety by two bands of Filipino guer-rillas.

Steel Helmet (1951)

Korea	Army	Cour	B&W 84 mins
Lippert	WV: 01-03-51		NYT: 01-25-51

DIR: Samuel Fuller. SW: Samuel Fuller. PRO: Samuel Fuller. STARS: Robert Hutton, Steve Brodie, James Edwards.

An early Korean War movie that started as a WWII "B" film and whose locale changed to exploit the new war. It focuses on a small unit, which allowed Fuller to develop the personalities of the soldiers. He made limited use of combat footage to complement the action he created on a sound stage.

Steele Justice (1987)

Vietnam	Army	NR	Color 95 mins
Atlantic	WV: 05-06-87		NYT: DNR

DIR: Robert Boris. SW: Robert Boris. PRO: John Strong. STARS: Martin Kove, Sela Ward, Ronny Cox, Bernie Casey, Joseph Campanella, Soon-Tek Oh.

In 1975 Vietnam, Kove as Lt. Steele and his buddy Kim survive an ambush by Oh, a Vietnamese general and supposed confederate, who leaves them for dead and heads for the United States with $20 million of "lost" CIA gold. Twelve years later, the same bad guy is heading the Vietnamese mafia in southern California and this time succeeds in killing Kim. Steele sets out to get justice, with the requisite violence.

The Story of Dr. Wassell (1944)

WWII	Navy	Full	Color 136 mins
Fox	WV: 04-26-44		NYT: 06-07-44

DIR: Cecil B. DeMille. SW: Alan LeMay, Charles Bennett. PRO: Cecil B. DeMille. STARS: Gary Cooper, Laraine Day, Signe Hasso.

Based on James Hilton's book, the film tells the true story of a Navy doctor who disobeys orders to leave his stretcher-bound patients behind during a medical evacuation and successfully gets them from Java to China. The film includes staged battle scenes and Navy ships.

The Story of G.I. Joe (1945) [G&G]

WWII	Army	Full	B&W 109 mins
UA	WV: 06-20-45		NYT: 10-06-45

DIR: William Wellman. SW: Leopold Atlas, Guy Endore, Philip Stevenson. PRO: Lester Cowan. STARS: Burgess Meredith, Robert Mitchum, Fred Steele, Wally Cassell.

Based on the writings of famed war correspondent Ernie Pyle, who died in the Pacific shortly before the film was released. Arthur Miller wrote the first draft of the script, but it required many rewrites before Cowan had an acceptable version. Wellman claimed to hate the infantry and refused the producer's efforts to hire him until Pyle convinced him to undertake the project. The Army provided soldiers who had actually fought in Italy, the location of Pyle's communiqués. After filming, the men went to the Pacific, where many died.

The Story of G.I. Joe remains one of the very best portrayals of men in combat, with none of Hollywood's clichés. In fact, the film has only one minor romantic episode in which one of the soldiers finally gets to marry his nurse girlfriend and has one night together with her in an ambulance. Then he dies, as do many of the men about whom Pyle wrote so lovingly.

The Story of Vernon and Irene Castle (1939)

WWI	Air Force	Unkn	B&W	90 mins
RKO	WV: 04-05-39		NYT: 03-31-39	

DIR: H. C. Potter. SW: Richard Sherman. PRO: George Haight. STARS: Fred Astaire, Ginger Rogers, Edna May Oliver, Walter Brennan, Lew Fields.

A musical, biographical tribute to dance partners and husband and wife Vernon and Irene Castle. Despite a flourishing career, Astaire (as Vernon) joins the Canadian Royal Flying Corps at the outbreak of WWI and flies in combat. After the United States enters the war, he returns home to become an Air Force instructor and dies during aerial maneuvers for a visiting general.

A Stranger in My Arms (1959)

Korea	Air Force	NR	B&W	88 Mins
Universal	WV: 03-11-59		NYT: 03-04-59	

DIR: Helmut Käutner. SW: Peter Berneis. PRO: Ross Hunter. STARS: June Allyson, Jeff Chandler, Peter Graves, Sandra Dee, Charles Coburn, Mary Astor.

Based on Robert Wilder's novel *And Ride a Tiger.* Air Force test pilot Chandler reluctantly comes to a memorial service for Graves, his long-dead navigator, knowing that he hated his possessive mother and had actually died a coward. The film contains some brief flying scenes and a flashback to the time the two men spent on a life raft after being shot down on a mission over Korea.

Strategic Air Command (1955) [G&G]

Cold War	Air Force	Full	Color	110 mins
Paramount	WV: 03-30-55		NYT: 04-21-55	

DIR: Anthony Mann. SW: Valentine Davies, Beirne Lay Jr. PRO: Samuel Briskin. STARS: James Stewart, June Allyson, Frank Lovejoy.

This was the first of Hollywood's Strategic Air Command (SAC) movies intended to show how the Air Force was using nuclear deterrents to keep the peace. General Curtis LeMay, the creator of SAC, gave his encouragement and blessings to the film and made sure the production received all the support it needed, including B-36s and the new B-47 jet bombers on the ground and in the air. Stewart, in real life a WWII pilot and then a reserve officer, plays a baseball star, recalled to active duty despite his age and lack of experience with jet planes. Hurt in a crash that cost him flight status, Stewart ultimately decides to remain on active duty to further the development of SAC.

Apart from the excitement of the aerial scenes, the film makes the pitch that the success of SAC depended as much on an understanding women as on the hardware, with Allyson representing the long-suffering wives. Lovejoy plays a fictionalized LeMay and is the general's surrogate in arguing for a large strategic bomber force. The Air Force band played at the premiere in Omaha, the home of SAC.

Streamers (1983)

Vietnam	Army	NR	Color	118 mins
UA	WV: 09-07-83		NYT: 10-09-83	

DIR: Robert Altman. SW: David Rabe. PRO: Robert Altman, Nick Mileti. STARS: Matthew Modine, Michael Wright, David Alan Grier, Mitchell Lichtenstein.

Rabe adapted his play for a one-set portrayal of five soldiers in a barracks waiting to be sent to Vietnam. They do all the things young men do when facing an unknown future while cooped up in a barracks. The Army drill team that opens and closes the film was actually the ROTC drill team from the University of Huntsville, in Texas.

Strike Commando (1987)

Vietnam	Army	NR	Color	90 mins
Flora Films	WV: 11-25-87		NYT: DNR	

DIR: Bruno Mattei. SW: Clyde Anderson, Bruno Mattei. PRO: Franco Gaudenzi. STARS: Reb Brown, Christopher Connelly, Alex Vitale, Loes Kamma, Alan Collins.

Spaghetti Vietnam genre film, with Brown headed out on a one-man mission to gather proof that the Soviet Union is aiding the Vietcong. His colonel, actually a KGB agent and traitor, complicates Brown's efforts.

Stripes (1981)

Peace	Army	Full	Color	105 mins
Columbia	WV: 06-17-81		NYT: 06-26-81, 07-09-81	

DIR: Ivan Reitman. SW: Len Blum, Dan Goldberg, Harold Ramis. PRO: Ivan Reitman, Dan Goldberg. STARS: Bill Murray, Harold Ramis, Warren Oates, P. J. Soles, Sean Young, John Candy.

Along with **Private Benjamin** and using the same plot line of joining the Army to escape from civilian problems, **Stripes** helped the rehabilitation of the military after Vietnam. Like other military comedies, the film does not portray the service at all accurately or even positively, but the Army and DoD provided full cooperation recognizing the value for recruiting purposes of showing that GIs could have fun in the service. As a result, the Army allowed the filmmakers to shoot the exterior military sequences at Fort Knox, where they had access to tanks, men, and other equipment.

Stryker's War (1985)

Vietnam	Army	NR	Color 84 mins
Renaissance Pic	WV: DNR		NYT: DNR

DIR: Josh Becker. SW: Josh Becker, Scott Spiegel. PRO: Shirley Becker, Scott Spiegel. STARS: Brian Schulz, Robert Rickman, Sam Raimi.

Opening scenes show Schulz taking two bullets in the leg while in Vietnam and one of his buddies carrying him back to safety. The movie hangs on the premise that returning Vietnam vets have trouble adjusting to civilian life and are outcasts until their firepower is needed.

Sub Down (1997)

Peace	Navy	Info	Color 93 mins
Carousel Picture	WV: DNR		NYT: DNR

DIR: Gregg Champion (Alan Smithee). SW: Silvio Muraglia, Daniel Sladek, Howard Chesley. PRO: Silvio Muraglia, Daniel Sladek, Jeffrey White. STARS: Stephen Baldwin, Gabrielle Anwar, Tom Conti.

Filmed in Luxemburg, the plot portrays a U.S. submarine getting stuck under the polar ice cap, pulling down an attached minisub manned by civilian scientists. The crew's survival depends on the civilians.

Submarine (1928) [SSS]

Peace	Navy	Full	B&W 103 mins
Columbia	WV: 09-05-28		NYT: 08-31-28

DIR: Frank Capra. SW: Winifred Dunn, Dorothy Howell. PRO: Harry Cohn. STARS: Jack Holt, Ralph Graves, Clarence Burton, Arthur Rankin.

The first of the major peacetime submarine movies, which faced the problem of creating drama without underwater combat. What to do? The loss of two U.S. subs to accidents during the 1920s inspired the story. Capra sinks a submarine and then stages a rescue. Although the Navy was still smarting from the criticism about the two disasters, it justified full cooperation on the theory that if submarines might sink, the service had to be able to rescue the suffocating sailors and the film would show the process.

In fact, Capra shows Holt making the deepest dive to date to attach an air hose to the sub but does not show how the Navy then rescued the men. Moreover, the story had Holt unknowingly embark upon an affair with his buddy's round-heeled wife. Despite such negative images, the service provided a submarine and scenes of Navy divers conducting their business. However, for Holt's dive, the director bought a toy sub and diver and filmed them through the glass of an aquarium.

Submarine Command (1951) [SSS]

Korea	Navy	Full	B&W	87 mins
Paramount	WV: 08-29-51		NYT: 01-19-52	

DIR: John Farrow. SW: Jonathan Latimer. PRO: Joseph Sistrom. STARS: William Holden, Nancy Olson, William Bendix, Don Taylor.

The film opens on the last day of WWII, when Holden, the executive officer, crash dives his submarine to escape a Jap airplane but has to leave the wounded captain and an enlisted man to die on the bridge. Although a hearing board exonerates him, Holden remains burdened by his action until his heroics as captain of the same submarine in Korea bring him peace of mind. Submarines actually had virtually no role in the Korean War, but the service provided a submarine for exterior shots.

Submarine D-1 (1937) [SSS]

Peace	Navy	Full	B&W	100 mins
WB	WV: 11-17-37		NYT: 12-30-37	

DIR: Lloyd Bacon. SW: Frank Wead, Warren Duff, Lawrence Kimble. PRO: Lou Edelman. STARS: Pat O'Brien, George Brent, Wayne Morris, Frank McHugh.

The movie portrayed the Navy's development of the McCann diving bell to rescue sailors from stricken submarines. Thanks to the service's providing men and ships, the film has a documentary flavor. Bacon did extensive filming at the New London, Connecticut, submarine base, where the diving bell was developed. He also shot the Pacific Fleet's battleships, cruisers, planes, and most important, a submarine that sank on cue. The suffocating men awaiting rescue while developers of the diving bell struggle to put it into operation created taut drama on the screen. The film proved strangely prophetic because the bell was used to rescue sailors from the stricken USS *Squalus* off the New England coast in 1939.

Submarine Patrol (1938)

WWI	Navy	Full	B&W	95 mins
Fox	WV: 11-02-38		NYT: 11-19-38	

DIR: John Ford. SW: Rian James, Darrell Ware, William Faulkner, Kathryn Scola, Jack Yellen. PRO: Darryl F. Zanuck. STARS: Richard Greene, Nancy Kelly, Preston Foster, George Bancroft.

Based on Ray Milholland's novel *The Splinter Fleet of the Otranto Barrage.* Ford combined comedy and combat in a story of small, wooden WWI sub chasers. The last four surviving craft, then berthed at the Naval Academy, played themselves in the film, which includes two battles with German U-boats.

A Submarine Pirate (1915) [SSS]

Peace	Navy	Full	B&W	4 reels
Triangle	WV: 11-19-15		NYT: 11-15-15	

DIR: Sydney Chaplin, Charles Avery. SW: Mack Sennett. PRO: Mack Sennett. STARS: Sydney Chaplin, Glenn Cavender, Wesley Ruggles.

This comedy used a U.S. submarine and gunboat as props. Chaplin, a waiter, overhears pirates planning to seize a gold-laden ocean liner using a submarine. Ultimately, he thwarts the scheme with the help of the Navy, which loaned Chaplin a submarine from the San Diego Navy Yard for two weeks and then extended assistance when filming took longer than expected. The Bureau of Navigation approved the completed film and the Navy liked it so much, it bought prints to use for recruiting purposes.

Submarine Raider (1942)

WWII	Navy	Ltd	B&W	65 mins
Columbia	WV: 06-24-42		NYT: 06-22-42	

DIR: Lew Landers. SW: Aubrey Wisberg. PRO: Wallace MacDonald. STARS: John Howard, Marguerite Chapman, Forrest Tucker.

A fictitious story portraying an American submarine that unsuccessfully tried to warn Pearl Harbor of the approaching attack and then successfully sank a Japanese aircraft carrier.

Submarine Seahawk (1959)

WWII	Navy	NR	B&W	83 mins
Amer-Intl	WV: 01-28-59		NYT: DNR	

DIR: Spencer Bennett. SW: Lou Rusoff, Owen Harris. PRO: Alex Gordon. STARS: John Bentley, Brett Halsey, Wayne Heffley, Steve Mitchell.

A "B" submarine story that uses stock footage, sets from more-expensive productions, and a hackneyed story about an officer who takes command of a submarine without actual leadership experience, causing the crew some concerns until his actions lead to the sinking of many Japanese ships.

Subway in the Sky (1959)

Cold War	Army	NR	B&W	87 mins
UA	WV: DNR		NYT: DNR	

DIR: Muriel Box. SW: Jack Andrews. PRO: Sydney Box. STARS: Van Johnson, Hildegard Knef, Albert Lieven, Cec Linder.

Set in postwar Germany. Johnson appears as an Army doctor falsely accused of drug dealing and murder. Linder, an Army investigator, pursues Johnson to Berlin, but Box fails to make the audience care about Johnson's innocence or guilt.

Suicide Battalion (1958)

WWII	Army	NR	B&W	79 mins
Amer-Intl	WV: 03-26-58		NYT: DNR	

DIR: Edward L. Cahn. SW: Lou Rusoff. PRO: Lou Rusoff. STARS: Michael Connors, John Ashley, Jewell Lain, Russ Bender.

Somewhere in the Philippines, a unit of specially selected demolition men attempts to demolish a former U.S. HQ building, which the Japanese have captured.

Suicide Fleet (1931)

WWI	Navy	Ltd	B&W	86 mins
RKO	WV: 12-01-31		NYT: 11-23-31	

DIR: Albert Rogell. SW: Lew Lipton. PRO: Charles Rogers. STARS: William Boyd, Robert Armstrong, James Gleason, Ginger Rogers.

Based on H. A. Jones's magazine article about Q-boats, which masqueraded as civilian ships not worth a German torpedo. When the U-boat would surface, the sides of the ship would drop, revealing cannons that actually outgunned the submarine's single naval gun. In this instance, however, three submarines approach the decoy and the captain of one discovers the truth. As he prepares to destroy the American ship, Navy destroyers come to the rescue in the nick of time.

The Sullivans (1944) [SSS]

WWII	Navy	Full	B&W	111 mins
Fox	WV: 02-09-44		NYT: 02-10-44	

DIR: Lloyd Bacon. SW: Mary McCall Jr. PRO: Sam Jaffe. STARS: Thomas Mitchell, Selena Royle, Edward Ryan, Trudy Marshall, John Campbell, Anne Baxter.

This film is more a biographical story of the five Sullivan brothers growing up in Iowa than a military movie. The brothers died aboard the USS *Juno* after the battle of the Guadalcanal Sea when a Japanese submarine torpedoed the crippled cruiser. However, the fictionalized death of the brothers and the parents' christening of the destroyer *The Sullivans* (the first ship the Navy named after more than one person) helped the war effort and still bring tears to viewers' eyes. The young men's deaths also led to the military order that brothers could not serve together, mentioned in *Saving Private Ryan*.

The Sum of All Fears (2002)

Terrorism	All	Full	Color	124 mins
Paramount	WV: 05-27-02		NYT: 05-31-02	

DIR: Phil Alden Robinson. SW: Paul Attanasio, Daniel Pyne. PRO: Mace Neufeld. STARS: Ben Affleck, Morgan Freeman, James Cromwell, Ken Jenkins, Liev Schreiber.

Based on Tom Clancy's best-selling novel but with changes—including making the story a prequel to other films portraying CIA man Jack Ryan instead of a sequel. This time, a would-be Hitler buys a long-lost Israeli nuclear bomb (as if Israel would not have searched high and low for the plane and the bomb) and attempts to use it to start a war between Russia and the United States. In the course of events, the terrorists detonate the bomb in Baltimore during the Super Bowl, with the usual visual carnage. In the end, Ryan barely averts the mutual launch of weapons by the two nations. All the services plus the CIA provided full cooperation, including an aircraft carrier, stealth bomber, Marines, and helicopters.

Summer Soldiers (1972)

Vietnam	Army	Unkn	Color	107 mins
Ronin Films	WV: 10-04-72		NYT: 10-02-72	

DIR: Hiroshi Teshigahara. SW: John Nathan. PRO: Yukio Tomizawa. STARS: Keith Sykes, Reisen Lee, Kazuo Kitamura, Shoichi Ozawa.

American Vietnam War deserters seek sanctuary in Japan among, and with the assistance of, peace-loving families. The film captures the horrors of war and the innocence of youth. The Japanese production company used a mixture of English and Japanese, as well as subtitles.

Sunday Dinner for a Soldier (1944)

WWII	Army	Full	B&W	86 mins
Fox	WV: 12-06-44		NYT: 01-25-45	

DIR: Lloyd Bacon. SW: Wanda Tuchock, Melvin Levy. PRO: Walter Morosco. STARS: Anne Baxter, John Hodiak, Bobby Driscoll.

Not appearing until the last third of the film, Hodiak, a B-17 waist-gunner invited to dinner, becomes romantically involved with Baxter. The film contains shots of an air base and military planes as background.

Suppose They Gave a War and Nobody Came (1970)

Vietnam	Air Force	Unkn	Color	113 mins
Cin	WV: 05-27-70		NYT: 09-12-70	

DIR: Hy Averback. SW: Hal Captain, Don McGuire. PRO: Fred Engel. STARS: Brian Keith, Tony Curtis, Ernest Borgnine, Suzanne Pleshette.

Filmed and released during the Vietnam War era, but the war is only briefly mentioned twice. The theme explores the antipathy between soldiers on a remote, missile silo base and the nearby town's citizens. The title was changed to **War Games** for television broadcast.

Surface to Air (1997)

Gulf Wars	Navy, Marines	NR	Color	93 mins
Artisan Enter.	WV: DNR		NYT: DNR	

DIR: Rodney McDonald. SW: Tony Giglio. PRO: Andrew Stevens, Ashok Amritraj. STARS: Michael Madsen, Chad McQueen, Melanie Shatner, Larry Thomas, Herb Mitchell.

According to all reports, a truly terrible movie. Navy pilot McQueen and Marine Gunnery Sgt. Madsen renew their sibling rivalry aboard an aircraft carrier in the Persian Gulf. When McQueen is shot down, Madsen joins in the rescue effort. Perhaps the opportunity to see Captain Kirk's daughter makes it worth the effort to find a video; otherwise, forget about it.

Surrender—Hell! (1959)

WWII	Army	Ltd	B&W 85 mins
Allied Artists	WV: 08-05-59		NYT: DNR

DIR: John Barnwell. SW: John Barnwell. PRO: Edmund Goldman. STARS: Keith Andes, Susan Cabot, Nestor De Villa.

Based on Philip Harkin's book *Blackburn's Headhunters*, the film tells the story of Army Lt. Donald Blackburn, who organized and led Filipino headhunters in guerrilla warfare against the Japanese. Despite being filmed on location, the interesting plot could not compensate for an inept script. Compare to *Farewell to the King*.

The Swarm (1978)

SciFi	Army	Full	Color 116 mins
WB	WV: 07-19-78		NYT: 07-15-78

DIR: Irwin Allen. SW: Stirling Silliphant. PRO: Irwin Allen. STARS: Richard Widmark, Michael Caine, Katharine Ross, Henry Fonda.

Based on Arthur Herzog's novel, the film is simply a silly disaster movie, sillier than most. Killer bees head north while the story heads south, and the cinematic military is ineffectual in trying to save the country, until the last possible moment. Nevertheless, the Army provided men and equipment to depict the military sequences.

Sweetheart of the Navy (1937)

Peace	Navy	Unkn	B&W 63 mins
Grand National	WV: 07-07-37		NYT: DNR

DIR: Duncan Mansfield. SW: Carroll Graham. PRO: B. F. Zeidman. STARS: Eric Linden, Cecilia Parker, Roger Imhof.

A trite romantic comedy in which enlisted man Linden is preparing to take his exam for Annapolis while his shipmates want him to fight the ship's commander to help get singer Parker out of a bad check writing mess. Complications almost cost him the chance to go to the Academy.

Swing It Sailor (1937)

Peace	Navy	Unkn	B&W 63 mins
Grand National	WV: 11-10-37		NYT: 12-13-37

DIR: Raymond Cannon. SW: Clarence Marks, David Diamond. PRO: David Diamond. STARS: Ray Mayer, Wallace Ford, Isabel Jewell.

A silly buddy film that uses the navy base at San Pedro, California, as a background and shows Pacific Fleet maneuvers.

Take the High Ground (1953)

Korea/Peace	Army	Full	Color	100 mins
MGM	WV: 09-23-53		NYT: 11-20-53	

DIR: Richard Brooks. SW: Millard Kaufman. PRO: Dore Schary. STARS: Richard Widmark, Karl Malden, Elaine Stewart, Russ Tamblyn.

The film focuses on the training of draftees to become tough fighting men. Schary initially wanted to feature the Marines, but the service objected to showing how the DIs turned boys into men. Moreover, the Marines had lost some men in a recent training accident and worried about the impact on viewers of the sometimes harsh training. On the other hand, as the least-glamorous service, the Army appreciated most opportunities to appear on the screen and so allowed the filmmakers to shoot at Fort Bliss, Texas.

Tank (1984) [G&G]

Peace	Army	Full	Color	113 mins
Universal	WV: 03-14-84		NYT: 03-16-84	

DIR: Marvin Chomsky. SW: Dan Gordon. PRO: Irwin Yablans. STARS: James Garner, G. D. Spradlin, Shirley Jones, C. Thomas Howell.

Garner, as a career sergeant major, takes his Sherman tank with him from post to post. When his son is arrested for a crime he did not commit, Garner uses the tank to rescue the boy from the local red-necked sheriff. Although Garner took the law into his own hands, the Army saw the overall portrayal as positive and so helped the service rehabilitate its image, which the Vietnam War had so savaged.

Tank Battalion (1958)

Korea	Army	NR	B&W	80 mins
Amer-Intl	WV: 10-29-58		NYT: DNR	

DIR: Sherman Rose. SW: Richard Bernstein, George Waters. PRO: Richard Bernstein. STARS: Don Kelly, Edward G. Robinson Jr., Frank Gorshin, Regina Gleason.

An unoriginal, low-budget war story of a tank crew lost in enemy territory, which made it possible for the producer to rent only one tank. The filmmakers also used stock footage. Nevertheless, the resulting film lacked reality.

Tank Commandos (1959)

WWII	Army	Full	B&W	79 mins
Amer-Intl	WV: 03-04-59		NYT: DNR	

DIR: Burt Topper. SW: Burt Topper. PRO: Burt Topper. STARS: Robert Barron, Maggie Lawrence, Wally Campo, Donato Farretta.

A mundane story in which an American demolition unit is sent to blow up a bridge that gives German tanks free access to the front.

Tanks a Million (1941)

Preparedness	Army	Full	B&W	50 mins
UA	WV: 08-06-41		NYT: 10-09-41	

DIR: Fred Guiol. SW: Paul G. Smith, Edward E. Seabrook, Warren Wilson. PRO: Hal Roach. STARS: William Tracy, James Gleason, Noah Beery Jr., Joe Sawyer.

A slapstick comedy about a recruit with a photographic memory that helps him get through training. Scenes of basic training helped pad this "C" movie.

The Tanks Are Coming (1951)

WWII	Army	Full	B&W	89 mins
WB	WV: 11-07-51		NYT: 12-06-51	

DIR: Lewis Seiler. SW: Robert Hardy Andrews. PRO: Bryan Foy. STARS: Steve Cochran, Philip Carey, Mari Aldon, Paul Picerni.

The story of tanks in the breakout from St. Lo, following the Normandy invasion. Seiler shot in part at the Fort Knox training center and combined this manufactured footage with stock combat footage into a portrayal of how the tank corps contributed to winning the war.

Taps (1981) [G&G]

Peace	Army	Full	Color	130 mins
Fox	WV: 12-09-81		NYT: 12-09-81	

DIR: Harold Becker. SW: Darryl Ponicsan, Robert Mark Kamen. PRO: Stanley Jaffe, Howard Jaffe. STARS: George C. Scott, Timothy Hutton, Ronny Cox, Sean Penn, Tom Cruise.

Based on Devery Freeman's novel *Father Sky*, the film tries to make an antimilitary statement by showing military academy cadets seizing their school when the board of trustees decides to turn the campus into a condominium development. Scott, as a retired general and the school's headmaster, dies early in the movie, but like Wayne in *Sands of Iwo Jima*, he has ingrained in his students the credo of honor, duty, and loyalty to flag and country, and they justify their actions on his discipline. The confrontation with the National Guard and civilian authorities lacks any real credibility, which mutes any antiwar statement. Given such images, the Pennsylvania National Guard wanted nothing to do with the project. But after the producer made the character of the unit's commander more sympathetic, the Guard agreed to provide men and equipment to portray the denouement.

Tarawa Beachhead (1958)

WWII	Marines	Full	B&W	77 mins
Columbia	WV: 11-05-58		NYT: DNR	

DIR: Paul Wendkos. SW: Richard Alan Simmons. PRO: Charles Schneer. STARS: Kerwin Mathews, Julie Adams, Ray Danton.

A low-budget Marine story set in the South Pacific with the climax during the battle for Tarawa. The film had more depth and character development than most such war films. The Marines cooperated despite the negative image of a Marine officer murdering an enlisted man.

Target Earth (1954)

SciFi	Army	Full	B&W 74 mins
Allied Artists	WV: 12-29-54		NYT: DNR

DIR: Sherman Rose. SW: William Raynor, James Nicholson, Wyott Ordung. PRO: Herman Cohen. STARS: Richard Denning, Kathleen Crowley, Virginia Grey, Richard Reeves.

The Army mobilized to fight alien invaders from Venus and ultimately developed supersonic sound waves that defeated the threat from space.

Target Unknown (1951)

WWII	Air Force	Full	B&W 90 mins
Universal	WV: 01-31-51		NYT: 03-05-51

DIR: George Sherman. SW: Harold Medford. PRO: Aubrey Schenck. STARS: Mark Stevens, Gig Young, Robert Douglas, Don Taylor.

The film contained an unusual story line, which looked at how the Germans tried to elicit information about future bombing raids from downed American pilots. Sherman made good use of combat footage and cinematic re-creations provided by the Air Force.

Target Zero (1955)

Korea	Army, Air Force, Navy	Full	B&W 91 mins
WB	WV: 11-23-55		NYT: 11-16-55

DIR: Harmon Jones. SW: Sam Rolfe, James Warner Bellah. PRO: David Weisbart. STARS: Richard Conte, Peggie Castle, Charles Bronson, L. Q. Jones.

A small American patrol links up with three British soldiers manning an American tank on the way to occupy a ridge. The usual American–British cinematic antagonisms fade under pressures of surviving a North Korean assault with the help of Air Force jets and Navy bombing.

Task Force (1949) [G&G]

Peace/WWII	Navy	Full	B&W/Color 116 mins
WB	WV: 07-20-49		NYT: 10-01-49

DIR: Delmer Daves. SW: Delmer Daves. PRO: Jerry Wald. STARS: Gary Cooper, Jane Wyatt, Wayne Morris, Walter Brennan, Jack Holt.

A fictionalized portrayal of the origins and development of naval aviation. The production had its origins during WWII and the script was ready to go into production in September 1945, when hostilities ended. The studio then canceled the project, believing people were tired of war movies and combat. Daves continued to collect combat footage and then shot his original script, with only minor changes, in 1949.

The film uses newsreel footage to show flying operations aboard the Navy's first carrier, the *Langley*, and then portrays the ongoing debate between the proponents of aviation and battleships during the 1920s and 1930s, replicating debates in congressional hearings. The film changes from B&W to color during World War II and uses the great Pacific naval battles to show how the aviation branch finally won the day over battleships.

Cooper rises through the ranks to become the commander of a fictional carrier, which suffered horrendous damage and barely survived, thanks to Cooper's leadership and the heroic efforts of the crew. To portray this, Daves used graphic footage from the attack on the USS *Franklin*, the most heavily damaged American ship to survive in WWII. With the war over, and his crusade for aircraft carriers having prevailed, Cooper retires as an admiral and the Navy begins to receive a new generation of carriers ready for jet plane operations.

The aviation branch naturally loved the story from its inception and provided Daves with information, access to the service's film archives, and access to Navy fliers both during the development of the script and ultimately during filming. Daves and his cast and crew went to sea on a training cruise aboard a carrier, where they filmed interior scenes as well as landings and takeoffs. In turn, the Navy received a recruiting tool and the arguments for more and larger carriers.

A Taste of Hell (1973)

WWII	Army	NR	Color	90 mins.
BxOfIntl	WV: 12-12-73		NYT: DNR	

DIR: Basil Bradbury, Neil Yarema. SW: Neil Yarema. PRO: John Garwood. STARS: John Garwood, Liza Lorena, William Smith.

The Japanese capture and torture Army officer Garwood. Left for dead, he recovers and organizes a guerrilla army to wage a war of revenge. The story has been done far better many times.

The Teahouse of the August Moon (1956)

WWII	Army	Full	Color	122 mins
MGM	WV: 10-17-56		NYT: 11-30-56	

DIR: Daniel Mann. SW: John Patrick. PRO: Jack Cummings. STARS: Marlon Brando, Glenn Ford, Machiko Kyô, Eddie Albert, Paul Ford.

From Patrick's play and Vern Sneider's book, the story takes place on Okinawa, where Army officer Ford tries to bring democracy and free enterprise to a small town in the postwar period. Incongruously, Brando plays a native translator. The service provided men and equipment as background.

Tears of the Sun (2003)

Peace	Navy	Full	Color 118 mins
Sony	DV: 03-10-2003		NYT: 03-07 & 04-14-2003

DIR: Antoine Fuqua. SW: Alex Lasker, Patrick Cirillo. PRO: Ian Bryce, Mike Lobell, Arnold Rifkin. STARS: Bruce Willis, Monica Bellucci, Cole Hauser, Eamonn Walker, Malick Bowens, Tom Skerritt, Johnny Messner, Nick Chinlund, Charles Ingram.

After years of trying to avoid appearances on the motion picture screen, and then only begrudgingly giving limited assistance to *Navy SEALS*, the SEALS finally agreed to provide assistance to a story about the rescue of a naturalized American citizen from war-torn Nigeria. What might have been simply a Bruce Willis action-adventure movie was instead a serious consideration of the limits of U.S. intervention in the affairs of a sovereign state, however brutal and repressive that government might be.

Willis, as a lieutenant, receives orders for his team to rescue Bellucci, a doctor running a hospital somewhere in the Nigerian countryside. When the good doctor refuses to leave her patients to the advancing government army, Willis tricks her into getting aboard a waiting helicopter. After seeing the murder, rape, and pillage being wrought, however, Willis returns with Bellucci and his men to evacuate the people to safety across the border.

Does Willis violate his orders to simply rescue the doctor? It might seem that way. However, his commander aboard an aircraft carrier off the coast, courtesy of the Navy, only recommends that Willis not go back, thereby freeing him to make his decision based on the circumstances on the ground. Willis plays it straight, with none of his earlier cinematic mannerisms. Although he is tired and weary of killing, much like Captain Miller in *Saving Private Ryan*, Willis does not have shaking hands or crying jags. He simply does what he thinks is right, and his men, trusting his leadership, follow him on their odyssey through scenes of unimaginable horror, into battle, and then a mad dash to safety.

Some live and some die, with the question of whether it was worth it left unanswered. Unfortunately, few people saw the movie and so were not even able to consider the question. Why? Given its visual images, *Tears of the Sun* was a very difficult film to watch and so would have limited appeal under any circumstances. But, like *Flight of the Intruder*, which came out the week the first Gulf War began, *Tears of the Sun* opened the week the second Gulf War started. So why pay good money to see fictional renderings of American fighting men in action when people could watch the real thing in real time on their TV sets? Consequently, apart from the serious issues the movie raised about the limits of U.S. power and ability to become the policeman of the world, people missed in Willis's portrayal perhaps the best rendering of military leadership since John Wayne in *Sands of Iwo Jima* and Gregory Peck in *Twelve O'Clock High*.

Tell It to the Marines (1926)

Peace/China	Marines	Full	B&W 97 mins
MGM	WV: 12-29-26		NYT: 12-24-26

DIR: George Hill. SW: Richard Schayer. PRO: George Hill. STARS: Lon Chaney, William Haines, Eddie Gribbon, Carmel Myers.

A Lon Chaney comedy about life in the peacetime Marines. As a sergeant, Chaney ultimately turns a lackadaisical young man into a good Marine. A requisite love triangle requires an expedition to China and a Marine battle with a bandit brigade before a happy ending. Along with **What Price Glory?**, the film helped cement the relationship between Hollywood and the Marine Corps. When Chaney died in 1930, the Marines acknowledged his influence on the Corps' image by sending an honor guard to the funeral, and a Marine chaplain conducted the service.

Telling the World (1928)

China	Navy, Marines	Full	B&W 72 mins
MGM	WV: 07-18-28		NYT: 07-16-28

DIR: Sam Wood. SW: Raymond Schrock. PRO: MGM. STARS: William Haines, Anita Page, Frank Currier, Polly Moran.

The Marines and Navy save the day by rescuing a cabaret girl from Chinese revolutionaries at the request of her journalist boyfriend. One reviewer noted that despite this, "it's still a good picture."

Ten Gentlemen from West Point (1942)

Preparedness	Army	Cour	B&W 104 mins
Fox	WV: 06-03-42		NYT: 06-05-42

DIR: Henry Hathaway. SW: Richard Maibaum. PRO: William Perlberg. STARS: George Montgomery, Maureen O'Hara, John Sutton, Laird Cregar.

A glorified preparedness film that mixes fact with fiction to portray the creation of West Point in the early 1800s. An Army unit at West Point and the first 10 graduates of the Academy head to Fort Harrison to help put down an Indian uprising. At the film's end, a voice-over recites the West Point graduates, including Lee, Grant, Custer, Pershing, and MacArthur, pictured over stock footage of contemporary cadets marching on the Academy's parade ground.

The Tents of Allah (1923)

Peace	Navy, Marines	Unkn	B&W 72 mins
Encore	WV: 04-05-23		NYT: DNR

DIR: Charles Logue. SW: Charles Logue. PRO: E. A. MacManus. STARS: Mary Thurman, Monte Blue, Mary Alden, Macey Harlam.

A clichéd desert story in which Marines are called to rescue a damsel in distress, with the usual complications.

Teresa (1951)

WWII	Army	Ltd	B&W 101 mins
MGM	WV: 02-28-51		NYT: 04-06-51

DIR: Fred Zinnemann. SW: Stewart Stern. PRO: Arthur Loew. STARS: Pier Angeli, John Ericson, Patricia Collinge, Richard Bishop.

As a soldier in Italy, Ericson falls in love, marries an Italian girl, and brings her home. The film has a brief military sequence, in which Ericson falters, setting the stage for his efforts to find himself and support his bride back home.

Terminator 3: Rise of the Machines (2003)

SciFi	Army, Air Force	Deny	Color	108 mins
WB	WV: 06-30-2003		NYT: 07-01-2003	

DIR: Jonathan Mostow. SW: John Brancato, Michael Ferris. PRO: Mario Kassar, Hal Lieberman, Joel Michaels, Andrew Vajna, Colin Wilson. STARS: Arnold Schwarzenegger, Kristanna Loken, Nick Stahl, Claire Danes, David Andrews, Mark Famiglietti.

Inferior third installment of the Schwarzenegger franchise. Hollywood has done the story before and far better in *The Forbin Project* and in *WarGames*, among other films. Here, the battles between good machine Schwarzenegger and the bad female terminator serve only as an excuse to put unrelenting, if sometimes humorous, violence on the screen. The Pentagon initially approved the script after the filmmakers made some minor changes to address the military's concerns. However, Mostow changed the benign character of the general, who inadvertently was responsible for the nuclear holocaust and rise of the machines, into a negative character, and the Pentagon withdrew its approval. Ironically, in the completed film, the general was returned to the positive portrayal of the original script. For all practical purposes, the general provided virtually the only visible uniformed person in the film, but he clearly represents the mentality that technology is better than a human finger on the button.

Test Pilot (1938)

Preparedness	Air Force	Full	B&W	120 mins
MGM	WV: 04-20-38		NYT: 04-16-38	

DIR: Victor Fleming. SW: Victor Lawrence, Waldemar Young, Howard Hawks. PRO: Louis Lighton. STARS: Clark Gable, Myrna Loy, Spencer Tracy.

Based on Spig Wead's story of civilian test pilots, the film acknowledges the assistance of the Army Air Corps and so, of necessity, the secrecy of some aspects of the test flights portrayed. However, in this context, the film is an early "preparedness" film, with its last third focusing on the development of the B-17 "Flying Fortress."

Them! (1954)

SciFi	Army	Ltd	B&W	93 mins
WB	WV: 04-14-54		NYT: 06-17-54	

DIR: Gordon Douglas. SW: Ted Sherdeman. PRO: David Weisbart. STARS: James Whitmore, Edmund Gwenn, Joan Weldon, James Arness.

The Army provided some material assistance since the military would in fact wage war against the giant ants, mutated by the residual radiation from the Trinity atomic bomb test in New Mexico on July 16, 1945.

There's Something About a Soldier (1944)

WWII	Army	Full	B&W 81 mins
Columbia	WV: 01-12-44		NYT: DNR

DIR: Alfred E. Green. SW: Horace McCoy, Barry Trivers. PRO: Samuel Bischoff. STARS: Tom Neal, Evelyn Keyes, Bruce Bennett, John Hubbard, Jeff Donnell.

This training camp genre film has little plot. The action takes place at an officer candidate training school for the Anti-Aircraft Artillery Command at Camp Davis, North Carolina.

They Came to Cordura (1959)

Mexican border	Army	NR	Color 123 mins
Columbia	WV: 09-23-59		NYT: 10-22-59

DIR: Robert Rossen. SW: Robert Rossen, Ivan Moffatt. PRO: William Goetz. STARS: Gary Cooper, Van Heflin, Tab Hunter, Rita Hayworth.

Based on Glendon Swarthout's book, the film follows the trek of five U.S. soldiers nominated for the Medal of Honor in a skirmish against Mexican bandits in 1916. Career officer Cooper, whose job it is to return the heroes to Cordura in New Mexico, has been branded a coward but must muster courage to succeed in his assignment as the situation deteriorates.

They Gave Him a Gun (1937)

Peace	Army	Unkn	B&W 93 mins
MGM	WV: 05-19-37		NYT: 05-13-37

DIR: W. S. Van Dyke. SW: Cyril Hume. PRO: Harry Rapf. STARS: Franchot Tone, Spencer Tracy, Gladys George, Edgar Dearing.

Tone, a returning, formerly peace-loving WWI doughboy, decides that as long as he is armed, he is as good as anyone around, and he pursues a life in racketeering. Tracy plays his buddy from the trenches of France, who is secretly in love with the girl Tone has married. Tracy's circus, an ex-sergeant who becomes a New York City police detective, a prison break, and a suicide highlight this melodrama.

They Were Expendable (1945) [SSS]

WWII	Navy	Full	B&W 135 mins
MGM	WV: 11-21-45		NYT: 12-21-45

DIR: Captain John Ford (U.S. Navy Reserves), Captain James C. Havens (U.S. Marine Corps Reserves). SW: Frank Wead. PRO: Captain John Ford. STARS: Robert Montgomery, John Wayne, Donna Reed, Jack Holt, Ward Bond, Marshall Thompson, Paul Langton, Leon Ames.

Based on William White's book of the same name. Ford made the movie during the closing days of WWII, while he was still in the naval reserves. The credits acknowledged the cooperation the film received from the Navy, Army, Coast Guard, and Office of Strategic Services. The plot traced the evacuation of MacArthur, his family, and other senior staff officers from Corregidor in Montgomery's PT-boat.

The Thin Red Line (1964)

WWII	Army	NR	B&W 99 mins
Allied Artists	WV: 04-22-64		NYT: 10-29-64

DIR: Andrew Marton. SW: Bernard Gordon. PRO: Sidney Harmon, Philip Yordan. STARS: Keir Dullea, Jack Warden, James Philbrook, Ray Daley.

Based on James Jones's 1962 novel, in which he poetically described his experience as one of the soldiers who replaced the Marines in the final days of the fighting for Guadalcanal in November 1942. Jones warned that he was not writing a history but an imossible cooperation, one producer asked about use of a ship: "Period or modern day? Can modern ships be modified to pass as WWII for filming purposes?" They also wanted help in obtaining WWII equipment and asked for technical advice about the fighting.

The Pentagon, of course, had no "antique" equipment or active duty soldiers who had served in WWII, not that it mattered. Jones had warned that he had not intended in his book to provide a historical record of the fighting on Guadalcanal. Still, one producer claimed that "we hope by all means to respect the historical accuracy of *The Thin Red Line*." In reality, Malick demonstrated little interest in portraying the war with any realism. Only one of his technical advisors had served in the military, and the director paid little attention to the advice the advisors offered. Instead, the director tried to replicate Jones's impressionistic narrative in a swirl of disconnected images and dialogue that ultimately provided no insights into the nature of war or men in combat, except perhaps that war was hell. And Malick returned to the anonymity he had apparently been enjoying during his 21-year absence from Hollywood.

Impressionistic account of the battle, and Marton took his cue from the novelist in creating a philosophical study rather than an epic war movie. In turn, Jones wrote to the director: "Very rarely can a writer sit down and write a letter to someone who directed a story of his and tell him that he came so close to the intention of the writer's ideas as any human being can." *The Thin Red Line* was one of the early American war movies made in Spain with help from the Spanish Army rather than the U.S. military.

The Thing, a.k.a. *The Thing from Another World* (1951)

SciFi	Air Force	NR	B&W 89 mins
RKO	WV: 04-04-51		NYT: 05-03-51

DIR: Christian Nyby, Howard Hawks. SW: Charles Lederer. PRO: Howard Hawks. STARS: Margaret Sheridan, Kenneth Tobey, Robert Cornthwaite, James Arness.

Scientists at an arctic research station discover a spaceship and accidentally thaw out the alien. All hell breaks loose, and the Air Force provides help in disposing of the threat.

Thirteen Days (2000)

Cold War	Army, Navy, Air Force	Full	Color	145 mins
New Line Cinema	WV: 12-04-2000		NYT: 11-05, 12-25-2000	

DIR: Roger Donaldson. SW: David Self. PRO: Armyan Bernstein, Peter O. Almond, Kevin Costner. STARS: Kevin Costner, Steven Culp, Bruce Greenwood.

Donaldson created a docudrama portraying the 13 days of the Cuban missile crisis in October 1962, from the perspective of the White House and the military. The film perpetuates the cinematic image of Gen. Curtis LeMay and his itchy trigger finger. Yet because of the Strategic Air Command, both sides blinked and the world survived to fight another day.

Thirteen Days (2000)

Cold War	Army, Navy, Air Force	Full	Color	145 mins
New Line Cinema	WV: 12-04-2000		NYT: 11-05, 12-25-2000	

DIR: Roger Donaldson. SW: Philip Zelikow, Ernest R. May, David Self. PRO: Armyan Bernstein, Peter O. Almond, Kevin Costner. STARS: Kevin Costner, Steven Culp, Bruce Greenwood.

Donaldson created a docudrama portraying the 13 days of the Cuban missile crisis in October 1962, from the perspective of the White House and the military. The film perpetuates the cinematic image of Gen. Curtis LeMay and his itchy trigger finger. Yet because of the Strategic Air Command, both sides blinked and the world survived to fight another day.

Thirty Seconds Over Tokyo (1944) [G&G]

WWII	Air Force, Navy	Full	B&W	138 mins
MGM	WV: 11-15-44		NYT: 11-16-44	

DIR: Mervyn LeRoy. SW: Dalton Trumbo. PRO: Sam Zimbalist. STARS: Van Johnson, Robert Walker, Phyllis Thaxter, Tim Murdock, Robert Mitchum, Spencer Tracy.

The film portrays Jimmy Doolittle's heroic raid over Japan in April 1942. Based on Ted Lawson's book, the movie follows his training, the raid, and his subsequent return to the United States. The service allowed the filmmakers to shoot the training sequences at Eglin Air Force Base in Florida, where Doolittle's men had trained, and provided 16 bombers for the flying sequences.

Because the Navy could not restage the actual launch of the B-25 bombers, MGM knocked out the wall of a sound stage to house three planes, which the Air Force had transported through the streets of Culver City. The studio then built a section of an aircraft carrier flight deck for filming, preparations for the launch, and other aboard-ship scenes. To stage the takeoffs, Buddy Gillespie, the studio's top art director, built a model aircraft carrier and model B-25 bombers, re-creating the launch in the studio. Scenes of the planes approaching the Japanese mainland were filmed over Long Beach with the short-term use of some B-25s.

Trumbo observed that he had to expand a two-act story into a three-act play since the visual climax was the bombing of Japan. The film remains historically accurate until the 15 planes reach China, where in reality the crews either crash-landed or bailed out. (The 16th landed safely in Siberia, where the Soviets interned the crew.) Trumbo acknowledged that showing Chiang Kai-Shek's loyalists rescuing Doolittle's men was historically inaccurate because the Chinese communists had actually guided Doolittle's men to safety.

Politics dictated that change as well as the inclusion of a scene on the carrier deck the night before the takeoff in which Johnson as Lawson and Mitchum as a fellow pilot agree that the Japanese people are not so bad and the bombing raid is a military necessity, not done out of hate or revenge. By the time MGM released the picture, the United States was well on the way to winning the war, and the government had decided the nation would need postwar allies, including Japan, to oppose the Soviet Union. In any event, the film reminded the American people of the bravery of Doolittle and his men and their contribution to victory. And even today, ***Thirty Seconds Over Tokyo*** still informs viewers of one of the greatest and most heroic military exploits of all time.

36 Hours (1964)

| WWII | Air Force | Ltd | B&W | 115 mins |
| MGM | WV: 12-16-64 | | NYT: 01-29-65 | |

DIR: George Seaton. SW: George Seaton. PRO: William Perlberg. STARS: James Garner, Eva Marie Saint, Rod Taylor, Werner Peters, John Banner.

Based on Roald Dahl's book, *Beware of the Dog*, the title refers to the hours before D-Day, during which this fictional story takes place. Garner plays a flier, with knowledge of the Allies' planned landing in Normandy, who becomes the prisoner of the Nazis. In order to learn the Allies' destination for the landing, they drug Garner and try to convince him that he has had amnesia for six years.

This Is the Army (1943)

| WWII | Army | Full | Color | 120 mins |
| WB | WV: 08-04-43 | | NYT: 07-29-43 | |

DIR: Michael Curtiz. SW: Casey Robinson, Capt. Claude Binyon. PRO: Jack L. Warner, Hal B. Wallis. STARS: Men of the Armed Forces, George Murphy, Joan Leslie, Lt. Ronald Reagan, Sgt. Joe Louis, Kate Smith.

Irving Berlin's music performed by stars and uniformed personnel. The box office gross benefited the Army Emergency Relief Fund.

This Man's Navy (1945)

| WWII | Navy | Full | B&W | 100 mins |
| MGM | WV: 01-10-45 | | NYT: 04-16-45 | |

DIR: William A. Wellman. SW: Borden Chase. PRO: Samuel Marx. STARS: Wallace Beery, Tom Drake, James Gleason, Selena Royle.

The Navy provided shots of blimps in action and access to Lakehurst Naval Station, New Jersey, for filming of blimp takeoffs and landings. Beery portrays an aviator who loves blimps and sinks a submarine from one.

The Thousand Plane Raid (1969)

WWII	Air Force	Full	Color 94 mins
UA	WV: 07-23-69		NYT: DNR

DIR: Boris Sagal. SW: Donald S. Sanford, Robert Vincent Wright. PRO: Lewis J. Rachmil. STARS: Christopher George, Laraine Stephens, Gary Marshal, J. D. Cannon.

Using both stock footage and newsreels, the film depicts the mass American bombing raids over German airplane manufacturing plants in 1943. The production was a throwback to WWII era film-making.

Thousands Cheer (1943)

WWII	Army	Unkn	Color 126 mins
MGM	WV: 09-15-43		NYT: 09-14-43

DIR: George Sidney. SW: Richard Collins, Paul Jarrico. PRO: Joseph Pasternak. STARS: Kathryn Grayson, Gene Kelly, Mary Astor, Ben Blue, and the MGM stable.

Nominally a story of new soldier Kelly's pursuit of the colonel's pretty daughter, but actually an opportunity for the studio's song and dance crew to strut their stuff in cinematic Army shows.

Three Brave Men (1957)

Cold War	Navy	Ltd	B&W 86 mins
Fox	WV: 01-16-57		NYT: 03-16-57

DIR: Philip Dunne. SW: Philip Dunne. PRO: Herbert B. Swope Jr. STARS: Ray Milland, Ernest Borgnine, Frank Lovejoy, Dean Jagger.

A semi-documentary treatment, based on Anthony Lewis's Pulitzer Prize–winning articles, of the trial and discharge of Abraham Chasanow, a longtime Navy Department employee, and his rein-statement with back pay after the accusation of Communist affiliation was proven false.

Three Kings (1999)

Gulf War	Army	NR	Color 114 mins
WB	WV: 09-27-99		NYT: 10-01-99,
			04-06-2003

DIR: David O. Russell. SW: David Russell. PRO: Charles Roven, Paul J. Witt, Edward McDonnell. STARS: George Clooney, Mark Wahlberg, Ice Cube, Spike Jonze, Nora Dunn.

The film combines drama, tragedy, action, and comedy in trying to make some sense of the Persian Gulf War. Clooney, a Special Forces major, recruits three gung-ho soldiers, who arrived too late to take part in the fighting, to help him retrieve millions in gold, which the Iraqis had stolen during their occupation of Kuwait. After enduring all manner of fighting, they find the gold and head home. However, the ending returns to the good old days when Hollywood portrayed American soldiers doing good deeds. In this instance, Clooney and his men give up their newly found wealth to the local people, whom the soldiers decide need the gold more than they do.

Three Stripes in the Sun (1955)

Peace	Army	Full	B&W 93 mins
Columbia	WV: 10-26-55		NYT: 10-24-55

DIR: Richard Murphy. SW: Richard Murphy, Albert Duffy. PRO: Fred Kohlmar. STARS: Aldo Ray, Philip Carey, Dick York, Chuck Connors.

Based on E. J. Kahn Jr.'s *New Yorker* article "The Gentle Wolfhound," the picture provides a slightly fictionalized story of Sgt. Hugh O'Reilly's transformation from a hater of Japan to the benefactor of a Japanese orphanage and his marriage to a Japanese worker. The 27th Infantry Regiment, known as the *Wolfhounds*, contributed their time and money to supporting the institution, which created a monument to the soldiers and O'Reilly in particular.

Thunder Afloat (1939)

WWI	Navy	Full	B&W 95 mins
MGM	WV: 09-20-39		NYT: 10-13-39

DIR: George Seitz. SW: Wells Root, Harvey Haislip. PRO: J. Walter Ruben. STARS: Wallace Beery, Chester Morris, Virginia Grey, Douglass Dumbrille.

Old sailor Beery and young rival Morris team up on a "mosquito" boat to chase German U-boats that were attacking U.S. shipping off the East Coast. The Navy provided a submarine for sequences shot at Annapolis and around Coronado Island. MGM released the film a month early to benefit from the interest in submarines following the outbreak of WWII in September.

Thunder Birds (1942)

WWII	Air Force	Full	Color 79 mins
Fox	WV: 10-21-42		NYT: 10-29-42

DIR: William Wellman. SW: Lamar Trotti. PRO: Lamar Trotti. STARS: Gene Tierney, Preston Foster, John Sutton, Jack Holt.

Based on an original story, the film does not do justice to the Army Air Corps flight-training base in Arizona. While Wellman did create a few impressive flying sequences, the ground story of the rivalry between an American instructor and a British flying cadet remains trite and clichéd. The film wasted the time and energy of the Air Corps and its assistance.

Thunderbirds (1952)

WWII	Air Force	Full	B&W 98 mins
Republic	WV: 11-26-52		NYT: 03-12-53

DIR: John H. Auer. SW: Mary C. McCall Jr. PRO: John Auer. STARS: John Derek, John Barrymore Jr., Mona Freeman, Ward Bond.

Using actual wartime clips of fighting at Salerno, Anzio, Cassino, and Sicily, the movie depicts the call up, training, European campaigns, and homecoming of Oklahoma's Thunderbirds, a National Guard Division. Derek and Barrymore are after the same girl, and Bond plays a court-martialed West Point grad who reenlists under a fraudulent name to regain his honor. He also turns out to be the biological father of Barrymore, who had been told his father was killed in WWI.

Thundering Jets (1958)

Korea	Air Force	Full	B&W 73 mins
Fox	WV: 04-16-58		NYT: DNR

DIR: Helmut Dantine. SW: James Landis. PRO: Jack Leewood. STARS: Rex Reason, Dick Foran, Audrey Dalton, Robert Dix, Lee Farr.

The training school for test pilots provides the background for this "B" film, which interweaves three subplots: two men in love with the same girl, an instructor who thinks he spends too little time on the ground, and a newly naturalized American student who previously flew for Germany in WWII.

A Ticklish Affair (1963)

Peace	Navy	Full	Color 88 mins
MGM	WV: 07-03-63		NYT: 08-22-63

DIR: George Sidney. SW: Ruth Brooks Flippen. PRO: Joseph Pasternak. STARS: Shirley Jones, Gig Young, Red Buttons, Carolyn Jones.

A lightweight romantic comedy, based on the short story "Moon Walk." Naval officer Young romances Navy widow Jones and her three boys. The fleet in San Diego served as background.

Tigerland (2000)

Vietnam	Army	NR	Color 100 mins
Fox	WV: 09-18-2000		NYT: 10-06-2000

DIR: Joel Schumacher. SW: Ross Klavan, Michael McGruther. PRO: Arnon Milchan, Steven Haft, Beau Flynn. STARS: Colin Farrell, Matthew Davis, Clifton Collins Jr., Thomas Guiry, Nick Searcy.

The story takes place in 1971, in Tigerland, the U.S. Army's Advanced Individual Training facility for infantry, where soldiers receive final indoctrination before heading to Vietnam. This reality overshadows the young men's entire existence, knowing death is lurking around the corner. Farrell, as Bozz, a rebellious, streetwise survivor who has no intention of going to Vietnam, becomes the fulcrum for all that happens during the training. The producers did not solicit assistance for obvious reasons.

Most likely, the Army would have given Farrell a dishonorable discharge, which seems to be his goal, due to his disruptive actions long before he reaches Tigerland. Likewise the service would undoubtedly have claimed that the film inaccurately portrayed the advanced training and lack of discipline. On the other hand, men who went through basic training in the film's time frame argue that Bozz's maverick personality contained signs of leadership that would have made him a good soldier, and the Army would have made every effort to change his nonconformist personality. Moreover, these veterans find the other assorted characters very genuine, much like the buddies with whom they served, and so see **Tigerland** as a refreshingly accurate look at training for Vietnam, rather than just another Vietnam War movie.

Till the End of Time (1946)

WWII	Marines	Ltd	B&W	105 mins
RKO	WV: 06-12-46		NYT: 07-24-46	

DIR: Edward Dmytryk. SW: Allen Rivkin. PRO: Dore Schary. STARS: Dorothy McGuire, Guy Madison, Robert Mitchum, Bill Williams, Tom Tully, William Gargan, Jean Porter.

From Niven Busch's novel *They Dream of Home*, the Marine version of **The Best Years of Our Lives**, which dealt with the problems returning soldiers had in adjusting to civilian life.

Till We Meet Again (1944)

WWII	Air Force	Unkn	B&W	85 mins
Paramount	WV: 08-30-44		NYT: 08-30-44	

DIR: Frank Borzage. SW: Lenore Coffee. PRO: Frank Borzage. STARS: Ray Milland, Barbara Britton, Walter Slezak.

Based on a play by Alfred Maury. Milland, an American flyer shot down over occupied France, receives help from Britton, a young, French nun, as he tries to escape from his German pursuers. Given the Production Code Office, the developing romance is doomed before it goes too far.

Time Limit (1957)

Korea	Army	Full	B&W	96 mins
UA	WV: 09-18-57		NYT: 10-24-57	

DIR: Karl Malden. SW: Henry Denker. PRO: Richard Widmark, William Reynolds. STARS: Richard Widmark, Richard Basehart, Martin Balsam.

Should an incarcerated officer cooperate with interrogators to save the other 16 men confined with him? This is the central question of the movie.

A Time to Kill (1996)

Peace	Army, NG	Ltd	Color	150 mins
WB	WV: 07-15-96		NYT: 07-24-96	

DIR: Joel Schumacher. SW: Akiva Goldsman. PRO: Arnon Milchan, Michael Nathanson, Hunt Lowry, John Grisham. STARS: Sandra Bullock, Samuel L. Jackson, Matthew McConaughey, Kevin Spacey.

Based on Grisham's bestseller about a Mississippi town thrown into turmoil when a black man murders two red-necks, who had raped his 10-year-old daughter. The Army approved use of the Mississippi National Guard for a few days to perform cinematic riot control.

To End All Wars (2001)

WWII	Army	NR	Color	125 mins.
Argyll Film	WV: 07-01 & 14-2002		NYT: DNR	

DIR: David L. Cunningham. SW: Brian Godawa. PRO: David L. Cunningham, Jack Hafer, Nava Levin. STARS: Robert Carlyle, Kiefer Sutherland, Ciarán McMenamin, Mark Strong.

Based on Ernest Gordon's memoir of his days in Burma, this British film portrays POWs building a railroad under the brutal hand of the Japanese. Sutherland, the lone American, is one of four Allied POWs who consider a foolhardy escape plan that Carlyle has drawn up. Cunningham does not solve the physical appearance of the men in POW movies because Sutherland looks too fit for someone who has been working for years with too little sustenance.

To Hell and Back (1955)

WWII	Army	Full	Color	106 mins
Universal	WV: 07-20-55		NYT: 09-23-55	

DIR: Jesse Hibbs. SW: Gil Doud. PRO: Aaron Rosenberg. STARS: Audie Murphy, Marshall Thompson, Charles Drake, Gregg Palmer, Jack Kelly, Paul Picerni, David Janssen, Denver Pyle.

The cinematic biography of Audie Murphy, the most decorated soldier in American history, stars himself. He had 24 decorations, including the Medal of Honor. Joining Company B of the 15th Infantry Regiment, Murphy fought in North Africa, Tunisia, Italy, France, Germany, and Austria, rising from PFC to company commander and surviving to the end of the war with only one other soldier of his original company. The Army provided tanks and other equipment.

To The Shores of Hell (1965)

Vietnam	Marines	Full	Color	82 mins
Columbia	WV: DNR		NYT: DNR	

DIR: Will Zens. SW: Robert Mc Fadden, Will Zens. PRO: Will Zens. STARS: Marshall Thompson, Richard Arlen, Robert Dornan.

A Marine officer leads a mission through the Vietnamese jungle to rescue his doctor brother, whom the Vietcong have taken prisoner. In its support of the war, the film presaged John Wayne's message in **The Green Berets** that the U.S. military can easily overcome a ragtag guerrilla army. The Marines allowed filming of their fleet exercise at Camp Pendleton in preparation for deployment to

Vietnam. The amphibious operations included men, armor, and helicopters, reminiscent of ***Devil Dogs of the Air,*** and anticipated the landing of the Marines through the surf when the first contingent of Leathernecks reached Vietnam.

To the Shores of Tripoli (1942)

WWII	Marines	Full	Color	82 mins
Fox	WV: 03-11-42		NYT: 03-26-42	

DIR: Bruce Humberstone. SW: Lamar Trotti. PRO: Darryl F. Zanuck. STARS: John Payne, Randolph Scott, William Tracy.

A peacetime story of Marine training at the Recruit Depot in San Diego with a tag added to acknowledge that war had begun. The film ends with Leathernecks boarding a troop ship and heading off to war with strains of "The Marine Corp Hymn" in the background.

Tokyo Joe (1949)

Peace	Army	Ltd	B&W	87 mins
Columbia	WV: 10-12-49		NYT: 10-27-49	

DIR: Stuart Heisler. SW: Cyril Hume, Bertram Millhauser. PRO: Robert Lord. STARS: Humphrey Bogart, Alexander Knox, Florence Marly, Sessue Hayakawa.

Occupied Japan provides the setting for this story, which showcases Bogart caught up in a web of Japanese organized crime characters trafficking in the return of Japanese war criminals to their homeland.

Tokyo Rose (1945)

WWII	Army	Unkn	B&W	70 mins
Paramount	WV: 12-05-45		NYT: DNR	

DIR: Lew Landers. SW: Geoffrey Homes, Maxwell Shane. PRO: William Pine, William Thomas. STARS: Byron Barr, Osa Massen, Donald Douglas, Lotus Long, Blake Edwards, Richard Loo.

In Japan, an escaped GI prisoner attempts to kidnap "Rose" from her radio station and get her to the United States via an American submarine.

Too Late the Hero (1970)

WWII	Navy	NR	Color	133 mins
Cin	WV: 05-06-70		NYT: 05-21-70	

DIR: Robert Aldrich. SW: Robert Aldrich, Lukas Heller. PRO: Robert Aldrich. STARS: Michael Caine, Cliff Robertson, Henry Fonda, Denholm Elliott.

Robertson portrays a lazy Navy officer whose military specialty is Japanese language translations. He is sent to the Pacific to join a British unit whose mission is to blow up an important radio transmitter.

Top Gun (1986) [G&G]

| Peace | Navy | Full | Color 110 mins |
| Paramount | WV: 05-14-86 | | NYT: 05-16 & 06-08-86 |

DIR: Tony Scott. SW: Jim Cash, Jack Epps Jr. PRO: Don Simpson, Jerry Bruckheimer. STARS: Tom Cruise, Kelly McGillis, Val Kilmer, Anthony Edwards, Tom Skerritt, Meg Ryan.

Once *An Officer and a Gentleman* became a box office hit and provided the Navy with a positive image despite its refusal to assist on the production, the service became receptive to again appearing on the screen. Consequently, when Bruckheimer and Simpson showed up in the Pentagon to pitch a story about the Navy's Top Gun school, the service quickly embraced the project even before the producers had a final script.

Portraying the post-Vietnam training of Navy aviators in a very positive light, the film completed the rehabilitation of the military image, which the Vietnam war, the media, and the initial wave of films depicting the war had savaged. The Navy allowed filming at Miramar, then home of the Top Gun school, and aboard an aircraft carrier. The plot contains a typical rite of passage in which Cruise develops from an undisciplined, arrogant pilot into a mature officer. In the course of events, he shoots down, off the coast of North Africa, two unidentified enemy MIGs, which breached the carrier's security perimeter, and lands to a tumultuous victory celebration worthy of a long touchdown run. Essentially a 1930s recruiting film, with the flier winning the girl, *Top Gun* had a powerful visual and aural impact, making it the top-grossing film of 1986, surpassing the Oscar-winning best picture, *Platoon*.

Top Sergeant (1942)

| Peace | Army | Ltd | B&W 58 mins |
| Universal | WV: 09-23-42 | | NYT: DNR |

DIR: Christy Cabanne. SW: Maxwell Shane, Griffin Jayne. PRO: Universal. STARS: Leo Carrillo, Andy Devine, Don Terry.

This "B" film used the Army as background for a cops and robbers and love story.

Top Sergeant Mulligan (1941)

| Peace | Army | Ltd | B&W 70 mins |
| Monogram | WV: 11-19-41 | | NYT: 11-12-41 |

DIR: Jean Yarbrough. SW: Edmond Kelso. PRO: Lindsley Parsons. STARS: Nat Pendleton, Carol Hughes, Sterling Holloway.

Trite, clichéd story of two drug salesmen who join the Army to escape the tax collector, only to find that he has also joined and has become their top sergeant. And, of course, there is a girl, a nightclub singer.

Tora! Tora! Tora! (1970) [G&G]

| WWII | Navy, Air Force | Full | Color 144 mins |
| Fox | WV: 09-23-70 | | NYT: 09-24 & 10-04-70 |

DIR: Richard Fleischer, Toshio Masuda, Kinji Fukasaku. SW: Larry Forrester, Hideo Oguni, Ryuzo Kikushima. PRO: Elmo Williams. STARS: Martin Balsam, Soh Yamamura, Joseph Cotten, Tatsuya Mihashi, E. G. Marshall, Takahiro Tamura, Jason Robards, James Whitmore.

Based on Gordon W. Prange's *Tora! Tora! Tora!* (published in Japan) and Ladislas Farago's *The Broken Seal*, the film remains the most accurate account of the Japanese attack on Pearl Harbor. Darryl Zanuck had hoped to duplicate the success of *The Longest Day* in an epic that would portray the events of December 7 from both sides, with Japanese filmmakers creating their story to be intercut with the American version. As he had done with the story of D-Day, Williams faced the daunting task of coordinating both productions, benefiting from his days as an Oscar-winning film editor (*High Noon*).

Unfortunately for audiences and their wallets, the filmmakers opted for a re-creation of history rather than for drama. As a result, the movie offers the standard interpretation of the attack on Pearl Harbor, showing how American intelligence ultimately failed to provide a warning of the imminent attack to Adm. Kimmel and Gen. Short in Hawaii. But the audience already knows that, and the film fails to create any dramatic tensions, in part due to the failure of any of the characters to become more than two-dimensional cardboard cutouts. So everyone waited for the explosions.

Visually, *Tora! Tora! Tora!* had much to offer. After long negotiations, the Navy allowed Williams to load his ersatz Japanese planes aboard the USS *Yorktown* in San Diego and then launch them off the coast to re-create the Japanese takeoffs on December 7. The service would not allow the old, fragile propeller planes to return to the carrier but did permit one of the aircraft to "touch and go," creating footage for post-attack landings. The film also brilliantly captures the arrival of the Japanese planes over Hawaii with a small, civilian plane passing through the formation in the other direction.

However, when the planes dive into Pearl Harbor, the illusion of reality collapses. The miniatures and painted backdrops look like miniatures and painted backdrops. In contrast, the full-sized mock-ups of a battleship used to portray the destruction of the *Arizona* and the other battleships do convey a certain reality as they explode and burn. Nevertheless, the action scenes cannot make up for the lack of human characters and drama. But they do raise the obvious question of why the Navy and the Pentagon would want to cooperate in the making of a movie that portrays the greatest military loss the United States had faced up to that time. Director Fleischer's answer? The film shows the value of a long-distance, aircraft carrier attack on enemy territory. They just happened not to be American aircraft carriers. Still, the Navy could use the success of the attack itself to support its argument for the building of more aircraft carriers.

Torpedo Alley (1952) [SSS]

Korea	Navy	Full	B&W	83 mins
Allied Artists	WV: 12-17-52		NYT: 12-20-52	

DIR: Lew Landers. SW: Sam Roeca, Warren Douglas. PRO: Lindsley Parsons. STARS: Mark Stevens, Dorothy Malone, Charles Winninger, Bill Williams, Douglas Kennedy, Charles Bronson (uncredited).

A WWII Navy pilot, responsible for the crash and subsequent deaths of two of his crew, rejoins the Navy during the "Korean police action" after not making a successful reentry into civilian life. He chooses the submarine service because he was rescued by a sub after his earlier crash. The film contains scenes of schooling received at New London, Connecticut, and submarines in action, even though submarines had no combat role in the Korean conflict. A romance is also mixed in for good measure.

Torpedo Run (1958) [SSS]

WWII	Navy	Full	Color 86 mins
MGM	WV: 10-22-58		NYT: 10-25-58

DIR: Joseph Pevney. SW: William Wister Haines. PRO: Edmund Grainger. STARS: Glenn Ford, Ernest Borgnine, Diane Brewster.

Set in the South Pacific, a submarine hunts a Japanese aircraft carrier and accidentally sinks the Japanese troop transport carrying American prisoners, including the sub commander's wife and daughter. The story portrays the commander's Ahab-like pursuit of the aircraft carrier.

Touchdown Army (1938)

Peace	Army	Cour	B&W 69 mins
Paramount	WV: 09-21-38		NYT: 10-28-38

DIR: Kurt Neumann. SW: Lloyd Corrigan, Erwin Gelsey. PRO: Edward Lowe Jr. STARS: John Howard, Robert Cummings, Mary Carlisle.

The colonel's daughter accidentally spills the beans, and the hero almost misses the big game when he innocently uses the information in an exam. Another football-at-West-Point "B" film, using stock footage for realism.

Toward the Unknown (1956)

Cold War	Air Force	Full	Color 115 mins
WB	WV: 09-26-56		NYT: 09-28-56

DIR: Mervyn LeRoy. SW: Beirne Lay Jr. PRO: Mervyn LeRoy. STARS: William Holden, Virginia Leith, Lloyd Nolan, James Garner.

Portrayal of a pilot, broken while a prisoner of the North Koreans, returning to the cockpit as a test pilot in the Air Force. Filmed mostly at Edwards Air Force Base, California. Their newest jets became the "stars" of the picture, which pleased the Air Force.

The Towering Inferno (1974)

Peace	Navy	Ltd	Color 165 mins
Fox, WB	WV: 12-18-74		NYT: 12-20-74

DIR: John Guillermin. SW: Stirling Silliphant. PRO: Irwin Allen. STARS: Steve McQueen, Paul Newman, William Holden, Faye Dunaway, Fred Astaire.

Navy helicopters fail to rescue trapped people from the roof of a San Francisco skyscraper (superimposed on the Trans America Building). The service determined that the movie showed what its aircraft would do in such a disaster. However, one helicopter crashes on the building. Not a very good image. The two studios split the production costs and distribution.

Town Without Pity (1961)

Peace	Army	NR	B&W 112 mins
UA	WV: 10-11-61		NYT: 10-11-61

DIR: Gottfried Reinhardt. SW: Silvia Reinhardt, George Hurdalek, Jan Lustig. PRO: Eberhard Meichsner, Gottfried Reinhardt. STARS: Kirk Douglas, E. G. Marshall, Robert Blake, Richard Jaeckel.

The defense of four GIs accused of raping a German girl raises ethical issues as the attorney determines how to destroy the prosecutor's German witnesses, including the innocent victim.

Toy Soldiers (1991)

Terrorism	Army, Air Force	Full	Color 112 mins
Tri-Star	WV: 04-22-91		NYT: 04-26-91

DIR: Daniel Petrie Jr. SW: David Koepp, Daniel Petrie Jr. PRO: Jack E. Freedman, Wayne S. Williams, Patricia Herskovic. STARS: Sean Astin, Wil Wheaton, Keith Coogan, Andrew Divoff, Louis Gossett Jr., Denholm Elliott, Jerry Orbach, R. Lee Ermey.

Colombian terrorists take over a prep school, and the rich students become bargaining chips because the terrorists' leader's father is being tried on drug cartel charges. The film portrays how the students defend themselves. The Army and Army National Guard gave assistance to the production after working out details of FBI/military command and control issues pertaining to use of U.S. military forces inside the United States. The production company also increased the military threat posed by the terrorists to justify the FBI requesting U.S. military involvement, creating a positive, reasonably accurate depiction.

Tracks (1976)

Vietnam	Army	Unkn	Color 90 mins
Trio	WV: 05-19-76		NYT: 02-16-79

DIR: Henry Jaglom. SW: Henry Jaglom. PRO: Irving Cohen, Bert Schneider, Ted Shapiro, Howard Zucker. STARS: Dennis Hopper, Taryn Power, Dean Stockwell, Topo Swope, Alfred Ryder, Zack Norman.

Hopper portrays an unorthodox Army sergeant, this time accompanying home for burial the body of his buddy. Along the way to California by train, the sergeant meets an assortment of symbolical characters, experiences flashbacks to the war, and hallucinates to the point that even the moviegoer has trouble distinguishing reality.

A Trooper of Troop K (1917)

Mexican border	Army	Unkn	B&W Unkn
Lincoln Motion Picture	WV: DNR		NYT: DNR

DIR: Harry A. Gant. SW: Noble Johnson. PRO: Noble Johnson. STARS: Noble Johnson, Beulah Hall, James Smith, VI.

The story of an irresponsible young, black man who joins the Army and, like his white counterparts in countless Hollywood films, becomes a man and a hero, this time in a battle against Pancho Villa's bandits. During fighting in Mexico, the hero saves his captain and returns home to win the girl. Retired officers and enlisted men portrayed the soldiers on the screen.

True Lies (1994) [G&G]

Terrorism	Marines	Full	Color	135 mins
Fox	WV: 07-11-94		NYT: 07-15 & 17-94	

DIR: James Cameron. SW: James Cameron. PRO: James Cameron, Stephanie Austin. STARS: Arnold Schwarzenegger, Jamie Lee Curtis, Tom Arnold, Bill Paxton, Tia Carrere, Charlton Heston.

Schwarzenegger, who is leading a double life as a computer salesman and a G-man who chases terrorists, receives help from the Marines to defeat a drug cartel. The film features a Harrier vertical takeoff plane. Initially, the service objected to the hero simply jumping into the plane and taking off to fight the terrorists. The filmmakers solved the problem by adding a line to the script that Schwarzenegger had once flown a Harrier in the Marines. The service then provided the plane, although Schwarzenegger flew a mock-up during the climactic battle.

True to the Army (1942)

Peace	Army	Unkn	B&W	76 mins
Paramount	WV: 03-18-42		NYT: 06-15-42	

DIR: Albert S. Rogell. SW: Art Arthur, Bradford Ropes, Edmund Hartmann, Val Burton. PRO: Sol Siegel. STARS: Judy Canova, Allan Jones, Ann Miller, Jerry Colonna, William Demarest.

In this song and dance comedy, Canova, trying to escape a gang of racketeers, hides in her boyfriend's Army camp disguised as a soldier. Jones, an ex-actor now soldier, puts together a camp show (the finale), during which Ann Miller tap dances and the racketeers arrive.

True to the Navy (1930)

Peace	Navy	Cour	B&W	70 mins
Paramount	WV: 05-28-30		NYT: 05-24-30	

DIR: Frank Tuttle. SW: Keene Thompson, Doris Anderson, Herman J. Mankiewicz. PRO: Paramount. STARS: Clara Bow, Fredric March.

An insignificant comedy, but one that makes the Navy seem like fun for potential enlistees. The film uses stock footage of battleship target practice, in a story about a girl with multiple Navy boyfriends who come to blows.

Twelve O'Clock High (1949) [G&G]

WWII	Air Force	Full	B&W	132 mins
Fox	WV: 12-21-49		NYT: 01-28-50	

DIR: Henry King. SW: Sy Bartlett, Beirne Lay Jr. PRO: Darryl F. Zanuck. STARS: Gregory Peck, Hugh Marlowe, Gary Merrill, Dean Jagger.

The classic portrayal of the U.S. Air Force battle for the skies over occupied Europe in the early days of WWII. More important than that, the film explores the burdens of leadership and the effects it can have on the mind and body of a leader. As a result, *Twelve O'Clock High* continues to be used in leadership training seminars.

In this case, Peck takes over a bomber command from his friend Merrill, who has become too involved with his men and so has difficulty ordering them into the skies and to possible death. As the squadron's new leader, Peck imposes a strong regime of discipline that has no place for slackers or incompetents. At first the men complain and even try to transfer. Ultimately, the fliers realize that Peck is training them to live, not to die. However, the general drives himself even harder than he pushes his men, and in the end he falls into the same trap that had snared Merrill.

Peck begins to see his fliers as men and even friends rather than flight crews whom he must send to their possible death. As a result, the day after a successful but costly mission over Germany in which he loses his best pilot, Peck finds himself unable to climb aboard his B-17 to lead a second attack on the crucial target. Instead, he goes into a catatonic state until the squadron returns. Lay and Bartlett, who flew on the first missions over Germany, used Gen. Frank Armstrong as their model for Peck's Savage, although Armstrong never had a breakdown as portrayed in the film.

The Air Force had some problems with the original script due to scenes in which the fliers drink at the officers club the night before a mission and with the general's breakdown. Given the credibility of the screenwriters and their combat experience, the service ultimately accepted their portrayals. Consequently, the Air Force helped round up and restore to WWII configurations 12 B-17 bombers for use in the flying sequences. King filmed exterior scenes at an inactive training base in Alabama, including the spectacular crash of one of the "Flying Fortresses," which renowned stunt flier Paul Mantz singlehandedly staged. The terse script, the fine acting, and the combat footage used only in the film's one grand aerial battle combined to create one of the greatest movies about war in the air and a cautionary tale about the burdens of leadership.

Twilight's Last Gleaming (1977) [G&G]

Vietnam	Air Force	NR	Color	146 mins
Allied Artists	WV: 02-02-77		NYT: 02-10 & 20-77	

DIR: Robert Aldrich. SW: Ronald M. Cohen, Edward Huebsch. PRO: Merv Adelson. STARS: Burt Lancaster, Richard Widmark, Charles Durning, Paul Winfield, Joseph Cotten, Richard Jaeckel.

Lancaster, as Gen. Dell, opposes the Vietnam War, which results in his being framed for murder. He escapes from prison, seizes a missile silo, and threatens to start WWIII unless the president, Durning, reads a secret memo detailing the reasons the United States went into Vietnam. In the end, the government again demonstrates its venal character by shooting the president, who had become Lancaster's hostage. Implausibilities and structural problems dilute the message. In fact, a general would not back himself into a corner from which he could not escape. Moreover, a general, with good intentions would most likely not be willing to start a nuclear war, whatever his goal. Nevertheless, the film does raise important questions about how a government should act but sometimes does not. Because of financial issues and the realization that SAC would not appreciate having one of its silos infiltrated, Aldrich shot the film in Germany.

Two Yanks in Trinidad (1942)

Preparedness	Army	Unkn	B&W 82 mins
Columbia	WV: 03-25-42		NYT: 04-06-42

DIR: Gregory Ratoff. SW: Sy Bartlett, Richard Carroll, Harry Segall, Jack Henley. PRO: Samuel Bischoff. STARS: Pat O'Brien, Brian Donlevy, Janet Blair, Donald MacBride.

O'Brien spats with Donlevy and escapes to an Army enlistment to avoid him. Donlevy and his racketeer body guards join up too, following O'Brien to Trinidad, where the pals bury the hatchet, save each other, and foil a Nazi spy.

U-571 (2000) [G&G]

WWII	Navy	NR	Color 116 mins
Universal	WV: 04-17-2000		NYT: 04-21-2000

DIR: Jonathan Mostow. SW: Jonathan Mostow, Sam Montgomery, David Ayer. PRO: Dino De Laurentis, Martha De Laurentis. STARS: Matthew McConaughey, Bill Paxton, Harvey Keitel, Jon Bon Jovi, Jake Weber.

In *U-571*, Mostow created one of the most exciting submarine movies ever made. But does that end justify the means the director used? And did he succeed in his goal of showing life aboard a WWII submarine? To those who complained that the director far exceeded the limits of dramatic license, he answered that he was simply telling a fictional story, not making a documentary. While that may give Mostow some wiggle room, it does not absolve him from having rewritten history or infused the film with distortions and combat implausibilities.

His story, an American submarine crew capturing an enigma machine from a German U-boat, falsifies the truth that a British destroyer actually seized the first decoder. That eight Americans could enter a disabled German submarine and get it underway, which its own crew could not do, lacks any believability. Showing a German destroyer and fighter plane operating in the North Atlantic ignores the reality that Hitler's destroyers did not venture that far afield and fighters did not have the range to reach anywhere near Greenland, etc. Do any of these shortcomings matter? After seeing the film, one young man observed that if he wanted to see the truth he would watch PBS. Nevertheless, accepting Mostow's fictions means that reality and history get lost, and truth may not matter to future generations.

U-Boat Prisoner (1944)

WWII	Navy	Ltd	B&W 66 mins
Columbia	WV: 08-16-44		NYT: DNR

DIR: Lew Landers, Budd Boetticher. SW: Malcolm Stuart Boylan, Aubrey Wisberg. PRO: Wallace MacDonald. STARS: Bruce Bennett, Erik Rolf, John Abbott, John Wengraf.

An absurd story glorifying the Merchant Marines' contribution to victory, with the hero performing ridiculous feats while a prisoner on a German U-boat.

The Unbeliever (1918) [G&G]

WWI	Marines	Full	B&W 7 reels
Edison	WV: 02-15-18		NYT: 02-12-18

DIR: Alan Crosland. SW: Unkn. PRO: George Kleine. STARS: Raymond McKee, Kate Lester, Erich von Stroheim, Marguerite Courtot.

Based on Mary Raymond Shipman Andrews's novel *The Three Things*, this seminal Marine film features the rite of passage of young dilettante McKee to manhood due to his wartime experiences. In addition to finding religion, tolerance, and equality, he saves Courtot, a young Belgian lass, sends her to his parents on Long Island, returns a wounded hero, and the couple walks off into the sunset. The Marines provided men (Third Battalion, Sixth Regiment) and equipment at their base in Quantico, Virginia, to stage battle scenes set in Belgium, even though the Marines ultimately fought only in France. In addition to portraying combat, the film serves as a propaganda piece as von Stroheim, playing a Prussian officer, commits atrocities and humiliates his men until they rise up and shoot him.

Uncommon Valor (1983)

Vietnam	Army	NR	Color	105 mins
Paramount	WV: 12-14-83		NYT: 12-16-83	

DIR: Ted Kotcheff. SW: Joe Gayton. PRO: John Milius, Buzz Feitshans. STARS: Gene Hackman, Robert Stack, Reb Brown, Randall Cobb.

A "Missing in Action" rescue film in which Hackman organizes a quasi-military expedition to locate his son and other POWs who may still be alive 10 years after the war in Vietnam ended.

Under Siege (1992) [G&G]

Terrorism	Navy	Cour	Color	120 mins
WB	WV: 10-12-92		NYT: 10-09-92	

DIR: Andrew Davis. SW: J. F. Lawton. PRO: Arnon Milchan, Steven Seagal, Steven Reuther. STARS: Steven Seagal, Tommy Lee Jones, Gary Busey, Erika Eleniak, Nick Mancuso.

Seagal, a disgraced Navy SEAL, is ending his career as a cook aboard the USS *Missouri* on its way to Hawaii to be decommissioned. At sea, terrorists commandeer the ship with the help of its rogue exec officer, who has created a plan to seize nuclear weapons and sell them to the highest bidder. Seagal uses all his martial arts to save the day. The Navy declined to provide assistance given the actions of the exec but did allow aerial filming of the *Missouri* underway and aboard ship during a ceremony in Pearl Harbor. Davis filmed exterior scenes on the USS *Alabama* in Mobile, Alabama.

The Unknown Soldier (1926)

WWI	Army	Full	B&W	82 mins
PDC	WV: 06-02-26		NYT: 05-31-26	

DIR: Renaud Hoffman. SW: E. Richard Schayer, James J. Tynan. PRO: Renaud Hoffman, Charles Rogers. STARS: Charles Emmett Mack, Marguerite De La Motte, Henry Walthall, Claire McDowell.

An American soldier in France meets an American entertainer, gets married by an impostor chaplain, goes off to battle, is wounded, spends two years in the hospital, and then is reunited with his wife and a nameless son. The closing sequence used actual footage of the burial of "The Unknown Soldier" with fictional scenes cut in.

Underwater Warrior (1958)

WWII	Navy	Full	B&W	90 mins
MGM	WV: 02-26-58		NYT: DNR	

DIR: Andrew Marton. SW: Gene Levitt. PRO: Ivan Tors. STARS: Dan Dailey, Claire Kelly, James Gregory, Ross Martin.

Based on the actual adventures of Navy officer Francis Fane, who championed the service's frogmen's combat abilities from before World War II to Korea. The story is better in the sea than on land but provided informational benefit to the organization that became the much more secretive SEALS.

Until They Sail (1957)

WWII	Marines	Unkn	B&W	94 mins
MGM	WV: 09-25-57		NYT: 10-09-57	

DIR: Robert Wise. SW: Robert Anderson. PRO: Charles Schnee. STARS: Jean Simmons, Joan Fontaine, Paul Newman, Piper Laurie, Charles Drake.

From a James Michener story, the film describes what happens to a female population (in this case in New Zealand) when all the marriageable men leave to fight a war and the American Marines arrive.

Up from the Beach (1965)

WWII	Army	NR	B&W	98 mins
Fox	WV: 06-09-65		NYT: 06-10-65	

DIR: Robert Parrish. SW: Howard Clewes, Claude Brulé, Stanley Mann. PRO: Christian Ferry. STARS: Cliff Robertson, Red Buttons, Irina Demick, Slim Pickens.

Based on George Barr's novel *Epitaph for an Enemy*, the film may have been intended as a sequel to *The Longest Day*. Instead, it turns into a complete mess as American soldiers, without any concern for their actions, herd French civilians from the coast on D-Day plus one.

Up Front (1951)

WWII	Army	Ltd	B&W	92 mins
Universal	WV: 03-07-51		NYT: 03-26-51	

DIR: Alexander Hall. SW: Stanley Roberts. PRO: Leonard Goldstein. STARS: Tom Ewell, David Wayne, Jeffrey Lynn, Richard Egan.

Based on Bill Mauldin's book of the same name, the movie showed war as it was for the grunts slogging through the mud, but as comedy, not drama.

Up in Arms (1944)

WWII	Army	Unkn	Color	106 mins
RKO	WV: 02-09-44		NYT: 03-03-44	

DIR: Elliott Nugent. SW: Don Hartman, Allen Boretz, Robert Pirosh. PRO: Samuel Goldwyn. STARS: Danny Kaye, Dinah Shore, Dana Andrews, Constance Dowling.

A musical comedy follows Kaye's induction into the Army and the romantic pursuits of the stars, including scenes on a troop transport ship headed to the South Pacific.

Up Periscope (1959)

WWII	Navy	Full	Color	111 mins
WB	WV: 02-11-59		NYT: 03-05-59	

DIR: Gordon Douglas. SW: Richard Landau. PRO: Aubrey Schenck. STARS: James Garner, Edmond O'Brien, Alan Hale Jr., Andra Martin.

Based on a Robb White novel, this straightforward submarine drama focuses on O'Brien as a by-the-book commander.

U.S. Seals (1999)

Peace	Navy	NR	Color	93 mins
Nu Image	WV: DNR		NYT: DNR	

DIR: Yossi Wein. SW: David Sparling. PRO: Danny Lerner. STARS: Jim Fitzpatrick, Greg Collins, Ty Miller, Justin Williams.

One of the worst, most incomprehensible military movies ever made. Heroes vaguely identified and portrayed as Navy SEALS receive orders from a civilian who seems tied to the military. Long shots of a U.S. battleship at sea attempt to connect the men to the Navy. Credits indicate that filmmakers used some footage from the earlier movie, *Navy SEALS*.

USS Teakettle. See You're in the Navy Now.

Verboten! (1959)

WWII	Army	Ltd	B&W	86 mins
Columbia	WV: 03-25-59		NYT: 07-12-60	

DIR: Samuel Fuller. SW: Samuel Fuller. PRO: Samuel Fuller. STARS: James Best, Susan Cummings, Tom Pittman.

Using old combat footage and newsreels from the Nuremberg War Crimes Trials, this "B" movie examines postwar Germany thru the romantic liaison of a wounded GI in the occupation forces and his German nurse, who reveals an underground neo-Nazi youth movement.

The Very Thought of You (1944)

WWII	Army	Unkn	B&W 99 mins
WB	WV: 10-18-44		NYT: 11-18-44

DIR: Delmer Daves. SW: Alvah Bessie, Delmer Daves. PRO: Jerry Wald. STARS: Dennis Morgan, Eleanor Parker, Dane Clark, Faye Emerson.

Morgan returns from 18 months in the Aleutians, meets Parker, and falls in love. Following a fast courtship and marriage, Morgan deploys to the Mediterranean, where he is wounded, and then returns home to his wife and new baby.

Via Wireless (1915) [SSS]

WWI	Navy	Full	B&W 5 reels
Pathé	WV: 09-24-15		NYT: DNR

DIR: George Fitzmaurice. SW: Ouida Bergere. PRO: Pathé. STARS: Bruce McRae, Gail Kane, Harry Weaver, Brandon Hurst.

Based on the Paul Armstrong and Winchell Smith play *Via Wireless*, the film dealt with the then timely subject of U.S. military preparedness. After President Woodrow Wilson calls for a strong defense, the War Department starts planning for large caliber coastal defense guns. The bad guy sabotages the first gun, and a Navy officer hero is blamed for an explosion that kills two operators. In the end, of course, the hero rescues the girl, and the bad guy is exposed and killed. The Army provided marching cadets at West Point and the Navy provided the Atlantic fleet cruising, the battleship *New York* in the Washington Navy Yard dry dock and at sea, and a coastal gun being fired.

The Victors (1963) [G&G]

WWII	Army	NR	B&W 175 mins
Columbia	WV: 10-30-63		NYT: 12-20-63

DIR: Carl Foreman. SW: Carl Foreman. PRO: Carl Foreman. STARS: Romy Schneider, Melina Mercouri, Jeanne Moreau, Elke Sommer, Eli Wallach, George Hamilton, George Peppard, Albert Finney, Vince Edwards, Peter Fonda.

The film takes a philosophical look at WWII, full of characters and their not-so-pretty stories. Foreman used newsreel footage to help bring British novelist Alexander Baron's *The Human Kind* to life. Even the Allies do battle with each other, and the behavior of the winners is sometimes no better than that of the losers, which was Foreman's point. The film includes a fictionalization of the execution of Private Slovak, the one American to be executed for desertion since the Civil War. (See chapter 2.)

Victory (1981)

WWII	Army	NR	Color 110 mins
Paramount	WV: 07-22-81		NYT: 07-31-81

DIR: John Huston. SW: Evan Jones, Yabo Yablonsky. PRO: Freddie Fields. STARS: Sylvester Stallone, Michael Caine, Pelé, Max Von Sydow.

Typical POW story that does not make life behind the barbed wire seem so bad. In this case, the Germans dream up the idea of a soccer match between their all-stars and the POWs led by Caine and Stallone, as if the prisoners would have the energy to compete in any competition. On their part, however, the POWs see the match as an opportunity to escape while in Paris. And they do.

Von Ryan's Express (1965)

WWII	Army	NR	Color	114 mins
Fox	WV: 05-19-65		NYT: 06-24-65	

DIR: Mark Robson. SW: Wendell Mayes, Joseph Landon. PRO: Saul David. STARS: Frank Sinatra, Trevor Howard, Brad Dexter, James Brolin, Vito Scotti, Sergio Fantoni.

This action picture depicts a massive escape of approximately 600 American and British POWs by train through occupied Italy in hopes of reaching a haven in Switzerland. The story has similarities to *The Great Escape*, of course, but the use of a train and the locale in Italy give it a different ambience.

The Wackiest Ship in the Army (1960)

WWII	Army	Full	Color	99 mins
Columbia	WV: 12-07-60		NYT: 02-09-61	

DIR: Richard Murphy. SW: Richard Murphy, Herbert Margolis, William Raynor. PRO: Fred Kohlmar. STARS: Jack Lemmon, Ricky Nelson, John Lund, Chips Rafferty.

Shot in Hawaii and using some battle footage, the film portrayed the Army's use of decrepit ships to move Australian "scouts" into coast watcher positions in the South Sea islands of the Pacific.

Wake Island (1942) [G&G]

WWII	Marines	Full	B&W	87 mins
Paramount	WV: 08-12-42		NYT: 09-02-42	

DIR: John Farrow. SW: W. R. Burnett, Frank Butler. PRO: Joseph Sistrom. STARS: Brian Donlevy, Robert Preston, Macdonald Carey, Albert Dekker, Barbara Britton, William Bendix.

The filmmakers based their story about the fight for Wake Island in the first days of WWII on both fact and fiction. They had radio dispatches and the account by a Marine officer who left the embattled island on the last plane out, under orders to bring back information about the Japanese tactics. From the time he left, however, Burnett and Butler had only a few radio reports, which ended before the final onslaught. So they had to fabricate the closing hours of the battle of the few Marines and civilian contractors against an overwhelming number of Japanese attackers. Despite the demands on its men and equipment during the first months of the war, the Marines provided assistance to the production at the Salton Sea, south of Los Angeles. Although the movie did portray a crushing defeat, it showed the Marines fighting bravely and so helped the war effort by instilling in the American people the goal of avenging the loss.

Wake Me When It's Over (1960)

| Peace | Army | Ltd | Color   126 mins |
| Fox | WV: 03-30-60 | | NYT: 04-09-60 |

DIR: Mervyn LeRoy. SW: Richard Breen. PRO: Mervyn LeRoy. STARS: Ernie Kovacs, Margo Moore, Jack Warden, Dick Shawn, Don Knotts.

Erroneously redrafted into the service, Kovacs is sent to a lonely Pacific island, where he develops a luxury hotel from war surplus materials while he waits for the Army to correct the error and discharge him. The resort is so successful, and notorious, that Congress investigates.

A Walk in the Clouds (1995)

| WWII | Army | NR | Color   102 mins |
| Fox | WV: 07-31-95 | | NYT: 08-11-95 |

DIR: Alfonso Arau. SW: Robert Mark Kamen, Mark Miller, Harvey Weitzman. PRO: Gil Netter, David Zucker, Jerry Zucker. STARS: Keanu Reeves, Aitana Sánchez-Gijón, Anthony Quinn, Giancarlo Giannini, Angelica Argón.

Reeves comes home from the war, a decorated hero, to find an unfaithful wife, but also the possibility of true love, albeit with a pregnant graduate student. The film opens with the return of soldiers from the South Pacific aboard a battleship to cheering relatives in San Francisco. Throughout the film, Reeves has brief realistic flashbacks to the horrors of combat against the Japanese, similar to the manner in which Hollywood portrayed Vietnam veterans trying to adjust to civilian life.

A Walk in the Sun (1945)

| WWII | Army | Full | B&W   117 mins |
| Fox | WV: 11-28-45 | | NYT: 01-12-46 |

DIR: Lewis Milestone. SW: Robert Rossen. PRO: Lewis Milestone. STARS: Dana Andrews, Richard Conte, Sterling Holloway, John Ireland.

Appearing shortly after the end of the war and based on veteran Harry Brown's novel, this film became one of the inspirations for Steven Spielberg's *Saving Private Ryan*. A unit of soldiers receives orders to advance to and occupy a lonely farmhouse. The film slowly follows the men's journey across the countryside and ends abruptly with a firefight at the farmhouse. However, the men talk more than they fight and what they say is not all that profound.

The Walking Dead (1995)

| Vietnam | Marines | NR | Color   89 mins |
| Savoy Pictures | WV: 02-27-95 | | NYT: 02-25-95 |

DIR: Preston Whitmore II. SW: Preston Whitmore II. PRO: Frank Price, George Jackson, Douglas McHenry. STARS: Allen Payne, Eddie Griffin, Joe Morton, Vonte Sweet.

The only new twist to this clichéd Vietnam movie is that four of the five Marines on their last mission, sent to rescue some POW officers, are black. The men meet unexpected resistance and realize they are expendable. They spend their time fighting the enemy and talking about their past and reasons for being in Vietnam, shown in flashbacks. Whitmore, who wrote the script in two weeks (it shows), filmed it in Florida without military assistance.

War Dogs (1942)

WWII	Army	Ltd	B&W 65 mins
Monogram	WV: 12-23-42		NYT: DNR

DIR: S. Roy Luby. SW: John Vlahos. PRO: George W. Weeks. STARS: Billy Lee, Addison Richards, Kay Linaker, Bradley Page, Ace as Pal the dog.

This film had its origins in a preparedness documentary on how the Army trained its canine corps. With the advent of WWII, the studio turned it into a feature movie. The plot involves a shell-shocked WWI Marine working in a defense plant who joins the Army and works with the dogs. Re-released as *Pride of the Army*.

War Hunt (1962) [G&G]

Korea	Army	Deny	B&W 81 mins
UA	WV: 03-14-62		NYT: 08-08-62

DIR: Denis Sanders. SW: Stanford Whitmore. PRO: Terry Sanders. STARS: John Saxon, Robert Redford, Sydney Pollack.

The Army denied a request for assistance because the film depicted a soldier, lauded as an efficient killer during the war, who continues to cross the ceasefire line to kill North Korean soldiers after the war is over. His commanding officer solves the "problem" by personally executing the warrior. This was Redford's first credited film appearance.

War Is Hell (1964)

Korea	Army	NR	B&W 81 mins
Allied Artists	WV: DNR		NYT: 01-23-64

DIR: Burt Topper. SW: Burt Topper. PRO: Burt Topper. STARS: Tony Russell, Baynes Barron, Judy Dan, Burt Topper.

This "B" film follows the sadistic actions of a GI seeking glory in Korea.

The War Lover (1962)

WWII	Air Force	Deny	B&W 105 mins
Columbia	WV: 10-24-62		NYT: 03-07-63

DIR: Philip Leacock. SW: Howard Koch. PRO: Arthur Hornblow Jr. STARS: Steve McQueen, Robert Wagner, Shirley Anne Field.

McQueen plays an emotionally ill pilot obsessed with killing.

War Nurse (1930)

WWI	Army	Unkn	B&W 79 mins
MGM	WV: 10-29-30		NYT: 10-24-30

DIR: Edgar Selwyn. SW: Joseph Farnham, Becky Gardiner. PRO: MGM. STARS: Robert Montgomery, Anita Page, June Walker, Robert Ames.

The tale of young Army nurses on the Western Front. Initially, they believe their jobs will be easy. The harsh reality of combat shows otherwise. Selwyn presented well the ambience of hostilities.

The War of the Worlds (1953)

SciFi	Air Force, Army, Marines Ltd.		Color 85 mins
Paramount	WV: 03-04-53		NYT: 08-14-53

DIR: Byron Haskin. SW: Barré Lyndon. PRO: George Pal. STARS: Gene Barry, Ann Robinson, Les Tremayne, Bob Cornthwaite.

Based on H. G. Wells's novel and the Orson Welles radio play, the film portrayed the U.S. military as ineffectual against the invading Martians. After failing to stop the Martians, the Army deferred to the Marines, who launched an artillery, tank, and rocket attack with no perceptible effect. The Air Force had no better luck with an atomic bomb, whose blast could not penetrate the Martian shields. The filmmakers requested footage of a bomber launching the nuclear attack. After long negotiations the Air Force allowed contractor Northrup to give the filmmakers a few feet of footage showing a flying wing.

Warbus (1985)

Vietnam	Marines	Unkn	Color 90 mins
Medusa	WV: DNR		NYT: DNR

DIR: Ferdinando Baldi. SW: Ferdinando Baldi, John Fitzsimmons. PRO: Unkn. STARS: Urs Althaus, Daniel Stephen, Rom Kristoff, Steve Eliot, Ernie Zarate, Gwen Cook.

This "C" feature filmed in the Philippines and quickly released to video tells the story of three Marines who commandeer a bus full of people escaping the advancing North Vietnamese army to get back to their base in De Nang.

WarGames (1983) [G&G]

Cold War	Air Force	Deny	Color 110 mins
MGM	WV: 05-11-83		NYT: 06-03-83

DIR: John Badham. SW: Lawrence Lasker, Walter F. Parkes. PRO: Harold Schneider. STARS: Matthew Broderick, Dabney Coleman, John Wood, Ally Sheedy, Barry Corbin.

Like *The Forbin Project*, this film offered the premise that a giant computer controls the nuclear arsenal of the United States. In this case, Broderick, a teenaged computer whiz, hacks into Norad's missile defense system but initially thinks he has just entered into a war game of mass global destruction. Once the reality intrudes, Broderick begins a race against time to stop an actual nuclear exchange. No such omnipotent computer exists, of course, but if it did, it would know better than to launch an attack when the geopolitical situation was calm. Likewise, the military officers controlling the computer would realize something had gone wrong with its "thinking" process because no global threat then existed. Given the fallacies driving the story, the DoD refused the request for assistance.

Warkill (1967)

WWII	Army	NR	Color	100 mins
Universal	WV: 06-28-67		NYT: DNR	

DIR: Ferde Grofé Jr. SW: Ferde Grofé Jr. PRO: Ferde Grofé. STARS: George Montgomery, Tom Drake, Paul Edwards Jr., Bruno Punzalan.

Montgomery, as an American colonel, leads a group of Filipino soldiers against isolated Japanese units in the last days of the war. His brutal tactics shock a journalist until he realizes that the Japanese are even more brutal and have committed appalling, horrendous atrocities. Closing combat sequences are impressive for such a low-budget film.

Welcome, Mr. Washington (1944)

WWII	Army	NR	B&W	95 mins
Brtsh Natl	WV: 06-28-44		NYT: DNR	

DIR: Leslie Hiscott. SW: Jack Whittingham. PRO: Elizabeth Hiscott. STARS: Barbara Mullen, Donald Stewart, Peggy Cummins, Leslie Bradley, Roy Emerton.

Based on Noel Streatfield's original story, the film portrays what happens when the overpaid, oversexed, over-here American GIs arrive in the English countryside. In this case, they do good deeds, for example, helping with the harvest, receiving the appreciation of the British country folk. (See *The Affair* in chapter 2 for the other side of the story.)

We Were Soldiers (2002)

Vietnam	Army	Full	Color	137 mins
Paramount	WV: 03-03-2002		NYT: 03-01-2002	

DIR: Randall Wallace. SW: Randall Wallace. PRO: Bruce Davey, Stephen McEveety, Randall Wallace. STARS: Mel Gibson, Madeleine Stowe, Greg Kinnear, Sam Elliott, Chris Klein, Keri Russell.

Based on the memoir *We Were Soldiers Once . . . and Young* by Lt. Gen. (Ret.) Harold G. Moore and journalist Joseph L. Galloway, *We Were Soldiers* portrayed the 1965 engagement between 400 soldiers of the Seventh Cavalry and 2,000 North Vietnamese regular soldiers in the Ia Drang Valley. When the script first arrived in the Pentagon, the public affairs office saw it as containing the first postwar story showing the United States winning in Vietnam. Since Moore and Galloway had spent eight years working with Wallace, the Army presumed the film would tell the story accurately and so quickly approved the script for assistance, including shooting at Fort Benning, where Gen. Harry Kinnard had developed the Air Cav tactics used in the battle and then throughout the war.

The Army also permitted Wallace to film the Vietnam sequences at Fort Hunter Liggett in central California, whose terrain closely resembled that of the Ia Drang Valley.

On their part, Moore and Galloway had no concerns about the accuracy of the completed film. *We Were Soldiers* did adhere reasonably well to the book despite Wallace's apparent lack of concern with history, as shown in his scripts for **Braveheart** and **Pearl Harbor**. In particular, he did convey the nature of the military mind before Vietnam, the men's religiosity, and their belief in American invincibility. Due to time limits and financial constraints, the film portrayed the fighting for only one of the two landing zones, which created the impression that Moore and his men alone fought against a superior force. And the film's final assault up the hill to the North Vietnamese headquarters never happened.

Despite these errors of fact and other changes in the name of dramatic license, the film contains one of the few positive portrayals of Americans fighting bravely and apparently winning on the Vietnam battlefield. But it also shows a North Vietnamese officer surveying the battlefield after Moore's men had been evacuated and observing that while his enemy thinks it has won the day, the results will be the same, that the United States will share the fate of the French in Indochina. Victory on the battlefield, however Hollywood chooses to portray it, could not and will not be able to hide the reality that in the end, Vietnam won and we lost.

We're in the Navy Now (1926)

WWI	Navy	Full	B&W	60 mins
Famous	WV: 11-10-26		NYT: 11-08-26	

DIR: A. Edward Sutherland. SW: John McDermott, George Marion Jr. PRO: Adolph Zukor, Jesse L. Lasky. STARS: Wallace Beery, Raymond Hatton, Chester Conklin, Tom Kennedy.

A prizefighter and his selfish manager accidentally end up in the Navy and spend their enlistment trying to obtain discharges. A former opponent is their petty officer. Famous Players released this comedy in the same year as **Behind the Front** and that featured some of the same cast.

Welcome Home (1989)

Vietnam	Air Force	NR	Color	87 mins
Columbia	WV: 05-24-89		NYT: 09-29-89	

DIR: Franklin J. Schaffner. SW: Maggie Kleinman. PRO: Martin Ransohoff, Don Carmody. STARS: Kris Kristofferson, JoBeth Williams, Brian Keith, Sam Waterston, Trey Wilson.

Kristofferson, shot down and declared missing, returns to the United States after 17 years in Cambodia. He had escaped from a POW camp, married a Cambodian woman, and fathered two children. When he finally remembers he had married before leaving for Vietnam, he returns to the United States to find his wife, now living in Vermont, and discovers how many lives he has complicated.

West Point (1928)

Peace	Army	Full	B&W	80 mins
MGM	WV: 01-11-28		NYT: 01-02-28	

DIR: Edward Sedgwick. SW: Raymond Schrock, Joseph Farnham. PRO: MGM. STARS: William Haines, Joan Crawford, Neil Neely, Ralph Emerson.

Using footage of the 1926 Army–Navy game, this coming-of-age film is set at the U.S. Military Academy, which provided colorful backgrounds of marching cadets, dining hall customs, and commencement ceremonies.

West Point of the Air (1935)

Peace	Army	Full	B&W 90 mins
MGM	WV: 04-10-35		NYT: 04-06-35

DIR: Richard Rosson. SW: Frank Mead, Arthur Beckhard. PRO: Monta Bell. STARS: Wallace Beery, Robert Young, Maureen O'Sullivan, Lewis Stone, James Gleason, Rosalind Russell.

Beery, an old Army sergeant, tries to make Young, his son, into an aviator. The film depicts the training school and features planes flying in formation, exciting stunts, and crashes. The aerial scenes are superior to the story line, in which two girls chase the pilot.

The West Point Story (1950)

Peace	Army	Full	B&W 106 mins
WB	WV: 11-15-50		NYT: 12-23-50

DIR: Roy Del Ruth. SW: John Monks Jr., Charles Hoffman, Irving Wallace. PRO: Louis F. Edelman. STARS: James Cagney, Virginia Mayo, Doris Day, Gordon MacRae, Gene Nelson.

A Jule Styne/Sammy Cahn musical in which Cagney plays an unlucky Broadway director who agrees to prepare the annual West Point show, discovers Cadet MacRae, and pursues him, hoping he will resign from the Academy and star in a big new Broadway production. His decision, of course, is predetermined.

West Point Widow (1941)

Peace	Army	Cour	B&W 63 mins
Paramount	WV: 06-11-41		NYT: 09-11-41

DIR: Robert Siodmak. SW: F. Hugh Herbert, Hanns Kräly. PRO: Sol C. Siegel. STARS: Anne Shirley, Richard Carlson, Richard Denning.

Shirley portrays a nurse whose annulled marriage to a West Point football star (he promised remarriage after graduation) produced a daughter. A doctor at Shirley's hospital uncovers the story and works to make Shirley and the baby his instant family.

We've Never Been Licked (1943)

WWII	Navy	Ltd	B&W 101 mins
Universal	WV: 08-04-43		NYT: 08-19-43

DIR: John Rawlins. SW: Nick Grinde. PRO: Walter Wanger. STARS: Richard Quine, Ann Gwynne, Noah Beery Jr., Martha O'Driscoll, William Frawley.

The film combines a college coming-of-age love story with military and spy dramas. Shot at Texas A&M University. Rawlins also used battle footage provided by the Navy. Frawley, of future *I Love Lucy* fame, played a Japanese spy.

What Am I Bid? (1967)

Peace	Navy	Ltd	Color 92 mins
Liberty	WV: 07-12-67		NYT: DNR

DIR: Gene Nash. SW: Gene Nash. PRO: Wendell Niles Jr. STARS: Leroy Van Dyke, Kristin Harmon, Stephanie Hill, Bill Craig.

Although the movie is essentially a country western musical, its final scene features a patriotic song and dance routine on a Navy aircraft carrier.

What Did You Do in the War, Daddy? (1966)

WWII	Army	NR	Color 115 mins
UA	WV: 06-29-66		NYT: 09-01-66

DIR: Blake Edwards. SW: William Peter Blatty, Blake Edwards, Maurice Richlin. PRO: Blake Edwards. STARS: James Coburn, Dick Shawn, Aldo Ray, Harry Morgan, Carroll O'Connor.

Ignoring the war as much as possible, this comedy pictures a battle-weary American unit ordered to take a town held by a large Italian force. The townspeople and the enemy soldiers are agreeable to surrender—but only after their wine festival. Lots of gags and hangovers.

What Next, Corporal Hargrove? (1945)

WWII	Army	Unkn	B&W 95 mins
MGM	WV: 11-21-45		NYT: 12-26-45

DIR: Richard Thorpe. SW: Harry Kurnitz. PRO: George Haight. STARS: Robert Walker, Keenan Wynn, Jean Porter, Chill Wills.

Walker and Wynn, assigned to an artillery division, take a shortcut, after being stuck in mud, to rejoin their outfit. As a result they "liberate" a small French village and, because of another mix-up, arrive in Paris in trouble with the military police.

What Price Glory? (1926) [G&G]

WWI	Marines	Ltd	B&W 110 mins
Fox	WV: 12-01-26		NYT: 11-24-26

DIR: Raoul Walsh. SW: James T. O'Donohoe, Malcolm Stuart Boylan. PRO: William Fox. STARS: Victor McLaglen, Edmund Lowe, Dolores Del Rio, William Mong, Phyllis Haver.

Based on the smash Broadway hit by Maxwell Anderson and Laurence Stallings, the film portrays the rivalry between Capt. Flagg and Sgt. Quirt for the love of a French girl during World War I. Unlike the antiwar tone of the play, the film focuses more on the pursuit than the hell of war. However, the film set the standard against which all future Marine movies would be judged. Actual combat scenes were limited in scope, and the Marines provided limited assistance.

What Price Glory? (1952)

WWI	Marines	Ltd	Color	110 mins
Fox	WV: 07-30-52		NYT: 08-23-52	

DIR: John Ford. SW: Phoebe Ephron, Henry Ephron. PRO: Sol Siegel. STARS: James Cagney, Dan Dailey, William Demarest.

A pale imitation of the original, turned more into a comedy with songs.

When Eagles Strike (2003)

Terrorism	Marines	NR	Color	88 mins
New Horizons	WV: Dnr		NYT: Dnr	

DIR: Cirio Santiago. SW: Michael Kinny. PRO: Roger Corman, Cirio Santiago. STARS: Stacy Keach, Christian Boeving, Davee Youngblood, Nate Adams.

What is a fine actor like Keach doing in a Santiago movie? Perhaps he had a mortgage payment due. Set this time in the Philippines, the director creates a hostage rescue story simply as a vehicle for continual action and violence. The timeliness of the subject of combating world-wide terrorism cannot compensate for the terrible acting, poor military tactics, and cliched story and the film quickly went to video.

When Hell Broke Loose (1958)

WWII	Army	NR	Color	107 mins
Paramount	WV: 11-05-58		NYT: DNR	

DIR: Kenneth G. Crane. SW: Oscar Brodney. PRO: Oscar Brodney, Sol Dolgin. STARS: Charles Bronson, Richard Jaeckel, Violet Rensing.

Bronson wants to avoid service but finally enlists near the end of WWII only to avoid imprisonment. While in Germany he hooks up with a German girl whose brother is in a group plotting the assassination of Gen. Dwight D. Eisenhower.

When Willie Comes Marching Home (1950)

WWII	Air Force	Full	B&W	82 mins
Fox	WV: 01-04-50		NYT: 02-18-50	

DIR: John Ford. SW: Mary Loos, Richard Sale. PRO: Fred Kohlmar. STARS: Dan Dailey, Corinne Calvet, Colleen Townsend, William Demarest.

Ford's comedy depicts a small town lad who is its first enlistee following Pearl Harbor. After training, the Army assigns him to a base near his hometown as a gunnery instructor, much to his chagrin. Late in the war he gets his chance to fly in the European theater, where his adventures win him first the disbelief of his town and then military honors.

Where Eagles Dare (1968)

WWII	Army	Unkn	Color	158 mins
MGM	WV: 12-11-68		NYT: 03-13-69	

DIR: Brian G. Hutton. SW: Alistair MacLean. PRO: Elliott Kastner. STARS: Richard Burton, Clint Eastwood, Mary Ure, Michael Hordern, Patrick Wymark, Robert Beatty.

Based on MacLean's novel, one of the many British commando operation films. In this case, American soldier Eastwood joins the unit to help rescue an American general held in a mountaintop fortress.

Where's My Man To-night? (see *Marhing On*)

White Christmas (1954)

WWII	Army	NR	Color	120 mins
Paramount	WV: date?		NYT: 10-15-44	

DIR: Michael Curtiz. SW: Norman Krasna, Norman Panama, Melvin Frank. PRO: Robert Emmett Dolan. STARS: Bing Crosby, Danny Kaye, Rosemary Clooney, Dean Jagger.

The opening sequence on Christmas Eve, 1944, takes place during the Battle of the Bulge. Crosby and Kaye put on a show for the troops before the Germans launch an attack. Curtiz filmed the sequence on a sound stage and did not require military assistance.

White Ghost (1988)

Vietnam	Army	NR	Color	95 mins
Gibralter Films	WV: DNR		NYT: DNR	

DIR: B. J. Davis. SW: Gary Scott Thompson. PRO: Jay Davidson, Barrie Saint Clair, William Fay. STARS: William Katt, Rosalind Chao, Wayne Crawford, Reb Brown.

Green Beret Katt did not return from his last Vietnam mission and roamed the jungles for 15 years collecting dog tags of dead American soldiers, hoping to ultimately return them to the families and thereby change their Missing in Action status. When he finally contacts U.S. intelligence sources and requests "extraction," the man in charge is a former superior, whom Katt had once accused of murdering women and children. He naturally tries to murder Katt to prevent the truth from coming out.

Who'll Stop the Rain? (1978) [G&G]

Vietnam	Marines, Navy	Ltd	Color	125 mins
UA	WV: 05-24-78		NYT: 08-26-78	

DIR: Karel Reisz. SW: Judith Roscoe, Robert Stone. PRO: Herbert Jaffe, Gabriel Katzka. STARS: Nick Nolte, Tuesday Weld, Michael Moriarty.

Brief Vietnam combat scene serves only as a springboard for this story of the war's impact on combatants and a drug deal gone wrong back in the States. The Navy reluctantly allowed limited filming at a West Coast facility, and the Marines helped stage a brief Vietcong attack.

Why America Will Win (1918)

WWI	Army	Full	B&W 7 reels
Fox	WV: DNR		NYT: DNR

DIR: Richard Stanton. SW: Adrian Johnson. PRO: Unkn. STARS: Olaf Skavlan, Harris Gordon, Ralph Faulkner, W. E. Whittle, Betty Gray.

Docudrama of the life of Gen. John J. Pershing from his boyhood in northern Missouri to his appointment as the commander of the American Expeditionary Forces in France during World War I. While in charge of the Presidio in San Francisco, Pershing lost his entire family in a fire. The film served to inform the American people of Pershing's character and leadership and so help the war effort.

Why Sailors Go Wrong (1928)

Peace	Navy	Full	B&W 6 reels
Fox	WV: 04-11-28		NYT: 04-09-28

DIR: Henry Lehrman. SW: Randall Faye. PRO: William Fox. STARS: Sammy Cohen, Ted McNamara, Sally Phipps, Nick Stuart, Carl Miller.

A Navy ship arrives in the nick of time to save Americans from the local natives on Pago Pago.

The Wild Blue Yonder (1951)

WWII	Air Force	Full	B&W 97 mins
Republic	WV: 12-05-51		NYT: 01-02-52

DIR: Allan Dwan. SW: Richard Tregaskis. PRO: Herbert J. Yates. STARS: Wendell Corey, Vera Ralston, Forrest Tucker, Walter Brennan, Phil Harris.

The B-29 Superfortress stars in this film, which details its development and use in the Pacific. A clichéd romantic triangle subplot involves two fliers pursuing the same Army nurse.

The Wild Bunch (1969)

Mexican Border		NR	Color 134 mins
Warner Bros.	WV: 06-18-69		NYT: 06-26, 07-06 & 07-20-69

DIR: Sam Peckinpah. SW: Walon Green, Sam Peckinpah. PRO: Phil Feldman. STARS: William Holden, Robert Ryan, Ernest Borgnine, Edmond O'Brien, Warren Oates.

While the film became a classic revisionist Western, the contemporary Army had no horse soldiers left to assist Peckinpah. In any case, the portrayal clearly did not burnish the cavalry's image, that Hollywood had created over the years.

The Wind and the Lion (1975)

Peace	Marines, Navy	NR	Color 119 mins
MGM/Columbia	WV: 05-21-75		NYT: 05-23 & 06-15-75

DIR: John Milius. SW: John Milius. PRO: Herb Jaffe. STARS: Sean Connery, Candice Bergen, John Huston, Brian Keith, Steve Kanaly.

When Berbers in Morocco abduct Bergen and her two children, Teddy Roosevelt sends in the Marines to rescue them. A fine action-adventure movie, with the Marines acquitting themselves admirably.

Windjammer (1958)

Peace	Navy	Full	Color 142 mins
National Theater	WV: 04-09-58		NYT: 04-10-58

DIR: Louis de Rochemont III, Bill Colleran. SW: Capt. Alan Villiers, James L. Shute. PRO: Louis de Rochemont III. STARS: Captain Yngvar Kjelstrup, Lasse Kolstad, crew of *Christian Radich*.

Described as a "dramatized" travelogue, the movie stars the famous tall ship *Christian Radich*, which is still used for training Norwegian sailors. The film features beautiful naval scenes, including a rendezvous with a U.S. aircraft carrier, destroyers, and a submarine. The latter was submerged with one of de Rochemont's cameras enclosed in a glass housing on its deck.

Windtalkers (2002)

WWII	Marines	Full	Color 134 mins
MGM	WV: 06-10-2002		NYT: 06-14-2002

DIR: John Woo. SW: John Rice, Joe Batteer. PRO: John Woo, Terence Chang, Tracie Graham-Rice, Alison Rosenzweig. STARS: Nicolas Cage, Adam Beach, Peter Stormare, Christian Slater, Noah Emmerich.

The highly fictionalized story of Navajo codetalkers who communicated in code and native language to thwart Japanese efforts to intercept Marine communications. The film posits that the Marines assigned bodyguards to each Indian with orders to kill him rather than allow the Japanese to capture him. The "peg" had no basis in fact, and the Marines and DoD negotiated with the filmmakers so that the order was not explicitly stated. However, the completed movie left no doubt of the order's intent.

At the same time, the Marine Corps insisted that the character of the dentist be removed from the screenplay, saying Marines could not be portrayed as extracting gold teeth from dead Japanese. In fact, this did occur. In any case, despite the Marine hope for a great story, the film deteriorated into Cage's battle with his demons for having lost 15 men under his command. His struggle was no more interesting than the cinematic combat.

Wing and a Prayer (1944) [SSS]

WWII	Navy	Full	B&W 96 mins
Fox	WV: 07-19-44		NYT: 08-31-44

DIR: Henry Hathaway. SW: Jerome Cady. PRO: William A. Bacher, Walter Morosco. STARS: Don Ameche, Dana Andrews, Charles Bickford, William Eythe.

A distorted and historically inaccurate narrative of the early days of naval aviation warfare in the Pacific following Pearl Harbor. Fox used footage it had taken during the shakedown cruise of the new *Yorktown* for the flying sequences. (The footage was first used to make *The Fighting Lady*. See chapter 3.) However, budget considerations dictated that the battle for Midway be portrayed only through the voices of the combatants broadcast over the cinematic carrier's loudspeakers. Despite its visual shortcomings, the film did provide good insights into how an officer leads his men. Like John Wayne in *Sands of Iwo Jima* and Gregory Peck in *Twelve O'Clock High*, Ameche drives his men to acquire the flying skills they will need to survive in combat. At first, the men rebel at the discipline Ameche is imposing, but as in the other portrayals of leadership, his fliers ultimately realize he is giving them the ability to remain alive.

Winged Victory (1944)

WWII	Air Force	Full	B&W	130 mins
Fox	WV: 11-22-44		NYT: 12-21-44	

DIR: George Cukor. SW: Moss Hart. PRO: Darryl F. Zanuck. STARS: Lee J. Cobb, Edmond O'Brien, Gary Merrill, Karl Malden.

From Hart's stage play, the film featured Hollywood stars who entered the service and received singing, dancing, and production assignments. It also showed Air Force training, and the box office revenues went to charity.

Wings (1927) [G&G]

WWI	Air Force	Full	B&W	139 mins
Paramount	WV: 08-17-27		NYT: 08-13-27	

DIR: William Wellman. SW: Hope Loring, Louis Lighton. PRO: Lucien Hubbard. STARS: Clara Bow, Charles "Buddy" Rogers, Richard Arlen, Gary Cooper, Jobyna Ralston, El Brendel, Hedda Hopper.

Wings set the standard against which all future movies about warriors in the sky would be measured. It also received the greatest amount of military assistance for the longest time of any movie about the U.S. armed services. The story itself is the standard issue of two boys chasing the same girl, with one conveniently dying, in this case shot down by his friend while trying to fly a hijacked German fighter back to his own lines.

Wellman used his own experiences as a WWI pilot to help him create the aerial sequences, coming to realize that he had to film planes in front of cloud formations to provide a proper sense of speed. The director spent nine months at Army bases around San Antonio shooting flying and infantry sequences and the climactic battle of St. Michel. The troops assumed not only the American role, but against regulations, the guise of the German soldiers. The key to the success of the film, of course, was the use of virtually the entire U.S. Air Corps, which played both sides in the fighting.

Ultimately, Wellman's own experiences, the advice of his military technical advisor, and the Army's men and equipment created an epic film that won the first best picture Oscar. More than that, it conveyed the excitement of war in the air, which was to help the Air Force in its recruiting and in obtaining congressional appropriations. So well did Wellman do his job that *Wings* remains a timeless film that still has the power to excite viewers—even those brought up on **Top Gun**, video games, and the computer-generated graphics of **Independence Day** and **Pearl Harbor**.

Wings for the Eagle (1942)

WWII	Air Force	Ltd	B&W 85 mins
WB	WV: 06-03-42		NYT: 08-01-42

DIR: Lloyd Bacon. SW: Byron Morgan, B. H. Orkow. PRO: Robert Lord. STARS: Ann Sheridan, Dennis Morgan, Jack Carson, George Tobias.

A defense plant essential employee tries to dodge the draft, but Pearl Harbor causes him to enlist in Army aviation. The film provides an inside look at airplane production in a defense plant.

The Wings of Eagles (1957) [SSS]

Peace/WWII	Navy	Full	Color 109 mins
MGM	WV: 01-30-57		NYT: 02-01-57

DIR: John Ford. SW: Frank Fenton, William Wister Haines. PRO: Charles Schnee. STARS: John Wayne, Dan Dailey, Maureen O'Hara, Ward Bond.

Ford is quoted as once saying that if he had a choice between the truth and legend, he would pick legend. In this film, he tried to create the legend of Frank "Spig" Wead, whose real life was far more interesting than Wayne's portrayal of him. Wead began life as a record-setting Navy flier in the 1920s. After becoming semiparalyzed in an accident at home, whether from falling down drunk or tripping over his daughter's toy (the movie version, of course), Wead went to Hollywood to write movies promoting the Navy, including **Submarine D-1** and **Dive Bomber**. After Pearl Harbor, Wead talked his way back into the service, despite his handicap and worked on war planning. There, he came up with the concept of the jeep carrier, which would deliver replacement aircraft to the fleet.

Ultimately, Wead received an assignment to the Pacific theater, braces and canes notwithstanding, and served aboard a carrier during combat. But unlike the film's ending, in which Wead suffers some unidentified illness and leaves the war in a breeches buoy, in reality, he returned to Hollywood. There he wrote **They Were Expendable** and **The Beginning or the End**, before dying in Ford's arms, or so they say. Wayne helped create the legend by playing Wead as a hell-raising flier who once landed in an admiral's swimming pool, while acknowledging he was a poor father and husband, but also a true Navy man to the end.

Wings of the Navy (1939)

Preparedness	Navy	Full	B&W 88 mins
WB	WV: 01-18-39		NYT: 02-04-39

DIR: Lloyd Bacon. SW: Michael Fessier. PRO: Lou Edelman. STARS: George Brent, Olivia de Havilland, John Payne, Frank McHugh.

The film could be subtitled, "Or why we need to build many additional planes and air bases," since it liberally displays scenes of Pensacola, San Diego, sea planes, and land planes. The unoriginal story portrays two brothers, who follow their dad into the Navy, love flying, and pursue de Havilland.

Wings Over Honolulu (1937)

Peace	Navy	Full	B&W 78 mins
Universal	WV: 06-02-37		NYT: 05-29-37

DIR: H. C. Potter. SW: Isabel Dawn, Boyce DeGaw. PRO: Charles S. Rogers. STARS: Wendy Barrie, Ray Milland, William Gargan.

A naval aviator marries a Southern belle and receives orders on his wedding day to report to Hawaii. She follows, but he spends most of his time on maneuvers. When the bride decides to visit a former boyfriend whose yacht shows up in the harbor, the flier pursues her in his plane but crashes and faces a court-martial. The bride intercedes with the admiral and all ends well.

Wings Over the Pacific (1943)

WWII	Air Force	Ltd	B&W 59 mins
Monogram	WV: 06-30-43		NYT: DNR

DIR: Phil Rosen. SW: George Sayre. PRO: Lindsley Parsons. STARS: Inez Cooper, Edward Norris, Montagu Love, Robert Armstrong.

A "B" melodrama of the clash between a Nazi flier (an advanced scout for the Japanese) and an American naval officer, who engages him in aerial combat.

Winslow of the Navy (1942)

Peace	Navy	Cour	B&W 19 mins per episode
Universal	WV: 01-07-42		NYT: DNR

DIR: Ray Taylor, Ford Beebe. SW: Paul Huston, Griffin Jay. PRO: Henry MacRae. STARS: Don Terry, Walter Sande, John Litel, Wade Boteler.

A serial, suggested by Lt. Cmdr. Frank Martinek's comic strip, portraying in 12 chapters the Navy's pursuit of a Japanese spy ring.

Womanhood, the Glory of the Nation (1917)

Preparedness/WWI	Army	Full	B&W 8 reels
Vitagraph	WV: 04-06-17		NYT: 04-02-17

DIR: J. Stuart Blackton, Earle William. SW: Helmer Walton Bergman. PRO: J. Stuart Blackton, Albert E. Smith. STARS: Alice Joyce, Harry Morey, Naomi Childers, Joseph Kilgour, Walter McGrail, Mary Maurice, Theodore Roosevelt, Woodrow Wilson.

Ruritania declares war on the United States and its army invades the East Coast, capturing New York. However, the American army counters with booby traps, trick fortifications, and aerial bombs, saving the day. Presidents Roosevelt and Wilson appear as themselves. The film featured glimpses of coastal artillery, and the Second Battery of Brooklyn participated in the battle scenes.

Women of All Nations (1931)

Peace	Marines, Navy	Full	B&W 72 mins
Fox	WV: 06-02-31		NYT: 05-30-31

DIR: Raoul Walsh. SW: Barry Conners. PRO: William Fox. STARS: Victor McLaglen, Edmund Lowe, Bela Lugosi.

Third in a series of movies about Marines Flagg and Quirt. This time they are on the move from Nicaragua, to Sweden, and finally to Turkey.

X-15 (1961)

Peace	Air Force	Full	Color 107 mins
UA	WV: 11-15-61		NYT: 04-05-62

DIR: Richard Donner. SW: Tony Lazzarino, James Warner Bellah. PRO: Henry Sanicola, Tony Lazzarino. STARS: David McLean, Charles Bronson, James Gregory, Mary Tyler Moore, Brad Dexter, Lisabeth Hush.

The film chronicles domestic problems of three test pilots and the flight problems of the X-15 rocket plane. The Air Force and NASA provided full cooperation on this docudrama concerning the X-15 program.

A Yank in Korea (1951)

Korea	Army	Cour	B&W 73 mins
Columbia	WV: 02-14-51		NYT: 04-02-51

DIR: Lew Landers. SW: William Sackheim. PRO: Sam Katzman. STARS: Lon McCallister, William Phillips, Brett King, Larry Stewart.

The film uses battle footage to trace the exploits of enlistee McCallister and re-upped Sgt. Phillips. McCallister, already tagged a hero, angers the men in his unit when his carelessness endangers them. He overcompensates by helping destroy an ammunition dump, aiding in the rout of North Korean tanks, and repairing a locomotive on an ambulance train.

A Yank in Viet-Nam (1964)

Vietnam	Marines	Unkn	B&W 80 mins
Allied Artists	WV: 02-05-64		NYT: 02-06-64

DIR: Marshall Thompson. SW: Jane Wardell, Jack Lewis. PRO: Wray Davis. STARS: Marshall Thompson, Enrique Magalona, Mario Barri, Drew Urban, Kieu Chinh.

The first movie portraying the American military in Vietnam. Thompson plays a Marine major whose helicopter is shot down. He then spends the rest of the film searching for a doctor whom the

Vietcong have captured. Along the way, accompanied by guerrillas, he falls in love with the doctor's daughter.

Yanks (1979)

WWII	Army	NR	Color 141 mins
Universal	WV: 09-19-79		NYT: 09-19 & 30-79

DIR: John Schlesinger. SW: Colin Welland, Walter Bernstein. PRO: Joseph Janni, Lester Persky. STARS: Richard Gere, Lisa Eichhorn, Vanessa Redgrave, William Devane, Chick Vennera.

"Overpaid and oversexed" Yanks in England awaiting the invasion of Europe embark on three intertwined love stores. Only occasionally does the director include Army business in boxing and training sequences (see also *The Affair* in chapter 2).

Yanks Ahoy (1943)

WWII	Army	Unkn	B&W 60 mins
UA	WV: 06-30-43		NYT: DNR

DIR: Kurt Neumann. SW: Eugene Conrad, Edward E. Seabrook. PRO: Fred Guiol. STARS: William Tracy, Joe Sawyer, Marjorie Woodworth, Minor Watson.

This "C" slapstick comedy portrays two Army buddies capturing a Japanese submarine while fishing from the rail of their troop transport ship. Absurd!

The Yanks Are Coming (1942)

WWII	Army	Unkn	B&W 62 mins
PRC	WV: 12-30-42		NYT: DNR

DIR: Alexis Thurn-Taxis. SW: Arthur St. Claire, Edith Watkins, Sherman Lowe. PRO: Lester Cutler. STARS: Henry King, Mary Healy, Jack Heller.

A stuck-up orchestra leader thinks all noncommissioned soldiers are "chumps." To irk him, his entire band enlists as soldiers, and the show they are rehearsing never opens.

You Came Along (1945)

WWII	Air Force	Full	B&W 103 mins
Paramount	WV: 07-04-45		NYT: 07-05-45

DIR: John Farrow. SW: Robert Smith, Ayn Rand. PRO: Hal Wallis. STARS: Robert Cummings, Lizabeth Scott, Don DeFore, Charles Drake.

Three pilot buddies barnstorm to stimulate war bond sales. Scott, the men's guide on the tour, falls in love with Cummings, who harbors a deep secret. The film includes a military funeral.

The Young and the Brave **(1963)**

Korea	Army	Unkn	B&W 84 mins
MGM	WV: 05-15-63		NYT: DNR

DIR: Francis D. Lyon. SW: Beirne Lay Jr. PRO: A. C. Lyles. STARS: Rory Calhoun, William Bendix, Richard Jaeckel, Richard Arlen.

Several GIs, escaping their communist captors, along with an orphaned Korean boy and his K-9 Corps police dog, try to get back to their unit through enemy lines. Some reviewers suggested the dog looked more frightened than the boy during the combat scenes.

Young Eagles **(1930)**

WWI	Air Force	Unkn	B&W 75 mins
Paramount	WV: 03-26-30		NYT: 03-22-30

DIR: William Wellman. SW: William S. McNutt, Grover Jones. PRO: Paramount. STARS: Charles "Buddy" Rogers, Jean Arthur, Paul Lukas, Stuart Erwin, Frank Ross.

Weekly Variety categorized this movie as the "pint-sized version of ***Wings***" because of its length, Wellman having directed both, and Rogers was still flying. This time, however, it is a comedy.

The Young Lions **(1958) [G&G]**

WWII	Army	Full	B&W 167 mins
Fox	WV: 03-19-58		NYT: 04-03-58

DIR: Edward Dmytryk. SW: Edward Anhalt. PRO: Al Lichtman. STARS: Marlon Brando, Montgomery Clift, Dean Martin, Hope Lange.

The film version of Irwin Shaw's best-selling novel changed the character of the dedicated Nazi officer at the request of the departments of State and Defense. As a result, Brando became a good, guilt-stricken German, and the portrayal helped the rehabilitation of Germany from wartime enemy to good ally against the Soviet Union. The Army also had problems with the anti-Semitism directed against Clift during basic training, and the filmmakers removed all but one instance. Given the new focus, it became more a buddy film of mismatched friends than a serious comment about man's inhumanity to man and the experience of combat.

The Young Warriors **(1967)**

WWII	Army	NR	Color 93 mins
Universal	WV: 04-12-67		NYT: 02-08-68

DIR: John Peyser. SW: Richard Matheson. PRO: Gordon Kay. STARS: James Drury, Steve Carlson, Jonathan Daly, Robert Pine.

Based on Matheson's novel *Beardless Warriors*, a clichéd treatment of the effect of warfare on the young. Borrowed footage from other films appears. The authenticity of the backlot fighting results from Peyser's previous direction of the television series ***Combat***.

You're in the Army Now (1941)

Peace	Army	Ltd	B&W 79 mins
WB	WV: 12-03-41		NYT: 12-26-41

DIR: Lewis Seiler. SW: Paul Gerard Smith, George Bentley. PRO: Ben Stoloff. STARS: Jimmy Durante, Jane Wyman, Phil Silvers.

Appearing the same month as the attack on Pearl Harbor, this slapstick comedy featured Durante and Silvers as a vacuum cleaner sales team who try to pitch their wares to a recruiting sergeant, only to discover that somehow they have enlisted in the army.

You're in the Navy Now a.k.a. *USS* **Teakettle** (1951)

WWII	Navy	Full	B&W 92 mins
Fox	WV: 02-28-51		NYT: 02-24-51

DIR: Lewis Seiler, Henry Hathaway. SW: Richard Murphy. PRO: Fred Kohlmar. STARS: Gary Cooper, Jane Greer, Eddie Albert, Jack Webb, Charles Bronson.

Cooper plays a newly minted officer, a "90-day wonder," who is assigned to an ancient destroyer that uses an experimental steam turbine. Although he studied engineering in college, Cooper unfortunately knows nothing about sailing or the sea. This becomes the springboard for the comedy that follows, including efforts to get the ship to move only to have it smash into an aircraft carrier.

Yours, Mine and Ours (1968)

Peace	Navy	Ltd	Color 111 mins
UA	WV: 04-24-68		NYT: 04-25-68

DIR: Melville Shavelson. SW: Melville Shavelson, Mort Lachman. PRO: Robert F. Blumofe. STARS: Lucille Ball, Henry Fonda, Van Johnson.

Naval officer Fonda, a widower with ten children, marries Ball, a widow with eight children, and together they produce at least one more in this comedy. The Navy provided some shipboard footage.

Zone Troopers (1986)

WWII/SciFi	Army	NR	Color 88 mins
Empire Pictures	WV: 04-09-86		NYT: DNR

DIR: Danny Bilson. SW: Danny Bilson, Paul DeMeo. PRO: Roberto Bessi. STARS: Tim Thomerson, Timothy Van Patten, Art La Fleur.

Clichéd characters and war-film plot changes after soldiers escape from the "Krauts" who had surrounded them. Then, the unit runs into a spaceship and *Combat* intersects *Star Trek*.

Television Films

The A-Team (1983)

Vietnam   Army   NBC   DIR: Rod Holcomb.

This pilot for a series, which NBC aired, starred George Peppard and Mr. T., who are on the lam, chased by an Army colonel for robbing the Bank of Hanoi, four days after the Vietnam War ended. When caught, they admit the robbery but claim to have been under orders to do so. Action and adventure fill the screen as the team is hired to find a reporter missing in Mexico on a big story. Only the pilot portrayed the characters in Vietnam in the Army. (VTR: 01-26-83.)

The Affair (1995)

WWII   Army   HBO   DIR: Paul Seed

The film provides a unique portrayal of the other Americans who came to England to fight Nazi Germany, the black soldiers who served, at least initially, as cooks and in other support positions for the white Americans preparing to invade the continent. Set in the months before D-Day, Courtney Vance plays a private who enters into a passionate love affair with a married woman. When her Navy husband returns home, he discovers his wife locked in an embrace with Vance and after beating the soldier, accuses him of raping his wife. Although he quickly realizes the truth, he forces his wife to testify against her lover who is found guilty and executed. The powerful story of love and betrayal reminds viewers of the prejudice that existed in the Army side by side with the effort to defeat Hitler and shows the danger people faced if they ignored society's strictures.

Afterburn: The Janet Harduvel Story (1992)

Peace   Air Force   HBO   DIR: Robert Markowitz.

A wife tries to clear the name of her fighter pilot husband, whom the Air Force blamed for the crash of his plane. The Air Force refused to cooperate on the story, which ran counter to its official position because of the premise that the service had covered up the causes for the crash of an F-16 in Korea. (DV: 05-29-92.)

American Caesar (1984)

| WWII | Army | History | DIR: John McGreevey. |

Canadian made, five-hour docudrama of the life and times of Gen. Douglas MacArthur. (VTR: 04-11-84.)

Asteroid (1997)

| SciFi | Army | NBC | DIR: Bradford May. |

Soldiers appear doing the jobs they would perform in any national emergency. (DVP: 02-14-97.)

Atomic Train (1999)

| Terrorism | Army | NBC | DIR: D. Jackson, D. Lowry. |

Terrorists seize a train carrying atomic missiles and then head toward Denver and an atomic holocaust. (DVP: 05-12-99.)

Baa, Baa Black Sheep (1976)

| WWII | Marines | NBC | DIR: Russ Mayberry. |

The pilot showcased the exploits of Marine flier Pappy Boyington and how he assembled his unit of misfits, which became known as the ***Black Sheep Squadron.*** (VTR: 09-29-76.)

Band of Brothers (2001)

| WWII | Army | HBO | DIR: Tom Hanks, David Frankel, Phil Alden, et al. |

Based on historian Stephen Ambrose's *Band of Brothers*, the 10-episode miniseries became the most expensive production ever made for cable. It follows Easy Company of the 101st Airborne Division from its training, through its parachute drops behind the Normandy beaches on D-Day and Operation Market Garden in Holland, to victory in Germany. Executive Producers Steven Spielberg, Ambrose, and Hanks were capitalizing on the success of ***Saving Private Ryan*** and the nostalgia that the film and Tom Brokaw's ***The Greatest Generation*** had generated. Most historians and veterans found that the series more accurately portrayed men in combat than Spielberg's earlier film. (DVP: 09-03-2001.)

Behind Enemy Lines (1985)

| WWII | Army | NBC | DIR: Sheldon Larry. |

WWII, OSS melodrama, set in wartime France, Norway, and England. Officers plan a daring rescue of a scientist who may or may not be working with the Germans. (VTR: 01-22-86.) (Broadcast 12-29-85.)

The B. R. A. T. Patrol (1986)

| Peace | Marines | ABC | DIR: Mollie Miller. |

"Born, raised and trapped" in childhood on a Marine Corps base and not old enough to belong to the Junior Marines club, the BRATs compete with their rival for the "Youth Service Award." Ultimately, they succeed in uncovering a plot to steal base equipment. Reviewers described this as one of Disney's worst television efforts. The Marines provided full cooperation. (VTR: 10-29-86.)

A Bright Shining Lie (1998)

Vietnam   Army   HBO   DIR: Terry George.

Bill Paxton portrays John Paul Vann, one of the first American military advisors in Vietnam, following him through the decade's loves and losses. The film has the same problem as Neil Sheehan's book in deciding whether it is telling a story of the Vietnam War or a psycho-history of a pedophile. (VTR: 05-27-98.)

By Dawn's Early Light (1990)

Cold War   Air Force   HBO   DIR: Jack Sholder.

Impressive special effects and a bevy of fine actors including James Earl Jones, Martin Landau, and Rip Torn create a cautionary tale that explores the issue of how nations, faced with an accidental nuclear launch, prevent it from escalating into a global holocaust. (VTR: 05-19-90.)

The Caine *Mutiny Court-Martial* (1988)

WWII   Navy   CBS   DIR: Robert Altman.

Courtroom drama, featuring Brad Davis as Captain Queeg, based on the court-martial segment in the Herman Wouk novel, the Broadway play, and Stanley Kramer's feature film. (VTR: 05-11-88.)

The Case Against Sergeant Ryker (1963)

Korea   Army   ABC   DIR: Buzz Kulik.

Lee Marvin, Bradford Dillman, Vera Miles, and Peter Graves appear in this pilot for a series renamed *Court-Martial*. Kulik and producer Frank Telford also adapted the story for a release as a feature film entitled *Sergeant Ryker* (see chapter 1). In Korea, Army lawyers Dillman and Graves prepare the trial of Marvin as Sergeant Paul Ryker, who stands accused of being a traitor.

The Children of An Lac (1980)

Vietnam   All   CBS   DIR: John Llewellyn Moxey.

Three women, including Ina Balin (playing herself), try to evacuate hundreds of Vietnam orphans from Saigon just prior to its fall in 1975.

China Beach (1988)

Vietnam   Army   ABC   DIR: Rod Holcomb.

Successful pilot for the series that introduced viewers to the doctors and nurses of the 510th Evacuation Hospital at China Beach, Vietnam. Some reviewers found it contained very sensitive portrayals of the soldiers and their caretakers. But the DoD denied WB cooperation because the military found the overall tone unacceptable. (VTR: 05-04-88.)

Carter's Army (1970)

WWII   Army   ABC   DIR: George McCowan.

Also known as **Black Brigade**, this was a pilot that Aaron Spelling hoped to turn into a multiracial TV series starring Richard Pryor. Led by Stephen Boyd, the unit included Pryor, Robert Hooks, Roosevelt Grier, Moses Gunn, and Billy Dee Williams. Despite the star power, the pilot, which showed the unit seizing a bridge from the Germans, was as far as the project went.

Chips, the War Dog (1990)

WWII   Army   Disney   DIR: Ed Kaplan.

Filmed at Fort Lewis, Washington, and based on a real war hero, this family film portrays the training in the Dogs for Defense program during WWII and re-creates some of the dogs' heroic feats. (VTR: 03-23-90.)

Code of Honor. See Sweet Revenge.

The Court-Martial of Jackie Robinson (1990)

WWII   Army   TNT   DIR: Larry Peerce.

Drafted into the wartime Army, Robinson left his four-sport stardom at UCLA to enter the segregated service. He fought the power structure to become an officer; he fought for equal Post Exchange benefits for Negro soldiers; and he failed to follow the "orders" of a civilian bus driver to ride in the back of an Army bus, for which he was court-martialed. Although he won his case, he resigned his commission and joined the Kansas City Monarchs of the Negro American League. The Army's loss was baseball's gain. (DV: 10-15-90.)

Court-Martial of Lt. William Calley (1975). See Judgment: The Court-Martial of Lieutenant William Calley.

Crash Dive (1996)

Terrorism   Navy   Video   DIR: Andrew Stevens.

Terrorists posing as victims of a boating disaster hijack a U.S. nuclear submarine intending to seize nuclear weapons. A former Navy SEAL undertakes the rescue and manages to board the submerged submarine.

Crash Landing: The Rescue of Flight 232 (1992)

Peace   NG   ABC   DIR: Lamont Johnson.

Charlton Heston, Richard Thomas, and James Coburn appeared in this docudrama about the stricken commercial airliner that crashed in Sioux Falls, Iowa, in 1989. The Air National Guard manned the fire station at the airport, and its members helped re-create the rescue it had carried out. (DV: 02-24-92.)

Day One (1989)

WWII   Army   CBS   DIR: Joseph Sargent.

Docudrama portraying the building of the atomic bomb. The Air Force and DoD denied material assistance and stock footage because they found the script contained too many inaccuracies. (DV: 03-03-89.)

DC/9/11: Time of Crisis (2003)

Terrorism   Air Force   Showt   DIR: Daniel Petrie.

Portrayal of President George Bush's reaction to the terrorist attacks in New York and Washington on September 11, 2001. Generally portrays a heroic president, perhaps in exaggerated terms given the conservative politics of producer-writer Lionel Chetwynd. The Air Force provided footage of *Air Force One* in flight accompanied by Air Force fighters. (WP: 09-06-2003.)

Decoration Day (1990)

WWII   Army   Unkn   DIR: Robert Markowitz.

Based on John William Corrington's novel. James Garner plays a recluse who rejoins the world and seeks to explain why his black childhood friend is refusing to accept a Medal of Honor for bravery in WWII, albeit more than 30 years after the action.

The Dirty Dozen: Next Mission (1985)

WWII   Army   NBC   DIR: Andrew V. McLaglen.

Sequel to the 1967 feature film, more like a remake, with a few surviving actors, including Lee Marvin and Ernest Borgnine, looking every bit their real age. Viewers might wonder if they will live long enough to accomplish their assignment. (VTR: 02-13-85.)

The Dirty Dozen: The Deadly Mission (1987)

WWII   Army   NBC   DIR: Lee Katzin.

Another dirty mission, with Telly Savalas taking over command from Lee Marvin with orders to destroy a German nerve gas plant before it can produce enough to become a viable weapon of mass destruction. At least the unit knew where to look. (VTR: 03-11-87.)

The Dirty Dozen: The Fatal Mission (1988)

WWII   Army   NBC   DIR: Lee Katzin.

The dirty misfits this time try to prevent the creation of the 4th Reich. A mercifully short series followed. (VTR: 02-24-88.)

The Dirty Dozen (1988)

WWII   Army   NBC   DIR: Kevin Connor.

Two-hour pilot for the series that followed. (VTR: 05-04-88.)

Disaster in Silo Seven (1988)

Cold War   Air Force   ABC   DIR: Larry Elikann.

True worst-case scenario docudrama about an accident in a liquid-fueled ICBM missile silo during routine maintenance. An explosion blew the warhead off the missile and into the nearby countryside. Despite the negative image of SAC that the mishap created, the Air Force permitted filming inside a missile silo at the Pima Air Museum in Arizona because the event actually happened and the script portrayed it with reasonable accuracy. (VTR: 11-30-88.)

Dress Gray (1986)

Vietnam   Army   NBC   DIR: Glenn Jordan.

West Point graduate Lucian Truscott IV set his murder mystery at the Military Academy (U.S. Grant Military Academy in the film). A cadet apparently had a homosexual lover or was raped shortly before he was killed. The search to find the perpetrator initially focuses on another cadet, who then joins with the victim's sister to solve the crime. Even the author's pedigree as the grandson of a leading WWII general and son of a West Point graduate could not help obtain assistance from the Army for such a negative story about the academy. (VTR: 03-19-86.)

The Enemy Within (1994)

Cold War   Marines   HBO   DIR: Jonathan Darby.

A poor remake of **Seven Days in May**. A Marine colonel discovers a conspiratorial group of senior officers intent upon staging a coup to remove the president from office because he had signed a nuclear disarmament treaty with the Soviet Union. Although the filmmakers visited the office of the Joint Chiefs of Staff to gather background information, the production never formally requested assistance. (VTR: 08-19-94.)

Enola Gay: The Men, the Mission, the Atomic Bomb (1980)

WWII   Air Force   NBC   DIR: David Lowell Rich.

Patrick Duffy portrays Colonel Paul Tibbets in a miniseries based on *Enola Gay* by Gordon Thomas and Max Witts detailing the training for and mission to drop the first atomic bomb on Hiroshima. The DoD allowed use of military installations since the portrayal was reasonably accurate.

The Ernest Green Story (2003)

Peace   NG   Disney   DIR: Eric Laneuville.

The DoD authorized 300 National Guardsmen to participate as extras in an off-duty status in this Disney re-creation of the integration of the Little Rock, Arkansas, high school. Green was one of the nine black students whom the National Guard escorted into the school. (VTR: 01-15-2003.)

The Execution of Private Slovik (1974)

WWII   Army   NBC   DIR: Lamont Johnson.

Martin Sheen portrays Eddie Slovik, the only American since the Civil War to be executed for desertion. General Dwight D. Eisenhower decided not to commute the sentence because he felt it sent a message to the troops during the harsh winter of 1944–45. (VTR: 03-13-74.)

Family Flight (1972)

Peace   Navy   ABC   DIR: Marvin J. Chomsky.

A family on a cross-country flight crash lands in the desert. The Navy provided an aircraft carrier for the search scenes. (VTR: 10-25-72.)

Fatal Vision (1984)

Peace   Army   NBC   DIR: David Greene.

Capt./Dr. Jeffrey MacDonald, a Green Beret surgeon stationed at Fort Bragg, claims that a hippie gang has murdered his wife and children. First responders find him injured at the scene, but Mrs. MacDonald's father does not believe his son-in-law's inconsistent statements about that night. MacDonald becomes the prime suspect and is ultimately convicted of the murders. The DoD found portrayal historically accurate but received the request for assistance too late to provide help. (VTR: 11-28-84.)

The Fifth Missile (1986)

Cold War   Navy   NBC   DIR: Larry Peerce.

Toxic poisoning from paint causes a submarine captain and his crew to run amok during a training exercise when the captain believes he has been given an order to attack the Soviet Union. Robert Conrad, Sam Waterston, Richard Roundtree, and David Soul star. (VTR: 03-05-86.)

Final Justice (1993). See *A Matter of Justice*.

Firehawk (1993)

Vietnam   Army   Video   DIR: Cirio H. Santiago.

Soldiers on a helicopter downed while on a mission in Vietnam believe the aircraft was sabotaged by one of their own. After fighting off capture by the Vietcong, they fight each other to discover and punish the traitor.

Flight of Black Angel (1991)

Peace   Air Force   Showt   DIR: Jonathan Mostow.

Deranged, but incredibly talented, fighter pilot believes his call sign of "Black Angel" is a message from God that he is to destroy America's most sinful city with a nuclear bomb. (VTR: 02-18-91.)

Fly Away Home (1981)

Vietnam   All   ABC   DIR: Paul Krasny.

Pilot for anticipated series set in Vietnam, shortly after the 1968 Tet Offensive. Included both American and Vietnamese characters and featured a journalist, his news-bureau chief, and medical and military personnel. First attempt by a television network to create a series based on the war, but ABC found discretion the better part of valor. (VTR: 09-23-81.)

The Forgotten (1989)

Vietnam   Army   USA   DIR: James Keach.

Shortly before international trade talks begin between Vietnam and a group of Western countries, Vietnam quietly releases six Green Berets who had been imprisoned for 17 years. CIA representatives, trying to shield the object of the soldiers' last mission, seclude them in Germany, planning to kill them. Another post-Watergate and Vietnam conspiracy film, painting the government black.

The Forgotten Man (1971)

Vietnam   Army   ABC   DIR: Walter Grauman.

With flashback scenes of his capture and imprisonment featured, Dennis Weaver portrays an American POW who was reported as killed in action. He escapes from North Vietnam and returns home to find his wife remarried, his daughter adopted, and his business sold. (VTR: 09-29-71.)

Frankie's House (1992)

Vietnam   Army, Marines   A&E   DIR: Peter Fisk.

Based on Tim Page's *Page After Page*, this Australian-produced docudrama follows the photojournalist's career in Vietnam beginning in 1964. He first learns about the war in Saigon and later on patrols with the troops. He meets up with the sons of Errol Flynn and John Steinbeck and forms a collegial bond with them at the local brothel, Frankie's House.

Friendly Fire (1979)

Vietnam   Army   ABC   DIR: David Greene.

Based on C. D. B. Bryan's *Friendly Fire*, this docudrama follows a family's efforts to gather the facts surrounding the death of their son in Vietnam. They push their investigation as they meet evasion and the Army's lies, until finding the truth, which does not make their pain any easier to bear. (VTR: 04-25-79.)

From Here to Eternity (1979)

WWII   Army   NBC   DIR: Buzz Kulik.

Three-part miniseries with big-screen cast including Natalie Wood, William Devane, Kim Basinger, and Peter Boyle. Based on James Jones's novel and Fred Zinnemann's feature film (see chapter 1), it shows life in prewar Hawaii. Why bother? Television would not permit the use of four-letter words or explicit sex any more than the film Code Office did in the classic original, of which this was a pale imitation. (VTR: 02-21-79.)

From Here to Eternity (1980)

WWII   Army   NBC   PRO: Carl Pingitore.

Two-hour pilot for what became a short-run series that followed old and new characters in the aftermath of Pearl Harbor. Most notably, Don Johnson appears as Prewitt's brother and becomes involved with Kim Basinger's Lorene Rogers, whom Donna Reed played in the original.

A Glimpse of Hell (2001)

Peace   Navy   Fox   DIR: Mikael Salomon.

Initial investigation of the explosion in a turret of USS *Iowa* places blame on a homosexual affair between two sailors. James Caan stars as an officer who digs deeper to set the record straight. (WV: 03-14-2001.)

The Great Escape II: The Untold Story (1988)

WWII   Army   NBC   DIR: Jud Taylor, Paul Wendkos.

This four hour, two-part sequel to the 1963 feature film includes all the stalag gags and stunts. Christopher Reeves and Judd Hirsch appear. (VTR: 11-16-88.)

Green Eyes (1977)

Vietnam   Unkn   ABC   DIR: John Erman.

Paul Winfield, a disabled Vietnam vet, still experiences flashbacks to battles and cannot find a job. He returns to Saigon to find the green-eyed child he fathered and left behind. One of Hollywood's few positive cinematic portrayals of Vietnam veterans.

Guts and Glory: The Rise and Fall of Oliver North (1989)

Middle East   Marines   CBS   DIR: Mike Robe.

Marine Lt. Col. North, while serving as a White House military aide, sold weapons to Iran for money that was passed to the Nicaragua Contras to continue their civil war against their government without direct support from the United States, which opposed the socialist government. (DV: 05-04-89.)

Heroes of Desert Storm (1991)

Gulf Wars Army, Air Force   ABC   DIR: Don Ohlmeyer.

Receiving full assistance from the military, Lionel Chetwynd, director of *Hanoi Hilton* and *DC/9/11*
and Hollywood's resident conservative, wrote the screenplay for this look at the Gulf War, which had
just concluded. The Pentagon's public affairs office reported a disappointing number of viewers.

Hiroshima (1995)

WWII   Navy, Air Force, Army   Showt   DIR: Koreyoshi Kurahara, Roger Spottiswoode.

This docudrama focuses on President Harry Truman's decision to use the secret weapon developed
by American scientists during the war without his knowledge. The film mixes newsreel footage
with new sepia-toned and color film as well as interviews with Hiroshima survivors and U.S. military personnel, although it did not receive formal assistance. It shows the Japanese diplomatic
corps wanting to sue for peace while the military fanatics would not even consider surrendering.
The Air Force provided stock footage and stills.

Ike: The War Years (1978)

WWII   Army   ABC   DIR: Melville Shavelson.

Original, condensed version of television miniseries broadcast in May 1979, focusing on Gen.
Eisenhower's wartime career and his love affair, chaste or otherwise, with Kay Summersby. The director explained he wanted to make Ike three dimensional, even if it might hurt Mamie, who was
still alive at the time. Robert Duvall and Lee Remick star.

Ike (1979)

WWII   Army   ABC   DIR: Melville Shavelson, Boris Sagal.

Three-part miniseries, with Robert Duvall as Eisenhower, expanding the earlier 1978 docudrama to
include Ike's entire career. Bonnie Bartlett, Dana Andrews, and Lee Remick appear as, respectively,
Mamie Eisenhower, George C. Marshall, and Kay Summersby. (VTR: 05-09-79.)

Ike: Countdown to D-Day (2004)

WWII   Army   A&E   DIR: Robert Harmon.

Recounts Eisenhower's preparations for the assault on Normandy. Shows his relationships with
Winston Churchill, Field Marshall Bernard Montgomery, and Gen. George S. Patton. However, the
movie does not portray Ike's involvement with his jeep driver, Kaye Summersby. (WP 05-31-2004.)

In Love and War (1987)

Vietnam   Navy   NBC   DIR: Paul Aaron.

Jane Alexander and James Woods provide sympathetic portrayals of Sybil Stockdale and James
Stockdale, the Navy's highest-ranking Vietnam POW. The Vietcong tortured the flier and end-

lessly questioned him about his role in the Gulf of Tonkin, while his wife organized POW wives to pressure the government to denounce publicly the North Vietnam treatment of the American captives. The Navy provided stock footage of carrier operations, although the military has continued to reject Stockdale's contention after he returned from captivity that no attack had ocurred in the Gulf of Tonkin in 1965, as the president and the government claimed. (VTR: 03-25-87.)

In Pursuit of Honor (1995) [G&G]

Peace   Army   HBO   DIR: Ken Olin.

Faced with a lack of funds to buy tanks to modernize the U.S. Army, Chief of Staff Douglas MacArthur, in 1935, orders the killing of most of the cavalry horses. A young lieutenant with an authority problem and four enlisted men, led by Don Johnson, portraying a Medal of Honor recipient for bravery during the 1915 incursion into Mexico, make a spur-of-the-moment decision to rescue 400 horses from the killing field and head toward Canada with the Army in hot pursuit.

Although the cable movie claims it is based on a true story, the Center for Military History, which provided informational help to the production, could find no record of the incident. Nevertheless, the film skillfully raises important questions about obeying orders, command and control, and issues of modernization of the military. It also captures well the manner in which senior sergeants take young officers under their wings and prepare them for leadership. Just as important, a fine script and excellent acting, especially by Johnson, combine to create a superb tale worth watching again and again. (DVP: 03-18-95.)

Interceptor (1992)

Terrorism   Air Force   Video   DIR: Michael Cohn.

An example of a film that can be made without military cooperation. The plot turns on the attempt of terrorists to steal one or more of our stealth fighters while they are in transit aboard a cargo plane. Filmmakers used computer-generated virtual reality images to create the hardware.

Intimate Strangers (1986)

Vietnam   Army   CBS   DIR: Robert Ellis Miller.

Teri Garr portrays Vietnam War nurse Sally Bierston, captured on the last day of the war and held as a POW for 10 years. She escapes to the Philippines and later reunites with Stacy Keach, her doctor husband. (VTR: 1-22-86.)

Judgment: *The Court-Martial of Lieutenant William Calley* (1975)

Vietnam   Army   ABC   DIR: Stanley Kramer.

Tony Musante, Harrison Ford, and Richard Basehart appear in Kramer's rendering of the trial that assigned responsibility for the Vietnam War's My Lai massacre of South Vietnamese civilians to one officer. On appeal his conviction was overturned. (VTR: 01-15-75.)

Just a Little Inconvenience (1977)

Vietnam   Army   NBC   DIR: Theodore J. Flicker.

Lee Majors portrays a friend of a soldier, James Stacy, who loses an arm and a leg to a land mine in Vietnam. Majors leaves his aerospace job to help his friend learn to ski on one leg and hopefully rejoin the living. The film includes some slickly shot battle scenes. (VTR: 10-05-77.)

Kent State (1981)

Vietnam   NG   NBC   DIR: James Goldstone.

Docudrama of the May 4, 1970, student protests against the U.S. invasion of Cambodia on the Kent State University campus, which led to the death of four students, the wounding of others, and the stigmatizing of the Ohio National Guard.

The Lost Battalion (2001)

WWI   Army   A & E   DIR: Russell Mulcahy

This is the TV remake of the 1919 film about a battalion of 500 American doughboys who became surrounded in the Argonne Forest in October 1918, during the final weeks of the war. The film portrays the soldiers's struggles to survive for six days until the Army units broke through German lines to rescue the trapped soldiers.

The Last Days of Patton (1986)

WWII   Army   CBS   DIR: Delbert Mann.

What happens after Gen. George Patton walks toward the windmill at the end of *Patton*? As this docudrama reveals, he suffers a paralyzing automobile accident and slowly dies as doctors and the family debate what to do with him. His mistress, a niece by marriage, comes to his side, an appearance the family feared would occur in the feature film. George C. Scott re-creates his Oscar-winning role and helps cement the general's mythical image. (VTR: 09-17-86.)

A Matter of Justice a.k.a. Final Justice (1993)

Peace   Army   NBC   DIR: Michael Switzer.

A young, naive soldier comes home on leave and introduces his new wife, considerably older than himself, to his mother. When he is killed, his mom works to solve the murder. (VTR: 11-05-93.)

Message from Nam (1993)

Vietnam   Army   NBC   DIR: Paul Wendkos.

When a journalism student's boyfriend dies in Vietnam, she travels to the war zone to learn for herself why the United States had become involved in Southeast Asia. There, she pursues the truth and has an intense affair with an officer. Also known as *Danielle Steele's Message from Nam*. (DVP: 10-19-93.)

Mission of the Shark: *The Saga of the U.S.S.* **Indianapolis (1991)**

WWII   Navy   CBS   DIR: Robert Iscove.

After delivering its secret atomic cargo to the scientists at Tinian Island, the USS *Indianapolis* heads to the Philippines by way of Guam. Along the way, a Japanese submarine torpedoes the ship, causing the Navy's greatest loss of life at sea. The film portrays the survivors' recollections of the sinking, including shark attacks and 96 hours of exposure in the water, which resulted in almost 900 deaths before rescue of the remaining 20 percent of the crew. Exteriors shot on the USS *Alabama* at Mobile, Alabama.

My Father, My Son **(1988)**

Vietnam   Navy   CBS   DIR: Jeff Bleckner.

The true story of Navy officer Elmo Zumwalt Jr., who commanded a river patrol boat in Vietnam and then developed two types of cancer, possibly as a result of exposure to Agent Orange, a defoliant used in Vietnam to provide better visibility for soldiers and fliers. Ironically, Adm. Elmo Zumwalt, later the Chief of Naval Operations and the officer's father, had approved the use of the chemical during his command of the Navy in Vietnam. (VTR: 06-15-88.)

Night of the Fox **(1990)**

WWII   Army   Syndicated DIR: Charles Jarrott.

George Peppard, as an American colonel assigned to British intelligence, arrives on a Channel Island off the coast of England to retrieve an American officer, whom the Germans captured when he washed ashore. Peppard must rescue him before he reveals the plans for D-Day. The DoD refused to provide stock footage because it concluded that the portrayals did not benefit recruitment and retention. (DV: 11-26-90.)

On the Beach **(2000)**

Cold War   Navy   Showt   DIR: Russell Mulcahy.

Remake of Stanley Kramer's 1959 film (see chapter 1) based on Nevil Shute's novel about the aftermath of a nuclear holocaust. Story is dated and lacks relevance in the post-Cold war period. (DVP: 05-26-2000.)

1,000 Men and a Baby **(1997)**

Korea   Navy   CBS   DIR: Marcus Cole.

True story of Amerasian orphan baby Dan Keenan, whom the crew of the USS *Point Cruz* rescued and brought to the United States. Because of the relatively accurate and positive depiction of the Navy, the Navy provided an amphibious carrier to portray the jeep carrier of the period. (DVP: 12-04-97.)

Op Center **(1995)**

Terrorism   Army, Air Force   NBC   DIR: Lewis Teague.

Based on Tom Clancy's novel. The DoD provided assistance to the production because portrayals of the military were positive even though the "Op Center" was fantasy. (BD: 02-26-95.)

Operation Delta Force II: *Mayday* (1998)

Terrorism   Army   Unkn   DIR: Yossi Wein.

Second in a series of films that rip off the Chuck Norris franchise (see *Operation Delta Force*, chapter 1). Delta Force is sent to rescue a U.S. submarine that terrorists have seized.

Operation Petticoat (1977)

WWII   Navy   ABC   DIR: John Astin.

Director/actor Astin was no substitute for Cary Grant in this two-hour pilot for a series about the pink submarine in search of the war, manned by misfits and carrying a cargo of nurses. (BD: 09-04-77.)

Pancho Barnes (1988)

Peace   Air Force   CBS   DIR: Richard T. Heffron.

Story of colorful early aviatrix, who once trained U.S. Air Force pilots. In later life, she ran a famous watering hole near Edwards Air Force Base frequented by Chuck Yeager and other test pilots and lovers of flying. The Air Force permitted filming on base. (VTR: 11-16-88.)

Pandora's Clock (1996)

Peace   Air Force   ABC   DIR: Eric Laneuville.

The DoD refused to provide assistance because the filmmakers portrayed Air Force personnel as callous and unprofessional. The story line featured a deadly virus on a jetliner, which the U.S. government intends to destroy while airborne to prevent contamination.

The Path to War (2002)

Vietnam   All   HBO   DIR: John Frankenheimer.

All-star cast and director dramatize the Johnson administration's internal debate concerning the escalation of or withdrawal from Southeast Asia.

The Pentagon Wars (1998) [G&G]

Vietnam   DoD   HBO   DIR: Richard Benjamin.

Based on an Air Force officer's memoir, the film uses a comedic approach to create a devastating portrayal of the Army's efforts to develop, test (or not test), and deploy the Bradley fighting vehicle. Kelsey Grammer, as the general in charge of the program, subverts the Air Force officer assigned to investigate the delays in completing the testing of the vehicle. Grammer ultimately receives promotion, while the Air Force officer's career comes to an abrupt end. For obvious reasons, the production did not request cooperation.

Perfect Crime (1997) a.k.a. *Hide and Seek*

| Peace | Marines | USA | DIR: Robert Michael Lewis. |

A military investigator uses interviews of military personnel and other circumstantial evidence to help convict a Marine officer as the murderer of his missing wife. The portrayals of the evil husband and angelic wife add no suspense.

Phantom Soldiers (1987)

| Vietnam | Army | Video | DIR: Irvin Johnson. |

Rogue soldiers, dressed in black chemical warfare attire, are operating in Vietnam and have captured a Texas Ranger's Green Beret brother. The Ranger heads to 'Nam, finds the "phantoms," and stages a Rambo-like rescue.

The Princess and the Marine (2001)

| Peace | Marines | NBC | DIR: Mike Robe. |

Based on a true story of a Marine on assignment in Bahrain who falls in love with a vivacious young woman, whom he discovers is a member of the country's royal family. The princess is not only resisting her parents' choice of her future husband but also knows they would never approve of her marriage to the Marine because he is a Mormon. The Marine races to get her out of the country to safety and marriage in the United States. Alas, they separated in 2004

The Promise of Love (1980)

| Vietnam | Marines | CBS | DIR: Don Taylor. |

Valerie Bertinelli stars as an 18-year-old widow of a Marine killed in Vietnam. The Marines provided assistance, including filming scenes on Camp Pendleton. The cooperation resulted in especially accurate portrayals of how the service helped families of men killed in action. (VTR: 11-19-80.)

Quantum Leap: *Genesis* (1989)

| SciFi | Navy | NBC | DIR: David Hemmings. |

Secret military project experiments with time travel. In this series pilot the scientist travels in the body of an Air Force test pilot, among other characters, as his invention malfunctions. Only the pilot contains military images and so qualified for inclusion in this guide.

Red Flag: *The Ultimate Game* (1981)

| Peace | Air Force | Video | DIR: Don Taylor. |

Six years before *Top Gun* flew across silver screens, this film, with a very similar story line and produced for television, sped directly to video. Two major stars, Barry Bostwick and William Devane, portray student and flight instructor, respectively, at the prestigious Air Force Fighter Weapons

School, known colloquially as "Red Flag," at Nellis Air Force Base, Nevada. As the student begins to outshine the instructor, tensions rise. The Air Force provided full cooperation.

Resting Place (1986)

Vietnam   Army   CBS   DIR: John Korty.

When a decorated black Vietnam lieutenant is denied burial in his hometown's all-white cemetery, John Lithgow, an Army officer, decides to use the man's hero status to convince the community to bury him honorably. In researching the awarding of the deceased's Silver Star, Lithgow suspects that the lieutenant's own unit may have killed him. The Army approved use of Fort McPhereson. (VTR: 05-14-86.)

Rocket's Red Glare (2000)

Peace   Air Force   Fox Family   DIR: Chris Bremble.

A troubled teenager restores a Mercury rocket as a science project, with the help of his ex-astronaut grandfather. When a shuttle is marooned in space, the boy's rocket is the only hope for rescue. The Air Force approved filming at Vandenberg Air Force Base because of the positive portrayal of the service and its involvement in the U.S. space program. (WV: 08-27-2000.)

Rough Riders (1997)

Spanish-American   Army   TNT   DIR: John Milius

Charge up San Juan Hill one more time, glorifying Teddy Roosevelt's formation of a volunteer regiment, which he then led into battle. Milius made his mini-series into a rousing celebration of masculinity, esprit de corps, militarism, and Manifest Destiny.

A Rumor of War (1980)

Vietnam   Marines   CBS   DIR: Richard T. Heffron.

Based on Philip Caputo's autobiographical novel. The author and John Sacret Young wrote a teleplay for this TV movie that probably should have been produced as a feature film. (In Europe, it was released theatrically.) Brad Davis, as Caputo, headed an all-star cast. The production company entered into lengthy negotiations with the Marines to obtain cooperation even though the service had significant concerns about Caputo's assertion that he had been involved in atrocities in country. Ultimately, Marine headquarters concluded it was in its best interest to cooperate to gain some leverage in improving their image. Major Pat Coulter served as technical advisor during production, which helped the miniseries to become one of the best portrayals of the American experience in Vietnam, along with the feature films **Go Tell the Spartans** (see chapter 1) and **Casualties of War** (see chapter 1). (VTR: 10-01-80.)

Sahara (1995)

WWII   Army   Showt   DIR: Brian Trenchard-Smith.

Cable remake has James Belushi in the Humphrey Bogart role of a tank commander lost in the North African desert, with cuss words thrown in to demonstrate the film's modernity. But why bother to remake one of WWII's classic portrayals? (See chapter 1.) (DVP: 07-31-95.)

Saving Jessica Lynch (2003)

Gulf Wars   Army   NBC   DIR: Peter Markle.

Rushed to the small screen with a patriotic portrayal of the capture and rescue of the West Virginia soldier. Unlike the first media stories that described how Lynch fought heroically to her last bullet, the TV story adheres as closely to the facts as possible under the circumstances. As a result, the Army provided assistance to the production. The question remains why Lynch became a hero when the media generally ignored other POWs, including a black female who had also suffered from similar injuries and captivity. (DVP: 11-05-03.)

Semper Fi (2000)

Peace   Marines   NBC   DIR: Michael Watkins.

Pilot for a series that did not get made, the film intended to introduce the male and female characters who were making their way through boot camp at Paris Island Marine Corps Recruit Depot. Stephen Spielberg's Dreamworks partnered with NBC Studios on the project.

She Stood Alone: The Tailhook Scandal (1995)

Peace   Navy   ABC   DIR: Larry Shaw

The portrayal of Lt. Paula Coughlin's sexual harassment at the 1991 Tailhook convention in Las Vegas had no up side for the Navy. The head of the investigation found the docudrama "surprisingly accurate."

Shooter (1988)

Vietnam   All   NBC   DIR: Gary Nelson.

Pulitzer Prize-winning Vietnam cameraman David Hume Kennedy created the story that described the everyday life of a group of combat photographers while in country. Originally made as a pilot for a series that was not produced, the film used locations in Thailand to re-create Saigon street scenes and combat in the countryside. (VTR: 10-05-88.)

Silent Night (2002)

WWII   Army   Unkn   DIR: Rodney Gibbons

Based on an actual story, a German mother convinces three American and three German soldiers to declare a truce on Christmas eve.

A Soldier's Girl (2003)

Peace   Army   Showt   DIR: Frank Pierson.

Based on a true story. A young soldier falls in love with a nightclub performer, who turns out to be transgendered. One of his fellow soldiers beats him to death believing he is a homosexual. The film conveys very well the homophobia within the armed services. (BD: 01-20-2003.)

Sole Survivor **(1970)**

WWII   Air Force   CBS   DIR: Paul Stanley.

This was inspired by the discovery of the B-24 bomber *Lady Be Good* in the North African desert. The film follows Air Force investigators as they study the crash of a fictional B-25 bomber and the efforts of the crew to survive in the Libyan desert. The ending helps raise the film above the usual TV fare.

South Pacific **(2001)**

WWII   Navy, Marines   ABC   DIR: Richard Pearce.

Remake of the 1958 movie (see chapter 1), starring Rade Sherbedgia as the French plantation owner Emile de Becque, Glenn Close in the Nellie Forbush role, and Harry Connick Jr. as Lt. Joe Cable, the young war hero, who falls in love with the native girl. No cooperation this time around, with the war more in the background and the hardware clearly of civilian origin. (DVP: 03-22-2001.)

Special Bulletin **(1983)**

Terrorism   Unkn   NBC   DIR: Edward Zwick.

Pacifists, resorting to terrorists' methods, seize a TV journalist and her cameraman and demand all nuclear detonators in the Charleston, South Carolina, area be collected and brought to them so they can destroy the devices at sea. If not, the pacifists/terrorists will detonate an atomic bomb they claim to have. The DoD did not provide assistance because it felt the film contained misleading information about military controls over nuclear weapons and the security of the materials critical to the manufacture of nuclear weapons. (VTR: 03-23-83.)

Submerged **(2001)**

Peace   Navy   NBC   DIR: James Keach.

In 1938 the USS *Squalus* sank after a mechanical malfunction during a test dive. This cinematic account of the first successful rescue of a trapped crew highlighted the use of the McCann rescue chamber.

Supercarrier **(1988)**

Cold War   Navy   ABC   DIR: William A. Graham.

Pilot, which received some cooperation from the Navy, for a series to which the Navy ceased to provide assistance because of the inaccuracies and implausibilities of subsequent scripts. Film featured stories of F-14 pilots and the crew of one of the Navy's nuclear carriers.

Sweet Revenge **a.k.a.** *Code of Honor* **(1984)**

Peace   Army   CBS   DIR: David Greene.

Convoluted soap opera with big-screen stars including Alec Baldwin. A major impregnates his commanding officer's daughter and convinces her to have an abortion. Unfortunately she dies; he panics and blames the pregnancy on a captain, whose life is ruined and who also dies. Fast forward several years to when the captain's sister, married to an Army major, finds that her husband is now under the command of the officer who falsely accused her brother. She avenges his death. (VTR: 11-07-84.)

Tail Gunner Joe (1977)

Cold War   Army   NBC   DIR: Jud Taylor.

Three-hour docudrama of Senator Joe McCarthy's life, including his army career and the hearings he chaired that led to his political demise after destroying many innocent people. (VTR: 02-09-77.)

Taken (2002)

SciFi   Army, Air Force   SFN   DIR: Breck Eisner, Felix Aleala.

Steven Spielberg's miniseries draws on his fascination with alien contacts with earth. Five decades of interaction between humans and aliens in 10 two-hour episodes. Although not about the military per se, aerial combat over France in WWII starts the story, and the military forms the framework in which the story progresses. (DVP: 12-01-2002.)

10.5 (2004)

SciFi   Army   NBC   DIR: John Lafia.

A 10.5-magnitude earthquake hits the West Coast of the United States. The Army becomes involved with rescue and evacuation activities.

Thanks of a Grateful Nation (1998)

Gulf wars   Army   Showt   DIR: Rod Holcomb.

Depicts the U.S. government's denial of troop exposure to toxic agents during the first Persian Gulf war and tells the stories of those who claim to have been affected. (DVP: 05-28-98.)

Tiger Cruise (2004)

Terrorists   Navy   Disney   DIR: Duwayne Dunham.

Following the attack on the World Trade Center a carrier is ordered into combat even though family members of the crew are taking a "Tiger Cruise," intended to show families how their loved ones serve aboard a ship.

To Heal a Nation (1988)

Vietnam   Army   NBC   DIR: Michael Pressman.

Story of Jan Scruggs, the embittered war veteran who conceived the need for a memorial to preserve the names of the thousands of U.S. service personnel who perished in Vietnam. The film captures his struggle to get the memorial financed and completed. The Air Force approved the use of stock footage. (VTR: 06-08-88.)

Too Young the Hero (1988)

WWII   Navy   CBS   DIR: Buzz Kulik.

Docudrama of 12-year-old Calvin Graham, played by Ricky Schroder, who enlists in the Navy after Pearl Harbor by forging his mother's signature and claiming he is 17. Scenes include boot camp at San Diego and Calvin's imprisonment in the brig for desertion. The Navy did not cooperate because they found the screenplay to be historically inaccurate in portraying specific characters and events. (VTR: 04-06-88.)

Tribes (1970)

Vietnam   Marine   ABC   DIR: Joseph Sargent.

Made while the Vietnam War was still in progress, the movie included location shooting at the U.S. Marine Corps Recruit Depot, San Diego. This provided an authentic ambience, unlike *The Boys in Company C* and *Full Metal Jacket* (see chapter 1), for which the filmmakers had to create their ersatz training facilities. In any case, the movie addressed the issue of how the Marines indoctrinated draftees into the previously all-volunteer service. Darren McGavin, in the guise of Sgt. Thomas Drake, regrets that the Corps now must accept draftees but understands that as a drill instructor, his job is to turn these reluctant recruits into warriors. Because the film was made for television, the dialogue lacks the realism of the profanity that actually existed and that R. Lee Ermey used so successfully in the two feature films, which also portrayed Marine basic training. (VTR: 11-18-70.)

The Tuskegee Airmen (1995)

WWII   Air Force   HBO   DIR: Robert Markowitz.

A docudrama, very long in the making, about a group of soldier-pilots who trained at the Tuskegee Air Force Base, Alabama, to become the first African American fliers in the U.S. Air Force, the "Fighting 99th." In action, the fighter squadron never lost a bomber it was escorting over enemy territory, earning the respect of white officers and men as well as giving pride to the black community. The movie combines fact and fiction, with Laurence Fishburne starring. Filmed at Fort Chaffee, Alabama, Fort Smith, Arkansas, and Davis Air Field, Muskogee, Oklahoma. (DVP: 08-25-95.)

Unnatural Causes (1986)

Vietnam   Army   NBC   DIR: Lamont Johnson.

John Ritter stars as a veteran, dying of cancer, who believes that his ailment is directly related to his exposure to Agent Orange while in Vietnam. He wants to track down other soldiers who were with him when they were accidentally sprayed while on patrol in the jungles. He links up with a veterans' counselor at the Veterans Administration and together they fight the bureaucracy. The ending title explains that while the veterans lost the court battle, the chemical companies established a $180 million fund in an out-of-court settlement.

Vietnam War Story (1989)

Vietnam   Army   HBO   PRO: Barry Jossen.

Six half-hour short stories dramatizing life among American soldiers in Vietnam. The first, "An Old Ghost Walks the Earth," recounts the activities of a soldier who spent three months in the field working with an advisory team helping the South Vietnamese clear out Vietcong from peasant villages. (VTR: 07-27-88.) Other titles in 1989 included "The Last Days," "The Last Outpost," "The Last Soldier," and "Dirty Work." (VTR: 08-19-89.)

War and Remembrance (1988)

WWII   Navy, Army   ABC   DIR: Dan Curtis.

This seven-part miniseries sequel to *Winds of War* received full cooperation from the DoD including facilities and stock footage. Based on Herman Wouk's novel, the $110 million TV epic follows the Henry family from a week after Pearl Harbor until the autumn of 1943. (VTR: 11-16-88.)

Welcome Home, Johnny Bristol (1972)

Vietnam   Army   CBS   DIR: George McCowan.

Broadcast shortly before the Vietnam war ended, the film tells the gripping story of a tortured Vietnam Veteran returning to a VA hospital in search of his home and childhood in Vermont. A VA nurse helps him find his way.

When Hell Was in Session (1979)

Vietnam   Navy   NBC   DIR: Paul Krasny.

Hal Holbrook portrays Cmdr. Jeremiah A. Denton, who was a POW for seven and a half years. The film documents much of the torture that he endured. The DoD approved Norton Air Force Base for locale shooting.

When Trumpets Fade (1998)

WWII   Army   HBO   DIR: John Irvin.

The director of *Hamburger Hill* (see chapter 1) re-created the little-known battle in the forests of Hurtgen in late fall of 1944, as the Allies pushed toward the Rhine. In a battle overshadowed by the Battle of the Bulge a few weeks later, the Army suffered staggering casualties, perhaps why the military avoided much mention of the fighting. Not your typical WWII or even post- WWII film, *When Trumpets Fade* has flying body parts and four-letter words in profusion. The DoD informally worked to provide less than 50 off-duty soldiers in the Bosnia region to work as extras. (DVP: 06-24-98.)

The Winds of War (1983)

WWII   Army, Navy   ABC   DIR: Dan Curtis.

Seven part miniseries for which Herman Wouk, the novel's creator, wrote most of the teleplay. Follows the activities of Pug Henry and his extended family during the years before the entry of the United States into WWII following December 7, 1941. The DoD and the Navy provided stock footage and location shooting, including Pearl Harbor. (VTR: 02-09-83.)

Women at West Point (1979)

Peace   Army   CBS   DIR: Vincent Sherman.

Story of the first women to enter the U.S. Military Academy at West Point and the resulting challenges facing both the female cadets and the school. The Army allowed filming on location.

Women of Valor (1986)

WWII   Army   CBS   DIR: Buzz Kulik.

A weak imitation of **Cry Havoc** and **So Proudly We Hail** (see chapter 1), the story follows 104 Army nurses captured by the Japanese in the Philippines at the beginning of the U.S. involvement in WWII. The DoD provided stock footage because of the positive images. (VTR: 12-03-86.)

Word of Honor (2003)

Vietnam   Army   TNT   DIR: Robert Markowitz.

From the novel by Nelson DeMille, this film is set three decades after the end of the Vietnam War. The Army accuses Don Johnson, a successful business executive, of taking part in or not stopping a massacre that his platoon committed in a Hue hospital. The service recalls him to active duty in order to put him on trial despite the time that has passed. The story captures the continuing impact the war has had on the American people and conveys the difficulty the soldiers had in separating friend from enemy. No military assistance, but well-done scenes of combat. (DVP: 12-03-2003.)

Young Joe, The Forgotten Kennedy (1977)

WWII   Air Force   ABC   DIR: Richard Heffron.

This docudrama tells the story of Joe Kennedy, who died in the explosion of his bomber during a secret mission over France.

Your Momma Wears Combat Boots (1989)

Peace   Air Force   NBC   DIR: Anson Williams.

Barbara Eden and her real-life son, Matthew Ansara, appear in this comedy that follows an overprotective mom who attempts to keep her son out of the Air Force, only to discover that somehow she has enlisted in the service herself. The DoD provided access to Fort Benning, Georgia, as well as Army and Air Force equipment.

Documentaries

Action at Angaur **(1945)**

WWII   Marines, Navy

A black-and-white, war-bond promotion film featuring Marine and Navy action in the Pacific, including training scenes and planning for the assault on the Peleliu Islands.

AFP: American Fighter Pilot **(TV) (2002)**

Peace   Air Force

A reality series that followed three Air Force officers attending flight school at Tyndall Air Force Base in Panama City, Florida. The film included the classroom training, interviews with their instructors, as well as the wives and families affected by the stresses of the training environment. CBS cancelled the series after three 60-minute episodes due to low ratings.

Air Power **(TV) (1956)**

WWI, WWII, Korea   Air Force

Walter Cronkite hosted this television series (1956–58), which portrayed the first 50 years of powered flight. It included a detailed look at the military use of airplanes during WWI, WWII, and Korea.

All This and WWII **(1976)**

WWII   All

Pop music selections from the Beatles, Bee Gees, and others provided the soundtrack for this documentary consisting of WWII clips. *Weekly Variety* believed the music arrangements detracted from the visual images in the 88-minute, color production. (WV: 11-17-76.)

America Goes to War (1990)

WWII   All

Public Broadcasting distributed this series, which described the U.S. involvement in WWII. The series began with the portrayal of the home front on the heels of the Great Depression, while the Blitzkrieg reigned terror on Europe. It then detailed how the United States entered the war.

America Is Ready (1917)

WWI   All

This depiction of America's preparedness included West Point cadets, sailors, and Marines with scenes of drill fields, artillery, coastal guns, mess halls, a simulated naval landing (probably Marines), and the stoking of the coal-fired ship's engines.

America Preparing (1916)

WWI   Army, Navy

The film portrayed young recruits training to become soldiers and sailors. The producers obtained footage from the government, including a Citizen's Soldier Camp at Plattsburgh, New York; the Military Academy; the Naval Training Station at Newport, Rhode Island; and the Naval Academy.

American Catholics in War and Reconstruction (1920)

WWI   Army

The Education Department of Famous Players-Lasky Company prepared this film under the supervision of the National Catholic War Council with the cooperation of the Knights of Columbus Committee on War Activities. It portrayed duties of the 1,525 volunteer Catholic chaplains under the direction of Archbishop Patrick Hayes of New York and included shots of soldiers in combat, Gen. Pershing marching down Fifth Avenue, and President Woodrow Wilson speaking.

The American Navy in Vietnam (TV) (1967)

Vietnam   Navy

Chet Huntley of NBC narrated this film, which depicted the Navy's involvement in the early years of the War in Vietnam, including scenes of Navy warships in the Gulf of Tonkin. It also portrayed the Marine landings at Da Nang and Chu Lai.

American Soldiers Defeating Filipinos Near Manila (1899)

SpAmer   Army

Lubin Company cameramen covered the Spanish American War. The company prepared a series of short films, which their catalog in the Library of Congress describes. When this movie approached 400 feet, the company hyped it as "the longest film of the war thus far produced." It featured coverage of American soldiers who, after stubborn resistance, vanquished the scantily clad Filipinos, who scattered in all directions.

American Valor (TV) (2003)

US Combat   All

Stories of Medal of Honor recipients unfold through newsreel footage, photographs, and interviews with recipients and comrades who witnessed the brave actions.

America's Answer: Following the Fleet to France a.k.a. America's Answer to the Hun (1918)

WWI   All   7 reels

The U.S. Committee on Public Information and the Army Signal Corps prepared these seven reels as the second release in the U.S. Government Official War Films series. The film featured the incredible complications of moving American men and resources across the ocean and to the French battlefields. It also included scenes of Red Cross activities, combat in the trenches, and aircraft in motion. The other two films in the series were *Pershing's Crusaders,* which portrayed our troops in France, and *Under Four Flags,* which showed the Allies' four military leaders: Foch, Diaz, Haig, and Pershing.

The Anderson Platoon (TV) (1967)

Vietnam   Army

CBS broadcast this French-made television documentary a year after its premier in France. For six weeks Pierre Schoendoerffer, the producer/director, his cameraman, and his sound engineer followed the 33-soldier unit led by Capt. Joseph B. Anderson, a recent West Point graduate. During that time, some platoon members were killed and others were injured. The movie received the Oscar for best documentary in 1967.

Appointment in Tokyo (1945)

WWII   All

This film covered the entire four years of the Pacific war, detailing the defeat of Japan, with MacArthur frequently appearing. It traced the fighting from Corregidor in 1942, through the naval victories in the Coral Sea, the land victory at Guadalcanal, and the Marines taking Iwo Jima, to the combined Army, Navy, and Marine forces assaulting Okinawa. It also included horrific footage from the Bataan Death March. Warner Brothers released the film in November 1945, after the Japanese surrender, for the War Activities Committee of the motion picture industry. The studio compiled the footage from the Signal Corp, the Air Force, and the Navy.

Army Champions (1941)

WWII   Army

A Pete Smith Special, one of a series of short films shown with MGM features. This one compared the physical characteristics of athletes with those needed for weapons training of American soldiers.

The Army-Navy Screen Magazine—Highlights (1943–1945)

WWII   All

The National Audio Visual Center selected segments that are representative of the major elements of the series, including features about the war. The film provides a sense of the most popular and fondly remembered series of films that the Capra unit made. The magazine was a biweekly news and information film that was shown before the feature films in all military motion picture theaters during the war. Capra said that after the Why We Fight series, he was most proud of the *Magazine.*

At the Front in North Africa (1943)

WWII   Army

Although his name did not appear in the credits, *Weekly Variety* stated that the industry referred to the film as "Colonel Darryl Zanuck's African pictures." Filmed in color, John Ford appears on a donkey in a scene with no explanation of why he was present or filmed. Tank battle forms the focus of the work. Signal Corps filmed and Warner Brothers distributed. (WV: 03-03-43, NYT: 03-19-43.)

The Atomic Café (1982)

Cold War   All

A collage of government-issued propaganda and commercial messages about the atomic age as it was portrayed during the 1950s and early 1960s. The film included the infamous cartoon character "Burt the turtle" of "duck and cover" fame (school children were drilled to hide under desks and tables when they detected a flash of light or explosive sound). A frightening look back at a more simple nuclear world.

The Atom Strikes! (1945)

WWII   Army

A 31-minute, official War Department film depicting the damage done by the atomic bombings of Hiroshima and Nagasaki in physical terms. It also contained an interview with a Jesuit priest who was present in Hiroshima on August 6, 1945, the day of the explosion.

Attack! The Battle of New Britain (1944)

WWII   All

While an officer in the Army, Frank Capra produced this 56-minute movie for the Office of War Information using Signal Corps personnel. It depicted one of the most significant early assaults against Japanese-held territory in the South Pacific theater. Gen. Douglas MacArthur, commander of the U.S. combined force, appeared, and the footage showed how the Air Force, Navy, and infantry supported each other to achieve victory. Used for the Fifth War Bond drive. (WV: 06-14-44, NYT: 06-21-44.)

Attack in the Pacific (**1944**)

WWII   Army, Navy

A 52-minute, armed forces information film that detailed, within the limits of security, the planning and battles that would lead to the defeat of Japan.

The Autobiography of a Jeep (**1943**)

WWII   All

A charming, lighthearted look at that most "all American" of vehicles, the Jeep.

Basic Training (**TV**) (**1971**)

Vietnam   Army

Frederick Wiseman's film followed draftees and enlisted men through the nine-week Army basic training program. His cameras captured the dehumanizing effects of recruit training at Fort Knox, Kentucky, while fighting was continuing in Vietnam. (VTR: 10-06-71.)

The Battle for Korea (**TV**) (**2001**)

Korea   All

Part of the PBS series *The American Experience*, the documentary explored the history of the Korean peninsula from the last days of World War II, when President Truman agreed with Joseph Stalin to a division into two separate countries at the 38th parallel, to the truce in 1953, after which the border became the existing battle line. It included significant combat footage, maps, and an excellent narrative. It also portrayed the first air war between U.S. and Soviet jet planes, some of which were manned by Russian fliers. The film detailed the Chinese involvement in the fighting after the United Nations troops, led by Douglas MacArthur as the supreme commander, had advanced north from Seoul toward the Yalu River, the border between North Korea and China.

The Battle for the Marianas (**1944**)

WWII   All

Marine Corps cameramen filmed the action depicted in this two-reel review of the battles, which resulted in the U.S. capture of Saipan, Tinian, and Guam, which then became bases for the U.S. bombing of Japan. (Compare to the postwar Marine film *Bombs over Tokyo*.) Six of the combat photographers died in action. The motion picture portrayed U.S. forces landing, tanks, dive-bombers, and flamethrowers used in mop-up operations. (NYT: 09-20-44.)

The Battle of Britain. See *Why We Fight.*

The Battle of China. See *Why We Fight.*

Battle of Manila Bay (1898)

SpAmer   Navy

J. Stuart Blackton reenacted the Naval battle using miniatures in what today would generously be called a docudrama.

Battle of Midway (1942)

WWII   Navy

John Ford directed and Henry Fonda narrated this account of the turning point in the Pacific war in June 1942. Patriotic and religious music provided emotional impact to the film, which won the 1942 Oscar for best documentary. (NYT: 09-15-42.)

The Battle of Russia. See Why We Fight.

Battle of San Juan Hill (1898)

SpAmer   Army

The Edison catalog describes this as creating great enthusiasm among viewers as the soldiers rushed up the hill, their ranks thinned by fire from a blockhouse, struggled with Spanish soldiers on the hilltop, and then raised the Stars and Stripes.

Battle of San Pietro (1944)

WWII   Army

John Huston's classic portrayal of combat in the Italian theater included some re-created scenes. President Franklin Roosevelt gave permission for the film to be made available to the general public. The Signal Corps shot the combat footage, and the film contained maps and diagrams showing the strategy of the battle and shots of soldiers' faces as fighting continued. Huston also included some of the first images of dead American soldiers, their bodies laid inside white bags like shrouds. Huston asked Gen. Mark Clark, the commander of the Italian campaign, to provide an introduction to the battle and provided him with some general ideas of what to say. Instead, Clark simply read Huston's notes.

Battle of Santiago Bay (1898)

SpAmer   Navy

J. Stuart Blackton, an early filmmaker and showman, created many of the early newsreels of contemporary events. Unfortunately some of his films were staged, including this one. Blackton pasted photographs of Navy ships onto pieces of wood, which he floated in a pool of water in his office for filming. Nevertheless, his creations incited patriotism within the audiences. Although he marketed his movie as a documentary, in today's terms it would be considered a docudrama.

Battleline (TV) (1963)

WWII   Army

Syndicated series about WWII battles as told by soldiers on both sides of the battlefield.

Beachhead to Berlin (1944)

WWII   Coast Guard

A two-reel, color film shot by Coast Guard cameramen, depicting the service's activities in support of the Normandy landings, including the movement of men and material across the channel and the return to England of the wounded and the dead. Frequently paired with the feature film *Hollywood Canteen* (see chapter 1). (NYT: 12-16-44.)

Berga: *Soldiers of Another War* (TV) (2003)

WWII   Army

Charles Guggenheim was ill and left behind when his unit moved to the front, where it was captured by Germans during the Battle of the Bulge. He saw the film, which PBS aired, as a tribute to his comrades. The movie describes how the German army separated 300 prisoners who were Jewish or "looked" Jewish and sent them to concentration camps rather than to a POW stalag. Many of these soldiers did not survive.

Beyond the Line of Duty (1942)

WWII   Air Force

Short documentary that Ronald Reagan narrated as an officer in Hollywood during the war. It told the story of flying hero Capt. Hewitt T. Wheless. Follows his training at Randolph Field; his career reached its climax in his aerial combat against 19 Japanese planes, for which he received the Distinguished Flying Cross. The film helped foster patriotism and the war effort.

Beyond the Wild Blue (1998)

Cold War   Air Force

This documentary series provided a history of the U.S. Air Force from the demobilization following World War II to its evolution as the principle weapon of the U.S. armed forces during the Cold War. The series, aired on the History Channel, included a survey of the aircraft and missiles in the U.S. arsenal in its confrontation with the Soviet Union.

The Bicycle Corps: *America's Black Army on Wheels* (TV) (2000)

SpAmer   Army

The film, aired on PBS, portrayed the journey of the black 25th Infantry, who left Missoula, Montana, on bicycles in June 1897 and completed their trek 1,900 miles and 41 days later in St. Louis.

The Army was considering replacing horses with bicycles, and the trip tested the feasibility of the idea. The documentary detailed the progress and challenges the soldiers faced.

The Big Picture (TV) (1951–1964)

WWII (primarily)   Army

Appearing in syndication or on ABC, the Army's Pictorial Center produced these 30-minute episodes to educate the public about their service's actions during the war. Segments included great battles, new weaponry, and historical roles played by the Army's various divisions. While generally employing footage from the Army's authentic and training film library, John J. Pershing's exploits during the segment covering the punitive expedition into Mexico used Hollywood footage from the feature film *They Came to Cordura* (see chapter 1).

Blackbird (1987)

Cold War   Air Force

The story of the building and flight of the Blackhawk SR-71 reconnaissance plane.

Bombs Over Tokyo (1946)

WWII   Marines

By late 1946, during the hearings on the unification of the armed services, the Marine Corps was fighting to survive as a separate service. To better explain their value, the Marines created this 20-minute movie to depict their important role in the bombing of Japan. In the film, the Marines pictured how their amphibious landings secured the remote island airbases in the Marianas from which the Air Force was able to unleash their bombers on Japan.

Brothers in Arms (2003)

Vietnam   Navy

Members of a Navy "fastboat" (river patrol boats) unit who served together on Vietnam's Mekong Delta visit the Vietnam Veterans Memorial in Washington. The film explores the impact that their shared experiences had on the development and life of their friendship.

Brought to Action (1945)

WWII   Navy, Marines

The War Activities Committee sponsored this film, which showed the naval battles that facilitated the allied landings on Mindoro. United Artists distributed. (NYT: 01-13-45.)

The Buffalo Soldiers (TV) (1992)

Nineteenth Century   Army

While portraying the story of the Afro-American 9th and 10th Cavalry during the latter half of the nineteenth century, the film opens and closes with footage at Fort Leavenworth, Kansas, during the 1972 dedication of the Buffalo Soldier monument. Nebraska Educational Television did an earlier four-part series using the same title.

Canal Zone (TV) (1977)

Peace   All

In this documentary broadcast on PBS, Frederick Wiseman portrayed both the functioning of the canal and the societies (business, military, and civilian) existing in the Canal Zone.

Carriers: A History of United States Aircraft Carriers (1990)

Peace/War   Navy

An Australian production traced the development and use of U.S aircraft carriers in 13 episodes for video release.

Cassino to Korea (1950)

Korea   Army

A Paramount documentary that attempted to create a tie between the WWII fighting in Italy and the then-contemporary war in Korea. Most of the combat scenes pictured came from WWII.

The Century of Warfare (TV) (1994)

WWI, WWII   All

Nugus/Martin Productions created this multipart television series about the wars of the twentieth century.

Citizen Soldier: The U.S. Army Story (*In Defense of Freedom*) (TV) (1985)

Cold War   Army

This documentary portrayed the history of the Army from its origins to modern times. *Weekly Variety* stated that the Turner Broadcasting filmmakers borrowed from Hollywood footage and government productions, using little original footage. This was the first of what was intended to be a series, each showcasing one of the services. (DV: 05-29-85.)

Clash of Wings (1999)

WWII   Air Force

This History Channel series provided a very detailed look at the great air battles of WWII. The production included never-before-seen footage and interviews with the participants.

Combat America (1943)

WWII   Army, Air Force

Clark Gable narrated this color film documenting the operations of the 351st Bombardment Group. It included footage of briefings and B-17 bombing missions over Germany. Gable was in the Air Force from 1942 to 1943 and flew as an aerial gunner in the Eastern Theater of Operations.

Counter Force (2001)

Peace   Army

The three-part documentary series portrayed the world's elite military units, including the U.S. Delta Force.

Crashing Through to Berlin (1918)

WWI   Army

Footage of troops on the road to Berlin, following an overview of the war.

Crusade in Europe (TV) (1949)

WWII   Army

Based on Gen. Dwight D. Eisenhower's memoirs of the same name, *Crusade in Europe* was the first documentary series produced for television. It consisted of 26 half-hour episodes using archival and newsreel footage. (VTR: 12-03 & 04-49, 05-11-49.)

Crusade in the Pacific (TV) (1952)

WWII   All

This series portrayed the entire war in the Pacific theater from the bombing of Pearl Harbor through the surrender of Japan on the USS *Missouri*. *Time* produced 20 black-and-white, 30-minute episodes.

D-Day (TV) (1962)

WWII   Army, Navy, Air Force

A presentation of the Du Pont Show of the Week produced by David Wolper. It contained an hour-by-hour account of the Allied invasion of France on June 6, 1944, and included captured German footage never before seen in the United States.

D-Day Remembered (1994)

WWII   All

Historian David McCullough narrated and provided the continuity in this 54-minute film that included interviews with more than 50 of the participants as well as footage and stills from British,

American, and German archives. Charles Guggenheim directed and Grace Guggenheim produced this film for the National D-day Museum, New Orleans. PBS also aired the film as part of its The American Experience (TAE) series.

Day after Trinity (1980)

WWII   All

Both a biography of J. Robert Oppenheimer and a history of the building of the atomic bomb. Detailed how the Army Corps of Engineers managed the Manhattan Project and how Gen. Leslie Groves worked with Oppenheimer to create the atomic bomb. Following the bomb's use, Oppenheimer, shown in archival footage, became a spokesperson against nuclear warfare. The title comes from the physicist's response to the question of when the nuclear arms race began.

Dear America: *Letters Home from Vietnam* (TV) (1987)

Vietnam   Army, Marines

Actors and actresses, including Tom Berenger, Ellen Burstyn, Willem Dafoe, Robert DeNiro, Michael J. Fox, and others, read letters from soldiers and Marines who fought the ground war in Vietnam. It included a final, emotional letter from a mother to her dead son. CBS broadcast the movie.

Death Rattlers (1995)

WWII   Marines

Story of VMF 323 U.S. Marine Fighter Squadron and its leader during the WWII battle for Okinawa.

December 7th (1943)

WWII   Navy

John Ford and photographer Gregg Toland restaged the bombing of Pearl Harbor and described the results, including the recovery of the ships, the improvements to the defense of Hawaii, and the immediate efforts to hold off and then attack the oncoming Japanese. The Navy confiscated the original version and then released a heavily censored version in 1943, which was understandable, since the war had not yet concluded. Subsequent feature films, including *From Here to Eternity* (see chapter 1) and documentaries of the attack on Pearl Harbor draw heavily on the documentary's footage, even though much of it consists of re-creation rather than original footage.

December 7: Day of Infamy (1963)

WWII   All

David Wolper produced this 60-minute film for telecasting in syndication. No new ground covered. (VTR: 12-18-63.)

***Diary of a Sergeant* (1945)**

WWII   Army

The autobiography of Harold Russell, a soldier who was fitted with artificial limbs after losing both hands in an explosion. Russell later appeared in ***The Best Years of Our Lives***, winning an Oscar for best supporting actor, as well as a special Oscar "for bringing hope and courage to his fellow veterans through his appearance in" the film.

Divide and Conquer. See *Why We Fight.*

***Eisenhower* (TV) (1993)**

WWII   Army

One of the PBS The American Experience presentations, in two parts: "Soldier" and "Statesman." The film examined Eisenhower's rise through the military ranks. Stalled in rank in the thirties as chief aide to Douglas MacArthur, during WWII Ike was able to seize the opportunity and benefit from luck to ultimately become Supreme Allied Commander. (DVP: 11-10-93.)

***A Face of War* (1968)**

Vietnam   Army

This 72-minute black-and-white documentary covered the daily experiences of Leathernecks in the Seventh Marine Regiment in Vietnam.

***Fahrenheit 9/11* (2004)**

Iraq   All

Michael Moore took dead aim at President George W. Bush in a documentary that might better be labeled as an old-fashioned political screed. Whatever else he might have to say about the president, Moore's focus remained on Bush's war in Iraq, and he was preaching to the choir. The critics, on the other hand, have forgotten or simply do not know that documentaries are not television news programs but rather historical or social events through the eyes of the director. Moreover, like most filmmakers, Moore is in the business to make money, whether or not he will admit it, and to succeed he must entertain. ***Fahrenheit 9/11*** does that, however painful the subject of the Iraq war and its human losses might be.

***15,000 Soldiers Reviewed by the President at Camp Alger May 28* (1898)**

SpAmer   Army

Predecessor of newsreels, this short film showed the faces of many of the soldiers who passed in review before President William McKinley as they prepared to leave the country to face the Spanish enemy, in this early Lubin release.

A Fighter Pilot's Story (1994)

WWII   Air Force

Originally conceiving the film as a legacy for his grandchildren, Quentin Aanenson produced, wrote, and narrated his own account of his experiences flying a P-47 Thunderbolt over Europe during the war. PBS broadcast the film in two 90-minute episodes.

The Fighting Lady (1944)

WWII   Navy

Twentieth Century Fox's Darryl F. Zanuck requested that the Navy allow him to place a camera crew aboard the second USS *Yorktown* during its shakedown cruise. The documentary depicted the role of the aircraft carrier, its planes, guns, and sailors. With a crew of 3,000 men, the Essex class carrier represented the Navy's carrier warfare in the Pacific and took part in the attack on Truk and the Marianas. The film opened with a brief re-enactment, but the rest utilized combat footage taken during the Pacific battles by cameras the filmmakers placed in the wings of the Hellcat planes. Robert Taylor, film star turned naval aviator, narrated. Because of its exploits in the Pacific, the carrier became known as *The Fighting Lady*. The ship now enjoys retirement in Charleston, South Carolina's Patriot's Point Museum. (WV: 12-20-44; NYT: 12-28-44 and 01-16-45.)

The First Forty Days (1950)

Korea   Army

The Army Signal Corps shot this detailed look at the foot soldiers as they rushed into Korea immediately after the communist North Korean invasion of South Korea. Despite the need to retreat, the GIs ultimately were able to maintain the Pusan perimeter until supplies and troops were delivered. Since the Army produced and distributed the film, the finished product does not include the contributions of the Air Force, Marines, or South Koreans. (WV: 10-11-50.)

First Kill (2001)

Vietnam   Army

Coco Schrijber directed this award-winning Dutch documentary about Vietnam, which included interviews with veterans who discussed their experiences and what it felt like to kill for the first time. Michael Herr, author of *Dispatches,* talked for the first time in ten years about his own dark experiences as a journalist in Vietnam.

The Fleet That Came to Stay (1946)

WWII   Navy

This 20-minute film was originally made for a war bond drive. It included footage of kamikaze attacks and a scene that shows a bomb that skips like a stone across the deck of a ship, passing personnel before dropping into the sea without exploding. (NYT: 07-27-45.)

Flying with the Marines (1918)

WWI   Marines

Filmed by Marines at their aviation camp in Miami, Florida, and edited by a Marine reservist, this film was among the first to take a camera on board a plane as it dived and performed tailspins, loop to loops, and other maneuvers.

The Fog of War: *Eleven Lessons of Robert S. McNamara* (2003)

Vietnam   All

Errol Morris crafted this feature-length documentary from his interviews with the then-85-year-old McNamara, the former Secretary of Defense under Lyndon B. Johnson. The film provided an insider's view of the misguided political, diplomatic, and military intervention into what had been a localized civil war. Despite his apparent openness to the camera, McNamara still did not apologize for his role in the tragedy that Vietnam became for the United States. Worse, he refused to explain why he did not speak out against the war after he left the cabinet. More than 22,000 men died in Vietnam while he was secretary of defense, and another 36,000 died afterward. How many would have lived if he had acknowledged what he had realized while still in the Pentagon, that the war could not be won? (WP: 12-21-03.)

A Force in Readiness (1961)

Cold War   Marines

Warner Brothers produced (at cost) this film, narrated by Jack Webb for the Marines. Congress saluted Jack Warner for his contribution, and the Motion Picture Academy presented a special Oscar to the film's producer, William L. Hendricks.

The Forgotten War (1974)

WWI   Army, Marines

PBS broadcast this BBC production about the Allied incursion into Russia after it withdrew from WWI. President Wilson ordered U.S. troops to protect the trans-Siberian railroad so that it would not end up in the hands of Germany or Japan and give them entry to the impending civil war there. The film made the case that the troops in Russia did not follow the noninvolvement orders, planting the seeds of the anti-American policies of the Soviet government. (VTR: 06-26-74.)

Four Years of Thunder: *Volume Four—Winged Victory: 1918* (TV) (1996)

WWI   Air Force

The History Channel's presentation depicted the development of the American aircraft industry, which began WWI in disarray. It included footage of naval aircraft and long-range bombing strategies.

F.T.A. (1972)

Vietnam   Army

The antiwar "FTA Tour" of Pacific Rim American bases provided the focus for this film. Dalton Trumbo penned the screenplay for the production, and Hollywood liberals, including Jane Fonda, Donald Sutherland, Holly Near, Peter Boyle, and others, appeared as themselves. FTA officially stood for Free Theater Associates and unofficially for "Free the Army." But the most commonly understood meaning, especially among the troops, was "Fuck the Army." (WV: 07-12-72, NYT: 07-22-72.)

Fury in the Pacific (1945)

WWII   Army, Air Force, Navy, Marines, Coast Guard

This 20-minute War Activities Committee film portrayed joint landings on a Japanese-held island in the South Pacific. (NYT: 03-23-45.)

George Stevens: D-Day to Berlin (1994)

WWII   Army, Air Force

George Stevens Jr. hosted and narrated one of the first color films documenting the movement of the Allied forces across Europe from D-Day to the end of the hostilities in Berlin. Along the way there was a lot of death, beside the roads, in the concentration camps, and in the towns and villages. His father, director George Stevens, took much of the footage.

The Great Air Race of 1924 (TV) (1989)

Peace   Air Force

Shown as a segment on the PBS series The American Experience. The filmmakers highlighted the round-the-world race undertaken by four airmen commissioned by the Army Air Service to test and promote air travel. It included archival footage.

Guarding Old Glory (1915)

WWI   All   5 reels

A preparedness film that showed the state of readiness, good and bad, of the armed services. The documentary contained scenes of heavy field artillery, recruits at training stations, the Signal Corps' wireless communications, Marines landing from a ship protecting them with its giant guns, and a submarine submerging. According to the American Film Institute's catalog, the release was held up for vetting by leading military figures. It eventually received endorsements from Secretary of the Navy Josephus Daniels, and Secretary of War Lindsey M. Garrison, among others, and was subsequently used in the war-effort campaign.

Hearts and Minds (1974)

Vietnam   All

Warner Bros. and Columbia produced and distributed this Oscar-winning portrayal of the impact the Vietnam War had on the United States and the men who fought in Southeast Asia. The film included statements by opponents of the war. Its most powerful sequence juxtaposed Commander in Chief of U.S. forces in Vietnam Gen. William Westmoreland's comment that the Oriental mind looks differently on death than the Western mind with a scene of Vietnamese women grieving over their dead sons, husbands, or relatives.

Here Come the Navy Bands **(1945)**

WWII   Navy, Marines

The film opens in a naval hospital in San Diego, California, and features a group of sailors and WAVES singing "Here Comes the Navy." Men and women of the Marines then sing with their band such tunes as "Oh I Love My GI Guy," "Semper Fidelis," and "Anchors Aweigh."

Hiroshima Nagasaki August, 1945 **(1970)**

WWII   Army

Producer Eric Barnouw discovered that the U.S. government possessed black-and-white, silent footage that the Japanese filmed shortly after the bombings in Hiroshima and Nagasaki, showing the destruction and injuries. Barnouw worked to have the film made available for public viewing. He edited it into a 16-minute short that included English voice-over narration and some scenes from American bomb footage.

History-Undercover: *One Hour Over Tokyo* **(TV) (2001)**

WWII   Air Force

The History Channel film used oral histories of the surviving Doolittle raiders, archival footage of Jimmy Doolittle, and narrative from Col. Carroll V. Glines's book *The Doolittle Raid* to tell the story of the first U.S. bombing raid on Japan.

How Uncle Sam Prepares **a.k.a.** *Uncle Sam Prepares* **(1917)**

WWI   Army, Navy   4–5 reels

President Woodrow Wilson and various other government officials appeared in this preparedness film. It included an all-black regiment training and drilling the same way as an all-white regiment. It also explained the tasks of Navy seamen. The film begins with Uncle Sam and President Abraham Lincoln discussing the European War and then switches to the documentary style.

The Hungnam Story **(1951)**

Korea   All

The documentary portrayed the near-disastrous evacuation of U.S. troops from the Chinese trap south of the Yalu River and the resulting long, slow hike to the beaches where the Navy rescued them. The film, which the Naval Photographic Center produced, included actual combat footage, shots of frostbitten body parts, and long lines of refugees.

The Hunt for Pancho Villa **(TV) (1993)**

Mexican Border   Army

The PBS series The American Experience aired this program, which portrayed Gen. "Black Jack" Pershing and his men pursuing Pancho Villa into Mexico after his attacks in New Mexico, which left 17 Americans and 67 Mexicans dead. This effort marked one of the last great cavalry mobilizations and the first use of "motorized" vehicles.

In the Year of the Pig (1968)

Vietnam   All

Many scholars describe Emile de Antonio's full-length film as an anti-American diatribe. Released during the escalating controversy about the Vietnam War, it found a receptive audience among anti-war forces and received an Academy Award nomination. Professionally and artistically crafted, the documentary included news footage, combat scenes, and interviews with prominent Americans, among them David Halberstam, author of *The Best and the Brightest*, Father Daniel Berrigan, and Senator Thurston B. Morton. (WV: 03-12-69.)

Kamikaze (1962)

WWII   Navy

Produced by Perry Wolff as part of a twin bill with *Smashing of the Reich*. It began at Pearl Harbor before the Japanese attack and followed events through the A-bombing of Hiroshima and Nagasaki. The film used Japanese home front scenes, including children playing "war games," and life in Hawaii before December 7, 1941.

Know Your Enemy, Japan (1943)

WWII   NA

In the style of Frank Capra's Why We Fight series, this film made more use of images than words. One of the last movies Capra's Army Signal Corps unit made. Strictly speaking, the film does not fall into the scope of this guide but was made by the Army for the same purpose as the seven films of the Why We Fight series.

Korea—The Unknown War (TV) (1990)

Korea   All

This six-part, PBS miniseries explained U.S. involvement in Korea after WWII, which led to the division of the Korean peninsula at the 38th parallel into the Communist North and the capitalist South. When the North Koreans invaded the South in 1950, the United Nations responded with an international coalition of troops fighting under U.S. command.

Efforts by veterans led to the creation of the Korean War Memorial on the Mall in Washington and a better understanding of events that led to the death of more than 35,000 American fighting men in three years in the "forgotten war."

Korea: *We Called It War* (TV) (2002)

Korea   Army

Denzil Baston, author of *We Called It War*, and his platoon buddies gathered together to recount their experiences as front line soldiers in Korea.

The Korean War: Fire and Ice (1999)

Korea   All

Oral histories from participants in the war, including Medal of Honor recipients Thomas J. Hudner and Raymond G. Davis, writers, and historians.

Last Reflections on a War (TV) (1968)

Vietnam   All

The Public Broadcasting Laboratory's documentary used reporter and scholar Bernard Fall's own words to describe the tragedy of Vietnam. Having covered the French involvement in Indochina, Fall returned to Vietnam to report on the American involvement in the war. In February 1967, less than a month after *Hell Is a Very Small Place,* his critically acclaimed account of the Siege of Dien Bien Phu, appeared, Fall was killed while on a patrol with U.S. Marines. In addition to Fall, the film used interviews with soldiers and villagers to depict the sorrows experienced by Vietnam's peasants. (VTR: 03-13-68.)

Let There Be Light (TV) (1946)

WWII   Army

John Huston directed this documentary while in the Signal Corps, but the Army did not allow distribution for 40 years even though it provided a sympathetic look into the psychological injuries that some WWII GIs suffered. Because the film shows patients' faces, the Army argued that its release would have constituted an invasion of the "patients' privacy." Huston told author Suid that he did, in fact, have signed releases from all the men who appeared in the film. In any case, the movie makes it clear that soldiers can suffer just as much mentally as from any wound on the battlefield. This antiwar statement undoubtedly contributed to the Army's efforts to suppress the film, which finally appeared on PBS.

The Liberation of Rome (1944)

WWII   Army

Portrayal of the British Eighth Army and the U.S. Fifth Army, from the landings on the Italian peninsula to the capture of Rome. The film contains scenes of aerial dogfights and the liberation celebration.

Liberators: Fighting on Two Fronts in World War II (TV) (1992)

WWII   Army

The "Two Fronts" in the title refer to the battlefield and to bigotry, not the usual reference to the European and Pacific theaters of operations. PBS broadcast the film as a part of its The American Experience series. While the bigotry was real, and probably even worse than reported, the film came under immediate attack, primarily from conservatives claiming that it contained a multitude of inaccuracies. Included among the questions raised were whether the black tank units shown liberating Buchenwald and Dachau had actually been anywhere near those concentration camps.

On camera, two concentration camp survivors described their rescue by black soldiers. Likewise, black tankers had testified they had helped liberate the two concentration camps. However, other black soldiers denied that their tanks had helped to liberate the two camps. In the end, PBS withdrew the film and investigated the accusations, concluding that the documentary did contain significant inaccuracies. PBS then requested the filmmakers to correct the misstatements. They refused, still claiming their account of events was accurate. Lost in the controversy were the very real contributions that black soldiers and sailors made to the war effort, which the documentary did show, including Joe Louis in uniform entertaining troops and Doris "Dorie" Miller, who was decorated for his bravery at Pearl Harbor.

The Marines Have Landed (1945)

WWII   Marines

This 10-minute documentary detailed the important contributions the U.S. Marines made during the war in the Pacific against Japan.

Marines in the Making (1942)

WWII   Marines

The MGM short showed Marines in training at a few, unnamed bases detailing how the United States would out-trick the "sneaky" Japanese.

MCRD, San Diego (1969)

Vietnam   Marines

The film depicted the training of Marine Corps recruits, referred to as grunts, at the Recruit Depot in San Diego, California, during the Vietnam War.

Masters of War (TV) (1994)

WWII to first Gulf War   All

U.S. News and World Reports made this multipart series for television focusing on the wars of the second half of the twentieth century.

Medal of Honor (TV) (1999)

WWII, Korea, Vietnam, Somalia   All

TNT prepared this film that told the story of six Medal of Honor recipients, the highest U.S. military honor. The Medal is awarded for acts of bravery that, had the person decided against acting, no one could blame him. About half of the awards have been made posthumously.

The Memory of Justice (1976)

WWII, Vietnam   All

Four-hour, monumental documentary from highly regarded and award-winning director Marcel Ophuls. He compares the Nazi War Crimes Trials in Nuremberg, his primary focus, with the American involvement in Vietnam and the French attempt to retain Algeria in a study of responsibility for the horrors of war.

The Memphis Belle: A Story of the Flying Fortress (1944)

WWII   Air Force

Considered one of the best WWII documentaries. Director William Wyler followed the *Memphis Belle*, a B-17 flying fortress, as its men became the first crew to complete 25 missions over enemy territory. For the first time in a WWII aerial documentary, Wyler used color combat footage, which his cameramen shot while on several combat missions on several planes during the early months of the air war over Europe. Despite the praise that Wyler received, he rewrote history in the film, reversing the last two missions of the *Memphis Belle*. The plane's pilot, Robert Morgan, told author Suid that Wyler believed the bomber's twenty-fourth mission over Germany would provide more drama than the plane's actual twenty-fifth flight over the German submarine pens on the French coast, which he thought would appear safer and therefore less dramatic. Much of Wyler's footage later appeared in Hollywood's portrayal of WWII in the air, including, most recently, the feature film *The Memphis Belle* (see chapter 1), which Wyler's daughter produced.

Men of Bronze (1977)

WWI   Army

The Harlem Hellfighters, the 369th Infantry Regiment, received the most American decorations of any unit in WWI, even though they fought under French command during the entire war. The documentary honors the all-black unit. (WV: 09-28-77, NYT: 09-24-77.)

The Mills of the Gods: Viet Nam (1965)

Vietnam   All

Shot entirely in country with Marines, soldiers, and air cavalry speaking for themselves and describing their experiences. The black-and-white documentary provided early insights into the American involvement in Vietnam. The film included scenes of dead Vietcong (VC) and one showed the drowning of a VC suspect to "aid interrogation."

Missile (1988)

Cold War   Air Force

Frederick Wiseman's film about the 4315th Training Squadron of the Strategic Air Command at Vandenberg Air Force Base in California, which trained Air Force officers to man the Launch Control Centers for the Minuteman Intercontinental Ballistic Missiles. Sequences included the discussion of the moral and military issues of nuclear war.

The Nazis Strike. See ***Why We Fight.***

The Negro Soldier (1944)

WWII   Army

Frank Capra produced and Stuart Heisler directed this 43-minute film for the War Activities Committee of the Motion Picture Industry while they were in the Signal Corps. The film showcased the contributions and achievements of blacks serving their country during the war.

Of Heroes and Helicopters (1993)

Vietnam   All

The helicopter became the icon and metaphor for much of the fighting in Vietnam. The film documented the stories of pilots and other heroic crewmen, including two Medal of Honor recipients.

Origins of the Motion Picture (1975)

SpAmer   Army

The film provided a history of the technological development of moving pictures during the nineteenth century. It included rare footage of American troops landing in Cuba in 1898.

Our Bridge of Ships (1918)

WWI   Navy

Under the auspices of Chairman George Creel and the Committee on Public Information, the film showed U.S. shipbuilding activities during WWI, including shots of torpedo boats and submarines.

Our Friend France (1917)

WWI   Air Force

The film showed the United States Army Air Corps and their involvement in France during WWI.

Our Job in Japan (1943)

WWII   Army

The 18-minute, black-and-white War Department film was produced to prepare U.S. soldiers for their tour of duty in the occupation of Japan after WWII.

Our Navy (1918)

WWI   Navy   12 reels

A two-color filter system added authenticity to the scenes of the Navy in action during WWI, including shipbuilding, repair and maintenance, the launching of torpedoes, and the preparation of decks for battle.

Our Time in Hell (1967)

WWII   Marines

The *Variety* reviewer criticized the film as being nothing more than a public relations plug for the Marines for which the 3-M Corporation, identified as a major contractor, paid. The critic observed that producer-director-writer Laurence Mascott's "usage of the often superb official films was sorely handicapped by the narrow limitations of his apparent recruiting poster (or appropriations committee) point of view and objective." In fact, *Our Time in Hell* captured very well the courage of the Marines as they staged their amphibious assaults on enemy-held islands, often suffering horrendous casualties. The film can also be considered an explanation for the need to use the atomic bomb, because it showed how Japanese soldiers and civilians committed suicide rather than surrender. (VTR: 03-29-67.)

Peleliu 1944—Horror in the Pacific (1991)

WWII   Marines

The film contained oral histories from the men (Company K, 3rd Battalion, 5th Marine Regiment) that fought for 28 days of unrelenting horror against the 10,000 Japanese troops who were dug into the caves of the island.

Pershing's Crusaders. See *America's Answer.*

Pistol Packin' Mama (1991)

WWII   Air Force

Five crew members of *Betty Boop/Pistol Packin' Mama*, a B-17 Flying Fortress, relate what it was like to fly daylight bombing missions over Europe during the early days of U.S. involvement in the air war.

P.O.W.—Americans in Enemy Hands: World War II, Korea, and Vietnam (1991)

WWII, Korea, Vietnam   All

Carol Fleisher fashioned a film that captures the experiences of nine prisoners of war, including capture, surrender, daily survival, torture, brainwashing, and homecomings. The stories made a strong, positive statement about America, its servicemen, and their families.

Prelude to War. See *Why We Fight.*

Proudly We Serve (1944)

WWII   Marines

The film illustrated the training of aerial gunners in the U.S. Marine Corps in WWII. Actors played the sergeants.

Radio Bikini (1987)

Cold War   DoD

In 1946 the United States tested atomic bombs on the island of Bikini, photographing the explosions and extent of destruction with more than 750 cameras. Using the Freedom of Information Act, documentary-maker Robert Stone obtained the footage and fashioned it to tell a story of science gone astray. Although originally thought to be harmless, the tests left the island uninhabitable for more than 40 years. The government films capture the sailors swimming in the warm waters surrounding Bikini, unaware that the radiation would cause the cancer that eventually claimed many of them. Although the government footage makes up over 90 percent of the documentary, the filmmaker also included interviews with the chief of the tribe that had to be relocated from the island and one of the sailors who developed cancer.

Radio Star—The AFN Story (1995)

WWII to the Present   DoD

This German documentary portrays the history of the U.S. Armed Forces Network, one of the branches of the Armed Forces Radio and Television Service. The film focused primarily on the effects of AFN on the German population in the two decades following WWII, including pop, rock, country music, and entertainment programs intended for American personnel. It described the continued popularity of the network during the Korean, Vietnam, and Gulf wars. It contained performance footage featuring stars such as Glenn Miller, Johnny Cash, and Judy Garland. (WV: 03-13-95.)

The Ramparts We Watch: *A Saga of Modern America* (1940)

WWI   All

The film shows how the United States reacted to World War I from 1914, through the U.S. declaration of war, to victory. The documentary includes scenes of U.S. industry converting to war and Assistant Secretary of the Navy Franklin Delano Roosevelt inspecting the front lines.

Reach for the Skies (1986)

WWII   Air Force, Navy

Virginia Bader produced this series of stories about air combat.

Regulus: *The First Nuclear Missile Submarines* (2002)

Cold War   Navy

The history of the Navy's Regulus Missile program described the development and deployment of the first U.S. nuclear missile submarines. Included interviews with Navy veterans.

Remember My Lai (TV) (1991)

Vietnam   Army

In 1968, American soldiers massacred over 500 men, women, and children in the Vietnamese hamlet of My Lai. PBS's *Frontline* aired the program, which explored the legacy of the men who were there and the Vietnamese survivors.

Report from the Aleutians **(1943)**

WWII   Army

John Huston directed this film that detailed the harsh conditions that U.S. soldiers faced when fighting the little-publicized war against Japan on the barren Alaskan islands. The Signal Corps filmed and MGM distributed it on behalf of the War Activities Committee of the motion picture industry.

The Return of Paul Jarrett **(1998)**

WWI   Army

Paul Jarrett enlisted in 1917 and earned a commission in the 42nd "Rainbow" Division, fighting in the major American battles in France. He was wounded three times and suffered from exposure to mustard gas. The documentary portrayed Jarret's return, with his grandson, to the battlefields of his youth.

Return to Iwo Jima **(1988)**

WWII   Marines

Gene Hackman narrated this reunion of American and Japanese veterans of the fight for Iwo Jima. The film contained interviews with Joe Rosenthal, the photographer of the Mt. Suribachi flag-raising, and Charles Lindberg, the sole survivor of the flag-raising, which became perhaps the most enduring image to come out of World War II.

Return with Honor **(1998)**

Vietnam   All

U.S. fighter pilots shot down over Vietnam and held as prisoners of war, including Everett Alvarez, John McCain, and James Stockdale, appeared in the film, recounting their experiences in the air and in the infamous "Hanoi Hilton." (DV: 10-26-98, NYT: 06-29-99.)

Riding the Tiger **(2000)**

Vietnam   All

The documentary included artistic visions of the war in Vietnam, the planes, armaments, and people and the voices of those involved, journalists, villagers, and soldiers, who speak to the viewer.

The Second World War in Colour **(1999)**

WWII   All

Actor John Thaw (Inspector Morse in PBS's Mystery series) narrated this British-made documentary containing three 60-minute episodes. It included portrayals of the battles between the American fleet and the German U-boats, the American invasion of Japanese-held islands, D-Day, the Holocaust, and Hiroshima.

The Secret KGB Sex Files (2001)

Cold War   Marines

Roger Moore hosted this documentary, which explained how the KGB used money and sex to gain U.S. secrets. Using KGB footage, it portrayed some of the compromised U.S. Marines who worked in security roles at our embassies.

Seized at Sea: *Situation Critical* (2000)

Vietnam   Marines

Forty Marines lost their lives six days after the end of the Vietnam War, as they attempted to rescue the crew of the U.S. merchant marine vessel *Mayaguez*, which the Cambodian Khmer Rouge had captured. The film used television network news footage and oral histories to tell the story of the failed mission.

The Selling of the Pentagon (TV) (1971)

Cold War   DoD

CBS produced this documentary examining how the Department of Defense conducted its public relations operations. It focused on three aspects of the Pentagon's activities: direct contacts with the public, DoD-produced films, and use of the commercial media. Ironically, the film said virtually nothing about the relationship between the film industry and the armed services. (The year before *60 Minutes* had done a segment on the assistance the Navy provided to *Tora! Tora! Tora!*) The documentary became controversial when it was revealed that the producers had "reconstructed" several of the interviews and taken statements out of context to support the goal of the program. Ultimately, television's freedom of expression was upheld after congressional hearings.

The Shores of Iwo Jima—Guadalcanal (1945)

WWII   Navy, Marines

The Office of War Information sponsored this portrayal of the amphibious invasion of Iwo Jima, including aerial bombing and rockets plus ground force action using flame throwers. United Artists distributed the documentary on behalf of the War Activities Committee of the Motion Picture Industry.

Smashing of the Reich (1962)

WWII   Army

Shown on a twin bill with *Kamikaze*, the film depicted the French Resistance helping to push the Germans out of Paris, the American–Soviet hookup at the Elbe River, and the liberation of the concentration camps. (WV: 10-03-62, NYT: 10-03-62.)

Soldier's Heart (1991)

WWII   Army

A WWII veteran returned to Normandy and talked on camera with other American and French veterans about the war that changed him forever.

Stillwell Road (1947)

WWII   Army

Described the crucial importance of the major supply road through the rugged mountains and jungles of Burma.

The Story of Cpl. Jolley (1945)

WWII   Army

A GI, who lost an arm during a Japanese aerial attack on Corregidor, narrated the story of the Bataan death march and the return of U.S. POWs to their families. This powerful firsthand account provided a portrayal of courage and endurance.

Submarine: Steel Boats, Iron Men (TV) (1989)

Cold War   Navy

Filmmakers were given a cruise aboard the nuclear-powered USS *Hyman G. Rickover* (SSN709) to obtain footage for this documentary, which also included discussions with retired submarine commanders and military experts about the strategy of underwater warfare.

Submarine Warfare (1945)

WWII   Navy

The film, in 53 minutes, detailed how submarine crews were fighting the war under the sea against Japan.

The Submariners (TV) (1958)

Peace   Navy

An "Omnibus" broadcast featuring Esther Williams and Alistair Cooke and shot on location at the Navy's New London, Connecticut, submarine base. Williams visited the submariners in their crowded quarters. Cooke visited the 112-foot water tank used for training men to escape from a sunken sub and the simulated docking of an underwater rescue craft to a crippled sub. (VTR: 11-12-58.)

Suicide Attack (1951)

WWII   Air Force

This documentary portrayed the war from the Japanese side with newsreel and combat footage. It included a small amount of footage of captured Doolittle raiders.

Surrender in the Pacific (1945)

WWII   All

Signal Corps black-and-white film showing the events in the Pacific at the end of the war, including U.S. troops occupying Tokyo and scenes from Hiroshima and Nagasaki as well as the surrender ceremony on the USS *Missouri*.

The 10,000 Day War (TV) (1980)

Vietnam   All

Journalist Peter Arnett wrote the narration for this comprehensive history of the American involvement in the Vietnam War, with reference to the French war in Indochina in the early 1950s. Ellsworth Bunker, Clark Clifford, William Colby, and John Ehrlichman appeared on the multipart series.

Theodore Roosevelt in the Great War (1930)

WWI   All

The film traced Theodore Roosevelt's concern before and during the U.S. participation in WWI. It included his visits to troops and soldiers visiting him at Sagamore Hill. The film also contained the victory celebration after the German surrender and TR's burial in Oyster Bay, New York.

They Drew Fire: Combat Artists of WWII (2000)

WWII   Army, Navy, Marines

Through oral history and archival footage, the film portrayed World War II combat artists and their representations of the war. Among other information, it explained that since all Marines are trained to fight, their combat artists were also considered combatants.

Thunderbolt (1947)

WWII   Air Force

Finally released two years after the end of the war, the documentary by directors John Sturges and William Wyler followed a fighter group based on Corsica to portray the P-47 Thunderbolt in aerial combat over Europe. Unlike most of the films about the war in the air that made combat seem glamorous, *Thunderbolt* illuminated the other side of the story, the youth of the pilots, the cold they experienced at altitude, and the real dangers they faced every day.

To the Shores of Iwo Jima (1945)

WWII   Marines

This 20-minute film, shot by Marine combat cameramen, depicted the Marine assault on Iwo Jima. Four lost their lives in the process, ten were wounded, and one was missing in action. The film's significance was not the portrayal of the battle but its emphasis on the nature of the fighting that American forces would be facing in subsequent battles. (NYT: 05-25 & 06-07-45.)

Torpedo Squadron (1942)

WWII   Navy

John Ford edited footage he took during the Battle of Midway into an eight-minute documentary showing the ill-fated fliers of the Torpedo Eight Squadron, aboard the USS *Hornet*, before they took off on their doomed mission. The planes reached their targets without fighter cover and the Japanese shot down all 15 planes, with only one pilot surviving. Although the Navy did not release the film for general distribution, Ford sent prints to each of the squadron members' families.

The True Glory (1945)

WWII   Office of War Information (US) and Ministry of Information (GB)

Compiled from footage shot by 1,400 cameramen, the 81-minute, black-and-white film presented the bravery of all who fought in the Allied armies in the European theater in WWII.

Tunisian Victory (1944)

WWII   Army

Directors John Huston and Frank Capra worked together to provide an in-depth look, in 77 minutes, at the planning and execution of the North African campaign by the Allies against the occupying German forces.

Turning Points of the Second World War (1990)

WWII   Navy, Air Force, Army

The filmmakers hypothesized that three battles significantly turned the tide of WWII: Midway, Stalingrad, and El Alamein. They made their case using footage from the battles.

24-Hour Alert (1955)

Cold War   Air Force

This short documentary looked at the objections citizens of a small town had to the intrusion of a nearby Air Force base on their lives. Made as a joint production by Walt Disney and Warner Brothers studios at the height of the Cold War, the film showed how the residents changed their attitude once they understood the role of SAC in keeping the peace. Jack Webb did the narration.

Uncle Sam Awake (1916)

WWI   Army, Navy

A preparedness film showing what the federal government was doing after the war started in Europe. It contained scenes of troops drilling at West Point, the Great Lakes Naval Training Station near Chicago, arsenals at Watervliet, New York, and a new kind of submarine.

The Uncounted Enemy: *A Vietnam Deception* (TV) (1982)

Vietnam   DoD

This 90-minute CBS documentary alleged that Gen. William Westmoreland, as commander of forces in Vietnam, had withheld information about the size of the North Vietnamese force in South Vietnam and so deceived the American people about the progress of the war. Westmoreland sued the network for libel, and *TV Guide* published a story that the TV report had violated the CBS News Standards. The controversy became one of the most bitter in television news history. In the end, Westmoreland dropped his suit after the trial had begun and CBS issued a statement saying the network had not intended to impugn the general's patriotism. Instead of contributing to the quality of TV documentaries, *The Uncounted Enemy* led to the decline of investigative journalism on television.

Under Four Flags. See *America's Answer*.

The United States Marine Band (1942)

WWII   Marines

The band and chorus performed music linked to the Marines while the images of various battle scenes and Washington, DC, monuments appeared on the screen.

The Unknown Soldier (1985)

WWII   All

Jason Robards, decorated veteran as well as a talented actor, narrated this tribute to the six representative profiles of WWII casualties. It included combat footage, personnel letters from those listed "Missing in Action," as well as interviews with family, friends, and fellow soldiers.

Unsung Heroes of Pearl Harbor (TV) (2001)

WWII   All

Historians, authors, and survivors of the Pearl Harbor attack described the little-known Americans who defended the island during the battle against the Japanese attackers on December 7, 1941.

Victory At Sea (TV) (1954)

WWII   Navy, Marines

NBC aired the 26, 30-minute programs that showed the battles in the Atlantic against the Germans and in the Pacific as, island by island, the United States advanced toward Japan. The filmmakers used combat footage from both Allied and enemy archives, as well as Richard Rogers's award-winning music to portray the drama of victory. The series was later edited into a 98-minute version, also featured on NBC.

Victory Through Air Power (1943)

WWII   Air Force, Navy

Disney produced this 68-minute, animated documentary based on the book by Major Alexander P. de Seversky to illustrate how air power was being used to defeat the Axis powers.

Vietnam (1972)

Vietnam   Air Force

Japanese-made film showing the war in the air from the North Vietnamese perspective. Although some of the scenes were apparently re-created, the movie did contain moving scenes of air raid victims and U.S. prisoners. (WV: 02-23-72.)

Vietnam: A Television History (TV) (1983)

Vietnam   All

PBS sponsored and aired the 13-part documentary series on the Vietnam War, combining oral interviews with archival footage to provide an in-depth history. Stanley Karnow, chief correspondent for the series, wrote the companion volume, *Vietnam: A History*, which remains one of the best sources of information about the war.

Vietnam Home Movies: Front-Line and Infantry Action (1990)

Vietnam   Army

The documentary used 8mm film shot by soldiers while on duty in country to create this video. *Variety* labeled the soldiers "natural historians and storytellers." Despite the title, most of the scenes were shot after combat had ended. Nevertheless, the images reveal what it must have been like living under fire. (VTR: 09-03-90.)

Vietnam! Vietnam! (1971)

Vietnam   All

Reputedly directed by John Ford for the U.S. Information Agency, this "documentary" imitated earlier government propaganda films of the 1940s and 1950s, taking a hard line against the communist North Vietnamese to justify U.S. involvement in Southeast Asia. The result was so extreme that the State Department directed the USIA not to release it. Debate still exists about the extent of Ford's actual contribution.

War Comes to America. See Why We Fight.

War Dogs: America's Forgotten Heroes (1999)

Vietnam   Army, Air Force

The documentary focused on the dogs MPs used for base security and other protective details in Vietnam. At the end of the war, the dogs were destroyed or simply left behind. In March 1984, the Air Force was appointed the executive agency for all military working dog matters throughout DoD. As a result, the U.S. no longer destroys dogs or leaves them behind.

War on Our Shores (1990)

WWII   Navy

German submarines (U-boats) worked off the East Coast of the United States during WWII, sinking U.S. and Allied merchant ships. In this film, German and American survivors told their stories about this warfare.

We Are the Marines (1942)

WWII   Marines

With full cooperation of the Marines and the camera work of staff from **The March of Time**, the movie served as a primer about the Marine Corps: their traditions, their training, their idiosyncrasies, and their battle accomplishments. Produced and directed by Louis de Rochemont, the film included a simulated attack featuring Marines who eventually landed on the Solomon Islands. *Weekly Variety* said, "It's a cinch to gain plenty of Marine recruits." (WV: 12-09-42, NYT: 12-14-42.)

Why Korea? (1951)

Korea   Army

Twentieth Century Fox used newsreel clips covering the Japanese invasion of Manchuria in 1931, Italy's attack on Ethiopia, Russia's aggression in Finland, and Germany's invasion of Poland to drive the point home: aggression unchecked places all free nations at risk.

Why Vietnam? (1965)

Vietnam   All

Intended to imitate Capra's WWII Why We Fight series. The military used the film for indoctrinating the troops during basic training. It purported to explain the history of the American involvement in Southeast Asia, with the "Domino Theory" being the central justification for the current war. The DoD filmmakers included comments by President Johnson justifying the conflict, despite earlier assuring the American people he would not send American soldiers 10,000 miles to fight. Those who supported the war embraced the film. Those opposing the war rejected its message. It was released overseas in U.S. Information Agency libraries and cultural offices. John Wayne incorporated the message into **The Green Berets** (see chapter 1).

The Why We Fight Series (1942–1945)

WWII   All

Army Chief of Staff Gen. George Marshall recognized the need to explain to new inductees into the armed services why they had to give up civilian life, go off to the far corners of the world, and perhaps die. At the beginning of the war, perhaps as many as 50 percent of young men could not read, so Marshall rejected the idea of providing them with books during basic training. Instead, he brought Frank Capra, then one of Hollywood's leading directors, into the Army and directed him to make a film series to indoctrinate the future soldiers with the need to fight Germany, Italy, and

Japan. While the series clearly contained a propaganda message, the term "propaganda" itself was not a pejorative in that context, and the series performed the necessary task of preparing young men to go to war. Although the Army intended the films to be shown only to men during basic training, the government ultimately distributed them to the public. The series included the following:

Prelude to War (1942)
The Nazi Strike (1942)
Divide and Conquer (1943)
The Battle of Britain (1943)
The Battle of Russia (1943)
The Battle of China (1944)
War Comes to America (1945)

Winter Soldier (1972)

Vietnam   All

A panel of Vietnam-era vets discussed in front of an audience and the camera their opposition to the war, describing their previous actions while in Vietnam, including the killing of civilians and torturing of prisoners.

With the Marines at Tarawa (1944)

WWII   Marines, Navy

Fifteen Marine combat cameramen, two of whom were killed, captured the images of the assaults shown in this documentary, edited at the Warner Brothers Studio and distributed by Universal under the auspices of the War Activities Committee of the motion picture industry. Some of the combat footage had also appeared earlier in newsreels and was to appear later in *Sands of Iwo Jima*. The film captured the desperate situation of the Marines as they were pinned at the seawall. It then portrayed their advance across the island and their ultimate victory. It received the Oscar for best documentary. (NYT: 03-03-44.)

With the Marines: Chosin to Hungnam (1951)

Korea   Marines

The documentary portrayed the Marine evacuation from Hungnam following the Chinese entry into the Korean War after U.S. forces had advanced to the Yalu River in December 1950. President Harry Truman decided not to escalate the war by using atomic weapons to stop the Chinese advance, a step many military men advocated. President-elect Dwight D. Eisenhower threatened to do so in order to pressure the North Koreans and Chinese to accept a truce, which happened soon after he entered the White House.

The World at War (1942)

WWII   Army

The film opened with the Japanese attack on Pearl Harbor and then used newsreel footage to cover the decade leading up to December 7, 1941. The U.S. Office of War Information produced and the War Activities Committee of the motion picture industry arranged distribution. (WV: 09-02-42, NYT: 09-04-42.)

The World at War **(TV) (1974)**

WWII   All

One of the most famous documentary miniseries, with more than 20 episodes. Very accurate and informative as it revealed the events in the 1920s that laid the foundation for WWII, then continued through the war's battles and into the Cold War in the 1950s.

World War I **(TV) (1964)**

WWI   All

CBS produced and broadcast this multipart series depicting the U.S. involvement in WWI. (VTR: 09-30-64.)

World War II: GI Diary **(TV) (1978)**

WWII   All

Time-Life TV supplied what was intended to be a new series for syndication. Lloyd Bridges provided narration and the Pentagon's film files provided beautiful footage, some of it in color. This first episode followed a B-29 attack on Tokyo and included scenes of daily life among the bomber crews. (VTR: 09-27-78.)

The Yanks Are Coming **(TV) (1963)**

WWI   Army

David Wolper produced and ABC broadcast this documentary that portrayed the U.S. role in the great battles of WWI after the nation entered the war in April 1917.

Films with Unseen Military Assistance

On nonmilitary projects, filmmakers have occasionally turned to the armed services for limited co-operation when they could not obtain locations, men, equipment, or advice from private industry. In each film listed, the military provided the needed assistance without being cinematically identified and in some cases without screen credit.

Batman and Robin (1997)

Peace	Army	Ltd	Color	130 mins
WB	WV: 06-16-97		NYT: 06-20-97	

DIR: Joel Schumacher. SW: Akiva Goldsman. PRO: Peter MacGregor-Scott. STARS: George Clooney, Arnold Schwarzenegger, Chris O'Donnell, Uma Thurman.

Filmmakers used an Army wind tunnel in Dayton, Ohio, to create the images of the caped duo swinging through the air.

The Birth of a Nation (1915)

Civil War	Army	Ltd	B&W	159 mins
Epoch	WV: 03-12-15		NYT: 03-04-15	

DIR: D. W. Griffith. SW: Thomas Dixon. PRO: D. W. Griffith. STARS: Lillian Gish, Mae Marsh, Henry Walthall, Miriam Cooper.

The first great epic film portraying the Civil War and its aftermath. The Army provided Griffith with a few old artillery pieces from West Point and some technical advice on how to re-create Civil War battles.

Hello, Dolly! (1969)

Peace	Army	Ltd	Color	129 mins
Fox	WV: 12-24-69		NYT: 12-18-69	

DIR: Gene Kelly. SW: Ernest Lehman, Michael Stewart. PRO: Ernest Lehman. STARS: Barbra Streisand, Walter Matthau, Michael Crawford, Louis Armstrong.

The Military Academy permitted filmmakers to build their wedding chapel on the Academy grounds overlooking the Hudson River.

Licence to Kill (1989)

| Cold War | Army (NG) | Cour | Color | 133 mins |
| UA/EON | WV: 06-14-89 | | NYT: 07-14-89 | |

DIR: John Glen. SW: Michael Wilson, Richard Maibaum. PRO: Albert R. Broccoli, Michael Wilson. STARS: Timothy Dalton, Carey Lowell, Robert Davi, Talisa Soto.

The Florida National Guard gave some help but insisted that no credit be given or military marking be shown on any personnel and equipment.

March or Die (1977)

| French Colonial | Marines | Cour | Color | 106 mins |
| Columbia | WV: 08-03-77 | | NYT: 08-06-77 | |

DIR: Dick Richards. SW: David Goodman. PRO: Dick Richards, Jerry Bruckheimer, Lew Grade. STARS: Gene Hackman, Terence Hill, Max Von Sydow, Catherine Deneuve.

Off-duty Marines from the embassy in Morocco portray foreign legionnaires.

Master and Commander: The Far Side of the World (2003)

| Napoleonic | Navy | Info | Color | 138 mins |
| Fox | WV: 11-03-2003 | | NYT: 11-14-2003 | |

DIR: Peter Weir. SW: John Collee, Peter Weir. PRO: Samuel Goldwyn Jr., Duncan Henderson, Peter Weir. STARS: Russell Crowe, Paul Bettany, James D'Arcy, Edward Woodall.

The U.S. Navy permitted the filmmakers to take laser measurements and photographs of the USS *Constitution*, the service's oldest commissioned ship. They used the information to build a replica of the *Constitution*. The cinematic ship then appeared in the movie as a French privateer, although such a ship would not most likely have been built along the lines of a U.S. 44-gun frigate.

Old Ironsides (1926)

| Revolutionary | Navy | Info | B&W | 117 mins |
| Paramount | WV: 12-08-26 | | NYT: 12-07-26 | |

DIR: James Cruze. SW: Dorothy Arzner, Walter Woods, Harry Carr, Rupert Hughes. PRO: James Cruze, B. P. Schulberg. STARS: Wallace Beery, Esther Ralston, George Bancroft, Charles Farrell, George Godfrey.

The Navy provided the original blueprints of the USS *Constitution* to help the filmmakers build a replica of "Old Ironsides" on the hull of an old sailing ship that the studio had blown up as part of the attack on Tripoli. The secretary of the Navy and other senior Navy officials attended the New York City opening of this very patriotic film. During the intermission the secretary spoke and unveiled a painting of the USS *Constitution*, prints of which were used to raise funds for the restoration of the ship.

Pursuit of the Graf Spee **(1956)**

WWII	Navy	Ltd	Color	119 mins
Rank	WV: 11-14-56		NYT: 12-27-57	

DIR: Michael Powell, Emeric Pressburger. SW: Michael Powell, Emeric Pressburger. PRO: Michael Powell, Emeric Pressburger. STARS: John Gregson, Anthony Quayle, Peter Finch, Ian Hunter.

The U.S. Navy provided the cruiser USS *Salem* to portray the *Graf Spee* even though all regulations relating to assistance say that American men and equipment cannot masquerade as the enemy. The movie is also known as ***The Battle of the River Plate***.

The Sound of Music **(1965)**

WWII	Navy	Cour	Color	174 mins
Fox	WV: 03-03-65		NYT: 03-03-65	

DIR: Robert Wise. SW: Ernest Lehman. PRO: Robert Wise. STARS: Julie Andrews, Christopher Plummer, Eleanor Parker**,** Peggy Wood.

The filmmakers requested that the Navy provide a sailor who could teach Plummer how to blow a bosun's whistle.

Tomorrow Never Dies **(1997)**

Peace	Air Force	Full	Color	119 mins
MGM	WV: 12-15-97		NYT: DNR	

DIR: Roger Spottiswoode. SW: Bruce Feirstein. PRO: Michael G. Wilson, Barbara Broccoli. STARS: Pierce Brosnan, Jonathan Pryce, Michelle Yeoh.

For this James Bond film, the Air Force permitted Brosnan to make a halo (high altitude/low opening) jump on a U.S. air base in England, but there is no indication of the military's involvement.

20,000 Leagues Under the Sea **(1954)**

SciFi	Navy	Full	Color	127 mins
Disney	WV: 12-15-54		NYT: 12-24-54	

DIR: Richard Fleischer. SW: Earl Felton. PRO: [Walt Disney]. STARS: Kirk Douglas, James Mason, Peter Lorre, Paul Lukas.

The Navy provided a submarine on which the set designer created the superstructure of the mythical *Nautilus* so that the filmmakers could take shots of Captain Nemo's submarine submerging and surfacing. Navy frogmen also served as lifeguards during filming of underwater scenes.

Films Considered but Deemed Ineligible

CRITERIA

This is a representative sampling of the films the authors considered but did not include in chapter 1. For each film listed below, we have provided a brief explanation. We believe this short listing will help readers to understand better the scope and intent of our study.

About Face **(1952)**

Action set at a Southern military academy and no active-duty Army personnel appear.

Act of Violence **(1948)**

Although Robert Ryan is seeking to kill a fellow former POW for informing the German commandant of an impending stalag escape, the escape is presented only through sounds on a dark screen, and the POWs are never seen.

Air America **(1990)**

The film portrays the air arm of the CIA as it operated in Laos during the Vietnam War. Despite the agency's involvement in the conflict over the border, no active duty U.S. military men appear on screen—at least not in uniform.

All Quiet on the Western Front **(1930)**

Although a film classic, all the characters are Germans and the American military does not appear. Delbert Mann's 1979 made-for-television version does not appear in chapter 2 for the same reason.

Assault at West Point: The Court-Martial of Johnson Whittaker **(Cable) (1994)**

The story of the first Afro-American cadet at the U.S. Military Academy. It takes place in the late nineteenth century. Filming occurred at the Virginia Military Academy in Lexington, Virginia, not at West Point, New York.

Black Jack a.k.a. *Wild in the Sky* (1973)

This comedy went through several titles before its release. At the heart of its satiric mess, three anti-war radicals hijack a B-52 bomber loaded with nuclear weapons. Filmmakers could not decide whether they were making a spoof of the military or a simple thriller; will the activists succeed in bombing Fort Knox? In any case, there is no actual military presence.

The Blue Max (1966)

A story of World War I in the air from the German perspective. Although a Hollywood film, it contains no American military portrayal.

Bomber's Moon (1943)

A routine melodrama about the escape of a Russian nurse and an American flier from a German prison camp and their journey to England. Although George Montgomery plays an American bomber pilot, he is flying for the RAF when he is shot down along with his navigator brother. The U.S. military does not appear in the movie.

Braddɔck: Missing in Action III (1988)

Chuck Norris returns to Vietnam to find his Asian wife and 12-year-old son, but the war is long over and the U.S. military is nowhere to be seen.

Brother Rat (1938)

Action set at the Virginia Military Academy and no active-duty Army personnel appear.

Buffalo Soldiers (TV) (1993)

Unlike the 2001 *Buffalo Soldiers*, this TV film does focus on the real buffalo soldiers, the all-black U.S. Cavalry Troop H that patrolled the Western territories in the years after the Civil War to safeguard settlers against Indian attacks. It portrays the racial tensions between the white and black soldiers. The title is not included because the action took place before 1898.

Captains of the Clouds (1942)

Americans Jimmy Cagney and his buddies join the Canadian air force and fight the Germans. U.S. military does not appear in the film.

The Clock (1945)

Robert Walker plays a soldier on a two-day pass in New York City, where he meets, courts, and weds Judy Garland. He is in uniform, but the film has no other images of the Army or the military in action.

Corvette K-225   1943

Although Universal made the film and Randolph Scott starred, it portrayed the Canadian Navy and one of its small escort ships.

The Crazy World of Julius Vrodder (1974)

A Vietnam vet makes his home in an underground dugout on the grounds of the local VA hospital. The comedy has no flashbacks to Vietnam or military presence. Moreover, VA hospitals are part of the Department of Veterans Affairs, not the Department of Defense.

The Day After (TV) (1983)

Done on the cheap, this doomsday story looks at how the residents of a small Kansas town deal with a nuclear holocaust, but the film contains no military presence.

Delta Force One: The Lost Patrol (1999)

Despite the title, the "soldiers" in this incomprehensible film are not active duty members of the U.S. Army but civilians recruited to rescue a peacekeeping force from a ruthless international arms dealer.

The Desert Fox (1951)

This classic film depicts Rommel's North African campaign against the British. Only Germans and British forces appear in the film, which provides a positive image of the Nazi general.

Desperate Journey (1952)

Errol Flynn plays an RAF pilot leading his downed crew through enemy territory back to England. Ronald Reagan played an American but was serving in the British Air Force.

Donovan's Reef (1963)

John Wayne plays a Navy destroyer hero who has settled on a South Seas island after WWII. The U.S. military does not appear.

Dumbarton Bridge (1999)

In this poorly acted film, an inarticulate Vietnam vet is confronted with the daughter he fathered and then abandoned while he served in country. No images of the military or combat are depicted.

Eagle and the Hawk (1933)

Although made in Hollywood, this antiwar film features British flyers in the Royal Flying Corps. The eagle squadron Americans fly for the RAF.

Fail Safe (TV) (2000)

A remake of the 1964 melodrama about a U.S. bomber accidentally ordered to attack Moscow. Although it used virtually the same script as the original, the program was broadcast live and so is not a motion picture.

Five Gates to Hell (1959)

Chinese mercenaries capture American nurses who suffer throughout their captivity. However, no U.S. troops come to the rescue.

Flying Ace (1926)

A black flier and WWI ace, now a railroad investigator, comes to a small Florida town to solve the mystery of a missing payroll. He fights the bad guys on the ground and in the air winning the girl. Although he arrives wearing his uniform and a newspaper article describes his wartime heroics, the pilot's plane is his own, not the Army's, and the film contains no military presence.

Flying Cadets (1941)

The story of a nonmilitary school that trains new pilots before Pearl Harbor—with no portrayal of the U.S. Air Force.

Flying Fortress (1942)

Although the B-17 Flying Fortress was an American bomber, a British crew flew the plane for the RAF.

Gettysburg (1993)

The Department of Interior's National Park Service provided assistance for this film set in the 1860s. Civil War reenactors appear as the troops.

Give Me a Sailor (1938)

Navy brothers pursue sisters. The whole story takes place on shore leave, with no images of ships or Navy activities.

Gods and Generals (2003)

As with *Gettysburg*, the Department of Interior provided assistance for this film set in the 1860s. Civil War reenactors appear as the troops.

The Guns of Navarone (1961)

The commando team sent to destroy the guns is British and Greek, with no American characters present.

Hail, Hero! (1969)

Michael Douglas, a pacifist, enlists in the Army to seek respect from his father and returns to the family ranch to tell his parents he will be shipping out to Vietnam. The film just shows the visit, not the soldier's life in the military. Notable only as Douglas's first screen appearance.

Hearts of Darkness (Cable) (1991)

Eleanor Coppola created this documentary for Showtime to portray her husband's struggle to make *Apocalypse Now* (see chapter 1). Although the movie was set in Vietnam, her images of the American military and the war came secondhand through excerpts from the feature film, so the documentary does not qualify as a portrayal of the Army or its activities in the war.

Hell and High Water (1954)

In this Cold War espionage film, Richard Widmark captains a private submarine with no connection to the U.S. Navy.

Hell's Angels (1930)

Howard Hughes directed and produced this self-indulgent epic about two brothers who flew for the RAF during World War I. Film has spectacular aerial scenes but no American military presence.

Her Sister's Secret (1946)

A Naval officer has a one-night stand with a girl he met during Mardi Gras and a planned second meeting does not take place because he receives early orders for overseas deployment. The girl gives the product of the tryst to her sister and several years pass before the officer finds her and all ends happily. The film has no portrayal of the officer in action.

The Hill (1965)

The movie portrayed a British Middle Eastern military prison and the punishment inflicted on its inmates.

It's a Wonderful Life (1946)

The classic Frank Capra film about Jimmy Stewart's search for self-worth contains only a few fleeting seconds of combat lifted from newsreels and a brief montage of home front scenes, including a draft board session. It also illustrates how the absence of a technical advisor can create mistakes. In the film, Stewart's brother receives the "Congressional" Medal of Honor, rather than the Medal of Honor.

I Won't Play (1944)

Joe Fingers claims to be a musician but will not play for his fellow Marines on a Pacific island until an entertainer arrives. Although the film won an Oscar for best short, at 18 minutes, it did not qualify as a feature film or even as a docudrama.

Lafayette Escadrille (1958)

Supposedly based in large part on the life of William Wellman, who flew in the Lafayette Escadrille and directed this movie. His son portrays him in the movie. Although the fliers were Americans, they flew in the French army, and the American military did not appear.

Last Flight Out (TV) (1990)

The TV film portrays the last chaotic days before the North Vietnamese army arrived in Saigon. By then the last American forces had departed, and there is no U.S. military presence in the film. Nor does the brief TV news footage of the final evacuation qualify as a cinematic portrayal of the military in action.

The Last Plane Out (1983)

Based on the experiences of journalist Jack Cox, who produced this film, which is set in Nicaragua during the last days of Somoza's regime. No American military presence.

Legends of the Fall (1994)

Three American brothers fight in World War I, but for the Canadian Army.

Megaforce (1982)

A future special forces unit travels the world eliminating evil, in this case a third-rate dictator. Film has no portrayals of the contemporary U.S. military.

Medal of Honor Rag (TV) (1982)

A Vietnam War Medal of Honor recipient has a difficult readjustment to civilian life and seeks help from a psychiatrist. No portrayals of the military in combat in country.

Miracle in the Rain (1956)

Van Johnson, a lonely soldier on leave in New York, meets Jane Wyman and they naturally fall in love. However, except for Johnson's uniform, the film has no military component.

My Old Man's Place a.k.a. Glory Boy (1972)

Michael Moriarty plays a Vietnam vet who returns home with two Army buddies, and trouble follows. No flashbacks to Vietnam and so no portrayals of the military in action.

No Leave, No Love (1946)

Van Johnson and Keenan Wynn are two discharged Marines in this unfunny comedy that has nothing to do with the war.

Oh! What a Lovely War (1969)

Set in WWI, the film contains only British and European characters.

Paths of Glory (1957)

Stanley Kubrick directed and Kirk Douglas appeared on screen. The characters are members of the French military, and no American military were included.

A Prize of Gold (1955)

Although Richard Widmark plays an American sergeant in occupied Berlin, the movie portrays his effort to hijack a gold shipment and his uniform is the only real connection to the U.S. Army.

The Purple Plain (1954)

Gregory Peck plays an RAF pilot in the Burma theater, with no American military presence.

Raid on Rommel (1971)

Film contained only British characters and recycled footage from earlier British commando raids, most particularly *Tobruk*.

Regret to Inform (1998)

Vietnam War widow Barbara Sonneborn made this documentary about the losses that she, other war widows, and the Vietnamese people suffered during the war. It does not deal with the military aspects of the conflict and contains no images of the American military.

Reunion in France (1942)

American flier John Wayne plays an RAF pilot shot down over France, but film has no American military presence.

Riders of the Storm (1986)

A World War II B-29 Super Fortress becomes the airborne home of seven Vietnam vets who fly endlessly (without landing—don't ask), beaming down antiwar dissent, jamming the airwaves. Occasionally included in the material are TV news reports from Vietnam, but the film in no way portrays the U.S. military either in Vietnam or after. Perhaps the most memorable scene occurs when, sweeping low over a city, the B-29 extends a rope ladder down to pick up a guest, waiting on the roof of a skyscraper. The next shot shows him climbing the ladder. The final shot in the montage shows a helicopter towing the ladder. In fact, the B-29 in flight is real and one of the few remaining ones in flying condition.

Rocket's Red Glare (2000)

A Vietnam vet is forced into the criminal world to support his handicapped brother. The film has no flashbacks to Vietnam or the military in action.

A Romance of the Air (1918)

The American characters flew for France's Lafayette Escadrille, and no American servicemen appear.

Sea Devils (1937)

Victor McLaglen and Preston Foster are rivals in the Coast Guard. Film shows the service's peacetime missions.

Secret Invasion (1964)

A British *Dirty Dozen* with no U.S. military presence.

Starship Troopers (1997)

The movie portrays future Marines, with no connection to the contemporary, or historical, service.

Submarine X-1 **(1968)**

A British captain loses his sub to a German ship and returns to fight the enemy with minisubs. Film has no U.S. military presence.

Tearing Down the Spanish Flag **(1898)**

Early propaganda film contained no actual people, just a hand tearing down the Spanish flag and had no U.S. military presence.

Thunderball **(1965)**

The parachuting of scuba divers into the ocean off Miami Beach, a Coast Guard helicopter rescuing James Bond, a destroyer pursuing SPECTRE's number 2 man Largo, and a credit to the U.S. Air Force all suggest that the American military appears in the fourth Bond movie. However, neither the dialogue nor visual images identify the frogmen or the warship as being from the Navy and the credits do not thank the service. The Coast Guard was a part of the Treasury Department; nowhere does the film identify Air Force men or equipment.

Tobruk **(1967)**

A 90-man British commando unit sets out to destroy Gen. Rommel's fuel depots near Tobruk. Although the film was shot in California with assistance of the 40th Armored Division of the California National Guard, its tanks masquerade as German and British tanks and the operation remains purely British, with no U.S. military contribution.

Two Girls and a Sailor **(1944)**

While on shore leave, the sailor helps the two girls set up a service canteen; no scenes of the Navy in action.

A Vestige of Honor **(TV) (1990)**

A former Green Beret struggles to keep a promise to aid a group of Montagnards trapped in Thailand following the war. The film does not harken back to the U.S. military in Vietnam.

Voodo **(1933)**

During the U.S. occupation of Haiti in 1925, a Marine sergeant befriended the natives on a nearby island who named him their king. After three years, he returned to the United States and made this documentary. The film focuses on how he ruled his subjects, not on his military career.

Week-end at the Waldorf **(1945)**

Van Johnson is on leave in New York in this musical comedy that has no military presence except his uniform.

A Wave, a WAC, and a Marine **(1944)**

Two girls and a guy make a movie in the two weeks before they join their respective services.

Warbirds (1988)

An Air Force general appears throughout the movie, and American pilots fly the F-16 jets against rebels in a small Middle Eastern country. However, the CIA recruits the men for the top-secret mission, and no U.S. military forces appear in action. In fact, the film is so bad, it probably does not even deserve this entry.

Which Way to the Front (1970)

Jerry Lewis stars as a 4-F billionaire who forms a private force of 4-F friends to fight Hitler.

Without Reservations (1946)

Action takes place on a cross-country rail trip when Marine flier John Wayne meets Claudette Colbert, a novelist headed to Hollywood to bring her book to the screen. Although Wayne and his buddy are in uniform, there is no portrayal of Marines in action, except for Wayne's falling in love with Colbert.

A Yank in the RAF (1941)

American flier Tyrone Power joins the RAF, but the film has no U.S. military presence.

Films Chronologically by Service

AIR FORCE

1911	*The Military Air Scout*
1927	*Wings*
1930	*Young Eagles*
1932	*Sky Devils*
1933	*Ace of Aces*
	Captured
	Hell Below
1934	*Crimson Romance*
1938	*Clipped Wings*
	Flight to Fame
	Men with Wings
	Test Pilot
1939	*The Story of Vernon and Irene Castle*
1941	*I Wanted Wings*
	Keep 'Em Flying
1942	*Flight Lieutenant*
	Flying Tigers
	Thunder Birds
	Wings for the Eagle
1943	*Adventures in Iraq*
	Aerial Gunner
	Air Force
	Bombardier
	A Guy Named Joe
	Pilot No. 5
	The Purple V
	The Sky's the Limit
	Stage Door Canteen
	Wings Over the Pacific

1944	*Hollywood Canteen*
	Ladies Courageous
	The Purple Heart
	Thirty Seconds Over Tokyo
	Till We Meet Again
	Winged Victory
1945	*Captain Eddie*
	God Is My Co-Pilot
	You Came Along
	China's Little Devils
1946	*Bamboo Blonde*
	The Best Years of Our Lives
1947	*The Beginning or the End*
1948	*Command Decision*
	Fighter Squadron
	Jungle Patrol
1949	*Twelve O'Clock High*
1950	*The Big Lift*
	Chain Lightning
	Operation Haylift
	When Willie Comes Marching Home
1951	*Air Cadet*
	Starlift
	Target Unknown
	The Thing
	The Wild Blue Yonder
1952	*Above and Beyond*
	The Devil Makes Three
	Invasion USA
	Thunderbirds
1953	*Clipped Wings*
	Fighter Attack
	Flight Nurse
	Island in the Sky
	Mission Over Korea
	Sabre Jet
	Sky Commando
	Stalag 17
	The War of the Worlds
1954	*Dragonfly Squadron*
	The Glenn Miller Story
1955	*Air Strike*
	The Court Martial of Billy Mitchell
	Hell's Horizon
	The McConnell Story
	Strategic Air Command
	Target Zero
1956	*Battle Hymn*
	Earth vs. the Flying Saucers

	On the Threshold of Space
	Toward the Unknown
1957	*Bailout at 43,000*
	Beginning of the End
	Bombers B-52
	The Deadly Mantis
	Jet Pilot
	Sayonara
	The Spirit of St. Louis
1958	*China Doll*
	The Hunters
	Jet Attack
	The Lost Missile
	No Time for Sergeants
	Thundering Jets
1959	*Here Come the Jets*
	It Started with a Kiss
	The Mouse That Roared
	Plan Nine from Outer Space
	A Stranger in My Arms
1961	*X-15*
1962	*Moon Pilot*
	The War Lover
1963	*A Gathering of Eagles*
1964	*Dr. Strangelove*
	Fail Safe
	Flight from Ashiya
	Kissin' Cousins
	The Starfighters
	36 Hours
1965	*McHale's Navy Joins the Air Force*
	Situation Hopeless . . . But Not Serious
1966	*Not with My Wife, You Don't*
	The Russians Are Coming, the Russians Are Coming
1968	*Bamboo Saucer*
	Battle Beneath the Earth
1969	*The Thousand Plane Raid*
1970	*Catch-22*
	The Forbin Project
	Suppose They Gave a War and Nobody Came
	Tora! Tora! Tora!
1971	*The Andromeda Strain*
1974	*Airport 75*
1976	*King Kong*
1977	*Close Encounters of the Third Kind*
	Rolling Thunder
	Twilight's Last Gleaming
1979	*Hanover Street*
1982	*Firefox*

1983	*Never Say Never Again*
	The Right Stuff
	WarGames
1984	*Brady's Escape*
	Red Dawn
	Starman
1985	*Cocoon*
1986	*Iron Eagle*
	The Manhattan Project
	Opposing Force
1987	*Amazing Grace and Chuck*
	Captive Hearts
	Good Morning, Vietnam
	The Hanoi Hilton
	Project X
1988	*Bat-21*
	Ernest Saves Christmas
	Iron Eagle 2
	Judgment in Berlin
	The Presidio
1989	*Jacknife*
	Welcome Home
1990	*Fire Birds*
	Memphis Belle
1991	*Final Approach*
	For the Boys
	Toy Soldiers
1992	*Into the Sun*
1993	*In the Line of Fire*
1994	*The Client*
1995	*Apollo 13*
	The Net
1996	*Broken Arrow*
	Fly Away Home
	Independence Day
	Larger Than Life
	Mars Attacks!
	Star Trek: First Contact
1997	*Air Force One*
	Tomorrow Never Dies
1998	*Armageddon*
	Godzilla
2000	*The Perfect Storm*
	Stealth Fighter
	Thirteen Days
2001	*Pearl Harbor*
2002	*Race to Space*
2003	*The Core*
	Terminator 3: Rise of the Machines

ARMY

1914	*Classmates*
1915	*Battle Cry of Peace*
	Via Wireless
1916	*Lieutenant Danny, U.S.A.*
1917	*The Man Who Was Afraid*
	Over There
	A Trooper of Troop K
	Womanhood, the Glory of the Nation
1918	*Draft 258*
	Hearts of the World
	Johanna Enlists
	Lafayette, We Come
	Over the Top
	Shoulder Arms
	Why America Will Win
1919	*The Fighting Roosevelts*
	The Lost Battalion
1923	*Quicksands*
1924	*America*
	Classmates
1925	*The Big Parade*
1926	*Behind the Front*
	The Flying Torpedo
	Her Man o'War
	The Unknown Soldier
1927	*Dress Parade*
	The Patent Leather Kid
	The Rough Riders
1928	*Buck Privates*
	Four Sons
	West Point
1929	*Blockade*
	Marianne
	She Goes to War
1930	*Anybody's War*
	Dough Boys
	Half Shot at Sunrise
	A Man from Wyoming
	War Nurse
1931	*Beyond Victory*
1932	*Pack Up Your Troubles*
1933	*Private Jones*
1934	*Flirtation Walk*
	Keep 'Em Rolling
1935	*West Point of the Air*
1937	*Sergeant Murphy*
	They Gave Him a Gun

1938	*Army Girl*
	Block-Heads
	Duke of West Point
	Flight to Fame
	The Invisible Menace
	Touchdown Army
1939	*Geronimo*
	Pack Up Your Troubles
	Panama Patrol
	The Real Glory
1940	*The Fighting 69th*
1941	*Buck Privates*
	The Bugle Sounds
	Cadet Girl
	Caught in the Draft
	Parachute Battalion
	Sergeant York
	Tanks a Million
	Top Sergeant Mulligan
	West Point Widow
	You're in the Army Now
1942	*About Face*
	Across the Pacific
	Army Surgeon
	For Me and My Gal
	Lucky Jordan
	Parachute Nurse
	Pride of the Army
	Private Buckaroo
	Remember Pearl Harbor
	She's in the Army
	Ten Gentlemen from West Point
	Top Sergeant
	True to the Army
	Two Yanks in Trinidad
	War Dogs
	The Yanks Are Coming
1943	*Bataan*
	Corregidor
	Cry Havoc
	The Human Comedy
	The Iron Major
	Marching On
	Rookies in Burma
	Sahara
	So Proudly We Hail
	Stage Door Canteen
	This Is the Army
	Thousands Cheer
	Yanks Ahoy

1944	*The Eve of St. Mark*
	Four Jills in a Jeep
	Hey, Rookie
	Hollywood Canteen
	In the Meantime, Darling
	Marine Raiders
	Mr. Winkle Goes to War
	See Here, Private Hargrove
	Something for the Boys
	Sunday Dinner for a Soldier
	There's Something About a Soldier
	Up in Arms
	The Very Thought of You
	Welcome, Mr. Washington
1945	*Back to Bataan*
	A Bell for Adano
	First Yank into Tokyo
	I Live in Grosvenor Square
	Keep Your Powder Dry
	Objective, Burma!
	Sergeant Mike
	The Story of G.I. Joe
	They Were Expendable
	Tokyo Rose
	A Walk in the Sun
	What Next, Corporal Hargrove?
1946	*The Best Years of Our Lives*
	The Courage of Lassie
	Little Mister Jim
1947	*The Beginning or the End*
	Buck Privates Come Home
	Courage of Lassie
	The Spirit of West Point
1948	*Beyond Glory*
	Homecoming
	The Search
1949	*Battleground*
	Francis
	Home of the Brave
	I Was a Male War Bride
	Tokyo Joe
1950	*At War with the Army*
	Breakthrough
	The Men
	The West Point Story
1951	*Bright Victory*
	Call Me Mister
	The Day the Earth Stood Still
	Decision Before Dawn
	Fixed Bayonets

Force of Arms
Four in a Jeep
G.I. Jane
Go for Broke
I Was an American Spy
Korea Patrol
Starlift
Steel Helmet
The Tanks Are Coming
Teresa
Up Front
A Yank in Korea

1952   *Back at the Front*
Because You're Mine
Eight Iron Men
Francis Goes to West Point
Glory Alley
Invasion USA
Jumping Jacks
Never Wave at a WAC
One Minute to Zero
Red Ball Express
Sound Off

1953   *Battle Circus*
Cease Fire
Combat Squad
Fear and Desire
From Here to Eternity
Glory Brigade
The Joe Louis Story
Off Limits
Take the High Ground
The War of the Worlds

1954   *Bamboo Prison*
Francis Joins the WACS
Night People
Prisoner of War
Silent Raiders
Target Earth
Them!
White Christmas

1955   *Battle Taxi*
House of Bamboo
The Long Gray Line
The Private War of Major Benson
Target Zero
Three Stripes in the Sun
To Hell and Back

1956   *Attack!*

Between Heaven and Hell
The Bold and the Brave
D-Day, the Sixth of June
Earth vs. the Flying Saucers
Giant
The Girl He Left Behind
The Lieutenant Wore Skirts
The Man in the Gray Flannel Suit
The Rack
Screaming Eagles
Somebody Up There Likes Me
The Teahouse of the August Moon

1957   *Beginning of the End*
The Deadly Mantis
Joe Butterfly
Men in War
Operation Mad Ball
Purple Heart Diary
The Sad Sack
Time Limit

1958   *Darby's Rangers*
Fraulein
Hell Squad
Imitation General
Kings Go Forth
The Last Blitzkrieg
The Lost Missile
The Naked and the Dead
Perfect Furlough
Suicide Battalion
Tank Battalion
When Hell Broke Loose
The Young Lions

1959   *The Bridge*
The Mouse That Roared
Never So Few
Operation Dames
Operation Petticoat
Paratroop Command
Plan Nine from Outer Space
Pork Chop Hill
A Private's Affair
Subway in the Sky
Surrender—Hell!
Tank Commandos
They Came to Cordura
Verboten!

1960   *Battle of Blood Island*
G.I. Blues

Heroes Die Young
I Aim at the Stars
Mountain Road
Ski Troop Attack
The Wackiest Ship in the Army
Wake Me When It's Over

1961   *Battle at Bloody Beach*
Dondi
Judgment at Nuremberg
Last Time I Saw Archie
On the Double
Operation Bottleneck
Sniper's Ridge
Town Without Pity

1962   *Hell Is for Heroes*
The Longest Day
The Manchurian Candidate
Merrill's Marauders
The Pigeon That Took Rome
War Hunt

1963   *Bye Bye Birdie*
Captain Newman, M.D.
The Great Escape
The Hook
Miracle of the White Stallions
The Quick and the Dead
The Raiders of Leyte Gulf
Soldiers in the Rain
The Victors
The Young and the Brave

1964   *Back Door to Hell*
Goldfinger
Man in the Middle
The Thin Red Line
War Is Hell

1965   *Battle of the Bulge*
Once Before I Die
Operation C.I.A.
The Satan Bug
Up from the Beach
Von Ryan's Express

1966   *Is Paris Burning?*
What Did You Do in the War, Daddy?

1967   *The Dirty Dozen*
Reflections in a Golden Eye
Warkill
The Young Warriors

1968   *Anzio*
Battle Beneath the Earth

	Commandos
	The Devil's Brigade
	The Green Berets
	In Enemy Country
	The Secret War of Harry Frigg
	The Sergeant
	Sergeant Ryker
	Where Eagles Dare
1969	*Baroque A Nova*
	The Bridge at Remagen
	Castle Keep
	Gay Deceivers
	Hannibal Brooks
	The Wild Bunch
1970	*The Forbin Project*
	Hornet's Nest
	Kelly's Heroes
	The Last Escape
	*M*A*S*H*
	Patton
	The Ravager
1971	*The Andromeda Strain*
	Johnny Got His Gun
1972	*Pancho Villa*
	Parades
	Summer Soldiers
1973	*A Taste of Hell*
1974	*Earthquake*
1976	*The Eagle Has Landed*
	Mean Johnny Barrows
	Tracks
1977	*A Bridge Too Far*
	The Cassandra Crossing
	Heroes
	MacArthur
1978	*Brass Target*
	The Deer Hunter
	Force Ten from Navarone
	Go Tell the Spartans
	Good Guys Wear Black
	The Swarm
1979	*Apocalypse Now*
	Hair
	1941
	Search and Destroy
	Yanks
1980	*Airplane!*
	The Big Red One
	The Exterminator

The Last Hunter
The Line
Private Benjamin
1981   *How Sleep the Brave*
The Soldier's Story
Southern Comfort
Stripes
Taps
Victory
1982   *Don't Cry, It's Only Thunder*
First Blood
Purple Haze
Some Kind of Hero
1983   *Blue Thunder*
Streamers
Uncommon Valor
1984   *Birdy*
Missing in Action
Red Dawn
A Soldier's Story
Starman
Tank
1985   *Cease Fire*
Invasion USA
Latino
Missing in Action 2: The Beginning
Operation 'Nam
Rambo: First Blood, Part II
Stryker's War
1986   *Death of a Soldier*
The Delta Force
The Forgotten Warrior
House
The Manhattan Project
Ordinary Heroes
Platoon
POW, the Escape
Zone Troopers
1987   *Gardens of Stone*
Hamburger Hill
Predator
Steele Justice
Strike Commando
1988   *Biloxi Blues*
Distant Thunder
The Expendables
Eye of the Eagle
Night Wars
Platoon Leader

	The Presidio
	Run for Your Life
	White Ghost
1989	*Casualties of War*
	84 Charlie Mopic
	Eye of the Eagle II: Inside the Enemy
	Fat Man and Little Boy
	Hell on the Battleground
	In Country
	Iron Triangle
	Nam Angels
	The Package
	Siege of Firebase Gloria
1990	*Cadence*
	Come See the Paradise
	Delta Force 2: Operation Stranglehold
	Dog Tags
	Eye of the Eagle III
	Fire Birds
	The Fourth War
	Jacob's Ladder
	Last Stand at Lang Mei
	The Lost Idol
	Operation War Zone
	Private War
1991	*Delta Force 3: The Killing Game*
	Field of Fire
	For the Boys
	Toy Soldiers
1992	*Beyond the Call of Duty*
	Forever Young
	A Midnight Clear
1993	*Hot Shots! Part Deux*
	Kill Zone
	Last Action Hero
	The Philadelphia Experiment II
1994	*Blue Sky*
	Clear and Present Danger
	Forrest Gump
	Guarding Tess
	In the Army Now
	The Next Karate Kid
	The Puppet Masters
	Renaissance Man
1995	*Goldeneye*
	The New World
	Operation Dumbo Drop
	Outbreak
	The Perez Family

	A Walk in the Clouds
1996	*Courage Under Fire*
	Executive Decision
	Independence Day
	Lone Star
	Sgt. Bilko
	A Time to Kill
1997	*Con Air*
	Contact
	Dead Men Can't Dance
	In & Out
	Life Is Beautiful
	The Peacemaker
1998	*Deep Impact*
	Ernest in the Army
	Godzilla
	The Patriot
	Saving Private Ryan
	The Siege
	A Soldier's Sweetheart
	Sphere
	The Thin Red Line
1999	*The General's Daughter*
	Three Kings
2000	*Cutaway*
	Thirteen Days
	Tigerland
2001	*Apocalypse Now Redux*
	Black Hawk Down
	Hart's War
	The Last Castle
	To End All Wars
2002	*We Were Soldiers*
2003	*Basic*
	Buffalo Soldiers
	The Core
	Hulk
	Saints and Soldiers
	Terminator 3: Rise of the Machines
2004	*The Day After Tomorrow*
	The Notebook
	The Manchurian Candidate
2005	*The Great Raid*

MARINES

1917	*The American Consul*
	Star Spangled Banner

1918	*The Unbeliever*
1919	*Bolshevisim on Trial*
1923	*The Tents of Allah*
1924	*Fools in the Dark*
1926	*Mike*
	Tell It to the Marines
	What Price Glory?
1927	*The Great Mail Robbery*
	Let It Rain
	Rookies
1928	*Moran of the Marines*
	Sadie Thompson
	Telling the World
1929	*Blockade*
	Cock-Eyed World
	Flight
	Flying Marine
	From Headquarters
	The Leatherneck
1930	*Leathernecking*
1931	*Cuban Love Song*
	Women of All Nations
1932	*Rain*
1933	*King Kong*
1934	*Come on Marines*
1935	*Devil Dogs of the Air*
	The Marines Are Coming
1936	*The Leathernecks Have Landed*
	Pride of the Marines
	San Francisco
1937	*Join the Marines*
	The Singing Marine
1938	*Air Devils*
	Cipher Bureau
	Come on Leathernecks
	Fighting Devil Dogs (serial)
	The Marines Are Here
1939	*Calling All Marines*
1940	*Isle of Destiny*
	The Marines Fly High
1942	*Atlantic Convoy*
	Buses Roar
	Call Out the Marines
	Iceland
	To the Shores of Tripoli
	Wake Island
1943	*Air Force*
	Guadalcanal Diary
	Gung Ho!

	Marines Come Through
	Salute to the Marines
	Stage Door Canteen
1944	*Abroad with Two Yanks*
	Hail the Conquering Hero
	Hollywood Canteen
	Marine Raiders
1945	*Pride of the Marines*
1946	*Till the End of Time*
1949	*Sands of Iwo Jima*
1950	*Halls of Montezuma*
1951	*Flying Leathernecks*
1952	*Battle Zone*
	Big Jim McLean
	Here Come the Marines
	Retreat, Hell!
	Stars and Stripes Forever
	What Price Glory?
1953	*China Venture*
	Crazylegs
	Girls of Pleasure Island
	Invaders from Mars
	Miss Sadie Thompson
	South Sea Woman
1954	*Beachhead*
	The Bob Mathias Story
	The Caine Mutiny
1955	*Battle Cry*
1956	*Earth vs. the Flying Saucers*
	Hold Back the Night
	The Proud and Profane
1957	*The D.I.*
	Heaven Knows, Mr. Allison
	Monkey on My Back
	Until They Sail
1958	*In Love and War*
	The Lost Missile
	Rascel Marine
	South Pacific
	Tarawa Beachhead
1959	*Battle Flame*
	The Mouse That Roared
1960	*All the Young Men*
	Hell to Eternity
1961	*Marines, Let's Go*
	The Outsider
	Steel Claw
1962	*The Longest Day*
	The Nun and the Sergeant

1963	*55 Days at Peking*
	Marine Battleground
1964	*The Brig*
	McHale's Navy
	Seven Days in May
	A Yank in Viet-Nam
1965	*In Harm's Way*
	None But the Brave
	Operation C.I.A.
	To the Shores of Hell
1966	*Ambush Bay*
1967	*Beach Red*
	First to Fight
	The Happiest Millionaire
1968	*Hell in the Pacific*
	Ice Station Zebra
1971	*Escape from the Planet of the Apes*
	Jud
1972	*Captain Milkshake*
1973	*The Last Detail*
1975	*The Wind and the Lion*
1976	*Baby Blue Marine*
1977	*MacArthur*
1978	*The Boys in Company C*
	Coming Home
	Who'll Stop the Rain?
1979	*The Great Santini*
	More American Graffiti
1980	*The Final Countdown*
	The Ninth Configuration
1981	*Inchon*
1982	*An Officer & a Gentleman*
1983	*The Right Stuff*
	Running Brave
1984	*The Killing Fields*
	Purple Hearts
1985	*Warbus*
1986	*Heartbreak Ridge*
	Invaders from Mars
	POW, the Escape
1987	*Death Before Dishonor*
	Full Metal Jacket
	Nowhere to Hide
1988	*Leathernecks*
1989	*Born on the Fourth of July*
	Cage
	Siege of Firebase Gloria
1990	*Delta Force 2: Operation Stranglehold*
1991	*Dogfight*

	For the Boys
1992	A Few Good Men
1993	Blood Warriors
	Heaven and Earth
1994	Chasers
	True Lies
1995	The American President
	Dead Presidents
	Major Payne
	The Walking Dead
1996	The Bloody Child
	Independence Day
	The Rock
1997	The Jackal
	Surface to Air
2000	Men of Honor
	Rules of Engagement
2001	Behind Enemy Lines
	The Green Dragon
	Jurassic Park III
	Quicksand
2002	High Crimes
	Windtalkers
2003	When Eagles Strike
2004	Stateside

NAVY

1915	Battle Cry of Peace
	Madame Butterfly
	Saved from the Harem
	A Submarine Pirate
	Via Wireless
1916	Hero of Submarine D-2
1918	Madame Spy
	No Man's Land
1919	Bolshevisim on Trial
1920	Behind the Door
1921	Sailor-Made Man
1923	The Tents of Allah
1925	Midshipman
1926	Blue Eagle
	We're in the Navy Now
1927	Convoy
	Let It Rain
	The Rough Riders
1928	The Fleet's In
	A Girl in Every Port

Wings of the Navy

1940   *Flight Command*

Murder in the Air

The Sailor's Lady

Seven Sinners

Son of the Navy

1941   *Dive Bomber*

A Girl, a Guy, and a Gob

In the Navy

Navy Blues

Sailors on Leave

1942   *Atlantic Convoy*

The Fleet's In

Hello Annapolis

The Navy Comes Through

Panama Hattie

Prisoner of Japan

Stand By for Action

Submarine Raider

Winslow of the Navy

1943   *Action in the North Atlantic*

Crash Dive

Destination Tokyo

Destroyer

Flight for Freedom

Gung Ho!

Minesweeper

Stage Door Canteen

We've Never Been Licked

1944   *The Fighting Seabees*

Here Come the Waves

Hollywood Canteen

Marine Raiders

The Navy Way

Practically Yours

The Story of Dr. Wassell

The Sullivans

Thirty Seconds Over Tokyo

U-Boat Prisoner

Wing and a Prayer

1945   *Anchors Aweigh*

A Bell for Adano

They Were Expendable

This Man's Navy

1946   *Gallant Bess*

It's a Wonderful Life

Out of the Depths

1947   *High Barbaree*

1948   *On an Island with You*

1949	*Lost Boundaries*
	On the Town
	Slattery's Hurricane
	Task Force
1950	*American Guerrilla in the Philippines*
	Flying Missile
	Mystery Submarine
1951	*Frogmen*
	A Girl in Every Port
	Let's Go Navy
	Navy Bound
	Operation Pacific
	Sailor Beware
	Submarine Command
	USS Teakettle
	You're in the Navy Now
1952	*Big Jim McLean*
	Flat Top
	Gobs and Gals
	Invasion USA
	Okinawa
	Skirts Ahoy!
	Torpedo Alley
1953	*Destination Gobi*
1954	*The Bridges at Toko-Ri*
	The Caine Mutiny
	Men of the Fighting Lady
1955	*An Annapolis Story*
	The Eternal Sea
	Francis in the Navy
	It Came from Beneath the Sea
	Mister Roberts
	Target Zero
1956	*Away All Boats*
	Battle Stations
	Earth vs. the Flying Saucers
	Navy Wife
	Sharkfighters
1957	*Don't Go Near the Water*
	The Enemy Below
	Hellcats of the Navy
	Kiss Them for Me
	The Monster that Challenged the Earth
	Three Brave Men
	The Wings of Eagles
1958	*The Deep Six*
	The Lost Missile
	Onionhead
	Run Silent, Run Deep

	South Pacific
	Torpedo Run
	Underwater Warrior
	Windjammer
1959	*Battle of the Coral Sea*
	Blood and Steel
	Don't Give Up the Ship
	John Paul Jones
	The Mouse That Roared
	On the Beach
	Operation Petticoat
	Submarine Seahawk
	Up Periscope
1960	*Atomic Submarine*
	The Crowded Sky
	The Gallant Hours
1961	*All Hands on Deck*
	Cry for Happy
	Parrish
1962	*The Horizontal Lieutenant*
	The Longest Day
	No Man Is an Island
1963	*Operation Bikini*
	PT-109
	A Ticklish Affair
1964	*The Americanization of Emily*
	Ensign Pulver
	Father Goose
	The Incredible Mr. Limpet
	McHale's Navy
	Seven Days in May
1965	*Bedford Incident*
	In Harm's Way
	McHale's Navy Joins the Air Force
1966	*Lt. Robin Crusoe, U.S.N.*
	The Russians Are Coming, the Russians Are Coming
	The Sand Pebbles
1967	*Easy Come, Easy Go*
	What Am I Bid?
1968	*Battle Beneath the Earth*
	Ice Station Zebra
	Nobody's Perfect
	The Private Navy of Sgt. O'Farrell
	Yours, Mine and Ours
1969	*The Extraordinary Seaman*
1970	*Patton*
	Too Late the Hero
	Tora! Tora! Tora!
1972	*Limbo*

Sphere
The Thin Red Line
1999 *Random Hearts*
U.S. Seals
2000 *Men of Honor*
Rules of Engagement
Stealth Fighter
Thirteen Days
U-571
2001 *Behind Enemy Lines*
Jurassic Park III
Pearl Harbor
2002 *Antwone Fisher*
K-19: The Widowmaker
2003 *The Core*
Tears of the Sun
2004 *In Enemy Hands*
2005 *Annapolis*
Stealth

Films by Subject or Period

CRITERIA

These films, whatever their historical accuracy, provide the cinematic perceptions that inform people about American military events and actions. Some films listed here do not fall into the scope of this guide because they do not portray the U.S. military from 1898 to the present. However, they have been included for informational purposes and are identified with an asterisk.

PRE-TWENTIETH CENTURY

Title	Subject/Period	Release Date
*The Alamo	Mexican War	1960
America	American Revolution	1923
Birth of a Nation	Civil War	1915
*Dances with Wolves	Civil War/frontier	1990
*Drums Along the Mohawk	Revolution/Indians	1939
*Fort Apache	Frontier	1948
*The General	Civil War	1927
*Gettysburg	Civil War	1992
*Glory	Civil War	1989
*An Occurrence at Owl Creek Bridge	Civil War	1963
*Old Ironsides	Barbary pirates	1926
*The Red Badge of Courage	Civil War	1951
*Rio Grande	Frontier	1950
*She Wore a Yellow Ribbon	Frontier	1949

WORLD WAR I

Title	Subject/Period	Release Date
*All Quiet on the Western Front	German Army	1930
The Big Parade	U.S. Army	1925

The Grand Illusion	POWs	1937
Johnny Got His Gun	U.S. Army	1971
Paths of Glory	French Army	1957
Sergeant York	U.S. Army	1941
Shoulder Arms	U.S. Army	1918
The Unbeliever	U.S. Marines	1918
What Price Glory	U.S. Marines	1926
Wings	U.S. Army Air Corps	1927

INTERWAR YEARS

Title	Subject/Period	Release Date
Devil Dogs of the Air	U.S. Marine aviation	1935
Dive Bomber	U.S. Navy aviation	1941
Flight	U.S. Marine aviation	1929
Hell Divers	U.S. Navy aviation	1932
In Pursuit of Honor	U.S. Cavalry	1995
I Wanted Wings	U.S. Army Air Corps	1941
The Sand Pebbles	U.S. Navy	1966
Submarine	U.S. Navy	1928
Submarine D-1	U.S. Navy	1937

WORLD WAR II

Title	Subject/Period	Release Date
Bataan	Pacific–Philippine invasion, U.S.	1943
Battle Cry	Pacific–Marine island hopping, U.S.	1957
Battleground	Europe–Battle of the Bulge, U.S.	1949
The Battle of Britain	Air War, Germans vs. RAF	1969
The Best Years of Our Lives	Returning veterans, U.S.	1946
Das Boot	Submarines, Germany	1981
The Bridge	German defenses	1959
A Bridge Too Far	Europe–Operation Market Garden	1977
The Caine Mutiny	Pacific, U.S.	1954
The Desert Fox	Gen. Rommel, German Army	1952
Destination Tokyo	Submarine warfare, U.S.	1944
The Enemy Below	Submarine warfare, U.S.	1957
From Here to Eternity	Prewar, U.S.	1953
Guadalcanal Diary	Pacific, U.S.	1943
The Longest Day	D-Day	1962
Patton	Europe	1970
Sands of Iwo Jima	Pacific, U.S.	1949
Saving Private Ryan	D-Day, Normandy	1997
The Story of G.I. Joe	Italian campaign	1949
They Were Expendable	Pacific, PT-boats	1945
Thirty Seconds Over Tokyo	Pacific bombing, U.S.	1944

Tora! Tora! Tora!	Pearl Harbor	1970
Twelve O'Clock High	European bombing, U.S.	1949
Wake Island	Pacific, Marines	1943

KOREA

Title	Subject/Period	Release Date
The Bridges at Toko-Ri	Navy aviation	1955
Men of the Fighting Lady	Navy aviation	1954
One Minute to Zero	Army, Air Force	1952
Pork Chop Hill	Army	1959
Retreat, Hell!	Marines	1952

THE COLD WAR

Title	Subject/Period	Release Date
The Bedford Incident	Navy	1965
The Big Lift	Air Force	1950
Dr. Strangelove	Air Force	1964
Fail Safe	Air Force	1964
I Aim at the Stars	Army	1960
K-19	Soviet Navy	2003
The Hunt for Red October	Soviet and U.S. Navies	1990
The Manchurian Candidate	U.S. Army	1962
On the Beach	U.S. Navy	1959
Pentagon Wars	U.S. Army	1998
Seven Days In May	All U.S. armed forces	1964
Strategic Air Command	U.S. Air Force	1955
WarGames	U.S. Air Force	1983

VIETNAM—COMBAT

Title	Subject/Period	Release Date
*Air America	CIA	1990
Apocalypse Now	U.S. Army	1979
Bat 21	Air Force	1988
Casualties of War	Army	1989
Flight of the Intruder	Navy aviation	1991
Go Tell the Spartans	Army	1978
The Green Berets	Army	1968
Hamburger Hill	Army	1987
Platoon	Army	1986
We Were Soldiers	Army	2002

VIETNAM—HOME FRONT

Title	Subject/Period	Release Date
Cease Fire	Veteran adjustment	1985
The Deer Hunter	Combat and home front	1979
Heroes	Veteran adjustment	1977
Limbo	Women in waiting	1972
Running on Empty	Antiwar activists	1988
Rolling Thunder	Veteran adjustment	1977
Same Time, Next Year	Civilian experience with Vietnam	1978
Taxi Driver	Veteran adjustment	1976

POST-VIETNAM

Title	Subject/Period	Release Date
Black Hawk Down	Somalia	2002
Courage Under Fire	Persian Gulf	1996
Independence Day	Alien invasion	1996
An Officer and a Gentleman	Peacetime military	1982
Tears of the Sun	U.S. intervention	2003
Three Kings	Persian Gulf	1999
Top Gun	Peacetime military	1986

TERRORISM

Title	Subject/Period	Release Date
Air Force One	Russian nationalists	1997
The Battle of Algiers	Algerian revolt	1965
Broken Arrow	Nuclear hijacking	1996
Clear and Present Danger	Drug Dealers	1994
Crimson Tide	Russian nationalists	1995
Executive Decision	Arab terrorists	1996
Firebirds	Drug dealers	1990
Navy SEALS	Arab terrorists	1990
Patriot Games	IRA	1992
The Peacemaker	Russian nationalists	1997
The Siege	Arab terrorists	1998
The Sum of All Fears	Arab terrorists	2002
True Lies	Drug dealers	1994
Under Siege	Nuclear hijacking	1992

POW FILMS

Title	Subject/Period	Release Date
The Bridge on the River Kwai	World War II, Japanese	1957
The Grand Illusion	WWI, German	1937

The Great Escape	WWII, German	1963
The Great Raid	WWII, Japanese	2004
The Hanoi Hilton	Vietnam, Vietnamese	1987
Hart's War	WWII, German	2002
The Last Castle	Peacetime, U.S.	2001

THE MILITARY & SCIENCE FICTION

Title	Subject/Period	Release Date
The Beginning of the End	Radiation mutation–grasshoppers	1957
Close Encounters of the Third Kind	Benign alien visit	1977
The Day the Earth Stood Still	Benign alien visit	1951
The Final Countdown	Time travel	1980
The Forbin Project	Computer takeover	1970
Independence Day	Alien invasion	1995
Invaders from Mars	Alien invasion	1986
King Kong (1933)	Local monster	1933
King Kong (1976)	Local monster	1976
The Philadelphia Experiment	Time travel	1985
Plan Nine from Outer Space	Alien invasion	1959
Starman	Benign alien visit	1984
Them!	Radiation mutation–ants	1954
WarGames	Computer takeover	1983
The War of the Worlds	Alien invasion	1953

BASIC TRAINING

Title	Subject/Period	Release Date
Battle Cry	Marines, WWII	1955
Born on the Fourth of July	Marines, Vietnam	1989
The D.I.	Marines, peacetime	1957
Full Metal Jacket	Marines, Vietnam	1997
G.I. Jane	Navy, peacetime	1997
An Officer and a Gentleman	Navy, peacetime	1982
Shoulder Arms	Army, WWI	1918
Stateside	Marines, peacetime	2004
Tigerland	Army, Vietnam	2000

25 Greatest American Military Films

CRITERIA

The first 15 films listed are classics, and anyone wishing to understand the genre should begin with these. Beyond the first 15, people may disagree about the rankings, but our criteria for selecting the films include the importance of their place in cinematic history, their portrayal of life in the military, their re-creation of history, and their continuing ability to move viewers.

1. *The Longest Day*
2. *Patton*
3. *A Bridge Too Far*
4. *From Here to Eternity*
5. *Twelve O'Clock High*
6. *Dr. Strangelove*
7. *Battle Cry*
8. *Wings*
9. *Sands of Iwo Jima*
10. *The Story of G.I. Joe*
11. *Go Tell the Spartans*
12. *The Enemy Below*
13. *Tears of the Sun*
14. *Air Force*
15. *Black Hawk Down*
16. *Thirty Seconds Over Tokyo*
17. *Battleground*
18. *In Pursuit of Honor* (cable)
19. *Beach Red*
20. *The Caine Mutiny*
21. *Casualties of War*
22. *Destination Tokyo*
23. *Wake Island*
24. *The Unbeliever*
25. *Retreat, Hell!*

OTHER CONTENDERS

The Big Parade
Gardens of Stone
Hiroshima (cable)
Sergeant York
Top Gun

The D.I.
Guadalcanal Diary
Rolling Thunder
They Were Expendable

Significant but Highly Flawed Military Films

The films listed here have some significance. Although the authors consider that these films lack redeeming features, they have created this category in recognition that their opinions may be in a minority.

For example, the authors are fully aware of the esteem in which most critics and Americans hold **Saving Private Ryan**. However, author Suid believes the film is essentially a lie and a slap in the face of the soldiers who landed on D-Day. Steven Spielberg claimed he was honoring these men, but peopled the film with cowards, mutineers, and a hero who is suffering from battle fatigue as a result of some unexplained combat. Moreover, the director has lifted most of his scenes from other films, including, most obviously, **The Longest Day** and **A Walk in the Sun**, but also **2001** and the German movie, **The Bridge**.

The Deer Hunter did, of course, win an Oscar for best film, so Michael Cimino did something right. Nevertheless, it is self-indulgent and totally false in its portrayal of the American experience in Vietnam. The same is true of **Apocalypse Now**. Although many Vietnam veterans say the film evokes memories of their time in combat, the reality remains that it portrays the actual experiences of few, if any, of the soldiers in the country.

Apocalypse Now	*Good Morning Vietnam*
The Beginning or the End	*The Green Berets*
Catch-22	*Platoon*
Coming Home	*Saving Private Ryan*
The Deer Hunter	*Tora! Tora! Tora!*
Fail Safe	*A Walk in the Sun*
Full Metal Jacket	*WarGames*

V

25 Worst American Military Films

CRITERIA

This list includes only films that had pretensions of social or artistic significance and intended to make meaningful comments about the human condition of men in the armed services. Some of these films have their supporters, such as ***In Harm's Way***. The French apparently love ***PT-109***, and *Midway* was one of the top 10 box office hits of 1976.

Except for the first twelve films on the list, the others are not necessarily in any descending order. The list does not include such films as ***Tora! Tora! Tora!***, which is devoid of believable characters and drama but does offer a reasonably accurate portrayal of Pearl Harbor—something that ***Pearl Harbor*** goes out of its way to avoid.

1. *Inchon*
2. *Pearl Harbor*
3. *Ice Station Zebra*
4. *Memphis Belle*
5. *Battle of the Bulge*
6. *Windtalkers*
7. *Midway*
8. *The Thin Red Line* (2001)
9. *The Boys in Company C*
10. *Navy SEALS*
11. *Hellcats of the Navy*
12. *Heartbreak Ridge*
13. *Gray Lady Down*
14. *PT-109*
15. *In Harm's Way*
16. *Sgt. Bilko*
17. *MacArthur*
18. *The Hunters*
19. *Tank*
20. *Independence Day*
21. *The Bridge at Remagen*
22. *Crimson Tide*
23. *The General's Daughter*
24. *Raise the Titanic*
25. *Firefox*

VI

Portrayals of Military Leadership

CRITERIA

Each of these films contains examples of military leadership or, in some cases, the absence of such leadership. Some show command and control, others the relationship between officers and enlisted men. In particular, *In Pursuit of Honor* contains one of the very best portrayals of how a young officer learns to lead from his sergeant. Despite its lack of any dramatic quality, *Hellcats of the Navy* does feature Ronald Reagan in an effective leadership role, which is why it is included on this list.

Above and Beyond	Great leader trains men to drop the A-bomb
Air Force	Pilot forges men into a cohesive crew
Battle Cry	Officer leads Marines by example
The Bedford Incident	Captain becomes an Ahab and loses control
The Big Red One	Sergeant turns boys into men
A Bridge Too Far	Plan goes awry, but officers maintain control
The Caine Mutiny	Captain loses control of his men and the ship
Casualties of War	Sergeant allows his men to commit atrocity
Destination Tokyo	Sub captain provides strong leadership
The D.I.	Superb example of Marine training
The Dirty Dozen	Officer molds misfits into crack commandos
The Enemy Below	Strong leadership on two opposing ships
Fighter Squadron	Commander leads by example
Flying Leathernecks	John Wayne leads men by example
From Here to Eternity	Strong sergeant, but ineffective officer
Full Metal Jacket	Paradigm of a DI, but second half fails
The Gallant Hours	Excellent portrayal of Navy admiral
Go Tell the Spartans	Officer leads despite an impossible situation
The Green Berets	Wayne does his thing in a bad movie
Halls of Montezuma	Officer leads men despite personal battles
Hellcats of the Navy	Submariner Reagan provides leadership
In Pursuit of Honor	Sergeant educates his new lieutenant
The Longest Day	Strong leadership all around
Patton	Perhaps the best U.S. military commander
Sands of Iwo Jima	John Wayne as the quintessential leader

Saving Private Ryan	Hanks battles his demons, men, and enemy
Tears of the Sun	Willis creates paradigm of twenty-first-century leader
Thirty Seconds over Tokyo	Doolittle commands heroic mission
Twelve O'Clock High	Film explores dangers inherent in command
A Wing and a Prayer	Officer teaches men how to survive in the air

Select List of Actors with Significant Credits in Military Films

Dana Andrews

Crash Dive	1943
Purple Heart	1944
Wing and a Prayer	1944
A Walk in the Sun	1945
The Best Years of Our Lives	1946
The Crowded Sky	1960
The Battle of the Bulge	1965
In Harm's Way	1965
The Devil's Brigade	1968
Airport '75	1974

Ward Bond

Devil Dogs of the Air	1935
The Leathernecks Have Landed	1936
Pride of the Marines	1936
The Devil's Playground	1937
Submarine Patrol	1938
Sergeant York	1941
Ten Gentlemen from West Point	1942
A Guy Named Joe	1943
The Sullivans	1944
They Were Expendable	1945
Operation Pacific	1951
Thunderbirds	1953
The Bob Mathias Story	1954
The Long Gray Line	1955
Mister Roberts	1955
The Wings of Eagles	1957
China Doll	1958

Ernest Borgnine

From Here to Eternity	1953
Torpedo Run	1958
McHale's Navy	1964

389

	The Dirty Dozen	1967
	Ice Station Zebra	1968
	McHale's Navy	1997
Marlon Brando		
	The Men	1950
	The Teahouse of the August Moon	1956
	Sayonara	1957
	The Young Lions	1958
	Reflections in a Golden Eye	1967
	Apocalypse Now	1979
Charles Bronson		
	You're in the Navy Now	1951
	Battle Zone (uncredited)	1952
	Torpedo Alley (uncredited)	1952
	Miss Sadie Thompson	1953
	Target Zero	1955
	X-15	1961
	The Great Escape	1963
	Battle of the Bulge	1965
	The Dirty Dozen	1967
James Cagney		
	Here Comes the Navy	1934
	Devil of the Air	1935
	The Fighting 69th	1940
	The West Point Story	1950
	Starlift	1951
	What Price Glory?	1952
	Mister Roberts	1955
	The Gallant Hours	1960
Montgomery Clift		
	The Search	1948
	The Big Lift	1950
	From Here to Eternity	1953
	The Young Lions	1958
	Judgment at Nuremberg	1961
Gary Cooper		
	Wings	1927
	A Man from Wyoming	1930
	Sergeant York	1941
	The Story of Dr. Wassell	1944
	Task Force	1949
	You're in the Navy Now	1951
	Starlift	1951
	The Court-Martial of Billy Mitchell	1955
Kirk Douglas		
	Town Without Pity	1961
	The Hook	1963
	Seven Days in May	1965
	In Harm's Way	1965

	Is Paris Burning?	1966
	The Final Countdown	1980
Robert Duvall		
	Captain Newman, M.D.	1963
	M*A*S*H	1970
	The Eagle Has Landed	1976
	Apocalypse Now	1979
	The Great Santini	1979
	Deep Impact	1998
Clint Eastwood		
	Francis in the Navy	1955
	Where Eagles Dare	1968
	Kelly's Heroes	1970
	Firefox	1982
	Heartbreak Ridge	1986
	In the Line of Fire	1993
R. Lee Ermey		
	The Boys in Company C	1978
	Apocalypse Now (uncredited)	1979
	Purple Hearts	1984
	Full Metal Jacket	1987
	The Siege of Firebase Gloria	1989
	Toy Soldiers	1991
Henry Fonda		
	Mister Roberts	1955
	The Longest Day	1962
	Fail Safe	1964
	In Harm's Way	1965
	Battle of the Bulge	1965
	Yours, Mine, and Ours	1968
	Midway	1976
	The Swarm	1978
	Battle Force	1978
Clark Gable		
	Hell Divers	1931
	San Francisco	1936
	Test Pilot	1938
	Homecoming	1948
	Command Decision	1949
	Run Silent, Run Deep	1958
John Garfield		
	Air Force	1943
	Destination Tokyo	1944
	Hollywood Canteen	1944
	Pride of the Marines	1945
James Garner		
	Toward the Unknown	1956
	Sayonara	1957
	Darby's Rangers	1958

The Great Escape	1963
36 Hours	1964
The Americanization of Emily	1964
Tank	1984
The Notebook	2005

Cary Grant

Madame Butterfly	1932
Destination Tokyo	1944
I Was a Male War Bride	1949
Operation Petticoat	1959
Father Goose	1964

Gene Hackman

First to Fight	1967
A Bridge Too Far	1977
Uncommon Valor	1983
No Way Out	1987
Bat-21	1988
The Package	1989
Crimson Tide	1995
Behind Enemy Lines	2001

Charlton Heston

The Private War of Major Benson	1955
The Pigeon That Took Rome	1962
55 Days at Peking	1963
Earthquake	1974
Airport '75	1974
Midway	1976
Gray Lady Down	1978
True Lies	1994

John Hodiak

Sunday Dinner for a Soldier	1944
A Bell for Adano	1945
Command Decision	1948
Homecoming	1948
Battleground	1949
Battle Zone	1952
Mission Over Korea	1953
Dragonfly Squadron	1954
On the Threshold of Space	1956

William Holden

I Wanted Wings	1941
The Fleet's In	1942
Submarine Command	1952
Stalag 17	1953
The Bridges at Toko-Ri	1955
The Proud and the Profane	1956
Toward the Unknown	1956
The Bridge on the River Kwai	1957
The Towering Inferno	1974

Rock Hudson

Fighter Squadron	1948
Air Cadet	1951
Giant	1956
Battle Hymn	1957
A Gathering of Eagles	1963
Tobruk	1967
Ice Station Zebra	1968
Hornet's Nest	1970

Richard Jaeckel

Guadalcanal Diary	1943
Wing and a Prayer	1944
Jungle Patrol	1948
Battleground	1949
Sands of Iwo Jima	1949
Fighting Coast Guard	1951
Attack!	1956
The Naked and the Dead	1958
When Hell Broke Loose	1958
The Gallant Hours	1960
Town Without Pity	1961
The Young and the Brave	1963
Once Before I Die	1965
The Dirty Dozen	1967
The Devil's Brigade	1968
Twilight's Last Gleaming	1977
Pacific Inferno	1979
Starman	1984
Delta Force 2: Operation Stranglehold	1990

Van Johnson

Pilot No. 5	1943
A Guy Named Joe	1943
The Human Comedy	1943
Thirty Seconds Over Tokyo	1944
High Barbaree	1947
Command Decision	1949
Battleground	1949
Go for Broke	1951
Men of the Fighting Lady	1954
The Caine Mutiny	1954
The Last Blitzkreig	1958
Subway in the Sky	1959
Yours, Mine, and Ours	1968
Delta Force Commando II	1991

Burt Lancaster

From Here to Eternity	1953
Run Silent, Run Deep	1958
Judgment at Nuremberg	1961
Seven Days in May	1964

	The Cassandra Crossing	1977
	Twilight's Last Gleaming	1977
	Go Tell the Spartans	1978
Victor McLaglen		
	What Price Glory?	1926
	The Cock-Eyed World	1929
	Women of All Nations	1931
	Call Out the Marines	1942
Fred MacMurray		
	Dive Bomber	1941
	Captain Eddie	1945
	The Caine Mutiny	1954
	The Happiest Millionaire	1967
	The Swarm	1978
Steve McQueen		
	Hell Is for Heroes	1962
	The Great Escape	1963
	The War Lovers	1963
	The Soldier in the Rain	1963
	The Sand Pebbles	1966
	The Towering Inferno	1974
Karl Malden		
	Winged Victory	1944
	Halls of Montezuma	1951
	Operation Secret	1952
	Take the High Ground	1953
	Bombers B-52	1957
	Parrish	1961
	Patton	1970
Fredric March		
	True to the Navy	1930
	The Best Years of Our Lives	1946
	The Bridges at Toko-Ri	1954
	The Man in the Gray Flannel Suit	1956
	Seven Days in May	1964
Lee Marvin		
	Eight Iron Men	1953
	The Caine Mutiny	1954
	Attack!	1956
	The Rack	1956
	The Dirty Dozen	1967
	Sergeant Ryker	1968
	The Big Red One	1980
Robert Mitchum		
	The Human Comedy (uncredited)	1943
	Gung Ho!	1944
	Thirty Seconds Over Tokyo	1944
	The Story of G.I. Joe	1945
	Till the End of Time	1946

	One Minute to Zero	1952
	Heaven Knows, Mr. Allison	1957
	The Enemy Below	1957
	The Hunters	1958
	The Longest Day	1962
	Man in the Middle	1964
	Anzio	1968
	Midway	1976
	Maria's Lovers	1984
Paul Newman		
	The Rack	1956
	Somebody Up There Likes Me	1956
	Until They Sail	1957
	The Secret War of Henry Frigg	1968
	The Towering Inferno	1974
	Fat Man and Little Boy	1989
Chuck Norris		
	Good Guys Wear Black	1979
	Missing in Action	1984
	Missing in Action 2: The Beginning	1985
	Invasion U.S.A.	1985
	The Delta Force	1986
	Delta Force 2	1990
Pat O'Brien		
	Here Comes the Navy	1934
	Flirtation Walk	1934
	Devil Dogs of the Air	1935
	Submarine D-1	1937
	The Fighting 69th	1940
	Flight Lieutenant	1942
	The Navy Comes Through	1942
	Bombardier	1943
	The Iron Major	1943
	Marine Raiders	1944
	Okinawa	1952
Gregory Peck		
	Twelve O'Clock High	1949
	The Man in the Gray Flannel Suit	1956
	Porkchop Hill	1959
	On the Beach	1959
	Captain Newman, M.D.	1964
	MacArthur	1977
Robert Ryan		
	Bombardier	1943
	The Iron Major	1943
	Marine Raiders	1944
	Flying Leathernecks	1951
	Men in War	1957
	The Longest Day	1962

	Battle of the Bulge	1965
	The Dirty Dozen	1967
	Anzio	1968
James Stewart		
	Navy Blue and Gold	1937
	The Glenn Miller Story	1954
	Strategic Air Command	1954
	The Spirit of St. Louis	1957
	The Mountain Road	1960
	Airport '77	1977
Spencer Tracy		
	San Francisco	1936
	They Gave Him a Gun	1937
	Test Pilot	1938
	A Guy Named Joe	1943
	Thirty Seconds Over Tokyo	1944
	Judgment at Nuremberg	1961
John Wayne		
	Salute	1929
	Men Without Women	1930
	Seven Sinners	1940
	Flying Tigers	1942
	The Fighting Seabees	1944
	Back to Bataan	1945
	They Were Expendable	1945
	Sands of Iwo Jima	1949
	Flying Leathernecks	1951
	Operation Pacific	1951
	Big Jim McLain	1952
	The Wings of Eagles	1957
	Jet Pilot	1957
	The Longest Day	1962
	In Harm's Way	1965
	Cast a Giant Shadow	1966
	The Green Berets	1968
James Whitmore		
	Battleground	1949
	Above and Beyond	1952
	Them	1954
	Battle Cry	1955
	The McConnell Story	1955
Richard Widmark		
	Halls of Montezuma	1951
	The Frogmen	1951
	Destination Gobi	1953
	Take the High Ground	1953
	Judgment at Nuremberg	1961
	Flight from Ashiya	1964
	The Bedford Incident	1965
	The Swarm	1978

VIII

Select List of Directors with Significant Credits in Military Films

Similar to what we did in appendix VII, we have identified major directors who made at least five military films during the course of their careers. Even with this minimal requirement, Frank Capra and John Huston qualified only with the inclusion of their wartime documentaries. Moreover, although the military genre has retained its popularity among audiences for most of the period that this guide covers, the list suggests that few directors made their reputation from portraying the armed services in war and peace. In the 30 years since the end of the Vietnam War, few directors have chosen to make more than one or two films set within the military.

Lloyd Bacon
Son of a Sailor	1933
Here Comes the Navy	1934
Devil Dogs of the Air	1935
Submarine D-1	1937
Wings of the Navy	1939
Navy Blues	1941
Action in the North Atlantic	1943
The Sullivans	1944
Captain Eddie	1945
The Frog Men	1951

Frank Capra
Submarine	1928
Flight	1929
Dirigible	1931
The Why We Fight Series (Documentaries)	1941–45

Delmer Daves
Destination Tokyo	1944
Hollywood Canteen	1944
The Pride of the Marines	1945
Task Force	1945
Kings Go Forth	1958
Parrish	1961

John Ford

Salute	1929
Men Without Women	1930
The Lost Patrol	1934
Submarine Patrol	1938
December 7 (Documentary)	1944
Midway (Documentary)	1944
They Were Expendable	1945
This Is Korea (Documentary)	1951
The Long Gray Line	1955
Mister Roberts	1955
The Wings of Eagles	1957

Samuel Fuller

The Steel Helmet	1951
Fixed Bayonets	1951
Verboten!	1960
Merrill's Marauders	1962
The Big Red One	1981

John Huston

Across the Pacific	1942
Report from the Aleutians (Documentary)	1943
Battle of San Pietro (Documentary)	1944
Let There Be Light (Documentary)	1946
Heaven Knows, Mr. Allison	1957
Reflections in a Golden Eye	1967
Victory	1981

Lew Landers

Submarine Raiders	1942
Cadets on Parade	1942
Atlantic Convoy	1942
U-Boat Prisoner	1942
A Yank in Korea	1951
Torpedo Alley	1953

Arthur Lubin

Buck Privates	1941
In the Navy	1941
Keep'em Flying	1941
Francis	1950
Francis Goes to West Point	1952
Francis Joins the WACs	1954
Francis in the Navy	1955
The Incredible Mr. Limpet	1964

Andrew Marton

Gallant Bess	1946
The Devil Makes Three	1952
Men of the Fighting Lady	1954
Prisoner of War	1954
Underwater Warrior	1958
The Longest Day	1962

	55 Days at Peking	1963
	The Thin Red Line	1964
Lewis Milestone		
	Rain	1932
	The Purple Heart	1944
	A Walk in the Sun	1945
	Halls of Montezuma	1951
	Pork Chop Hill	1959
Mark Robson		
	Home of the Brave	1949
	Bright Victory	1951
	I Want You	1952
	The Bridges at Toko-Ri	1955
	Von Ryan's Express	1965
	Limbo	1972
	Earthquake	1974
Cirio Santiago		
	Kill Zone	1984
	Eye of the Eagle	1986
	The Expendables	1988
	Nam Angeles	1989
	Last Stand at Lang Mei	1990
	Field of Fire	1991
	Beyond the Call of Duty	1992
Lewis Seiler		
	Murder in the Air	1940
	You're in the Army Now	1941
	Guadalcanal Diary	1943
	Breakthrough	1950
	The Tanks Are Coming	1951
	Operation Secret	1952
	The Bamboo Prison	1955
	Battle Stations	1956
Raoul Walsh		
	What Price Glory?	1926
	Sailor's Luck	1933
	You're in the Army Now	1937
	Objective, Burma!	1945
	Fighter Squadron	1948
	Battle Cry	1955
	Marines, Let's Go!	1961
William Wellman		
	Wings	1927
	Men with Wings	1938
	This Man's Navy	1945
	The Story of G.I. Joe	1945
	Battleground	1949
	Darby's Rangers	1958

Fred Zinnemann

Little Mr. Jim	1946
The Search	1948
The Men	1950
Teresa	1951
From Here to Eternity	1953

Academy Award®-Winning Military Films

The films listed here have received Oscars® from the Motion Picture Academy. We have included recipients' names for acting, directing, and screenwriting. For the other awards, we have only included the category, such as documentaries, sound and film editing, art direction, cinematography, and music.

Year	Title	Awards
1927–28	*Wings*	Picture
1936	*San Francisco*	Sound Recording
1941	*Sergeant York*	Actor (Gary Cooper) and Film Editing
1941	*I Wanted Wings*	Special Effects
1942	*Battle of Midway*	Documentary
1942	*Prelude to War*	Documentary
1943	*Air Force*	Film Editing
1943	*This Is the Army*	Scoring of a Musical Picture
1943	*Crash Dive*	Special Effects
1943	*December 7*	Documentary (Short Subject)
1944	*With the Marines at Tarawa*	Documentary (Short Subject)
1944	*The Fighting Lady*	Documentary (Feature)
1944	*Thirty Seconds Over Tokyo*	Special Effects
1945	*Anchors Aweigh*	Scoring of a Musical Picture
1945	*The True Glory*	Documentary (Feature)
1946	*The Best Years of Our Lives*	Picture, Director (William Wyler), Actor (Fredric March), Supporting Actor (Harold Russell), Screenplay (Robert E. Sherwood), Scoring of a Dramatic Picture, and Film Editing
1948	*The Search*	Writing Story (Richard Schweizer and David Wechsler)
1949	*On the Town*	Scoring of a Musical Picture
1949	*Twelve O'Clock High*	Supporting Actor (Dean Jagger) and Sound Recording
1949	*Battleground*	Writing screenplay and story (Robert Pirosh) and B&W Cinematography

1950	*Why Korea?*	Documentary (Short Subject)
1953	*Stalag 17*	Actor (William Holden)
1953	*From Here to Eternity*	Picture, Director (Fred Zinnemann), Supporting Actor (Frank Sinatra), Supporting Actress (Donna Reed), Writing Screenplay (Daniel Taradash), B&W Cinematography, Sound Recording, and Film Editing
1953	*War of the Worlds*	Special Effects
1954	*The Glenn Miller Story*	Sound Recording
1955	*The Bridges of Toko-Ri*	Special Effects
1955	*Mister Roberts*	Supporting Actor (Jack Lemmon)
1956	*Somebody Up There Likes Me*	B&W Cinematography and Art Direction
1957	*The Bridge on the River Kwai*	Picture, Actor (Alec Guinness), Director (David Lean), Adapted Screenplay (Carl Foreman, Michael Wilson, Pierre Boulle), Cinematography, Score, and Film Editing
1957	*Sayonara*	Supporting Actor (Red Buttons), Supporting Actress (Miyoshi Umeki), Sound, and Art Direction
1957	*The Enemy Below*	Special Effects
1958	*South Pacific*	Sound
1961	*Judgment at Nuremberg*	Actor (Maximilian Schell) and Adapted Screenplay (Abby Mann)
1962	*The Longest Day*	B&W Cinematography and Special Effects
1964	*Father Goose*	Screenplay (S. H. Barnett, Peter Stone, and Frank Tarloff)
1964	*Goldfinger*	Sound Effects
1967	*The Anderson Platoon*	Documentary (Feature)
1967	*The Dirty Dozen*	Sound Effects
1970	*Patton*	Picture, Director (Franklin J. Schaffner), Actor (George C. Scott), Original Screenplay (Francis Ford Coppola, Edmund North), Art Direction, Sound, and Editing
1970	*Tora! Tora! Tora!*	Special Visual Effects
1970	*M*A*S*H*	Adapted Screenplay (Ring Lardner Jr.)
1974	*The Towering Inferno*	Cinematography, Song, and Film Editing
1974	*Earthquake*	Sound
1974	*Hearts & Minds*	Documentary (Feature)
1977	*Close Encounters of the Third Kind*	Cinematography
1978	*Deer Hunter*	Picture, Director (Michael Cimino), Supporting Actor (Christopher Walken), Sound, and Film Editing
1978	*Coming Home*	Actor (Jon Voight), Actress (Jane Fonda), and Original Screenplay (Waldo Salt, Robert Jones, and Nancy Dowd)
1979	*Apocalypse Now*	Editing and Sound

1982	*An Officer and a Gentleman*	Supporting Actor (Louis Gossett Jr.) and Song
1983	*The Right Stuff*	Sound, Original Score, Sound Effects Editing, and Film Editing
1984	*The Killing Fields*	Supporting Actor (Haing S. Ngor), Cinematography, and Film Editing
1986	*Platoon*	Picture, Director (Oliver Stone), Editing, and Sound
1986	*Top Gun*	Song
1989	*Born on the 4th of July*	Director (Oliver Stone) and Film Editing
1989	*The Abyss*	Visual Effects
1990	*The Hunt for Red October*	Sound Effects Editing
1994	*Forrest Gump*	Picture, Actor (Tom Hanks), Director (Robert Zemeckis), Adapted Screenplay (Eric Roth), Film Editing, and Visual Effects
1994	*Blue Sky*	Actress (Jessica Lange)
1995	*Apollo 13*	Sound
1996	*Independence Day*	Visual Effects
1998	*Life is Beautiful*	Actor (Roberto Benigni), Original Score, and Foreign Film
1998	*Saving Private Ryan*	Director (Steven Spielberg), Cinematography, Sound, Sound Effects Editing, and Film Editing
2000	*U-571*	Sound Editing
2001	*Black Hawk Down*	Sound and Film Editing
2001	*Pearl Harbor*	Sound Editing
2003	*The Fog of War*	Documentary (Feature)

TV Series Featuring Significant Military Characters/Themes

American Dreams (2002)

Vietnam	Marines	Color

Series provides a nostalgic look at the 1960s, the changing societal values, the cultural changes, and, of course, the Vietnam War as the catalyst for all that transpired. The heroine's brother ultimately goes off to the war, which is portrayed in combat sequences.

American Family (2002–03)

Second Gulf War	Army	Color

Broadcast on public television stations, this drama series was the first to feature a Latino cast. During the second season in 2003, one of the sons participates in the 2003 Iraq War.

Baa Baa Black Sheep (1976–78) (Retitled *Black Sheep Squadron*, 1977–78)

WWII	Marines	Color

Based on Gregory "Pappy" Boyington's book about his exploits, first in the Flying Tigers, and then as a Marine flier in the Pacific, where he became a multiple ace and Medal of Honor recipient.

The Blue Angels (1960)

Peace	Navy	B&W

Fictional stories about the Navy's acrobatic flying team and its adventures in the air and on the ground.

Broadside (1964–65)

Peace	Navy	Color

Comic spin-off from *McHale's Navy* in which women maintain a Navy ship.

Call to Glory (**1984–85**)

Cold War	Air Force	Color

Series drew on patriotism emanating from the Los Angeles Olympics. Featured the Air Force's role in the Cuban Missile Crisis and the Cold War.

China Beach (**1988–91**)

Vietnam	Army	Color

Dramatic series in which the lives of the doctors, nurses, and soldiers intertwine at an Army evacuation hospital on China Beach in Vietnam.

Combat (**1962–67**)

WWII	Army	B&W, Color

Longest-running TV series about the Army in WWII. Followed a unit on its trek through France and Germany to ultimate victory. Series created a realistic portrayal of men trying to maintain their humanity, and their lives, in desperate situations.

Convoy (**1965**)

WWII	Navy	B&W

Short-lived series portraying action in the North Atlantic, set aboard a U.S. destroyer escort responsible for protecting a convoy and on a freighter within the flotilla.

Court-Martial (**1964–65**)

WWII/Korea	All	Color

A 26-episode series with hour-long segments that described cases investigated and sometimes tried by a crack team of lawyers from the Army's Judge Advocate General's office. Bradford Dillman and Peter Graves reprised their attorney roles from the earlier 1963 pilot film. Successful Hollywood directors, including Alvin Rakoff, and stars, including Sal Mineo and Donald Sutherland, participated in individual episodes. The pilot was also later adapted and released as a feature film in 1968. (See chapter 1.)

C.P.O. Sharkey (**1976–78**)

Peace	Navy	Color

Don Rickles as Chief Petty Officer Sharkey tries with little success to turn raw recruits into competent sailors.

The Dirty Dozen (**1988**)

WWII	Army	Color

One feature film and four made-for-television movies preceded this series based on the same premise that bad guys with a good goal can be rehabilitated. Hour-long format that lasted only one year.

Emerald Point N.A.S. (1983–84)

Peace   Navy   Color

Sordid soap opera set on a Navy air station in the deep South. Admiral heads dysfunctional family of wanton hussies.

Ensign O'Toole (1962–64)

Peace   Navy   B&W

Comedic adventures of a young naval officer and his shipmates aboard a destroyer.

Flight (1958)

WWI, WWII, Korea   Air Force   B&W, Color

Stories about the U.S. Air Force in war and peace.

From Here to Eternity (1980)

WWII   Army   Color

Misguided attempt to continue the story of Sgt. Milton Warden, with William Devane in the role Burt Lancaster made famous. Using the TV miniseries (see chapter 2) as its starting point, production attempted to graft new stories onto the James Jones characters who survived the attack on Pearl Harbor. Better they should have been left in peace.

Gallant Men (1962–63)

WWII   Army   B&W

Similar to *Combat*, but lasted only one year, so the soldiers did not make it to Germany and victory.

Gomer Pyle, U.S.M.C. (1964–70)

Peace   Marines   B&W, Color

The trials and tribulations of a bumbling, Southern-hick Marine on a base near Los Angeles. He was clearly not a favorite character with the Marine Corps public affairs office.

Hogan's Heroes (1965–71)

WWII   Army   B&W, Color

Typical POW story in which the camp more resembles a country club than the desperate circumstances that American captives actually endured. None of the characters showed signs of malnutrition from which POWs actually suffered. Instead, Hogan and his men conducted espionage and sabotage under the nose of the camp's commandant. Ludicrous (see **Berga** in chapter 3).

I Dream of Jeannie (1965–70)

Peace   Air Force, Army   B&W, Color

Adventures of an Air Force astronaut and his genie, named Jeannie, whom he released from her bottle-prison when he discovered the bottle while stranded on a desert island awaiting recovery/rescue after his space capsule landed. Series set in NASA/military context.

JAG (1995–)

Peace   Navy, Marines   Color

As Judge Advocate General attorneys, Harm Rabb and Sarah Mackenzie defend and prosecute Navy and Marine officers and men. Although an injury removed Harm from flying status, he manages to occasionally return to the cockpit in both Navy fighters and nonmilitary planes, including the landing of a C-130 aboard an aircraft carrier. Impossible, except that a similar plane did land aboard the USS *Forrestal* in 1963. Otherwise, the Navy would not have allowed the portrayal on a series that greatly benefits the service. The question remains as to whether Harm and Sarah will ever get beyond the sexual tension they create and end their chaste relationship.

The Lieutenant (1963–1964)

Peace   Marines   B&W

Set at Camp Pendleton, series portrayed the training of Marines as they struggle to achieve military perfection.

McHale's Navy (1962–66)

WWII   Navy   B&W

Ernest Borgnine, as Lt. Cmdr. McHale, commands a motley crew of misfits as they battle their superiors and the enemy, first in the South Pacific and later in Italy, of all places. Series spun off two feature films set in the military (see chapter 1).

Major Dad (1989–93)

Peace   Marines   Color

By-the-book Marine Corps major meets and marries in one day a pacifistic, liberal journalist and single mother with three children. Officer has to quickly learn how to be a father to his ready-made family. The DoD and Marines provided assistance during the series' four-year run since it provided a very positive image of the Marine Corps and the compromises needed to combine a military career and family life during peacetime.

M*A*S*H (1972–83)

Korea	Army	Color

TV series about a Mobile Army Surgical Hospital (M*A*S*H) behind the battlefield, except that like the 1970 feature film (see chapter 1), the show had virtually nothing to do with war. The hospital tents could just as easily be situated on the side of the Hollywood freeway ministering to automobile accident victims. The gallows humor relieves the tension of treating gravely injured people, not of the war being fought somewhere up the road. A fine medical series, but not a military series.

Men of Annapolis (1957)

Peace	Navy	B&W

Dramatic anthology series of 39, 30-minute episodes set at the Naval Academy; not very different from Hollywood's military academy movies of the 1920s and 1930s. Exteriors filmed on location at Annapolis, Maryland.

Navy Log (1955–58)

WWII, Peace	Navy	B&W

Stories about the Navy and its fighting men in war and peace, appearing first on CBS and then ABC. Approximately 104, 30-minute episodes.

Navy NCIS (2003–)

Peace	Navy	Color

Naval Criminal Investigative Service (NCIS) investigates criminal activity within the Navy and Marines.

No Time for Sergeants (1964)

Peace	Air Force	B&W

Sammy Jackson, as Airman Will Stockdale, a country hick from Georgia, finds himself in the Air Force, where he regularly runs into trouble with the rigid military discipline and conservative community.

Operation Petticoat (1977–79)

WWII	Navy	Color

Following from the feature film and the two-hour TV-movie pilot, the series focused on one crew member each week in a 30-minute comedy format.

Pensacola: Wings of Gold (1997–00)

Peace	Navy, Marines	Color

Set at the Pensacola Naval Air Station, the series followed the adventures of young Marine fliers, whom their commander selects to become an elite military unit.

The Phil Silvers Show a.k.a. *Sgt. Bilko* (syndication title) (1955–59)

Peace   Army   B&W

Sergeant Bilko could be viewed as the poster boy for the Army's slogan "Be All You Can Be," becoming the consummate con man as he runs the motor pool at an Army camp in Kansas.

Private Benjamin (1981–83)

Peace   Army   Color

Spoiled, young Jewish princess enlists in Army and struggles to win friends and survive despite her lack of discipline. Hollow shell compared to original film in which Benjamin becomes a mature woman in a typical military rite of passage.

The Silent Service (1957–60)

WWII   Navy   B&W

Dramatized true stories of the submarine service in WWII. Admiral Thomas Dykers, a highly decorated submariner, hosted the program, which included interviews with actual participants in the portrayals.

The Six O'Clock Follies (1980)

Vietnam   DoD   Color

Comedic portrayal of Armed Forces Radio and Television service and its production of the evening news and sports program in Saigon in 1967. Similar to *Good Morning, Vietnam* (see chapter 1).

Stargate SG-1 (1997–)

SciFi   Air Force   Color

The spin-off of the 1994 feature film *Stargate* began on Showtime and later moved to the SciFi channel. Unlike its inspiration, the TV series has received assistance from the Air Force, beginning with season one. The help has included character and story line development, costume assistance, and script review. Both Gen. Michael Ryan and Gen. John Jumper, the previous and current Air Force Chiefs of Staff, have appeared in cameo roles playing themselves. For the first time, the Air Force permitted the production company to do some limited shooting at Cheyenne Mountain, and it uses the entrance of the underground facility as an establishing shot for virtually every episode.

Steve Canyon (1958–60)

Cold War   Air Force   B&W

Based on Milton Caniff's comic strip, series began with Canyon as an Air Force officer on special assignment; he subsequently became commanding officer of an Air Force base. Approximately 39, 30-minute, black-and-white episodes.

Supercarrier (1988)

Cold War   Navy   Color

After assisting on the pilot, the Navy backed away from the series production because of the fraternization, sexism, and negative images of its officers. The service did allow the producers to do some filming aboard naval ships for early episodes of the series but then terminated all connections.

Tour of Duty (1987–90)

Vietnam   Army   Color

Followed an Army unit in the field during Vietnam, necessarily sanitized because of TV regulations.

Twelve O'Clock High (1964–67)

WWII   Air Force   B&W, Color

Continued the story of the American war in the air over Europe from the 1949 feature film. Series explored the fliers' efforts to survive aerial combat and the men's courage and fears. Used stock footage to advantage.

The Wackiest Ship in the Army (1965–66)

WWII   Army   Color

Dual command of an old sailing ship the military uses to deliver spies behind enemy lines. A Navy officer is in charge while at sea and an Army officer while in port, resulting in expected conflicts between the men.

West Point (1956–58)

All   Army   B&W

Dramatized stories of people and events that occurred at the U.S. Military Academy.

The West Wing (2000–)

Peace   All   Color

Although ostensibly about politics in the White House, the Pentagon and the services regularly intrude into the highest realms of the executive branch's decision-making processes, including responses to terrorist acts and threats from rogue nations, real and fictional. Action often takes place in the war room, located somewhere in the depths of the White House. Marine guards do appear doing their normal jobs, and the services provide, on occasion, material assistance. In one of the most powerful and Emmy-winning episodes, a homeless Korean War veteran is buried in Arlington National Cemetery with full military honors befitting a medal winner, which the Fort Myer burial detail performed for the cameras.

Bibliography

Adair, Gilbert. *Hollywood's Vietnam from the Green Berets to Full Metal Jacket.* London: Heinemann, 1989.

Adams, Michael. *The Best War Ever: America and World War II.* Baltimore: Johns Hopkins University Press, 1994.

The American Film Institute Catalog of Motion Pictures Produced in the United States. Berkeley: University of California Press, 1993.

Anderegg, Michael. *Inventing Vietnam: The War in Film and Television.* Philadelphia: Temple University Press, 1991.

Auster, Albert, and Leonard Quart. *How the War Was Remembered.* New York: Praeger, 1988.

Baker, M. Joyce. *Images of Women in Film: The War Years, 1941–1945.* Ann Arbor: University of Michigan Press, 1980.

Barsam, Richard M. *Nonfiction Film: A Critical History–Revised and Expanded.* Bloomington: Indiana University Press, 1992.

Basinger, Jeanine. *The World War II Combat Film, Anatomy of a Genre.* New York: Columbia University Press, 1986.

Bayles, Martha. "Portraits of Mars." *Wilson Quarterly* (Summer 2003): 12–19.

Beigel, Harvey. *The Fleet's In: Hollywood Presents the U.S. Navy in World War II.* Missoula, MT: Pictorial Histories, 1995.

Birdwell, Michael E. *Celluloid Soldiers: Warner Bros.'s Campaign Against Nazism.* New York: New York University Press, 2001.

Black, Gregory D., and Clayton R. Koppes. *Hollywood Goes to War.* New York: Free Press, 1987.

Braverman, John. *To Hasten the Homecoming: How Americans Fought World War II Through the Media.* Lanham, MD: Scarecrow Press, 1996.

Butler, Ivan. *The War Film.* South Brunswick and New York: A. S. Barnes, 1974.

Butler, Lucius, and Chaesoon Youngs. *Films for Korean Studies: A Guide to English-Language Films about Korea.* Honolulu: Center for Korean Studies, University of Hawaii, 1978.

Callaghan, David Scott. "Representing the Vietnamese: Race, Culture, and the Vietnam War in American Film and Drama." PhD dissertation, City University of New York, 1998.

Campbell, Craig. *Reel America and World War I: A Comprehensive Filmography and History of Motion Pictures in the United States, 1914–1920.* Jefferson, NC: McFarland, 1985.

Chambers, John Whiteclay II, and David Culbert. *World War II, Film, and History.* New York: Oxford University Press, 1996.

Colldeweih, Jack. "Napalm in the Morning: the Vietnam War Film." In *A Vietnam Reader: Sources & Essays*, edited by George Moss, 217–43. New York: Prentice Hall, 1991.

Cripps, Thomas. *Making Movies Black.* New York: Oxford University Press, 1993.

Cross, Robin. *The Big Book of B Movies, or How Low Was My Budget?* New York: St. Martins, 1981.

Davenport, Robert. *A Complete Guide to Movies about Wars of the 20th Century*, New York: Facts on File, 2003.

Debauche, Leslie Midkiff. *Reel Patriotism: The Movies and World War I*. Madison: University of Wisconsin Press, 1998.

Dick, Bernard. *The Star-Spangled Screen: The American World War II Film*. Lexington: University Press of Kentucky, 1985.

Dittmar, Linda, and Gene Michaud, eds. *From Hanoi to Hollywood: The Vietnam War in American Film*. New Brunswick, NJ: Rutgers University Press, 1990.

Doherty, Thomas. *Projections of War: Hollywood, American Culture and World War II*. New York: Columbia University Press, 1993.

Dolan, Edward F. *Hollywood Goes to War.* Twickenham, England: Hamlyn, 1985.

Donald, Ralph. "Hollywood and World War II: Enlisting Feature Films as Propaganda." PhD dissertation, University of Massachusetts, 1987.

Donald, Ralph R. "Savages, Swine, and Buffoons: Hollywood's Selected Stereotypical Characterization of the Japanese, Germans, and Italians in Films Produced During World War II." In *Race/Gender/Media: Considering Diversity Across Audiences, Content, and Producers,* edited by Rebecca Ann Lind. Upper Saddle River, NJ: A. B. Longman Books, 2003.

Edwards, Paul. *A Guide to Films on the Korean War.* Westport, CT: Greenwood Press, 1997.

Eiserman, Frederick. *War on Film: Military History Education.* Historical Bibliography No. 6. Fort Leavenworth, KS: U.S. Army Combat Studies Institute, 1987.

Epstein, Edward, John Griggs, and Joe Morella. *The Films of World War II.* Secaucus, NJ: Citadel Press, 1973.

Evans, Alvin. *Brassey's Guide to War Films.* Dulles, VA: Brassey's, 2000.

Evans, Joyce A. *Celluloid Mushroom Clouds: Hollywood and the Atomic Bomb.* Boulder, CO: Westview Press, 1998.

Farber, Manny. "Movies in Wartime." *New Republic*, September 7, 1942, 16–20.

Farmer, James. *Celluloid Wings.* Blue Ridge Summit, PA: TAB Books, 1984.

Fulbright, J. William. *The Pentagon Propaganda Machine.* New York: Liveright, 1970.

Furhammar, Leif, and Fulke Isaksson. *Politics and Film.* New York: Praeger, 1971.

Fyne, Robert. *The Hollywood Propaganda of World War II.* Metuchen, NJ: Scarecrow Press, 1994.

——. "The Unsung Heroes of World War II." *Literature/Film Quarterly* 6 (1979): 148–57.

Gallagher, Tag. "John Ford: Midway (The War Documentaries)." *Film Comment* XI (September–October 1975): 40–46.

Garland, Brock. *War Movies: The Complete Viewers Guide.* New York and Oxford: Facts on File Publications, 1987.

Gilman, Owen, and Lorrie Smith, eds. *America Rediscovered: Critical Essays on Literature and Film of the Vietnam War.* New York: Garland, 1990.

"GIs Versus Hollywood." *Time*, September 11, 1944, 9.

Goodman, Ezra. "Hollywood Belligerent." *Nation*, September 12, 1942, 213–14.

Guttmacher, Peter. *Legendary War Movies.* New York: Michael Friedman, 1996.

Guy, Rory. "Hollywood Goes to War." *Cinema* 3, no. 2 (1966): 22–29.

Hellman, John. *American Myth and the Legacy of Vietnam.* New York: Columbia University Press, 1986.

Hemenez , Richard. *The United States Marine Corps in Books and the Performing Arts.* Jefferson, NC: McFarland, 2001.

Higashi, Sumiko. "World War II Newsreels and Propaganda Film." *Cinema Journal* 37 (Spring 1998): 38–61.

Hillstrom, Kevin, and Laurie Collier Hillstrom. *The Vietnam Experience: A Concise Encyclopedia of American Literature, Songs, and Films.* Westport, CT: Greenwood Press, 1998.

"Hollywood and the War." *Newsweek*, September 18, 1939, 38–39.

"Hollywood Goes to War." *Time*, December 22, 1941, 46.

Holsinger, M. Paul, and Mary Anne Schofield, eds. *Visions of War.* Bowling Green, OH: Bowling Green University Popular Press, 1992.

Hoopes, Ray. *When the Stars Went to War: Hollywood and World War II.* New York: Random House, 1994.

Hughes, Robert, ed. *Film: Book 2, Films of Peace and War.* New York: Grove Press, 1962.

Hunter, Jack, ed. *Search and Destroy: Vietnam War Movies.* New York: Creation Books, 2003.

Hurd, Geoffrey. *National Fictions: World War II on Films and Television.* London: British Film Institute, 1984.

Hyams, Jay. *War Movies.* New York: Gallery Books, 1985.

Isenberg, Michael T. *War on Film: The American Cinema and World War I, 1914–41.* East Brunswick, NJ: Associated University Presses, Fairleigh Dickenson University Press, 1981.

Jacobs, Lewis. "World War II and the American Film." *Cinema Journal* 7 (1967): 1–21.

Jeavons, Clyde. *A Pictorial History of War Films.* Secaucus, NJ: Citadel Press, 1974.

Jones, Dorothy. "Hollywood Goes to War." *Nation* 27 (January 1945): 93–95.

Jones, Dorothy. "War Films Made in Hollywood, 1942–44." *Hollywood Quarterly* I (October 1945): 1–19.

Jones, G. William. *Black Cinema Treasures Lost and Found.* Denton: University of North Texas, 1991.

Jones, James. "Phony War Films." *Saturday Evening Post*, March 30, 1963, 64–67.

Jones, Ken D., and Arthur F. McClure. *Hollywood at War: The American Motion Picture and World War II.* South Brunswick and New York: A. S. Barnes, 1973.

Kagan, Norman. *The War Film.* New York: Pyramid Publications, 1974.

Kane, Kathryn. *Visions of War: Hollywood Combat Films of World War II.* Ann Arbor, MI: UMI Research Press, 1982.

Kelly, Thomas O. "Race and Racism in the American World War II War Film: The Negro, the Nazi, and the 'Jap' in Bataan and Sahara." *Michigan Academician* 24 (Summer 1992): 571–84.

Klozoff, Max, William Johnson, and Richard Corless. "Shooting at Wars: Three Views." *Film Quarterly* 2 (1967): 27–36.

Koppes, Clayton R., and Gregory D. Black. *Hollywood Goes to War: How Politics, Profits and Propaganda Shaped World War II Movies.* New York: Free Press, 1987.

———. "What to Show the World: The Office of War Information and Hollywood, 1942–1945." *Journal of American History* 64, no. 1 (1977): 87–105.

Langman, Larry, and Ed Borg. *Encyclopedia of American War Films.* New York and London: Garland, 1989.

Lanning, Michael Lee. *Vietnam at the Movies.* New York: Fawcett Columbine, 1994.

Lingerman, Richard R. *Don't You Know There's a War On? The American Home Front, 1941–45.* New York: Putnam, 1970.

Lipschutz, Ronnie. *Cold War Fantasies: Film, Fiction, and Foreign Policy.* Lanham, MD: Rowman & Littlefield, 2001.

Look Magazine, eds. *Movie Lot to Beachhead: The Motion Picture Goes to War and Prepares for the Future.* New York: Doubleday, 1945.

McAdams, Frank. *The American War Film.* New York: Praeger, 2002.

Mackenzie, S. P. *British War Films, 1939–1945.* Hambledon and London, New York: 2001.

Malo, Jean-Jacques, and Tony Williams. *Vietnam War Films.* Jefferson, NC: McFarland, 1994.

Manvell, Roger. *Films and the Second World War.* New York: Dell Publishing, 1974.

Marill, Alvin H. *Movies Made for Television: The Telefeature and the Mini-Series, 1964—1986.* New York: Baseline, 1987.

Maslowski, Peter. *Armed with Cameras: The American Military Photographers of World War II.* New York: Free Press, 1993.

Matelski, Marilyn J., ed. *War and Film in America: Historical and Critical Essays.* Jefferson, NC: McFarland, 2003.

Maynard, Richard. *Propaganda on Film, A Nation at War.* Rochelle Park, NJ: Hayden Buck, 1975.

Mayo, Mike. *Video Hound's War Movies: Classic Conflict on Film.* Detroit: Visible Ink Press, 1990.

McClure, Arthur F. "Hollywood at War: the American Motion Picture and World War II, 1939–1945." *Journal of Popular Film* 1, no. 2 (Spring 1972): 123–35.

Meerse, David E. "To Reassure a Nation: Hollywood Presents World War II." *Film and History* 6, no. 4 (December 1976): 79–91.

Mintz, Steven, and Randy Roberts, eds. *Hollywood's America: United States History Through Its Films.* New York: Brandywine Press, 1993.

Moeller, Susan. *Shooting War: Photography and the American Experience of Combat.* New York: Basic Books, 1989.

Morella, Joe, Edward Z. Epstein, and John Griggs. *The Films of World War II.* Secaucus, NJ: Citadel Press, 1973.

Murphy, William. "John Ford and the Wartime Documentary." *Film & History* VI (February 1976): 1–8.
——. "The Method of 'Why We Fight.'" *Journal of Popular Film* (Summer 1972): 185–96.
Muse, Eben J. *The Land of Nam: The Vietnam War in American Film.* Lanham, MD: Scarecrow Press, 1995.
National Audio Visual Center. *Documentary Film Classics.* Washington, DC: U.S. Government, n.d.
The New York Times Film Reviews, 20 volumes plus index of films, 1913–1968. New York: New York Times Company, 1913–1998.
Nichols, Dudley. "Men in Battle: A Review of Three Current Pictures." *Hollywood Quarterly* I (1945): 34–39.
Nornes, Abe Mark, and Fukushima Yukio, eds. *The Japan/America Film Wars: Propaganda Films from World War II.* Chur, Switzerland: Harwood, 1993.
O'Connor, John, and Martin Jackson, eds. *American History/American Film.* New York: Fredrick Ungar, 1979.
O'Neill, William. *A Democracy at War: America's Fight at Home and Abroad in World War II.* New York: Free Press, 1993.
Orris, Bruce. *When Hollywood Ruled the Skies.* Hawthorne, CA: Aero Associates, 1984.
Paris, Michael. *From the Wright Brothers to Top Gun: Aviation, Nationalism and Popular Cinema.* Manchester, UK: Manchester University Press, 1995.
Palmer, William. *The Films of the Eighties: A Social History.* Carbondale: Southern Illinois University, 1994.
Parish, James Robert. *The Great Combat Pictures: Twentieth-Century Warfare on the Screen.* Metuchen, NJ: Scarecrow Press, 1990.
Pendo, Stephen. *Aviation in the Cinema.* Metuchen, NJ: Scarecrow Press, 1985.
Perlmutter, Tom. *War Movies.* Secaucus, NJ: Castle, 1974.
Polan, Dana. *Power and Paranoia: History, Narrative, and the American Cinema, 1940–1950.* New York: Columbia University Press, 1986.
Quirk, Lawrence J. *Great War Films.* New York: Carol, 1994.
Ray, Robert. *A Certain Tendency of the Hollywood Cinemas: 1930–1980.* Princeton, NJ: Princeton University Press, 1985.
Renov, Michael. *Hollywood's Wartime Woman: Representation and Ideology.* Ann Arbor, MI: UMI Research, 1988.
Ricci, Mark, Boris Zmijewsky, and Steve Zmijewsky. *The Films of John Wayne.* Secaucus, NJ: Citadel Press, 1973.
Richards, Larry. *African American Films Through 1959.* Jefferson, NC: McFarland, 1998.
Robb, David L. *Operation Hollywood.* Amherst, NY: Prometheus Books, 2004.
Roeder, George H., Jr. *The Censored War: American Visual Experience during World War II.* New Haven, CT: Yale University Press, 1993.
Rollins, Peter, ed. *Hollywood as Historian: American Film in a Cultural Context.* Lexington: University Press of Kentucky, 1983.
Rollins, Peter, and John O'Connor. *Hollywood's World War I: Motion Picture Images.* Bowling Green, OH: Bowling Green State University Popular Press, 1997.
Rubin, Steven Jay. *Combat Films, 1945–1970.* Jefferson, NC: McFarland, 1981.
Sampson, Henry. *Blacks in Black and White: A Source Book on Black Film.* Metuchen, NJ and London: Scarecrow Press, 1995.
Schatz, Thomas, ed. *Boom and Bust: The American Cinema in the 1940s.* New York: Scribner, 1997.
Serene, Frank, com. *World War II on Film: A Catalog of Select Motion Pictures in the National Archives.* Washington, DC: National Archives, 1994.
Shain, Russell Earl. *An Analysis of Motion Pictures Released by the American Film Industry 1930–1970.* New York: Arno Press, 1976.
Shindler, Colin. *Hollywood Goes to War: Films and American Society 1939–1952.* Boston: Routledge, 1979.
Short, K. R. M., ed. *Feature Films as History.* Lexington: University Press of Kentucky, 1981.
——. *Film & Radio Propaganda in World War II.* Knoxville: University of Tennessee Press, 1983.
Shull, Michael, and David Edward Wilt. *Hollywood War Films 1937–1945: An Exhaustive Filmography of American Feature-Length Motion Pictures Relating to World War II.* Jefferson, NC: McFarland, 1996.
Simone, Sam P. *Hitchcock As Activist: Politics and the War Film.* Ann Arbor, MI: UMI Research Press, 1986.
Sklar, Robert. *Movie-Made America.* New York: Vintage Books, 1975.
Slide, Anthony. *The New Historical Dictionary of the American Film Industry.* Lanham, MD: Scarecrow Press, 1998.

Small, Melvin. "War Films Made in Hollywood, 1942–1944." *Hollywood Quarterly* I (1945): 1–19.

Smith, Julian. *Looking Away: Hollywood and Vietnam.* New York: Scribner, 1975.

Smith, Paul, ed. *The Historian and Film.* New York: Cambridge University Press, 1976.

Soderbergh, Peter A. "The Grand Illusion: Hollywood and World War II, 1930–1945." *The University of Dayton Review* 5, no. 3 (Winter 1968–69): 13–21.

———. "The War Films." *Discourse* II (1968): 87–91.

Spiller, Robert J. "War in the Dark." *American Heritage* (February/March 1999): 41–51.

Suid, Lawrence. *Air Force.* Madison: University of Wisconsin Press, 1983.

———. *Guts & Glory.* Lexington: University Press of Kentucky, 2002.

———. *Sailing on the Silver Screen.* Annapolis, MD: Naval Institute Press, 1996.

Television Programming Source Books 2002. 3 vols. Philadelphia: North American Publishing, 2001.

Thompson, Lawrence, Richard Welch, and Phillip Stephens. "A Vietnam Filmography." *Journal of Popular Film and Television* 9, no. 1 (Spring 1981).

Variety Film Reviews: 1907–1996. 24 vols. New Providence, NJ: R. R. Bowker, 1997.

Variety Television Reviews: 1946–1994. Edited by Howard Prouty. 18 vols. New York: Garland, 1991.

Vidal, Gore. *Screening History.* Cambridge, MA: Harvard University Press, 1992.

Violence and the Media: A Report to the National Commission on the Causes and Prevention of Violence. Washington, DC: Government Printing Office, 1969.

Virilio, Paul. *War and Cinema: The Logistics of Perception.* New York: Verso, 1989.

Walker, Mark. *Vietnam Veteran Films.* Metuchen, NJ and London: Scarecrow Press, 1991.

"War, Film, and History." [Special issue]. *Historical Journal of Film, Radio and Television* 14, no. 4 (October 1994): 353–478.

Wetta, Frank, Frank Joseph, and Stephen Curley. *Celluloid Wars: A Guide to Film and the American Experience of War.* New York, Westport, CT, and London: Greenwood Press, 1992.

Wetta, Frank & Martin Novelli. "'Now a Major Motion Picture': War Films and Hollywood's New Patriotism," *Journal of Military History*, Vol. 67, (July 2003): 861–82.

White-Hensen, Wendy, and Veronica Gillespie. *The Theodore Roosevelt Association Film Collection.* Washington, DC: Library of Congress, 1986.

Woll, Allen L. *The Hollywood Musical Goes to War.* Chicago: Nelson, 1983.

About the Authors

Lawrence Suid is a military historian. He received his BA in history from Western Reserve University, an MA degree in Russian history from Duke University, an MFA in film studies from Brandeis University, and his PhD in American studies from Case Western Reserve University.

His first book, *Guts & Glory* (1978), remains the definitive study of the symbiotic relationship between the film industry and the United States armed services. *Sailing on the Silver Screen* (1996) provides an in-depth study of the making of the U.S. Navy's image in motion pictures. The revised, expanded edition of *Guts & Glory* (2002) carries the story of Hollywood and the military up to *We Were Soldiers* and *Windtalkers*. His next book, with his coauthor Dolores Haverstick, will be a biography of Fred Zinnemann, the director of *High Noon, From Here to Eternity, The Nun's Story,* and *A Man for All Seasons*. His website address is www.lawrencesuid.com. He may also be reached at lhsuid@aol.com.

Dolores Haverstick received her B.A. in history from William Jewell College. She worked for the federal government for 32 years, mostly for the Department of Labor. Her last position held was in the Office of Inspector General as director of human resources. She has worked with Dr. Suid for more than 15 years, helping to edit his books and articles. She retired to help research and write this book and the biography of Fred Zinnemann.